HOME AND COMMONWEALTH AFFAIRS	FOREIGN AFFAIRS

1947

	Oct. 29 Benelux customs union established
	Oct. 30 General Agreement on Tariffs and Trade signed at Geneva
Nov. 13 Cripps replaces Dalton as Chancellor of the Exchequer	
	Dec. 30 Michael of Roumania abdicates. 'People's Republic' established

1948

Jan. 1 Rail and road transport nationalised	
Jan. 4 Burma leaves Commonwealth	
Feb. 4 Ceylon becomes a Dominion	
	Feb. 25 Communists seize power in Czechoslovakia
	March 17 Brussels Treaty organisation – France, Britain, Benelux
April 1 Electricity nationalised	
	April 16 O.E.E.C. established
	May 7–10 Congress of Europe at The Hague
	May 14 Israel proclaims her independence British mandate for Palestine ends
	May 15 Arab League invades Israel
	June 18 Soviet blockade of West Berlin begins
	June 28 Yugoslavia expelled from Cominform
July 5 Start of National Health Service	
	Nov. 2 Truman elected President of U.S.A.

£5.00

S/4

1949

	Feb. 24 Israeli–Egyptian armistice
March 15 Clothes rationing ends	
	April 4 North Atlantic Treaty signed
April 18 Eire leaves Commonwealth	
April 28 King recognised as 'Head of the Commonwealth'	
May 1 Gas industry nationalised	
	May 5 Council of Europe established
	May 12 Soviet blockade of Berlin ended
	May 23 Federal German Republic established in West Germany
Sept. 18 Devaluation of the pound	
	Sept. 22 U.S.A. claims that U.S.S.R. has exploded an atomic bomb
	Oct. 1 Chinese People's Republic proclaimed in Peking
	Oct. 7 German Democratic Republic established in East Germany

1950

Jan. 26 India becomes a Republic	
	...na and
Feb. 23 General Election Labour Government Prime Minister: Attlee Foreign Secretary: Bevin Chancellor: Cripps	
	May 9 Federal German republic joins Council of Europe as associate
	May 25 U.S.A., Britain, France issue Tripartite Declaration on Middle East
May 26 End of petrol rationing	
	June 25 N. Korea invades S. Korea U.N. organise resistance

D1326294

TIDES OF FORTUNE

WINDS OF CHANGE
1914-1939

THE BLAST OF WAR
1939-1945

TIDES OF FORTUNE
1945-1955

Foreign Secretary, April 1955

TIDES OF FORTUNE

1945–1955

HAROLD MACMILLAN

* * *

LONDON

MACMILLAN

MELBOURNE · TORONTO

1969

Published by
MACMILLAN AND CO LTD
Little Essex Street London WC2
and also at Bombay Calcutta and Madras
Macmillan South Africa (Publishers) Pty Ltd Johannesburg
The Macmillan Company of Australia Pty Ltd Melbourne
The Macmillan Company of Canada Ltd Toronto
Gill and Macmillan Ltd Dublin

Printed in Great Britain by
ROBERT MACLEHOSE AND CO LTD
The University Press, Glasgow

Contents

Part Three: OFFICE AGAIN, 1951–1955

List of Illustrations

List of Cartoons

The first three cartoons are reproduced by courtesy of the
London Express News and Feature Services and the fourth by
courtesy of *Punch*.

Acknowledgements

I HAVE to record my debt to a number of histories, biographies, and autobiographies, which I have consulted, especially to those specified in the footnotes.

I am greatly indebted to Miss Anne Glyn-Jones, who has carried out all the research work among my own papers and other books and documents, as well as to Miss Anne Macpherson, Miss Bunty Morley, Miss Penelope Mumford and Mrs. Christine Deman, who have typed and retyped the text with skill and patience.

December 1968   H.M.

Preface

T H E German surrender in May 1945 was generally regarded as the effective end of the Second World War. The campaign in the Far East had still to be brought to a conclusion, but from the British point of view, although our forces employed against Japan were by no means negligible, by far the greater burden lay upon our American allies. We could not know that the end would come within a few months, still less that it would be hastened by the first use of the new atomic power, of which only a few of us had even heard the vaguest whispers. In the development of this terrible invention, the Western Allies had only beaten the Germans by a narrow margin.

In the midst of their rejoicing in those spring days, most of our fellow countrymen and women so long and so devotedly engaged in the daily tasks of war found it difficult to look ahead to the problems and issues of peace. Whether on overseas service or at home, almost every man and woman, young and old, had been sucked into the machinery of warfare to a degree unequalled in any other country. Even the boasted German efficiency was never able to mobilise man- and woman-power on anything approaching the scale achieved in Britain. Therefore, with few exceptions, our eyes were so closely restricted to the immediate scene that we had neither time nor inclination to scan the distant horizon. Yet during the war itself, as the years passed, some of the outstanding peaks began to emerge. When victory came, and we had a little more chance for reflection, they stood out more clearly.

It is difficult even now to realise the enormous price paid by humanity as the result of German aggression and brutality. In Europe alone, twelve and a half million fighting men had been killed and civilian deaths had reached the appalling figure of over twenty-nine and a half million, including six million Jews, two-thirds of all the Jews in Europe. In addition seven millions of both sexes and all ages had been enslaved and subjected to appalling hardships. Similarly, the Far Eastern war had left its trail of loss of men and material, widespread destruction and hideous barbarity. It seemed impossible that this gulf of hatred and resentment could easily, if ever, be bridged. Yet, after a few years, these bitter memories between former enemies were quenched in a still greater fear. The bond of common danger was to bring new alliances into being.

Meanwhile, there were plenty of reasons for anxiety at home. Whatever might be the character of the Government—Conservative, Labour, or even Coalition—which would emerge from the General Election which clearly could not be long delayed, the economic and financial prospects were frightening. Apart from the cost of maintaining the maimed, the widowed and the orphaned, added to the still heavy pension commitments resulting from the First World War, we had to shoulder a new burden of debt and oppressive taxation. Moreover, it was clear that the vast expenditure which Britain had incurred whilst she stood alone against Hitler's onslaught had once again involved the sacrifice of the bulk of her foreign investments. While the internal debt, disruptive as it might prove of established social conditions, could be and was cheerfully met by our people, grave external problems loomed ahead. Almost without exports, visible or invisible, and deprived of the income on our foreign investments, the British economy would have faced bankruptcy but for Lend-Lease. What was now to replace it? If, in the event, a generous American loan came to our immediate rescue, this was but a temporary alleviation necessarily adding after the first few years to the obligations of interest and capital repayment. The fundamental problems remained.

British industry had been ruthlessly adapted to war production at whatever expense to exports by painful and often arbitrary methods. The price had now to be paid. Indeed, as it proved, we were to be worse off than either our allies or our enemies. The vast scale of American production had increased capacity to such an extent that they had no difficulty in combining the demands of civilian needs with all military requirements. Germany, and later Japan, having had most of their industrial equipment destroyed, were in due course to see this rebuilt largely by the assistance of their former enemies. Thus, without an internal or an external debt, without any expenditure on defence and with new and modern plants, the vanquished could, after the first few years of difficulty and confusion, challenge the victors in the markets of the world.

At the same time, the social changes initiated by the First War would clearly be hastened. The rate was to exceed even the most confident expectations of those who in the later years of the war were making the plans for what was known as 'Reconstruction'. In spite of a certain scepticism which lingered in the minds of those who remembered the fate of Lloyd George's election promise of 'homes fit for heroes' in 1918, there was a general hope that, somehow or other, in spite of all the difficulties and pitfalls, peace would lead to progress. The vision of a new Utopia, to be based on the Beveridge Plan and supported by a Socialist or semi-Socialist economy, had already begun to enthral a large proportion of civilians and Servicemen alike. There were to be disappointments and delays. Yet, by a strange irony, this social revolution was destined after some hesitations and set-backs to find its apogee under a series of Conservative administrations. The 'Affluent Society', as it came to be called, was to become a cause of congratulation, denigration or envy according to the interests or prejudices of the critic. But it was secured and will remain.

This vast social and economic revolution has brought with it many problems, spiritual as well as material. Yet few who criticise it today can realise or even remember the harsh and often primitive conditions which have been superseded.

When we reflected on the situation which would face us after the war, most of us realised that the partial breakdown of what might be called a class society which had to some extent resulted from the First War must be enormously enhanced and hastened by the Second. The high rates of taxation on accumulated wealth and current income, in addition to the changed habits and desires of all, must involve radical alterations in the structure of society in town and country alike. These changes would affect every aspect of our national life.

At the same time, the Second War, like the First, had already resulted in prodigious strides forward in technology, notably in specialised fields. It is a sad truth that the exigencies of war result in expenditure of effort and money on many kinds of research on a scale that no peace-time budget can sustain. In aerodynamics and in many other sciences the advance is specially rapid. Even today, both in the Western countries and in Russia, a high proportion of scientific research must be classed under the heading of defence. British industry, as we well knew, would have to face a major effort of adaptation and modernisation. Its success is shown in the enormous increase in exports which has been achieved. Its failure has perhaps resulted from its intense conservatism, especially in outmoded restrictions and conventions. But, as we foresaw, there would be the overriding need of earning sufficient on visible and invisible exports to pay for our imports, and also to maintain the overseas investment which, while it sometimes puts unwelcome pressure upon the balance of payments, is the traditional and indeed the only method by which an island power can maintain and develop its strength.

Amid so many uncertainties, we could not tell what would be the future of our defence—Army, Navy and Air Force. In the later stages of the campaign I used sometimes to talk over these matters with the high-ranking officers with whom I was brought in contact. The relative roles of the three Services were a matter of constant discussion and argument. We knew well enough that American and Russian strength, based on their vast populations and huge industrial potential, had already altered the balance of power. But it was also clear that the development of the aeroplane would prove of additional weight in this inevitable transformation. When the sea has been the only method of communication, the lead has rested with small sea-going nations. The aeroplane is at once the instrument and creator of continental power.

If in the last years of the war the change in the balance of power became apparent as the leadership in the struggle began to pass out of our hands, it equally began to be clear that the old Imperial and Colonial system which had stood so many strains in two world wars must now undergo radical and even revolutionary development.

The battlefields of the Second War mark the end of the heroic age of the British Empire. In Africa, in Italy, in France, in the Far East, great armies had gathered and fought under British command. These forces comprised not merely men of British and European origin and descent—from Australia, New Zealand, Canada and South Africa—but the natives of almost every colony, great and small, throughout the world.[1] Yet we were conscious that this was likely to be the final, if splendid, scene in a drama which had been played through the centuries. Even the Coalition Government, in spite of Churchill's own restraining hand, had held discussions with Indian leaders which made it clear that a substantial measure of independence was on the way. Where India led, others would surely follow. While we could not foresee, even at the end of the war, the rapidity with which the dissolution of the old system would come about, we knew in our hearts that the process was inevitable, and right.

Furthermore, although we hoped for an early conclusion to the Eastern war, it was clear that the prestige of Britain, and indeed of all European peoples, had been much injured by the ease with which Japanese forces had overrun immense territories—Burma, Malaya, Indo-China, Indonesia. These conquests had been accompanied, unhappily, by the unprecedented and large-scale surrender of British troops. Many discussions took place, in any spare moments that we might have, on the future of these territories. None of us was optimistic enough to believe that the old system could be restored, untarnished and unchanged. If we could not see clearly the course of events, we knew that it could 'never be the same again'. The cataclysm was too dramatic and engulfing to be treated as an episode.

Yet while Britain was ready, from the highest motives and with the best intentions, to direct into a new channel the stream of her Colonial and Imperial story, she was all the time—both during and after the war—to be the subject of self-criticism at home, and denigration abroad. Not the least wounding attacks were those by our friends and allies. Deceived by a false analogy drawn from their own independence, the Americans were from ignorance or prejudice unable to understand the British theme and purpose. In contrast,

[1] See *The Blast of War*, p. 170.

while the process of transforming the British Empire was to
proceed, some will say too precipitately, but at any rate inexorably,
the Russian Empire was to grow at a startling pace in all directions,
partly by direct annexation and partly by the imposition upon many
limitrophe countries of Communist regimes under the control of
Moscow. While the Western nations were rapidly to demobilise
their forces, in Asia, as well as in Central and Eastern Europe,
the Soviet armies were to consolidate and extend their authority.

What of Europe? Germany destroyed—without Government,
Army, industrial or financial structure, the prey to bitter recrimination and the object of universal detestation; France, only lately
liberated, without a clear political or economic future; her industries
destroyed or removed; much of her manpower transported to
Germany; her finances in disorder; Italy, the scene of nearly two
years of bitter warfare, following on the follies and disasters of
Mussolini and Fascism; Belgium and Holland only lately freed
from the ruthless exactions of their conqueror. Europe lay prostrate
and bleeding from her wounds. How was the old—or, indeed, any—
Europe to emerge from these long years of horror? Drawing on the
memories of the inter-war years, I knew that recovery could only
come through prolonged and consistent American help. How generous that would prove to be lay hidden in the future. Meanwhile, over
all these countries, even in Western Europe, the dark shadow of
Communism was beginning to fall.

Much of Western Europe's revival (although many of the
countries concerned would not feel very anxious later to acknow-
ledge the debt) we were to owe to the foresight of a few great
Americans. Yet by a curious twist of events, faulty American
strategy was to prove responsible for the domination by Russia over
a great part of Central and Eastern Europe. Had Field-Marshal
Alexander been allowed to develop the plans which he put before
Churchill, and for which Churchill pleaded so loyally with Roosevelt,[1] the dominating position of Stalin and his armies could have
been forestalled and frustrated. If, instead of the unnecessary
landings in the south of France, which gravely weakened Alexander's
armies without any corresponding effect upon the fortunes of the

[1] *The Blast of War*, chap. xviii.

battle in this theatre, the Americans had accepted the plan to move rapidly through the Ljubljana Gap, to occupy Vienna, and to secure a great part of what is now Communist Europe, the history of the world would indeed have been changed. The life and strength of Western Europe, which was so greatly impaired by the events of the last year of the war, would have been correspondingly nourished. But these, alas, were by now but vain regrets.

For many months, both during and after the war, I was obsessed with this vital problem. What would Russia do? By what motives would she be swayed? This was the 64-dollar question. I had, of course, been aware of Churchill's forebodings. At the Cairo Conference in 1943 he had lifted the veil.[1] He had realised that with the power of Germany destroyed, our main concern must be the new Soviet threat. The Soviet menace had already, in his eyes, begun to replace the Nazi foe.[2] But the Americans were still in the mood of fellowship and camaraderie; and British influence in great decisions had already begun to decline. I had not forgotten that it was only with sullen American acquiescence that we had been able to rescue Greece from Communism a few months before.[3] Owing to the thrust forward of the Russian armies while the Allies were still on the lines of the Po and the Rhine, the future of Roumania, Bulgaria and Hungary seemed almost hopeless, even that of Austria precarious. Yugoslavia was in the hands of the strongest and most effective of the Communist leaders in the Balkans. We could not foresee that Tito's firmness of character would lead him ultimately to assert his independence of orthodox Marxism and Moscow domination. What we saw immediately before us was a demonstration of Yugoslav irredentism and imperialistic expansion which was already an embarrassment and even a menace.

In the concluding months of the war Churchill became increasingly distressed by the apparent blindness of Roosevelt to these new dangers. But the President, like his advisers, could think of little beyond the German campaign. Moreover, in his anxiety not to

[1] *Winds of Change*, p. 14.
[2] Winston S. Churchill, *The Second World War*, vol. vi: *Triumph and Tragedy* (London, 1954), p. 496.
[3] *The Blast of War*, chaps. xxi–xxiii.

'gang up' with his British ally, an attitude which Truman was also to adopt, at least initially, he seemed ready to abandon his long affection for Churchill in order to win Stalin's smiles. At the Yalta Conference, where the President, thin and frail, was unable to cope with the vast questions looming ahead, Churchill had found himself in an increasingly isolated position. On his return, he had given large hostages to fortune by his assurances to the House of Commons that he believed that Russia would meet her undertakings towards Poland. But Russian promises had soon begun to wear rather thin, and the fate of Poland was destined to be the first disillusionment that led ultimately to the breakdown of the Grand Alliance. Yet at Yalta Stalin had been in a friendly mood, with a general attitude towards post-war problems in which he seemed to welcome and indeed desire the maintenance of close Anglo-American-Soviet co-operation. Certainly, in the last stages of the war Russian armies had occupied all eastern Germany, and Berlin had fallen into her physical control. But all this was in accordance with arrangements reached long before. These unlucky agreements—negotiated in very different conditions—were scrupulously observed by the British and the Americans. Nevertheless, their results proved tragic.

At Allied Force Headquarters in Caserta, watching day by day the conflict of wills of our masters, we were conscious in general terms of the diminishing influence of British diplomacy even under Churchill's strong direction. Roosevelt, an ageing man, had, partly from weakness and partly from vanity, fallen victim to the notion that he could bend and charm the Man of Steel. Russian statesmen cannot be cajoled; but being strong realists they can be dealt with on a basis of frankness and truth. We had already seen the terrible blow to Poland implicit in the Yalta decisions, even with their minor concessions. We had little expectation of the Russians carrying out either the letter or the spirit of the bargain. My meetings with General Anders, Commander of the Polish forces in Italy, had convinced me that any more hopeful view was mere wishful thinking.[1] It was therefore apparent that an East—West conflict was about to begin which has in practice dominated world politics since

[1] *The Blast of War*, pp. 496, 497, 694–6.

the end of the Second War. This division has still prevented signature of a German peace treaty. It has hampered and frustrated the work of the United Nations, for the foundation of which negotiations were already under way in the spring of 1945. The Security Council, which was intended to be a kind of Cabinet of world powers, with the General Assembly as a consultative Parliament, has become impotent. The ideological split has vitiated the whole concept of a world order. It has moreover excluded both Germany, still partitioned, and China, with a population greater than that of Western Europe and the United States put together, from even being members of the United Nations Organisation.

When the war ended, these troubles lay ahead. We only dimly sensed the dangers. Yet we were perhaps more aware of them from our resentment at the frustration of Alexander's ambitious and imaginative plans. I knew, from Churchill's own lips, his regrets and anxieties. If the Americans had been to some extent responsible for the Russian extension of power so far to the west, with the partitioning of Germany and all that followed from it, yet with their wonderful resilience and idealism they were to do much to redeem this tragic error. The maintenance of large forces overseas; diplomatic support; treaty commitments unbelievable to former generations of Americans: all these in the next few years were to be generously accepted and scrupulously observed. From my own experience in the Mediterranean campaign I had rejoiced in the fullness and genuineness of Anglo-American co-operation. Whatever else might fail, this could be maintained.

The seeds of all these changes at home, in the Empire and throughout the world had indeed been planted after the First War. As the result of the Second they were now to ripen. If in 1939 I had sensed something of the developing future, yet in 1940 and in the next two years we were all obsessed by the only issue at stake— survival. Great as were the difficulties of the modern world, they would have been greater still if Britain had not stood successfully, and stood alone, against the triumph of Hitler. This is not always remembered by the beneficiaries of our resistance. Nevertheless, in the last years of the war, when it was clear that the victory of the Allies was assured, however long and bitter the struggle might be, we all knew that the future was dark and uncertain. If the First War had shaken the old internal and international systems to their very foundations, the Second was to destroy the concept of the political and economic independence of nations, however powerful. Isolationism was dead, in America as in Britain. Some believed that, shocked by the frightful destruction of life and wealth, the nations would accept something like a world Government in the shape of an effective United Nations system. If this were to fail, then at least alliances over wide areas must be created and preserved. At the end of the war we could see something of where the dangers were to lie if only as through a glass, darkly. The nationalism of the African and Asiatic peoples must break out in a wave of emotion. The Communist pressure would be difficult to resist. Equally determined would be the aspirations and demands of our own people for a fuller life.

If Alexander and I were given little opportunity for relaxation after the German surrender, we were at least spared that flatness of mind and spirit that sometimes follows the end of great and exciting conflicts. The great storm was over; but there were threatening clouds on the frontiers of Italy, which presaged new dangers. These we had now to meet.

PART ONE

Last Months of Office

1945

CHAPTER I

End of a Mission

THE German forces in Italy capitulated to Field-Marshal Alexander on 29 April 1945. The total German surrender on all fronts took place on 8 May. On 26 May I laid down my duties as British Resident Minister in the Mediterranean, Political Adviser to the Supreme Allied Commander and Acting President of the Allied Commission for Italy. Thus ended an assignment which had begun in January 1943.[1] Yet within these last weeks we were called upon to face some problems as difficult and as delicate as any in the previous years. Although I left before they were all resolved, I was able to take some part in the initial stages.

In the last months of the war in Italy we had been deeply concerned about the situation in northern Italy and the threat which the large forces of armed partisans might present. Nobody knew what would be the state of these areas, so long under the nominal control of Mussolini's rump republic and his German allies, when the enemy had been driven out, or what difficulties would face us during the interval between the German retirement and the arrival of the Allied armies with their attendant apparatus of military government. Many of us—with recent events in Greece in mind—feared that a series of Communist *coups* would take place, at least in some of the great cities. The imposing body of partisans which had been armed and equipped from Allied sources might prove unwilling to accept the alternatives of enlistment in the Italian Army or returning to private life. Elaborate arrangements had been made for their demobilisation. Special messages had been prepared from the Field-Marshal, conveying his admiration and gratitude to the patriot forces. All our Military Government officers were fully briefed, and ready to act.

[1] *The Blast of War*, p. 219.

In the event, everything went better than we had expected. Ceremonial parades were held in Milan and Turin in the first week of May at which the partisans were thanked for their services and the handing-in of arms was begun. These proved reasonably successful. Both in the north-western and in the north-eastern districts, French intransigence and Yugoslav infiltration made it difficult for the partisans to abandon their formations and relinquish their arms. But elsewhere, although no doubt at the formal parades only a proportion of their equipment was in fact surrendered, the general situation in the weeks immediately following the German surrender was better than we had dared to hope. The arrangements for feeding the population of the north worked out well, in spite of transport difficulties. Both in the Fifth and Eighth Army zones a satisfactory distribution of rations was possible, and the approaching harvest justified us in taking some risks with our stocks. Conditions were not easy, but they were tolerable. Although the Committees of National Liberation, who were responsible for the Resistance, had in many cases installed a system of local administration, and the predominance of Communists in these cadres was a cause of anxiety, yet the rapidity with which the patriots accepted the situation and the northern populations settled down under the guidance of the Allies to something like normal life was greatly to their credit. Thus conditions in northern Italy, which at one time had been a major source of concern, proved to be easily manageable. But the situation on the frontiers was to prove delicate and dangerous.

It was clearly the duty of the Supreme Allied Commander, acting as the agent of the British and American Governments, to preserve the integrity of the Italian frontiers as they had stood at the beginning of the war. Any rectification should take place only as the result of agreement. At that time we believed that the negotiation of a general peace treaty over all Europe would be practicable and rapid. These expectations were to be disappointed and a formal peace treaty even with Italy was not possible until February 1947. Nevertheless this was the principle upon which we were instructed to act, and it accorded with our concept of our duty. It is true that these frontiers represented, especially in the north-east, a settlement highly distasteful to some neighbouring countries and, in some areas, to the majority of populations involved. But our position was clear. Negotiation, not force, should decide any contended issues. Meanwhile, we were in the position of trustees.

The first conflict came in the north-west, especially in the Val d'Aosta. After the armistice in September 1943, the Italian military forces, which had been in occupation of south-eastern France, naturally melted away. Subsequently, partisan movements became active in harassing the Germans on both sides of the Franco-Italian frontier. The Italian partisans and the French *maquis* were in close and friendly contact. Since these forces could only be sustained by the Allies, either from French or Italian territory, we were well acquainted with all that was going on.[1]

In the spring of 1945 regular French forces were being rapidly collected on the frontier, and the Italian Foreign Minister delivered to the Allied Commission a formal memorandum protesting against these developments. The Italian Government feared that the French intended to annex the Val d'Aosta and certain other territories east of the old border. Nevertheless, so long as the battle continued, Alexander felt, and with good reason, that if French troops could help to keep engaged a number of German divisions on this border it would assist him in the final battle which he was now fighting with forces hardly equal to the task. It was therefore agreed that regular French formations should move temporarily across the frontier as an operational need. Of the wisdom of this I had some difficulty in persuading the British and American Governments,[2] but I felt that Alexander was entitled in all the circumstances to any military assistance that he could obtain by these means. There had been no reason at this time to believe that when the Germans had been defeated, the French troops would not retire into French territory. When the time came, they did no such thing. They even penetrated beyond the limit of twenty kilometres which had been approved. Nor was the French intervention confined to the normal activities of military occupation. Strong efforts were made to promote in the civilian population a desire for annexation

[1] C. R. S. Harris, *Allied Military Administration of Italy, 1943–1945* (London, 1957), pp. 317–18.
[2] *The Blast of War*, pp. 690–1.

to France, and many somewhat dubious means were used to foment such a movement. French troops actually reached a point as far east as twenty kilometres west of Turin, and even reached Savona on the Ligurian coast.[1]

All this had taken place before General Clark's Fifth Army could arrive in these areas. As the Americans advanced, clashes seemed inevitable. Even before the final German defeat General Devers, commanding the Sixth Army Group, who had been in charge of the Allied landings in the south of France under General Eisenhower, ordered General Doyen, the commander of the French troops on the Franco-Italian frontier, to halt his offensive and withdraw as soon as was militarily possible. On 7 May General Eisenhower asked General Juin, the commander of the French forces in the field, to send firm instructions to this effect. After some delay a reply was received in rather intransigent terms. General Doyen argued that as active operations were now over, French troops no longer fell within the strategic sphere of General Eisenhower's command. The question of the frontier was no longer a military one; it must be dealt with 'on the diplomatic level'. Until the Governments decided, his troops would stand firm. Alexander, in commenting to the Combined Chiefs of Staff on this development, wisely added his view that the British and American Governments would have to act firmly in Paris if they were to achieve their purpose.

Meanwhile, the Fifth Army was ordered by Alexander to move forward as rapidly as possible. Allied Military Government was to be set up in all territory whether French-occupied or not, and a frontier control was to be established. Armed conflict should be avoided if possible. But pressure must be maintained. Nevertheless, it was clear that, so far as the French were concerned, the ultimate decision would rest with General de Gaulle, whose orders the local commanders would unswervingly obey.

During the weeks that followed the end of the campaign, this dispute caused Alexander and myself increasing trouble. But the final stages were not reached until after I had left Allied Force Headquarters. During the last days of May, General Doyen sent a

[1] Harris, p. 318.

disagreeable, and even menacing, message to the American General
Crittenberger, commanding IV Corps:

> I have been ordered by the Provisional Government of the
> French Republic to occupy and administer this territory. This
> mission being incompatible with the installation of any Allied
> administrative agency in the same region, I find myself obliged
> to oppose it. Any insistence in this direction would assume a
> clearly unfriendly character, even a hostile character, and could
> have grave consequences.[1]

On 2 June a still more intransigent communication was sent.
Alexander's reaction was rapid and decisive. He recommended
that the Combined Chiefs of Staff should instruct him 'to complete
the occupation of north-west Italy and to establish Allied Military
Government there, using force if necessary'.[1] Churchill had already
sent an appeal to President Truman asking for his support. But
he had no need to press Truman, who was already indignant over
this affair. He sent a personal message to de Gaulle, stating that
unless the French forces withdrew from north-west Italy, no more
equipment or military supplies of any kind would be given to the
French. This immediately produced the required result. De Gaulle
climbed down, and protested that there had never been any intention to oppose by force the presence of American troops in the
small areas occupied by the French east of the 1939 frontier. Juin
was sent to Alexander's headquarters to study the matter 'in the
broadest spirit of conciliation'.[2]

Finally, on 10 June an agreement was made that all French
troops should retire behind the 1939 frontiers by 10 July. Thus
what Churchill called a 'vexatious dispute' came to an end. But it
left an unpleasant taste. Moreover, considerable embarrassment
was caused to the Allied Military Government because during
these uncertainties the difficulty of disarming partisans in Piedmont
and Liguria had correspondingly increased.[3] On the other side, we
must admit that the French had, like ourselves, every reason to
feel bitterly against Mussolini's Italy. France, like Britain, had
been stabbed in the back. De Gaulle may have thought that, as in

[1] Harris, p. 320.
[2] Churchill, *Triumph and Tragedy*, p. 494.   [3] Harris, p. 321.

1859, the French were entitled to some price for the liberation of Italy. Yet on this occasion victory had been achieved primarily by British and American forces, who asked neither compensation nor reward.

The issues involved in the struggle over the north-east provinces were more serious and more dangerous. The territorial advantages gained by Italy after the First World War had been bitterly resented by many of the inhabitants of Udine, Venezia Giulia and Istria. Only the break-up of the Austro-Hungarian Empire and the firmness with which the Italian Government demanded their price for having abandoned their two allies led to the extension of the frontiers so far to the east. The Istrian peninsula was largely Croat. In Udine and Venezia Giulia the races were mixed, partly Slovene and partly Italian. The towns were mainly Italian, the hinterland Slovene.

We had been concerned with this problem as early as August 1944, when General Wilson, Alexander's predecessor, warned Tito that the Allies would require their own Military Government in the whole area, whatever might be the final peace settlement. As the campaign developed, it became clear that the Yugoslavs would in fact be in occupation of large parts of the territory in dispute. Alexander, although realising the political dangers, was also acutely aware of the military difficulties. A rough division of Venezia Giulia into two spheres, together with control of the city and port of Trieste and perhaps of Pola, would adequately safeguard his communications into Austria. But there was, of course, the risk that any such temporary division would prejudice the question of ultimate sovereignty. An alternative might be some joint occupation with Russia participating, on the analogy of the arrangements being made for Austria.

Eventually, after discussions with London and Washington which lasted all through the winter, the Americans maintained their strong objection to any solution except that of total occupation by the Allies. Alexander had for long been anxious for a direct discussion with Tito; but this had to be postponed. He still felt that the Combined Chiefs of Staff were evading the real problem: how were Tito's forces to be ejected from areas which they occupied? It was finally agreed that Alexander should meet Tito for a general discussion. But since Washington still demanded Allied Military Government in all the areas which had belonged to Italy in 1939, the Field-Marshal was forced to confine his conference to exploratory talks. Tito made it clear that he was only willing to grant our control of the necessary lines of communication and the operation of Allied Military Government within this zone, provided the Yugoslav civil administration, already or about to be installed, remained intact. He would probably be willing to place this under Allied Military Government. But he could not admit full Allied Military Government throughout. He particularly objected to the inclusion of the Istrian peninsula.

As the weeks passed, Tito's partisans were moving rapidly forward. At Allied Force Headquarters we began to feel that the only thing to do was to seize all the territory we could, including Trieste and the port of Pola; and to set up military government over as wide a territory as possible, operating wherever practicable through local groups, whether Italian or Yugoslav, at the same time informing Tito that any armed forces in the whole area must come under our command. But with this the Combined Chiefs of Staff were not satisfied. Peremptory orders were given on 28 April to occupy and administer the whole area. The Russian Government would be asked to bring pressure on Tito to withdraw. Nevertheless, before any actual conflict Alexander should communicate with the Combined Chiefs. This seemed to us a somewhat unrealistic approach.[1] Eden equally thought that these instructions could not be implemented, at least in their entirety, and so informed Edward Stettinius, now in charge of the State Department.

While our masters argued, Alexander decided to press his armies forward with the greatest possible speed. He informed Tito on 30 April of his intention to occupy Trieste and secure his lines of communication. In return, Tito informed the Field-Marshal of his own plans. He could not accept Allied troops or Military Government east of the Isonzo river. Sir Ralph Stevenson, our Ambassador in Belgrade, feared that a clash was unavoidable.

[1] *The Blast of War*, pp. 693-4.

But President Truman now became anxious, and the Americans seemed to be less firm than before. Churchill, meanwhile, tried to bring some pressure upon Tito by cutting off all military supplies, not a very effective weapon in the circumstances, for the partisans were well supplied not only with British equipment but with all that they had captured from both the Italians and the Germans.

Next came the question as to the approach to Russia. The President was very keen on this. Eden and I were on the whole against it. Stevenson, who kept admirably calm throughout this critical period, now believed that Tito did not wish to press things to an extreme. He also thought that there was an element of bluff in his protestations. Our discussions at Caserta were continuous through these days. I noted the position at the time as follows:

> Unfortunately, the Americans began by taking a very pedantic attitude. They thought we must occupy and govern all Venezia Giulia. . . . Last February, I think the F.M. when he visited Tito could easily have got a purely military agreement as to a line of demarcation between our forces and his. This would have given him Fiume and Pola, and us Trieste. Italian opinion would have been satisfied and things could have been kept quiet till some final peace settlement. I am not sure that this is now possible. . . . Now the Americans (through State Department) demand the whole. But the War Department wants to use *no* American troops and the President is beginning to take fright. Unless we are very careful, it will be another Greece—with us carrying the baby, as usual.[1]

I was still anxious for a direct agreement between our Headquarters and Tito on a purely military basis. But I began to fear that it would be too late: 'As usual, no instructions from U.S. and U.K. Governments—only vacillation or silence.'[1] However, the race for Trieste at least proved not unsatisfactory. General Freyberg, with his New Zealanders, had received the surrender of 7,000 Germans and was in occupation of the docks and harbour, while the Yugoslavs held the town. In a similar dash for Gorizia we were able to employ an

---

[1] 5–6 May 1945. These quotations are taken from a series of letters that I wrote home to my wife, and which were in effect a journal. Subsequent quotations from my journals and diaries are indicated in the footnotes by the date of the entry alone.

American division attached to the Eighth Army. This was a valuable piece of reinsurance, since all the burden would otherwise have had to be borne by British troops.

Alexander remained calm though anxious. He never wavered in expressing his view that the orders of the Chiefs of Staff, if interpreted literally, could not be carried out without force. But I continually urged him not to act without clear and unequivocal instructions endorsed by our Governments. There was now revealed one element in this tangle which might prove of importance. Stevenson in Belgrade reported that the Yugoslavs seemed not altogether sure of Russian support. The Russians had many clients to satisfy. We heard from Rome that a hint had been given to the Italian Government by the Soviet representative that his Government might be willing to mediate between the Italians and the Yugoslavs on the question of Trieste if the Italians would recognise the Polish Government at Warsaw. The Italians were also deeply interested in the fate of 100,000 prisoners held in Poland, yearning to return home. To secure their return would be a feather in the cap of Ivanoe Bonomi, the Italian Prime Minister. At the same time the Russians themselves realised that the question of the north-eastern frontier was putting the Italian Communists in a very unhappy position. Soon there would be elections in Italy, and many people thought that the Communists would prove the strongest party. Yet if they could be accused by their opponents of lack of patriotism over this question, to which all Italians attached so much importance, they would be much weakened. This situation was to be exploited by Bevin some years later over this very problem of Trieste. Meanwhile, could not this information somehow be leaked to the Yugoslavs?

On 7 May the situation was unchanged:

> The race continues. No incidents at present, but we have had to abandon any attempt to set up Allied Military Government even in those areas where our troops are. The Yugoslavs are in control, with a civil and military organisation. (All very like Greece!)[1]

A number of sharp messages now passed between Alexander and

[1] 7 May 1945.

Tito, each expressing astonishment at what the other was doing. Tito made no attempt to conceal his political motives and claimed that Venezia Giulia had been unjustly annexed by Italy after the First World War. However, he agreed to Alexander's proposal that their respective Chiefs of Staff should meet. Accordingly, on 8 May General Morgan went to Belgrade to see what he could effect. He was to propose a temporary military agreement dividing Venezia Giulia into two sections, with the Allied Military Government in the west and leaving the Yugoslavs to the east. Pola and Trieste must be in our control. Alexander, Morgan and I went over in detail what he should say and the arguments he should use. We were acting beyond, or even contrary to, our instructions, but by now we had some experience of this. However, events were taking charge.

The problem was indeed baffling:

> Neither British nor American troops will care for a new campaign in order to save Trieste for the 'Eyeties'. On the other hand, to give in completely may be a sort of Slav Munich.[1]

At the same time it was difficult to know exactly what advice to send to London. At the Commander-in-Chief's conference on 10 May there was a long discussion but little progress:

> The chief object of these large and formal conferences is that of a Cabinet—to let everyone know what is happening and have his say. A long dispute between Ambassador Kirk[2] and General McNarney[3] was very illuminating. The State Department violently anti-Tito and demanding strong action; the War Department much more temperate and thinking of the Far East.[4]

We had now received Tito's counter-proposals, which would meet our immediate military needs as regards communications. But they could obviously not be accepted as a whole by the Field-Marshal,

[1] 9 May 1945.
[2] Alexander Kirk combined the posts of American Ambassador to Italy and political adviser to SACMED.
[3] American second-in-command to Field-Marshal Alexander.
[4] 10 May 1945.

since they are founded on the political assumption that all territory east of the Isonzo is *de facto* and *de jure* under Yugoslav
sovereignty. He offers, in exchange, free user rights of Trieste
and the lines of communication and a kind of military 'condominium' [west of the Isonzo]. The rest of the area he claims,
and will occupy and govern himself.[1]

We decided to tell Tito that since he had raised a vital political
issue the matter was out of Alexander's hands and must be settled
by the Governments concerned. At the same time, our planners
were to set about a full military appreciation of the forces that would
be required in order to throw the Yugoslavs out altogether.

General Morgan returned on the afternoon of the same day,
much impressed by Tito's determination and strength of character.
Stevenson, however, still thought that Tito would not press his
demands to the point of war. Unfortunately, since his troops were
largely in possession, the responsibility was on our shoulders. The
spate of telegrams continued. In one of his messages to the Combined Chiefs of Staff, Alexander included a paragraph which I felt
would satisfactorily flutter the dovecotes in Washington:

> In the event of hostilities against Yugoslavia, I must know
> on what Divisions I can rely. I would be glad if you would
> consult the U.S., U.K., New Zealand, South African, Indian,
> Brazilian, Polish and Italian Governments.[2]

Sir Noel Charles, British Ambassador in Rome, began to fuss
about the possible fall of Bonomi and his Government over this
affair. I urged him to emphasise the other argument—the political
embarrassment of the Communists:

> If he plays his cards well, [Bonomi] can turn the tables on the
> Italian Communists. They are on the horns of a dilemma and
> they should be firmly impaled.[2]

I was becoming more and more anxious about the British position.
General McNarney, who in addition to his position as second-in-
command was responsible for the U.S. forces in the area, told me

---

[1] 10 May 1945.   [2] 11 May 1945.

quite frankly that his orders were not to allow himself to be embroiled in the Yugoslav row. Yet the State Department was taking exactly the opposite line.

At this time a new difficulty arose. The Yugoslavs were claiming and invading not only Italian but also Austrian territory, both in Styria and Carinthia. The Foreign Office had instructed Stevenson in Belgrade to request the withdrawal of their forces, since this area was to be in the proposed British zone of occupation. On this issue Eden sought support, both from the Russian and the American Governments. Truman expressed his determination to remain firm on both questions, and Churchill accordingly began to bring increasing pressure on Alexander.

Robust messages now began to pass between the President and the Prime Minister. But I had an uneasy feeling all the time that while Churchill would always be willing to take strong action, the Americans would shrink from it when it came to the point. In reality, the Americans had again begun to shift their ground. In his message of 12 May, the President demanded that Alexander must obtain 'complete and exclusive control of Trieste and Pola, the line of communication through Gorizia and Monfalcone, and of a big enough area to the east to ensure proper communication'. But this was by no means clear. On the face of it, the occupation of *all* Venezia Giulia, and of course of Istria, was tacitly abandoned.

I immediately sent a message to Churchill, repeating my doubts and emphasising the change of position:

> Many thanks for letting me see the President's telegram to you . . . of 12 May. This of course radically changes the position in which we have hitherto found ourselves here. On 10 May General McNarney, Deputy Theatre Commander, informed us categorically that he had specific instructions not repeat not to allow American troops to be involved in the Yugoslavian affair. There was some trouble about General McCreery[1] sending a battalion of the American Ninety-first Division which was under his command to Trieste.[2]

In spite of all this talk about refusing to yield to 'force, intimidation or blackmail', the President had in his last message suggested a *de*

---

[1] Commander of the Eighth Army.   [2] 13 May 1945.

facto arrangement on the lines that we could easily have negotiated in February and which had been rejected as weak and unprincipled. I could not resist a final sentence in my reply to Churchill:

> You will remember that the line to which the President refers is roughly the line which Field-Marshal Alexander wanted to negotiate with Tito in March. We then had to abandon this plan owing to American objections.[1]

Alexander had suggested that I should go up north and see what was really happening. Accordingly I left Caserta early on the morning of 12 May accompanied by Philip Broad, a member of my staff. We arrived at Treviso by 10.30 a.m., where I was met by General McCreery. We were joined by his Chief of Staff, Brigadier Floyd, and by Con Benson, the commander of the Military Government section. General McCreery was worried, and a little sore over his lack of information. I therefore gave him a full account of the situation with all its problems and difficulties. In return, he informed me of his position:

> Naturally, coming so soon after their victory, it is disappointing for them and their troops to find themselves in such a difficult and delicate situation. They are not allowed to exercise any authority by force of arms. So they have to sit by and watch the Yugoslavs set up a local government of their own, seize all the public buildings in the areas into which they have [been] and are still infiltrating, and conscript villagers, requisition food and transport and the like. Not only are they in effective control of the territory east of the Isonzo (we have a brigade in the dock area of Trieste, the Yugoslavs control the town) but they have also made A.M.G. unworkable in certain areas west of the river. The British soldier can only lean up against them (like the London policeman) and there are many more of them than of us.[2]

I had brought with me the relevant files, and showed the General the most recent interchange of telegrams from different capitals in the world. This at least was helpful from the psychological point of view, since it put the General and his staff in the picture.

After lunch we flew (by 'whizzers') to a strip near Monfalcone

[1] 13 May 1945.   [2] 12 May 1945.

where we were met by an old friend, General John Harding, formerly Chief of Staff at A.F.H.Q. and now commanding XIII Corps. He had installed himself in a splendid castle with a delightful garden and a wonderful view. General Harding was as usual firm, confident and robust. He did not like his position, since everywhere his troops were more or less on sufferance. But he thought he could, if necessary, maintain this uneasy balance for several weeks while negotiations proceeded. I got back to Eighth Army airfield by 7.20 p.m., feeling that at least these visits had done some good in explaining to the commanders in the field all the issues involved.

In the evening we drove to Venice. It was a great thrill to go down the Grand Canal, past the Casa d'Oro and the great Renaissance palaces, and stop opposite the Salute and Custom House—all happily intact.

The next day, Sunday 13 May, we flew to Klagenfurt in Austria.

> It was an absolutely perfect day—very hot indeed on the ground; nice and cool at about 10,000 feet. The flight across the Alps was really magnificent. The Apennines seemed like modest hills in comparison with these tremendous mountains, with their great jagged peaks and cliffs, some still snow-clad.[1]

At Klagenfurt we were met by General Keightley of V Corps and some of his staff. Klagenfurt and the district constitute

> a beautiful Alpine valley, of fair size, with lakes, etc., and Alpine fir plantations. The only access to the south lies through the great mountain passes and winding road which leads through Villach and Graz. Hence since the only effective line of communication into this part of Austria lies through these towns and is best served by Trieste (rather than Venice), the problem of our occupation of an Austrian zone is intimately linked up with that of Venezia Giulia.[1]

The Yugoslavs were claiming part if not all of the province of Carinthia. Believing possession to be nine-tenths of the law, they had raced us into Austria, just as they had raced us into Venezia Giulia. They actually reached Klagenfurt after us, so we had been

[1] 13 May 1945.

able to secure the best buildings and put sentries in them. But we had not enough men to guard every place.

> The Yugoslavs are bringing in considerable numbers, partly regulars and partly irregular forces—and repeating the Venezia Giulia tactics. We put up A.M.G. notices. They pull ours down and put up their own. They requisition and loot and arrest so-called Nazis and Fascists. We have to look on, more or less helplessly, since our present plan is *not* to use force and *not* to promote an incident.[1]

In this conflict for the possession of Klagenfurt and its surrounding area we had a few brigades to match 30,000–40,000 Yugoslavs. But there were other complications.

> [General Keightley] has to deal with nearly 400,000 surrendered or surrendering Germans, not yet disarmed (except as to tanks and guns), who must be shepherded into some place or other, fed and given camps, etc. On his right flank Marshal Tolbukhin's armies have spread into what is supposed to be the British zone in Austria, including the important city and road centre of Graz.[1]

With the Russians there were considerable Bulgarian forces, who added to the general confusion. Among the surrendering Germans there were about 40,000 Cossacks and White Russians, with their wives and children. These were naturally claimed by the Russian commander, and we had no alternative but to surrender them. Nor indeed had we any means of dealing with them had we refused to do so. But it was a great grief to me that there was no other course open. At least we obtained in exchange some 2,000 British prisoners and wounded who were in the area and had been in German hands. We also persuaded the Russians to deliver them immediately instead of sending them, as was the routine practice, through Odessa, which involved great personal hardship.

> We have already found a good number (I think over 1,000) British prisoners (many of them sick and wounded) in the Klagenfurt area. I watched the ambulances bringing them into

[1] 13 May 1945.

the airfield. They are flown straight away in Dakotas to Naples or other hospitals or camps in southern Italy.[1]

Among the refugees were many thousands of Ustashi or Chetniks (anti-Communist Yugoslavs), mostly with wives and children, fleeing in panic into the area in front of Tito's advancing troops. These included

> anything from guerrilla forces raised by the Germans from Slovenes and Croats and Serbs to fight Tito, and armed and maintained by the Germans; to people who, either because they are Roman Catholics or Conservative in politics, or for whatever cause are out of sympathy with revolutionary Communism and therefore labelled as Fascists or Nazis. (This is a very simple formula, which in a modified form is being tried, I observe, in English politics.)[1]

This visit impressed upon me once more the turmoil and misery resulting from war. It was heart-breaking; but we could do nothing to mitigate the suffering of all these unhappy people.

When I got back to Caserta on the evening of 13 May, I found that a joint Anglo–American declaration had been agreed and presented in Belgrade. On 17 May Tito replied to this Note. In effect, he merely reiterated the counter-proposals which he had already made to General Morgan. The position seemed to be drifting dangerously towards something like war.

Alexander, a few weeks before, had expressed his anxiety about the effect of any use of force on the morale of the troops under his command:

> Before we are committed I think it as well to consider the feelings of our own troops in this matter. They have a profound admiration for Tito's Partisan Army, and a great sympathy for them in their struggle for freedom. We must be very careful therefore before we ask them to turn away from the common enemy to fight an Ally.

But he now (18 May) believed that feeling against the Yugoslavs was growing stronger. Our troops did not like being pushed around. Nor did they relish their inability to intervene to prevent actions

[1] 13 May 1945.

that offended their sense of justice. After some discussion we both felt that Alexander should send a new signal to the Combined Chiefs setting out what he really meant by his reference to the morale. Apart from anything else, if we were to ask our soldiers to undertake this new task whole-heartedly, we must let them know what it was all about. B.B.C. and Press propaganda must be good. There must be no division in Britain—or, if possible, in America—as over Greece, and there must be absolutely clear instructions as to what forces were to be used and how far all the troops, of whatever nationality, were to be made available.

On 18 May I received a telegram instructing me to return to London. I arrived on the 19th and spent the next weekend at Chequers with the Prime Minister. But although many other subjects of great interest to me were discussed, this meeting did not greatly advance the situation with which I was chiefly concerned. I returned to Italy on 22 May.

While I was in England some indication had been received that the Yugoslav Vice-Premier, Kardelj, seemed ready for an accommodation and was anxious to open discussions on certain conditions. But since these were not regarded as satisfactory, Truman, with Churchill's approval, now sent a strong message to Stalin asking for his support. Stalin's reply, after arguing the Yugoslav case for the final settlement of the territorial dispute, and stating that the Yugoslav Army had a moral right to the occupation of the territory which they had captured from the enemy, made a not unhelpful suggestion:

> The following seems to me a just solution of this question. The Yugoslav armed forces and the Yugoslav administration now functioning in that region should remain on the spot. Simultaneously, supervision and control of the Allied Supreme Command should be established in this region, and a demarcation line defined by mutual agreement between Field-Marshal Alexander and Marshal Tito. By adopting these proposals the question of administration in the region of Istria—Trieste would also find a just solution.

In fact, he proposed a demarcation line—a solution which the Americans had appeared in some moods to favour.

Although during the next few days there were some unpleasant incidents–for instance the peremptory orders communicated by the commander of a Yugoslav division to a United States General to withdraw his forces (which was indignantly refused)–and a number of similarly belligerent communications between local commanders, I felt that with Stalin's message we were 'over the hump'.

On 21 May the Yugoslav Foreign Office sent a Note to the British and American Ambassadors in Belgrade in which–like the Americans–they in effect reversed their former policy. They now agreed on the establishment of Allied Military Government west of the demarcation line proposed. They made certain conditions as to the inclusion of Yugoslav officers in the military administration and the retention of military units in the area, although these would be under Alexander's command. They also demanded that the A.M.G. should operate through the civil authorities already set up in the area. No doubt the Russian Government, faced with a number of conflicting interests, had advised them to yield. Although the conditions as they stood were unacceptable, it needed less than three weeks' negotiation to reach a settlement.

In its final form, the agreement placed the portion of all Venezia Giulia west of the 'Morgan Line', as well as the port of Pola, under the Supreme Allied Commander. Any Yugoslav forces west of this line were to be withdrawn, except for a detachment of 2,000, who were to be under Alexander's command. It made clear that A.M.G. would be in full control of the Allied sectors, although use would be made of any civil administration which seemed to be working satisfactorily. Tito would withdraw all his regular forces from the Allied zones by 12 June, and all irregular forces would surrender their arms. It was also stipulated that the Yugoslav Government should return all former residents whom they had arrested or deported to the Allied area, and restore all property which they had confiscated or removed. It was finally declared that the agreement in no way prejudiced the ultimate disposition of the territories on either side of the line.[1]

This agreement was signed on 9 June. It is somewhat ironic to observe that after all these dangers and threats this settlement was

[1] Harris, p. 342.

almost exactly what could have been obtained in February, had it not been so summarily rejected by distant Governments in London and Washington unacquainted with the difficulties and dangers on the spot.

To finish the story, the Allied zone continued under Allied administration until the Peace Treaty with Italy in 1947, when, with the exception of Trieste, it became incorporated with Italy. The Yugoslav zone, as well as Pola, was at the same time annexed to Yugoslavia. But the problem of Trieste itself remained unresolved, and was a subject of international friction and negotiation for many years. Anglo-American occupation troops were still there almost ten years later; but at last, in October 1954, Italy and Yugoslavia agreed to rest content with the existing zones, and, subject to some minor border adjustments, the district was partitioned on lines very similar to those delineating the Military Government boundaries. Italian troops then replaced the Allied Forces in the Western Areas.

On my recent visit to England Churchill had told me of the approaching end of the Coalition and had offered me a post in the Government he proposed to form. Before leaving, there were many farewells to be made both in Rome and Naples. The next few days were spent largely in entertainments to this end. Among these was a party in our offices in the Palace of Caserta to all those British and Americans who had helped us in our work either at A.F.H.Q. or in the many proliferations of Anglo-American co-operation. All our staff—typists, cipherers, clerks, etc.—were included. Alexander came early and stayed to the end, thereby giving great pleasure to all.

The next day, 25 May, I flew to Rome in the early morning and at 11 a.m. was granted a farewell audience with Pope Pius XII, who presented me, on leaving, with a fine silver medallion.

> He is, of course, much concerned and saddened; the future seems dark. But one cannot help being impressed by his saintliness and goodness of heart. Poor, solitary figure![1]

[1] 25 May 1945.

I had also to take leave of my colleagues in the Allied Commission, British and American. After a farewell audience with Prince Umberto, the Regent, I called on Bonomi, the Italian Prime Minister.

> He doubts whether he will survive the present crisis, but he does not despair. Undoubtedly, the Trieste affair is a set-back to the Communists in Italy.[1]

On 26 May I left finally for home, accompanied by John Wyndham, who had been with me from the start to the finish of my strange adventure, and Robert Cecil, who had recently joined my staff.[2] My little party left in the Field-Marshal's Dakota from the airfield at 10 a.m.

> A very good send-off—the Field-Marshal and lots of officers, British and American, were at the airfield. It has been a great rush, but I think I have forgotten nobody. John and Robert have been excellent.[3]

After so long and so enthralling an assignment, the final scenes were rather saddening. At any rate it had been a unique experience.

> It is the end of a chapter—'Mediterranean merry-go-round or from DARLAN to TITO'.[3]

[1] 25 May 1945.   [2] *The Blast of War*, p. 705.   [3] 26 May 1945.

CHAPTER II

General Election, 1945

CHURCHILL, once engaged in a party battle, was a resolute and resourceful fighter. But, like his great ancestor Marlborough, he was not essentially a party man. Occupied all his life with great affairs, he was at his happiest in a Coalition of all parties or, at least, a concentration of moderate and central opinion. Before the First War he was concerned with Lloyd George and F. E. Smith[1] in tentative negotiations for the formation of a central Government to meet the growing German menace with a programme of military preparation. This must have involved agreed solutions of some of the issues which were so bitterly contested at the time between the two great parties. After the war he remained faithful to the second Coalition until it was broken up in 1922 by the decisive vote of the rank and file of the Conservative Party at the famous Carlton Club meeting.[2] Seeing the Liberal Party, for which he had abandoned his earlier Conservative allegiance on the Free Trade issue, weakened and divided as a result of the split between those who followed Asquith and those who supported Lloyd George, he had gradually moved back into the Conservative fold. In 1924, although nominally elected as a 'Constitutionalist', he was given high office in Baldwin's second administration. From 1931 onwards, when the National Government was formed from which he was excluded, he separated himself increasingly from the official Conservative hierarchy. As the German threat once more began to cast its dark shadow across Europe, he launched his campaign for rearmament and a strengthening of our old alliances. But he was to plough a lonely furrow. With but a small following in the House of Commons and without any organised support in the country, his career seemed doomed to end in frustration and failure. On the

[1] Later Lord Birkenhead.　　　　[2] *Winds of Change*, p. 128.

outbreak of the Second War in 1939 he joined Chamberlain's Government and served with characteristic loyalty until the collapse of that administration. But his finest hour, like that of the nation, was not to come until May 1940, when he was summoned by acclamation to the highest post as a truly national leader. For five years he presided over the greatest and most powerful Government in Britain's history. In the inscription on the bronze medal which he distributed to all those who had served with him, he rightly called this administration 'the Great Coalition'.

It is true that after Chamberlain's death in the autumn of 1940 he accepted, against the advice of a great part of the Press and many personal well-wishers, the leadership of the Conservative Party. He had not forgotten that in the closing years of his career Lloyd George was rendered politically impotent by the lack of any effective party at his disposal. Churchill was shrewd enough not to be deluded by those who at the moment of crisis rightly claimed him as a national figure above all parties. He knew that when the mood changed, the traditional system under which Britain had been so long governed would reassert itself. It would be wise for him, therefore, like a prudent general, to secure a firm base for the future. Nevertheless, at heart he cared little about parties as such. Like a great number of his countrymen his feelings were partly Conservative and partly Radical. His father's aims and ambitions were never out of his mind. If Lord Randolph's political career had ended in disaster, the son remained loyal to the main themes which had inspired the father.

Instinctively, therefore, as the end of the war approached, Churchill, although he accepted the necessity of a new Parliament to replace one elected nearly ten years before, would have preferred to postpone the election and carry on the Coalition till it had completed its tasks. Alternatively, he had visions of re-forming a central Government after the election had been fought. Had it resulted in only a narrow majority for either party, this might indeed have proved a feasible plan.

Already in the summer and autumn of 1944, when it was clear that the final defeat of Germany could not be far away, the thoughts of men both inside and outside the Government inevitably began to turn towards future political alignments. The attention of Cabinet Ministers themselves could not be wholly concentrated on the remaining tasks of the Coalition. The problems of reconstruction and the divergent points of view from which post-war questions would be approached occupied more and more of their attention. The more active party leaders like Attlee and Morrison could not fail to think in terms of a revival of the strength of their party, whose numbers in the existing House of Commons were clearly out of line with public opinion in the fighting services as well as among civilians. The more active partisans on the Left had for some time begun to agitate for freedom to pursue policies based on Socialist principles. Moreover, the Labour Party was still broadly based upon the trade unions, whose structure had been fully maintained and whose influence had been strengthened rather than weakened by the war, while the Conservative political organisation had almost melted away. It was clear therefore that an election, whatever its result, must increase the representation of the Labour Party in the House of Commons. The 1935 election had been held in conditions very unfavourable to Labour, and reflected the confusion in their ranks following Baldwin's ingenious tactics. Thus, as the months passed, the members of the Government began to separate themselves into their different groups. In Churchill's own words, 'Instead of being comrades in arms, we became rivals in power.'

In the autumn of 1944 it became necessary once more to prolong the life of the existing Parliament by legislation. At that time it was generally assumed that, although the German war would end by the spring of 1945 at the latest, to deal with the Japanese would take some eighteen months after the fall of Hitler. In moving the necessary Bill on 31 October 1944, Churchill declared that since this Parliament was already almost in its tenth year it would be wrong to prolong its life beyond the period of the German war. By these words, which I think he afterwards regretted, he committed himself more than was necessary or prudent. It would not have been unreasonable for the Coalition to continue until the defeat of the Japanese; and, as Churchill himself pointed out, it would be possible during this period to carry forward an ambitious and agreed programme of reform and social progress. The preliminary steps had been taken, even under the stress of war. Comprehensive plans had been widely publicised by the Beveridge Plan and the White Paper on Full Employment, as well as other wide-ranging declarations of policy. To have presided over the fruition of these projects would have been Churchill's natural desire. As he observed with some candour in his autumn speech, he found the Coalition Government very satisfactory: 'Having served for forty-two years in this House I have never seen any Government to which I have been able to give more loyal, confident and consistent support.' Nevertheless, his words were on the record limiting the life of the Parliament to the period of the German war.

When I was at Chequers on my short visit in May, I found that there was more discussion about this problem than of my anxieties about Venezia Giulia. There was only a small party on the first night—Churchill, Lord Cherwell and I, together with Jock Colville, one of the private secretaries:

> At dinner a lot of talk—chiefly on the political situation at home. The P.M. has written a letter to Attlee, suggesting that the Coalition should go on till *after* the Japanese war. If necessary, a referendum to take place on the question of continuing the life of Parliament. The letter was produced and read. . . .[1]

At that time Churchill believed that Attlee and Bevin, especially the latter, would be able and willing to carry such a plan through the Labour Party conference. I was not so hopeful:

> I do not believe it. The Labour Party are much more suspicious of Bevin than of Churchill.[1]

When I returned to Chequers two days later, Attlee's answer had come:

> P.M.'s proposal to continue the Coalition has been rejected. Of course they want an October election; but it is quite impossible to go on till then, with a Government in effect in dissolution. Winston was hurt at the unnecessarily waspish and even offensive tone of Attlee's reply. It arrived during dinner. . . .
>
> Most of the evening was spent in drafts and re-drafts for the P.M.'s reply to Attlee, at which we all tried our hand.[2]

[1] 19 May 1945.   [2] 21 May 1945.

In rejecting Churchill's plan of holding together until the end of the Japanese war, Attlee made a counter-proposal, in which he made it clear that they were only prepared to go on until October. Still believing that the Japanese would hold on for at least another eighteen months, Churchill was deeply disappointed. The alternative, which was strongly urged by leading Conservatives, was an immediate election. This would be better than an uneasy five months of electioneering. From June to October was too short a time to achieve any effective work upon the home front by way of legislation; yet it was too long to keep Ministers, Members and, above all, the nation in a condition of political tension, increasing week by week. Apart from any considerations of party advantage as to the state of the rival political organisations, Churchill was surely right to decide that if an election must come in 1945, the sooner the better.

Curiously enough, the early collapse of Japan in August 1945 made the whole argument seem in retrospect unnecessary and pointless. Attlee naturally complained that we were rushing the election, to which Churchill equally naturally replied that so far from rushing it he was prepared not only to grant the normal twenty days between dissolution and polling, but an additional three weeks' notice.

Difficult as it is for a party Government to operate effectively under the shadow of an approaching election, it would be almost impossible for a Coalition to do so. Moreover, there were great issues at home and abroad that required resolute decisions. These could only flow from a Government conscious of its power and able to rest upon the full strength of a Parliamentary majority. Of course there was an awkward period to be got through. Churchill handed his resignation to the King on behalf of himself and the whole Government on 23 May. Since there was a Conservative majority of some 180 over all parties combined, the task of forming a new administration was entrusted to Churchill. Although its composition was mainly Conservative, the Prime Minister did his best to give it a less partisan flavour by the retention of non-political figures such as Sir John Anderson, Lord Leathers, Sir Andrew Duncan, Lord Woolton, Sir James Grigg, Sir Arthur Salter and Lord Cherwell.

Gwilym Lloyd George also remained and certain others of strong Liberal traditions, such as Ernest Brown, William Mabane, and Leslie Hore-Belisha. Thus it was by no means a wholly Tory Government that succeeded the Great Coalition. Unluckily, it was immediately dubbed by the discouraging title of the 'Caretaker' Government.

While I was at Chequers, Churchill suggested I should become Minister of Labour, but I said that I thought I had been too much out of politics for the last two or three years for such a post. However, I left it to him. In the event, I found myself Secretary of State for Air. The Cabinet appointments were out the very day that I left Italy for good.

It has often been stated that Churchill was under heavy pressure from Beaverbrook and Brendan Bracken to insist upon the break-up of the Coalition, the formation of a broadly Conservative Government and an immediate dissolution. But Morrison was clear that there could be no question of extending the Coalition after the defeat of Germany. It is true that he records that Bevin was on Churchill's side, and that Bevin came out in the Labour Party executive in favour of Churchill's scheme.[1] But Attlee and Morrison were easily able to get their way. Certainly Churchill never ceased to hanker after the continuance of the Coalition. That was what he really wanted and honestly thought would be best for the country, as perhaps it might have been. But once that plan was rejected, his intimates were equally right to press for an early election. Any other course would have proved intolerable and unworkable.

Although polling took place on 5 July, the results could not be declared until the 26th, because of the difficulties about counting the Service vote. My tenure, therefore, of my new office lasted for two months, much of which was taken up in electioneering. It was clearly impossible, indeed improper, to attempt anything more than day-to-day administration. Owing to my many contacts with the Air Force in the course of the Mediterranean campaign, I found myself happy in my post. I was indeed proud to be responsible for so great a department, and the administration of such a magnificent

---

[1] Lord Morrison of Lambeth, *Herbert Morrison: An Autobiography* (London, 1960), pp. 234-5.

Service. But there was nothing much to be done in the way of forward planning.

I made one interesting and pleasant visit to the Air Force in Germany and renewed many old contacts. I was hospitably entertained by their commander, Air Marshal Coningham. I was also able to see something of Eisenhower and Tedder on my way back through Paris.

But these eight weeks were an unhappy interlude. I felt myself almost a stranger at home, and it was so long since I had given any thought to political questions in the narrow sense that I was a little at sea. For two and a half years I had concentrated on urgent daily tasks at the Ministry of Supply and at the Colonial Office. Then for another two and a half years I had struggled with the baffling and tortuous problems that presented themselves in novel and unprecedented conditions, with strange conflicts and excitements, in North Africa, Italy, Greece, Yugoslavia. Even during recent months I had neither the leisure nor the inclination to read the Government White Papers about the new reconstruction plans. I was remote from the influence of the political issues which were beginning to be discussed at home and the atmosphere of electioneering which was developing. When I found myself a member of the new Government there was a certain flatness and frustration. The Prime Minister was away at Potsdam, dealing with enormous questions of which we heard only distant and occasional echoes. Cabinets were few and uninspiring. We knew that we were indeed 'caretakers' and that our main task was to do our best to keep the house in order until the duly elected tenant—whoever he might be—returned to claim his rights.

Nevertheless, the Government had a good reception from the Press as a whole, and the general view prevailed that the Conservatives would be returned to power by a small majority—something between thirty and fifty. Even the Labour leaders did not anticipate the landslide which actually took place. I was quite unable, after so long an absence, to form any opinion. I had received a request from the Foreign Office, shortly before I left Italy, to forecast the likely result of the referendum on the future of the monarchy. I replied by saying that if the Foreign Office would tell me who would win the next General Election at home, I would do my best to risk a similar prophecy about public opinion in Italy. I received no answer.

While I was in Italy I had received a very tempting invitation to abandon Stockton in favour of an absolutely safe seat—St. George's, Westminster. This flattering proposal was made to me unanimously by the committee concerned. But the same reasons which had actuated me fifteen years before at Hitchin[1] weighed with me now. Moreover, it is one thing to look for another seat after dismissal at the hands of the electors. This had been my position in 1929, and I had every right to seek another constituency. Even then, after much thought I decided to return to my old love. The experiment had been successful; I was re-elected in 1931 and again in 1935. It was quite another thing to give up Stockton without even a fight. It did not take me long to make up my mind. Accordingly, I wrote a letter to the chairman of the St. George's Conservative Association expressing my gratitude but declining the invitation. This decision was formally announced on 26 April, and on the same day I sent a letter which was read to a meeting of the organisation in Stockton, stating that if it was in accordance with the wishes of my friends in Stockton and Thornaby, I would be proud to offer myself for re-election when the time came. Meanwhile, I must remain at my post overseas.

Although at the time of my decision I did not foresee how formidable would be the swing to Labour, I felt in my own mind doubtful of my personal success. For five years I had been forced to neglect the constituency. Although all necessary correspondence and the details of individual requirements of my constituents were dealt with by my secretary and with the help of fellow Members, my visits to Stockton had been rare, even when I was working in London. During the last two and a half years when I was abroad I only managed to appear on one occasion. My wife had worked hard and with her usual devotion. But a Member's prolonged absence, even on duty, is not understood or forgiven. In addition, our local organisation had almost completely disappeared in the turmoil of war. However, I had such a fondness for the North-East Coast that

[1] *Winds of Change*, pp. 251–2.

I thought I would at any rate wait to be turned out. I did not like the idea of running away.

As soon as electioneering began in earnest I knew what the result would be. Three weeks of campaigning passed quietly, much too quietly. My meetings were well attended, but dull and uneventful. This was my sixth contest in the constituency, and it had been my experience that when my opponents felt confident of victory they treated me with special courtesy and consideration. Questions were few, interruptions negligible. When, however, they began to think it not unlikely that they would lose, or when as the election proceeded they began to face defeat, the atmosphere changed. The meetings became rowdy and violent. On such occasions it was often impossible to speak except by a series of replies to questions. Enthusiasm grew on both sides; parades of supporters marched through the streets; a sense of excitement developed. Since the wireless played a comparatively small part and television none, in the average constituency the local fight was insulated from outside interference. Nevertheless, in some mysterious way waves of emotion to the Left or to the Right usually followed the same general pattern throughout the country.

We carried through the campaign as best we could, but I had little hope of success. Many people believed that Churchill's first speech on the wireless was a turning-point to our disadvantage. It was certainly unbalanced and ill-advised. He prophesied a growing control of all our lives if the Socialists won. He attributed to the ultimate realisation of Socialism in Britain the kind of political features that we associated with the Gestapo. But the use of this terrible word in connection with his opponents was a grievous error. Moreover, it was easy to deride as an outrage the implied attack on colleagues with whom he had been working in perfect amity for the last five years—men of moderate opinions such as Attlee, Morrison and, above all, Bevin. Of course, if this passage was studied quietly and carefully its meaning was clear. Churchill was only saying what he believed to be the inevitable result of a system of State control developed with increasing ruthlessness over a period of years. Churchill had been much impressed by some foolish statements of Professor Laski's, who held an important position in the executive of the Labour Party but carried little weight with any of the leading Labour politicians. He had been fortified in his apprehensions by reading Professor Hayek's *The Road to Serfdom*. Thus, with his usual artistry, he painted what seemed to many a fantastic picture of the future. Whether it would seem quite so exaggerated to a later generation may perhaps be doubted. But at the time it shocked as well as angered ordinary folk. I do not believe, however, that this incident was in any way decisive. The election, in my view, was lost before it started.

Churchill was buoyed up by the enthusiastic reception which he received in his thousand-mile electoral tour. Vast crowds, who had hardly seen him in person since the beginning of the war and had only heard his voice through those famous broadcasts, by which they had been sustained in times of disaster and inspired at moments of success, turned out in flocks to see and applaud him. They wished to thank him for what he had done for them; and in that all were sincere. But this did not mean that they wished to entrust him and his Tory colleagues with the conduct of their lives in the years that were to follow. They had been persuaded, civilians and Service-men alike, during the last years of the war, that immediately the struggle was over there would follow a kind of automatic Utopia. The British people would move with hardly an effort into a Socialist or semi-Socialist State under their own leaders, which would bring about unexampled prosperity in a world of universal peace. Nor had they forgotten or been allowed to forget the years before the war. Pamphlets and books attacking the 'guilty men of Munich' were published and circulated in vast numbers. It was not Churchill who lost the 1945 election; it was the ghost of Neville Chamberlain.

The drabness of the election continued until the closing scenes. Instead of a declaration of the poll to cheering crowds in the High Street between 11 p.m. and midnight on polling day, we had to wait for three weeks. Then the candidates, accompanied by a few of their friends, went to the Town Hall in the afternoon to hear the result. No crowds, no enthusiasm; it was a dull formality.

At least the figures in my case were decisive. There was nothing that I could have done which would have altered the result. My Labour opponent, George Chetwynd, a young man of conspicuous charm and distinction, who had served in the Army Education Corps, was well known in the constituency. He won easily, by a majority of 8,664 votes. (Incidentally, my son Maurice, who stood in a hopeless fight at Seaham against Emanuel Shinwell, did relatively better than most of us.) Discouraged, but not surprised, my wife and I returned to London on the night train as we had so often done before. At any rate my record was not lacking in a certain symmetry. In the course of twenty-two years I had fought six elections at Stockton. I had won three and lost three. I have since observed of this experience that when one loses an election one is apt to become sceptical of the value of the democratic system, based on a universal franchise. 'Counting noses! What a way to elect the Government of a great empire.' But when one wins, there is quite another feeling. 'I always knew,' declares the victorious candidate, 'that the British people were sound at heart.' Such at any rate are the vagaries of political life.

The next day the Cabinet met at No. 10–a rather grim affair. Against 166 Labour Members in the old Parliament there were now 393. The 398 Conservatives had fallen to 213. The Labour triumph had indeed been overwhelming. There were no excuses and no post-mortems. Churchill seemed still somewhat dazed by the blow, but not a word of recrimination escaped him. I felt that he owed no apology to the party. It was not he who had dragged us down. It was we who had somehow hoped to get through by cling-ing to his coat-tails. As to the future, we could only wait upon events. Churchill himself recalls his wife's consoling thought: 'It may well be a blessing in disguise.' He replied, 'At the moment it seems quite effectively disguised.'[1] Nevertheless, I soon began to feel that she was right. The immediate post-war years were bound to be a period of serious economic and financial difficulty at home and of grave problems abroad. In both spheres it may well be that by a sound instinct the British people felt that it would be wiser for a Government of the Left to be in control. Certainly, so far as the Russian threat was concerned, the last-minute change by which Bevin went to the Foreign Office instead of the Treasury was provi-dential. He would be disappointed, but he would be firm. Stalin

[1] Churchill, *Triumph and Tragedy*, p. 583.

would not be at all impressed by what must have seemed to him a pinkish type of Socialism. But Bevin would not be bullied. If many mistakes were to be made in the ensuing years in other fields, some changes were brought about which could not and ought not to be reversed. At the same time the electors were to learn many salutary lessons. They would soon be ready for a more pragmatic and less doctrinaire approach to the nation's difficulties.

The loss of my seat was naturally a personal blow, all the more because it was clear that it would end my long association with the North-East Coast. Both my wife and I had made genuine friendships with many people in every walk of life, and formed a real affection for the industrial North. I seriously considered whether I should try to find another seat, or accept the position and confine my future activities to the family business with which I had been so long connected. I was fifty-one years old. I had not very happy recollections of party politics before the war. During the war I had been lucky to have played a minor but not insignificant part in great events. Prudence and personal convenience seemed to recommend 'calling it a day'. However, I soon began to reflect upon the strange experiences through which I had passed before and during the war, and upon the feelings which had urged me to enter politics after the First War. So I became determined to continue if at all possible. It seemed to me that the problems which lay ahead, although frightening in their magnitude, were fascinating in their perplexities. Large and almost unprecedented as was the Labour majority, it would not be likely to last for more than one or at the most two Parliaments. I might still have an opportunity to serve. In this decision I was encouraged by Churchill, who ridiculed my hesitations, and confidently set about the last phases of his own political career at the age of seventy.

Accordingly, with the help of Churchill and the Conservative Central Office, my name was put forward for a seat which had suddenly and tragically become vacant by the death of the recently elected Member. This was the constituency of Bromley, Beckenham and Penge, which had long been represented by Sir Edward Campbell. Although his majority had fallen from 27,941 in 1935 to a mere 6,259, and in view of the general and no doubt continuing swing the seat could not be regarded as absolutely secure, yet it was as good a chance as I was likely to get. The local committee were already searching for a successor. After some manœuvring and the generous withdrawal by Randolph Churchill in my favour from the list of aspiring suitors, I was duly nominated as prospective candidate at the end of August. Since the local organisation was still very weak, it was thought wiser not to apply for the writ until later in the year. Several months of hard preparatory work followed. With my wife's help we began to make new friends and had everywhere a most generous reception. But it was a very different kind of constituency, and we found some difficulty in adjusting ourselves. It was also very large, covering Beckenham and Penge in addition to Bromley. Before the next General Election two seats were carved out of it, and Bromley became smaller in size and electorate and thus more manageable.

The by-election when it came was rather anxious work. I decided to stand unashamedly on my old pre-war views, and circulated as my election address a pamphlet based on *The Middle Way* and other pre-war writings. This no doubt puzzled the electors, but I think impressed them. The only dramatic incident was a visit by Churchill from Chartwell, for which I was grateful. He drove to my headquarters, where he made a short speech. In his tour of the constituency he was received with tempestuous enthusiasm. When the polling was declared the vote was not dissimilar from that of the General Election. Sir Edward Campbell had polled 26,108 votes. I polled almost the same—26,367. The Liberal and Labour votes had divided somewhat differently, and a large proportion of Liberals had clearly abstained. My majority, therefore, was 700 less than Sir Edward's; but at 5,557 it was quite satisfactory.

When I came to take my seat in the House on 20 November, I was introduced not by the Whips (as is the usual practice) but by Harry Willink, ex-Minister of Health, and Harry Crookshank, ex-Postmaster-General. Both of them had been at Eton with me, in the same election to College, and both were valued friends. This was a repetition of a procedure which Crookshank and I had adopted for Willink five years previously. I do not think there has ever been a case of three exact contemporaries as Eton Scholars sitting in two successive Parliaments and being Members of two successive Governments. So we thought we would celebrate by this gesture so unusual an event.

I missed, of course, the earlier and turbulent scenes when the House had met with its overwhelming Labour majority. No wonder they believed so fervently that they would be in power for twenty years or more. No wonder they sang the 'Red Flag' with such enthusiasm. No wonder one of the new Ministers so exuberantly declared, 'We are the masters now.'

Some of the younger members of our party, both in and outside the House, indulged in the usual recriminations that follow defeat and seemed almost to fear that the new House of Commons would prove the end of Parliamentary government. But the older hands, including, of course, our experienced leader, knew better. 'What goes up, must come down,' or, in Canning's famous phrase, 'I do not fear firebrands in this House. As soon as they touch its floor they hiss and are extinguished.'

PART TWO

Opposition

1945–1951

CHAPTER III

Parliamentary Personalities

D ISRAELI wrote in 1868, after the defeat of the Conservatives following his first short Premiership, 'there are few positions less inspiriting than those of a discomfited party.' He had certainly good reason to know the disappointments and troubles which face every Opposition leader. For with two short intervals he had spent twenty years or more of his life in this depressing task. Indeed, it is a tragedy that the only man of genius among the politicians of his century should not have reached real power until he was too old either to enjoy it or to use it to the full.

With Churchill it was different. Although he was seventy when he adopted this new role, he could look back with a satisfaction vouchsafed to few men to five laborious but splendid years of a unique Premiership. Defeated at the polls, he was still enthroned in the hearts of the voters. Although Churchill's appeal for continued support had been answered favourably by only two-fifths of the electors, yet what seemed a crushing political defeat was not a personal censure. Throughout the campaign the Liberals, the Independents and even the Labour candidates were anxious to pose as his admirers. If they attacked the Conservatives, it often suited them to do so by quoting from Churchill's pre-war speeches. It was almost certain that under a presidential system Churchill would have been triumphantly returned to power. In many parts of the country—so it was said—the electors were persuaded that they could vote for Liberal and Labour candidates without in any way interrupting the continued Premiership of Churchill. It was, at any rate, by such arguments that we tried to comfort him in the first moments of disappointment. By the time, however, that I had got back to the House of Commons, Churchill had begun to settle down to his new duties.

One of the melancholy aspects of Opposition, especially to anyone who has enjoyed high office and likes responsibility and power,
is the sense of futility. After a similar rebuff Disraeli wrote to a
friend, 'Kicking against the pricks is neither dignified nor useful.'
Therefore he thought the Opposition's part should be 'one of reserve
and quiescence'. Nor was he easily moved from this attitude. A
powerful Government with a large majority could not be destroyed
by the Opposition any more easily in 1945 than in 1868. Gradually
it might destroy itself; but while the Parliamentary fight had to be
continued with reasonable assiduity it was in the country that the
test would come. Churchill was determined to fight his way back to
power, however long and arduous the struggle might prove. When
he had to leave Downing Street, he was without a London home.
But he soon got himself established in a charming house in Hyde
Park Gate which he was to occupy until his death. For the purposes
of his office and secretaries he bought the house next door, and
soon, as was always his custom in or out of power, a private office
began to be organised on a generous scale. It soon became a hive of
activity.

When he settled in Hyde Park Gate, Churchill was always
explaining to us its proximity to the House of Commons. He
seemed to fear lest we felt his living so far away might indicate an
attitude of remoteness. 'I assure you,' he would tell me many times,
'I can get to the House in under fifteen minutes.' However, as if to
compensate for this laxity, on the days on which he entertained his
colleagues or at periods when late nights or special pressure might
be expected in the House, he moved to what he called his 'forward
headquarters'—a large and no doubt expensive suite in the Savoy
Hotel. I think he felt that this gesture got him nearer to the battle,
and with his 'forward headquarters' in Westminster, as opposed to
his 'rear headquarters' in Kensington, he was following the example
of Alex or Monty in their caravans.

Churchill's leadership of the Opposition was neither exclusive nor
all-absorbing. He had plenty of other things to do. There were
world problems, chiefly the growing menace of Russia, which
occupied much of his thoughts. There were the six volumes of the
great history of the Second World War to be planned and written.

(The first five volumes were actually completed before he returned to office in 1951.) There were pictures to be painted. There were holidays to be enjoyed. Some of his energy was devoted to physical recovery which, even with his strong constitution, was necessary after the fearful demands of five years of war. But this did not prevent him from becoming one of the planners and promoters of a completely new venture—the European Movement.

In the House of Commons Churchill's prestige, although shaken, was still strong. He did not make the mistake of too many interventions, either by formal speeches or at Questions. When in the mood, his interruptions could be frequent, truculent, and sometimes embarrassing to those who confused greatness with pomposity and did not realise the schoolboy element in their hero's character.

In every Parliament the House of Commons soon develops a special character of its own. This is indefinable, subtle, but real. It is necessary, in order to manage it effectively as a Government or appeal to it with success as an Opposition, to study and understand its peculiar and distinctive moods. The Parliament of 1945 must have recalled to Churchill something of the Parliament of 1906, when the Radical tide had swept all before it. The Labour Members enjoyed the giddy experience of unexpected triumph. They were proud, overweening, offensive and ungenerous—looked at from our point of view. Looked at from their own, they were 'exalted, dedicated, walking on air, walking with destiny'.[1] Although the first enthusiasms gradually began to wear off under the dull routine of Parliamentary life, with its slow formalities, it was a House impatient of anything that seemed to recall the traditional methods either of conduct or of debate. It was intolerant of lengthy speeches, however eloquent, delivered in the old Parliamentary style. Nor was this spirit confined to the dominant party. Churchill found it at first difficult to adapt himself to the changed conditions. He would deliver from time to time a long oration—a set piece—that would have been received with attention and applauded with rapture only a few months before. But its form was sometimes too ponderous and even the attacks or rebukes too stylised to please this assembly, so large a part of which were wholly unaccustomed to the usages or

[1] Hugh Dalton, *Memoirs, 1945–1960: High Tide and After* (London, 1962), p. 3.

methods of Parliament. Moreover, the Prime Minister, Attlee, who seldom spoke for more than twenty minutes, had adopted a low tone in speaking, with a simplicity verging on banality and a certain pawkiness which proved very acceptable to his followers and seemed much in the spirit of the new approach to affairs. On the occasion of a vote of censure or a similar attack on the Government by the Opposition he usually managed to follow the first speaker. Churchill would generally open with a speech of great vigour and nobility, often illuminated by some novel and suggestive concepts, with here and there a touch of inimitable humour. But it was too carefully composed, too classic, and above all too long. When Attlee got up to answer he was unexpectedly effective, like a small boy successfully puncturing with a few darts or stones a ponderous balloon. Beneath his curiously matter-of-fact and pedestrian replies, the whole great Churchillian fabric began to waver and collapse. Before his sarcastic and down-to-earth approach, imagination, romance, grandeur seemed to wither away.

On one of these occasions, while the Government's reputation was still very high and the beautiful morning had not yet begun to be overclouded by the fogs of trouble at home and abroad, Churchill had delivered a well-rehearsed and much advertised attack, only to be put aside—his arguments not answered but disregarded—by just such a technique from Attlee as I have described. When we went into the smoking-room to the table at which Churchill always sat, and several Members gathered round him, I could see that he was depressed, angered and puzzled by what had happened. He knew that he had made a fine speech to which he had devoted a great deal of thought and work. But it had misfired. Somehow Attlee, with hardly a finished sentence or a sentiment of any value, had outmanoeuvred him. At this point a popular, but not always tactful, member of our party joined us. 'Don't you think it is extra-ordinary, Mr. Churchill, how tremendously Attlee has come on? It is quite remarkable. Look at his speech today. He has come on tremendously.' 'Oh, you think so,' replied Churchill, in a gruff voice. 'Yes indeed, Prime Minister, I mean Mr. Churchill. Attlee has come on in an extraordinary way.' 'Oh,' answered Churchill. 'Have you ever read Maeterlinck, Major?' For this clumsy if candid friend had, naturally, that military rank. 'Oh no, I have not read Maeterlinck.' (Indeed, I doubt whether he had ever heard of Maeterlinck.) 'Well, if you read Maeterlinck,' was the answer, 'you will learn that if you feed a grub on royal jelly you may turn it into a queen bee.' Never was the effect of power on personality better described. Churchill was comforted. But the Major seemed puzzled.

The House of Commons before and immediately after the Second War was less highly organised or regimented than it is today. Nowhere was this more marked than in the conduct of the Opposition. There were a number of advisers to the leader (often a former Prime Minister), which the Press had christened after 1929 by the name of 'Shadow Cabinet'. But its members were not—as in a real Cabinet—allocated to particular posts. In selecting this body Churchill followed the traditional system, for he was a great believer in precedent. It consisted of Privy Councillors who sat by right on the Opposition front bench. Others, not Privy Councillors, he gradually promoted; or, since our numbers were so thin at the beginning of the Parliament before such defeated ex-Ministers as Bracken, Richard Law and I began to get back, one or two were asked to help from the very start. All these met each Wednesday in the Leader of the Opposition's room to discuss the immediate business and to allocate the different tasks accordingly. The chief members were, from the Commons: Eden, Oliver Stanley, Oliver Lyttelton, R. A. Butler, 'Shakes' Morrison (afterwards Speaker), Harry Crookshank, Lord Winterton, Ralph Assheton, James Stuart, David Maxwell Fyfe and I; from the Lords, Salisbury, Swinton and Woolton. In addition, Sir John Anderson, although unwilling formally to enrol himself as a Conservative in view of his long and distinguished career as a public servant, generally joined our counsels. But none of us were designated by the title of 'Shadow' Minister of this or that. In the work of dealing with the main Bills, both on Second Readings and in Committee as well as in more general debates, some of us concentrated on particular issues. In foreign affairs Anthony Eden naturally took the lead in the House of Commons and Salisbury in the Lords. Financial and economic questions were divided between Stanley,

Lyttelton, Butler and me. But there was no precise or exclusive designation. The incongruity of calling someone 'Shadow' Minister of Transport or 'Shadow' Postmaster-General was avoided. The new fashion, which has sometimes included appointing even Shadow' Under-Secretaries, was adopted by the Labour Party in their long years of Opposition from 1951 to 1964, and was later followed by the Conservatives. There are grave disadvantages in this formality. Only from the Opposition benches is it possible for Members, including ex-Ministers, to speak on a whole variety of subjects. The chief compensation for a party being in Opposition is that it can train individuals in a wide range of subjects, so that they obtain practice and experience over a broad field. In office men have to be, to some extent, circumscribed within the walls of their own Ministry. Out of office let them wander free and unencumbered. This at least was Churchill's plan. Once a fort-night he entertained us—about fourteen in all—at an imposing luncheon at the Savoy Hotel. This sometimes took the place of and was sometimes followed by the more formal Wednesday meet-ing. Naturally conversation was sometimes more about the im-mediate past than about the immediate future; but these were occasions not to be forgotten, forever cherished by those few who can remember them, where we could enjoy the genius as well as the hospitality of our beloved leader.[1]

Nevertheless, there were, as was no doubt to be expected in view of the magnitude of our defeat, some grumbles. Some complained of the laxity of Churchill's attendance at the House. He certainly did not think it necessary to intervene every day at Questions or to make a statement in the country every weekend. These were, of course, the days before television and the fashion for 'instant' politics. Others thought he had lost touch with the House and that his speeches no longer struck a modern note. Yet as he gradually attuned himself to the spirit of the new House and when he spoke in the country, more especially at the great party conferences, his power and authority were easily re-established. Sometimes even his closest friends deplored his love of a verbal tussle, either with the Speaker or with Herbert Morrison, the Leader of the House.

[1] *Winds of Change*, p. 29.

The Bromley by-election, 1945
'The only dramatic incident was a visit by Churchill'

Conservative leaders in Opposition
Macmillan, Salisbury, Crookshank, Woolton, Maxwell Fyfe, Eden, Butler

Whether he was successful, or—as often happened—worsted in these engagements, the boyish enthusiasm with which he plunged into these affrays disarmed criticism. He loved a good Parliamentary row. Nor was there any occasion, whether in public speech or private conferences, which was not illumined by some pregnant phrase which showed how carefully he was studying the present and the future in the light of the past. In many ways this old man was the youngest and the most up-to-date of us all.

Throughout these years, Churchill remained the dominant figure in Britain, in Europe and in the United States. Many of his Parliamentary speeches, especially those on the broad themes in which he took the deepest interest—Europe, Russia, America—found a responsive audience, even in a House so dominated by his opponents, and a wide circulation outside. In the realm of foreign affairs, while sometimes critical in detail, he proved a firm supporter of the main policies for which Bevin struggled so stoutly. On economic and financial questions Churchill's interventions were not so happy. He could always make fine 'knock-about' speeches in the old Parliamentary style and thus do much to restore the spirits of his own supporters inside and outside the House. But stripped of the splendid phraseology, the content seemed often uncreative and unimaginative, in marked contrast to his contributions on wider issues. In reality his general views on economic affairs had not substantially changed from those he had absorbed from his Victorian upbringing. While he was always ready to study new ideas, and generously accepted the suggestions of his followers, he was not capable or desirous of initiating new concepts of financial, monetary or economic policy. He could certainly criticise with vigour the results of the Government's action or inaction. But he seemed less able to enquire effectively into the roots of our maladies or to propose novel remedies. It was clear that his chief prescription was to turn out the Government as soon as possible; form a new one himself; collect round him all the most intelligent people he could find; and somehow deal with the problems of peace as he had attacked those of war. Thus this indomitable old man continued, in spite of some criticisms inside the party, steadily upon his course. In the end he was to have his way.

c

In the party, both in and out of Parliament, Eden ranked un-questioned as second-in-command. There was never any doubt of this or any attempt by any of his colleagues to challenge his position. All this made for great goodwill and friendly co-operation. There was no question of personal rivalries; the two highest posts were already decided in the event of our returning to power. Nor were we all so completely involved in politics as to allow them to absorb our whole thoughts. After six years of war it was quite agreeable to enjoy whatever private life and entertainment remained. I personally was fully employed, since I had the care of my own publishing business to share with my brother, as well as the pleasures of family life and of a wide circle of friends.

From a Parliamentary point of view we were a strong team. Apart from the heavy guns which Churchill could bring into play when required, Eden was a practised and skilled performer, particu-larly in winding up a debate. He was the best exponent of that art that I have ever known. When required to speak he always did so with common sense and wisdom as well as with moderation. The House listened to him attentively. It was the fashion to say that he only shone in debates on foreign affairs. In fact he often made a far more profound contribution to the solution of our many economic problems than appeared from his modest and debonair approach.

On economic and financial questions Oliver Stanley was incom-parably our most able and most agile speaker. He never overstated a case. He was never ruffled or thrown off his stride. He would put his probing finger with uncanny accuracy upon the real point—especially the weak point. But here, too, his speeches did not seem to give a very clear or creative lead. Perhaps this is not the duty of Opposition leaders, certainly in the House of Commons. But of the more limited function of a Parliamentary party, out of office and weakly represented in Parliament—that is brilliant and piercing criticism—Stanley was the acknowledged master. He was one of the most polished of Parliamentary speakers whose lambent wit delighted all sides of the House. I remember a typical example of his lightness of touch in a sad affair which, like all personal questions, was distasteful to all those of whatever party who cherished the traditions of Parliament and sympathised with a fellow Member in trouble. It was to do with an unhappy Minister who had been compromised by designing men. The question had to be sent to a tribunal presided over by Mr. Justice Lynskey. When the report was made it had to be debated. The chief villain had changed his name from its somewhat exotic original and taken what he no doubt thought would be a more respectable cognomen. He called himself Stanley. It fell to Oliver to speak on our behalf. It was an awkward affair in which everyone felt uncomfortable. He wisely did not press the issue too hard or make too heavy weather about an unfortunate incident. The Government side were naturally nervous and anxious. I remember Oliver telling them that much to his pleasure this gentleman had brought at last some temporary notoriety to his name. This delighted and relieved a tense and anxious House.

Stanley's danger was that his audience, delighted by a series of epigrams, remained dazzled but unimpressed when he spoke on serious issues. The very brilliance of his wit impaired the weight of his argument. Nevertheless, he was a fine Parliamentarian. A certain shyness and diffidence made some think him stand-offish and even proud; but by his friends he was loved as well as respected. Alas, he was struck by a terrible disease in the prime of life, and died in 1950 after a long and painful illness. Had he lived it is probable that Churchill would have appointed him Chancellor of the Exchequer in 1951. He would thus have become the most powerful member of the Government, for next to Eden he had the longest experience of public life. After Eden's illness he would no doubt have succeeded him as Prime Minister.

Butler spoke less frequently than some of us, but always with effect. He was listened to with interest and respect by the Government benches, for what he had to say was always significant and often profound. But he gave much of his time to the rebuilding of the philosophy of the party, and was largely responsible for its intellectual activity.

Oliver Lyttelton, although coming too late into the House of Commons ever to learn the true Parliamentary style, was a power of strength in counsel and, on occasion, effective in debate. One of the best and most consistent performers was Harry Crookshank. He had been a Member since 1923 and was deeply versed in the procedure of the House, ready to seize any advantage based upon this knowledge. He was a witty, entertaining speaker, often interrupted, but never thrown off his balance.

In the rough and tumble of debate and the long process of committee work we had two distinguished lawyers who later reached the top of their profession—David Maxwell Fyfe and Reggie Manningham-Buller, both of whom later became Lord Chancellor. Bracken could always be relied on for a fighting, truculent speech; the more infuriated the Government benches became, the more imperturbable was his manner. We were soon reinforced by some of our younger Members, notably Quintin Hogg, Peter Thorneycroft, Selwyn Lloyd, Anthony Head and Nigel Birch.

Thus our debating strength, in spite of our pitifully small numbers, was never negligible and became, as the years passed, increasingly effective.

Nevertheless, Opposition in Parliament cannot be said to be a very enthralling affair. The various Government Bills have to be fought both in the great Second Reading debates and point by point through Committee. For the first two years the Government were triumphant and seemed unshakeable. For myself, I did not much enjoy the work, for my whole life has been directed, whether in business or politics, to trying to create rather than to destroy. Criticism without the opportunity of effective action becomes— especially after a taste of real power—tedious and uninspiring. However, I did my part and tried to enliven my contributions as much as possible. These were useful years for me, since I began to learn the moods and study the temper of the House in the post-war world. The fault of my speeches at that time was that they were over-prepared and indulged in too many paradoxes and epigrams. Nor was this a Parliamentary situation which favoured detached or philosophic speculation. It was a battle which we had to do our best to fight against very superior forces. I had to try to encourage the spirit of my own side, and not be afraid of occasional Parliamentary conflicts. One of my self-appointed biographers has accused me of being at that time 'flippant, supercilious, superficial and arrogant'.

However, with characteristic generosity, he adds that the Conservatives thought me 'clever, hard-hitting, forceful, eloquent'. The standard of debate was high, but the methods would today no doubt seem out of fashion and incongruous. Carefully prepared speeches were already unpalatable unless the preparation could be as carefully concealed. Equally, taunts and gibes, perhaps pardonable in view of the inferiority of our position, have come to be less acceptable when parties are more nearly matched or when the seriousness of successive crises makes them seem inappropriate and almost indecent.

Against us there was ranged one of the most able Governments of modern times, which until it began to disintegrate from external blows and internal dissensions was also one of the most powerful. It had been a useful if not a very generous argument in pre-war elections that the Labour Party, even after their two short experiments—in 1924 and in 1929–31—had no outstanding leaders fit for the trials of office. But this certainly did not apply in 1945. In the course of the War Coalition Government several great figures had emerged, well known to and admired by the public.

Clement Attlee had shown himself an efficient and loyal colleague to Churchill through five testing years. During Churchill's frequent absences he had presided over the War Cabinet with quiet authority. Ernest Bevin commanded widespread respect among the trade unions and the employers alike. He had mobilised the whole man- and woman-power of the country for the tasks of war. Herbert Morrison, as Home Secretary, and charged with Home Security, had added to the stature which he had already acquired in the London County Council, with a reputation for successful organisation and administration. Sir Stafford Cripps had come into prominence and had apparently been transformed from a wild man of the Left to a sound and diligent Minister. Hugh Dalton, who had been charged with a department connected with a vital aspect of war—the Ministry of Economic Warfare—had proved himself in government, as well as in the House. Thus they had plenty of men who had undergone the most rigorous training under the vigilant eye of Churchill. In stature, therefore, with the exception of Churchill who was unique, they were certainly equal to

us. In argument and Parliamentary gifts they were in some ways
superior. Moreover, they were backed by a large majority—with a
sense of triumph added to a sense of mission.

Attlee, the Prime Minister, has often been much underrated—
not least by some of his colleagues. He was one of the best chairmen
I have ever sat under. He listened to other people's arguments and
put forward very few opinions himself, and that, from the point of
view of a member of any committee, makes a perfect chairman.
At the end he would sum up shortly, succinctly and decisively.
It is true that one sometimes had the feeling that he was watching
for other people's opinions, seeking to find where the majority lay.
Nevertheless, this is a useful gift, at any rate in ordinary times. In
addition, he was cool and unexcitable and never lost his head. In
the war, of course, the main burden had lain on stronger and
broader shoulders. But in the six years of his Premiership he was
forced, like all Prime Ministers, to undergo a series of crises and
difficulties, some of them personal, some of them public. The
country's position after the war was financially and economically
very feeble. If in the earlier years the underlying weaknesses did
not show themselves, and if after the beginning of 1946 they were
relieved by the vast American loan, yet the steady drift towards
something like collapse must have been painful to him. The convertibility crisis of 1947 and the final devaluation of 1949 were the
outstanding points in this process of decline.

At the same time he had many irritating personal difficulties to
overcome. But he seemed to ride over all these troubles with remarkable self-control—even nonchalance—at least outwardly. In
Parliament he stood up to Churchill and often gained substantial
tactical victories over him. His dry, precise and unemotional method
enabled him sometimes to reply to Churchill's arguments with a
bleak detachment which was all the more impressive because it was
done so quietly and easily. All this was much to the taste of his
followers, whom he kept well in hand. He was also, for all his lip-
service to the more unpractical aspects of the Socialist creed,
capable of making firm decisions in the national interest at moments
of crisis. The American decision to use the atomic bomb in order to
bring the Japanese resistance to an end did not seem to concern

him unduly. He succeeded in the important and invaluable task of making the atomic bomb for Britain without even informing Parliament, by hiding away by some manipulation of the Estimates the necessary £100 million. He got the job well under way before he could be restrained by the less robust members of his party. When NATO had to be implemented and Britain, contrary to her long tradition, entered in peacetime into a firm defensive alliance involving the stationing of a large army in Europe, he seemed hardly conscious of the revolutionary character of the policy which he was advocating. At the outbreak of the Korean war he did not hesitate, and appropriate contributions to this long-drawn-out and bitter contest were made by British, as well as by Commonwealth forces. At the same time he was ruthless in his relations with his colleagues. He was 'a good butcher', a quality said to be essential for a good Prime Minister. If he could not be said to have contributed much to the moulding of great events, he was imperturbable in handling difficult and dangerous issues as they arose.

An acute observer and a trained critic has described him thus:

> small and spare in person; quick and alert in his movements; a mongolian impassivity in his facial expression, a flat voice and a hurried, staccato articulation—all combined to disguise rather than disclose his real quality. He was like a tactful and reserved manager among prima donnas, over whom his influence was the greater because of his difference from themselves.[1]

There had been a contest, the details of which are somewhat obscure, about the beginning of his Premiership. Although Herbert Morrison denies that he tried to seize the leadership for himself, undoubtedly he proposed that Attlee should not answer the King's summons after Churchill's resignation without a conference of the Parliamentary Party. The method of choosing a Prime Minister has of course developed like every other part of the British constitution over the years. When the time came for me in the throes of illness to abandon my task, there was much debate over the procedure adopted. Even in 1922 Bonar Law, at his first audience with King George V, refused to kiss hands until after a party meeting

[1] Lord Salter, *Memoirs of a Public Servant* (London, 1961), p. 285.

had elected him as leader. Nevertheless, this was regarded as a breach of tradition and can perhaps only be excused by the peculiar circumstances of the case. For when Bonar Law destroyed the Lloyd George Government at the Carlton Club meeting, he was an independent Member and he was acting contrary to the advice given by the leader of the Conservative Party, Austen Chamberlain.[1] But in 1945, since Attlee had acted as leader of the party since 1935 and had been Deputy Prime Minister for five years of war, the plan to force an election proved abortive. If it was a formality, it was unnecessary; if it was a plot, it failed, coming up against the solid common sense and profound loyalty of Ernest Bevin.

Throughout Attlee's six years as Prime Minister, there were movements against his leadership, as always happened, even with Churchill. In the winter of 1947, when the glamour of success had begun to wear off, the combination of a fuel crisis and a food shortage had given the Opposition an easy cry, 'Starve with Strachey and shiver with Shinwell'—Ministers of Food and of Fuel and Power respectively. At the same time, national bankruptcy was beginning to loom ahead. There were many doubts then expressed as to whether Attlee had 'the personality, or the strength of popular appeal, to be the Leader in these increasingly critical months'.[2] But of his possible contenders Morrison was already a sick man, Dalton was to fall from office before the end of the year, and Bevin, although often critical of Attlee's dilatoriness and of his Ministerial appointments, was too loyal ever to enter any intrigue against him.[3] His only possible rival as Bevin's health also began to fail could have been Cripps, always busy with new ideas and new political combinations. But Attlee, who had much more political sense than Cripps, could easily outmanoeuvre him. In these difficult months 'Cripps was toying with the idea of resigning alone, on the ground that Attlee was no use as Prime Minister in this crisis. He would tell him this, and it would be recorded in a published exchange of letters.'[4]

Although in the Opposition we heard some rumours of all these

[1] Robert Blake, *The Unknown Prime Minister* (London, 1955), p. 460.
[2] Dalton, p. 236.　　　　[3] Ibid., pp. 239–40.　　　　[4] Ibid., p. 241.

dissensions, I was never conscious at any time from the moment he became Prime Minister until the day that he retired from the leadership of the party that Attlee was not in full command of the situation.

At the same time, Attlee was somewhat of a mysterious figure and often seemed rather aloof. Herbert Morrison, who must have known him longer than almost anyone in the Labour Party, records his own judgement:

> Despite these close contacts over a period of more than thirty years I regret to say that I cannot claim really to know Clement Attlee. Nor indeed could I name anyone, living or dead, in the Labour Party who has managed a real degree of intimacy with him.[1]

This reticence, as Morrison complains, made him distant and unapproachable:

> In his attitude to his colleagues Attlee was strangely like Ramsay MacDonald in that there was a remoteness about him so that it was quite impossible to approach near enough to get inside his mind and to know what he was really thinking. . . .[1]

To sum up: if Attlee lacked charm, he did not lack courage. If he drifted into difficulties, he generally found a way out of them. He was adroit; he was also firm. His reputation in Parliament and his stature in the country grew rather than diminished as the years passed. He commanded, if not affection, admiration from his opponents as well as from his supporters. His place in history, like the achievements of his Government, is assured.

Herbert Morrison, Lord President and Leader of the House of Commons, was the most experienced politician of all the Labour leaders. If he had not had the misfortune to lose his seat by a narrow margin in 1931, he would undoubtedly have been the leader of the Parliamentary Party at the outbreak of the war and so succeeded almost automatically to the Premiership in 1945. He was thus a victim of pure bad luck. His work on the London County Council had put him in a commanding position in the Labour world; he had long led the London Labour Party, and had acquired an

---

[1] Lord Morrison, *Autobiography*, pp. 294–5.

intimate knowledge of local government. His place in national politics was equally assured, and as a skilful manager of the party machine he could claim to have been 'the chief organiser of victory' in the election of 1945. His record in the Second War was good. Although his tenure of the Ministry of Supply was undistinguished, it was short; and the public remembered only his fine work at the Home Office where he was responsible for Home Security. The Morrison shelter thus became a household word. He was a good administrator and a man of very considerable charm. When I served under him in the Ministry of Supply I found him an agreeable, understanding and loyal chief. But his special attraction for me was that he personified the London Cockney, being almost a Dickensian character. He sported a quiff of hair like a street urchin, and his accent was undisguised and perhaps even exaggerated.

Morrison represented the Centre, even the Right, of the Labour Government. Although I had often to cross swords with him in debate, our views were not very far apart. He believed in 'public control of public utilities'—such as railways, gas, electricity and the like. In road transport, he preserved the C licence system, which has proved an essential aid to modern industry and commerce. Coal was an exceptional case, based on a long and unhappy history. But there he would have stopped. He fought hard against steel nationalisation, and when that became politically necessary he was the protagonist of a workable compromise, thus offending the Socialist zealots. Morrison could boast a long record of service to Labour. He was, next to Lord Woolton, the greatest party manager in political history. He led a triumphant party with tact and moderation and thus was able, without undue pressure on the House, to ease through a prodigious amount of highly controversial legislation. He was well liked by the Opposition. He neither boomed at us, like Dalton, nor lectured us like Cripps. He was a good Leader of the House because he was good-humoured and 'jollied it along' in a friendly way. Phrases like 'a good time was had by all' would be his description of a bitter debate or an all-night sitting. He was a practised Parliamentary speaker; although he made no pretensions to oratory and still less to style, he was all the more effective because much of his speaking was extempore. But the qualities which served him well as a Leader of the House were not so useful when he became Foreign Secretary in March 1951 after Bevin's illness and retirement. His methods, both in the control of an office and in the exposition of a policy, were unsuited to his new tasks. A Foreign Secretary, for instance, when asked about the situation in the Korean War, can hardly maintain his dignity if he replies in the following gem which has stuck in my mind: 'I think that if a cease-fire were arranged, it must mean that everybody ceases fire, otherwise the fire will not cease.' Nevertheless, if his language was pedestrian, his speeches generally achieved their purpose, for they were dexterous and gay. 'His flights were like those of the swallow—very quick but often very near the ground.' If he did not aspire to soar to great heights of thought or expression, he usually got where he wanted to go.

In the early years of the 1945 Parliament Morrison dominated the House and exploited his great majority with good humour and without unfairness. He was popular on all sides. A serious illness in 1947 sadly reduced his strength, but left him otherwise as jaunty as ever.

But the most powerful figure in the new administration was undoubtedly Bevin. It was he who commanded the confidence not merely of organised Labour but of that great mass of central opinion on which Governments must depend for their ultimate strength. When the Government was being formed, Bevin had wanted to go to the Treasury, leaving Dalton to occupy the Foreign Office. But Attlee yielded to the King's suggestion or protest. Thus, greatly to the national advantage, Bevin was to preside over foreign policy during the difficult and formative years that followed the end of the war. Like many others he had indulged in the sanguine hope that post-war Russia would follow new and less aggressive policies. In the election he had exploited this argument to the full. A Socialist Government, he would declare, would get on better with Communist Russia than the Tories: 'Left will look to Left with confidence and hope.' Alas, his confidence was soon to be shattered and his hopes prove vain. But with him disillusionment did not mean despair. His strong character and resolute spirit enabled him to accept and endure the inevitable. Except in Palestine, where he yielded unduly to his advisers in their pro-Arab and anti-Zionist views, he presided with broad success over the evolution of these troubled years. The Brussels Treaty; the NATO pact; the immediate welcome to Marshall Aid: all these bear upon them the stamp of Bevin's imagination and authority. As the greatest trade unionist of the day, and indeed the trusted representative of the unions in high office, he commanded special authority in the party and the nation. His massive personality, which made him the second man to Churchill in the war in public estimation, now made him one of the most powerful figures in the post-war world. He did not affect the delicacies of diplomacy. In Lord Salter's words, 'he used a truncheon rather than a rapier'. Perpetually harassed by his own Left wing, whom he accused of stabbing him in the back, he received the consistent support of the Opposition. Few Foreign Secretaries were more beloved in the office than he. Coming with some natural bias against the members of the Foreign Service, he was quick to recognise their quality as well as their devotion. He did much to make effective a useful and comprehensive reorganisation of the Foreign Office and the Diplomatic Service and has left behind him to this day a cherished memory.

As Minister of Labour during the war, his interventions had always carried great weight. For he had a profound knowledge of his subject based upon long experience. Even when he was led into novel fields he could speak with authority. As Foreign Secretary he was less effective in debate, except in reply. It is the practice of the Foreign Office, as I was to learn during my short tenure, to serve up to the Secretary of State on the occasion of a general discussion a long, elaborate, but somewhat jejune document composed in the most correct officialese and more like a memorandum than a Parliamentary speech. Bevin would read this out from start to finish, stumbling over the difficult words but plodding on manfully, often regardless of sense and punctuation. This *tour d'horizon*, as it was called in the office, was based on separate drafts from the different departments and seldom followed any single theme. It was boring to read, tedious to deliver, and intolerable to hear. Occasionally Bevin would depart from the text into a few homely sentences. But normally these performances followed their sad and wearisome course to the predestined end. When, however, it came to answering a debate on great issues such as NATO or Germany or Marshall Aid, Bevin could make a fine speech in his own way and in his own words, unburdened by the 'brief'. Then he let himself go, and demolished his critics and delighted his friends.

Naturally those of us who had served in Churchill's War Government preserved our amicable relations with our old colleagues—Attlee, Morrison and the others. But for Bevin we had a particular and lasting regard. Nor did he ever forget these heroic days. He would have occasional tiffs with Churchill, whose provocative methods he sometimes resented; but these two great men retained for each other genuine affection as well as respect.

Perhaps the most testing crisis that Bevin had to endure was the Soviet blockade of Berlin, which lasted from the middle of June 1948 until the following May. Here, as at the time of the outbreak of the Korean War, he did not hesitate. In both cases he was criticised, sometimes bitterly, by the Left wing of his own party, and sustained by his opponents. Unhappily, during his last months of office his health began to fail. It was sad for all of us to watch his gradual decay—the literal withering away of his life and strength. He was able to hold on beyond the election of 1950. But the strain was too great. He could, with difficulty, be kept going by drugs and stimulants. But he finally resigned on 9 March 1951. Five weeks later he died. Never did a man more truly give his life for the cause which he served.

The next in importance and influence of the Ministers of the triumphant Labour Government of 1945 was Hugh Dalton, who, hoping for the Foreign Office, found himself somewhat unexpectedly Chancellor of the Exchequer. I had always liked Dalton, although to many people he was unattractive and even repellent. I liked him because in the years before the war he had been a robust patriot. He had done his best to persuade his own party to abandon their foolish views about rearmament and move away from their pacifist traditions. I had been on good terms with this jovial, rollicking extrovert in those grim years of Chamberlain's rule. He had helped me at certain important moments by giving me information of the Labour Party's likely attitude, and by his assistance at some critical moments. His memoirs, based almost exclusively upon his diaries, are of intense interest and reveal even in their published form more about the workings of Labour politicians behind the scenes than almost any other source. In contrast to the many Socialist Malvolios, like Cripps, he was the Sir Toby of the Labour Cabinet. He always regarded politics and life as great fun. He never lost his exuberance, except in the concluding stages of his career at the Treasury when he began to be oppressed by the financial results of his policies. He was wildly indiscreet, and since his booming voice could be heard from almost one end of the Palace of Westminster to the other, his indiscretions were widely advertised. Yet he did a great deal to build up the Labour movement, in particular by his encouragement of young men of ability. Under his influence, the middle-class intellectuals soon began to equal and then outnumber the 'horny-handed sons of toil'. Dalton was the son of a dean—and a royal dean at that. He was also a great intriguer. Attlee, Bevin and Morrison all knew this. Yet his machinations were so open and ingenuous as to be almost pardonable. His mood of ebullience and gaiety suited his period as Chancellor, for it corresponded with the early years of triumph, at any rate on the home front.

As one nationalisation scheme followed another, Dalton never ceased to gloat in a series of bellowing speeches, which, much as they annoyed—and almost deafened—the Opposition, raised great enthusiasm in his own benches. He had succeeded in launching an undated loan at $2\frac{1}{2}$ per cent (the famous, or infamous, 'Daltons'), and fortified by immense borrowings from America and Canada, he habitually went about, in his own words, 'with a song in his heart'. He even, as a by-product, abolished the perpetual pension to Earl Nelson's family. He tells us somewhat naïvely of an intrigue in which (although he had little inkling of all its ramifications) he indulged with Cripps in an attempt to blow up the leadership in a manner almost worthy of Guy Fawkes himself. As George Brown, his Parliamentary Private Secretary, reported to him:

the boys all talked, during the all-night sitting this week on the Transport Bill, about the lack of leadership.

(How well I was later to recognise this phrase! This is what 'the boys' habitually do in every administration.)

> Most were in favour of substituting Bevin for Attlee; they seemed to think that these two could just swop jobs. Failing this, he said, mine was the only name mentioned as a possible new Leader! They thought that I was the Minister who, until now, had shown himself clearly 'on the top of the job'. There was, he said, no other strong candidate. It was generally felt that Morrison was a sick man and couldn't do it. No one else, and neither Cripps nor Bevan, was mentioned.[1]

But this was not to be. One fatal, although really venial, error brought Dalton's career effectively to an end. It was a tragic story, in which he became a victim, to my mind rather unfairly, to the strict and traditional conventions about the Budget. On 12 November 1947 a supplementary Budget was to be introduced in view of the increasing financial stress. On his way to the Chamber he passed the *Star*'s Lobby correspondent and had a few words with him about some of its contents. As a result, a small edition, and a very small one, of this paper—now defunct—was published just *before* the Budget statement had actually been made. The next day a Question was asked. Dalton made a frank explanation, offering 'deep apologies to the House' for what he called 'a grave indiscretion'. Churchill's immediate reaction was typical of his generosity. He acknowledged 'the very frank manner in which the Chancellor had expressed himself and his sympathy for the misuse of his confidence'. That evening there was a general view that the slip would be passed over. I think it was Churchill's own wish not to press the point. Much as the rank and file of the Conservative Party disliked and even feared Dalton, they found him a convenient target for their own week-end speeches. Indeed, they had a sort of queer liking for the man who at least showed them good sport. Thus the general sentiment was well summarised, when the resignation was announced, by Nigel Birch's famous cry of pain, 'My God! They've shot our fox.' The majority of Churchill's colleagues would have preferred to let the matter drop, for the threatened punishment

[1] Dalton, p. 238.

for his lapse seemed altogether disproportionate. But a feeling in the party began to develop in the course of the evening in favour of exploiting our advantage. No doubt under its influence and following the advice of our Whips, Churchill wrote that night a letter in which he made it clear that while he acknowledged the frankness of the Chancellor of the Exchequer's apology, he must ask for the appointment of a Select Committee to enquire and report on the facts. Before, however, this communication had been delivered Dalton's proffered resignation had been accepted by Attlee. Perhaps he had heard something of the Dalton–Cripps manœuvres to remove him from the leadership!

For many reasons, of which the memory of our pre-war co-operation against 'appeasement' was the most potent, I felt sorry about this affair. When we had both become members of the Council of Europe at Strasbourg I was glad to be able to renew my friendship with Dalton and to work with him in an agreeable and amicable spirit.

The fall of Dalton led to the rise of Cripps. This strange and eccentric character had first come into notoriety before the war as a 'parlour Bolshevist' of a high intellectual order. He had infuriated the Conservatives and alarmed many of his own party by the extravagance of his views and the bitterness of his attacks upon all established institutions. He had insulted the Crown; made it clear that he wished to reduce Parliament to a mere rubber stamp of a Socialist dictatorship; and in the most critical years of Hitler's threats to the peace of the world had urged the workers of Britain to refuse to make munitions to defend a capitalist society. Combined with these public activities, which led him at one time to be ejected from the Labour Party, he was a most successful barrister enjoying one of the largest practices of his day. In this country businessmen are no fools. The same instinct which made Churchill welcome Stalin as an ally against Hitler induced leading companies and individuals to retain the services of Cripps—in spite of the dislike and disgust they felt for his political views—in private or corporate actions where large sums were at stake. For they respected his qualities as an advocate. A malignant rebel with Marxist leanings, the most highly paid advocate at the Bar, born from a rich and noble family, Cripps was in addition a devout Christian. In private life he was a delightful companion, except at meals—for he did not eat or drink, but only smoked. I got to know him fairly intimately in 1942, on his return from Russia, before I left for the Mediterranean.

At that time he had, or thought he had, too little to do as Leader of the House of Commons—a post he held for a few months only.[1] So he would make a practice of calling upon his colleagues, young and old, as part of his parochial duties. I remember long conversations with him in which he explained the future liquidation of the Colonial Empire and what we ought to do or not do meanwhile. I was never offended at these intrusions. You could not be angry with Cripps for long because he was so sincere. Like all eccentrics, he had a slightly White Knight side to him, detached from reality. He was so devoted to the cause which he served that he had no hesitation in taking actions that in any other man would have been thought thoroughly disloyal.

At the time we did not know the full story of the intrigues of the summer of 1947, of which Dalton has given us so vivid a picture.[2] Only vague rumours had reached us. Cripps had come to the conclusion that 'Attlee must go', and a most complicated plot was entered into between him and Dalton to substitute Bevin for Attlee. In their view only Bevin would manage the economic situation into which the country was then drifting and ride the threatening storm. Cripps believed that unless Attlee were immediately replaced by Bevin 'the Party and the country were all sunk'.[3] Bevin should become Prime Minister, Cripps his Chief of Staff as Lord President, and Dalton should go to the Foreign Office. Morrison would remain as Leader of the House and act as Deputy Prime Minister. Unhappily, there was a hitch:

> Morrison fully agreed about Attlee, but not about Bevin. He thought that he [Morrison] should be Prime Minister. Anyhow, leading the House wasn't a full-time job. He wouldn't serve under Bevin, and he had charged Cripps with putting a pistol at his head.[4]

[1] *The Blast of War*, p. 182. [2] Dalton, chap. 29.
[3] Ibid., p. 240. [4] Ibid., p. 242.

The plan faded out in the way these things generally do. I feel doubtful whether Bevin, although possibly willing to accept the Premiership if it were handed to him on a plate, would have entered into any such intrigue.

Attlee, when met with the proposal that he should make way for Bevin, handled the matter with consummate skill. He did not think Bevin would want to leave the Foreign Office. With some finesse Attlee suggested that Cripps should himself become Minister of Production; and so in fact it was decided. His new duties were announced in the autumn of 1947, when he became Minister of Economic Affairs. Morrison was now altogether shorn of the vital functions of 'Central Planning' for which he had, up to now, been responsible. Some of these manœuvres were reported to me and my friends, but all we could do was to watch for the unfolding of this personal drama. When, at the critical moment, Dalton's resignation followed his unlucky mistake, Cripps's supremacy became assured. For without surrendering his post as Minister for Economic Affairs and Planning, he now succeeded to the Treasury. He thus became the most powerful single figure in the Government, at any rate on the home front.

During the next few years many of us began deeply to regret Hugh Dalton. It was like Solomon and Rehoboam. The former had chastised us with whips; the latter chastised us with scorpions. He was a strange contrast to Dalton, the jolly Friar Tuck of the Labour movement. The austere Cripps was in reality no sour Puritan, but he seemed nevertheless almost to revel in the tale of woe and suffering which he was unfolding day by day. But the strength of his position was based on certain special qualities. His legal training gave him a power of exposition which was unique. Even the most complicated series of figures were reduced by him to an intelligible form. But it was not merely by this intellectual display that he imposed his personality. His sincerity, his ascetic fervour, his dramatic appeals to a Higher power, in terms which from any other man would have been intolerable, deeply impressed the House. In the course of the next period he was to reach a position in which it was regarded almost improper, if not sacrilegious, to interrupt him or even to question his pronouncements. His more loyal acolytes surrounded him like a troop of devout worshippers. This identification of economics and religion, which some of us found somewhat nauseating, was successful only because Cripps had persuaded himself that his policies were not merely based on sound material arguments but rested on moral truths. He now became inspired with an extraordinary white heat of devotion, even fanaticism. Inheriting from his predecessor a desperate financial position, he struggled to restore it by a regime of austerity for the mass of the population which surpassed even the privations of war. The song in the old Chancellor of the Exchequer's heart now became a melancholy dirge, which the new Chancellor repeated with all the penetrating clarity of his brilliant mind. The British people, who had put up with having little to eat in the years of Woolton, when shortage was sold with a smile by this best salesman in the world, became deeply incensed when rations were continued and even reduced some years after the war by a Minister who appeared almost to enjoy their privations with all the emotion of an anchorite. Cripps drank no alcohol and was believed to live on nuts and watercress, and as the terrible strain of his dedication to work began to tell upon his health, he seemed more and more to resemble an Indian fakir.

The collapse of his hopes through the unavoidable devaluation of sterling in 1949 told hard upon him. Moreover, since he was an honourable man (even in his plots against the Prime Minister he was straightforward enough to inform his threatened leader of the plans for his demotion), he suffered greatly during the long months when he had to repudiate any question of the de-valuation of sterling, although he and his advisers must have known that this was becoming inevitable. He did not like it; he felt ashamed that such prevarication had been forced upon him. Before his enforced resignation through ill-health, the harsh pressure of events and the weight of responsibility had begun to wear him down. But he struggled on. When I first got to know him in the war years he could reveal an occasional gleam of humour and even fun. These moods now seemed blighted. His appearance began to betray the burden under which he laboured. In the end his body revolted against the strains he had put upon it, and he died on 21 April 1952 in a Swiss clinic. Beyond the narrow circle of his intimate friends he was mourned by many who recognised his selflessness and devotion to what he conceived to be his duty. His deep Christian faith undoubtedly inspired his life. Yet like all men who have a high sense of vocation, he was an egoist. But Dalton was right. He had ability, amounting almost to genius, but little judgement.

These five men constituted a body of Ministers as talented as any in the history of Parliament. Nor, as so often happens when a party long out of office returns at last to power after an interval of many years, were they untried. All of them had considerable experience both of legislation and administration. All had served in the Great Coalition and survived the harsh test of war. All of them, with the exception of Bevin, who never learned its ways or understood its character, had shared in the life of the House of Commons and were sensitive to its strange and uncertain moods.

In 1945 there was added to this constellation an eccentric and uncontrollable star—perhaps almost a comet. Yet in many ways he was the most brilliant and the most memorable of them all—Aneurin Bevan. I first got to know Bevan in those dreary Parliaments before the war when I was struggling to persuade my leaders to do something more than record the numbers and relieve the barest necessities of the unemployed. Bevan himself was a product of those nightmare days. He could not forget and never wanted to forget the sufferings which he had seen in the mining valleys of South Wales. This passionate and dedicated young man stormed into the debates of those dull times with a fervour which was irresistible to any man of feeling. As he grew older he mellowed; some, I suppose, might say he became corrupted. He grew to love the amenities of life as well as kick against its pricks. He even became a farmer in a small way, and a modest collector of pictures. But already in his earlier days Bevan stood apart from the other protesters of the time. He was as fervent and as moving as any in his declarations against the social structure which had allowed such conditions to exist. But he was more than a mere demagogue. He studied and learned Parliamentary methods. He became as agile and as nimble in debate as any other of the great Parliamentarians. Like Churchill, he used his slight physical defect to enhance the impact of his speeches. His stammer had an attraction all its own. He was gifted with an acute sensitivity. When we used to sit and argue in the smoking-room for long hours, he would always pick out with accuracy and distinguish between the Conservatives who he felt were doing their best and for whom he had a certain sympathy, as against those he regarded as the enemies of society. On the whole, his judgements in this matter always struck me as pretty correct. He had, of course, little sense of balance and was easily swept away by his emotions. During the war this often made him appear unpatriotic and almost to deserve the reproach of 'squalid nuisance', which Churchill in a mood of exasperation once applied to him. Naturally, being out of office and with the leading figures in the Labour movement serving in Churchill's Government, Bevan had forced upon him the role of critic, similar to that adopted by Shinwell on the Left and Winterton on the Right.[1] But the difference was that Bevan had real genius. He was a poet as well as a Jacobin. After the war, he became from the Labour Government's point of view a dangerous colleague. For his mind moved so rapidly from point to point and he was so enamoured of paradox that he was often an unconscious help to us Conservatives in our weakness. You could be sure that he would say something that we could take hold of and exploit.

The first of these errors was the famous tirade against exports delivered during the 1945 election: 'By some twist of the Tory mind it is good trade to persuade someone in a remote part of the world to buy our goods, but ruinous to allow the same goods to be consumed by our own people.' But this heresy was as nothing to the famous 'vermin' speech. These silly words—'I regard the Tories as lower than vermin'—which came out at some obscure meeting in an extempore speech, were of course a gift to the cartoonists and to an Opposition making at that time very little headway in the country. We formed Vermin Clubs all over the country, and poor Morrison was so deeply hurt and shocked that he never got over it.

Nevertheless, these indiscretions were only the products of momentary impulse. Bevan had declared the Tories to be lower than vermin; but in fact he only thought this about Tories in the bulk. To all men as individuals, including Tories, he was a kind

[1] *The Blast of War*, pp. 121–2.

and sympathetic friend. Even when he called Morrison 'a third-rate Tammany boss,' the most wounding part of it was the qualification.

Bevan was in many ways much the most exciting of all the Labour team. Unexpectedly he proved to be a good administrator and a good Minister. He failed over his housing policy for the simple reason that the Ministry over which he presided was too wide in its responsibilities. The chief task of the Ministry of Health in this Parliament was the initiation of the Health Service, based upon the Beveridge Report; but housing was also included in its scope. Therefore, while inaugurating the vast scheme of social services for which Bevan managed somehow to extract almost endless amounts of money in spite of the financial difficulties, first from Dalton and then from Cripps, he could hardly ask for the same indulgence for his housing plans. Moreover, he was apt to take too seriously what he was told by his civil servants. The fault of most Ministers is not kicking over the traces; it is running too easily in the harness of Whitehall. When I succeeded him in Housing, I found how wrong the so-called experts of the Treasury and of the Ministry had been about the potentialities of the building industry when given encouragement and freedom.

If Bevan was an *enfant terrible*, he was certainly a very attractive child. He was human. Even when his resignation came in 1951, backed by Harold Wilson, then a cool and calculating rebel, I felt that Bevan had acted in accordance with his inmost nature. Bevan, like all poets, and particularly Celtic poets, was no doubt easier for his nominal opponents to admire at arm's length than for his friends to work with in close proximity. Whatever may be said about some of his occasional outbursts, he was free from cant and hypocrisy. Of course, like many Socialists, he was at heart and in character a supreme individualist.

When he died in 1960 he had been out of the limelight for several years; but suddenly, and in a sense unexpectedly, the House and the country were conscious of something like a personal loss. In paying tribute to his memory in the House of Commons, I thought it might be wondered why a man who had been all his life a some-what controversial figure should have ended by commanding such general admiration and even affection:

First, he was a genuine man. There was nothing fake or false about him. If he felt a thing deeply, he said so and in no uncertain terms. If he had strong opinions—even prejudices—he expressed them strongly, but sincerely. Secondly, he was a bonny fighter— and a chivalrous one. If he struck blows which sometimes aroused angry retaliation he was always ready to receive them in return. Moreover, if he sometimes spoke violently, he was never dull. He was sometimes harsh; he was never trite.

Finally, he expressed in himself and in his career, in his life, some of the deepest feelings of humble people throughout the land. Unlike many prophets, he was specially honoured in his own country. He was a keen politician, but he never played at politics. He was something of a revolutionary; he was always a patriot. And, beneath the charm and ebullience of his Celtic temperament, he was a deeply serious man.[1]

Taken as a whole, therefore, the political personalities in this Parliament on both front benches were certainly equal to their predecessors, of whatever epoch. In days when Parliament, and not the wireless or the television, still formed and dominated political thought and action, they constituted as notable and memorable a group as any in our history.

[1] *Hansard*, 7 July 1960.

CHAPTER IV

Labour Triumphs and Tribulations

THE first in a long series of 'Socialist' measures introduced by the new Government, in the full flush of their electoral triumph, was well chosen. It was the Bill to nationalise the Bank of England. This was doubly welcome to their own supporters. In the first place, the memories of 1931—the 'Bankers' Ramp' and all that—still rankled. It was the Bank which had seduced Ramsay MacDonald into 'the great betrayal' of the movement of which he had been almost the founder. Secondly, it was the sinister influence of the Governor, Montagu Norman, who had so long been the virtual dictator of policy, which had led to, or at least prolonged, the years of the great depression between the wars. Now had come, at last, the day of reckoning. The choice was a shrewd one. It confounded and divided the Opposition from the start. For while Churchill had taken the first opportunity—in the debate on the Address—of declaring that in his view the matter involved 'no question of principle', some of his colleagues were distressed at this Laodicean attitude and determined strenuously to oppose the Bill when it should be introduced. Thus, at the very first stage of implementing the 'nationalisation' programme, the Opposition, already weak, was divided and made to cut a somewhat ludicrous figure. Moreover, it was well known that strong Chancellors of the Exchequer (like Lloyd George and Bonar Law in the First War) had succeeded in imposing their will on a recalcitrant Governor. If Churchill had been overborne in 1926, it was from ignorance of the dangers of a return to gold at the old parity, not from weakness.

The grounds for opposing the Bill were twofold. First, it was claimed that the special connection of the Bank of England with and responsibilities for the Sterling Area made ownership by the United Kingdom Government inappropriate, and likely to cause a lack of confidence in sterling. Secondly, and somewhat in contradiction to the first argument, the change was unnecessary. For it was clear that the shareholders had never exerted any influence on the policy of the Court of Directors, still less on that of the Governor. Nevertheless it was on these grounds that Oliver Stanley, supported by Sir John Anderson, did his best to oppose the Bill at the end of 1945.

In reality this was something of a sham battle. For the Socialists, the nationalisation of the Bank of England was chiefly important as a symbol of the new era. The State must own the State Bank—the Central Bank which controlled monetary policy. For many of the Conservatives, it seemed that the formal transfer of the equity and of the right of appointing successive Governors would be of minor importance. If and when the test came, the strength of sterling would be decided by events. Fortunately, I was not involved in this controversy, for I had only just been re-elected to Parliament.

Looking back over the years, which include those of my direct responsibility for these grave matters, as Chancellor of the Exchequer and Prime Minister, I do not believe that the new system has been of great significance. Every Governor has thought it his duty to give his advice and express his anxieties or even his fears with an independence which every Government has in turn respected. Nor has he generally found any difficulty in getting support from the Treasury. If there has been a change of emphasis it has not arisen from the fact of the Government having become the proprietors of the shares of the Bank. It has been a natural process in a period when the importance of monetary policy in the economic life of the nation has become generally recognised. In the old days, these were mysteries which the public and even the Press hardly ventured to discuss. Between the wars the curtain was to some extent pulled aside by critics like Keynes and his followers. Yet it was still thought somewhat indecent to reveal these hallowed secrets. In recent years such matters have become subjects of daily discussion and debate. No Government, whether of the Right or Left, whether armed with new powers or not, can be content to leave the ultimate control in any hands except its own. Nevertheless, I would not go so far as to accept the view expressed to me by one of the leading merchant bankers in the country that the Bank of England has little importance today, being, to use his own words, 'merely the East End office of the Treasury'. The Bank and the Governor have still a certain independence and feel their responsibility to the nation. The resignation of a Governor would be an event which any Government would be most anxious to avoid. The Governor, like the Chiefs of Staff, has access not only to his own Minister, the Chancellor of the Exchequer, but also to the Prime Minister. His authority, as before, depends essentially on his personality.

This incident, however, did to some extent weaken the Conservative leaders, already suffering from the violent shock of their election defeat. As a result, the normal practice was followed in order to rally the back-benchers—a vote of censure was proposed at the end of the year. This was moved by Oliver Lyttelton, and I was invited by Churchill to wind up for our side. I am bound to say I did not find it a very easy task. The Government was equally strong in the House and in the country and the timing of the debate seemed to me premature. Nevertheless, after my long absence, for three years had passed since I had spoken in Parliament, this occasion gave me an opportunity for reappearing on the stage. My speech was well received by my fellow Members and widely praised in the Press. In this, as in the other speeches which I had to make during the period of the apparent unassailability of the Government, I tried to criticise and even attack their policy without abandoning the progressive policies which I had preached in the past. In order to achieve this uneasy balance with any success, I had to seek to present my views with as much lightness of touch as possible. This led me into the error, which with greater experience I learned to eschew, of attempting too many jokes. While Members on all sides like a sharp and witty approach, it is important to avoid the danger of being accused of levity. Nevertheless, it is difficult to attack a majority of two to one against you with a bludgeon; the rapier seems to be the only available weapon. In this debate, as in others, Attlee began to demonstrate his great supremacy over his party and a growing mastery over the House. Morrison and Cripps were both admirable, Cripps impressive with his fierce fanaticism and Morrison effective with his cocky and genial banter. Our efforts fell rather flat.

There now began a period when the Government's Bills followed each other with ruthless rapidity. The nationalisation of civil aviation was adumbrated on 24 January 1946; the Second Reading of the Coal Industry Nationalisation Bill took place on 30 January and the Third Reading on 20 May. Cable and Wireless were also to be taken over by the State. I had to take part in the first three of these debates, and here again, since I felt the issues were really settled beyond recall, it was best to attempt some philosophic approach to the general problems which we had to face in the post-war world and to lighten the heaviness of my argument with a certain amount of banter.

As regards civil aviation, the Coalition Government had agreed to what was known as the Swinton Plan. This was a scheme which combined in a sensible compromise the benefits of public and private ownership and management. But it was thrown over by the new Government in spite of its having been approved by all the leading Ministers in the old. I could not help observing how politic was their attitude to agreements reached during the Coalition. When it was a scheme which they wished to promote they appealed to the unanimity reached with their old colleagues; when it was something different they repudiated their former views. Their memories seemed to be sometimes singularly tenacious, sometimes conveniently weak. Surely this matter ought to be treated purely on a pragmatic basis:

> I understand now—I have always understood—that the orthodox or what I might call the 'high and dry' Socialists, believe, or affect to believe, in the whole dogmatic creed of 'national ownership of all the means of production, distribution and exchange'. Yet now, under the high authority of the Lord President, expressed frequently in Canada and even occasionally in England, a more latitudinarian interpretation is being gradually accepted.... He has adopted the theme that there is, in the great range of the economic life of the nation, a sphere both for public and private effort. What at any given time the precise delimitation is to be is a matter for argument and adjustment. Even the virgin purity of the President of the Board of Trade [Cripps] has yielded to this

seductive conception. He boasted that even when he and his friends have done their worst, 80 per cent of the total production of the country will still be in private hands. Of course, it is patent that the free sphere must remain large, for how else are we to find the personnel fit and trained to manage the nationalised sector?[1]

Or, I might have added, the profits to sustain it. Over twenty years later this seems still to be more or less the situation. It may even be thought that of the orthodox and traditional nationalisation plans, that for iron and steel is the last remnant—a kind of survival from this 1945 period. But the danger of the literal interpretation of dogma was at the time very great and still persists. It was therefore of some importance to try to fix a frontier and defend it.

On the Second Reading of the Coal Bill I did my best to make the case for an alternative plan. This had been embodied in what was known at the time as the Reid Report, and might or might not have functioned successfully. Knowing the very strong feelings of the many Members representing mining constituencies and of the sad history of the industry, at least during certain periods, I tried to argue my case against the particular form of State corporation (without any representation of the workers) which the Bill proposed. Another danger was involved in the attempt to bring into a single unit 850 undertakings at one fell swoop, without any preliminary process of regional amalgamation. None of us of course then anticipated the necessity for so drastic a reduction in the output of coal and the redeployment of miners as became necessary during the next generation owing to the competition of atomic energy and oil. Perhaps the greatest justification of national ownership has been that—assisted by conditions of full employment—it has provided the means of reducing the human suffering involved in this process.

When we came to the Third Reading, I had to conclude the debate. I prophesied, and I think with some reason, that the anonymous members of the Coal Board would prove no more popular with the miners and would be far more distant from effective criticism than the old owners—'new presbyter' being 'but old priest writ large'.

[1] *Hansard*, 24 January 1946.

Indeed, until my appointment of Lord Robens in 1961, very little progress was made with the human side of the mining problem. But at any rate it was clear that the new structure was not one of co-partnership or participation of the mineworkers in the affairs of the industry. It was pure State capitalism. However, I accepted the fact that this controversy must now be settled, and that it must be settled broadly to the satisfaction of the Government and its supporters, as well as to the miners:

> I recognise how great must be the emotion, even the jubilance, of hon. Members opposite, especially those who have sat for long years for mining constituencies and who are among the oldest and most respected Members of this House. This must be for them a great day. The achievement of their great objective seems at hand; their triumph is complete, and we cannot withhold from them, if we have any feelings of magnanimity, a tribute of respect and of admiration. They have toiled hard, sacrificed much in this long struggle for nationalisation.[1]

I concluded by reminding them that if theirs was the triumph, theirs, also, was the responsibility. If the Conservative Party felt it their duty to formally oppose the Bill at this last stage, we could still join in wishing Godspeed to all those who lived and worked and had their being in and about the mines.

The drive for nationalisation continued through 1946 and 1947 at a remarkable pace. Nobody could complain that in this respect at any rate Ministers were not carrying out their promises. In addition to the nationalisation of the Bank of England and the coal industry, cable and wireless communication, rail and road transport, electricity and gas were all brought under the same system of State-capitalised control. The whole of this process was completed by the end of 1950. Only steel remained over for final passage into law. On this industry, so different in character from the others, opinion among the chiefs of the Labour Party was notoriously divided, and the operation of the Act was postponed until after the General Election.

There was one common feature in the form in which all these

---

[1] *Hansard*, 20 May 1946.

Bills were drafted which at that time was widely criticised. They left a great number of points uncertain—partly, no doubt, in order not to give what Whitehall is apt to regard as unnecessary information to Members of Parliament and the public; partly because final decisions had not yet been reached on many important questions. This tendency has, alas, continued, and has perhaps become inevitable in view of the complexity of modern legislation. But at that time it was unusual, even novel. In one of these debates I drew attention to this departure from old practice:

> The Minister has great reserve power. The Minister may direct; the Minister may make regulations. All that is common form nowadays. Indeed, if only Moses could have known this technique, he would never have committed himself to anything so precise and, occasionally, so inconvenient as the Ten Commandments. When he came down from Mount Sinai he would have taken powers to make regulations.[1]

With the exception of steel and road transport, the nationalisation battle, apart from the question as to whether the management structure was likely to prove effective and other important details, was to some extent unreal. Many of us on the Conservative side had long recognised that for a variety of reasons certain undertakings—the coal-mines on historic and sentimental grounds; the railways on financial; and the public utilities and other monopolies like gas and electricity on technical—stood in a wholly different category from the great mass of productive industry and commerce. In my own writings, which were naturally freely quoted against me by Morrison and Shinwell, I had frankly admitted the necessity of public ownership and control in this field. What was more doubtful was the policy of cramming into so short a period such great changes without any chance of learning from experience. Moreover, the financial effects of large sums being paid out in compensation, thus turning fixed into liquid assets, added to the requirements for capital investment on Government account, were bound to prove serious additional causes of the inflation which was soon to menace both the Government and the country.

[1] *Hansard*, 20 May 1946.

Nevertheless, the achievements of the Labour Party in this Parliament have stood. It has perhaps proved unfortunate from the point of view of those anxious to extend the process that so many of these industries were already declining in the immediate post-war period. The mining industry, which was then thought to have all the advantages of a monopoly, has been increasingly supplanted by other methods of producing heat and power, and indeed has had to be partially sustained by a protective duty against oil. Similarly, the railways passed to the State at the very moment when the monopoly which they had enjoyed throughout the nineteenth century was about to disappear, and by a full turn of the circle the road was to regain its supremacy. In other spheres a considerable degree of competition, even between industries publicly controlled, has certainly had healthy results. It has been the competition between atomic power, oil and coal which has resulted in the continual improvement in the design, with a corresponding fall in the cost and an increase in the efficiency, of power plants. The competition between gas and electricity, although both publicly owned, has been equally valuable.

The triumph of nationalisation in this Parliament left the Labour Party exhausted; and as time has passed, this classical form of State capitalism seems out of date and certainly unsuited to the industry, trade and commerce on the strength of which, especially the export market, the life of the nation depends. It did not pass without remark—indeed, it was a continual point made by Opposition speakers—that even the most extreme Socialists seemed very unwilling to disturb any enterprise which operated chiefly in the export market. In particular, in spite of the talk of some hot-heads, there was no question of interfering with the vital earners of invisible exports—banking, insurance and the like.

The first years of Attlee's Government were thus, from the legislative point of view, successful and productive. On the administrative side they could also claim to have handled effectively the most urgent problems that had followed the end of the war.

But in dealing with the financial problems they were less fortunate. They had certainly inherited a frightening situation. For over four years we had in effect been kept going by the Lend-Lease system. By this alone had the vast military expenditure of Britain and the Empire been sustained. Yet seven days after the end of the Japanese war, President Truman signed an order directing that steps be immediately taken to discontinue all Lend-Lease operations and to notify foreign Governments accordingly. All outstanding contracts were cancelled. This devastating blow, struck without warning and without any attempt at negotiation, was wholly unexpected. Nor was the order limited or moderated in its operation. All shipments to Russia and other European countries were at once embargoed, and some ships were actually turned back and unloaded. However, as soon as Truman realised what he had done—or been induced to do—he took steps to modify the impact of his action. Hasty discussions now followed. The final settlement, accompanying the proposed Loan Agreement, was not ungenerous. All orders that had been or were on the point of being placed prior to Japan's defeat were honoured. Large stocks of goods already in Britain or in the Empire which had been delivered were handed over without payment. In addition, the various cross-claims were written off.

But even with this amelioration of the position, the financial difficulties seemed almost insurmountable. With huge sterling balances in favour of many Allied and the leading Commonwealth countries—the bitter price of having saved them from enslavement by Hitler which, by a strange inversion of equity, we now had to pay— with small reserves, and large military commitments overseas, it seemed a choice between bankruptcy and borrowing. The Government opted—not without good reason—for the second.

This was the urgent issue which I found, on my return to the House at the end of 1945, was being discussed with great animation in every quarter. There were strong feelings on all sides. The sum to be borrowed was large—$3,750 millions. The conditions as to interest and repayment were onerous, in spite of certain concessions regarding postponement in any time of special crisis. Other clauses in the agreement were harsh and indeed contrary to the Bretton Woods Agreement.[1] We were held to the acceptance of convertibility

---

[1] Forty-four nations attended the conference at Bretton Woods in July 1944. The agreements reached were ratified by Britain in December 1945 and became operative on 27 December 1945. They resulted in the creation of the International Monetary Fund

Ernest Bevin, 'the
strongest figure in the
Labour Government',
and Clement Attlee,
'imperturbable in handling
difficult and dangerous
issues', at the United
Nations, January 1947

Aneurin Bevan, 'much
the most exciting of all the
Labour team'

Hugh Dalton, 'the Sir Toby of the Labour Cabinet' and Herbert Morrison, 'almost a Dickensian character', at a Labour Party Conference

Sir Stafford Cripps 'seemed almost to revel in the tale of woe and suffering which he was unfolding'; with Harold Wilson

of sterling, but we were to be deprived of the five-year transitional period available to the other signatories. Britain's interval of grace was to be cut down to twelve months from the ratification of the agreement. Again, we alone were to surrender the benefit of the 'scarce currency clause' in managing our sterling control. We alone were prevented from regaining freedom of action by resigning from the 'International Fund' system and its obligations.

The negotiations with the American Treasury had been conducted by Keynes, and the agreement was recommended as the best obtainable by the full force of his authority. His speech in the House of Lords, replying to Beaverbrook, was one of his last public pronouncements before his death and carried immense weight. Meanwhile, it was known that many Ministers were disturbed—and even disgusted—by the harshness of the terms and the arrogant tone of the American administration. The Opposition leaders were equally divided and their discussions in council prolonged.

One of the advantages of office is that however divided internally on any issue, short of a total break-up or the resignation of particular Ministers, the Government must present an unbroken front. With an Opposition this is not so. Without responsibility there is not the same pressure for unanimity. Churchill was instinctively for taking the American money, partly because he believed strongly in Anglo-American co-operation, which had served us so well in our dire straits in war, and partly because he was sufficiently practical to be confident that if anything went seriously wrong another arrangement would no doubt have to be made. Beaverbrook, who although not sharing our formal counsels still had a considerable influence, opposed the loan violently. He was supported with equal vigour by Bracken. Among the rest of us, Stanley was in favour of acceptance of the loan in spite of the drawbacks, and most of us were content to follow Churchill and Stanley. The party as a whole made rather a poor show, for sixty or seventy Conservatives went into the Lobby

---

and the International Bank. Proceeds of international transactions were to become freely convertible within five years. The initially established par value of a currency was not to be changed without prior consultation with the Fund, and was to be expressed in terms of gold or U.S. dollars.

D

against the agreement, with a handful in favour. The rest of us, including the front bench, were put into the disagreeable and inglorious position of abstaining. So we got the money—and a short respite.

Without the American loan our situation would be hopeless; with it, unless some spectacular adaptations of policy were made, it would be almost hopeless. For we were spending about £2,000 million a year more on external account than we were earning. We had only about £500 million left in the reserves. Certainly, a large part of the overseas expenditure went on the pay and supply of the Services and occupation forces in every part of the world. But this did not account for more than perhaps £700 to £800 million. How were the other £1,200 or £1,300 million spent? Alas, upon imports. These, even under a tightly controlled system and restricted by the world-wide shortage of shipping, were still greater than any exports we could supply to meet them, in spite of exceptional demand from every quarter, at any rate until our forces could be demobilised and our industrial capacity restored to its peace-time pattern. What, therefore, could we do? The Labour Government were right, in my view, to accept the loan even on these rough terms. Where, perhaps, they were not so prudent was, having taken the loan, to forget all about it, continue their nationalising policies at an almost desperate rate and wait in a resigned mood for the inevitable crash. At this moment in our history we needed almost as great a combined national effort as we had made in 1940. But whereas in 1940 we had created a united Government before meeting Hitler's challenge, we had now destroyed it and reverted prematurely to party politics.

Yet amidst all these details of exports and imports, dollar loans and dollar debts, and all the rest of the complicated economic and financial arguments which seemed at this period to be the daily food of the House of Commons, there lingered in many minds the thought that perhaps the true solution lay elsewhere. Socialism or State capitalism as against private enterprise could be argued interminably, and often unprofitably. But many on both sides of politics began to wonder whether this was the real problem. These men were beginning to feel that the vital questions were how to apply the

most modern methods; how to induce men to work, if not necessarily harder, at least more intelligently; how to make technology
serve the needs of production; how to sweep away all the old and
reactionary restrictions of the past, only applicable to a period when
unemployment was the chief danger. In a word, the financial
problem was really only to be resolved by facing the problem of
productivity. This is still true.

Even by the end of 1946, and in spite of fierce political battles,
this view was beginning to emerge. At the deliberations with my
colleagues towards the end of this year I was able to persuade them
that an amendment to the Address could be used to raise a valuable
discussion on these issues. It was to be a debate of two days; I was to
move the amendment on the first day. More than twenty years later
it is perhaps worth recalling some of the arguments.

Throughout each phase of our long political and social history, a
single dominant theme seemed usually to emerge. On this men's
hopes and fears, aspirations and disappointments, struggles, controversies, failures, partial successes, were concentrated in each succeeding generation. During the twenty years that I had sat in
Parliament, this major role had been played by the question of
employment. Every Government in turn had suffered under the
curse of heavy unemployment. Each had tried to ameliorate its
hardships or remove its causes—with varying fortunes, though never
with success.

The new monetary policies, associated with the name of Keynes
and expanded and adopted by the general agreement of all parties in
the War Coalition, had not yet been put to the test. For so large was
the immediate need for goods and services all over the world and so
great the gap between supply and demand that there did not seem
to be any danger of over-production for many years to come.
Exports should therefore flourish. Of course the prices and the
quality must be right. There were many handicaps and troubles
so soon after the war, including shortages of supply, especially of
raw materials. But broadly speaking the new economic policy held
the field, and I sincerely believed that it would succeed. For the
next generation it would not be unemployment and deflation, but
inflation and all its attendant dangers, which would be our trouble.

This was particularly dangerous in a country like ours, which depended on maintaining a reasonable balance between exports and imports.

> . . . in this period on which we are now embarking the problem of unemployment will be replaced by the problem of production—success or failure in raising production, in overcoming scarcity, in increasing both visible and invisible exports. This will be the test. By this measuring rod Governments will be judged; by this criterion they will stand or fall.[1]

It would be a sad look-out for us all if we were to spend our time on obsolete and fruitless discussions about private enterprise, Socialism, free trade and all the rest. These conflicts and arguments were out of date. In the years between the wars the restriction of production had been fostered by Governments of all parties to meet the lack of balance between production and demand:

> On the employers' side, new entrants were discouraged and competition reduced. By internal selling arrangements many methods tending towards monopoly or quasi-monopoly were developed, and those were justifiable, given the conditions and knowledge of the time. They were supported by Conservative and Socialist Governments alike. In the same way, the restrictive practices of trade unions were developed in order to make the job last as long as possible, since there was a grave risk that when one job was finished it would not be followed by another.[1]

All these practices, whatever may have been their justification in the past, were now surely indefensible. They must somehow or another be abolished or at least modified. This would be the problem of this Parliament and its successors for many years to come.

Morrison, in answering, took a very friendly and constructive line, his chief criticism being a doubt as to how far I was speaking for the party and how far only for myself. Although the debate ended with a wrangle between Morrison and Churchill and a good deal of purely party skirmishing, the Press and the public followed my main theme with interest and approval. Trite as it now seems, it had then a certain novelty.

[1] *Hansard,* 20 November 1946.

Again, in March 1947, there was another long debate on the economic situation, in which I developed further the same arguments and tried to put forward my view as to the form of planning, based upon a partnership between the Government and industry, which was the only workable solution in a democratic society. A purely authoritarian method attracted many minds, including the extreme Left of the Labour Party, and Cripps himself. In the course of the discussion, which was prolonged over three days, in spite of the normal political charges and counter-charges the general tone was appropriate to the crisis which was now approaching. The debate was indeed revealing. I had repeated the argument that no Government of whatever complexion could dissociate itself from a large degree of intervention and indeed strategic management in the economic life of a modern State. We could never return to the old classical *laissez-faire*. After all, the Conservative Party had been opposed to this doctrine for over a century. The question was surely the method, the level and the purpose which the Government should adopt in playing its part.

In November 1946 I had used these words:

> A compromise must be devised between the extreme individualism of the early nineteenth century and the totalitarian tendencies of modern Socialism. Such a compromise is, surely, in the British tradition, but if a right solution is to be found, it must be based upon the right division of functions. In a word, we have to evolve a system whereby public design by the Government is combined with private initiative, and whereby order and freedom can march together.[1]

I repeated them again. It was clear to me by the end of the debate that with the exception of the extreme Right of the Conservative Party and the extreme Left of the Labour Party, there was a general acceptance of something like the Middle Way which I had preached so long. All the arguments that have since followed have been on the methods rather than on the principle. It is true that recently it has been rather fashionable to turn against all 'planning'. But it is difficult to take this reaction too seriously. The old liberal concepts of the nineteenth century cannot be revived. Sometimes these

[1] *Hansard*, 20 November 1946.

criticisms have resulted from planning being misapplied or misused. Sometimes they are more a pose than a policy.

The winter of 1946–7 proved one of the most terrible for many years. As the bitter frost gripped the whole country, the social and industrial mechanism which Hitler and his bombing had failed to destroy seemed suddenly to break down. This of course was bad luck; but it was also partly bad management. The Government naturally accentuated the first and the Opposition equally emphasised the second explanation. Unfortunately, Shinwell, who was the Minister primarily concerned, had taken a fairly nonchalant line in the summer of 1946 when the disquieting figures of coal stocks, both actual and prospective, began to be known. Six weeks of frost, snow and fog completed the general confusion. The coal industry was in its period of transformation from one system to another. This, together with the difficulties of rail and road, produced a situation altogether unprecedented in our history. Power was completely cut for the industrial, and ruthlessly restricted for the private consumer. By 2 February 1947, unemployment had risen to over two and a quarter million. Even by the middle of March it was still over three-quarters of a million. In other words, from $2\frac{1}{2}$ per cent, then regarded as more or less normal, it had risen to 15 per cent. Even when the physical difficulties had been overcome, it remained at 5 per cent.

It is difficult now to recall the mood of the people in this unhappy year, struck by such disasters within so short a time of so great a victory. Fog had followed the frost, and with the thaw came devastating floods. Never had there been anything like it in human memory. By a cruel irony, even the water supply of London was threatened by the polluted reservoirs. Exports had been dramatically affected by the fuel shortage—the loss was estimated at some £200 millions. Worst of all, the figures of coal production continued to fall. A certain divergence had shown itself among Ministers at this time, some pleading for national unity, others continuing to exploit the class war. Bevan's 'vermin' speech was not delivered till the next year (May 1948). Meanwhile, Shinwell's famous declaration that everyone who was not a worker 'did not matter a tinker's cuss', subsequently interpreted to mean that he 'did not care two hoots' about such people, added insult to injury at a time when he had been singularly unsuccessful in his own department. He was the Minister of Fuel.

This seemed to be the turning-point of the Government's hitherto unbroken spell of good fortune, although the electorate remained remarkably faithful. Indeed, the Conservatives never won back a single seat in all the by-elections from 1945 to 1950. Yet somehow, after these winter discontents, Ministers seemed to waver a little in their own self-confidence. Although few of us were conscious of the rapidity with which the inexorable financial crisis was approaching, the leading members of the Government must have been aware of the facts. Dalton's first Budget in October 1945 and his second Budget in the spring of 1946 had been notable performances, well received by the City, the Press and the public. In spite of the enormous expenditures which were still necessary before war commitments could be reduced and the main armies demobilised, the Chancellor of the Exchequer was able to claim that within the coming year we would be in striking distance of a balanced Budget. Naturally, the war and immediate post-war years had been years where Budget deficits had been unavoidable. But in his third Budget, introduced on 15 April 1947, Dalton was able to claim a surplus of just under £300 million. This was a heartening result. Both the Press and public opinion recognised with admiration not merely the lucidity of the Chancellor's exposition but his robustness and confidence.

Yet in his heart he must have known that it was not the stabilising of the Budget in terms of internal expenditure that was his main anxiety. It was the heavy deficit in the balance of payments and the eating up of the dollar loan. Eden appealed to the Government to 'stop galloping ahead down nationalisation avenue' and concentrate 'their attention on food which was threatened, fuel which was gravely short, houses where the programme was deficient, agriculture harshly hit by loss of stock and flooding and, above all, the problem of the trade balance'.

Regardless of approaching danger, the nationalisation machine was driven ruthlessly forward from target to target, with all its accompanying inflationary expenditure on compensation and on new capital investment. The National Health Service—the crowning achievement of many years of gradual approach to the Welfare State —was due to begin in July 1948, with an ever-increasing burden of cost to the Exchequer. During 1947 it was clear that the dollars which were being spent largely upon consumer goods would soon be running out. What Dalton has called, in his most revealing reminiscences, the problem of 'the vanishing dollar' began to become increasingly menacing.

Yet Dalton still maintained, with unflinching resolution, his cheap money policy. If inflation was to be restrained by new taxation, even by some £200 million in a full year, could this policy be effective with money so cheap and so readily available? Why was Bank Rate kept throughout all this period and that of his successors at 2 per cent? The answer lay no doubt in the memory of the years of deflation and restricted credit which had accompanied, and perhaps been the cause of, the bitter years of unemployment. But a new paradox had taken the place of the old. Between the wars, we complained of 'starving in the midst of plenty'. Now with less food available than in war-time, with almost everything rationed or 'in short supply', and with a terrifying housing shortage, nothing was cheap or readily obtainable except money.

All through the spring and summer of 1947 the crisis moved inexorably forward. The American loan had been intended to last, together with the Canadian credit, until 1949 or 1950, by which time it was hoped that all would be well with our balance of trade.

We used to put down questions, which were sometimes answered and sometimes evaded, as to what the dollar credit had been spent upon and how much remained. Alas! Thirty per cent or more of it had melted away through a rapid depreciation in the value of the dollars lent to us owing to the rise in prices. In addition, something of the order of $120 million a year was going to feed the Germans. All this meant that the terms which we had agreed at the end of 1945 had become impossible for us to honour by the summer of 1947. We were pledged to make sterling freely convertible for all current, as opposed to capital, transactions by 15 July. We duly carried out our obligation. By the end of July 1947 only about $1000 million out of the $3,750 million remained. There was also the bullion reserve of £600 million, soon in its turn to be depleted. The import programme, already restricted, was heavily cut again. This necessitated a reduction in the meat ration to a point lower than during the war. Yet since world prices were rising rapidly, the relief to the exchange was small. All through this critical time the continued lag in coal production caused the gravest concern. In addition to a general slowing down, unofficial strikes had caused additional loss in certain areas. As production fell and the intake of labour was reduced, even the most credulous began to wonder whether the psychological effect of nationalisation was likely to be so great as had been claimed.

After six weeks the effort proved too great. The world, starved of dollars and replete with sterling, drew heavily upon us, as might have been foreseen. On 20 August, after frantic negotiation, convertibility had to be abandoned. What was perhaps more serious was that after the beginning of September 1947 $400 million would be all that remained of the American loan or line of credit. It therefore became necessary to introduce still stronger measures, and to revert to some of the classical methods for restoring confidence.

At the end of the summer, as the drain on dollars continued, the country waited for the Government's plans. The total adverse balance of the Sterling Area against the dollar was now said to be in the region of £10,000 million. Yet Ministers seemed still to have no firm grip on the situation. At last, in October, some more resolute action was announced by Cripps, in his capacity of Minister for Economic Affairs. Taking account of the cuts already announced, the dollar deficit would be running at £475 million (nearly $2000 million) a year. Further restrictions on raw materials and tobacco, as well as on the armed forces overseas, would yield another £100 million savings. A £200 million reduction in capital expenditure at home would be made 'as a first step'. New starts in house building would be postponed, and only factory building for export purposes would be allowed. (Practically no private building of houses was at this time permissible.) He hoped that as a result of various international agreements exports would rise. In addition, the announcement of the Marshall Aid offer by the Government of the United

States, another example of the remarkable foresight and generosity of American statesmen when the true facts were fully understood, was bringing a new hope to Europe. If, as we believed likely, aid to Europe itself were not to be restricted to dollar purchases, the outlook for British exports would be encouraging. All these steps were preliminary to Dalton's last Budget. Yet when this was introduced on 12 November it was well described by a Member who said that the nation needed and was prepared for a shock and received a sedative. A greater shock was in store.

At this stage in its life, the prestige of the Labour Government had fallen to its lowest point. Confidence had been gravely shaken. As a sign of the gravity of the situation the Government had taken powers unprecedented in peace-time. The Transitional Powers Bill, including direction of labour (though this was sparingly used), introduced in August, seemed to place unlimited authority in their hands. It was aptly described by Churchill as 'a blank cheque for totalitarian government'. But neither Attlee nor Morrison was the kind of man who would form a deep plot to conduct a social revolution by ministerial order. The danger was rather that they would hesitate to act with sufficient decision. Nor were the electors, though stunned and disillusioned, yet in the mood to transfer their allegiance to the Opposition. The Gravesend by-election, for which we had high hopes, proved a disappointment. There was a swing of votes here as in two other places, but not enough to win the seat.

This, then, was the situation at the end of 1947. Attlee still presided over the Government with apparent nonchalance and in this storm of trouble bravely kept his head. The attempts to unseat him failed dismally. But the collapse of all the Socialist plans, culminating in the eclipse of Dalton, whose buoyancy had up to now seemed symbolic of the once triumphant mood of Labour, led to the emergence of one man of outstanding quality and peculiar gifts. On Cripps and his power to ride the storm all the hopes of the Labour Party and even of the nation were now to be concentrated.

In the middle of the economic stresses and anxieties of 1947 the Government suddenly introduced a strange diversion. In the King's Speech on 21 October, reference to a Bill to amend the Parliament

Act revived a controversy which had slumbered for thirty-six years. The Lords' power of veto was to be reduced from two years to one. Since nobody suggested that the House of Lords had misused its powers or had conducted itself in anything but a responsible manner, it was difficult for the Government to rebut the charge that this was an ingenious political device, the purpose of which was to allow the Steel Bill to be postponed to a later part of the session without the danger of being too late to overcome the Lords' veto. In the spring of 1948 it became clear that this was the true motive. An inter-party conference was held on this question in March, which reached agreement on the constitution of a new House of Lords, but failed to agree as to the period of delay which any suspensory veto might impose on a particular measure. I have always felt that the Conservative leaders made a mistake in not accepting the period twelve months from Second Reading, which the Government proposed, and by insisting on eighteen months from the Second Reading or twelve months from the Third. In the event, the new Parliament Bill was forced through and the House of Lords was weakened as to its powers, without attaining the advantage of improving its public 'image' by a modification of its membership. Unfortunately this and other controversies raised the temperature of party dispute in the remaining years of the Parliament. Conservative bitterness was accentuated by the Government's somewhat dubious device of arranging a short Parliamentary session in the autumn for the sole purpose of passing the new Parliament Act under the provisions of the Act of 1911 before the dissolution of Parliament.

The year 1948 included a Reform Bill abolishing not merely the last relics of plural voting but also the university representation and one of the two City Members, and making a large redistribution of seats. It is perhaps worth recalling in connection with Morrison's Reform Bill that the use of motor-cars at elections raised a violent if rather ludicrous controversy. In 1948 it was assumed that the Conservatives would gain largely by the right to take voters to the poll in motor-cars, and elaborate provisions were passed to restrict or prevent this well-known practice. Today it seems incredible that this issue could even be raised. But these were days when motor-cars were still regarded as the privilege of the rich. The 'affluent society' had to wait for thirteen years of 'Tory misrule' to become effective.

But these were distractions. Throughout 1948 the attention of Parliament was concentrated almost entirely upon economic and financial matters. During the fifteen months after the disasters of 1946–7 –that is, from the end of 1947 to the spring of 1949–the strength of the Government slowly increased and the spirit of the country recovered. Indeed, mesmerised by the skill and determination shown by Cripps, a mood of confidence began to return. If Dalton's emergency Budget at the end of 1947 could be criticised as not sufficiently severe to meet the economic situation, the same accusation could not be brought against Cripps's Budget of 1948. Indirect taxation was heavily increased, additional imposts on beer, spirits and tobacco being the chief method of reducing the excessive purchasing power of the mass of consumers. But Cripps, while giving certain concessions to the lower income groups, appeased his party by swingeing demands upon the surtax-payers. His plan in fact amounted to a capital levy, for it was an additional 'once and for all' tax on the larger incomes by which one extra year's surtax was extorted. It was clear, therefore, that with income tax at 9s. in the £ and with surtax running up to very high levels, the extra tax on investment income could only be paid out of capital. This plan, although it infuriated Mr. Bernard Shaw, satisfied the Left wing of the Labour Party. At the same time, so great was the effect of the conversion of the 'authorities' to the Keynesian doctrine, as it was generally understood by these recent converts, that Bank Rate remained at what seems to us now the incredibly low figure of 2 per cent.

For the coming year, in what he called 'the battle for solvency', Cripps was more hopeful. The problem was that although the Budget had a surplus of £700 million to the good, the trade balance was about the same amount to the bad. But one was in pounds, the other in dollars. Much depended upon the effect of Marshall Aid during the year; and although Congressional approval was not given until the middle of 1948, Cripps had no hesitation in prophesying that the pressure would be relieved and the deficit on the exchanges reduced if the country would support him in the combination of high taxation and low living. One concession was, however, made in the spring of this year. Petrol rationing was modified to the extent that the public were given at any rate the opportunity of travelling ninety miles in a month! This standard ration was not, however, additional to the various special allowances already in force.

But Cripps could not—or did not—halt the policies which were to some extent responsible for these troubles. The continual flow of nationalisation plans went on, notwithstanding the weakness of already nationalised industries. Great inflationary outpourings of capital could not be sufficiently balanced by Cripps's measures in other fields. He made exports his main theme, and there were many on our side of the House who criticised him for his emphasis on this urgent need. For they felt that he did not sufficiently realise that in mass-production industries a buoyant home market is an essential basis for high exports. Yet Cripps was broadly right, and under his strong lead there was a sense of improvement. The reserves at any rate would now be likely to last till the end of 1949. The net drain in 1946 had been £226 million; in 1947, £1023 million. It was hoped to reduce this to £222 million for the first six months of 1948. The total disappearance of the reserves in a couple of years did not seem to strike the country with any particular alarm. They thought that somehow or other America would come to the rescue again. These were dangerous illusions. The promotion of wage stability and the first steps towards an 'incomes policy', together with the fixing of prices and the restriction of profits and dividends, were preached by Cripps with increasing fervour, and absolute, even moving, sincerity. If they were not more effective, it was because the Government did not practise what it preached.

As the year passed, the failure of John Strachey's grandiose scheme for feeding Britain by growing groundnuts in the African bush began to be apparent and was soon to recoil on the Government as a ludicrous fiasco. Dalton joined in our discussions, after a year's silence, with an accusation of conspiracy in the City and in the financial Press to defeat his cheap money policy. But now that 'Daltons' stood only at 76 and it was generally believed that the trade union funds had been invested heavily in this type of security, there was a certain resistance to his reappearance. Meanwhile,

Cripps had recorded his pleasure at certain signs of 'disinflation' such as consumer resistance to luxury goods as 'the first step in the direction in which we want to go'.[1] In this phrase can be summed up at least a part of his philosophy; by reducing lower and lower the general standard of living and avoiding the temptation presented by indulgence in minor luxuries, it might be possible to win through. But alas, while he could partially control consumption by fiscal and other methods, the problem of increasing production was not so easily resolved.

Although the finances of Marshall Aid (known officially as the European Recovery Programme) were somewhat obscure, with complicated provisions regarding what Britain would draw direct from the United States and what cross-payments backwards and forwards we would make with Europe, it was nevertheless clear that in one way or another we should be likely to benefit to the tune of some £300 million. Thus as 1948 passed, prospects improved. Cripps began the first of his long series of declarations that there could be no question of the devaluation of the pound. Our position was further strengthened by a series of bilateral agreements with various countries. Although these were sadly out of tune with the hopes for multilateral trade with which the world had confidently set out immediately after the war, they were useful and profitable in the short term.

By the spring of 1949 the tide seemed to have turned and the vision of the future to be brightening. In the early part of 1949 the Government could claim that the prospects of finally stabilising the British economy were in sight. All the people had to do was to accept, with a good grace, temporary hardships and restrictions.

Perhaps the most disagreeable of these was the reduction of the meat ration still further to 8d a week, the lowest point ever reached in the history of the country. But this was not wholly due to lack of money but to the delay in reaching agreement with the Argentine Government and the inability of that Government to carry out its undertakings. In other respects there were alleviations. The petrol ration was doubled for the summer months of 1949, and on the historic First of May–Labour Day–the restrictions on street

[1] *Annual Register, 1948* (London, 1949), p. 42.

lighting were removed. Great crowds stood in Piccadilly Circus to watch the blaze of lights which had been extinguished on the outbreak of war ten years before. There was an increased ration of paper; by the spring of 1949 even clothes, as well as textiles, could be freely purchased.

In this situation in the early months of 1949 our Conservative outlook seemed rather grim. We could protest against Cripps and his philosophy, but it certainly seemed to be winning through. We had continued to fail in Parliamentary by-elections. We had gained no great advantages in the local elections. As the date of the General Election approached, in spite of the great progress which we had made in the reorganisation of our party, our immediate prospects were not hopeful. So matters stood in April 1949.

In the early months of 1949 the Government were still riding high upon the world-wide reputation of Cripps as a kind of a cross between a priest and an economist, both being professions generally admired as influential and powerful. In January Cripps was able to assure the public that the visible adverse balance of trade in the previous December had been the lowest for more than two years. We were making progress, and with unremitting efforts we should be able to reach our goals. He still urged restraint both in wages and profits. Morrison campaigned vigorously on the same lines, and it certainly looked as if the Labour leaders had grounds for their confidence. As usual, corresponding dissatisfaction began to spread among the less stout-hearted of our supporters in and out of Parliament. People began to talk more openly of the failure of the leadership. Their doubts were confirmed by the loss of a significant by-election in South Hammersmith which we had been confident of winning. Mutterings began again about Churchill's age, incapacity and unsuitability to modern life. All these, as I have often noticed, were merely the nervous reactions of those about to plunge into another electoral contest.

Everything seemed to be moving along quietly with debates on the Lynskey Tribunal (a fairly solid mountain which gave birth to a very modest mouse), the abolition or the prohibition of hunting and coursing, and the need for spelling reform. While the foreign situation was still confused, it no longer seemed quite as menacing as before. On the home front, strikes or threatened strikes in the transport industry were troublesome rather than dangerous. In the trade union world Arthur Deakin's firm stand succeeded once again in blunting the Communist attack. His allegation that the month of August 1949 had been chosen for a fierce onslaught on the British economy by the Communists, with methods similar to those employed in France a year before, attracted much notice and helped to strengthen public confidence in the management of the trade union movement and its ally, the Labour Party. That Harry Pollitt—the Communist leader—categorically denied all these accusations seemed to confirm their truth.

On the economic front the delicacy of presenting our case for Marshall Aid to the United States was emphasised by the reactions to a rash statement by an Under-Secretary declaring that our recovery was complete and that we were in sight of balancing overseas payments. Opponents in Washington at once seized upon these boasts and decided to reopen hearings on Britain's need for $940 million in the second year. Poor Cripps had now to issue a statement saying that we had only recovered in a 'Pickwickian' or 'Crippsian' sense. We had passed our pre-war production level, but we needed at least $1000 million of aid across the exchanges. This little squall which blew up so rapidly was symptomatic. Yet we still hardly realised the truth or understood the dangers which lay ahead.

Thus all seemed to be progressing towards a year of quiet progress, culminating in a General Election in which it would be difficult, if not impossible, for the Conservative Party to recover anything like parity. Harold Wilson, President of the Board of Trade, had recently assured the drapers of Britain that it was not in the mind of the Government to nationalise the retail drapery trade. On this low note the stage was set for the high drama of the concluding months of the Parliament. The Budget was introduced on 6 April. It was to be a milestone to Conservative victory and a tombstone in the Socialist graveyard. Now at last the tide of our fortunes was to turn and flow in our favour. The ebb was not to come for nearly fifteen years.

The Budget proved to be neither what is called 'hard' nor 'soft'. It was neutral. It became known as a 'consolidating' Budget. In

May 1949
'Great crowds stood in Piccadilly Circus to watch the blaze of lights which had been extinguished on the outbreak of war ten years before.'

other words, since it did what most of the orthodox authorities had regarded as likely and even salutary, it pleased nobody. Had Cripps embarked upon a new set of savage attacks on the 'rich'—that is, had he imposed increased burdens on the higher range of incomes, already taxed almost to extinction—he would have delighted most of his own supporters. Had he given any sign of adopting a policy of 'incentives' to encourage production, or included some measures towards greater freedom with a view to facilitating industrial expansion—above all, had he made significant cuts in Government expenditure—his proposals would have been welcomed by the Conservatives and no doubt by many moderates on all sides. As it was, although introduced with all his customary clarity and sincerity, and inspired, no doubt, by a sense of approaching danger, the Budget of 1949—after the first gasp of disappointment—was greeted by a wave of general indignation. It was attacked with violence and persistence from all sides. Moreover, since this was the last Budget likely to be introduced before the General Election, it allowed him and his colleagues no room for further manœuvre.

A 'flat' Budget introduced early in a Parliament may achieve strategic, if not tactical, advantages for a Government if it can secure the base from which to develop an effective advance in the concluding stages. But as the last financial exercise of the great Socialist Parliament elected in 1945 with such high hopes, it seemed weak and defeatist. The 'special contribution' of 1948, which had raised surtax almost into the form of a capital levy, could hardly be repeated, even if the promises then given could be disregarded or evaded. The Government supporters were scarcely compensated by some addition to the death duties imposed on large estates, or even by the increase of the levy on pool betting. The food subsidies, which had risen to £485 million and if left unchanged were estimated to reach £568 million in the coming year, must be reduced. A limit of £465 million was to be imposed regardless of the rise in the cost of living which must follow. Some increases in postal charges were matched by the exemption of income tax in respect of certain social benefits and a relief to industry by increasing the allowances for new plant. But all this, after the excitements of the last few years, was very tame stuff.

The Labour back-benchers, led by George Wigg, called it a Tory Budget. The Opposition, led by Oliver Stanley, called it 'the end of an era of Socialist policy and Socialist propaganda'. Some complained that the Treasury and the Bank of England had won their long campaign against Socialist finance. Others declared that the trade union leaders could no longer sustain a policy of wage restraint and that all hopes of continued wage and price control were now vain. History repeats itself; and some of these complaints, then so novel, have become sadly familiar. Had the Budget contained a startling development of Socialist policy it would have been violently opposed but strongly, even enthusiastically, defended. Now, for the first time, even the Crippsian mystique had failed. The magician's wand had lost its power. The spell seemed broken.

The first effect was shown in the local elections. Lancashire had already gone Tory, but after the Budget Labour lost heavily all over the country. The elections for the London County Council produced a dramatic and quite unforeseen result. In place of a Labour majority of nearly sixty, the parties were now absolutely equal and a single Liberal councillor held the balance. This unexpected role fell to a respected if unexciting Member of the House of Commons, Sir Percy Harris. The flood of propaganda in preparation for an early election began to pour out in ever-increasing streams. Labour morale, which a few months before had been so high, became rapidly depressed; that of the Opposition rose correspondingly.

We now moved into the long dollar crisis which was to dominate British politics during the summer and autumn of this year. While it would be tedious to recount all the details of this now only too familiar problem, a short account is necessary to give a picture of the new blows which fell upon our much tried people.

The trouble began with a deadlock between the Finance Ministers of the leading nations of Europe meeting in Brussels on the question of the convertibility of the drawing rights of the Marshall Plan debtor countries into dollars and their free transferability within the European zone. After prolonged negotiations, now renewed in Paris, a compromise was reached; but it was clear that the inevitable dollar losses involved in the settlement would put a heavy strain upon the already depleted reserves of the Sterling

Area. A minor recession in America was producing, as so often before, unduly large repercussions on Europe, especially on Britain. The resulting fall in exports to America was accentuated by the continuing obstacles to trade which resulted from excessively high American tariffs, coupled with the restrictions on the importation of important raw materials, notably raw rubber. This protectionist device to support the manufacture of artificial rubber involved the Sterling Area in a loss of at least £100 million a year—a sad response to the exertions of the Colonial Empire during the war.[1] As usual, many plans were discussed in official and unofficial circles alike: an increase in the price of gold; the reduction of tariffs; a new system of world liquidity. As usual, none was adopted. While the discussions were prolonged, the crisis deepened. The arguments for and against the devaluation of sterling now became clamorous.

The American, Canadian and British Finance Ministers met in London in July, and the customary communiqués were given out, vague but anodyne, including the formal repudiation of any question of devaluation. It was agreed that there should be fresh talks in Washington in September between the same Ministers. Meanwhile, all possible short-term expedients were set in motion unilaterally by the British Government. Licences for imports from dollar sources, already limited, would now be further reduced. (It is worth remembering that we were still working under a strict system of licensing and control inherited from the war.) There would be cuts in the import of machinery, timber, pulp, non-ferrous metals, steel and tobacco. The sugar ration would be lowered to 8 oz., and since sweets had anyway disappeared from the shops, the war-time system of rationing would be revived. However, none of these measures would be effective unless exports could be increased by some means, or further large loans could be made available. But after the huge American loan of 1947, new borrowings seemed 'unthinkable'.

All this time the party pamphlets poured out. 'Labour Believes in Britain' was countered by 'The Right Road for Britain'. Churchill made two or three powerful speeches in the country in his most combative mood. These were answered by Attlee with sprightly

[1] *The Blast of War*, p. 168.

accusations of Conservative 'window-dressing'. So it went on until the public confusion was so great and the sense of uncertainty so harmful that the Prime Minister took the unusual step of announcing on 13 October that he had no intention of advising the King to dissolve Parliament during the current year.

But the fateful decision on sterling had already been taken. The position had become untenable, and the run on the reserves had begun to grow from a trickle to a flood. There was a hold-up of forward contracts and current payments in view of likely devaluation, as well as a mass (or so Cripps alleged) of 'black market' and 'cheap sterling' transactions at home and overseas. Accordingly, on 18 September, in a famous broadcast, Cripps announced that the pound would be devalued from $4.03 to $2.80. After considering the relative advantages of a floating or fixed pound, the Government had determined to revalue to the highest point at which sterling could reasonably be held. In this broadcast Cripps used an unlucky phrase which was much quoted against him. In reviewing the history of recent years, he declared that 'we have tried to overcome our series of difficulties by a series of expedients which led to a series of crises as each expedient became exhausted'.

Parliament was recalled for a short but unproductive session at the end of September. The relative advantages and disadvantages of the step which had been taken under duress were debated at length, but without any very clear conclusion. The Government maintained that the only alternative to devaluation was deflation, mass unemployment and poverty. Meanwhile wage increases must still be foregone; dividends must not be allowed to rise; savings must be encouraged; exports must at all costs be increased. The Opposition declared, with equal fervour, that it was all the Government's fault.

The arguments proved little except that it was high time for the nation to be consulted as to the Government which they preferred to steer them through the crisis. Although, when Parliament met in the normal way at the end of October, fresh cuts in expenditure were announced by the Prime Minister and the Government's record was further denounced by the Opposition leaders, there was a general and growing sense of unreality.

Before the end of the Parliament brought all these now fruitless debates to a conclusion, there was a strange sequel to the dispute about the Steel Bill. It was agreed that the House of Lords would pass the Bill on the understanding that the new State body would not be incorporated until October 1950 and the Act not become effective before 1 January 1951. In other words, the expected election would amount to a referendum on this issue. This compromise was accepted by both parties without enthusiasm, but with relief that at least some degree of good sense had entered into this controversy at a time when much more serious issues were at stake.

On 16 December Parliament was at last prorogued. Many Bills, mostly of minor importance, duly reached the Statute Book. But there was a general understanding that a dissolution would soon follow, and our discussions would be transferred from the Senate to the hustings. Like my colleagues I was filled with ardour for the coming political battle, although it seemed hardly possible that we should be able to eliminate in one election so great a majority as that with which we were faced. Nor, indeed, on reflection did the prospects of victory seem very attractive. We could only inherit a dark and almost desperate situation.

So ended the story, at least on the financial and economic side, of the great Labour Parliament. It was one of mixed triumphs and tribulations. Many of the questions raised in these five years are still with us. How to get expansion without inflation; how to carry the burdens as well as enjoy the advantages of a reserve currency. Immediately following the Second War, which had lasted six years and involved such terrible losses, moral and material, these were especially urgent and baffling problems. Even now, with many more favourable and alleviating conditions, it is not easy to keep to the narrow path between undue expansion on the one hand, leading to excessive wages, salaries and profits, with all the attendant perils of inflation, and, on the other hand, deflationary measures which involve the waste of resources, both human and material, and the danger of stagnation.

In one respect our position is greatly changed. It is difficult now to recall the degree of restriction and control which still remained in the first years after the war. With all this vast apparatus at hand it had been impossible to avoid first the 'convertibility' crisis and then the 'devaluation' crisis. Then, as later, a Government of the Left was forced to abandon many of the hopes which it had rashly raised in the ardour of election promises and disappoint the great body of its followers by bowing to the harsh realities of a situation for which they were partly responsible. Yet the survivors of that Parliament can look back to a great period in the history of the Labour movement. The Government of 1945 was established by a substantial popular majority, and enjoyed an impregnable position in the House of Commons. This Labour administration—unlike those of 1924 and 1929—was 'in power' as well as 'in office'. Its supporters can regard with satisfaction the changes carried through within our mixed economy by large measures to bring under public ownership and control some of the most important industries and services of the country. These decisions once taken have been accepted or only partially reversed. They can claim, too, to have presided over a rapid advance of the social revolution and the swift development of the Welfare State, the foundations of which had been laid by their predecessors.

In the latter years of this Parliament there had also been, perhaps unavoidably, a sense of frustration among many of those, whether managers or workers, most concerned with the development of production and the future of British industry and commerce. This, combined with the inevitable, but unpalatable, weakening of Britain's relative strength in terms of wealth and military power, may have sometimes led to a certain melancholy among the more thinking men of all parties. It was not defeatism, but disillusionment. The struggle had been so hard. The fruits of victory seemed so bitter. I had, perhaps foolishly, expressed some of these sentiments in a talk with Field-Marshal Smuts in the summer of 1949. I still cherish a letter which he wrote shortly after his return, repeating his more robust views. It ended with these words:

> I feel deeply the heavy onus on us. The Battle of Britain is still on, but in a deeper sense than in 1940. It is also the battle of the world, the battle for humanity. It is in that sense of urgency that I said the few things I did say on that occasion.
>
> Here in South Africa things have gone wrong far more than I had believed possible. But here, also, the fight is on, and will

continue until once more the cycle changes, and the people see the light again. It is this fight which keeps me in the battle line, in spite of the years.

Now that he, like Churchill, is no longer with us, we need more than ever to look back for inspiration to the indomitable spirit of such men.

CHAPTER V

The Russian Aggression

IF the Labour Government elected by so triumphant a majority in the summer of 1945 was destined to suffer under a number of pressing internal difficulties which impeded the successful application of many parts of their Socialist creed, the problems which faced them overseas proved even more baffling. As in the realm of home affairs, the immediate dangers were masked at the beginning by the illusions as well as the triumphs of victory. Yet the leading Ministers in the new administration did not come into office without knowledge and experience. Many of them had played a conspicuous role in Churchill's Government, and had shared the anxieties which began to oppress Churchill in the concluding years of the war. Although they still hoped against hope that a Socialist administration in Britain would be able to get on terms with a Marxist Government in Russia, they could not have shut their eyes to the signs of growing Russian intransigence.

The governing agreement between the Western Allies and the Russians was that concluded at Potsdam in August 1945. In the first stages of this conference Churchill had represented Great Britain and President Truman the United States.[1] Since the outcome of the General Election in Britain could not yet be known, Churchill had invited Attlee and Bevin to accompany him, in order that whatever might be the result there should be no breach of continuity. It was during this meeting that the news of a successful test explosion of the new atomic bomb was received, on 17 July. A week later, by agreement with Churchill, the President informed Stalin of this tremendous event.

The main issue at Potsdam, apart from a good deal of wrangling about the administration of Germany and the question of repara-

[1] President Roosevelt died on 12 April 1945.

tions, was the Polish claim to annexation of German territory up to the line of the Oder–Western Neisse. This demand was supported –and indeed inspired–by the Russians and sustained by the argument that the Poles had already occupied the area. But Churchill in previous discussions on this matter had only intended that the western frontier of Poland should reach the Oder–Eastern Neisse. He strongly opposed this additional claim, since it would involve moving another three million Germans from their homes, making eight or nine million in all. Furthermore, these refugee Germans would swell the population which would have to be fed in western Germany by the Western Allies, while the land which normally supplied their sustenance would be lost to them. In Churchill's words, 'they would have the food while we would have the mouths'.

The Russians justified their demand by the argument that 'the Germans have all gone', a statement not supported by the information available. The Russians, by way of compromise, proposed that a final adjudication should be left for the peace conference; but this was an illusory concession, since by the time any conference might meet, possession would have become nine-tenths of the law. Therefore Churchill obstinately refused to agree. After Churchill had left, Attlee and Bevin took his place as sole negotiators. They were finally overborne by the argument that there was a 'vacuum' left by the fleeing Germans which the Poles might as well fill, at any rate 'for the time being'.

Within a few days of the end of the Potsdam conference, the world was staggered by the shattering news of an event unprecedented in history, and to the vast majority wholly unforeseen. An atom bomb was dropped on Hiroshima on 6 August, and three days later another on Nagasaki. The effects were devastating. On 14 August the Japanese surrendered and the Second World War was now formally at an end. In these strange and sombre circumstances mankind moved towards the Nuclear Age.

Yet the immediate situation which confronted Britain was by no means desperate. In spite of the ambivalence of the Russian position on Poland, it was still possible that things would work out better than we feared. In July 1945 a Polish administration was formed which included Stanislaw Mikolajczyk, the leader of the Peasant

Party. The Yalta Agreement had at least resulted in the formal organisation of a united national government. In spite of many disquieting developments, there was still a belief that by friendly negotiation, pursued by Bevin with remarkable patience as well as persistence, conditions would improve. For the Russian intentions, although suspect, were not yet clear.

Britain's position, objectively considered, was certainly not encouraging. Our fundamental weakness had been temporarily concealed by the glamour of victory. During the war our authority had been enhanced, first by our single-handed resistance to Hitler in 1940 and 1941 and secondly by the disproportionate number of forces which Great Britain and the Empire had put into the field, and their splendid feats of arms. Yet our enfeeblement, although masked, was real. Apart from the strain upon our whole people involved in the long struggle, we had effected a complete diversion of our economy to war purposes on a scale far beyond that which America had attempted or Germany accomplished; we had suffered the loss of £1000 million of our foreign assets; we had incurred an external debt of at least £3000 million. Our export trade had been largely abandoned, and we had lost many of our best customers either because of their own ruin or because of our inability to supply their needs. In the East, the victory over Japan, won largely by American forces, had failed to restore our old prestige. All this amounted to a dramatic declension in British power. This was to some extent revealed in the economic crises which struck us one after another in the following years. Moreover, although at first we did not realise its import, our traditional policy of granting full independence to the White Dominions—which reached its final fruition after the First War—was now to move forward with inevitable and inescapable momentum to include our Asiatic and African possessions. At the same time, the United States, in accordance with Roosevelt's declaration at Yalta that all American troops would have left Europe two years after victory, seemed about to return to their traditional policy of isolation. Meanwhile, demobilisation both of British and American forces proceeded rapidly. Since the Russian armies remained, in undiminished strength, in control of half of Europe, the power of the Western Allies had begun to wane while that of the Soviets still waxed. Yet within a few short years all this was to be reversed. The Russian aggression was to result in a radical change in American opinion and a corresponding alteration of the foreign and military policy of American Governments.

There was an important difference between the situation in 1945 and that in 1918. Western and Central Europe were ruined by both wars; but at the end of the First War Russia had been prostrate as well as Germany. Now Russia, in spite of heavy losses in men and material, was victorious and triumphant, with immense manpower available and great supplies of arms. Nor had a Russian Government to fear any public opinion demanding rapid return to peace conditions. Moreover, the Russians held the central position, poised to exert their pressure on limitrophe countries and to pursue their political aims with ever-increasing authority.

After 1945 the main British purposes and objectives must be to rebuild the economy; to secure Dominion and later Commonwealth support for British foreign policy; to reduce our inflated forces as far as was consistent with maintaining our influence; to obtain all the help we could from the United States without provoking a relapse into isolation; and by every means in our power, short of wilful blindness to realities, to remain on good terms with the Soviet Union. This mood was dominant throughout the first two years.

On 20 February 1946 I was selected to open a two-day debate on foreign affairs. Bevin, as Foreign Secretary, chose to speak at the end and no Minister spoke in front of me, an unusual procedure which put me in some difficulty. After welcoming the first meeting of the United Nations—an historic event—I felt it right to say that we should not disguise from ourselves the other side of the picture. The relations between the Great Powers were now greatly, even alarmingly, strained. New groupings of minor satellites round one or other of the Big Three were taking shape. Soviet diplomacy, for whatever reason, seemed to be concentrating upon outward pressure in the Mediterranean and the Middle East against well-recognised and established British interests. The same technique was being followed in the Security Council—to attack all the weak links in the chains of world security and peace:

It would be folly not to recognise that the Anglo-American-Russian Alliance that held so firmly, in spite of so many difficulties throughout the years of war, is virtually, if not formally, in abeyance.[1]

Naturally I devoted part of my speech to a description and defence of British policy in Greece, now triumphantly vindicated. I was also anxious about Italy. The recovery of Italy as a stable and democratic power in the Mediterranean was a British interest and a world interest:

It is nearly two and half years since the Armistice was signed. They have been a long way to work their passage home. The Americans and ourselves have made great efforts for Italy, but it is now essential that a formal peace shall be made and made quickly.[1]

(In fact, peace was not made for another year.) I went on to express my fear that Italy would become just a diplomatic pawn in the great game, to her detriment and ours. All these uncertainties were creating an atmosphere of suspicion and distrust. I was reminded of Metternich's famous reception of the news of the death of the Russian Ambassador at the Congress of Vienna. 'Ah,' he exclaimed, 'is that true? What can have been his motive?' I had to admit that perhaps the anxiety—not to say the growing scepticism—of opinion at this time was healthier than the facile optimism that had followed the First War. Nevertheless, in spite of our anxieties, it was clearly still right to work for some accommodation and not yet abandon the attempt. I had therefore no hesitation, on behalf of my party, in giving our full support to Bevin in his struggle to halt the drift into a final division of Europe.

In the concluding part of my speech I tried to penetrate the mystery which then surrounded, and still to some extent surrounds, Soviet policy. What, I asked, did Russia really want? What was the motive behind all these manœuvres? Were they a manifestation of the expansionist policy which had inspired Tsarist Russia—greatly to the alarm of the European powers—during the greater part of the nineteenth century? Had this urge, temporarily sus-

[1] *Hansard*, 20 February 1946.

pended during the revolutionary period, once more taken control? Had Russia, yielding to those recurrent forces which seemed to seize nations in turn, Spain, France and Germany, made up her mind to dominate the world? Was it a new Imperialist drive? Or was it, as many believed, a return to the proselytising fervour of international Communism? There were many possible explanations. If we were to be victims of a new aggression of either kind, we would do our best to defend both our interests and our spiritual heritage. But, if it were at all possible, we must try to learn the truth:

> These matters are too grave to be dealt with on party or preconceived lines. We cannot be pro-Russian or anti-Russian; we must be pro-mankind. This is the situation. If it drifts on, it is full of danger threatening ultimate disaster.[1]

In the search for a possible explanation, I raised a point which had been much emphasised to me by Russians both in the Mediterranean campaign and later. I felt that we had sometimes made insufficient allowance for the psychological background of the Russian people:

> All through her history, in early, medieval and modern times, Russia has been invaded, both from the East and from the West, by a succession of enemies. It is no accident that her recent propaganda—by film, by the written and spoken word, and by orders of chivalry and the like—has all been concentrated upon the heroic figures of Russian resistance in preceding conflicts. Whether it be Demetrius Donskoi or Kutuzov or Suvarov, it is significant that all these great names are now brought back to the public mind. Each of these successive invasions of Russian territory—and in the last 130 years there have been four, the Napoleonic, the Crimean and the two German onslaughts—has caused immense suffering and loss of Russian life and property. The last has been the most devastating, to a degree that we perhaps hardly realise.[1]

What was the reaction to all this? Surely it was the search for security. The French had followed it after the last war when they sought the Rhine frontier. But when denied both this and the American

[1] *Hansard*, 20 February 1946.

guarantee which was to have been its substitute, they had to set in train a whole diplomatic campaign, in order to build a structure of alliances designed to isolate Germany. Might it therefore be that the apparent chauvinism of Soviet policy was a form of insurance, not of expansion; that security, not imperialism, was their instinctive goal? Was it not for this purpose that

> a new *cordon sanitaire* is being created of States made satellite and dependent, both by power and doctrine, partly dominated, partly converted? These are to form a kind of defensive *glacis* of small nations looking to the Kremlin for political and economic theory, and to the local Russian commander for material support, and using their arms and police forces, rather than the ballot box, as the instrument of power.[1]

If this interpretation of Russian motives was right, it need not be fatal if it were dealt with in time. Drift and delay might well lead us into the abyss. The instrument of the Security Council had already become a mere forum for public debate. Sooner or later we must break through and re-establish a method of genuine negotiation both by diplomatic means and by personal contacts.

Within a fortnight of this debate came Churchill's Fulton speech. With his famous phrase, 'From Stettin in the Baltic to Trieste in the Adriatic an iron curtain has descended across the continent', he shook and even shocked American opinion. It was true that events in Poland had proved a great disappointment to all those who had believed in Stalin's good faith. It was not so much the changes of frontier as the gradual Bolshevisation of the country which caused first concern and then anger. Poland after all was a friendly country whose security and freedom had been the occasion if not the cause of the Second World War. Polish armies had fought loyally throughout the long Italian campaign under Allied command. The Polish Air Force had won well-deserved renown. It is true that the Russians were also beginning to exert pressure both in Bulgaria and Roumania. But, at any rate on a narrow view, these might be treated as ex-enemy countries, with no claims on our conscience or right to ask our help.

[1] *Hansard*, 20 February 1946.

Thus the reception of the Fulton speech was mixed. His American hosts, enthusiastic about the man, were reserved about the theme. The comparison between Communism and Fascism seemed lacking in courtesy to our recent allies. Surely the Second War, at least, was to be the war to end war. What was the old statesman doing? Was it restlessness? Was it disappointment over his loss of power? Or—unpleasant thought—could he perhaps be right? After all, he had been right before.

At home, the leaders of opinion, official and unofficial, affected to be pained and shocked—perhaps more pained than anything else. The Prime Minister, the Foreign Secretary and all the Labour Members took great pains to dissociate themselves from this troublesome fellow and his disturbing ideas. Many went further and demanded his public repudiation and even censure. All this Churchill must have foreseen. Yet he deliberately decided to dramatise a menace which almost all Americans, in and out of positions of responsibility, had up to now decided to play down or ignore.

Although I accepted Churchill's diagnosis of the facts—who could resist his battering-ram of argument?—I was not quite certain as to whether he had not over-simplified the moods and motives of those who controlled the great Russian people. Was Stalin really so powerful as to be able to promote his own policy by purely autocratic means? I remembered having been much impressed in March 1945, just before the end of the war, with a visit from Edward Flynn, one of the many personal representatives of President Roosevelt 'swanning' about Western Europe at the time, who had visited me at Caserta. He was, or had been, a political campaign manager, or super-boss, by profession; he was also a man of fine presence, considerable charm and great acuteness:

> Flynn's views on Russia were interesting and rather unexpected. He admired enormously the political machine which controls the U.S.S.R. 'Those are "some" boys.' But he thinks we are all apt to over-estimate the supremacy of Stalin. He does not regard him (as it is now fashionable to do) as a sort of Bonaparte—first consul, if not Emperor. In Flynn's view, a political machine is only as strong as the pillars which support it. The 'boss' must have first-class 'deputy-bosses'. These must be strong,

active, intelligent, hard. If not, the 'boss' will himself be endangered. Nor can he rely on a spiritual sanction (like the Pope) or a ritual and sanctified tradition (like an anointed King or Tsar).

In Flynn's view, the Politbureau (or whatever it is called) is still very strong. And he thinks that the 'boys' were not too pleased by Stalin's concessions at Yalta. Many thought he went too far in conciliation over Poland, Roumania, and liberated territories generally. And ever since he returned to Moscow the 'boys' have been 'stalling on the deal'. They have (with Molotov's active co-operation, M. being jealous of Stalin) done everything to prevent carrying out the agreement reached. And, in Flynn's view, Stalin does not venture to take any active steps, although he personally would like to carry out his word. Stalin, like Roosevelt and Churchill at these conferences, likes to pose as all-powerful. Although the forces controlling (and often opposing) the President and the Prime Minister are overt, they are not much stronger than those which secretly and privately exercise considerable power over Stalin.[1]

Certainly there was good reason for thinking that many changes had taken place in Russia as the result of the great and heroic struggle in which they had been all but overwhelmed, and from which they had emerged only by supreme efforts and superb devotion.

The German attack in 1941 was a bitter blow to Stalin and Molotov, all the more so because it was unexpected. Neither of them had believed the clear evidences of Hitler's purpose.[2] But apart from the military and economic confusion which the war produced, there was a subtler and more dangerous source of concern to the rulers of Russia. The invading German troops had actually been welcomed by much of the population when they entered the Ukraine. Had the Germans behaved with reasonable prudence they might well have succeeded in establishing a powerful separatist movement. However, with their usual brutality, they had alienated the people instead of wooing them by concessions.[3] But the first phase, when the advancing Germans were greeted as

[1] 21 March 1945. [2] *The Blast of War*, p. 148.
[3] R. W. Pethybridge, *A History of Postwar Russia* (London, 1966), pp. 23 ff.

liberators, had shocked and frightened Moscow. Later, when the end of the war came and the Russian peasant armies began to move across Western Europe, they obtained for the first time some glimpses of the outside world which, even after years of war, revealed a higher standard of living and many novel refinements of civilisation. All this had made a deep impact on the soldiers. Finally, the patriotic appeals to Russia's splendid past which became necessary during the war had stirred old and dormant emotions. The concept that Russian life and glory had begun only with the Bolshevist revolution was correspondingly weakened. The idea of Holy Russia re-emerged from limbo. In a sense, there had always been an 'iron curtain' since 1917; in the last months of the war it was temporarily lifted. Perhaps—or so it seemed to me—it was fear of internal reaction rather than a desire for fresh conquests that was at the root of the new aggression.

Yet the Russian armies were powerfully poised. Not only had they the effective occupation of eastern Germany and growing control over Poland, but as a result of the faulty strategy of the Western Allies they had been allowed to occupy a commanding position at Vienna.[1] To what extent Stalin planned world revolution was, and remains, obscure. World revolution had been Trotsky's great cry, and Trotsky had been Stalin's most dangerous enemy. Stalin's reply had been 'Socialism in One Country'. Now it was being extended on a systematic basis to 'Socialism in One Zone'.[2] The control of this zone would certainly be stubbornly defended as essential for Russia, partly to prevent the poison of Western thoughts seeping into Marxist territory and partly as military security against capitalist aggression.

I was not able then and have found it difficult since to make up my mind how genuine was this last fear. Certainly the Russian Government must have known that the Americans would never launch a pre-emptive war. In any event, there was a change in the Russian outlook since 1918. After the First War, the Communist regime in Russia had only just survived a civil war fomented and fortified by foreign intervention. Then, encouraged by the full blast of revolutionary enthusiasm, the emphasis was on world

---

[1] *The Blast of War*, chap. xviii.　　　[2] Pethybridge, p. 38.

E

Communism, almost as a weapon of defence for the survival of the Revolution. After the Second War the Soviet motives were more complex. First was the need to protect the virginity of Marxist Russia threatened by the dangerous seduction of bourgeois concepts. Secondly there was the instinct to build up powerful defensive positions and to make sure that if any war ever took place again it would not be fought on Soviet territory—that is, a policy of defence in depth. Thirdly, there was a revival of the old imperialist designs which had dominated Russia for many centuries. Finally, Germany and the danger of a German revival were a major preoccupation of Stalin and his successors.

By the spring of 1947 it was becoming clear that the prospects of continued unity between the old Allies were dark indeed. Fortunately, peace treaties could still be agreed to which Russia, as well as the three Western Allies, were parties. These were now signed with Italy, Bulgaria, Roumania, Hungary and Finland. But the effect was very different in the various countries. The withdrawal of the Allied Control Commissions had already left Italy virtually free. Finland was able by that skilful balancing which has characterised the policies of successive Governments of that brave nation to keep some measure of independence, although only at the cost of serious territorial losses and heavy indemnities to Russia. The Finnish Government had also been forced to agree to severe punishment of some of her leading Ministers, including Vaino Tanner, one of the heroes of the Winter War. Nevertheless, Finland was still free. But with Bulgaria, Roumania and Hungary the withdrawal of the Allied Commissions was to be followed by a steady tightening of the Soviet grip. We watched helplessly as the opponents of Communism in Eastern Europe were gradually eliminated, with exile the privilege of the more fortunate.

Thus gradually, as the months passed, the old hopes faded. Bevin struggled manfully and never became enfeebled in his nerve or weakened in his determination. He still resisted the Churchill doctrine, as expounded at Fulton. But at the Moscow Conference in March-April 1947 no progress was made with any of the outstanding problems of Europe. As so often before, Churchill's warnings and forebodings proved to be right. The United States began gradually to be drawn into the next stage of the world contest. American opinion came only reluctantly to accept the stark reality of the division of Europe. All through 1946, British troops overseas were equal in numbers to the American forces, and in spite of all our economic difficulties there was talk of still more rapid American withdrawal in the autumn of 1946. At that time the American mood was that in the event of a Russian aggression Europe should be abandoned, not defended. But in the spring of 1947—largely as a result of the futile arguments in Moscow— there was a radical change in policy. President Truman's message to Congress in March of that year called for military and financial aid for the free but threatened peoples of Europe. This was to include a gift of $400 million for Greece and Turkey.

Bevin had always stood firmly for striving patiently for a Four-Power agreement even when the chances seemed doubtful. The official policy of the Labour Party as broadcast by him on 22 December 1946 made it clear that British Socialists still hoped to act as 'mediators' between the East and the West—between Russia and America. Britain, he declared, approved neither the unbridled capitalism of the United States nor Russian Communism. He opposed altogether any thought of an alliance with America such as Churchill had demanded. His purpose was to bring Russia and America into co-operation. Even after the disappointments of the Moscow Conference, Bevin did not despair.

On 15 May 1947 there was a major debate in the House of Commons. The Foreign Secretary opened our discussion in his own highly personal and inimitable style. He began by reminding us that there was no German Government to deal with and that 'the result of the war was a tremendous smash'.[1] There was therefore no pre-cedent to guide him. Nevertheless the problems were urgent. If the tasks of reconstruction were to be unduly delayed, the difficulties would get worse, not better. If the main issues, Germany, Austria and the relations between East and West, were not brought to a satis-factory conclusion in the next conference (to be held in November), then no one could prophesy the course that world events might take.

[1] *Hansard*, 15 May 1947.

Meanwhile, he deplored charges being passed backwards and forwards. For instance, we had been accused by the Russians of employing and protecting former Nazis. All this was quite false and could be proved by the facts and figures:

> When one examines the enormous task that the Control Council [in Germany] and the administration were given to do, in rooting out the worst elements of Nazism after the indoctrination carried on by Hitler, one realises that they have done a great job.[1]

I felt much sympathy for this, for we had met exactly the same trouble in Italy, and similar accusations had been levelled against me when I had been acting as President of the Allied Control Commission. Bevin's main point was that the Potsdam Agreement had been made and ought to be carried out without qualification and without selection.

At that time one of the chief issues in dispute was that of the industrial plant to be left in Germany and its future use, as well as the level of steel output to be allowed or encouraged. The Russians were, not unnaturally, torn between the desire to seize everything of capital value for their immediate use and the need to keep going some current production in order to secure a continual flow of reparations. All this had led to long, tedious and unprofitable disputes—at least, unprofitable for all except the West Germans, who at the end of some years of suffering were able to re-equip themselves with modern plant largely by the help of their old enemies. Meanwhile, since the Potsdam Agreement was not really functioning, the economic fusion of the Anglo-American zones had become essential. This was naturally not welcome to Moscow, but Bevin stoutly defended it:

> Apart from food, the remedy for the present difficulties of Germany lies in the successful fusion first of the British and American zones, and then of the other two zones with the combined British and American zones, as soon as they are ready. The fusion agreement as I have stated so often is open for the

1 *Hansard,* 15 May 1947.

others to join. Ultimately, I hope and believe it will lead to the creation of a unified Germany.[1]

Although the French zone was soon to be amalgamated with the Anglo-American, Bevin's wider hopes were to remain unfulfilled.

On Austria he had nothing encouraging to say. He had hoped that an agreement could have been reached in Moscow on the terms of a treaty. This was still frustrated by the question of German assets in Austria. Although it had been accepted at Potsdam that reparations should not be exacted from Austria herself, it had also been agreed that German assets in Austria should be included in the list of properties available for this purpose. But no definition of German assets had been formulated at Potsdam. The argument about this and other minor matters was to continue for another eight years.

Although the Foreign Secretary was subjected to a certain amount of sniping from his Left-wing critics, the majority of Members, on both sides, were still not without hope of some improved situation later in the year. Churchill's main theme was still regarded with some suspicion even among Conservatives.

When I came to wind up the debate on behalf of the Opposition, it was upon the dramatic change in American policy that I concentrated. To balance our many disappointments there had been one great and outstanding gain—an immense contribution to the profit side of the ledger. This was the recent American initiative:

> We cannot but be glad that the United States have taken a decision, a non-party decision, binding equally upon Republicans as upon Democrats, to abandon isolationism, and to recognise the truth that the safety and prosperity of the New World is inextricably bound up with the restoration and reconstruction of the Old.[2]

It was irresistible to recall the situation at the time of the Greek Revolution in the winter of 1944–5, and to contrast it with the position now. When the Communists had tried to seize power by a *coup de main*, Great Britain had stood alone in saving the freedom of

[1] *Hansard*, 15 May 1947.   [2] *Hansard*, 16 May 1947.

the Greek people. We had met both the relief and the military burden from our own resources. To this end, Field-Marshal Alexander had been forced to detach British and Indian divisions from his army at a time when he was already preparing the final battles of his campaign in Italy:

> While his headquarters was integrated with the American headquarters in every sphere by sea, by land, by air, in the economic field and in the harassing and expensive field of relief, our American Allies were, on instructions from a higher level, scrupulously neutral [as regards Greece]. Neutrality of comrades in a siege is not very pleasant. Meanwhile, a flood of ill-informed attacks upon the honour and integrity of British policy was let loose from a considerable part of the British Press.[1]

It was a great tribute to their good temper and common sense that during this period the relations between British and Americans in the field were never unduly strained. Each had understood and accepted the position of the other. Now the position was radically changed:

> Has there ever been a more dramatic reversal of policy than that of the United States towards Greece in two short years? Has there ever been a more complete endorsement of British policy? Has there ever been a more sensational justification of the wisdom of what we did then? The revolutionary Communist fire was lit in Athens in the winter of 1944, and but for us, but for the British, that conflagration might have spread throughout what was left of free and democratic Europe. If we now pass to the United States, our great Ally, some part of the duty we first accepted, and which we carried out loyally and to the full, we hand it on in pride, and not in shame, 'Our task accomplished and the long day done'.[1]

Although it was gratifying to see our policy vindicated, unhappily we could not conceal from ourselves the reasons for the conversion of our critics. They arose not from an improvement but from a serious deterioration in the state of the world. America had now been forced to stake out strategic positions in Europe as her defence

[1] *Hansard*, 16 May 1947.

against the potential thrust of an expansionist Russia. These were of course precautionary measures, but nevertheless they were defence measures. It was not necessary for me to underline the gravity of the situation, although it seemed only just to be dawning on many people inside and outside the House. The Russian attitude towards Germany and the tactic of procrastination were clearly meant to prevent the re-emergence of Germany and certainly its unification. The failure to agree upon an Austrian treaty; the Sovietisation of the Danube which seemed now to be threatened, rather than the internationalisation which had been virtually agreed; indeed, the massive pressure upon Central and Eastern Europe, clearly marked the beginning of a new struggle. Yet there was even then in my mind a feeling that sooner or later some accommodation had to be made. We must not ignore the danger of the Russian aggression, but we must not exaggerate it; we must try to seek again for the motives, fears and inhibitions which underlay their stubborn truculence:

> It is no doubt, in an exhausted and shattered world, only a war of nerves; but a war of nerves may be very dangerous. Unless within some reasonable time a genuine accommodation can be found between the Communist world and the democratic world, who can say that the same tragedy which we have seen twice in our lives may not be repeated, this time finally and fatally?[1]

On 5 June 1947, Secretary of State George Marshall, in a famous speech at Harvard, made his memorable proposal for Marshall Aid. First Lend-Lease, a pooling of resources unprecedented in history; then the UNRRA contributions and numerous American loans; then Marshall Aid. This was indeed a splendid sequence of wise and generous acts of policy, 'in their purpose, scale and magnanimity, in their freedom from restrictive conditions ... beyond precedent in the history of war and peace'.[2]

Certainly, the effect of Marshall's speech was immediate and dramatic. It was at once welcomed both by Bevin on behalf of the British and Georges Bidault on behalf of the French Governments.

[1] *Hansard*, 16 May 1947.
[2] Lord Salter, *Memoirs of a Public Servant*, p. 311.

Within a few weeks, on 18 June at Paris, they agreed to send an invitation to the Soviet Government to join in a meeting to discuss the whole question of European reconstruction and the American offer. The Russians accepted, and tripartite discussions between Britain, France and Russia began on 27 June. But within a few days it was apparent that the Russians would have nothing to do with the Marshall Plan. Their formal reason was their objection to the suggested procedure. The proposals required European nations to examine their own resources to see what they could provide out of their own production to meet their needs, and that help should then be sought from the United States to meet the gaps which would be revealed by these preliminary enquiries. Molotov, however, took the view that the United States ought to state what amount of money they were prepared to provide, how long it would last and what would be the conditions. Then each country should give a list of its requirements. It was soon apparent that Russian opposition was really due to the fear that any form of joint examination of their needs would be bound to result in a form of European union, at least on economic questions, covering East and West. The excuse was that the Marshall method involved an interference with national sovereignty and national plans for recovery. But this was thin and unconvincing. It was the all-embracing character of the plan, intended to include all the countries of Europe, Communist and non-Communist alike, which was offensive to Soviet policy. Molotov, in his anger, went so far as to accuse the Americans of merely being interested in expanding their own external market in view of 'the approaching crisis of capitalism'.

As a result, the Marshall Plan became not merely decisive in the history of Europe, but divisive. The Russians seemed determined to play their hand in their own way—to collect round them the largest possible group of satellite countries to protect their military security and the Communist ideas to which they were wedded. The Iron Curtain, therefore, was not something which America and Western Europe imposed upon them. Indeed, our statesmen had hoped against hope that it could somehow be lifted or pierced. It was the expression of policies which Stalin either determined himself or had forced upon him by his most intimate advisers. Nor did Molotov content himself with dissociating Russia and her friends from Marshall Aid. He ended his speech with a warning to Britain and France of the grave consequences that would follow: Russia had faced 'threats' before and would not be deterred from doing what she considered her duty. This was indeed 'double talk', when American generosity was twisted into a menace to peace.

As soon as these discussions broke down, the British and French Governments issued an invitation to all other European countries to attend a conference on 12 July to consider Marshall's proposals. They set out, in addition, the first plans for an organisation to make the scheme effective. This became the famous Organisation for European Economic Co-operation, destined to preside over the most critical period of Europe's recovery. Russia's satellites, much against their will, were forced to refuse. But Italy, Belgium, Holland, Luxembourg, Austria, Norway, Sweden, Denmark, Iceland, Greece, Portugal, Switzerland, Eire and Turkey accepted the invitation.

Within a year of Marshall's famous speech, both Houses of Congress voted for 'aid' a sum of over $6000 million, of which $4000 million was for the European Recovery Programme. This immense effort did not exhaust the generosity of the United States, for in addition to direct dollar aid, provision was made for the granting of loans to a number of countries. In the changed conditions of today it would be wise to remember this story with gratitude. There are many who now find it convenient to forget, or even to resent, benefits which they have received.

As was not unexpected in the light of events, when the Council of Foreign Ministers met again in London in December 1947 complete deadlock was reached. Molotov once again demanded that a central German Government should be set up immediately and declared this to be an essential preliminary to any peace conference. Since neither frontiers, powers nor methods of election had been agreed, this seemed a somewhat unreal proposal. Nevertheless, it put Russia into the tactical position of being apparently in favour of a united Germany and placing the odium of prolonging the division upon the Western powers. As the long weary days of talk proceeded, even Bevin's patience began to fail. 'Every time we ask for information,' he declared, 'we get insults, insinuations, or accusations....'

In the British zone no German firms or factories had been sold for reparations; no profits had accrued to the British Government from the sale of Ruhr coal or German timber. Russia, on the other hand, had carried off material to the value of at least $7000 million since the war ended. At the Conference a long battle raged; but it was a battle of words, for it was clear by now that Churchill had been right after all. For the future, be it for a short or long period, the fateful division of Europe had in fact taken place.

When the House met on 18 December 1947 there was a general sense of frustration and failure, but also a recognition of the calm dignity with which Bevin told the sorry story. He had hoped that the four Great Powers would meet in an increasing spirit of friendship and understanding. Unfortunately, this had not been the case. The peace treaties had taken far too long, especially the Italian treaty, although that and those with the satellite nations had at last been concluded. There was no reason for the delay in the Austrian treaty except a squalid dispute about German assets in Austria. The Russian demands were indefensible, and amounted to a permanent hold upon the Austrian economy by the Soviet Government. As regards the German settlement, Bevin protested that he had tried at Moscow earlier in the year to reach agreement by every means in his power. Then had come the Marshall Aid proposals, welcomed by all European States, involving no interference with their independence and sovereignty, but met by a campaign of misrepresentation by the Russian Government. He reminded us that in October the Cominform had been established as an instrument of Russian aggression and disruption. At the same time, the Security Council of the United Nations had been used as a platform for misrepresentation. To all these attacks and provocations he had made no reply. He had gone on hoping for agreement; and now it had failed. Even so he would not close the door but, and this was the phrase which impressed the House, 'We cannot go on as we have been going on.'[1]

By the time Parliament met in January 1948 Bevin himself, who had shown all through an almost excessive patience and willingness to put the best possible interpretation on the Russian attitude, seemed finally to have made up his mind to face reality.

[1] *Hansard*, 18 December 1947.

He declared that there was no doubt that it was the policy of the Soviet Union 'to use every means in their power to get Communist control in Eastern Europe and, as it now appears, in the West as well'. One had only to look at the map and see the great expansion of Soviet power since the end of the war. Now in Greece the same pressures were being exerted, 'where it is not a question between a Royal, Socialist or Liberal Government; it is a question of power politics'. As regards Germany, we had honestly tried to produce step by step, on a Four-Power basis, a situation which would lead to a peace treaty and a competent German Government. But the Russian idea of a German Government was very different from ours and very sinister.

Bevin still disclaimed the old policy of the 'balance of power'. But it was difficult to see from his analysis how this was now to be avoided. Meanwhile, the Left was suspicious and bitter. Churchill's mood was sombre, but his speech was relieved by some constructive thoughts. He did not adopt a wholly pessimistic view. People were asking 'Will there be war?'

> When this Parliament first assembled, I said that the posses-
> sion of the atomic bomb would give three or four years' breathing
> space. Perhaps it may be more. . . . But more than two of those
> years have already gone.[1]

But we had drifted too long; and the best chance of preventing war was to bring matters to a head and come to a settlement with the Soviets before it was too late:

> It is idle to reason or argue with the Communists. It is, how-
> ever, possible to deal with them on a fair, realistic basis, and, in
> my experience, they will keep their bargains as long as it is in
> their interest to do so, which might, in this grave matter, be a
> long time, once things are settled.[1]

These sentiments were unexpected and deeply impressed the House. They were later to occupy much of his thoughts. I did not forget his words.

The Prime Minister, Attlee, contributed a somewhat novel, and to the extreme Left of his party a disturbing view. He declared

[1] *Hansard*, 23 January 1948.

Communism to be 'an economic doctrine . . . which has but very slight appeal to those who have experience of Western civilisation but makes a strong appeal to backward peoples who have never known anything better'.[1]

Through all these critical years, there remained the problem of Germany, obscure to many of us but charged with dire foreboding. Even as early as the debate in February 1946, which was mainly devoted to the growing concern about Russian policy, Germany had been much in my mind. I had always felt that since the rise of Bismarck Germany, not France or even Russia, had been, and remained, the key of Europe. I had therefore declared, less than a year after the defeat of Hitler and his forces, that apart from the countries which we were then discussing there was another great nation, with a large population, great agricultural and mineral resources, great in industrial capacity, with great intellectual and organising power, and with great past achievements. For the moment it was wrapped in mystery and darkness. We had practically no information of what was happening; there was a statistical and international blackout. Yet that country lay at the centre of Europe and at the centre of the European problem. Her name was Germany:

> What is our policy towards Germany? Unless an accommodation can be found, and a formula established between the Eastern and Western hemispheres, you can have no sound policy regarding Germany. If that accommodation is reached Germany, so often the scourge of Europe, can in due course be transformed into a healthy and valuable member of the European family. Only so, can the soul of the German people be saved. But if not, if there is dispute and acrimony and intense feeling between the East and the West, she will once more become a menace to peace. Nothing can prevent the inevitable and logical development of this situation. Germany, now cast down, despised, shunned like an unclean thing, will once more be courted by each of the two groups, and from a starving outcast she will become the pampered courtesan of Europe, selling her favours

[1] *Hansard*, 23 January 1948.

to the highest bidder. She will once more have lost the war and won the peace, and Hitler's dream and mad prophecies will have come true. Therefore, before it is too late let us act.[1]

By the summer of 1947 the responsibility for the British Control Commission, which had hitherto rested with the Chancellor of the Duchy under a separate office, had been transferred to the Foreign Office. The previous Minister had been pensioned off—or rather had become Minister of Pensions. But by this time, although nearly a year had passed since we had debated the German question, all that we had been vouchsafed was a series of Supplementary Estimates, first £80 millions and then £39 millions, as well as £58 millions lost in the currency racket, which we had to pay for the needs of our zone in Germany, out of our own reserves or our dollar borrowings. Parliament had become very critical of this continued strain on us, without apparently any corresponding benefit even for the unhappy people of Germany. It is difficult, more than a generation later, to recall the problems and sufferings of that time. The miracle of German economic recovery has certainly been mainly due to the patient efforts of the German people, under the leadership of brilliant public servants and Ministers. But it is fair to recall how much poor Britain, amidst her own difficulties, contributed to that end.

In an important debate, which took place at the end of the summer of 1947, I was again entrusted with the task of speaking for the Opposition. I maintained that one of the reasons for this vast expenditure falling upon the Allies was that the economy of Germany had been reduced to a state of near-paralysis. All this, apart from the heavy loss to ourselves and the grievous human suffering involved in Germany, carried with it great dangers:

If some would assess the dangers of militant Communism as the greater, and others would put the dangers of a revived militant Nazism as the greater, I think all must agree that the greatest danger of all would be an aggressive combination of the two.[2]

[1] *Hansard*, 20 February 1946.
[2] *Hansard*, 4 August 1947.

At this time I had tried hard to obtain what figures were available from various friends, official and unofficial. This had been a difficult operation since the Government were very cagey about releasing information. Fortunately, a most illuminating article had appeared in *Lloyds Bank Review*. It was both well documented, objective and factual:

> Industrial production in Germany fell by the end of 1946 to 35 per cent of pre-war production. I am speaking of the British and American zones only. By February 1947, it had fallen to 25 per cent of pre-war. The production of consumer goods, which in October 1946 was running at about 23 per cent of pre-war, was, by the winter, reduced practically to zero. The food production of the zone is only sufficient, if it stood alone, to supply about 1000 calories per person. Therefore, the double pressure to which we are so sadly accustomed—the shortage of food, which leads to low production, and the shortage of consumer goods, which leads to an unwillingness of the farmers to grow or to part with their food—all this vicious circle is going on at full swing.[1]

I went on to argue that equally serious had been the complete breakdown of any incentive in Germany. Surely we had ourselves begun to learn that whereas controls might be a convenient way of mitigating, they could not cure a shortage. Only more production could do this, and at the present time nobody in Germany felt it worth while to produce. The possession of money gave no title to goods or services, since everything was rationed and controlled. There was therefore no incentive to earn money. Indeed, the only truly free market in Germany was for postage stamps and antiques.

Unhappily, both in the American and British zones we had introduced our own battle of dogmas. The British Government wanted to nationalise everything; the Americans were in favour of complete free enterprise. Meanwhile, there had been no currency reform. This could have been undertaken in 1946, because at that time there were goods and services available to launch a new currency. Now there was a vast accumulation of money competing with current wages for the reduced quantity of goods and services:

[1] *Hansard*, 4 August 1947.

Even the black market does not afford a great outlet, for the present price of ten cigarettes on the black market is a month's work at present value, while a woollen overcoat is a year's work for the ordinary wage-earner.[1]

The reason for the delay in tackling vital and urgent problems was now clear. It was because, not perhaps without good reason, the Western Allies had gone on hoping against hope that it would be possible to create a united Germany on some kind of democratic basis. I then made a statement for which I was much blamed at the time, but which twenty years later seems not unreasonable:

> We must recognise that partition now [exists] *de facto*. I would not recognise it *de jure*.[1]

Of course, neither the British nor the Americans could be held responsible for this event; they must now recognise it as a fact. We should do everything possible to keep an Allied Control Commission, including Russia, in Berlin, as well as maintain our own rights in Berlin. Even in its most ineffective form the Commission still allowed some contact with the Russian control of Eastern Germany and some machinery for improvement if Russian policy should ever change. Nevertheless, I urged that the British, American and French zones must now be joined to form an effective and workable economic and administrative unit. Since only the Americans could provide the capital, the inclusion of Western Germany in the preparation of Europe's proposals for the Marshall Plan provided an opportunity which should not be lost.

I ended with a plea which was certainly not so popular in 1947. I felt the time had come to put an end to the de-Nazification procedure, or at least to put some limit to its operations.

I had always felt somewhat doubtful as to the policy of the political trials which culminated in the long drama of Nuremberg. Hitler, fortunately for us all, had committed suicide; Mussolini had been done to death by Italian partisans. We were thus relieved of the major burden of dealing with the Heads of State. But what could we have done with them had we captured them alive? To have sent them to St. Helena would have been far too flattering a

[1] *Hansard*, 4 August 1947.

fate; to have killed them in cold blood would have been discreditable; to have put them on trial might have helped to foster rather than to destroy the mystique of their strange reigns.

The arguments for the trials were nevertheless strong. Both Roosevelt and Churchill had repeatedly declared our intention to bring the war criminals of all kinds to justice. In this Stalin had joined enthusiastically. But there seemed to be a distinction between internal crimes and brutalities on the one hand and the waging of war and the invasion or conquest of other countries on the other. For these latter acts of policy, however deplorable, there were plenty of precedents throughout history. Indeed, the Nuremberg procedure nearly collapsed on this very ground—that war, even aggressive war, had not been and could not be a criminal charge. Goering's defence of himself on this point was brilliant, and he scored heavily over the American prosecutor, Judge Robert Jackson. Goering was well able to show that Bismarck, Frederick the Great, Napoleon, Louis XIV and indeed almost every ruler of Europe through two or three hundred years could have been assailed under the strict code of the indictment on these high political issues. But when he fell under the merciless and tireless cross-examination of David Maxwell Fyfe, who pursued him relentlessly not so much upon the questions of high State decisions but upon the almost unmentionable horrors of Nazi persecution, Goering collapsed. The British case had been prepared with a most careful analysis of official archives and records. The story of the concentration camps, of the calculated genocide and all the other terrible crimes committed under Nazi rule was illustrated by precise and careful examination of a vast mass of documentary evidence 'not only from Nazi orders and minutes but from their own films, by which they feasted their eyes on their own atrocities, and our stark documentaries of the concentration camps as we found them'.[1]

Remembering the falsification of history which had been the basis of Hitler's political success, including the myth that the German Army had not been beaten in the First War but stabbed in the back, as well as the delusion about the brutality of Versailles, the so-called 'Carthaginian Peace', there was a powerful argument for

[1] The Earl of Kilmuir, *Memoirs: Political Adventure*, p. 111.

making sure that after the Second War the rottenness, as well as the criminality, of the Nazi regime should be established beyond dispute. If apologists for Hitler should ever appear in post-war Germany, or movements revive with the object of justifying and re-establishing a new Nazi doctrine, the unimpeachable records, documents and films produced at Nuremberg stand as evidence for ever and cannot be controverted.

Considering the immensity of the task, the Nuremberg trials were carried out with reasonable expedition. They were begun in November 1945 and finished before the end of 1946. On the other hand, in spite of our recent enthusiasm for our Russian allies, it had seemed somewhat cynical to informed British opinion that Russian judges could solemnly be associated with the task of punishing mass deportations, mass imprisonment and mass liquidation of fellow citizens or subjects of conquered territories. If Saul had slain his thousands, David had slain his tens of thousands.

On the whole, therefore, I felt at the time, and still feel, that in view of the gain for the future (and it was only the future that mattered, both for the Allies and for the German people growing up in the generations to come), the Nuremberg trials were justified and salutary. This was not because anyone could take much pleasure in the capital punishments of some of the leading criminals, still less in the terrible sentences of life imprisonment imposed on others. It is this great volume of evidence which no critics can ever successfully overthrow, standing on the record, that forms the real value of the Nuremberg trials.

But I was never happy about the prolonged process of de-Nazification. I had found in Italy that when a regime had lasted as long as that of Mussolini it was almost impossible to find anyone in any position of trust or with the necessary technical qualifications who had not been appointed by the Fascists and in some way or other associated with the Fascist Party. Of course, there was nothing in Mussolini's rule to equal the horrors of Hitler's regime. Nevertheless, after removing the main party leaders, *Gauleiters* and all the rest, it seemed difficult to see how this process could be carried on without injury to German recovery and without the danger of stimulating some eventual reaction.

Throughout the early post-war years de-Nazification proved a very thorny problem, creating much unrest and resentment. Moreover, the methods varied in the different zones. In both the British and American zones the procedure was inevitably very slow. Nominally, thousands and even millions of the population fell within the ambit of the de-Nazification laws. But in practice attention was focused on the most prominent personalities. It also seemed strange to many people that certain individuals such as von Papen and Schacht, who had been acquitted by the Nuremberg tribunal, should now be retried in a de-Nazification court in the American zone.[1] All this appeared distasteful and even dangerous for the future. Gradually the matter was handed over to the German administrations, and the German courts began to play a role. Yet the process dragged on year after year and became an increasing burden both to the Allies and those Germans who were trying to co-operate loyally. It was a shock to me to hear two years after the end of the war that Field-Marshal Kesselring, who conducted a brilliant defence against Field-Marshal Alexander's campaign throughout Italy, was condemned to death by a British military court. Although his sentence was commuted, nevertheless it seemed a proceeding of somewhat doubtful value. I expressed some of these views, although they were not very well received, in the debate, and nothing that happened subsequently made me change my opinion.

Apart from this odious question, there was the need to create some kind of German administration. One of the great difficulties was the shortage of capable men, both in industry and local government. The vast officialdom by which the Allies were trying to control almost every detail of German life must be speedily reduced. From my experience in Italy I knew well how easily this machinery swelled and how dangerous it could be in preventing the growth of any real self-reliance and the development of genuine self-government:

Germany must govern herself to a far greater extent than she is being allowed to do at present. From top to bottom, from the

[1] Franz von Papen, Chancellor November 1932–January 1933, Vice-Chancellor 1933–4; then Ambassador to Austria and Turkey. Dr. Hjalmar Schacht, President of the Reichsbank 1923–30, 1933–4, Economics Minister 1934–7.

federal top . . . to the much smaller regional councils and county councils, there must be real self-government. The traditional boundaries of Germany should be revived, as far as possible. Regional patriotism should be allowed to flourish, but it should not be allowed to lead to economic separation. The Germans must be responsible, and must be made to feel responsible.[1]

There were too many reserved subjects, too many British officers, in our zone at any rate, in a parallel position to that of German functionaries, preventing any real responsibility. It is true that there had been some improvement. In 1946 there had been 42,000 officials in our zone alone. Now, in 1947, there were said to be 20,000; but that was still far too many. The Allies should not be day-to-day administrators; a small body of expert advisers would be sufficient. Nor was there any reason why the occupying forces should not be drastically reduced. Our authority—in Germany at any rate—depended not upon the military forces but upon the economic sanctions at our command, for without British and American imports German mouths could not be fed. Above all, there should be no interference and no preference or favouritism shown to German political parties. We must let Germany develop her own freedom and her own life:

> After the last war, we tried to force liberalism upon the Weimar Republic, and we killed both liberalism and the Weimar Republic because they became associated with defeat and dishonour in Germany. In the same way, if we now try to force social democracy upon the Germans they will react as soon as they are free to do so.[1]

Finally, I made a plea for an immediate currency and taxation reform. There could be no return to any kind of healthy life without these; incentive must be brought back. The German economy must be so far as possible free. There must be a complete integration of the Anglo-American-French zones.

Some of these matters were dealt with reasonably rapidly. During 1948 currency reform was successfully introduced, and from that moment the whole life of Germany began to change. The final breakdown of the pretence of co-operation with the

[1] *Hansard*, 4 August 1947.

Russians had at least the benefit of allowing the Western Allies to handle German problems themselves without any inhibitions. The rupture between the war-time allies was symbolised in a most dramatic way by the Russian blockade of Berlin and the long and successful struggle of the Berlin airlift. Before June 1948 Russian interference in various ways with access to Berlin had begun, and after June it became intensified. From 18 June until the Russian acceptance of defeat almost a year later this struggle continued, watched with growing excitement throughout the world as the first great test of will. By a remarkable joint Anglo-American effort, over 200,000 flights carried over a million and a half tons of supplies during these months.[1] In one of his most robust speeches, Bevin claimed that what the British and American air forces had achieved in ordinary conditions of peace could be compared with some of the highest exploits of the war; we had indeed every reason to be proud of them. But the moral effect was greater still:

> It showed conclusively that the people of Berlin did not want to fall into dependence upon Soviet Russia, since they knew that this was the first step of subjection.[2]

The German people had responded and had realised that we could not be driven out of Berlin in defiance of international agreements. The American share of the work had been 60 per cent, ours 40 per cent. Partnership had been as complete as in the years of war.

On 6 July, a few weeks after the beginning of the blockade, the formal instrument was signed for economic co-operation in support of the Marshall Plan. This gave effect to the consolidation of Western Europe, and involved the recognition of the division between East and West. The way was now clear for the formalisation of the situation in Germany. By the end of 1948 the whole apparatus of Four-Power rule had collapsed. Berlin was isolated and besieged. But in the three Western zones, as a result of the currency reform and the aid now forthcoming under the Marshall Plan, a remarkable economic revival had begun. All the preparations were now being

---

[1] Though the blockade was lifted on 12 May 1949, the airlift was continued as a precaution until 6 October 1949.

[2] *Hansard*, 22 September 1948.

made for the establishment of a federal Parliament and Government; its headquarters were provisionally to be fixed in Frankfurt.

Although there were still some intricate problems to be resolved and many disagreements over the allocation of powers between the central, or federal, Government and the separate states or *Länder*, the drafting of a constitution for the new Western State was set in hand, following the promulgation of an Allied Occupation Statute, adjustments of Western Germany's frontiers, tri-zonal administrative fusion and the creation of an Allied Military Security Board. The most troublesome matter still in dispute was the International Ruhr Authority. This question, combined with the policy of dismantling, led to many difficulties in the spring of 1949. Allied counsels were divided, and the Germans succeeded in exploiting these differences with some skill. But in the end, after months of negotiation and as the result of a conference of the three Western Foreign Ministers in Washington in April 1949, all the problems were resolved. A new Occupation Statute was issued in a simplified form, and the three powers agreed upon the new 'deal' for Germany. As a result, the basic law was formally adopted. On 23 May 1949 the Federal Republic of Germany came into being with a constitution which has remained broadly unchanged until the present time. All the *Länder*, with the exception of Bavaria where there were strong separatist leanings, voted in its favour. Bonn was now chosen as the provisional capital. Elections took place in August, and the new Parliament was formally opened in September, when Professor Theodor Heuss was chosen as the first Federal President. Dr. Konrad Adenauer, elected as Chancellor by a narrow majority, formed a Government which was destined to last for many years. Thus, scarcely more than four years after the end of the war, after all the confusions and troubles of a Germany beaten, disheartened and largely destroyed, there was born a new democratic State, which has since proved its strength and power of survival.

These developments in Germany were largely the Allied answer to Russian aggression. All through 1947 and 1948 there had been a steady tightening of the Russian grip on Poland, Hungary, Roumania and Bulgaria. At the end of 1947 King Michael of Roumania was forced to abdicate, and a Republic was proclaimed under Russian control. Poland was now a wholly Communist State, although the people were loyal to the Catholic Church. Hungary had fallen altogether into the hands of the Soviet Government and, like Bulgaria, was largely occupied by Russian troops. This steady erosion of any form of freedom or democracy in the Eastern European countries was accepted, though with regret and with resentment, as inevitable. In Yugoslavia, Tito, while maintaining an intransigent position on Trieste, greatly to the embarrassment of the Italian Communist Party, had ended the monarchical system, and established the 'dictatorship of the proletariat' on orthodox lines with himself in the dominant role.

But the final blow, the news of which was received with special bitterness and anger in the West, was what became known as the Rape of Czechoslovakia. This event took place in February 1948. The process of setting up Communist rule in Czechoslovakia proceeded, under Russian influence, along lines similar to those already effectively followed in other countries. It was not the result of an independent or indigenous revolution. Indeed, Stalin had no particular affection for such developments. In Poland, Hungary, Roumania and Bulgaria, as earlier in the Baltic States, Communist systems had been set up through a combination of external pressure and internal subversion. But no country—except Russia herself—had gone Communist without external pressure. Nor indeed would the Soviet authorities have looked with any great favour on anything of the kind. In Yugoslavia, where no effective Government had survived, even in exile, which commanded the support of the people, and power fell almost naturally into the hands of the partisans, a certain independence of spirit soon began to develop and led later to bitter quarrels between Belgrade and Moscow. However genuine may have been the Soviet desire in theory to see Communism spread throughout the world, any independent Communist country was bound in practice to adopt a form of gallicanism. This was all the more likely if Communism had come about through internal methods alone, unaided either by Russian armies or by the infiltration of Russian agents. Such converts were not to be trusted. A genuine ultramontane spirit was more likely to flourish if the true religion of Communism had resulted from external pressures. In other words, important as Communism was to Moscow, it was more important as an instrument either of imperialism or of security than merely as an expression of the true faith.

The methods adopted for bringing Czechoslovakia under full control were not dissimilar to those used in Poland.[1] Here the Communists had carved out enclaves from the border areas, that is in the lands east of the Oder–Neisse line. In Czechoslovakia they did the same, concentrating on Bohemia. In both cases they succeeded in enforcing a rigid totalitarian control. These were used as a base for extension over the whole country. In Czechoslovakia, Eduard Beneš, the successor of the great Thomas Masaryk, had always shown a certain pliancy. He had yielded, under almost intolerable pressure, to the Germans in 1938. He did not succeed in resisting the Russians. After the war he accepted the People's Front Government, largely though not exclusively Communist. But the Communist bid for complete control was already foreshadowed in 1947, and it even seemed as if they would be able to secure their purpose by at least nominally constitutional methods. By the spring of 1948 it seemed more prudent for the Communist leaders to take power by a *coup d'état*, to be followed by the usual controlled form of elections to ratify their authority. Beneš at first seemed firm; but matters were brought to a head at the end of February 1948 when the remaining non-Marxist Ministers were excluded. By a series of complicated and ingenious manœuvres the Communists consolidated their power, and by the time the representatives of the Soviet Government arrived in Prague the game was lost and won. Beneš, a sick man, having lost all real authority, finally gave his signature to an instrument appointing a new Communist-dominated Government. On the very day that the unanimous vote of confidence was given to the Communist Klement Gottwald and his Government by the Constituent Assembly, Jan Masaryk, a worthy son of a great father, was found dead under his window in the Czernin Palace. His murder, or suicide, caused a wave of horror throughout the free world.

Thus, by the early spring of 1948, Russia had organised and

[1] Pethybridge, p. 86.

enforced a Communist seizure of power in a country whose liberalism and democratic traditions had long been recognised in the West. These events made a tremendous impact upon European and American public opinion. They were especially resented in Britain, where the memories of Munich were still strong. A sense of shock and almost despair ran through the country, with a corresponding impetus for the unity of Western Europe and close alliance with America. Russia's forward march appeared to be no longer confined to the security of her immediate frontiers or the domination of ex-enemy countries. A whole grand design seemed now to be unfolding. In addition to the annexation of the Baltic States as well as part of Finland and Eastern Poland, Bulgaria, Roumania, Hungary, Albania, the new Polish State and now Czechoslovakia had become Russian-controlled satellites. Yugoslavia, although restless, was still Communist. In a few months the blockade of Berlin emphasised the clear design of regarding Eastern Germany as finally annexed to the Russian sphere. Where was all this to stop? What limit was to be set on the Russian advance? These moves, so relentless and so ruthless, could no longer be explained as the search for security. They were the familiar products of imperialist ambition or Communist fanaticism. Thus, within less than three years after a desperate struggle against Hitler's aggression, it seemed now our destiny to be locked in conflict with a new aggression arising from the East.

Unable any longer to persuade himself of the value of the 'Third Force', Bevin had called in January 1948 for a 'new adjustment of power'. In the previous March Britain and France had signed the Dunkirk Treaty, an alliance of mutual aid against any renewal of German aggression. On 17 March 1948 this instrument was superseded, in the face of the threat from further east, by the Brussels Treaty, to which Belgium, Holland and Luxembourg also adhered, which guaranteed all parties to the treaty against any armed attack, and set up a permanent Consultative Council with periodic meetings of Ministers. The Rape of Czechoslovakia was to have still wider repercussions, for in the spring of 1949 there took place a dramatic reversal of American policy. On 15 March 1949 the Atlantic Pact was signed. This remarkable instrument marked a complete abandonment of the traditional American attitude towards the out-side world, for by its terms the United States and Canada joined the Brussels Treaty powers. A few weeks later, on 4 April 1949, came the North Atlantic Treaty. Norway, Denmark, Iceland, Italy and Portugal now joined the Atlantic organisation and the purpose of the alliance was more accurately defined. The formal treaty con-tained this vital clause: 'An armed attack against one or more of them in Europe or America shall be considered an attack against them all.' Neither Greece nor Turkey was invited to join at this stage, but both countries were included in February 1952.

The leadership of the United States as the founder and head of a new Grand Alliance was generally welcomed throughout Western Europe. Few voices then were raised against American interference, or complained of American domination. The morbid jealousy of America which was to develop in later years had not arisen even in France. Meanwhile America had then the monopoly, or virtual monopoly, of the new atomic power. Britain had indeed started to develop atomic weapons of her own through the patriotic enthusiasm of Attlee and his colleagues, but this was unknown to Parliament. In any event, only by American military and economic help did it seem that a fresh barbaric invasion of Europe, apparently imminent, could be successfully resisted.

Later, with NATO firmly established, it seemed both prudent and possible to find some kind of working solution by which the two sides of a divided world could live together, if not in true peace, at least without conflict. In this new phase, a balance of destructive power had been secured, since the Russians had now armed themselves with formidable nuclear weapons. On this uneasy, but perhaps convenient, basis of mutual fear some more constructive policies might be built. But in 1948 and 1949 the aggressive thrust, not content with Eastern and Balkan countries, began to spread into Western Europe. The clear intention seemed to be to undermine France, Italy and other Western European countries, using the same techniques of subversion and infiltration. There was thus no alternative to the reply firmly and decisively given by the foundation of the North Atlantic Treaty Organisation. Indeed, only through the wholehearted entry of the United States into world politics and the final abandonment of isolationism could the balance of power be maintained and the peace and freedom of the West defended.

This great reversal of British policy was not achieved without much searching of hearts and much agony of conscience, especially among Labour and Socialist enthusiasts. Just as in the realm of home affairs the bright triumphs of 1945 soon began to be tarnished by a succession of financial and economic crises, so the high hopes, that Socialism in Britain would be the natural and sympathetic ally of Communism in Russia, had faded in the course of two or three years into dark despair.

The Labour Party as a whole now became more and more alarmed and even angered by the developing situation. In a debate on Germany early in 1949, I had quite a rough time from the extremists. They did not like to be reminded of the inexorable march of events, the breakdown of the policy of appeasement and the collapse of the promises which they had held out to the electors. After the signing of the North Atlantic Treaty in April 1949, the Government asked for the formal support of Parliament. Once again, Bevin did his best to win over the doubters in his own party. These were in fact more numerous than appeared from the division, when only six Members, with two tellers to assist them, went into the Lobby against the signing of the treaty. The most effective in argument were D. N. Pritt and Konni Zilliacus. Pritt was a K.C. of distinction, with a wide practice, who had already made himself pretty troublesome in the war and now seemed to aspire to the position of spiritual heir of the Cripps of the thirties. Zilliacus was more sprightly and more engaging. Bevin could only rehearse once more the gloomy story of the last four years and the catalogue of Soviet iniquities. Step by step the indictment went on. Poland, Bulgaria, Roumania, where 'the Government was wiped out and the new regime was established with a ruthlessness with which we are all familiar'; Hungary, where the Smallholders' Party had won the election but were ejected from power; until the final seizure of Czechoslovakia. Once again, regardless of the views of many of his party, he defended the actions of Britain and America in support of Greek liberty during and after the war. He reminded us of our

efforts to create order out of chaos in Germany, to introduce currency reform and to revive trade. Week after week and month after
month the Western Allies had been blocked by Russian intransigence. We therefore had to make our own plans for Western
Germany, and the answer to this had been the blockade of Berlin,
'an attempt to cut off two and a half million people with a view to
driving the Western Allies out of Eastern Europe and to deny our
rights which were a part of the Occupation Settlement'.[1] This
blockade had happily now been raised.

He then defended the Atlantic Pact in a detailed argument
which is chiefly of interest because it reveals the strong opposition
and fear of America that existed even then among 'progressive'
politicians and publicists. The Atlantic Pact, he declared, was not
aggressive and would not bring war. At any rate its absence had not
stopped war in 1914 or 1939. People living round the Atlantic
Ocean of common origin, common moral and ethical standards and
institutions derived from common traditions, would regard this new
system as a deterrent and not a threat.

Prolonged and somewhat technical discussions followed as to the
relations between the Atlantic Pact and the United Nations Charter;
but it was clear to most of us that the whole structure of the Security
Council had already fallen into disrepute, with a permanent veto
available in Russian hands. Churchill in his reply was short and
appreciative of Bevin's efforts. He was glad that the lifting by the
Soviet Government of the blockade of Berlin a few weeks before
had not been taken as a peace gesture:

> Before the last war, I do remember how, every time Herr
> Hitler made some reassuring statement, such as 'This is my last
> territorial demand', people came to me and said, 'There, now,
> you see how wrong you have been; he says it is his last territorial
> demand'; but the bitter experience we have gone through . . . has
> made us more wary of these premature rejoicings upon mere
> words and gestures.[1]

He gave a cordial welcome on behalf of himself and his party to the
Atlantic Pact and our special thanks to the American people for the

[1] *Hansard*, 12 May 1949.

splendid part they were so determined to play in the world. He would have been hardly human had he not referred to the views he had put forward at Fulton in March 1946. At that time—as he reminded his audience—a motion of censure against him had been placed on the Order Paper and signed by 105 Members of the Labour Party. It was unusual for such a motion to be put down against an individual private Member or a Minister out of office; but there it was. Among the 105 there must have been a large-scale process of conversion:

> ... naturally, I welcome converts, and so do His Majesty's Government. They say that 'there is more joy over one sinner who repenteth than over ninety and nine just persons who need no repentance'. Here, we have got about a hundred in a bunch, so far as I can make out, although some of them have emphasised the change of heart which they have gone through by a suitable act of penance by abstaining from attending this Debate.[1]

He added a plea for a better organisation of the military forces. Something like the Supreme Headquarters under Eisenhower, which had been created in the war, was needed now; the staff, however, must be fully representative of all the constituent nations. Once again Churchill proved to be right, although there was the usual delay in carrying out the plans which he foreshadowed. NATO became formally effective in August 1949, but it was not until February 1951 that SHAPE, the successor to SHAEF, came into being.[2]

There were many jeers from the extreme Left about the surrender of the Government to Churchill's demands. The North Atlantic Treaty, declared one Socialist orator, was merely a concrete expression of what Churchill had uttered in his Fulton speech three years ago. We were now being asked to vote for Fultonism; not Fultonism and water, but Fultonism unadulterated.

In these distracting years British foreign policy was guided almost entirely by Bevin, a massive figure who earned, as he deserved,

---

[1] *Hansard*, 12 May 1949.
[2] SHAEF: Supreme Headquarters, Allied Expeditionary Force. SHAPE: Supreme Headquarters, Allied Powers in Europe.

the general support of Parliament and the country. Dangerous and difficult as were the rapids through which he had to steer, he never lost his general sense of direction. He began by trying, loyally and patiently, to carry out the Potsdam agreements. As these hopes steadily faded, following the aggressive actions of the Soviet Union, he took a full part in what might be called a policy of containment, resting upon defence alliances aimed at preserving the balance of power in the world. These reached their culminating point in NATO.

By the end of the Parliament Bevin was an ageing man. But he held on with splendid courage for more than a year. In March 1951 he was forced by failing health to retire. He died in April. In spite of certain weaknesses and prejudices, he was the strongest figure in the Labour Government. At the same time he commanded the sympathy and even affection of the Conservatives, among whom he had many intimate friends. It was not his fault that in the immediate post-war years foreign affairs had taken a disastrous course. He may perhaps be blamed for clinging too long to the illusion that he could reach accommodation at that period with the Soviets. Yet it was not easy for him to abandon these hopes. In the end, by his work as Foreign Secretary, in spite of some blemishes, the nation and the Free World were encouraged and strengthened.

> He has done one immense service to Britain and the world. He has imposed upon an unwilling and hesitant party a policy of resistance to Soviet Russia and to Communism. A Tory Foreign Secretary (in the immediate post-war years) could not have done this.[1]

Nevertheless, powerful as was Bevin's personal hold upon Parliament and the nation, once again the task of inspiring British, Commonwealth and even American opinion fell to Churchill. As before, he proved the true prophet, leading and not following public sentiment. The Fulton speech was justified by the logic of events, since it was followed within three years by the Atlantic Pact. Once again he had seen and proclaimed the needs of the hour.

During all this period the danger of major war was averted by the

[1] 16 April 1951.

fact that atomic and nuclear power lay in American hands. In October 1951 the Russians admitted to the world that they had succeeded in exploding an atomic bomb. Thus this frightful destructive power would no longer be the monopoly of the Western Powers, and it was under the shadow of this appalling menace to the life of the world that the search, if not for peace at least for co-existence, must now begin.

CHAPTER VI

East of Suez

WHILE the menace of Russian aggression overshadowed the life of Europe, Soviet activities in Asia, at least for the first few years after the end of the war, were comparatively restricted.

Russia's Asian frontiers were substantially strengthened by the concessions obtained at Yalta in 1945. The Soviets were promised, and were soon able to secure, southern Sakhalin and the Kurile Islands. Their authority in Outer Mongolia was extended; in addition they gained naval bases in Korea and Manchuria. After the failure of the Council of Foreign Ministers in Moscow in December 1945, the Soviet Government set up a puppet Government in North Korea, following the pattern of subversion and infiltration which they operated so successfully elsewhere. This was destined to lead within a few years to tragic consequences, and a long and bitterly contested war.

Manchuria afforded an opportunity for almost blatant loot; the country was thus stripped of every kind of industrial equipment under the pretence of reparations. But in China the complicated situation between the Nationalists and the Chinese Communists led the Russians to adopt, at least at first, a vacillating policy. It was not Russian support that led to the triumph of the Chinese Communists. The fall of the Nationalists was due partly to their own weakness and corruption, partly to the devotion and courage of the Communist armies. Nor has this been forgotten by the new rulers of China. Meanwhile, by holding Outer Mongolia and by the consolidation of the Mongolian People's Republic, Soviet control on this vital border was considerably strengthened.[1] In this respect, Russian objectives were not dissimilar from those pursued in Europe. The Soviet

[1] Pethybridge, pp. 106 ff.

Government were determined to secure their vital frontiers and protect important economic interests. But elsewhere in the Far East they were content with operations on a comparatively minor scale.

Similarly, in these years, the Soviet interest in the Middle East was slight. In Iran, indeed, they suffered a serious setback, having been induced in May 1946 to withdraw all their troops, who had occupied northern Iran during the war, and even to abandon the claims which they had tried to establish in the province of Azerbaidjan. Turkey next became the principal target of Soviet propaganda and pressure, since Turkey's alliance with the West and acceptance of American aid were a cause of anger in Moscow. There followed insistent but unsuccessful demands to obtain new rights of passage through the Dardanelles. At the same time Russia, equally unprofitably, tried to claim a mandate over Tripolitania.

Strangely enough, in the light of later events, Russian policy at this time was pro-Israel and anti-Arab. When the Arab League countries invaded Palestine in 1948 Russia called upon them to withdraw, or at least to 'exercise restraint', and the new State of Israel was immediately accorded recognition. The reasons for a later change of policy are not perhaps far to seek. Israel, when it emerged as a nation, not only acted as a rallying point for Jewish nationalism inside the Soviet Union but, in spite of all the bitter recollections of the dispute with Britain as the mandatory power, continued, spiritually and materially, to be attracted to the West. Meanwhile, the Arab League came to be no longer regarded by the Soviet Government as a 'tool of British imperialism'.

Thus, during the greater part of this period, from 1945 to 1950, Russian influence both in the Middle East and the Far East, although important and often distracting, was not able to achieve such conclusive results as those which had crowned Soviet success in Eastern and Central Europe.

In the Middle East, Britain was still a Great Power. In Iraq, as in Libya, we maintained considerable forces and held important air bases. Our influence was supreme in Transjordan. In Egypt, by the treaty of 1936, we controlled the Canal Zone. The Sudan was still under our authority. The Americans showed no jealousy of our strength and prestige throughout the area. On the contrary, they were ready enough to leave Britain to look after this part of the world. Nor were we, in general, unsuccessful. In the same year as Russia suffered her serious reverse in Iran, Transjordan was formally constituted as an independent nation and a treaty of alliance was signed with Britain, enabling British forces to be stationed there, thus assuring our influence in an area of considerable strategic importance.

But if, throughout the Middle as well as the Far East, Soviet pressure constituted no serious embarrassment, there was one painful and hideous problem which faced the British Government after the war. It was that of Palestine.

Throughout these years it was this difficulty which was the most intractable and in the end proved insoluble. The British people sincerely desired to carry out their duties under the original Mandate which required the creation of a national home for the Jews, in accordance with the famous Balfour Declaration. There would in addition be substantial political and strategic advantages if we could find a method of reconciling opposing interests, and thus constitute a peaceful and independent State, closely allied to us by genuine sympathy and perhaps gratitude.

For many years there had been intense interest in this question in Parliament and outside. Before the war the majority of the Labour Party had been strongly pro-Zionist. In the Conservative Party, the position was reversed, and pro-Arab sentiments had predominated. In the spring of 1939, when it became apparent that war with Germany was now almost inevitable, it became a matter of urgency to ensure that the Arabs should not be thrown into the arms of Germany. Chamberlain accordingly summoned the Jewish and Arab leaders to London and tried to get agreement upon a joint policy, the terms of which were laid down in a famous White Paper. Both the Arab and the Jewish representatives refused to accept these proposals. Although the Arabs rejected this plan, it was obviously in their favour. The White Paper appeared almost to close down on future Jewish immigration, at a time when it was the most urgent need of that persecuted race, and in such a way as to close the door against Jewish hopes and ambitions. Only 75,000 victims of persecution

F

were to be admitted over the next five years, after which Arab consent would be required. In other words, the British Government, by this decision, seemed to declare that with this final number of immigrants the obligation to create a national home in Palestine would be adequately if not completely fulfilled. Yet the proportions of the population were now about two-thirds Arab and one-third Jew; when, therefore, independence came in due course to be granted, an overwhelming Arab majority would be consolidated.

The Mandate had always hitherto been interpreted to mean that Jewish immigration should be allowed up to the limit of 'economic absorptive capacity'—a formula coined by Churchill himself in 1922. In addition to an immigration system which seemed wholly incompatible with the Mandate, it was proposed to impose restrictions on the sale of land to the Jews. Churchill, supported by Leo Amery and a number of other Conservatives, of whom I was one, joined with the Labour leaders in strong protest against the White Paper. It was even stigmatised as a 'Middle Eastern Munich'. It was, however, supported on military and strategic grounds by the bulk of Conservative Members, who felt it to be more important in the threatening condition of Europe to avoid further Arab antagonism than to stand by the policy to which the British Governments had been committed for nearly twenty years.

Then came the years of war, with the fluctuating struggle throughout the Middle East. Large numbers of the Jewish community in Palestine were recruited and armed by Churchill's authority, and Jews were encouraged to play their full part in the defence of the area against a German invasion likely to strike through Turkey, Syria and Palestine towards the Suez Canal. Meanwhile, in Iraq, there had been a revolt of the pro-German Arabs which had been subsequently quelled. Syria had been liberated; Iran had been safeguarded. But when the war ended the problem of Palestine remained unresolved.

It is hardly necessary to describe in detail the different plans and proposals that were devised, each of which in turn held the field for a few months, only to be abandoned as impracticable. In January 1946 an Anglo-American committee was appointed by Attlee and Truman to consider what should be done, with regard both to

Palestine itself and the situation of the surviving Jews throughout Europe. The main recommendation was to allow the immediate admission into Palestine of 100,000 Jewish immigrants. At the same time the committee recommended that the Mandate should be continued and no separate Arab or Jewish State created. It looked forward, with hardly justified optimism, to Arab–Jewish co-operation under the mandatory power. A degree of separate autonomy was proposed for each community, but no political independence for either people. The report was obviously a compromise. But the main issue which emerged was that of the early admission of 100,000 immigrants.

Through many months of negotiation the British Government tried to find some comprehensive solution. Their first step was to appoint in agreement with the U.S. Government a number of 'expert'–or at least official–representatives. These devoted themselves to a review of the report of the original committee, and it was not until the end of July 1946 that the British Government was able to inform the House of their recommendations. The experts had recognised that the pressure of Hitlerism had led to an immense problem of Jewish refugees throughout Europe. The best means of dealing with this would be for every country to find new homes for the resettlement of these unhappy people either in Europe or overseas. An elaborate scheme was prepared which in the event proved almost completely ineffective. In any case it did not meet the passionate desire of a great number of Jews to enter Palestine, or our obligation to allow them to do so, subject to the power of the country to absorb them without injury to the economy. The experts had gone on to accept the principle that Palestine as a whole should be neither a Jewish nor an Arab State, and that neither of the two communities should dominate the other. Consequently some form of central Government must continue. Nevertheless, they felt that the feelings were so bitter between the two communities that the only hope was to develop a system where each in practice could manage its own local affairs. They therefore proposed a form of devolution. Palestine should be divided into an Arab province and a Jewish province. The district of Jerusalem would be under independent control, and the Negev, being largely uninhabited, would be treated separately. A central Government representing and responsible to the mandatory power would have exclusive authority on defence, foreign relations, customs and excise. Only if this plan were put into operation, and each province managed its own affairs, including immigration, could the movement of 100,000 Jews from Europe to the Jewish area of Palestine prove acceptable.

The debate took place under the shadow of increasing terrorism by various Jewish organisations, culminating in the destruction of the Government offices in the King David Hotel in Jerusalem, where nearly a hundred people were killed and many wounded and missing. In this connection, Morrison, in the absence of Bevin who was detained in Paris by the Foreign Ministers' meeting, stated that the greatest obstacle to success in restoring order had been the refusal of the Jewish population of Palestine to co-operate with the British authorities. In the course of a carefully prepared and lucid speech, Morrison said that the British Government accepted the experts' report, at least as a basis of action. It was therefore proposed to bring together a meeting of Jewish and Arab delegations to discuss a constitutional scheme on these broad lines. This system, which was sometimes called 'local home rule' and sometimes 'cantonisation', was accepted by Oliver Stanley, who spoke in the first day of the debate on behalf of the Conservative Party. His speech was well informed (he had himself been Colonial Secretary for several years) and followed the same tone of moderation as that which had characterised Morrison's.

Both that day and when the discussion was resumed on 1 August many powerful protests were made, chiefly from the Labour side, against the scheme. They naturally concentrated on the failure to carry out effectively the most important proposal of the original Anglo-American committee—that is, the immediate admission of 100,000 immigrants.

But, as so often, the speech which most impressed, if it did not yet convince, the House was that which Churchill himself delivered on the second day. He made it clear that while he accepted Stanley's speech as representing a large body of opinion in the Conservative Party, he wished to express his own views and deploy his own story. This long and fascinating review, though not altogether to the taste of his followers, was one of the most powerful and courageous that I have heard him deliver. It lasted an hour and covered the whole field. He reminded us that, although it was true that largely because of persecution in Europe the Jewish population in Palestine had grown in a quarter of a century from 80,000 to nearly 600,000, with a notable expansion of industrial and agricultural production, yet it must be remembered that the Arab population had doubled during the same period. This showed the great economic advantages which both sides had obtained from British assistance, guidance and support. He recalled his strong objections to the White Paper of 1939 in which the principle of absorptive capacity had been abandoned and under which after a five-year interval all Jewish immigration would have been brought to an end, except by an unobtainable agreement with the Arab majority. He thought then and believed now that this was a breach of all our honourable obligations. After reviewing the events of the war and referring to the changed condition of affairs, he made clear his position and the course which he would have followed had political power remained in his hands. He condemned like every other speaker, the terrible atrocities of the Jewish extremists. But he by no means abandoned the full obligations of the Mandate and the Zionist cause which he had always supported. Yet he felt that an unfair burden was being thrown upon Great Britain by our having to carry the whole weight of this commitment, with the resulting estrangement and alarm in many Arab and Moslem countries so vital to our own Empire, as well as by its heavy drain on our resources:

> Therefore, I had always intended to put it to our friends in America, from the very beginning of the post-war discussions, that either they should come in and help us in this Zionist problem, about which they feel so strongly, and as I think rightly, on even terms, share and share alike, or that we should resign our Mandate, as we have, of course, a perfect right to do.[1]

This firm pronouncement somewhat shocked the great majority of Members on all sides. But he made it with such fervour and determination that I was persuaded that in his hands the plan might have

[1] *Hansard*, 1 August 1946.

been successful. He might have been able, by personal negotiation, to induce the Americans to share this burden, as they were, within a year, to accept the obligations of defending the freedom of Europe. Nevertheless, at this time American opinion had still hardly begun to move from the isolationist position, and even later it was not possible to achieve the necessary co-operation. In that event Churchill would have insisted on giving up the Mandate and withdrawing both our civilian administration and our armed forces.

When the Government's scheme was put to the Arabs and Jews, both rejected it. Indeed, whatever course we proposed seemed now to be equally opposed by the Jewish and Arab populations and their leaders. As a result, large numbers of troops had to be kept in the area and heavy expense incurred. Painful military and civilian casualties from terrorism continued. By the end of 1947 a breakdown was inevitable. The position of the Jews and Arabs was wholly irreconcilable, since the Jews demanded a separate Jewish State and the Arabs, trusting to their majority, insisted that no such State should come into existence but clamoured for independence. Nor did the terms of the Mandate give us any real authority to accept or impose partition. The Government, therefore, in despair, appealed once more to the United Nations. In Palestine itself violence and terrorism increased. An Arab economic boycott of Jewish industry and commerce was declared and was largely effective. Efforts were made to bring in other countries such as France, and especially the United States, to help us. When the issue was thrown to the United Nations, a special committee was appointed to report. But by the time the Assembly met in September to consider its recommendations, the British Government made it clear that whatever might be the result of its deliberations Britain had at last determined to withdraw. Much scepticism was expressed by Arabs and Jews alike as to the genuineness of this threat or promise. This was shared by many other countries, so convinced were they that Britain would never surrender her 'Imperialist policy'. Little gratitude was shown then or since for the devoted work of British administrators and the courage of British troops, or for the large sums expended for the benefit of both communities in Palestine for the preservation of order and for the development of the economy.

The Assembly of the United Nations, by a majority vote, declared on 29 November 1947 in favour of partition, though on a basis far less favourable to the Jews than they later achieved by war. Nevertheless, the Government had at last reached a decision to which they were determined to hold. This was formally announced to the House of Commons in December by the Colonial Secretary, Arthur Creech Jones, who made it clear, as he had done to the United Nations Assembly, that the Mandate would be terminated not later than 1 August 1948 and the troops withdrawn. In fact, the target date, subject to negotiation with the United Nations Commission which was to be sent out to preside over the partition, was 15 May. This decision, unpalatable to many members on both sides of the House, was accepted as unavoidable. Once again, in default of any plan carefully devised and energetically carried out by a British and American partnership, Churchill's conclusion, ill-received as it had been in the summer of 1946, by the end of 1947 was agreed to be inevitable.

The first six months of the next terrible year, 1948, proved a period when the declining authority and power of the British under an expiring Mandate led to continuous guerrilla warfare on both sides. While conditions in Palestine were lapsing into anarchy and civil war, the unhappy British forces did their best to maintain some kind of order. But as their numbers began to dwindle and come under increasing attack, our authorities drifted into the position of little more than spectators of events. The British officials did their best to negotiate local truces and reduce by every possible means the suffering involved. Meanwhile, the Arab countries were disunited and irresolute, and great numbers of Arab refugees, alleged by some to number 600,000, fled from areas occupied by the Jews. Immediately on the end of the Mandate, the Jewish National Council and the General Zionist Council declared the establishment of a Jewish State to be called Israel. Dr. Chaim Weizmann, the world-famous scientist, became the President of the Provisional Council, and David Ben Gurion the first Prime Minister. President Truman immediately announced the recognition by the United States of the *de facto* authority of the new State of Israel. This was on 14 May 1948. The Soviet Government followed within three days.

The rapid decision of the American Government can be explained partly by sentiment and partly by internal political pressures. That of the Soviet Government shows how firm at that time was their support of the Jews and their opposition to the Arab claims. The British Government refused to follow the example in which the great protagonists of Capitalism and Communism were so strangely joined. With our many commitments to the Arab countries and our important interests in the Middle East, we were in a difficult position. It was not until after the termination of the subsequent Arab–Israeli war and the coming into effect of the armistice in the spring of 1949 that British recognition was accorded.

In the vacuum left by our withdrawal a bitter war between Arabs and Jews immediately broke out. It was widely rumoured at the time that British military experts were of the opinion that once the British had left Palestine the Arabs would easily overcome the Jews. Indeed, it was believed that by the end of May at latest they would have captured Tel Aviv and cut the country in half. Nor was this feeling confined to military circles. Many observers, including experienced diplomats, shared this view. Morrison states categorically that this was Bevin's own opinion.[1] Yet in spite of some early successes, including an advance almost reaching Tel Aviv, the Arabs failed to achieve a decisive result, despite their preponderance in arms and men. A month's truce was negotiated by the United Nations Committee on 11 June; but on the day before it was due to terminate the Arabs made a further attack, hoping by their assault to bring about a final victory. They were, however, completely defeated on all fronts, and by the time a second truce was established the military position of the Jews had greatly improved. All through the year operations continued with varying degrees of violence. By the beginning of 1949 the Israeli forces seemed poised for a successful and overwhelming assault. But they, too, were unable to exploit their successes to the full.

Great pressure was brought by the United Nations to bring hostilities to an end, and to arrange at least an armistice. The Egyptian Government were the first to ask for this, and under the chairmanship of a U.N. mediator a series of armistice agreements were also signed with the other Arab States during the spring of

[1] Lord Morrison, *An Autobiography*, p. 272.

1949. The Arab part of Palestine on the west bank of the Jordan was subsequently incorporated in Transjordan—which in June 1949 changed its name to Jordan.

Thus ended a vital phase in the story of Palestine—not, alas, by the adoption of any agreed method of conciliation or even by the signature of a final peace.

For the moment the concern of the House of Commons at this time was relieved, even if its anxieties were by no means removed. This protracted crisis naturally fell most heavily upon the Government of the day and their supporters, for upon them lay the full responsibility. But the Opposition also was unhappy and divided. Although my sympathies were with Churchill on this issue, as they had been before the war, it was clear to me that the majority of his supporters did not share his approach. Yet he maintained his opinions and set them out where necessary with his usual clarity and vigour, without in any way impairing his general relations with his colleagues. Never did I more admire his combination of determination and fairness.

After the Armistice of 1949, Britain began to supply arms on a limited scale to the Arab States, and the sense of uncertainty and crisis continued. By 25 May 1950 the three Western powers—Great Britain, the United States and France—agreed on the famous Tripartite Declaration. In this they gave warning of the dangers of a Middle East arms race and set up a committee amongst themselves to regulate the flow with a view to keeping stability and balance. The Declaration also included an important statement of policy—that the three Governments, should they find any of these States preparing to violate the frontiers or armistice lines, would, consistent with their obligations as members of the United Nations, immediately take action both within and without the United Nations to prevent such a violation. The Declaration was of course fiercely denounced by the Arab States who were thirsting for the renewal of the war. Unhappily, this policy, unlike that of the Atlantic Alliance, was not supported by any effective defence organisation.

These were years of confusion and disorder in many of the Arab countries, during which the British people became painfully aware that their easy assumptions of Arab friendship were misplaced. In

F2

March 1949 there was a revolution in Syria. In March 1951 the Prime Minister of Iran was assassinated, and in May the new Government announced the nationalisation of the Anglo-Iranian Oil Company, which supplied about 25 per cent of British oil, and the seizure of Abadan, the biggest refinery in the world. In July King Abdullah of Jordan was assassinated, and a year later came the overthrow of King Farouk of Egypt, with all that it was to entail for the future of the Suez Canal.

If the troubles of the Middle East were to prove a source of persistent difficulty and even danger during this period, in the Far East our problems were relatively less acute. Yet British and even Western power and influence had begun to decline. It is true that Japan remained friendly, largely under American influence. But the British grip on the East was seriously weakened. India, Pakistan and Ceylon exchanged the direct rule of Britain for the weaker ties of the Commonwealth. Burma passed altogether out of our sphere. In Malaya we were faced with a Communist guerilla war which was destined only gradually to be overcome by the combined efforts of a notable British commander, loyal troops and skilful administration. In China the Communist People's Republic had won complete authority over almost all the country by the autumn of 1949. In the same year, the countries of Indo-China, including Laos and Vietnam, became independent, although still within the French Union. Soon a more spectacular crisis was to break upon the world. On 25 June 1950 South Korea was invaded by the Soviet-inspired and Communist-controlled Government of North Korea. The British people were now to face a new test, with widespread political, military and economic repercussions.

CHAPTER VII

The Council of Europe

THE concept of a united Europe is almost as old as Europe itself. For many centuries, statesmen and philosophers have dreamed of a day when the countries of Europe, conscious of their common heritage, could forget their animosities and rivalries and join together for peace and prosperity. The rise of the spirit of nationalism from the ruins of the Roman Empire had been accompanied, no doubt, by an extraordinary development of vigour and power in many European nations, with a corresponding expansion of their world influence. But, in modern conditions, the clash of conflicting interests and the fierce jealousies of the Great Powers seemed now to threaten their very survival. In the year 1897, when the British Empire reached its apogee of glory and power in the celebrations for the Queen's victorious Diamond Jubilee, her Prime Minister, Lord Salisbury, was thinking in larger terms. Surveying the European scene he made this declaration:

> The federated action of Europe, if we can maintain it, is our sole hope of escaping from the constant terror and calamity of war, the constant pressure of the burdens of an armed peace, which weigh down the spirits and darken the prospect of every nation in this part of the world. The Federation of Europe is the only hope we have.[1]

It was in this spirit that in 1930 Aristide Briand, then French Prime Minister, had put forward an ambitious project to the League of Nations at Geneva, at a memorable meeting. But the response was hesitant; the moment was lost. Europe soon plunged into economic disaster, following the great American collapse. Then

[1] A. L. Kennedy, *Salisbury, 1830–1903, Portrait of a Statesman* (London, 1953), p. 273.

came the rise of Hitler and the Second World War. Yet the initiative taken by Briand, one of the most imaginative of French statesmen, was not altogether lost.

During the war itself the European idea had found many sympathisers, both in the underground movements fighting Hitler and among leading members of the exiled Governments. Thus United Europe to some extent became a symbol of resistance to Hitler's New Order. One of the most prominent in this work was General Sikorski, the former Prime Minister of Poland, assisted by Dr. J. H. Retinger, who afterwards became an important figure in the European movement. It was during these terrible years that the first outline of the customs union which was to become Benelux was devised, and two eminent Belgian statesmen, Paul van Zeeland and Paul-Henri Spaak, were equally active in the development of the European ideal. They were joined by such men as Jan Masaryk from Czechoslovakia, Dr. Eelco van Kleffens from the Netherlands and M. Trygve Lie from Norway (later to be the first Secretary-General of the United Nations).

Similar thoughts were in many of our minds, however imperfectly expressed, even at the beginning of the Second War. For instance, I have found among my papers a reply to a questionnaire on war aims at the end of October 1939 in which I seem boldly to have declared my firm, if uninstructed, faith:

> Many people are asking what kind of Europe one could expect to emerge out of the chaos of today. The picture can only be painted in the broadest colours. But if western civilisation is to survive, we must look forward to an organisation, economic, cultural, and perhaps even political, comprising all the countries of western Europe.[1]

A much greater mind and a much more significant authority was at work in these early years. In the autumn of 1942, a few days before the battle of Alamein, when the fate of our armies was still in the balance, Churchill wrote a minute to Eden, then Foreign Secretary, of extraordinary foresight:

> I must admit that my thoughts rest primarily in Europe—the

[1] *Picture Post*, 28 October 1939.

revival of the glory of Europe, the parent continent of the modern nations and of civilisation. It would be a measureless disaster if Russian barbarism overlaid the culture and independence of the ancient States of Europe. Hard as it is to say now, I trust that the European family may act unitedly as one under a Council of Europe.[1]

This remarkable document continues as follows:

I look forward to a United States of Europe in which the barriers between the nations will be greatly minimised and unrestricted travel will be possible. I hope to see the economy of Europe studied as a whole.[1]

Even at this anxious and critical moment, Churchill had begun to consider the formation of a Council of European Governments. It might consist of

perhaps ten units, including the former Great Powers, with several confederations—Scandinavian, Danubian, Balkan, etc.—which would possess an international police. . . .[1]

The next sentence is of particular interest in view of the later anxieties and suspicions of the French:

Of course we shall have to work with the Americans in many ways, and in the greatest ways, but Europe is our prime care. . . .[1]

Six months later, on 21 March 1943, Churchill delivered a famous broadcast much of which was devoted to a plan for the reorganisation and reconstitution of Europe. The creation of a Council of Europe was the first practical task to be tackled. He devoted a considerable part of his address to a detailed consideration of the place of such an organisation within the framework of whatever might prove to be the new form of a post-war League of Nations. The revival of Europe seemed to him to harmonise with the permanent interest of the United States and Russia, which could only gain from a revived and strengthened Europe. Although many of his listeners may have felt that these ideas were somewhat remote from the hard practical problems by which they were at that time oppressed, yet he did not hesitate to dwell on this theme. I remember

[1] Winston S. Churchill, *The Second World War*, vol. iv: *The Hinge of Fate* (London, 1951), p. 504. The relevant extract is printed below as Appendix One.

hearing the broadcast after dinner in General Alexander's camp. It was a Sunday; a great battle had been raging for the last two days on which was to turn the outcome of the African campaign and the possibility of an early landing of our armies on the continent of Europe. Both of us were enthralled by Churchill's ideas—for the future. We little knew that within two years Alexander was to accept the surrender of all the German forces opposed to him in the Mediterranean area.

After the General Election of 1945 and Churchill's loss of any direct political power, his prestige and authority in the world were still immense. The following year—1946—was one of the most productive in his life. In March 1946 he delivered the Fulton speech, which was followed in September by a speech in Zürich, the results of which were to prove almost as spectacular. He did not attempt to expound a detailed plan. He contented himself with a broad and general appeal for European unity: 'When the Nazi power was broken I asked myself what was the best advice I could give my fellow citizens in our ravaged and exhausted continent. My counsel to Europe can be given in a single word: Unite!'

Organisations of different kinds sprang into being with great rapidity during 1946 and 1947. One of the earliest was the European League for Economic Co-operation (ELEC) under the chairmanship of Paul van Zeeland, a former Prime Minister of Belgium. This was founded in May 1946; a year later a British committee came into being, which was to have important results during the next few years. Sir Harold Butler was the first chairman; Walter Layton, Roy Harrod, Paul Chambers, Edward Beddington-Behrens and others did a great deal of detailed research; the devoted secretary was Lady Rhys Williams. This body can even claim that the creation of the European Payments Union, which played such an important role in restoring the economic life of Europe during the fifties, was largely due to the work of Sir Roy Harrod and his colleagues. In France, a similar movement was formed under Raoul Dautry's chairmanship and received great support. On the broader aspects of the European problem varying objectives, ranging from federalism to what became known as the 'confederalist' approach, came rapidly under discussion. In these different efforts many distinguished Europeans played a notable role—Robert Schuman, van Zeeland, André Philip and, above all, Paul-Henri Spaak.

At home, Churchill founded the United Europe Movement at the beginning of 1947. Among his Conservative colleagues he invited David Maxwell Fyfe and myself to join the managing committee, which was 'non-party' and included such well-known figures as Walter Layton, Lady Violet Bonham-Carter and Robert Boothby. But the success of the organisation was primarily due to the tenacity of Duncan Sandys, who proved able to enlist the services and command the respect of a great variety of individuals and organised bodies. The inaugural meeting to launch this new and exciting project took place at the Albert Hall on 14 May. There was a packed hall and a distinguished platform. The Archbishop of Canterbury presided, and messages were received from many leading statesmen at home and abroad.

It is difficult now to recall the state of collapse and misery into which the countries of Europe had sunk. Churchill was guilty of no exaggeration when he declared that

> in our task of reviving the glories and happiness of Europe and her prosperity, it can certainly be said that we start at the bottom of her fortunes.

Comparing the state of Europe in the past with its present diminished and impoverished condition, he went on:

> Here is the fairest, most temperate, most fertile area of the globe. The influence and the power of Europe and of Christendom have for centuries shaped and dominated the course of history. The sons and daughters of Europe have gone forth and carried their message to every part of the world. Religion, law, learning, art, science, industry, throughout the world all bear in so many lands, under every sky and in every clime, the stamp of European origin, or the trace of European influence.

What was Europe now?

> It is a rubble-heap, a charnel-house, a breeding-ground of pestilence and hate. Ancient nationalistic feuds and modern ideological factions distract and infuriate the unhappy, hungry

populations. Evil teachers urge the paying off of old scores with mathematical precision, and false guides point to unsparing retribution as the pathway to prosperity.

He went on to ask a question which may seem over-dramatised now, but struck then a respondent chord:

Has she nothing to give to the world but the contagion of the Black Death? Are her peoples to go on harrying and tormenting one another by war and vengeance until all that invests human life with dignity and comfort has been obliterated? Are the states of Europe to continue for ever to squander the first-fruits of their toil upon the erection of new barriers, military fortifications, tariff-walls and passport networks against one another?

Churchill, and perhaps it was the weakness as well as the strength of his approach, made no attempt to devise a constitution for Europe, whether political, military or economic. It was not for us at this stage to attempt to define a complete structure or design a perfected constitution. Within the United Nations system a united Europe would form one important regional entity, and Britain could in his view play a full role in Europe without loss or disloyalty to the traditions of her Empire and Commonwealth. Perhaps the most striking of his appeals was that for the restoration of Germany:

Germany today lies prostrate, famishing among ruins. Obviously no initiative can be expected from her. It is for France and Britain to take the lead. Together they must, in a friendly manner, bring the German people back into the European circle.

To this end he was to make a dramatic gesture at Strasbourg two years later. Meanwhile he contented himself with setting out the broadest principles and the most flexible methods.

All parties and all interests, including the trade unions, were represented at this meeting. Next to Churchill's perhaps the most eloquent speech was that delivered by Lady Violet Bonham-Carter. Oliver Stanley spoke at the end of the meeting, fully associating himself with the purposes of the movement.

I have never understood why Anthony Eden stood aloof. It may well be that Churchill shrank from trying to commit too specifically a friend and colleague who must, in the event of a Conservative

Government returning to power, become either Foreign Secretary or, in the event of Churchill's death or illness, Prime Minister. It may be that Eden felt himself unable, with his long experience at the Foreign Office, to share his leader's enthusiasm. He must certainly have realised the immense difficulties to be overcome if even the most modest of our objectives was to be reached. But I felt then, and still more later, how much we had lost. The history of the subsequent years might well have been different had Bevin, and later Eden, been more ready not merely to give a beneficent approval to the coming together of the continental nations of Europe, but also to bring Britain into active participation at an early stage.

With so many separate organisations coming into being almost spontaneously in different countries, there was an obvious danger of confusion and even contention. Finally, after long negotiations, there was established in December 1947 an international committee under whose guidance all these various activities could be co-ordinated. The whole was now to be known, in every country, as the 'European Movement'. As is so often the case with voluntary organisations, this unification was not achieved without considerable difficulty, and many conflicts both of personality and principle had to be resolved. That this was achieved was largely due to the soothing influence of Spaak, supported by the persistence and per-severance of Duncan Sandys. Sometimes these two strong personali-ties disagreed; but when, as nearly always, they worked together they were irresistible. The stage was now set for the 'Congress of Europe', which was organised by the whole European Movement and met at The Hague at the beginning of May 1948.

Meanwhile the march of world events had led to important measures of co-operation between the nations of Western Europe, at least upon the governmental level. Secretary Marshall had announced his European Recovery Programme—Marshall Aid—in June 1947. At the end of October of the same year the Benelux customs union, between Belgium, the Netherlands and Luxem-bourg, had come into being. On 17 March 1948 the Brussels Treaty Organisation, consisting of the United Kingdom, France and the Benelux countries, had been formed. This was to include a consultative council composed of the five Foreign Ministers meeting at least once every three months, as well as a permanent commission of ambassadors and officials. A military committee would also be called as required. By this treaty Britain—so Bevin claimed—'became in reality a part of Europe'. Indeed, this substantial progress on a basis between Governments was used by the Foreign Secretary and many others to deplore any question of the transfer of sovereignty in any form to some wider organisation. Effective unity, it was argued, could be created without any formal institutions, certainly of a popular or even of a Parliamentary kind. In addition, in order to perfect the arrangements for distribution of Marshall Aid, the Organisation for European Economic Co-operation (O.E.E.C.) had been set up, comprising the fourteen Governments concerned. This important event took place on 16 April, only a few weeks before the meeting of the Hague Congress. On the military side, negotiations had already begun which were to result in the creation of the North Atlantic Treaty Organisation.

It was therefore in a mood of hope and even exultation that the delegates came to this historic gathering. It was indeed one of the most remarkable and representative collections of famous European personalities ever brought together. Altogether eight hundred delegates attended, some representing various voluntary organisations, others being attracted by or interested in the Movement. There were several former Prime Ministers, twenty-nine former Foreign Ministers, and some Ministers actually in office. So far as the European representation was concerned little difficulty arose—all political parties, except Communists, were represented; all walks of life, all shades of opinion. This was equally true of the British delegates other than Members of Parliament. There were churchmen of all denominations, industrialists, trade unionists, administrators, economists, professors, scientists, poets, artists. Nor had we any reason to be ashamed of our contingent; a great proconsul and administrator like Sir John Anderson seen side by side with John Masefield, the Poet Laureate, and Charles Morgan, the famous novelist. Catholic bishops, leading Anglicans, nonconformist ministers, Fellows of the Royal Society were present. The great chemical industry was represented by Lord McGowan and Paul Chambers, and the Chemical Workers' Union by its General

Secretary, Bob Edwards. Among the many economists were Arthur Salter and Roy Harrod.

As regards our Parliamentary representation, however, Churchill was in a somewhat delicate position. He enjoyed of course an un-rivalled position as the war leader who had helped to save Europe. But he was also a party politician, an active and sometimes truculent leader of an Opposition anxious to weaken and as soon as possible take the place of the existing Government. As a party leader he could not fail to recognise that a considerable portion of the Con-servative Party were doubtful and even anxious about this new movement. They feared, and not unnaturally, that in one way or another, both on the political and on the economic side, Britain's position as head of the Empire and Commonwealth might be prejudiced. These doubts were to remain, and it was not until many years later that they could be substantially removed. The Liberal Party was small, and on this matter united. But the weight that they could give either in Parliament or outside was limited. The Labour Party, or at least its chiefs, was undoubtedly suspicious if not opposed to the whole affair. They were not unnaturally jealous of Churchill's unique position, which they believed him to be exploiting. Although the Labour Party was represented on our committee by several Labour Members, including the Rev. Gordon Lang, a much respected Member who shared the secretaryship of the British section with Duncan Sandys, yet the administration as a whole, fortified no doubt by the then prevailing sentiments in Whitehall, especially in the Foreign Office and the Treasury, was uneasy or hostile. Those temporarily in power, equally with the majority of those exercising the permanent authority of officialdom, joined in looking with some suspicion at any movement which might involve a European institution composed of demo-cratically elected bodies or even representatives of democratically elected Parliaments. Why should such persons take any part in these high matters? Anything that needed to be done for European unity could surely be better done by Governments working through Ministers, ambassadors and officials. It was a matter for the bishops and the clergy; the laity had better keep out of it.

Moreover, there was an attempt among Socialists generally,

both at home and in European countries, to promote the concept that the liberties and prosperity of Europe were only safe in Socialist hands. When it became known that no less than forty Members of the Labour Party intended to participate in the Hague Conference, the National Executive of the party wrote to them deprecating their decision. On 27 February, after a meeting attended by Attlee as Prime Minister, the Executive issued a statement to the effect

> that the survival of democratic Socialism as a separate political form was bound up with the survival of Western Europe as a spiritual union, and that the concept of European unity 'might be corrupted in the hands of reaction'.[1]

Coalitions, it would seem, were pardonable in order to survive in war, but not to preserve peace and restore prosperity.

Speaking at this time at a meeting in the Central Hall, Westminster, I ventured to protest against this narrow attitude:

> The next few months will be critical, for the Communist attack, hitherto contained, will be reopened both in France and Italy. In Czechoslovakia it seems to have begun.

Europe was already, I declared, divided by the line from Stettin to Trieste. It would indeed be folly to erect a new division, in which all who were not Socialists were to be regarded as pariahs :

> No illusion is more dangerous than that of a Socialist united front to resist Communism. It must be a democratic, united front, of all parties and personalities who believe in freedom and democracy. We shall never unite Europe by dividing ourselves.

These unhappy hesitations, on the Right and on the Left, were to survive and do great injury to the unity of Europe in the formative years. Conservative fears and Socialist suspicions were destined to prevent Britain playing her full role in the great adventure.

Next to Churchill, perhaps the most romantic of the many notabilities attending the Hague Conference was Édouard Herriot, the famous Radical President of the French Assembly and a former Prime Minister who had stood resolutely by the cause of the Republican tradition against the treason of Vichy. He was chairman

[1] *Annual Register, 1948*, p. 9.

of the French Council for United Europe. The federalists were represented by Dr. Hendrik Brugmans, a Dutch Socialist. The leader of the 'Nouvelles Équipes Internationales', composed chiefly of Christian Democrats, was Robert Bichet, a former French Minister. The presence of a small German delegation, led by Dr. Adenauer, was a striking demonstration of the deep purposes which inspired the gathering.

The conference, like all bodies of this size, proved somewhat unwieldy. Three committees were formed—political, economic and cultural—presided over by suitable figures of distinction, each aided by its managing 'bureau' and attended regularly by a solid core of devotees. Others of us wandered about, like students at a university, from one classroom to another, attracted by some notable speaker or by some specially keen debate. To most of us, again like undergraduates recently released from school, the chief attraction was the opportunity for making new and renewing old friendships. Many of our number had scarcely been out of our beleaguered island for nearly ten years, except on active service. It was agreeable to escape for a few days from the restrictions and hardships of our somewhat arid regime at home into the easier conditions of Continental life. Of course, we had no money, or very little—there was an economic crisis 'on' at the time. So we had a very meagre allowance of currency. But we were given food tickets by some of our European friends and hospitably entertained by others. Such are the fruits of victory.

The task of organising a conference on this scale, on what might be called an amateur basis, without the assistance of civil servants and diplomatic functionaries, was a heavy one. It would scarcely have been possible if the European Governments had treated the meeting with the same aloofness and even hostility as the British Government displayed. In the event, the three days passed without any serious breakdown. The delegates were successfully housed and fed; the necessary halls and meeting-places were available; the appropriate documents were printed. Even the final resolutions which emerged, after prolonged discussion and many amendments, were ready for the plenary meeting. The extravagances of some of the younger enthusiasts had naturally to be restrained by the efforts of the more experienced and prudent members. However, as with amateur theatricals, everything was all right 'on the night'. The political and economic committees succeeded in framing ten resolutions. These, like the Ten Commandments, were of varying importance and difficulty. When they were brought down from the heights of the drafting committee they were unanimously approved by the whole body of delegates. But the main proposal, on which the chief attention of those present at The Hague and outside was concentrated, was that for a European Assembly, to be convened as soon as possible. This was recommended to the final meeting by Churchill in a speech of remarkable vigour and eloquence. Its effect was rather enhanced than diminished by the accompaniment of a formidable storm of thunder and lightning. In this somewhat Wagnerian atmosphere the 'Congress of Europe' closed.

For our return, Beddington-Behrens had hired a Dove aeroplane and invited me to join him. The other passengers were Harold Butler, Walter Layton, Lady Violet Bonham-Carter, and Peter Thorneycroft. We took off successfully, in spite of the storm, but when we got to Croydon our host informed me that the pilot was unable to lower the undercarriage. After several attempts to shake it free by swooping rapidly down as if to land had proved ineffectual, the only course was to fly round for an hour or more to use up all the petrol and then land as best we could. Beddington-Behrens seemed to fear that his guests might be surprised, or even alarmed, by the delay and the prolonged circling round the airfield. I took a different view. As I expected, Lady Violet and Layton happily discussed the future of the Liberal Party for over an hour, scarcely noticing that anything was amiss. Butler and Thorneycroft argued about economics. My host and I watched the familiar rolling out of the fire-engines and the ambulances with what nonchalance we could assume. All this nostalgically recalled to me my Mediterranean days. In the end we landed without disaster and jumped out safely. Peter Thorneycroft and I gallantly cried out 'Women and Liberals first'. If the worst came to the worst, they would provide a convenient cushion.

The proceedings of the Hague Congress were derided in some quarters as amateurish and often disorderly. It was followed by two other meetings, on a more limited scale, at Brussels and at West-minster. These were certainly businesslike and efficient. The first, which was held in February 1949, was chiefly devoted to matters of organisation and to definition of the immediate programme of propaganda. I had undertaken in the preceding autumn lecture tours both in Germany and Italy, where I found growing enthusiasm for the European idea. I was therefore able to contribute something to the plans which were formulated at Brussels.

The Westminster Conference, in April 1949, was held under the auspices of ELEC and was devoted to economic and financial problems. It was attended by a large number of distinguished economists, British and European, both from inside and outside our membership. The chief questions discussed were currency con-vertibility, European payments, the organisation of basic industries and the refugee problem. But, of course, these were but prelimin-aries to the long-expected convening of the Council of Europe.

Shortly after our return from The Hague, Churchill summoned his committee to discuss the next step. It was decided to ask Attlee to receive a deputation to put before him the results of the con-ference and the main proposals, so far as they affected Governments. The Prime Minister's consent was obtained and the day and hour fixed.

I shall never forget this somewhat bizarre affair. We all met in Churchill's room in the House of Commons, to the number of a dozen or more. After agreeing our procedure, we marched in solemn procession, through New Palace Yard, across Parliament Square, up Whitehall till we reached Downing Street. Churchill led, with the usual cigar and the equally inevitable V-signs. The policemen on duty seemed a little surprised, as we dutifully followed our leader, two by two, like a school crocodile. But the traffic was stopped for our benefit, and we reached No. 10, into which I do not suppose Churchill had entered since the summer of 1945, in reasonably good order.

The Prime Minister and the Foreign Secretary (with a number of other Ministers) received us with appropriate courtesy and gravity. Churchill deployed the case with eloquence, concentrating on the main point—our request that the Governments primarily concerned, that is the five Governments signatory to the Brussels Treaty (Britain, France, Belgium, Holland and Luxembourg), should agree to study the question of a European assembly and take the initiative in constituting it on as wide a basis as practicable.

In October, these Governments agreed to appoint a Commission to examine the plan. After much discussion, and in spite of Bevin's reluctance, the Foreign Ministers of the five powers finally decided on 28 January 1949 to call the Council of Europe into being. On 18 March they invited five other States, Italy, Eire, Norway, Denmark and Sweden, to join. All consented, and at a constituent conference in London on 5 May, agreement was reached on the text of the necessary statute setting up the Council.

Although the British Government tried to rule out defence from the scope of the new body (as being dealt with by NATO) and economic questions (as falling under O.E.E.C.), leaving us, apparently, only empowered to discuss legal and cultural matters, none of us felt any doubt that once the Assembly met, there would be little difficulty in debating whatever the members might decide. And so it was to prove.

Meanwhile, we waited anxiously and hopefully for the first meeting, to be held in Strasbourg, of the long-awaited Council of Europe.

The Council was to consist of two organs: a committee of Foreign Ministers and a Consultative Assembly of Parliamentarians from the constituent countries. In this body the larger countries were allotted eighteen representatives and the smaller either six or eight. The first act of the committee of Ministers, which met on 8–13 August 1949, was to admit Greece and Turkey. This brought the total number of countries to twelve and of Assembly members to 101.

The British Parliament had already been informed, at the beginning of June, that in accordance with the arrangement by which each Government should decide the composition of its representatives, there were to be eleven Socialists, six Conservatives and one Liberal. The Socialists included Morrison, Dalton and William Whiteley, the Chief Whip. Since Dalton had recently re-entered the Government as Chancellor of the Duchy, the Labour group included three Ministers—an arrangement avoided by most other countries, and one which put Morrison in a somewhat embarrassing position in relation to Bevin, the Foreign Secretary. Among others prominent in the Labour team were Maurice Edelman, R. W. G. Mackay—an ardent 'European'—and others who have since played a considerable part in politics, including Fred Lee and Lynn Ungoed-Thomas. The Conservative team was composed of Churchill, David Maxwell Fyfe, David Eccles, Boothby, Ronald Ross (representing Ulster Members) and myself. Sandys was not appointed a member of this first gathering, but operated from the offices of the European Movement. Since a very large number of the members of the Assembly were well known to him, he exercised much influence behind the scenes, in addition to acting as Chief of Staff to Churchill.

A preparatory commission had met earlier in May to work out the draft rules of procedure both for the Committee of Ministers and the Assembly, and to agree a budget of expenditure. The Assembly's 'standing orders' had been provisionally drawn up with the assistance of the former Chief Clerk of the House of Commons, Sir Gilbert Campion. The plan finally agreed on was a compromise between British and Continental methods. The hall was to be semi-circular, as in most European Parliaments. But members were placed neither by the countries they represented nor by parties, but alphabetically. There were therefore no national 'blocs', and no 'Right, Centre and Left'. This was to have a salutary effect upon our debates, by adding to the spontaneity and tending to depress a purely partisan or national approach to the emerging problems. Churchill, if I remember right, was placed between two Italians with whom he conversed volubly and audibly in his characteristic French. At the same time the lobbies' restaurants and bars became of even greater importance than at home.

Although the form of the hall was Continental, the method of speaking followed English practice. There was no tribune; each member spoke from his place as in our Parliament. Many of our Continental friends who found this somewhat disconcerting at first seemed later to appreciate this method as tending to produce less declamation and more discussion. The guidance of the Assembly was to be provided by a President assisted by four Vice-Presidents; these together acted as the managing 'Bureau'. Broadly, the general procedure for the wording of resolutions and motions and the calling and voting on amendments was a compromise between British and European methods. Nevertheless, Sir Gilbert Campion succeeded in imposing a great deal of his own ideas upon the organising committee and was held in the deepest respect by all. Calm, elegant, impervious to any emotion, with apparently as complete a knowledge of the rules that had just been adopted as if he had been operating under them all his life, he had already become the Erskine May of the Assembly. He was generally known among all the members as 'Monsieur "Pas en Angleterre" ', this being his invariable answer to any proposal of which he might disapprove.

In addition to the members, the Governments had the right, if they so chose, to appoint alternates or substitutes (*suppléants*) who could exercise the full right of sitting, speaking and voting in the absence of their principals. With characteristic pettiness, the British Treasury, supported by Morrison, prevented us taking full advantage of this arrangement by refusing any allowances to the alternates except when actually functioning. Yet obviously, if the Assembly was to be useful, the more Members of Parliament who shared this experience the better.

It was certainly a thrilling moment when we all gathered at Strasbourg. Why exactly this city had been chosen as the seat of the Council of Europe was obscure. It had poor communications at that time, since the airfield was small and unsuitable for large machines, and the train journey from Paris took at least six hours. Some people thought that Strasbourg had been selected because of its symbolic position, in the very centre of Western Europe and more suitable therefore than any national capital. Others suspected that those Foreign Ministers who were least favourable to the European concept thought its inaccessibility would be of some advantage in preventing its undue popularity. Certainly, many of my French friends seemed to find it very difficult to stay long at Strasbourg, but returned continually to Paris. Nevertheless, Strasbourg was in many ways well fitted to our purpose. Had the meetings taken place in a great metropolitan city like Paris or London, there would have been little opportunity for developing a sense of unity and comradeship. In Strasbourg there were few distractions. We lived together in the Assembly or its committees during many working hours. In our leisure, we shared an agreeable atmosphere of social recreation and informal discussion.

During the three years that I sat on this body I got to know almost every distinguished personality in Europe. Since the Ministers in most countries seemed to change more rapidly than in ours, there was a constant flow in and out. For instance, by a happy chance there was a change of Government in Belgium a few days before our first meeting. This freed Spaak from his position as Foreign Minister and enabled him to be elected first a member of the Assembly and afterwards, by unanimous vote, President. This proved to be of great value to our work:

> With no other President could the first five weeks' session have been such a success. For in the first Assembly—as in the early British Parliaments—the Speaker must not be content merely to follow precedents. He must make them. He must not preside in the sense in which, after generations of experience and the emergence of an elaborate code of procedure, the Speaker presides over a British House of Commons—that is, do anything except speak. President Spaak talked a great deal, with wit and wisdom. He had to guide the members through a procedure which had to make itself.[1]

I must honestly confess that one of the attractions of Strasbourg to the British members, regardless of party, was the chance to escape for a few weeks from the austere regime ruling at home—which I once somewhat flippantly described as one of 'fish and Cripps'. Now we could enjoy the fleshpots of Alsace. Indeed, all of us had got so accustomed to the minute rations of meat and other foods which we were allowed at home that our shrunken stomachs were quite unable to deal with the vast helpings with which we were now provided in the hotels and eating-houses of the city. Until we began to get into practice one portion of meat was generally enough for three of us. Strasbourg food, even apart from the

[1] Harold Macmillan, *The Spectator*, 16 September 1949.

famous *foie gras*, was noted both for its elegance and abundance—
especially the latter. It could be summed up in a remark of an
Alsatian worthy, with whom I became acquainted : 'Mon esprit est
français, mais mon estomac est allemand.' The weather was fine—
usually hot, sometimes disagreeably so—but with my North African
experience I had become accustomed to this. Since my wife had to
be at home, I brought out my daughter Catherine, who was with me
throughout on this first occasion. My wife came in the following
years. Thus, although we all worked hard, we all enjoyed ourselves.

Apart from these material and even gross pleasures, we met in a
real atmosphere of spiritual excitement. We really felt convinced
that we could found a new order in the Old World—democratic,
free, progressive, destined to restore prosperity and preserve peace.
While nearly all of us were averse to the federal concept which a few
extremists enthusiastically promoted, we accepted that sincere
partnership in the common task of rebuilding Europe must involve
some surrender of sovereignty and the creation of some form of
political organisation, if European institutions were to avoid a regime
of pure technocracy. In these early days, therefore, in spite of all the
difficulties, we were hopeful and confident. Much, of course, of the
sense of unity and goodwill which the Council of Europe was
founded to create still remains. Much good work is still being done.
But the European concept, especially on the economic side, has
passed into a different system and into other hands than ours. This
was largely our fault; and when we tried to retrieve the position it
was too late. Meanwhile, we were sanguine and expectant.

Most of the British were lodged at one or other of two main hotels
and comfortably looked after. The Treasury paid for our accommodation and we were given cash for our meals on a modest but not
ungenerous basis. Churchill lived in a villa, with his usual 'court'.

The Assembly met officially for the first time on 10 August 1949.
Since no President had yet been elected, the first session took place
under the chairmanship of M. Herriot.

M. Herriot made an 'allocution' and we then adjourned. The
fun started later.

The trouble began with poor Herbert Morrison and his team.

Having absolutely no knowledge or experience of foreigners, and little imagination, Herbert clearly thought that he would reproduce Westminster at Strasbourg. He would 'lead' the House; we should be a docile and patronised Opposition. The 'foreigners' would stand in awe of British prestige and the power of a great British Minister (none of the other countries, with rare exceptions, have sent Ministers to the Assembly).[1]

On the first afternoon Morrison called a meeting of all the British 'delegation', as he somewhat incorrectly termed us. We did not regard ourselves as a national delegation but as individual representatives chosen by our own Governments to attend a European Parliament:

> He was going to alter the rules; he was going to elect the officers; he would rearrange the seating (which is alphabetically arranged and not by countries or even by parties). He would make his Chief Whip (Whiteley) Vice-President of the Assembly (as Caligula made his horse Consul).
> We (Tories) would bow to his superior authority here (as at Westminster) and get a small dose of patronage in exchange (a little whisky and an entertainment allowance).
> Churchill was not at this meeting and . . . I took a very reserved view.
> Within a day or two the fat was in the fire.

After the election of Spaak as President, which was unanimous, there came the question of the Vice-Presidents. There were no difficulties about three out of the four; Stefano Jacini (Italy), François de Menthon (France) and Ole Björn Kraft (Denmark) were proposed and proved generally acceptable. The fourth Vice-President must clearly be British. But this election led to an exciting and even bitter contest. Morrison insisted on nominating Whiteley, a charming man and a popular Chief Whip. He had acted as colleague to James Stuart in the War Coalition and was deservedly liked and respected by all those who knew him. But for this particular post he was really not acceptable. The Vice-President not only had to take the chair in rotation and guide the debates, but also had to

[1] This, and subsequent passages, are taken from letters which I wrote to my wife at the time.

assist in much of the work of the committees and in organising the effective functioning of the Assembly. This was of especial importance in its early days. Morrison was determined to run his candidate, and a contest ensued:

> We put up Layton; and canvassed freely for him. L. was terrified and wanted to withdraw. Churchill seized the trembling L. during an interval and thundered at him 'If you retire now, I will never speak to you again. You will have betrayed me. You will have betrayed the whole Liberal Party.'

The canvassing now began in full earnest:

> All the Socialists in the Assembly had made a deal with Herbert Morrison at a stormy meeting the night before. Herbert had to agree to his rival André Philip[1] becoming chairman of the international Socialist movement, in order to buy the Vice-Presidency for Whiteley. (Philip told me this, with tears of shame and indignation—'Que voulait-vous? Il m'a fallu marchander avec ce Mor-r-r-r-ison. J'en suis dégouté.').

We polled all the Italians except two; the Greeks and Turks were solid—their orders were to follow Churchill. The voting was secret, by a ballot paper dropped in an urn. Two tellers were chosen by lot. By an extraordinary chance the lot fell on Churchill, which somehow seemed to accentuate the drama. The excitement and the heat were intense. It proved a 'damned close-run thing', for Layton was elected by 52 votes to 47:

> The canvassing pro and con poor old Whiteley was of 18th-century intensity and carried on by everyone—journalists, secretaries, etc. Randolph [Churchill] and Ali Forbes acted more or less as Whips. It was like Fox and the Westminster election. It was freely rumoured that Whiteley (in spite of two wars in his lifetime) had never till today crossed the Channel. . . . The Whiteley partisans repudiated this with indignation. On the contrary, he *had* been abroad before. Many years ago he had gone on a day trip from Folkestone to Boulogne.

All this was perhaps rather reprehensible, but it was very enjoyable. Naturally, after the election there was an adjournment. One of the

---

[1] A distinguished French Socialist, who had joined de Gaulle in Algiers.

most agreeable features about the Continental Parliamentary system is that when anything interesting or exciting happens you adjourn for a drink, gossip or repose. I therefore escorted Churchill back to his villa, which had been given to him, with food, wine and servants all included, by the people of Strasbourg. The city had indeed reason to be grateful to him, for at a most critical moment in the last stages of the war, during the German counter-stroke in the Ardennes, Eisenhower had authorised the withdrawal of the American armies from the Rhine to the Vosges. This would have involved leaving Strasbourg open to a return of the enemy to exact frightful vengeance, for the population had welcomed their earlier deliverance with passionate emotion. Churchill, who chanced to be at Eisenhower's Headquarters at this time, appealed to the Commander-in-Chief not to take this action, and as a result of his plea Eisenhower cancelled his instructions. The people of Strasbourg knew this story, and will never forget their second deliverance.

Churchill was in a most happy and exultant mood, like a schoolboy:

> He was so tired that he lay on his bed—fully dressed—but declaring repeatedly, 'This is the best fun I've had for years and years. This is splendid. This is really fun.'

Thus Morrison suffered his first Parliamentary defeat since 1945.

In spite of his exhaustion, the result partly of the extreme heat and partly of the morning's agitations, Churchill returned with me to the afternoon meeting. The first half-hour was devoted to an admirable presidential address by Spaak, both practical and inspiring. We then turned to the question of our future discussions and the compilation of something like a Parliamentary Order Paper. When the Consultative Assembly was created by the Governments, it was clearly the intention of the Foreign Ministers to restrict its scope as far as possible. This indeed was not unreasonable as regards powers. But of course the Assembly had no powers; it was consultative in the strict sense; its functions were to deliberate and advise. There seemed to be no reason why its discussions should be so confined as to reduce its proceedings to a farce. It was therefore round this issue —the right of the Assembly to debate what it wished—that the battle was next joined.

Churchill's position was not altogether easy, although his purpose was fixed. He asked me to raise this broad question as a matter of urgency. This I did, after prior agreement with Spaak. While it was clear that we wanted to discuss vital issues, such as the economic and political problems facing Europe, as well as juridical questions, such as human rights, we were not yet ready to bring up the matter about which Churchill was at this time most exercised—that of the future of Germany. The West German elections were now going on, and it would clearly be wise to wait until after they were finished, which would be the following Monday, 15 August. Yet according to the rules, the Assembly could not discuss anything without the leave of the Ministers, and their permission must be sought and obtained within three days of the opening, 10 August. It was now the 12th. If we waited, and the rules were strictly applied, we should be too late. In any case, the Committee of Ministers would shortly be dispersing. After a long debate the Assembly decided to appeal to the Ministers, through the President, for greater latitude. We of course did not at this stage raise specifically the German question, but merely demanded the right to raise new matters during the course of the session:

> Churchill more or less 'led' the Assembly in all this—much to Morrison's discomfiture. Every time M. opened his mouth, somebody jumped on him—usually a French Socialist.

At the end of the discussion a most painful incident took place, embarrassing to us all. It had now been agreed by Whitehall that one 'substitute' Conservative would be allowed to come, since Churchill did not expect to attend every meeting himself, or remain for long. For this purpose the appointment of John Foster had been approved. But the prospect of his allowance still appeared to rankle. The Treasury view was that he could not be paid except while he was actually functioning. £2 a day was at stake:

> Morrison foolishly came up to Churchill in the Assembly chamber (just after the President had left the chair but when the hall was full of members and public making their way out) and attacked him for staying on and asked about Foster's allowance.
> 'I do not wish to speak to you. Pray write to me.' 'Yes; but we

Three views of Europe: Schuman of France, Bevin of Britain and Stikker of the Netherlands

Speaking at the Council of Europe, Strasbourg, August 1949
'Members were placed neither by the countries they represented nor by parties, but alphabetically . . . This was to have a salutary effect upon our debates.' Maxwell Fyfe is beyond Macmillan, and Morrison is at the end of the row.

cannot pay Foster his £2 a day.' 'Oh—it's your money is it? Well you can take your money and put it where you like—don't speak to me. Please let me leave. You may write to me or to Macmillan.'

So the meeting broke up. We have repaid a few pounds to the Treasury, and I hope Herbert is satisfied.

The French and other foreigners were amazed.

On the next day there was no meeting in the morning, but in the afternoon Spaak informed us that the Committee of Ministers had capitulated:

> An arrangement is agreed that *at any time* during the session a new subject may be proposed. It will be referred (by telegraphic or other means) to the Committee of Ministers for permission to discuss it and they undertake to give their decision within five days.

This marked a substantial victory for the Assembly, but I found the greatest difficulty in persuading Churchill to accept it. Since we were separated by some distance, I had to keep moving from my seat to try to press my moderating views upon him by whispering in his ear. Finally, after many interventions, he accepted the new arrangement but grudgingly, and with dark mutterings.

> 'He is an obstinate old man', somebody said to me. 'But that is no doubt how he beat Hitler.'

So ended the second round. On the next morning the additional agenda, already agreed, was sent to the Foreign Ministers for their approval. All the motions which the Conservatives had proposed were accepted. But although these were broad enough to raise the German question, no specific proposal could yet be included.

The Assembly was now adjourned until the following Tuesday, but the intervening days were active and interesting:

> On Friday evening—after the debate—an immense public meeting took place in the great square (Place Kléber) at which nearly 20,000 people must have been present. This ... was organised by the European Movement and addressed by Spaak, Reynaud, Kraft and Churchill. Churchill received a tremendous welcome and made an extremely effective speech—written in

G

English, translated into French—and delivered with a better accent than usual. Every part of the huge square was filled. At every balcony and every window were massed spectators—*except one*. That, of course, was the window of Bevin's sitting-room window [in] the hotel overlooking the square.[1]

Much of my time was spent in going out to the 'Villa Churchill' for luncheon or dinner. The evening hours were as usual very late. He showed at this time astonishing activity:

> How he can stand it, I cannot imagine. He is entertaining very freely—Americans, French, Belgians, Dutch, Italians—all who can in any way be flattered or cajoled.

Meanwhile, a committee on detailed procedure was working away all Sunday and Monday:

> David [Maxwell] Fyfe represents us on this. Morrison was elected chairman, in deference to his Ministerial rank, but has apparently had a very bad time, being quite unused to the logical and persistent Continental mind. He tries to be jaunty—but the French and others hate jauntiness. And, of course, without a tame majority to carry all his points, he is lost. In this Parliament there is no majority; no Government; no Opposition; no Whips. You have to rely on persuasiveness and the weight of argument. . . . It strikes some of us as very queer and rather alarming !

Monday 15 August was a holiday. On this day Churchill received the freedom of Strasbourg. I think he was under the impression that the public holiday was in his honour. When it was explained to him that it was for the Feast of the Annunciation, he seemed rather put out.

Finally, on Tuesday and Wednesday, a full-dress debate took place upon the political future of Europe. In the course of it there were some truly remarkable speeches. Both Georges Bidault and Paul Reynaud, who seemed younger than ever, were particularly effective. But when Churchill rose to speak after these preliminary days of skirmishing, the excitement in the hall and in the galleries

---

[1] Bevin had arrived for the meeting of the Committee of Ministers.

was intense. I began to realise the tactics that he had been pursuing:

This extraordinary man, during the early sittings, seemed to come down almost too rapidly to the level of normal political agitation. His intervention in the Layton–Whiteley incident and his several short speeches on the question of the powers of the Assembly to fix its own agenda, were all calculated–perhaps intentionally–to reveal him as a Parliamentarian, rather than as a great international figure. You can imagine that we were all a little alarmed at this. For our pains, we were treated with a firm and even harsh refusal to accept our advice. He certainly took more trouble to listen to the debates than I have ever known him do in the House of Commons. He walked about, chatted to each representative, went into the smoking-room, and generally took a lot of trouble to win the sympathetic affection of his new Parliamentary colleagues. This was done with much assiduity. He used his villa for entertaining the more important to luncheon and dinner; and he took much trouble over all this determination to charm them as well as impress them.

Now all these minor manœuvres seemed to be put aside. He rose to an altogether different plane. Yet this speech, long awaited, must have been to the majority of those present a disappointment, or at least seemed inopportune. Already Western Europe had begun to be darkened by a new shadow, not merely the fear of Russia but the fear of a remilitarised and revived Germany. Some people did not like to think much about this or want to talk about it. Yet perhaps it was the most immediate of European problems. How could it be resolved? Only by making European unity a reality and making it as inclusive as possible. Only so could the danger of a new militarism be avoided or contained. Churchill knew this and was not afraid to speak out. With the wonderful combination of prophetic foresight and moral courage which so often inspired him, he avoided the temptation of making a speech much more to the taste of his audience than that which he delivered. On this occasion he could have been excused for putting popularity before truth; for, after all, the foundation of the Council of Europe was largely the result of his efforts. In a sense, today was his 'benefit'. He could easily have won applause by some well-phrased generalities. Undeterred, he made the question of Germany the main and almost the sole theme of his speech. He shocked some; he almost bullied others. In a dramatic outburst, looking round the hall, he demanded almost fiercely, 'Where are the Germans?' He pressed for an immediate invitation to the West German Government to join our ranks. Time was passing. There should be no delay. 'We cannot part at the end of this month on the basis that we do nothing more to bring Germany into our circle until a year has passed. That year is too precious to lose. If lost, it might be lost for ever. It might not be *a* year. It might be *the* year.'

He was to hold to this position while he remained at Strasbourg, and we were to carry on the struggle in his absence. This speech could not have been delivered by any other man. Although not so long or so closely argued or so copiously developed, it ranked in its effect with those at Fulton and at Zürich.

The next day Churchill left by air for Monte Carlo. He intended to stay for a week or ten days in the south of France and hoped to return for the purpose of pressing to a conclusion a resolution on the subject of German entry. He put me in charge of our group, with instructions to send him a daily report of the situation and to press on with his German proposal.

In the general political, economic and legal work which now followed I was wonderfully helped by David Maxwell Fyfe, a tower of strength in all subjects, as well as by David Eccles, who spoke with real knowledge and brilliance in economic debates. Behind the scenes, Duncan Sandys continued to pull the strings. We had substantial success. Maxwell Fyfe achieved something of a real triumph on the subject of human rights and the proposal of enforcing them in Europe by a special court. There had been long, complicated arguments in committee. Now, with the help of M. Teitgen, he had carried through his proposals and

> made a massive and impressive speech in winding up the debate. The more of him I see, the more I like and admire him. He is a remarkable character—loyal, honourable, intelligent and modest.

The debates both in committee and in full session were both entertaining and instructive. I spoke in several, not without some success. On one of these occasions I was particularly gratified by a double compliment:

> One of my Italian friends congratulated me on my speech, saying 'You are a fortunate man. You have made the best speech of the debate, and you have the prettiest daughter—like an angel.'

Even the procedural questions, which would be dull at home, I found fascinating. These discussions revealed the differences in temperament and approach between the different countries:

> The Latins are clearly shocked by the sloppy way we think; we—and the Scandinavians—are bored by the Latin logic.

Our form of humour, too, was a failure. Rather jaunty chaff was much resented; wit, certainly, but not banter.

In the general economic debate Dalton spoke extraordinarily well, by far the best of all his colleagues; but even he fell into the error of introducing jibes against Churchill. André Philip, Reynaud and some of the Italians were especially good. At the same time we had new additions to our little team. Freddie Birkenhead and his wife arrived, he being one of our 'substitutes'.

The first meeting of the Council of Europe was still a novelty. Diplomats, politicians, supporters of the Movement, journalists, American observers were accordingly attracted to Strasbourg in large numbers. There was a flow of formal and informal entertainments. So the days passed pleasantly enough.

But the task which Churchill had entrusted to me during his absence was not altogether easy to carry out. His formal request that the Assembly should ask the Ministers to take the necessary steps, either by an immediate communication to the German Government or by calling a special Assembly early in the New Year for the purpose, had been reluctantly refused by Spaak, as President, as 'out of order' at that stage in our proceedings. He had, however, suggested that the Assembly would probably have a chance of debating the matter in one form or other before the end of the session. But I found myself puzzled as to how the German question could be brought to a head. We were in something of a dilemma as to whether to raise it under the five days' rule or to introduce it into the discussions of the political committee.

Bidault, who carried considerable weight at that time as the leader of the largest party in France, was sympathetic; but he had his own anxieties and reservations. The Italians, too, were nervous about their home opinion. In any case the question remained—by what means were we to impress the Ministers with the Assembly's views? Apart from the procedural difficulty, it can well be imagined that it was not easy for the representatives of nations so lately occupied and oppressed by Nazi cruelty (we were still only four years from the end of the war) to rally with immediate enthusiasm to the idea of welcoming in our midst eighteen German representatives. They might prove a discordant element, just as we were all settling down happily together. There was an additional complication. The French at that time were anxious to do nothing which would prejudge the final decision as to the future of the Saar territory. Moreover, we had been informed on good authority that the Committee of Ministers before adjourning had decided to oppose the inclusion of Germany in our agenda. It was said that Bevin and his advisers believed that they could obtain the necessary two-thirds majority to block any such proposal.

There were various possible courses. We could force the issue by persuading our colleagues to give the necessary five days' notice and thus obtain the Ministers' permission to discuss the whole question. We could then propose a formal resolution, and try to persuade the Assembly to add it to the final resolutions which would be presented to the Council of Ministers as the result of our labours at the end of the session. Alternatively—and that seemed agreeable to the French—instead of raising the matter specifically as to Germany, the text might be widened to include 'the question of new entrants'. I reported this to Churchill, adding 'the majority of French opinion is still divided and public opinion is nervous with the tone of the new German Government still unknown'. I added that I felt sure that the French would insist on reserving the future of the Saar as their price of agreement to discuss Germany, either with or without the permission of the Ministers.

Ultimately a formula was agreed with our French and Italian colleagues which seemed to meet the case. We would ask permission to debate, either in the present session or in an extraordinary session to be invoked under the appropriate article, 'the position of the German Federal Republic and the Saar territory in relation to the Council of Europe'. On 22 August I received Churchill's approval of my proposal. At the same time, he stated his intention to be back in Strasbourg on the afternoon of Wednesday, 24 August, and he invited us all to dine with him to discuss the situation. Meanwhile, a great deal of pressure was being brought by Morrison and his supporters to find some way of delaying or frustrating our plans. I was confident, however, that Churchill's own authority when he returned would carry the day.

All was now set for the final stages of the session and the passing of substantive resolutions, when on 25 August we received the shattering news of Churchill's illness:

> We got the most exaggerated stories—he had pneumonia, he had had a stroke, he was gravely ill. However, Duncan Sandys came in to me early in the morning, to say that he had talked with him on the phone and he seemed in good form. It seems that he has certainly got a chill, and since Moran is with him, it is probable that he will not be allowed to return here—at least for some days. Naturally, the rumours spread throughout the day, and were not altogether dispelled by a reassuring bulletin.

In fact, as I was afterwards to learn, Churchill had suffered from one of those minor attacks which were to threaten him for the rest of his life. This one, happily, proved slight, and by careful control of the news was effectively concealed. This indomitable old man was still destined to fight two General Elections and form another Government which was to last nearly four years.

As soon as he began to recover, the telephone began to ring with increasing urgency. I remembered only too well the long conversations which had passed between Algiers and Marrakesh after his previous illness.[1] Once more it was difficult to explain to him, at a distance, the changing complications of the scene. But I was able to assure him that in one form or another we would be able to carry out his wishes.

Meanwhile, we had considerable success in the final stage of the

[1] *The Blast of War*, p. 439.

economic resolutions when they came back from committee for the approval of the whole Assembly—a kind of Third Reading. Eccles, who had been elected *rapporteur*,

> carried out his task with quite remarkable skill. There [had been] literally 80 or 90 amendments proposed, some of them of a wrecking character. The British Socialists, annoyed at finding themselves without their regular parliamentary majority and having failed (although they tried to push the Committee) to carry their main points, made every effort to destroy the report.

At the end of the first day, Dalton tried to 'move the report back', a procedure which shocked and antagonised the Continental Socialists. Failing in this, he and his friends tried obstruction. Fifty or sixty amendments had to be voted on without any system of selection by the chair or of a 'guillotine'. But these Parliamentary methods, so familiar at home, proved unacceptable at Strasbourg:

> By overdoing it, they put the Assembly against them. By the end, they voted alone, abandoned in disgust by the Continental Socialists. On some issues, even old Whiteley voted against Dalton!
>
> It was a most interesting example of how a Parliament *can* work, and no doubt used to work in England, before the rigidity of parties and the growth of the power of the Whips.
>
> Another important point is that there is no division bell. Only those vote who have heard the arguments! Almost no one leaves his seat for this reason during the whole sitting.

I was not sorry to witness this exhibition. It would serve to weaken the position of the British Socialists for the next contest.

All this brought us to Saturday, 3 September. In order to obtain what Churchill wanted, everything depended upon the report of the political committee, which was to come forward on Monday. For after much deliberation we had thought it wise not to raise the German question separately but to include it in the set of resolutions which would come out as the work of the political committee for the Assembly to adopt. In this we were successful. Nevertheless, when the text was published, it was difficult to make the Press understand its implications:

Although I did not think it possible to carry a motion in committee in favour of admitting Germany as such, I carried unanimously a proposal for (*a*) an emergency session early in 1950;
(*b*) the discussion of new members of the Council of Europe at
this extraordinary session.

I shall have to make this clear on Monday, so that the Press
will not report it as a rebuff to Churchill. At the same time, I must
be careful not to put it in such a way as to alarm the French, who
have agreed to this formula.

In view of his inability to attend the final meeting himself,
Churchill had wished to send a message to be read out on his behalf.
This plan was likely to raise many difficulties, including objections
from the British Labour Members. Such an application would
certainly put Spaak in an embarrassing position, and it would be
hard for him to make a precedent which might be troublesome in the
future. After discussion, therefore, with Duncan Sandys and David
Maxwell Fyfe, I sent Churchill a discouraging reply. It was agreed
that in the final debate I should make a short speech expressing
Churchill's regrets at his absence. In order to heighten the effect I
proposed to read passages from the Minute which he had written to
Eden in October 1942.[1] After a telephone conversation on the
Sunday night (4 September) with Churchill, who had now returned
to Chartwell, he readily approved.

The debate on Monday 5 September was the culminating point
of the first session of the Strasbourg Assembly. Since we had succeeded in our first object—that is, a unanimous recommendation
from the political committee to the plenary meeting of the Assembly
on the question in which Churchill was chiefly interested and to
which he had devoted all his energy, I felt confident of success.
Nevertheless, I was conscious that a heavy responsibility lay upon
me. In the morning I had given copies of my speech to the Press.
They included the Churchill Minute. Since it had never been
published it naturally had considerable news value.

I began my speech at 4 p.m. I had changed from my old
flannel suit into a black suit and a stiff white collar (I have a feeling
that when one is to speak, one should be properly dressed—

[1] See pp. 152–3 and Appendix One.

especially if one is to make a speech of dramatic importance). The perspiration was dripping from me at every pore—but fortunately my speech was short.

I reminded the members that the phrase employed—'new members and new associate members of the Council of Europe'—covered the whole German problem. This paragraph, after much debate, had been carried unanimously by the Committee; I trusted it would have the same reception from the whole Assembly. I continued as follows:

> It will be remembered that during our general debate on the political structure of Europe the question of Germany was brought forward in a short, but striking, contribution by Mr. Winston Churchill.
> Unfortunately, he is not able to be with us today; he has therefore left the matter in my hands. I must ask the indulgence of my fellow members in my task. But I will be brief.

I recalled that after Churchill's original intervention on 14 August, Bidault had responded with a speech characteristically generous and statesmanlike. He had raised, as he had both a right and duty to do, the position of other territories—notably the Saar. It was also pointed out that in due course Austria might appropriately become a candidate. It was for this reason that the committee had unanimously recommended a phrase broad enough to cover not only the urgent case of Germany but all other claims and contingencies. This proposal, coupled with that recommending an extraordinary session early in 1950 to deal with the question of new entrants, was indeed very close to the appeal made by Churchill three weeks before in this very hall. I continued:

> There is certainly no man whose views are more entitled to our respect. For they are not based on recent or opportunist decisions, but on long study and deep reflection.
> In the last few days he has sent me some notes on these important matters, including a Minute from which I have his permission to quote a short, but I think most relevant passage. It was written by him as Prime Minister of Great Britain seven years ago

—in October 1942. I ask the Assembly to note the date: October 1942.

I then read out the text.[1] I added that these words had never before been published and nowhere could they be more suitably made known than in the first session of the Assembly.

The reading of this document made a great sensation, especially when I reminded my fellow members of the date on which it had been composed—a period when the issue of the war was still uncertain, 'before the end of the beginning and long before the beginning of the end'.

Two French speakers, both favourable, followed. Jacini, who also spoke, was very helpful. The necessary resolutions were carried unanimously and the session ended at 6.30 p.m. The British Socialists made no effort to oppose, either by speech or by vote. It got hotter and hotter as the day went on, and we ended with an immense party given by the European Movement at which Spaak was the chief guest. When Churchill rang up later in the evening, he seemed more than satisfied.

There was little work now for the Assembly to do except pass all the final resolutions which had emerged from the various committees. These included a project for a convention on personal and political rights—the so-called 'Human Rights' declaration—with a machinery for a European committee and court, and various proposals for co-operation in the economic sphere, in the field of social security and in cultural matters. Naturally, on the political structure of Europe and the methods for achieving greater unity there was a certain ambivalence. Neither Churchill nor Morrison wanted anything in the nature of federal union on the basis of a United States of Europe. With few exceptions, however, all wanted to strengthen the power and reality of the Assembly and bring it into closer touch and co-operative working with Ministers and Governments.

Before we finally returned home I had a talk with Dalton, who had long been a good friend of mine. Morrison had by now gone home and left him in charge. As a result the situation was more relaxed. Dalton was fundamentally a friendly soul. I was glad, therefore, when he proposed that the British should give a party on a generous scale to everyone concerned—members of the Assembly, officials and other notabilities, Press, and leading citizens of Strasbourg. Since funds appeared to be available from Government sources, I readily agreed, and on the last day he and I acted as hosts to a large and happy gathering. It was pleasant to be able to drown our differences so agreeably at the taxpayers' expense.

In the event, the German question was finally resolved without the necessity for convening a special session of the whole Assembly. A 'standing committee' had been created, before we parted, which was empowered to deal with the Committee of Ministers on behalf of the whole body of members. In the debate in the House of Commons on 17 November, Bevin expressed his willingness to try to get the matter agreed as rapidly as possible. For technical reasons, since Germany was still nominally under the control of the occupying powers, she would have to be elected as an 'associate' member. Accordingly, following a short session of the Committee of Ministers on 30 March 1950, a formal invitation was issued to the German Federal Republic. This was accepted and became effective in May. At our next meeting at Strasbourg we were able to welcome the German representatives as colleagues. Whatever might be the future role of the Council of Europe, a decisive step had been taken towards reconciliation and unity.

CHAPTER VIII

Europe: Federal or Confederal?

THE admission of the Federal Republic to the Council of Europe marked a determination to bring the German people back into association with Western Europe and to end by a dramatic gesture the isolation from which they had suffered during the years of occupation. The German Government and people were no longer to be suspect or treated as pariahs; they were to be welcomed into the European community. Nevertheless, many urgent problems had still to be resolved if confidence was to be restored and maintained. The lifting of the restrictions which the Allied Governments had necessarily and properly imposed upon Germany after the war was inescapable. But it would not remove—it would even enhance—the fears of the French and other peoples who had suffered so much from German militarism for three generations. Men's minds, therefore, began to turn to methods of integrating Germany into the economic life of her Western neighbours and of sharing their common defence. These took shape in proposals which were soon to be popularly known as the 'Schuman Plan' and the 'European Army'.

As far back as the debate in the House of Commons on 23 March 1949 I had discussed, at least in general terms, the first of these questions. There was much talk at the time of the advantages of an early withdrawal of the Allied occupying forces. This had many attractions, but some dangers. Much turned upon the future of the Ruhr, with its vast arsenal of power. I reminded the House that although under the Trusteeship Law the ownership of the Ruhr industries was eventually to be decided by a German Government, this was not the real issue. Whether the industry was in private hands, or nationalised, it would be equally dangerous if the wrong kind of German Government ever took power again: 'There must be guarantees—for the French, but equally for ourselves.' But what guarantees could be effective once the occupation ended? Paper guarantees were valueless:

> The only guarantee is if the soul of the German people is won for the West. If Germany enters a Western European system, as a free and equal member, then indeed German heavy industry can be subjected to control; but not an *invidious* control directed against Germany alone, but to exactly the same regulations as to quantity, planning, development and so forth, as the coal and iron and steel industries of Belgium, Holland, Luxembourg, France, Italy and Britain.[1]

An internationalised control of these industries could doubtless be justified on economic grounds; it was essential on security grounds.

These ideas were rapidly followed up by a conference organised by ELEC, which considered a report on the European coal and steel industries, stressing the need for their co-ordination on a supra-national level. Robert Schuman, then French Foreign Minister, welcomed these suggestions and hoped that in due course the Assembly of the Council of Europe would consider them. Accordingly, the economic committee of the Assembly at its meeting in December 1949 recommended a scheme for intra-European organisations for coal, iron and steel, as well as in due course for electricity and transport. Informal discussions continued among economists and politicians interested in these affairs throughout the opening months of 1950. But the world was startled when on 9 May Schuman suddenly announced his famous plan.

Robert Schuman was a man of remarkable moral and intellectual power. A prominent member of the M.R.P., the Christian Democrat party of France, he had much in common with the leaders of sister movements in Germany and Italy—Dr. Adenauer and Alcide De Gasperi. All three, one from the Rhineland, one from the Tyrol, and the third from Alsace, came from regions which had been the subject of bitter national rivalries throughout history, and were truly imbued with the European spirit. By a strange chance, De Gasperi had sat in an Austrian Parliament, and Schuman had in his youth,

---

[1] *Hansard*, 23 March 1949.

when Alsace was a German province, served in the German army. No one proclaimed his faith with greater fervour or maintained his proposals with more intellectual vigour than Schuman, who sprang at this moment into the very first rank of European statesmen. It soon became clear that he was actuated not so much by economic motives, important as these were, as by the political aim of linking France and Germany in an indissoluble association which would replace the old hostility by a new partnership.

The Allied control of the Ruhr could not continue indefinitely. Sooner or later Germany must regain her independence in this sphere. But if she regained it in isolation, all the old suspicions and all the old fears would revive in France. It would be the same in Britain, too, for Britain had suffered no less severely than France from German aggression. Since production of steel is the vital basis of military power; since Germany seemed determined to control her own steel industry and to set no limitations to its productive capacity; since the German problem had been for generations the dominating danger in Europe, here was a plan, bold, imaginative and practical. Germany could regain her position of equality; Europe would obtain security.

The Schuman Plan, although primarily based upon the pooling of the coal and steel resources of France and Germany under a joint high authority, contemplated an organisation in which all other European countries could participate. It may well be argued that Schuman was wrong in bursting this bombshell without full diplomatic preparation. No doubt he feared that so novel a plan would be whittled away or lose itself in the sands of prolonged negotiation. The Foreign Ministers of Britain, the United States and France were due in any case to meet two days later, on 11 May, to discuss a number of problems, chiefly arising from the tense situation created by Russian pressure. As a result of their conference a communiqué was issued, declaring the Western Powers' determination to uphold their rights in Berlin and protesting against the Soviet Government's attitude towards the repatriation of German prisoners of war. But it was also stated that Schuman had explained his proposals for the coal and steel industries of France and Germany. Although no serious discussion then took place, it became known that Bevin had sharply criticised Schuman's plan in language which surprised and even shocked his French colleague. Nevertheless, Attlee gave a formal welcome to the French initiative in a statement in the House of Commons on 11 May, at the same time emphasising 'the far-reaching implications of the future economic structure' proposed. Jean Monnet, who had been Schuman's chief adviser and was now Chief Commissioner for Planning in France, came privately to London a few days later to explain the details.

No man could have been better qualified for this purpose. In the days when I had spent long hours discussing with Monnet in Algiers successive French crises I had learned something of his constructive and far-seeing views on the emerging post-war problems. When I met him early in July 1944, he had just returned from Washington and was full of the importance of dealing with the German problem:

> In his view the whole future of Europe depends upon the solution of the German problem and the effective reduction, not merely for the first few years when peace is assured but over a long period, of the German war potential.
> In his view a full United States of Europe is still beyond realisation; but he feels that a strong League; possibly combined with inter-State trade and monetary arrangements, could be made effective among the Powers of Western Europe.
> In this England must take the lead and France must support her. The smaller States – Belgium, Holland, Denmark, the Scandinavian Powers, Spain, Italy—must be both contributors to and beneficiaries of this Western system.[1]

Could Germany, deprived of her capacity for making war, be led to accept, genuinely and sincerely, a more peaceful and civilised conception of life?

Although it was known that discussions were going on privately, the British Government delayed any formal reply. This of course caused my friends and me much anxiety, for there seemed insufficient reason for hesitation. It was true that Bevin was now a sick man; but there were other Ministers quite capable of grasping and dealing with the situation. Accordingly, in a speech in London

[1] Record of conversation of 7 July 1944.

on 17 May, I expressed alarm at the somewhat tepid reception given so far in British official circles to the Schuman proposals:

> I trust this does not mean that the British Government intend to keep out of the plan themselves, or still worse—to kill it in committee.
>
> In my view, M. Schuman's proposals are an act of high courage and of imaginative statesmanship. They may prove a real turning-point in the long and tragic story of Franco-German relations. Every Frenchman may well be proud that the initiative has come from a French statesman.
>
> I hope that British statesmanship will at least be equal to this new responsibility and this new opportunity. For Europe cannot return to the position before the French offer.
>
> If the plan is pursued and implemented, it will be a wonderful step forward. But if it fails, it will mean a serious deterioration. It will be more than a set-back. It will be a disaster.

I followed this up, with other members of the committee of ELEC, in a letter to *The Times* on 22 May 1950 in support of the plan. This at least received sufficient attention to justify a violent attack the following day in a leading article in the *Daily Express*. I was always amused by Lord Beaverbrook's ambivalence over the European question. His whole mind and soul reacted violently against any co-operation with European countries, which he regarded as a betrayal of the great Imperial concept to which he had devoted his life. At the same time, he had so deep and sincere an affection for Churchill that while he attacked violently those who supported Churchill in the European Movement, he never mentioned his great friend by name in this connection.

It was not until 25 May that the British Government made their first formal communication to the French. This expressed readiness to enter 'exploratory' discussions with France and Germany. It added the hope 'that it might be found possible' for this country to join the scheme when a clear picture had emerged of how it would work. From now on there was an almost ludicrous confusion, largely as the result of the British insistence on negotiation by interchange of written memoranda. The British Note had crossed with the French Note asking Britain to subscribe to a public statement of agreement with the proposals contained in Schuman's statement of 9 May. A further British note then reaffirmed their view that participation in negotiations must be without any definite commitment. However, by this time both the West German and the Italian Governments had accepted the French request. On 4 June, when the British Government's refusal was already widely known, the Belgian, Dutch and Luxembourg Governments expressed their general consent. However, a few days later, the Dutch Government added a further reservation, on which much of our discussion in Parliament was later to turn. The Dutch Government wished

> to reserve its freedom to go back on the acceptance of these general principles during the negotiations, if, contrary to what it hoped, it should prove in the future that the application of these principles raises serious objection in practice.

Nevertheless, the British Government were determined on maintaining their position, and on 13 June the Prime Minister made a formal statement to the effect that they were not willing to join the discussions which were due to open on 20 June. They were unable in advance either to reject or to accept the principles underlying the French proposal. He added that there was 'no question of putting forward any alternative British proposal at the present time'. The Prime Minister's statement was naturally received with a good deal of concern on all sides of the House. But since the White Paper was due to appear that afternoon and the debate was promised for an early date, there the matter rested. There was some acid criticism when the British White Paper on the whole question, quoting a large number of documents and communications which had passed between the two Governments, was published.[1] Here, although in its original form the Prime Minister's statement appeared to be confirmed, an erratum slip to paragraph 2 of one of the documents was soon circulated in which the following phrase occurred:

> They themselves are actively engaged in working on proposals inspired by the French initiative of 9th May, in order that they may be ready to make such a contribution.

[1] *Anglo-French Discussions Regarding French Proposals for the Western European Coal, Iron and Steel Industries*, Cmd. 7970 (H.M.S.O., London), published 13 June 1950.

In the subsequent discussions there was much confusion as to the point upon which the breakdown had finally taken place. To some it seemed fundamental, to others almost trivial. The original French proposal was that the Government should be asked to accept the plan for the pooling of coal and steel production and the constitution of a higher authority with binding decisions 'in principle'. But the British Government still felt unwilling to accept so drastic a transfer of sovereignty without knowing the full scheme. The full scheme, they said, had not been worked out. Yet how could we join in a discussion of the plan without some prior commitment to the principle of the plan? The French were determined to secure that the negotiations should be approached positively and not negatively. Above all, they were anxious to keep Germany on the hook, fully committed to what the French regarded as vital both for their economic and military security.

The British attitude caused widespread disappointment. Yet many felt that our Government was justified, at least in not publicly committing themselves to the main basis of the scheme by agreeing 'in principle' to the pooling of coal and steel resources. But it is difficult to see how, except upon a very narrow interpretation of language and perhaps some understanding of the different attitude that British and Continental statesmen are apt to take in these matters, why we could not have attended the conference with the six other countries who ultimately came into the discussions— France, West Germany, Italy and the three Benelux nations. In reality, behind the superficial argument, as it was publicly presented, there lay much deeper feelings and perhaps differences. Certainly, to the Continental mind the acceptance of the plan 'en principe' would not preclude any participator in any negotiations from honourably retiring at the end if he felt that the scheme worked out was impracticable or impolitic.

I had to speak in my own constituency and had no hesitation in stating my views:

> This has been a black week for Britain; for the Empire; for Europe; and for the peace of the world.
> The political importance of the Schuman Plan far outweighs

its economic or industrial aspects. Its purpose is the unity of France and Germany. With British participation, this will secure peace; for Russia will be unable either to seduce or to attack any of these countries separately. But without British participation, Franco-German unity may be a source not of security but danger.

In the not too distant future, we may have to pay a terrible price for the isolationist policy which British Socialism has long practised and now openly dares to preach. . . .

If the Government were confronted with the problem of making an immediate and effective decision on the question of whether or not to join in the discussions on the formula proposed, to a lesser degree the Opposition faced an equal dilemma. Nor were we in a position to disclaim responsibility in the same way as we had some-times been able to do in the years immediately succeeding the war. We were no longer a tiny body of defeated and dispirited troops facing an overwhelming superiority on the Ministerial benches. Only a few months before, a General Election had taken place, and we had now nearly three hundred Conservative Members. In this situation, therefore, an even greater sense of responsibility was felt by all Conservatives in the House of Commons, both in the directing circles and in the rank and file. In our own small group of Churchill's intimate advisers, there were differences both on the immediate problem and the general approach to the vital issues. Churchill of course was deeply committed to the principles which he had preached to the United Europe Movement. Eden, who had not taken any active part in this organisation, was nevertheless, as always, tolerant and fair. Nobody realised more than he the im-mense opportunities either for success or failure in the restoration of European strength and world peace which were involved. Some of our colleagues were definitely opposed to any 'surrender of sovereignty', or rested upon the practical difficulties and disadvan-tages for the British economy. After all, the British steel industry was the most efficient in Europe; it could produce better and cheaper steel at this date than our competitors. Our coal, if we could produce it, was readily saleable overseas. What, then, was there to be ob-tained in exchange for our existing position? Others joined me in feeling strongly that whatever might be the difficulties or dangers, by far the greatest loss would be if European industries were to be remodelled without Britain even being present to take part in the discussions.

A remarkable contribution to the general discussion had been made by the publication of a pamphlet entitled *European Unity*. This statement by the National Executive of the British Labour Party was thought to be inspired, if not written, by Dalton. It had almost certainly not been read or approved by the Prime Minister. But the reactionary, unimaginative, and even defeatist attitude which it represented was both a shock to many Labour Members and a grave embarrassment to the Government. So far as the Labour Party could be committed by such a body, it had pronounced clearly against any form of co-operation between European countries unless upon a planned Socialist basis. This was certainly discouraging. But I was more concerned about what line the Conservative Party should take, which was still undetermined when I had to leave for Strasbourg on 20 June to attend a committee of which I was a member. Deeply disturbed lest my colleagues should reach no effective decision, or even support the Government on the narrow position on which they had chosen to rest, I sent an urgent minute to Churchill. It ran as follows:

1. The situation created by M. Schuman may well be a major turning-point in European history. It is certainly a turning-point in the fortunes of the Tory Party. This issue affords us the last, and perhaps only, chance of regaining the initiative. . . .

2. While there is a natural—and understandable—resentment against the rather harsh and pedantic attitude of the French, we must remember:

(*a*) That they were very anxious to pin the Germans down to something definite.

(*b*) That the Latin peoples always think *a priori* and by deduction. This is the tradition of Aristotle and St. Thomas Aquinas. Since the Reformation Anglo-Saxons think *a posteriori* and inductively.

(*c*) The French have a very natural suspicion of Bevin, Morrison, Dalton & Co., based on the experience of recent years.

(*d*) They would not have tried this on you. For they trust you.

3. There is, of course, no Schuman Plan in existence. . . . There is a plan to have a plan.

4. But this is the very reason why Britain should be in from the start. Then we can mould the plan to our pattern.

5. If we are not in:

either (i) the whole thing will collapse, and with it all real hope of European co-operation,
or (ii) the Germans will, in due course, get complete control. . . .

6. It is now widely reported that the British Government will make an immense (and probably successful) effort to reopen negotiations. . . . In that event, it is *absolutely vital* that this should come about as the result of pressure from the Tory Party and from you.

7. For this reason, you must give the lead for which *Britain, the Empire, Europe* and *the world* have been waiting. Everyone looks to you. They feel entitled to look to you. They have, up to now, been disappointed and are getting a little restive at your inaction. They will soon get suspicious.

8. It is said that the British Embassy in Paris (and no doubt other Embassies elsewhere) has been instructed to spread the story that, under the influence of some of your advisers and fearing to lose votes, you are preparing a retreat from the whole concept of United Europe, now that practical decisions have to be made. 'Winston is selling out Europe' is the phrase being spread everywhere. This propaganda is causing much anxiety and darkening of counsel.

9. You started United Europe. Without you, there would be no Council of Europe, no Committee of Ministers, no Consultative Assembly, no Strasbourg. This is the first and supreme test. You cannot let down all Europe.

10. . . . I beg you to consider putting down a *motion, as soon as possible—today, if practicable*. . . This motion may still be in time to forestall a new Government move.

11. But whatever the Government may or may not do, we shall have to define our policy soon. The modern Conservative Party is tough and imaginative. But it expects and respects firm and decided leadership, not trimming. It would be distasteful to the electorate to see Conservative leaders going through a sort of balancing 'Balfourian' tight-rope programme.

12. The Socialists have got, and look like keeping, the immense advantages of full employment and high pay-packets. So far, we have only *cost of living* and the *housing muddle* against these.

13. We must raise the whole issue to a new level; we must support the principles of the Schuman Plan on two sorts of grounds:

> (*a*) To support expanding demand, but on an *orderly* basis and to safeguard *full employment* for workers in industry, and thus maintain *wage-rates*.
>
> (*b*) But much more to secure the *peace* of Europe.

This is a great strategic conception which should command general support. In any case, *with* British participation, a great step to peace will have been taken; without it, we face great risks. On this point, nobody has a greater right to be heard than you.

14. Of course, the Schuman Plan is not a new idea. It was discussed before the war; it was discussed widely after the war; it was the subject of much debate at Strasbourg last summer and was included in a resolution which commanded almost unanimous support.

15. On the Socialist manifesto *European Unity*, you will no doubt have observed that the recantations are almost as remarkable as the heresies. The 'third force' idea has gone....

16. This is a crisis for Europe. It is also a crisis for you and the Party. But make no mistake, this is a new Tory Party, impatient of political tactics and manœuvring, but absolutely ready to follow a great cause.

I went on to describe a meeting held by the appropriate committee of Conservative Members in the House of Commons which had met the night before. Eighty or more were present. Of the speakers, twenty-three were in favour of the Plan and only two or three against. There was an overwhelming majority that the party should give a lead and that a motion should be tabled. Some who afterwards spoke in the debate and were believed to have special knowledge of the industries concerned had given their support. The younger elements were anxious for a clear and positive attitude. I also sent Churchill the draft of a resolution urging the Government to re-open their discussions with the French Government with a view to joining in the conference on the conditions which have been accepted in the case of the Netherlands Government and thus take a constructive part in the formulation of proposals calculated to promote full employment, and protect wage levels for British workers and at the same time contribute to the maintenance of the peace of Europe and the defence of free democracy.

When I got back from Strasbourg, I learned that Churchill had made up his mind, and would be followed with different degrees of enthusiasm by all his colleagues and the party as a whole. An amendment was therefore tabled broadly in the terms which I had suggested.

The debate held on 26 and 27 June 1950 was conducted on two levels. There was first the narrow issue as to whether or not the British Government should have joined in the negotiations on the basis of a broad acceptance of the principle, safeguarding itself by a declaration on similar lines to that of the Dutch Government. Against such a course the arguments were clear and simple. It was contrary to our whole tradition to tie ourselves beforehand to a formula which we might find in practice unacceptable. Moreover, it was wrong for us to take any step which would tend to reduce rather than enhance the chances of agreement between other powers in Europe on the basis of the principles laid down by Schuman. This was argued in a most powerful speech by Cripps, now Chancellor of the Exchequer, but in terms which many people thought more suitable to a court of law than to a senate. If it was true that in the end no British Government would be able to persuade our people to accept whatever degree of surrender of sovereignty was involved in any plan of this kind, then no doubt it was arguable that our position of detachment was the right one. But Eden had made it clear that this argument of sovereignty was of very doubtful value. The Soviet Government certainly made use of it continually. On this basis they had opposed a plan for an international atomic authority; on this ground they had persuaded many countries to reject the benefits of Marshall Aid. Yet it was evident that the narrow concept of sovereignty was one which in recent years we had agreed radically to amend. We had joined the Atlantic Pact, under which there was to be 'a pooling in times of peace of military information and resources which would certainly have been considered a surrender of sovereignty even a few years ago'. The NATO organisation was now coming into being. Many new organisations were thus being created in which, in Eden's words, 'we have undertaken direct or implied commitments, without regarding them as incompatible with our sovereignty or incompatible with our position as the heart and centre of the British Empire and Commonwealth'.

On the Labour side, the broader case was powerfully argued. There was in many parts of the House and in the country a fundamental reluctance to place under any 'foreign' control such vital British interests as the management of coal and steel. Apart from social and economic questions, there was the problem of employment. Were we to allow British pits to be closed or the output of British steel plants to be reduced at the behest of a Higher Authority, operating with a kind of Papal detachment from the control of Governments? Was this authority to be purely bureaucratic in character? Where were the independent members to be found to serve it? What was this new Parliament, or body of Parliamentarians, effectively to perform? Was there to be a proliferation of such authorities and such Parliamentary institutions as part of the New Order of Europe? At this time British coal and steel could find ready markets. There was a fear that some restriction, in the interests of the weaker Continental producers, would result from the new scheme and that this restriction would be fatal to the financial interests of our nation as well as to the rights of our workers.

Bevin was unfortunately away through illness, and we missed his robust and uninhibited counsels. As the debate proceeded, many back-bench Members on the Conservative side, several of whom afterwards rose to high Ministerial rank, made speeches of marked value. These included David Eccles, Quintin Hogg, Harold Watkinson and Julian Amery. There were a few speeches expressing doubt from the Conservative benches, but the great body rallied to the lead which Churchill and Eden gave. A maiden speech much impressed the House, from a newly elected Member, strongly urging co-operation with Europe. It came from Edward Heath.

On the Government side, Crossman delivered a discourse of remarkable fluency and variety—fascinating in its erudition and skill in argument, but marred by almost Gladstonian convolutions and reservations.

Thus apart from the question of the wisdom, or otherwise, of the Government's decision on formal grounds and the skill, or clumsiness, with which the negotiations had been managed, there was an underlying issue which came more and more to the fore as the debate proceeded. Eden contented himself with an appeal; Churchill passed rapidly to the attack. He was especially scornful of the legalistic argument. There was 'no excuse for the British Government piling their own prejudices on the top of French pedantry'. All these difficulties ought, among friends, to have been smoothed away. He frankly deplored the attitude of the French in springing this large and far-reaching proposal on us so suddenly and making precise stipulations before taking counsel with their war-time comrades. Perhaps this might be regarded as a retaliation for the way in which we had disrupted their whole economy and financial structure by devaluing sterling without a word of warning. Nevertheless, he regretted the lack of close friendship which all this confusion made evident. There was a typical Churchillian passage objecting to the new phrases which tended only to darken counsel—'the usual jargon about "the infra-structure of a supranational authority" '. These must surely have been introduced into our current political parlance by the band of intellectual highbrows who were naturally anxious to impress British Labour with the fact that they learned Latin at Winchester. (Churchill had been somewhat nettled by Crossman's speech, and this was a characteristic riposte.) He then made tremendous play with the Labour Party's pamphlet which had been the cause of so much trouble. The Dalton theme was that if a united Europe was to succeed it could only do so if all the countries first committed themselves to Socialism. He made great fun of this 'insular' Socialism, pointing out that of course there was one exception to their condemnation of capitalism :

. . . the outstanding, mighty, capitalist, free-enterprise United States. That is the exception. But then, of course, they are paying us the heavy subsidies upon which the Socialists' claim that they are able to maintain full employment is founded. But, apart from this important exception, it would be a lonely pilgrimage upon which we are to be led.[1]

While he did not underrate the technical argument about the prior commitment to principles, or objectives, he posed the question on which we would have to vote in simple language:

> Every Member should ask himself two simple practical questions: 'Do I wish to see the unity of Western Europe advanced?' and anyhow, apart from that, 'Had we not better take part in the conference subject to the reservations which the Dutch have made?' These are the issues before us tonight.[1]

On the question of sovereignty he repeated Eden's words. He was prepared without any hesitation to consider, and if convinced to accept, the abrogation of national sovereignty involved, provided the conditions and the safeguards were satisfactory. His final passage made a great impact upon the House. With that remarkable capacity for striking every note—argument, humour, criticism and appeal—in the course of a single speech, he ended with words which should be rescued from the vast and often repellent accumulation of *Hansard*:

> Nay, I will go further and say that for the sake of world organisation we would even run risks and make sacrifices. We fought alone against tyranny for a whole year, not purely from national motives. It is true that our lives depended upon our doing so, but we fought the better because we felt with conviction that it was not only our own cause but a world cause for which the Union Jack was kept flying in 1940 and 1941. The soldier who laid down his life, the mother who wept for her son, and the wife who lost her husband, got inspiration or comfort, and felt a sense of being linked with the universal and the eternal by the fact that we fought for what was precious not only for ourselves but for mankind. The Conservative and Liberal Parties declare that national sovereignty is not inviolable, and that it may be resolutely diminished for the sake of all the men in all the lands finding their way home together.[1]

[1] *Hansard*, 27 June 1950.

ANOTHER ATTEMPT TO SWIM THE CHANNEL—*Cartoon by Vicky*

In a curious and impressive interlude in the last stages of the debate when the Prime Minister rose to answer Churchill, he asked permission to make a statement on Korea. It was the first announcement of the invasion of South Korea by the Northern forces and the decision of the Security Council to recommend all members of the United Nations to furnish such assistance to the Republic of Korea as might be necessary to repel armed attack. Apart from the tremendous consequences of this event, the economic situation was about to be altogether transformed. Shortage would rapidly take the place of feared over-production in the basic industries.

Attlee, after his dramatic announcement about Korea, contented himself with a very short answer. As to the famous pamphlet, *European Unity*, he was in considerable difficulty, more especially, as he frankly admitted, because it had obtained the enthusiastic support of Lord Beaverbrook. But in the main he merely repeated the statement that we could not enter into negotiations bound to a principle which had not been fully examined and which he and his friends at this stage were not prepared to accept. In lowering the temperature and bringing the matter back to the narrowest point, he showed his usual Parliamentary skill. In the final vote, the Government carried their own amendment by 309 votes to 296. But it seemed sad if this was to be the final British attitude towards the most important event in the post-war history of Europe.

My friends and I who had worked closely together at Strasbourg and in the European Movement felt unhappy and dissatisfied. We could not accept this as the last word. Yet we could not but recognise the objections which could be brought against the plan as it stood. The Six-Power Conference had already opened in Paris, and vital decisions would no doubt be taken during the next few months. Could we not use the opportunity of the next meeting of the Consultative Assembly in August to propose some compromise? It was as the result of much hard work and much assistance, particularly from such organisations as ELEC, that we were in a position when the Assembly met on 15 August to put forward a British alternative plan which became popularly known as the 'Macmillan–Eccles Plan'. By far the greater part of the constructive work was due to David Eccles, but we also owed much to a band of keen and expert advisers. One of the most enthusiastic of these was Lady Rhys Williams. Only those who were her close friends realised the immense contribution which she made during her active life to the work of ELEC, as well as to many other social and economic discussions. She combined the most acute intelligence and profound knowledge with simplicity and charm. She had sent me some valuable suggestions in July when our plan was being drafted. In thanking her, I observed:

> The 'Schuman' plan seems to grow in complexity and vagueness the more one tries to study it. 'For the Snark was a Schuman, you see.' Nevertheless, I am sure we are under an obligation to hammer out something intelligent, if we can. I am hoping that with all your excellent work and with the help of my colleagues, like David Eccles, we shall have something to propose at Strasbourg. If we can do that, it will be a great coup.

The chief purpose of our proposals, which were set out in a formal resolution, was to meet British apprehensions without injury to the main feature of the plan. Our people were afraid of 'putting our key industries in the hands of foreigners', especially in the hands of foreign bureaucrats. Our scheme differed from Schuman's in three respects:

> 1. The experts who co-ordinate the coal and steel industries will be responsible to a Committee of Ministers, and therefore the link with the underlying Parliaments is kept.
> 2. The basic social, economic and strategic interests of each country are safeguarded from encroachment by the experts.
> 3. Any member can withdraw on giving 12 months' notice; and any member can be expelled by the others.

Clauses were introduced to ensure that wage standards should be safeguarded from the effects of pulling down barriers between the markets in different countries; that collective bargaining should be retained; that there should, if possible, be separate boards of coal and steel respectively, a point to which British industry attached importance. We also proposed that if it became necessary to reduce overall production any Government would be allowed to stockpile a surplus, should it choose to do so. Other safeguards were included.

The Imperial Preference system should not be impaired so far as British exports to the Commonwealth were concerned; the authority should only have powers to advise in regard to capital investment in Britain; the voting powers of the members of the authority should be in proportion to the production and consumption of coal and steel in the member countries. Finally, Britain's association and signature when the whole scheme had been agreed would require the approval of Parliament.

The night after our arrival in Strasbourg, Churchill invited some of us to his villa for dinner. The guests included David Maxwell Fyfe and Duncan Sandys, as well as Lady Tweedsmuir. A long discussion followed on our proposals:

> Eccles and I have been at work on them for some time, but could not get the job done in time for me to submit to the Shadow Cabinet. However, since Oliver Lyttelton has approved them, and since I had sent copies before leaving London to all our leading colleagues, W.S.C. is fairly satisfied. The only question is whether his name is to be put to this or not. If not, he will give them a broad paternal blessing in his speech. This problem of how far we can operate here without precise prior agreement with our colleagues at home is a permanent and often an acute one. But I am convinced that the Macmillan–Eccles plan can do nothing but good on the home front. For it will show that Conservatives are as determined as anyone else to protect British interests, while willing to co-operate with Europe on a reasonable basis.[1]

I was also able to tell them of my talks with Eden, who thought our contribution was helpful from the European view and beneficial from the party view. Nevertheless, he preferred that Churchill should not actually put his name to our resolution, partly because there had been no time to consult the Shadow Cabinet and partly because it was felt that Churchill should stay out of detailed controversy. It was, however, agreed that he should give general approval and blessing to our initiative.

I had some further correspondence with Monnet, to whom I sent a copy of our document. He naturally, and from his point of view rightly, disliked the idea that any Government could retain even a

[1] 6 August 1950.

formal right to withdraw. In a letter to me of 8 August, his opinions were stated with his usual clarity and logic:

> The Schuman proposals are revolutionary or they are nothing. For centuries we Europeans have tried to solve our common problems either through diplomacy or through war, but, in the context of present-day Europe, agreements between national states for the preservation of strictly national interests are wholly inadequate. Co-operation between nations, while essential, cannot alone meet our problem. What must be sought is a fusion of the interests of the European peoples and not merely another effort to maintain an equilibrium of those interests through additional machinery for negotiation.

He went on:

> The Schuman proposals contemplate the resolution of the ancient difficulties between Germany and France by the creation of a community superior to national antagonisms which can provide a new focus for the energies and aspirations of the peoples of Europe.

On the afternoon of 10 August, Schuman gave to the Assembly

> his 'explanation' or 'exposé' of his plan. It was a strange performance. There is something very attractive about the man, half hermit and half Buchmanite!
> He did not really explain the details of his plan, only the 'mystique'.[1]

I was hopeful that since the whole matter was still in the early stages, some compromise might be reached:

> I cannot help feeling that there is a great possibility that one or both of two things may happen. When the Governments (especially Holland and Belgium) get the Monnet proposals, which are still up before the experts only, they will shrink from some aspects of the plan. Secondly, when the French Parliament and people realise that it means going in *without* Britain, they may shrink from handing over their rather weak and largely obsolescent industry to German control. For, in a few years, that is what

[1] 10 August 1950.

Churchill at the Council of Europe, August 1949
'in a most happy and exultant mood, like a schoolboy'

Place Kléber, Strasbourg, 12 August 1949
'Churchill received a tremendous welcome and made an extremely effective speech.'

it will mean. In any case, I feel sure we shall have done no harm, either at home or abroad, by putting forward our proposals.[1]

On 15 August I spoke in the resumed debate on the Schuman Plan. My speech lasted about twenty-five minutes and the reception was friendly and appreciative. I began by a general welcome to the Schuman initiative and to the imaginative character of his proposals:

> It is not, in the essentials, an industrial or economic conception. It is a grand design for a new Europe. It is not just a piece of convenient machinery. It is a revolutionary, and almost mystical, conception. It is perhaps because the British Government failed to appreciate this element in the Schuman Plan, that there have been so many tragic misunderstandings.

For whatever reason there had been a sad set-back in our hopes:

> No doubt there were mistakes and misunderstandings on both sides. I must allow myself this comment. When I read the pages of telegrams between London and Paris; notes, *aide-mémoires*, *démarches* and all the rather rusty weapons in the diplomatic armoury solemnly deployed between Britain and France, I felt some surprise and real sorrow. Surely, after an alliance of nearly half a century—after so many sorrows suffered together, after such triumphs shared together—we might act more as partners and brothers, and less as performers in a diplomatic minuet. Why were there no personal contacts? Why were there no intimate talks? After all, it is not necessary to swim the English Channel in order to cross it.

After describing the traditional difference of approach inherent in the Latin and Anglo-Saxon temperament, which was the result of the long divergence of two streams of thought and methods of argument, I went on to apply this to the present situation:

> It naturally occurs to us to say—'Well, what exactly is it that we want to do together? When we have decided that, we will set up a Committee and write the rules.' You are apt to say (or so it seems to us)—'The first thing is to have the Committee. The Committee

---

[1] 10 August 1950.

H

will write the rules. Then the Committee will decide what it is that we want to do together.'

I added, in an attempt to soothe my audience, a further preliminary:

> The very words 'en principe' send a shudder—a sort of spasm of horror down every Anglo-Saxon spine. Of course, the Scottish people (who are the intellectuals of Britain) know that there is nothing to be frightened of. One should accept everything 'en principe'; get round the table; and start the talks.

There was another difference. British opinion had approached the plan almost entirely from the economic point of view, regarding it as an industrial contrivance for the orderly management of the basic industries to avoid slump, over-production, price-cutting followed by wage-cutting—all of which we remembered only too vividly. While the plan had many attractions, we were frightened of technocrats, especially international technocrats. We had not destroyed the divine right of kings in order to fall down before the divine rights of experts. But we had not sufficiently appreciated the political purposes which lay behind the supporters of the plan—the resolving of the deep conflicts so repeated and so recent which had threatened and destroyed the peace of Europe. How, then, could we marry these different points of view? The so-called Macmillan–Eccles proposals were a genuine attempt to put forward a solution. We preferred a governmental to an expert authority, not for detailed control but for broad direction of policy. We therefore proposed a Ministerial committee of the contracting powers. But such a committee should not operate in the void. It should be attached to one of the organisations of the Council of Europe—the Committee of Ministers. It should not operate in secret. We asked therefore for periodical reports and debates in the Consultative Assembly.

Certain changes Schuman had already made. He had accepted, in addition to the High Authority, a Committee of Ministers and an Assembly of Parliamentarians, but these were both to be attached to the countries which were parties to the agreement. We wished these to be attached to the Council of Europe. We had two reasons for this. The consumer countries, as well as the producers, had a right to be heard. The Council of Europe was the proper forum for this purpose. In addition we asked that there should be, at least in the initial stages, the right for a nation to resign as well as a corresponding right for nations to expel. We also included some definite directives to the High Authority, especially as regards collective bargaining, the levelling-up, not down, of living standards, and to ensure short- as well as long-term planning. The principle of Imperial Preference as far as Britain was concerned had already been accepted in the previous year by the Assembly.

I then paid a tribute to Monnet for the work which he had done for Britain, as well as for France, in the testing years of war. He also knew our particular problems. While he longed for permanence, he knew our desire for a trial run:

> He believes in a certain hierarchical and classical order. He knows our passion for improvisation. But he also knows, at least I hope so, that we are quite a reliable folk; that if we dislike tying up ourselves in too tightly drawn contracts, we try to carry out our obligations with a certain tenacity.

The French had a saying 'Ce n'est que le provisoire qui dure'.

> In the face of the huge tasks which await us, at home and abroad, we shall need many provisional arrangements—in defence, in rearmament, in shipping, in raw materials, in food, in manpower. To meet this crisis, whether it is called war or not, we British will certainly be prepared to accept the merging of sovereignty in practice, if not in principle.

The Korean War had of course made a vast alteration in the background against which all these proposals were now under discussion. But we were confident that if we could only make a start we should achieve success:

> For the provisional structure will in fact—if it works—have become permanent. Practice will have grown into principle. We shall have made Europe without knowing it. I admit that to do so in a fit of absence of mind and by a series of improvisations would be particularly gratifying to my countrymen. But if it works, is it not also logical to let it work? If we can thus save Europe and at

the same time make Europe, we shall all, in different ways, have done our duty.

I was supported by my colleagues in many admirable speeches, notably that delivered by David Eccles, and as the result of the discussions at this meeting of the Assembly we were satisfied that the course we had pursued had been valuable. We were met not merely with courtesy but with understanding by the members of the Assembly as a whole. Many of the countries outside the inner core of Europe, especially the Scandinavians, shared our views and gave us active support. At any rate we had preserved some tenable position for Britain and, incidentally, for our own party.

Maurice Schumann spoke after me, and although he naturally did not accept my main thesis, he was most friendly and appreciative. It was clear, as indeed he told me afterwards, that he intended to reprove Monnet for being too rigid.[1]

The final debate in the August session took place on the 24th. When the report of the Committee came before the whole Assembly it was not possible for us to accept the French resolution, and we therefore decided to put down an amendment. It ran in the following terms:

'That a renewed effort should be made forthwith by all the governments concerned to find a basis for an agreement which will enable all the principal coal- and steel-producing countries of Europe to participate fully in the scheme, and stresses the importance of bringing this, like other functional schemes, within the framework of the Council of Europe.'

I hear from Maurice Schumann (who is always very friendly) that an effort is to be made to call the Economic Committee together to discuss and perhaps agree. This will be excellent, but perhaps a little optimistic.[2]

The debate on the Schuman Plan was held the following day. My speech was well received, although Reynaud argued that since the agreement would be signed in a few weeks there was nothing further

[1] 15 August 1950. Maurice Schumann was Chairman of M.R.P. in 1949 and became Foreign Minister in 1951.
[2] 24 August 1950.

that the British could do. He appealed to me to withdraw our amendment. I was forced to reply as follows:

'Well—it suits us. I want it. I think after what Churchill has done for you all, I have a right to ask it' (very stiff and formal). Then Maurice Schumann said 'Yes; and Macmillan has a right to ask it in his own name. He has done more for France than any man, even including Churchill.'[1]

After a number of other speeches (the British Socialists lay low and none of them spoke except Mackay, well known as a keen Federalist),

Reynaud got up. It was really beautifully done. He agreed the general case for Schuman; he abandoned no position; yet—with a most handsome tribute to me—if we would help him over part of his difficulty, he would help us. The deal was not only done, but carried out.[1]

In the end, the vote was quite good. We got 66 for our amendment, 19 against and 19 abstentions.

After that, more excitement and confusion. The British Socialists had announced their intention (with much sanctimonious righteousness) of voting for the two 'recommendations' of the Economic Committee. Now was added the third (the Macmillan amendment). What were they to do on the 'ensemble'— that is, when the whole resolution, now including three parts, was put. Usual result, when they have no Whip to rely on, and sitting in different parts, they can only watch Dalton's gestures. Some voted no; others abstained. The whole was carried, with 32 abstentions. . . .

I had a press conference and a B.B.C. conference immediately after the division. Of course, I know that all this is only small beer and no one at home takes the slightest interest, but it is rather fun![1]

I was told that evening by some of the news representatives that in fact the negotiations were not going well and the French might well require a withdrawal proposal to save their face.

[1] 26 August 1950.

When the Assembly met again in November 1950 the plan was still under discussion, and I could only speak in general terms, regretting that Britain was not a founder member and hoping that some of the alleviations and amendments which we had suggested would prove useful.

> It was opened by Reynaud, in a brilliant and convincing speech. I followed. It was not an easy speech to make, but it seems to have been a success and generally approved. The British Socialists were really rather impressed and took a very friendly line—far different from that adopted in August. Dalton was very moderate and even expansive.[1]

But either because of the political situation at home or for whatever reason, the British Government made no further move to take any part in this great affair.

The negotiations between the six powers continued all through the winter and spring, resulting on 18 April 1951 in the signature of the treaty by the six countries setting up the European Coal and Steel Community. Although the actual inauguration of the new structure was not to take place for at least a year, there was little more that we could do. When the Consultative Assembly met in May 1951 I could only congratulate the experts and Governments concerned. I paid a further tribute to Monnet:

> All of us who recall his work during the war remember him as a good friend of Britain in dark days. He has now achieved permanent renown as a great European.

I went on to say how deeply I deplored Britain's policy of abstention. However, we had three days of stimulating discussion. The first day (8 May) was made memorable by a truly magnificent speech by Lord Layton:

> I have never heard him speak so well. He spoke 'as one having authority'.[2]

He was followed by Edelman, who moved a much advertised resolution, signed by all the Socialists in the Assembly:

[1] 21 November 1950.   [2] 8 May 1951.

[This] is an attempt to rebuild that international Socialist front which Bevin, Morrison, Dalton and Co. have shattered since 1945. It was a gallant attempt; but rather thin. The truth is that there is no future for Socialism in countries where Communism has seized the Left's position. It can only continue (as in Scandinavia, etc.) by abandoning Socialism and becoming a sort of mild radicalism. Perhaps this is now happening in Britain ?[1]

Lady Tweedsmuir spoke after him, and scored a great success by her charm:

'Mais elle est épatante !', etc., etc. French senators seemed particularly susceptible.[1]

This was the last stage of our discussions on the Schuman Plan. The report of the Committee and the appropriate resolution was introduced by André Philip in a fine speech, one of the best I had ever heard him make. I had to follow, and did my best with a speech which seemed well received enough:

I tried to set out the Conservative attitude, and was able to have a little fun with the extraordinary phenomenon by which modern Socialism, both in Britain and now in Germany, had become nationalist and isolationist.[2]

William Blyton, speaking for the British Labour Party, made a curious contribution. After a few minutes of a robust and amusing attack on me (in his own language), he read out thirty minutes

of a jesuitical and casuistic essay [obviously] written [for him]. . . . What had [been] composed for Mr. Blyton was so ridiculously out of character as to be comic. B. is a good honest miners' member from County Durham. He could not be guilty of the subtleties . . . supplied to him.[2]

This was followed by a brilliant Parliamentary speech by Reynaud, summing up the whole discussion. It was

witty and charming, but also deadly in its analysis of modern Socialism in Britain and in Germany. He ended with a moving

[1] 8 May 1951.   [2] 10 May 1951.

peroration, in the best style. Duncan Sandys made a short but crushing reply to Blyton, quoting the famous resolution of the Socialist Party in 1948, demanding a supranational authority for steel and coal![1]

It was indeed a tragic decision when the British Government refused to join in the initial discussions at least on the same basis as the Netherlands Government. Had they done so, I believed that a plan might have been agreed acceptable to British opinion. Nor could the six signatory Governments be altogether happy with a plan which did not include a country which was the greatest manufacturer of steel in Europe and which produced as much coal as all the others in the scheme put together. Nevertheless, my colleagues and I could take some satisfaction in the final form in which the Schuman Plan had now been agreed. For instance, if the High Authority was still supranational, it was certainly not supreme; it was not a tyranny but a constitutional monarchy. Subject to the approval of the Common Assembly, the Consultative Committee would now be drawn from both consumer and producer interests and armed with substantial powers. The Ministerial Committee, which had hardly emerged last August, was to play a vital and even decisive role. The unanimity rule, in spite of all that had been argued against it, was preserved. Finally, some relationship had been created between the new authority and the Council of Europe by admitting the right of the Assembly to receive and debate the annual report. What could Britain do? There were two things, both practical and urgent. The British Government had a juridical position as one of the countries concerned at the time in the Ruhr Authority. If this new system was to work, the Allied High Commissioners must now abandon their rights and functions. To this we ought readily to agree. Secondly, we must find some way of becoming an associate, if not a full member, of the Community. Here, at any rate, we were able to keep our word. For when the Assembly met in the following November a change of Government had taken place, and David Maxwell Fyfe was authorised to inform the Assembly that as soon as the High Authority became operative, a permanent British mission would be appointed.

[1] 10 May 1951.

Thus ended the first stage in a long and disappointing episode in the story of European co-operation, with many melancholy consequences.

If the question of the co-ordination of the basic industries of Europe held the field of public discussion during 1950, the equally vital problem of defence was brought urgently before the Consultative Assembly, largely by Churchill's own initiative, in the same year.

The chief concern of Britain and France was to form some permanent system of common defence against a revived German aggression. The occupation of Germany could not continue for ever; and it was against the possibility of a new German militarism that the Dunkirk Treaty was negotiated by Bevin in March 1947. Fear of Russia soon came to rival, if not to obliterate, fear of Germany, and the moves which led to the founding of NATO followed.[1]

But it must be remembered that at this date no steps had been taken to create any coherent force in Europe other than that maintained in Germany by the occupying powers. It was not until later that some attempt was made to put teeth into the Atlantic Treaty by NATO; that is, by the creation of a definite Allied force, composed of contingents of the Allied nations, with a united system of command and an operating headquarters. The outbreak of the Korean War in June 1950 was a new cause of alarm, spotlighting the weakness of our military preparations. A Communist army from North Korea rapidly overran the southern half of the country. If a direct conflict between the Communist and the free world had been so far avoided in the West by the rallying of the nations through the Atlantic Pact, in the Far East the uneasy truce had now been broken. It was no wonder, therefore, that through the summer of 1950 the European countries felt naked and unprotected, living under a sense of real danger. Protection, adequate and urgent, was the first issue.

In this mood the Consultative Assembly met in August 1950. In spite of the rival attractions of the Schuman Plan as a subject for discussion, the whole mind of the Europeans was now concentrated

[1] See above, p. 133.

on defence. In the opening day of the debate, members were deeply moved by a brilliant speech from André Philip. Defence could no longer, he declared, be regarded as a question of small national armies, which from their size and character were nothing more than expensive, but inefficient, toys. Something more was required: a European army must be created, financed by the European nations, under a European Minister, and subject to the democratic control of a European Assembly. It was essential that such a force should be available immediately, before the assembling of the great Allies could be organised. Churchill had not been present on this occasion. I therefore sent him a minute giving my impressions:

> It is clear that the dominant motive in Europe today is fear. The most applauded part of André Philip's speech was when he said 'We do not want to be liberated again.'[1]

Included in Philip's plan was the suggestion that a German contingent should form part of the European army. It was little more than five years since the Nazi jackboots had bestraddled all Europe, and emotions still ran high, not in the occupied countries only, but in Germany too.

My minute to Churchill continued:

> The Germans are shy about German rearmament for two reasons.
>
> (a) They fear that what they may be allowed will be insufficient to protect them from the Russians but sufficient to provoke them.
>
> (b) Liberal-minded Germans fear renascent militarism in the old sense, the revival of O.K.W. and all that this implies.
>
> But the Germans can probably be got to welcome a German contingent (even a very strong contingent) in what is called 'a European army'.[1]

I went on to express the hope that, swayed by the sense of danger and living in this twilight between peace and war, the Europeans might develop a sufficient sense of urgency and unity to bring about some agreement for common defence without becoming lost in a

[1] Minute to Churchill, 8 August 1950.

maze of constitution-making. Alas, this hope was to prove illusory. For the same pressure, both from those who wished to create a system which would prove permanent, and from those who passionately desired a form of federalism for Europe, as had shown itself in the developments of the Schuman Plan, soon became noticeable in the discussions about the European army.

To this project, stated in general terms, and on the understanding that German contingents should be included, Churchill agreed, after much thought, to give the weight of his supreme authority. This decision was not reached without much reflection and discussion with his colleagues. On the night of the opening debate I was summoned to his villa after dinner, where I found a large party of Germans whom he had been entertaining. As usual, there were some of his family, his private secretaries and all the usual apparatus to which he had been accustomed as Prime Minister. He only lacked—and it was a considerable handicap—the means of communicating by cyphered telegrams with his colleagues at home. In other respects, I was reminded of the scene at one of the great war conferences, Casablanca or Cairo:

> A long and vitally important discussion followed till after midnight. It was really rather moving. The Germans behaved with simplicity and dignity. They made their position quite clear, which was useful. They do *not* want a German army; they would join a European army.[1]

The next day was one of alarms and excursions:

> Mr. Churchill will speak—no, he will not—yes, he will. I went round in the morning, before the session. He was in bed and working on a speech. He will speak tomorrow, Thursday; Spaak should be so informed. The truth is that he is in one of those moods, preparatory to some creative effort, when the artist is anxious, nervous, dissatisfied with himself, and everyone else—a good sign on the whole.[2]

Reynaud's was the main speech of the second day:

> He is an absolute master—witty, precise, limpid. We have nothing like it now. Perhaps Asquith was the nearest.[2]

[1] 8 August 1950.   [2] 9 August 1950.

He repeated the figures of Russian strength, which were indeed alarming. But perhaps the most important speech was that of the first German to address the Assembly, Eugen Gerstenmaier. He was to play an important role in politics during the next few years:

> While disclaiming any German wish for a German army, he accepted the need for a German contribution to European defence. This is the view of the C.D.U. and other parties of the Right and Centre. It is not the view, I fear, of the Social Democrats. . . .
> Well, if the Germans won't fight, they will be in no-man's-land; this means they will be 'atom-bombed'.[1]

The debate was resumed on 11 August. On the evening before I went to Churchill's villa to go through yet another version of the speech:

> This is now getting much better. One cannot but admire his extraordinary attention to detail and desire to perfect and improve. I then had to go on a mission of friendship to Dalton. For W.S.C. has now decided on risking everything on carrying his motion in favour of the immediate creation of a European army. This I did; with a mixture of gin (supplied by him) and bitter (supplied by me) the Dalton–Macmillan front was made unusually coherent. I think he and [James] Callaghan . . . will abstain; the rest of the British Socialists will be allowed a free vote.[2]

The session opened at 10.30 a.m.

> Churchill spoke—for about 25 minutes—at 11.30, and moved his resolution. His speech was impassioned, both in manner and matter. The little touches of humour found their mark, although the technique of speaking to an audience the greater part of which is listening to an indifferent translation through earphones is not an easy one. It is really more like a broadcast than a speech. But then the truth is that W.S.C.'s broadcasts *are* speeches.[3]

He made it abundantly clear that he was not seeking to undermine the Atlantic Treaty Organisation, which indeed—at that time—had yet neither shape nor head. His purpose was to call attention to the

[1] 9 August 1950.   [2] 10 August 1950.   [3] 11 August 1950.

present weakness of the West. In addition, in the presence of the first official German delegation at a post-war conference of Allied and neutral countries, he wished to emphasise the need for welding the new Germany not merely into the economic and cultural life of Western civilisation, but into its active defence. He began by reminding the Assembly that it had no executive responsibility or power; but it was bound to give its warning and its counsel. An effective defensive front must be built up in Europe in the shortest possible time:

> Great Britain and the United States must send large forces to the Continent. France must again provide her famous Army. We welcome our Italian comrades. All—Greece, Turkey, Holland, Belgium, Luxembourg, the Scandinavian States—must bear their share and do their best.

He therefore proposed that

> We should now send a message of confidence and courage from the House of Europe to the whole world. Not only should we re-affirm, as we have been asked to do, our allegiance to the United Nations, but we should make a gesture of practical and constructive guidance by declaring ourselves in favour of the immediate creation of a European army under a unified command, and in which we should bear a worthy and honourable part.

At that stage, as indeed in many other aspects of his European policy, Churchill had no clear or well-defined plan. He was then in Opposition, deprived of the vast machinery at the disposal of Ministers. He was an old man trying to give a new lead to the world which he had helped to save. He therefore did not consider this question as a Minister introducing the second reading of a Bill. His purpose was to throw out general ideas and give an impetus towards movements already at work. It was for others to find detailed solutions. Nevertheless, it was clear from his words that he contemplated a system in Europe in which Britain should play a leading role, not merely cheer from the side-lines.

This debate, which continued till late in the evening, was, of course, technically outside the 'statute' of the Consultative Assembly, which was specifically debarred from the discussion of defence matters. Nevertheless, neither then nor later did the Council of Ministers insist upon their rights:

> Dalton spoke in the afternoon, and [his] was the only other speech of great importance. He was trying, I think, to be friendly. Some almost thought that the coalition was forming. The debate lasted with the usual interval for luncheon and other adjournments for 'lobbying' until about 9 p.m. Throughout the day there was a great conflict of view as to whether Churchill would carry the day. The French would run out, torn by internal dissensions. The Germans would run out, for similar reasons. All the Scandinavians would be hostile. The British Socialists would also be opposed.[1]

All this uncertainty and these continual changes of front formed part of the interest of this Assembly. When the vote was taken, at about 9 p.m., 89 voted for the motion, 5 against. There were 27 abstentions.

> The fact that all the French and a great number of the Germans voted in favour was the true significance of the vote.[1]

The process of preparing elaborate legislative proposals, to which the Assembly was much addicted, soon began to go forward with enthusiasm, if not always with discretion, both in the lobbies and through the machinery of a special committee. Thus a provisional scheme defining the structure of a European army and the functions of any European Defence Minister was rapidly prepared by Duncan Sandys, who had been appointed *rapporteur* of the sub-committee. Churchill was rightly anxious to use the Strasbourg machinery to bring pressure on the Ministers of the different European countries, not to usurp their functions. He never liked all this detailed planning. He had now left Strasbourg, and I sent him on 17 August a message describing the fevered activity and constitution-making enthusiasm which were developing, and asked for his guidance. He replied as follows:

> I am sure it would be a mistake to get involved in details. Council of Europe can never at this stage in affairs deal with

[1] 11 August 1950.

problems which belong to executive Governments. It may point the way and give inspiration. We cannot possibly do better than by our resolution.[1]

Meanwhile, discussions on Germany's contribution to Western defence were taking place in a different sphere. The NATO Council met in New York in September. The American and Canadian Governments had decided not merely to 'come to the assistance of any signatory State in the event of war', but to provide American and Canadian troops for a joint defence force and to send them to Europe in the immediate future in order to preserve peace. This was a very positive and even revolutionary undertaking, and the announcement sent a thrill of relief and confidence throughout Western Europe which can hardly be imagined today. It was believed that the United States was pressing for a German contribution to this joint defence force of some ten German divisions. The French Government was unwilling to agree to German units larger than battalions. The British Government, in the teeth of disapproval from much of the Labour Party, had acquiesced in the American suggestion, but too late to avoid new difficulties with the French, and deadlock was reached:

> All this comes from Attlee's inertia and Bevin's jealousy. If Britain had taken a hand a year ago, when Churchill first raised the question of Germany's contribution to defence, all these matters might have been handled successfully. Now I am afraid that we are once more in the old dilemma. Are we to woo Germany or to repel her? It is the same problem as was unresolved after the first war and led inevitably to the second.[2]

The French were indeed in a difficult, almost desperate, position. That part of her armies which was not stationed in Germany or devoted to the protection of the French Colonial Empire was becoming increasingly involved in the almost hopeless task of recovering and maintaining French control of Indo-China. But the memory of two wars was strong, and the brutalities of the German occupation of France still resented. A new German army might help to restrain Russia—if indeed Russia was the most dangerous

[1] 17 August 1950.   [2] 23–30 October 1950.

aggressor. But who would restrain a new militarised Germany? American and British soldiers could not be relied upon to remain on guard forever. Could not Continental Europe, by some means, be at once armed against external aggression and yet organised to prevent a revival of nationalist ambitions?

On 24 October, Pleven, at this time Prime Minister of France, presented his plan for a European Army to the French National Assembly. Its purpose was to meet the American demand for German rearmament without incurring the dangers of a German revival as a military power.

Under the Pleven plan, national contingents would be incorporated 'in the smallest possible units'. German combat teams were to be created to integrate into divisions made up of predominantly non-German forces. His scheme involved a supranational 'authority', with a European Minister of Defence, a European Budget, and a European Parliament for Defence. All this was based upon the Schuman Plan for coal and steel.

It was apparent that this scheme was more calculated to alleviate the fears of the French than to strike terror into the Russians. Those who had any knowledge of military problems, of organisation and supply as well as of strategic and tactical control, realised that quite apart from the difficulties of language, the morale of such a force would be low and that it would be of little military value. It would be a crusade, not an army. This vast Foreign Legion was deprecated by Churchill as a 'sludgy amalgam'. His mind had always worked upon the lines of an alliance such as we had known in the war. Divisions and even corps would operate under their own commanders, although under the direction of a supreme commander responsible to the Governments concerned. At the same time, to enhance the authority of the European community, supply would be centralised. There would be standardisation of arms and ammunition. All this, in Churchill's view, could be achieved by agreements between Governments. They needed no more elaborate, and certainly no 'supranational', machinery.

Nevertheless, French public opinion was hostile to the raising of German troops except upon these or equally strict conditions. They must be incorporated in one way or another in an integrated

European organisation, and not permitted to develop a staff or command system of their own. Although French Ministers and perhaps the greater part of the French public were not particularly attracted to the concept of a federal United States of Europe, they were ready to welcome a structure, however elaborate, whose main purpose was to imprison any new German formations in a tight European organisation. With their long and bitter experience, they were even then thinking of the day when the Soviet menace might disappear, American troops be withdrawn from Europe, and the Atlantic Pact command dissolved. Without a truly European military system, what could prevent a reversion to the separate national forces which had so often been the curse of Europe? What, indeed?

In Britain, too, Press and Parliamentary comment at that time showed that public opinion was almost as apprehensive about the danger of revived German militarism as about the threat from Russia. Many of the Germans felt this themselves, and were as anxious about German rearmament as the French or the British. At the same time, Dr. Adenauer had made it clear that while he welcomed for this very reason an international force, a German contingent must enjoy a status of complete equality with those of other nationalities. This was generally accepted by the politicians at Strasbourg.

When the Council of Europe met again in November 1950, Robert Schuman, as French Foreign Minister, was invited to address the Assembly on the Pleven plan, and the debate immediately followed. I had to sum up on behalf of my Conservative colleagues on 24 November and had to tread warily. The greater part of the discussion had turned upon Germany; many of the German delegates had repeated their fears of what they called 'the dangerous rivalry of a German National Army while democracy and Parliamentary institutions and even free Governments are still young'. The German Socialists had accordingly decided to vote against the recommendation for a German participation. I reminded them that their objections were somewhat contradictory. Most of the Germans had declared that what Germany needed was the withdrawal of our occupation troops.

Surely what is really meant is that Germany requires that their function should be changed and that they should be immensely strengthened and reinforced.

They would thus become not enemy, or ex-enemy, but allied forces. Moreover, the willingness of the Atlantic powers, the United States and Canada, to join us in an active defence organisation had really changed the whole position:

This is an immense decision, and it is all the more remarkable when we remember the background of this pact. The New World is to be called in to redress the balance of the Old, not after the catastrophe, but before. It promises not liberation, but security.

If Germany did not accept her part she would become not a neutral territory but a vast no-man's-land, subjected to the terrible disruption of modern war. As regards the German question, I had Churchill's authority for saying that if the Germans were to join they ought to be received as comrades 'with the same and equally honourable military status' as the contingents of any other country.

On the more complicated issue of how the European army, if it came into being under the Pleven or any other plan, could be fitted into the new and wider concept, I could only issue some warnings as to the technical difficulties, with the hope that in some way or another they might be surmounted under a European army fitted into the framework of the Atlantic system and under a single command. It was on this note of uncertainty, both as to the structure of a European force and as to the German part in it, that the Assembly contented itself with a reaffirmation of the original resolution passed in August. Only the German Social Democrats voted against.

But progress was being made within the framework of NATO. The Council of Deputies, the chairman of which was my old friend of Algiers days Charles Spofford, drew up a proposal on the lines suggested by Pleven for the incorporation into NATO of a 'European Army' including German combat units of some 6,000 men in divisions made up of predominantly non-German forces. This scheme was accepted by the French Government and finally confirmed by the North Atlantic Council at its meeting in December

1950. At the same meeting General Eisenhower was appointed Supreme Commander, and his headquarters were established in February of the following year, in Paris.

There were therefore two great gains, in spite of so much confusion, in this formative year. First, the North Atlantic Treaty had moved in the course of eighteen months from a general undertaking to give support in the event of attack to the decision to create a combined force, with a unified command, ready to prevent aggression. Secondly, since this force was to include at least a contingent of German troops, the principle of German military co-operation, leading necessarily to German rearmament, was accepted. But the plan had still to be clothed with reality. The Continental powers, inspired by France, continued to seek a method of creating a system which would combine the advantages of promoting a permanent European structure and finding the appropriate function for a reviving Germany, while at the same time ensuring that Europe should play its full part in the joint defence of Western civilisation against the Soviet threat.

Churchill's initiative and the long discussions at Strasbourg were therefore not altogether fruitless. If in the event the project for what later became known as the European Defence Community, first suggested by the French, was to prove a source of much confusion and many new difficulties and burdens for Britain, a strong impetus had been given to the willingness of the United States and Canada to join in immediate and not merely contingent defence.

At the beginning of 1951 I was still hopeful that a more practical plan for the 'European army' might emerge. On 3 January I dined with René Massigli.

> A discussion took place on the 'European army' as the conception has emerged from Strasbourg and as it has been presented by Schuman. I urged with all the strength I could command that the French Government should abandon all the complicated constitution with which the French Foreign Secretary had tried to surround this simple conception. The British would never accept a Parliamentary control by a sort of sub-committee of the European Assembly. What was important was that a British contingent should be included in the European army, even if the

greater part of the British contribution was made direct to the Atlantic force. If we were to persuade our people to accept this, the system must be simple and elastic.[1]

I still felt that British co-operation in some form was vital if French suspicions were to be allayed. But it was not to be.

To complete the story of this period, it is only necessary to recall that in February 1951 a conference was held in Paris where the five powers—France, Belgium, Luxembourg, Italy, West Germany—met to discuss the formation of a European army. Schuman was in the chair. All the other signatories of the North Atlantic Treaty, including Holland and Britain, sent observers. The discussions were long and complicated. The plan agreed followed the broad lines of that which had already been developed for the Iron and Steel organisation, and was intended to operate first under a Council of Defence Ministers and then ultimately under a European Defence Minister responsible to a Parliamentary organisation. The five powers met again on 24 July in Paris and agreed that whatever armed forces of the member countries were allocated for European defence, these should be fused under a common supranational, political and military authority. There should be a common equipment policy and a common fund. The military authority should conform to the views and directives of the Supreme Headquarters Allied Powers Europe (SHAPE). In November, Schuman reported to the NATO Council, then meeting in Rome, that some progress had been made in working out the military objective of the European force—namely, 43 divisions, including armoured and mechanised divisions, as well as an international air force and the establishment of a common budget and a common method of production of armaments. Finally, in December 1951, the participating powers announced that they agreed to the creation of a European Defence Community. Already, on 14 September, Herbert Morrison, then Foreign Secretary, had declared that Britain, while unable to join any such body as a full member, was anxious to establish a close and effective association.

Thus ended an important—though by no means decisive—phase in

[1] 3 January 1951.

the birth-pangs of the new Europe. The foundations were laid for a common economic and defence policy. During the next period many difficulties were to follow, and many complications in which Britain was to be closely involved. But these were to be the responsibility of a new Government at home.

During these years, I devoted much time and effort to various aspects of the European Movement. In addition to the activities which I have described, there were the conferences organised by ELEC, including an important Commonwealth conference in May 1951, the work of which was of the greatest value to me in later years. Apart from the constructive results of these meetings, a number of distinguished economists from many different countries were brought together. Although many of the subjects were rather beyond my limited grasp of economic and currency theory, I was conscious both of the skill and of the fervour with which all these notabilities pursued their labours.

One further aspect of the work was the creation in August 1949 of a section to deal with Central and Eastern Europe. Of this Beddington-Behrens was the indefatigable founder. The first meeting was held in Strasbourg in August 1949, and delegates attended from Poland, Hungary, Czechoslovakia, Bulgaria, Roumania and Yugoslavia. Later we accepted members from the Baltic States. Whatever may have been the practical value of this group, it had some propaganda importance in the Cold War. We succeeded in persuading the Consultative Assembly to establish a special committee to ensure that the interests of nations 'which are precluded from participating in the work of the Council' were considered in every proposal formulated by the Assembly or its committees. We also may have brought some comfort to many aching hearts. The Foreign Office, not unnaturally, was somewhat tepid in giving its support. But as an instrument for at least giving some hope to the countries behind the Iron Curtain and in the moral defence of the Western position in the Cold War, what we did had perhaps its place. Although I gave much time to this committee, of which I was chairman, I never put very high hopes upon what it could achieve. Any body of this kind, doomed to depend largely upon *émigré* groups, must have serious limitations. Yet we may have helped to some extent to preserve the tradition of European culture in those countries then so oppressed.

In addition, I undertook a number of journeys to promote the European idea. I visited Germany and Italy. In the spring of 1951 I made a tour in both Sweden and Norway, accompanied by Dr. Gordon Lang, the secretary of the British side of the Movement. In Stockholm we were received by my friend Senator Karl Wistrand with almost overpowering hospitality, and we carried through a heavy programme of public and private meetings. In Norway Dr. Herman Smitt-Ingebretson looked after us with equal kindness. The Scandinavians naturally sympathised with the British in favouring the so-called 'functional' approach, as against the federalist tendencies of some of our Continental friends. But nowhere were there more devoted partisans of the general concept of Europe's unity in defence of her safety and her culture.

Similarly, all through these years we received much help and support from America, both among Democrats and Republicans. Some, with characteristic enthusiasm, argued that we ought to be able within a very short period to create a United States of Europe on the same basis as the United States of America. Others understood the long and tangled history of European countries; the differences of language and tradition; the struggles, rivalries, ambitions, hatreds; and thus estimated more practically the obstacles to such a course. Many Americans remember these years, when they sometimes felt a not unnatural impatience with the varying and uncertain policies recommended or pursued by European Governments. Others were more understanding. I recall a conversation with Bill Donovan in Strasbourg in 1950. I had known him in the war as the indefatigable head of O.S.S. His impressions were clear and candidly expressed:

He had just been in Asia. The Americans are feeling rather lonely. The fact is that they are for the first time experiencing the burdens of world responsibility. Being unaccustomed to reverses, they are irritable and impatient. They have conveniently forgotten incidents like Greece, when we fought the Communist revolution of 1944 and they were neutral. They are also beginning to regret all they did to help break up the British Empire in Asia and their abandonment of the Dutch.[1]

But Europe's difficulties were—alas—inherent in the situation. When Churchill raised his Zürich cry, 'Let Europe Unite', it was an emotional appeal. The problem of translating an ideal into reality, whether in the economic, financial or defence spheres, has indeed proved baffling. Sometimes the federalist dream dominated European opinion, sometimes a more practical 'functional' approach. Sometimes a somewhat inward-looking course has been followed by the inner ring of European countries, leading to a further division of an already divided Europe. Sometimes the emphasis has been upon co-ordination of Governments; sometimes upon the creation of European Parliamentary institutions. The full story has still to be unfolded, for its course is not yet run. Here I have only tried to describe the early stages of a movement which was inspired not merely by a natural reaction from the horrors of war, but by a genuine search after a nobler role for the countries of Europe in a common desire to promote their own strength and to contribute to the peace and happiness of the world.

[1] 9 August 1950.

CHAPTER IX

Empire into Commonwealth

WHEN the first British Empire was brought to an inglorious end by the loss of the American colonies, the pattern of the second British Empire was already taking shape:

A vast land mass in North America, larger in area than the United States; great islands in the Antipodes; a firm if anomalous position in the Indian sub-continent, and a strong hold upon the southernmost part of Africa from which to make further annexations; these were the basis of our imperial power and to them were added such isolated jewels as possessions in the China Seas, in South-East Asian waters and in the Caribbean.[1]

There was built upon this edifice a world-wide commercial and industrial influence. At the same time a strong instrument was forged for the preservation of peace and the spread of civilisation throughout a great part of the globe. This imperial system, which reached its apogee at the end of the nineteenth century, was threatened, but not overthrown, by the shock of the Boer War, which threw a lurid light on the inefficiency and weakness of Britain as a military power. The First World War, however, restored her prestige; nevertheless, in the course of the war and in the years that followed, the structure of the Empire underwent a significant change, with a division into two separate groups—the independent and the dependent. While India and the Colonial territories remained under the ultimate control of the Government and Parliament of the United Kingdom, the self-governing Dominions— Canada, Australia, New Zealand, South Africa, Eire—obtained full autonomy and complete independence both in their internal affairs and their external relations. The Statute of Westminster in 1931

[1] Sir John W. Wheeler-Bennett, *A Wreath to Clio* (London, 1967), p. 21.

gave legislative force to a characteristically ingenious formula which was the product of one of the most subtle and experienced of British elder statesmen, Arthur Balfour, and had been approved at the Imperial Conference in 1926. It ran as follows:

> The Dominions are autonomous communities within the British Empire, equal in status, in no way subordinate one to another in any aspect of their domestic or internal affairs, though united by a common allegiance to the Crown, and freely associated as members of the British Commonwealth of Nations.[1]

There were some who feared that this Statute, together with the India Act of 1935 which in effect recognised the inevitable end of our Imperial mission in the sub-continent, marked the passing of the British Empire. As regards the Dominions of British descent, the Statute did little more than recognise the facts which had emerged from the First War. The India Act, as Churchill rightly saw, was bound to be the precursor of a movement towards a similar degree of independence, not merely in India, but in all Colonial territories, as each in turn became fitted for self-government, or at least claimed it in the name of progress and freedom. Yet when the Second War came, the whole vast structure, independent and dependent, responded to the call with astonishing unanimity and resolution. This was due to instinctive rallying of the 'old Dominions' to the Mother Country in her hour of danger. It no doubt also resulted from a moral and intellectual revolt against the Nazi doctrines and all that flowed from them, although this was not sufficient to affect decisively the policy of the United States. Even in South Africa, with its strong German traditions and no doubt some sympathy for the racial doctrines which Hitler proclaimed, Smuts had little difficulty in obtaining the mastery and bringing his people into a declaration of war in the first weeks of September 1939. Equally the diverse armies of India fought with conspicuous gallantry and played an important role in the campaigns both in the West and in the East. Nor were the contributions of the Colonial Empire any less remarkable.

Nevertheless, it was clear throughout the war years that the pre-war processes would be accelerated and intensified. The very

[1] *Winds of Change*, p. 112.

principles for which Britain and her Allies claimed to be fighting seemed to involve the recognition of the right of all peoples, of whatever colour or creed, to advance with the greatest practicable speed to self-government and to enjoy the full authority and prestige belonging to nationhood. These pressures were fortified by the somewhat naïve attitude to 'Imperialism' or 'Colonialism' of our American allies and, above all, by the policies of President Roosevelt himself. There was hardly any moment in the war, however grave, at which the President did not find an opportunity to drag in his anti-colonial bias, based on very little real knowledge but much vague prejudice. Basing himself upon the success by which immigrants from many different countries had been welded together to form the proud and self-confident American people, he, like Woodrow Wilson, underestimated the age-long national problems even of Europe. He altogether ignored the religious, racial, tribal and national tensions and complexities of Asia and Africa.

The centrifugal forces were at work before the war. They were stimulated by the events of the war, including the collapse of European authority in South-East Asia, with the fall of Burma, Malaya and Indonesia at least temporarily into the hands of the Japanese. They were sustained and fomented by American pressure, at many levels. They became irresistible when hostilities ended. Yet few if any of those elected to the Parliament of 1945 realised how rapid would be the change. If these years marked a great watershed, few of us could foresee how swiftly—some would say how disastrously —the stream would swell into a torrent.

The first question which demanded urgent solution was that of India. Although I had little knowledge or experience of Indian affairs, I had some contact with individual Indians from my early years. My father, in the course of a prolonged tour in the 1880s, had laid the foundations of our Indian business and established in due course printing and publishing branches in Calcutta, Bombay and Madras. He had many Indian friends, chiefly in the educational and literary world, who often stayed with us in our country home or were entertained in London.

Between the wars, when I held no office and devoted a great part of my time to business, I naturally had much to do with Indians of all types. My father, although reticent about expressing strong political opinions, always held the view that the proper aim of British rule in India was to prepare that vast continent for self-government. With his knowledge of the many conflicting facets of Indian life, he fully realised the complexities and difficulties. But he would have agreed with the view of a modern writer about the decision of 1835 to carry out the proposals of Macaulay's famous minute on education:

> It opened the floodgates of European thought and literature, and subjected the best brains of India, from their childhood onwards, to the powerful influence of English liberal and scientific thought.[1]

Indeed, the rapid extension of educational facilities in India—in primary and secondary schools, as well as in crowded universities—had been the basis for the growth of our own business and that of our English competitors.

I remember many ardent discussions on what were called the Morley–Minto Reforms in 1909, which my father approved. When these were followed by the Montagu–Chelmsford constitutional changes, my father and his colleagues gained some experience of the system of 'diarchy' which was set up under the Government of India Act, 1919. Education became a 'transferred' subject, under the control of Indian Ministers. We had close and friendly relations with the new authorities and were able to see something of the healthy effect of administrative responsibility in turning many moderate Indians from revolutionary plans to the practical facing of day-to-day problems. When the crisis in the Conservative Party came about in 1929 over Lord Halifax's statement that it was implicit in the declaration of 1917 'that the natural issue of India's constitutional progress as there contemplated is the attainment of Dominion Status', my sympathies were with the Viceroy. Nevertheless, I did not follow with any great attention the disputes about the precise effect of this declaration upon the work of the Simon Commission, although I watched with regret the virtual breakdown of the Round Table Conference in 1931.

[1] Sir Percival Griffiths, *Modern India* (London, 1962), p. 55.

During the years when these issues first became prominent (1929–31) I was out of the House of Commons. But when I returned in 1931 the problem of India once again raised bitter conflicts in the Conservative Party. These originated with the publication of the White Paper of 1933, and were only ended by the final passing of the Government of India Act in 1935, steered through many difficult crises by the ingenuity and patience of Sir Samuel Hoare.[1] On this question, at any rate, I supported the Government throughout. That it had led to a final breach between Churchill and the leaders of the Conservative Party was to me a tragic event, for the time was approaching when the rise of the Nazi Party and the seizure of power by Hitler began to cause me and many of my friends increasing anxiety. On this issue I was soon to range myself with Churchill. But on India I felt instinctively that he was wrong and strangely reactionary. My sympathies were with Baldwin, who on great occasions spoke with a persuasive force which has seldom been surpassed. I remember especially his speech at a party meeting in December 1934. These were his words:

> Remember: what have we taught India for a century? We have preached English institutions and democracy and all the rest of it. We have taught her the lesson and she wants us to pay the bill. There is a wind of nationalism and freedom blowing round the world and blowing as strongly in Asia as anywhere in the world. And are we less true Conservatives because we say: 'the time has now come'? Are those who say 'the time may come—some day', are they the truer Conservatives?[2]

When, many years later, I used the phrase 'wind of change', it may well have been an unconscious echo of Baldwin's words.

Before the outbreak of the Second World War there was a general agreement among the leaders and rank and file of all parties, with a few notable exceptions, that the march of progress could not be indefinitely delayed. All the 'Dominions'—the old 'colonies' of British descent—had achieved their full ambitions in 1931. Even in the most backward territories of the 'Colonial Empire' some of the first forward steps were being taken by the addition of 'elected

[1] Afterwards Lord Templewood.   [2] *Winds of Change*, p. 318.

members' to the officials of the Governors' councils. How then could the genuine rise of Indian nationalism be permanently obstructed, in a country which could boast so long a history and was being so rapidly educated towards the prospect of self-government? Naturally, although there was a general agreement in principle that this hard road must be trod, with all its obstacles and pitfalls, there was much uncertainty in practice as to precise plans and detailed timing. The India Act of 1935 had, in effect, satisfied nobody, and resolved none of the real problems.

Whatever might be urged against the history of British rule in India, which had followed on the breakdown of the Mogul Empire, we had at least brought to the vast and varied populations of the sub-continent peace and substantial material progress. It was this task which occupied us for many generations; one which Macaulay described as 'the stupendous process of the reconstruction of a decomposed society'. It was therefore of vital importance, if we were to complete our work honourably and leave behind us a legacy of which our successors could be proud, that the unity of India should be preserved. It followed, and was accepted by all with any knowledge of Indian conditions, that a single unitary State was out of the question. There must be a Federation of India. The various provinces, each with local self-government, must be united under a central legislature and Government. We would transfer full responsible government in the provinces to Indian Ministers. The central legislative assembly would be Indian. But in the Viceroy's council (composed partly of British and partly of Indian members) would remain the ultimate residuum of power until the last stage was reached.

But if this plan was to operate, it involved two further essentials. Somehow or other, the Indian States must be brought into the Federation with British India. These were very numerous and covered, taken together, very large areas. In most of them there was still purely personal rule by the princes, and there was little sympathy between these rulers, fortified by the panoply of ancient tradition, and the modern forces of Indian nationalism. It would be a marriage of oil and vinegar. But even if this difficulty could be overcome, there remained another and more perilous division.

Disregarding Buddhist and other religions with smaller followings, and even overlooking the many millions of the 'depressed classes', there remained the great gulf between the Moslems and the Hindus. It was easy to hold out the promise of Dominion status. But the task of creating an All-India Federal Government to comprise both the Indian States and British India, and to resolve the bitter communal antagonisms of the followers of the two great contending religions, would be long, difficult and perhaps in the end impossible. So it was to prove.

When the Second War began, in spite of the repudiation of the Act of 1935 by the nationalist leaders—Gandhi, Nehru and the rest— some progress had been made. The war years afforded a triumphant vindication of the skill and sympathy of those few but devoted British civil servants who, working with their Indian colleagues, were able to maintain under the Viceroy a reasonable degree of peace and order as well as give splendid assistance to the Allied cause. It is an equal tribute to the loyalty and martial valour of many of her peoples that India's contribution to the war effort, though bitterly impeded by Congress—the strongest political party in the country—proved so notable. Two and a half million men and women were enrolled in the fighting forces, an almost unprecedented voluntary recruitment. Another eight million Indians were engaged in auxiliary work; five million served in war industries. The Indian armies fought with conspicuous gallantry in every part of the vast front and suffered heavy casualties. Not less remarkable was the increased production, both agricultural and industrial. Yet when the Germans were defeated in Europe and the Japanese surrender followed a few months later, the problem of India's political future, which most of us had disregarded with so many other distractions during the war years, came once more ineluctably to the front.

When I was serving in the Ministry of Supply in the first two years of the war, I had some connections with the munitions and industrial effort that was being made in India. In the spring of 1942, although I was not a member of the Cabinet, I heard of the effort which had been made to reach some co-operation with the Congress leaders. It was indeed launched at a terrible moment in our history. On 15 February Singapore had surrendered, and the advance of

Japan into Asia, coupled with the loss of Hong Kong, had been a serious blow to our prestige:

> The security of the Indian sub-continent was now directly endangered. The Japanese Navy was, it seemed, free to enter, almost unchallenged, the Bay of Bengal. India was threatened for the first time under British rule with large-scale foreign invasion by an Asiatic Power. The stresses latent in Indian politics grew. Although only a small extremist section in Bengal, led by men such as Subhas Bose, were directly subversive and hoped for an Axis victory, the powerful body of articulate opinion which supported Gandhi ardently believed that India should remain passive and neutral in the world conflict. As the Japanese advanced this defeatism spread. If India, it was now suggested, could somehow throw off British connections, perhaps there would be no motive for a Japanese invasion. The peril to India might possibly only consist in her link with the British Empire. If this link could be snapped surely India could adopt the position of Eire. So, not without force, the argument ran.[1]

At the same time, President Roosevelt was only too ready to offer counsel on Indian affairs. As Churchill grimly writes:

> States which have no overseas colonies or possessions are capable of rising to moods of great elevation and detachment about the affairs of those who have.[2]

This critical situation was the origin of the Cripps mission to India. No man could have set out more fitted for his task or endowed with greater sincerity of purpose and sympathy for the Indian claims. His object was to seek India's full co-operation in the war against Japan and to persuade the leaders of the Congress Party to accept a proposal which he was empowered to put forward on behalf of the whole National Government of Britain. It was made abundantly clear by him that we were prepared to grant full independence to India, if asked for by a Constituent Assembly, to be held immediately after victory. The document, which had been drafted by

[1] Winston S. Churchill, *The Second World War*, vol. iv: *The Hinge of Fate*, pp. 182–3.
[2] Ibid., p. 185.

all parties in the Government, had been devised not only with the hope of rallying support in India to her own defence but to prove our sincerity before world opinion. It was rejected out of hand. The necessary preliminaries were unacceptable, and Congress demanded the immediate formation of a National Government to which power should be transferred; even the necessary reservations for defence were put aside. Nevertheless, the Cripps mission achieved something. Apart from the moral effect in India and throughout the world, at least it led Nehru to revolt against the blind pacifism of many of the Congress leaders. He declared that in spite of the failure of the negotiation the war against the Japanese invader must be won and that the British war effort in India should not be embarrassed.

At the time I was not in a position to know much more of the details of this affair than was given by Churchill and his Ministers to Parliament. Nevertheless, there was a lesson to be drawn from the utter failure of even so sensitive and friendly a missionary. Bitter as was the feeling of Indian nationalist opinion against Britain, the internal conflict of Moslem and Hindu was even more virulent. It was convenient then, as in the years when Halifax and his successors had struggled to bring reason to the Indian extremists and had pleaded for the end of communal outrages, to put all the blame upon the Viceroy and the British Government. But many of those who knew India best feared that this violent reaction against any British proposal was partly, if not entirely, intended to conceal the unbridgeable chasm between Indians themselves.

In the concluding stages of the war the situation in India remained tense but not unmanageable. Lord Wavell,[1] who had accepted the Viceroyalty in 1943, preserved throughout these years his wonderful combination of good humour, patience and resilience. In spite of continual unrest and communal disturbances, the war effort of the sub-continent was fully maintained. At the same time, under agreements made during the war, a vast amount of expenditure within India became debitable to the British exchequer. Thus India was transformed from a debtor to a creditor nation, the so-called 'sterling balances' reaching a figure of some £1,250 millions.

[1] Field-Marshal Lord Wavell, Commander-in-Chief Middle East 1939–41; Commander-in-Chief India, 1941–3; Viceroy of India 1943–7.

It was upon this form of aid, sometimes known as 'unrequited exports', that the economies of India and Pakistan were to be supported for many years, with corresponding burdens upon British production and consequential strains upon the balance of payments.

In the spring of 1945—the year of victory—Wavell did his best to constitute an Executive Council drawn from the leaders of political life. In order to facilitate this process the principal members of the Congress Party, still under detention, were released. At a great conference at Simla in June it seemed likely that Wavell would succeed, and that a purely Indian Executive Council could be created as a preliminary to the discussion of the future. Unhappily, the Moslem League, under Mohammed Ali Jinnah's influence, demanded that no Moslem other than members of the League should take part in any governmental institution, temporary or permanent. Over this condition, Wavell's bold initiative was frustrated and failed.

So matters stood when the result of the General Election in Britain became known. Attlee, now Prime Minister, had some experience of Indian affairs. He had served on the Simon Commission between the wars, and had taken a considerable part in the discussions in the War Cabinet which led to the Cripps mission of 1942. He was a man of firm determination—a quality sometimes cloaked under apparent diffidence.

After a visit of the Viceroy to London, the Government's plan was announced. Elections, both to provincial and central legislatures, postponed in the war, would be held as soon as practicable. A constituent assembly would then be called together. Meanwhile, the Viceroy would hold preliminary talks to see how far the Cripps plan of 1942 might prove acceptable or what amendments might be required.

This proposal met with little response in India. It was violently attacked in the Nationalist Press. Congress had no better contribution to put forward than a reaffirmation of the notorious 'Quit India' resolution of 1942. Violent agitation followed, led by Nehru and Sardar Patel, who did their best to foment ill-feeling and lawlessness. Congress need not have been so anxious. Attlee had already made up his mind to quit.

I

There was to follow a period of tragi-comedy, for the next eighteen months were to be taken up with almost frantic efforts by the British Government to extricate themselves from any further responsibility for Indian affairs. Indeed, never was a great empire brought to an end in such a peculiar and unexpected fashion. Proposal after proposal was put forward: for the holding of elections; for the creation of a constitution-making body; for the transfer of power to an All-India Central Government. All these originated from a British Government who seemed bent on ridding themselves of their responsibility at almost any price and on any conditions. The representatives of the Indians, whether formally elected or leaders of the rival bodies, Congress and the Moslem League, seemed to refuse the gift of freedom and independence so feverishly pressed upon them by the masters of India. In the event, every plan for orderly transfer of power and the preservation of the unity of India was to founder on the rock of the Hindu–Moslem conflict. Wavell remained patient and persistent, but seemed helpless. When at the end of 1945 the elections took place for the Central Assembly, the Congress Party made a clean sweep of all the 'open' constituencies, completely eliminating every other party, while the Moslem League won every 'reserved' Moslem seat. Thus the Hindu–Moslem conflict was brought into still sharper relief.

In an attempt to find some solution another Cabinet mission was announced in February 1946. Cripps would set out again, but this time he would be accompanied by Lord Pethick-Lawrence, the Secretary of State, and A. V. Alexander, First Lord of the Admiralty and later Minister of Defence. At the same time, Attlee made it clear that immediately after the central and provincial elections had been completed, positive steps would be taken to frame a constitution, and to bring into being a Government to whom the transfer of power could be made. Since some kind of machinery was necessary for the purpose, it was Britain's desire to help with the setting-up of the various institutions. He also stated categorically that whether or not India wished to remain in the British Commonwealth would be entirely a matter for India herself. He was well aware of all the difficulties of a vast area containing such a multitude of races, religions and languages; but he declared that their future was not a matter for the British Government but for the Indians to settle.

I remember feeling, when I heard this statement, astonished at a situation almost without parallel in history. I shared the general view that India ought to obtain self-government. But that a British Government should be so determined to abandon its responsibilities, while the Indians seemed equally unwilling to accept the obligations placed upon them, appeared to most Conservatives an outrageous paradox. For Britain, it seemed an abdication of duty as well as of power.

All through 1946 Wavell tried to find a solution to what proved to be an insoluble problem. Our desire to bring to fruition in an orderly way the policy of full autonomy for a united India was frustrated not by the Viceroy or by the British civil service or any vested interests based upon the long British rule. Its failure was due to Moslem–Hindu animosity and to no other reason. Yet the continual manœuvrings and almost monthly announcements of a new plan weakened the Viceroy's position. The elections for the Central Assembly at the end of 1945 had already proved that the two hostile forces–Congress and the Moslem League–had swept away every other political grouping. This was repeated in the elections for the Provincial Legislatures held in the spring of 1946. On the other hand, it now became possible to operate the Governors' Provinces for the first time since the outbreak of war by the appointment to the ministerial positions of elected members, instead of relying on the reserved powers of the Governor.

The Moslem League had by now categorically put forward their claim to what became known as Pakistan–that is to say, they demanded the partition of India, with sovereign power in north-west and north-east India for a Moslem State. Naturally, all those who loved and cared for India fought desperately against this outcome of the struggle, for it seemed destined to destroy one of the greatest benefits which British intervention in the anarchy of India two hundred years before had been able to secure. Cripps and his colleagues, with the consent of the Cabinet, put up an ingenious counter-plan for dividing India into three major groups and giving to the All-India Central or Federal Government only minimal powers, but providing for a legislature constituted both from British

India and from the Indian States. There was to be a Constituent Assembly elected by the existing Provincial Legislatures and a number of other proposals by which a loose federation, giving maximum authority in their own areas to Moslems and Hindus, could at least secure the survival of a united India. Out of this there might gradually develop a growing degree of respect and authority for the Federal centre.

The discussions on this imaginative if complicated plan continued for many months. Further proposals were made for an Interim Government—or Executive Council—to consist of five Congress Party and five Moslem League nominees, with some representatives of other interests. All these schemes broke down in turn and the Viceroy was forced to rely on an Executive Council of officials. At the end of August, however, an Indian Executive Council was created, in which Nehru accepted the position of Vice-President. But now the Moslem League held aside. Disorder and communal riots followed. In the next months there were violent conflicts in Calcutta and throughout Eastern Bengal, spreading to the United Provinces and Bihar. At last, in October 1946, the Moslem League decided to enter the Interim Government. But it was a Government without any unity of purpose or understanding.

At the end of the year the Viceroy came to London, accompanied by Jinnah and Liaqat Ali Khan, as well as Nehru. Long discussions, mostly of a highly legalistic and argumentative character, took place with the Prime Minister, turning on the precise interpretation of this or that paragraph in the Cabinet Mission's scheme for the three regional groups.

Just before Christmas, following the return of the Indian leaders after their fruitless talks in London, the British Government issued a statement which seemed to imply a firmer policy. They declared that the presence of both major political parties was essential for the success of any plan, which could not proceed without Indian co-operation. At the same time the Constituent Assembly, still without the elected Moslem League members or any representatives of the States, met and adjourned until the third week of January 1947.

Out of all this confusion there rose more and more clearly the separate contending figures of Gandhi on the one side, supported by

Nehru, and of Jinnah on the other. The British Government tried by every means to convince the Indians of their own sincerity. Even before our final withdrawal a High Commissioner was appointed to deal with purely British interests; no further recruitment was made to the Secretary of State's Service or for British officers in the Indian forces. Diplomatic arrangements were made at the United Nations to try to create the illusion that an independent Indian Government already existed.

During all this time, there was much discussion among the Opposition leaders as to the course they should pursue. Churchill, from his temperament and his memories of the past, felt unhappy and angry about the development of affairs in India. Although he loyally accepted the policy of leading Indians along the path to self-government, he felt dismayed and dishonoured by the terrible situation which appeared to be developing and threatening anarchy and even civil war. From such an inglorious end to the noble story of Britain's imperial rule he shrank with horror. In the eighteen months since the election, in spite of Wavell's well-meant efforts, the authority of the central and to some extent the provincial Governments of India was beginning to break down. The sense that 'we were on the way out' made it difficult for our hard-pressed officials, from the Viceroy to the youngest member of the Service, to command the traditional respect of the people. If we were really on the way out, what mattered to them was 'who would be on the way in?' Meanwhile, how were we to command the continued support and loyalty of the moderates whom we were about to desert and hand over to the tender mercies of the extremists? Thus all our traditional friends began to fall away; all our long-standing enemies began to exult. As a consequence, there were troubles and something like mutiny in certain Indian military and naval units. Serious food shortages, following on several bad seasons, began to affect some areas, at a time when the normal machinery for relief was weakened. There was nothing, of course, approaching the famine conditions that have since oppressed whole states, but there was enough to cause anxiety and grief to the attenuated body of British officials whose responsibility was great and whose devotion to India was unshaken. All this news was continually reported to us from many sources. Among our colleagues 'Rab' Butler was particularly well informed and kept us in close touch with each development in turn. The long connections of his family with India, as well as his special knowledge, made him a most valuable adviser. Yet there was little that we could do. We were equally weak in the House of Commons and the country. We could only give our support to each well-meant move of the Government to find some way out of this fantastic dilemma. Here was an Imperial power attacked, abused and calumniated for many years by the critics of the Left as brutal exploiters of conquered peoples, trying by every means to extricate itself from the obligation to decide the future of 400 million people who looked to them for succour. Here were the British politicians of the Left, who had for years supported in principle the immediate transfer of authority and were only too anxious to do so, placed in the embarrassing and almost ludicrous position of being unable to surrender power in practice without creating not freedom but anarchy. For many months they tried to find an orderly method of handing over their responsibilities. In the end they were to abandon them in despair.

At the end of 1946 the deadlock was complete. It seemed to me, therefore, that it might be interesting to pay a short visit to India to see what was going on. I had, in addition to the political interest, the practical need to visit our various establishments if only to bring some comfort and cheer to our loyal British and Indian employees, and to deal with some urgent problems with which we were confronted. At the same time I would no doubt be able to see something of the state of affairs over a wider field. John Wyndham travelled with me. He showed the same qualities of organisation and care for my comfort that he had displayed during the war and was generously to devote to me in the years which still lay ahead.

We had indeed chosen a critical month for our visit. For before we returned the tremendous decision was taken in Whitehall to put a definite term to British rule in India. This was to lead to a year which even the objective compilers of the *Annual Register* described as

the most momentous in India's history since the battle of Plassey. It saw her partition into two independent nation States, the end of

British rule, and a mass migration, millions strong, preceded and accompanied by hideous slaughter and destruction.[1]

We arrived in Bombay on 24 January 1947. Although the Moslem League was still boycotting the Constituent Assembly, they shared posts as Ministers in the Interim Government at Delhi with the Congress representatives. On 22 January Hindu members of the Assembly had asserted their firm and solemn resolve to declare India an independent and sovereign republic. Its boundaries were to comprise all the territories of the sub-continent in a union where they should 'possess and retain the status of autonomous units'. This somewhat obscure statement had only one positive result. The working committee of the Moslem League passed a resolution on 31 January declaring that the British constitutional plan had failed, and that the proceedings of the Constituent Assembly should be regarded as invalid. There naturally followed a period of growing and almost intolerable tension.

Yet, as has often been my experience at moments of crisis, everything on the surface seemed reasonably quiet. Naturally, I spent most of my time in Bombay talking to Indian authors, teachers, educationalists and administrators, all of whom seemed extremely friendly and expressed genuine gratitude to their British friends and colleagues. The fact that education had been in Indian hands for a considerable time had no doubt made relations easier. Moreover, the natural courtesy of Indians played its part. But I was struck by the fact that of the many whom I saw, young and old, few expressed bitterness, or even criticism, about the long years of British rule. There was, however, a genuine and almost pathetic sense of enthusiasm about the future:

> One cannot help being impressed by the keenness and even excitement of these educationalists. They are all obviously in a mood of elevation at the thought of India's 'liberation' and the strides which she will now make.[2]

Our own managers, as well as our Indian authors, foresaw a greatly increased market, both in the higher educational field and for the

[1] *Annual Register, 1947*, p. 145. [2] 27 January 1947.

teaching of literacy to adults. There was certainly no sign of panic, or even nervousness, about the immediate future.

There was much discussion, but little agreement, about the future of the English language in education. Most of the practical educationalists were sceptical about the substitution of Hindi, or any other language, except in primary schools. I visited in the course of the week a large number of schools and colleges, as well as the Department of Chemical Technology and the Institute of Science. I was received with special kindness by the Vice-Chancellor of the University of Bombay, and everyone whom I met seemed far less concerned with the political situation as such than with the pursuance of their own educational plans.

> It is really very interesting to compare all the nonsense in the papers, breathing hatred and bitterness, with the attitude of these educated men—most of whom are probably (at least nominally) nationalist.[1]

At the same time I saw a number of British businessmen, representing the larger firms. A dinner was given for me on our last evening in Bombay at which a considerable number attended:

> A really interesting evening, with a long and frank argument. The general view is pessimistic, although some feel that if—a big if—the country holds together at all, we should be able to trade after the British authority is withdrawn.[2]

A few days previously I had attended a conference arranged by the Bombay Chamber of Commerce:

> A long discussion—interesting but rather inconclusive. It is clear that the general view is (a) that it would be quite impossible to go back; (b) that very little good is likely to come of going forward. The atmosphere is just one of hoping for the best. Many of the large interests are selling out.[3]

During all our visit we stayed at Government House. The Governor, Sir John Colville, was an old friend and House of Commons colleague. Those who have travelled in India in the old days will remember the high standard of comfort and hospitality.

[1] 30 January 1947.   [2] 31 January 1947.   [3] 29 January 1947.

We occupied a small house or bungalow in the Government compound, with a mass of servants ready to attend to every possible want and sometimes even seeming to suggest them. Many years later, when I visited India as Prime Minister, I was to receive the same generous entertainment.

The Governor asked a number of Indians to meet me at informal luncheons and dinners. These included Mr. Morarji Desai, who was then Minister for the Interior in Bombay:

> Able, fluent, plausible, very well educated (at Wilson College). . . . As member of Congress Ministry now in power in Bombay (after three years or more of Governor's administration under Section 93) Mr. Desai has the unenviable task of being responsible for law and order in the province.[1]

Although the Governor would readily have brought me into contact with all the leading politicians, we agreed that in the existing situation it would be wiser for him only to invite a few old and trusted friends. Broadly, I found those whom I met friendly but unhappy. I also had some long talks with the Governor and his staff. The older members of the Indian Civil Service were naturally saddened at the state of affairs, but I found the Governor calm and resolute:

> Colville feels that Wavell and H.M.G. have gone further and more rapidly than was necessary. But as things are, it is almost impossible to reverse the policy. We can only 'wait and see'. But Colville is not as defeatist as some here. He thinks the situation may develop in a way which would at least keep India in the Commonwealth in spite of all the protestations of Congress.[2]

We arrived in Delhi on 1 February and stayed for five days as guests of the Viceroy. I will not try to describe New Delhi, so well known to many British visitors and illustrated by so many books on art and architecture. It certainly seemed strange at that moment to stay in the Viceroy's extraordinary palace—an Indian Versailles—erected by some almost inexplicable act of pride or folly at the very time when British rule was reaching its end. It was of course a wonderfully impressive edifice inside and out, with splendid reception

[1] 25 January 1947.   [2] 31 January 1947.

halls and saloons and decorated in a magnificent and luxurious style. The gardens, both in design and execution, were a miracle of skill and beauty. Ten years later I was to revisit the palace when it was the residence of the President of India. Now I was to be received by almost the last of the Viceroys.

I had not met Lord Wavell in the course of the war, for he had left the Middle East before my arrival in North Africa. He had accepted his task in India much against his will and yielding only to the demands of duty. He had now been there some five years. I was impressed, as everyone who met him must have been, by his combination of simplicity and dignity. It was clear that he had a strong sense of service and was guided by a spiritual power which preserved him through many troubles. In our first short talk, he asked me to see as many people as possible and give him any impressions before I left. Nevertheless, I came away somewhat baffled from this first meeting:

> Talk with Viceroy after luncheon. It is difficult to get much out of him. He clearly feels that we must go. The only question is how. I asked him what he would need to re-establish British Raj. He said five divisions and 1,000 administrators. This astonished me by its moderation. Think of what we have in Germany, Trieste, Greece and Palestine.[1]

The physical conditions in Delhi were more pleasant than at Bombay. Here it was cool enough to need fires at night, and by day it was agreeably warm, like a fine June day at home. I called on a number of educationalists, including Sir John Sargent, Educational Adviser to the Central Government, who was sceptical about the use of the 'mother tongue', Hindi, in universities throughout India, but believed that a successor Government would try to force it through. I also saw Maulana Azad, a great Sanskrit and Arabic scholar, who was full of praises for the work that Macmillans were doing in India and plied me with flattering hospitality. But of course in Delhi, and especially at this critical moment, the political situation was the only subject of discussion. I was invited to dinner by Nehru, whom I met for the first time. But since there were several other guests, British and Indian,

[1] 1 February 1947.

the conversation was light, flitting from point to point, adroit and courteous. (The continual references to prison experiences were the only jarring notes, but these were made lightly and humorously.)[1]

I recorded then my first impressions of this remarkable man with whom I afterwards formed a close friendship and who was to play so great a role in guiding India through the first years of independence:

Pandit Jawaharlal Nehru—high-class Brahmin, of Kashmir; intellectualist, philosopher, writer; nationalist, socialist, revolutionary; exquisite and even flowery in taste, is an admirable and charming host. Many years of prison life—or rather preventive detention—have left a mark upon him. He is, I should judge, torn between bitter hatred of the British and a desire to be fair and objective. He struck me as very nervous, jumpy and strained. For some months now he has had some experience of power. Even with the support of what remains of British authority—and it is not inconsiderable—this has taken a good deal out of him. He has found that government is not as easy as criticism.[1]

I recognised that Nehru was a man of first-class intellectual powers. I felt less certain that he

would stand up to the rough and tumble of ... trouble. He is not a man for storms; only a stormy petrel.[1]

I was wrong. For Nehru's courage and perseverance proved to be no less than his ability.

The next morning I spent an hour with a figure of almost equal authority, Sardar Patel:

A very impressive man—the only Indian I have seen so far who struck me as having character and courage. He looks rather like a Roman Emperor, this effect being accentuated by the sort of white rug which is worn in cold weather by Hindus. He spoke bitterly of the Communists—a movement which was un-Indian and should be resisted. He did not allow the conversation to take any course except as he chose and he terminated the interview rather abruptly, but without actual discourtesy. He did not

[1] 3 February 1947.

mention Nehru, etc., by name, but made one or two contemptuous references to 'those who trusted more to talk than action'.
P. is the Bevin of India.[1]

There could be no greater contrast to Patel than Liaqat Ali
Khan, the Moslem League representative in the lately formed
Interim Government. I was impressed by his peculiar charm and
admirable courtesy. He reminded me of a cultivated country
gentleman at home, with good education, a good library and fondness for field sports. But even his temper was ruffled by a sense of
grievance which he did not try to disguise:

> He spoke with more bitterness than I expected, for he has the
> reputation of being a moderate man. He blamed the Cabinet
> Mission and the Viceroy for having allowed themselves to be
> deceived time after time by the trickiness of Congress. At every
> stage, there had been mental reservations and casuistry, instead of
> frankness. He felt that Mr. Jinnah's last pronouncement placed
> upon H.M.G. the duty of making a decision. The whole plan
> had failed.[1]

I suggested that this might not be the reaction of moderate public
opinion either in India or in the rest of the world. The intricacies of
the argument on the precise form of the Cabinet Mission's plan
would be forgotten. But the outstanding fact would emerge that
Congress had entered a Constituent Assembly and the League had
refused. He did not demur at this, but

> felt that the League could not allow itself to get deeper and deeper
> into the trap which Nehru had prepared with the connivance of
> H.M.G.[1]

He then set out with remarkable clarity the three courses which in
his view were open to the British Government:

1. To continue her efforts to get an equitable settlement, thus
   starting an independent India on her course with a fair prospect of success.
2. To abandon the task and leave India at a fixed date, leaving
   Indians to settle affairs by agreement or by civil war.

[1] 4 February 1947.

3. To allow things to drift, until all administration collapsed, at the centre and in the provinces, so that neither British nor Indian rule existed in India, but chaos.

It appeared to him that (1) was the right course – the only one worthy of our past. (2) was, however, logical and might be justified if we felt unequal to the burden. (3) was ignoble.[1]

He next spoke indignantly about the situation in the Punjab. Although the Moslem League had won 79 out of 86 Moslem seats, the 'weighting' system for the Sikhs and a few 'quisling' Moslems had enabled the Governor to form a coalition Government without genuine Moslem support. He ought first to have called on the League, as the largest party. He should only have fallen back on a coalition if a League Government had been defeated. He seemed very bitter about this decision of the Governor, which he regarded as unfair and only to be explained as part of a definite bias, almost plot, against the League.

I asked if he thought the Central Interim Government could last, in view of such divergencies. He replied that it was not a Government, in the true sense. It was a Viceroy's council; the Viceroy presided over it; the Ministers looked after their portfolios; but it did not act as a Government in any sense of the word.[1]

I continued to argue the unwisdom of the League in refusing to enter the Constituent Assembly, and warned him that British public opinion would not understand their attitude:

It would be better to enter the 'Assembly' and produce a minority report or leave at a later date, if they could not get satisfaction. He said 'Ulster will fight, and Ulster will be right' or words to that effect.[1]

During my few days in Delhi, I was fortunate in being able to attend a session of the Central Assembly. The procedure was familiar, being based on ours in the House of Commons. The hour of meeting was 11 a.m.:

Questions for an hour. Then motions to adjourn the House 'on matters of urgent public importance' – nearly 20 such motions

[1] 4 February 1947.

were proposed. The Speaker allowed a good deal of talk but ruled them out of order.

This afternoon was taken up with a Bill to reduce corruption in the public services! This was introduced by Patel–the Home Member. Curiously enough–instead of attacking the British–all the speakers engaged in an orgy of self-reproach and intellectual masochism which was quite remarkable.[1]

Before leaving for Lucknow I had a long and revealing conversation with Wavell:

He told me that he recognised now his mistake in accepting the original Congress agreement to the [Cabinet Mission] plan in May 1946. The mental and other reservations made it not a genuine acceptance; but he was persuaded, against his better judgment, by the Cabinet Mission. He had hoped that if he could once get the parties together, the logic of facts would keep them together. Even Alexander (who generally supported him against Cripps) had joined in persuading the Viceroy.[2]

Wavell feared that Congress would soon demand the dismissal of the League Ministers from the Interim Government or, if this was refused, their Minister would resign. Altogether, I felt him an almost pathetic figure, alone, with few advisers or confidants, with no clear knowledge of what he ought to do or what course the British Government intended to follow. He seemed like a man resigned to fate. He finally impressed upon me that

things were moving rapidly–more rapidly than people at home realised. Although it would still be possible to re-establish their authority, it was becoming more difficult every day.[2]

In the afternoon we left Delhi, but I continued to be haunted by the tragic figure of the Viceroy.

At Lucknow we were again guests at Government House. After calling upon the Vice-Chancellor of the University, Raja Bisheshwar Dayal Seth, who showed me great courtesy but was reticent on public affairs, I had a useful and entertaining talk with the Lieutenant-Governor of the United Provinces, Sir Francis Wylie:

[1] 3 February 1947.   [2] 4 February 1947.

He is an Ulsterman, with a Southern Irish wife. Racy, full of wit and humour, vigorous in expression, energetic in action—he impressed me most favourably.[1]

As for the political situation, he saw no solution:

He regards Parliamentary democracy as quite unsuitable to India. India is a country of minorities—with bitter differences and permanently fixed divisions. A Parliamentary system depends on first one party, then another winning power. With fixed minorities, this is impossible. At the same time he thinks we have lost the will to govern and are no longer welcome. The struggle in India is simply what Raj will succeed to the British Raj.[1]

On the following day I called on Dr. Sampurnanand, the Minister of Education in the Congress Government which was now in office. He explained to me his views on primary, secondary and university education with an impassive face but embittered words. The British teaching of history in the schools was all wrong and inspired by an 'unforgivable' bias:

At present children are taught that there was a Hindu, a Moslem and then a British epoch. They must be taught the nationalist creed—there is only one India.[2]

Alas, in his hopes for 'one India' he was soon to be disillusioned.

My next visit was to Mrs. V. L. Pandit, Nehru's sister, who at the time was Minister for Local Government. It was my first meeting with this highly educated and attractive lady, who later became an intimate and valued friend.

She explained to me quite frankly that the Congress Party could only be held together until the British had gone. After that, the older elements who were Right-wing and capitalist-minded would fade out and the Left take control. (This, of course, reflects the deep struggle between Nehru and Patel.)[2]

I was impressed by Mrs. Pandit's genuine desire that the Congress Party should not be regarded as a Hindu party but as a national party. In her view a secular State must take the place of a religious

[1] 4 February 1947.   [2] 5 February 1947.

State. It is only fair to say that Nehru and his intimates were to struggle honourably to achieve this end.

> The rest of the morning we spent at the Residency, making a tour of the whole grounds and each strongpoint in the famous siege. Thanks to Lord Curzon, the whole place is splendidly preserved. This is the only place in the world where the Union Jack is flown by night and day. It is never hauled down.[1]

Whatever might have been my conviction of the inevitable progress towards India's independence, it was a sad and moving experience to visit this unique monument at such a time.

From Lucknow we went by train to Calcutta. On the first day (6 February) I went to our business office, where I was received, as at Bombay, with the usual ceremonies of welcome by the staff, including speech-making and garlanding. These courtesies are a pleasant feature of Indian life.

In Calcutta we stayed first at a hotel and later at the famous Government House, built in the style of Kedleston Hall. During the last few days there had been severe Hindu–Moslem riots, with many killed on both sides. This tragic, but all too common, conflict had rather a macabre result, which threw something of a shadow over a most hospitable party given to me in the famous Botanical Gardens by Dr. Biswas, a friend and colleague of Mr. Brimble, the editor of *Nature*, a Macmillan publication. The list of guests was representative and distinguished, and I felt that high honour was being paid me:

> I had a sort of royal reception, each guest being brought up for a few minutes' conversation in turn. It is really queer how (politics apart) they are really gratified to meet Englishmen and how pleased they are by minor courtesies.[2]

As we sat out on the terrace by the river in the shade of the famous banyan tree, dead bodies kept floating down in different stages of decomposition. These were attacked by numbers of vultures. Since, however, the vulture is not an aquatic bird, it had some difficulty in securing the delicacies by which it seemed most attracted—that is,

---

[1] 5 February 1947.   [2] 7 February 1947.

the faces and especially the eyes of the corpses—without considerable risk to itself. A vulture would dive boldly and grab at the face; but as the corpse began to sink, the bird had hurriedly to take off to avoid drowning. Wyndham and I, with natural politeness, affected not to notice the gruesome scene, although it had a certain fascination, especially as a background to the very highbrow and intellectual level of our discussions. Apart from these interruptions, the general tone of my fellow guests was optimistic. They all seemed to hope that a way would be found to keep India both united and a loyal member of the Commonwealth. Most of the talk, however, was on science and education, and similar topics.

The day ended with a dinner in our honour given by the European members of the Legislative Assembly. Sir Edward Benthall, an old school-friend, struck me as head and shoulders above the others:

> Almost 20 were present and the arguments for and against this or that course went on till after midnight. As usual, nothing very new or very helpful emerged. The trading community is very nervous of discriminating legislation.[1]

As at Bombay, I called upon a number of educationalists, including some of our authors. One of the most pleasant visits was to the house of Dr. H. C. Raychaudhari:

> He and Dr. R. C. Majumdar are co-authors of an Indian history which has at last been published. Dr. R. is an invalid. He received me in bed—Dr. Majumdar was present, as well as numerous sons, sons-in-law, daughters, daughters-in-law, etc. Much high talk—valuation of Herodotus as a historian—and much tea and sweets—an odd party....
>
> It was really an interesting insight into a typical Hindu intellectual household.[2]

In the afternoon, Dr. M. M. Bhattacharyya, head of the Department of English, took me to Calcutta University where I was received by the Vice-Chancellor, Professor P. W. Banerjee, and all the professors at a formal conference:

> Tea was served; speech of welcome; a few intelligent questions by me; statements in reply by the V.-C. and others; more

[1] 7 February 1947.   [2] 8 February 1947.

speeches and then a tour round some of the University buildings.
The University is, of course, almost entirely Hindu-controlled.
It is very alarmed at what a Moslem Government of Bengal
may do.[1]

Here again I was struck by the moderation of the views of these
professors and teachers, by whom I was received with almost
embarrassing consideration and respect. This experience, so often
repeated, confirmed me in my view that the great hope for the future
lay in the influence of these highly educated and responsible men.

We now moved from the hotel to Government House, which was
much more comfortable and where there was a room set aside for me
to receive my callers. Among these was Dr. S. P. Mookerjee, one of
the most powerful figures in Bengal. He had been three times Vice-
Chancellor and seemed more or less to control the University:

> From the political point of view he is a considerable power,
> although he has temporarily quarrelled with Congress. An
> orthodox Hindu and a Brahmin, he is the Bengal leader of the
> Mahasabha (the sort of Hindu counterpart to the Moslem
> League). They were beaten in the election, although he has a seat
> in the Bengal Assembly. He has always been in and out of
> politics. A fine figure (very tall and well built), very plausible, very
> subtle–he reminded me of some of the French or Italian poli-
> ticians with whom I used to deal. His plea was that the Bengal
> position should be really understood at home. The Moslems have
> a small numerical majority (53 per cent against 47 per cent),
> chiefly based on Eastern Bengal. But all the culture, all the
> wealth, and the greatest part of Calcutta is Hindu.[2]

It was rather unusual to hear of the pleas for a minority being
made by a Hindu, since in most places the boot was on the other
foot.

> He argued *against* any form of communal representation, as
> contrary to the whole spirit of Parliamentary system and leading
> necessarily to an intensification of the communal feeling. He
> traces this error to Lord Minto (Lord Morley never liked it), and
> the MacDonald Award concerning Bengal was (in his view) a
> fatal error.[2]

[1] 8 February 1947.   [2] 9 February 1947.

I replied that in logic, of course, his arguments were correct, but they seemed to lead to the conclusion that the British should stay in India as the only sanction for the protection of minorities. Dr. Mookerjee's view was, however, quite clear:

> ... the only thing we can now do is to allow the [Constituent] Assembly (even without the Moslem League) to frame a Constitution. He says we should reserve the right to amend it for two purposes and two only: (*a*) proper safeguards for minorities; (*b*) protection of British trading interests. We should then pass it into law and allow an Indian Government to take over. I asked if this would lead to civil war. He said—perhaps. But we should have done our best and could leave with a clear conscience! At present, he feared the policy of drift would lead to a general collapse of all administration, and chaos.[1]

I also saw Mr. Rowan Hodge, the chairman of the European Group. He was a very intelligent man and quick to seize new points, but it was

> clear to me that the European Association and Chambers of Commerce have not really thought out the implications of independence, as distinct from Dominion status. Nor has H.M.G. If there is really to be independence, no treaty will be worth anything unless it is negotiated *after* the separation, with an independent Government. If there is to be Dominion status, the trade safeguards can be incorporated in an Act and enforced.[1]

We dined alone with the Governor, Sir Frederick Burroughs, slow-minded but sensible. He had been a Great Western Railway man, and a sound trade union leader. He held somewhat reactionary views, in particular disliking all politicians!

> He took us to his room after dinner and delighted us with a refreshingly racy account of his experiences here. Stolid, slow, but very acute, this old trade union official can see through hypocrisy and plausibility. A very staunch man.[1]

On 10 February we flew to Madras, where we were hospitably entertained by Sir Archibald Nye, former Deputy C.I.G.S., who was now the Governor. At dinner I was glad to meet again

[1] 9 February 1947.

General Sir Richard O'Connor (Adjutant-General) whom I had not seen since he and General Neame, V.C., arrived at my villa at Algiers having both escaped from Italy....[1]

There were also present a number of Madras notabilities. During the next few days I had many visitors, the most important being the Vice-Chancellor of the University, who, however, preferred to talk politics rather than education. I was amused by the views of a most charming and cultivated Indian, who could only deplore the folly of the newly-elected Government if they were going to sacrifice the greater part of their revenue by introducing prohibition. How then could education go ahead?

Madras was full of wonderful memories. We visited the Fort, one of the first British strongholds in India, and the old St. Mary's Church, built in 1680. This part of the city is strangely beautiful, full of romance and redolent of history. At lunch on 13 February, apart from the Governor and Lady Nye, there was only the Prime Minister, Mr. T. Prakasam. He seemed very concerned about a complicated intrigue against him which could only be settled by the Congress High Command. He was therefore about to leave, first for Delhi and then for Eastern Bengal:

> In the final analysis, the decision as to which set of 'Congress Whigs' shall govern Madras will be made by old man Gandhi, now engaged in his walking pilgrimage (with Press, radio reporters, photographers, police and bearers) in the villages of East Bengal.[2]

Madras seemed much calmer than Calcutta or Delhi, and nobody appeared to realise the rapidity with which the crisis was about to develop. From Madras we returned to Bombay, this time staying at the Taj Hotel:

> 6.30. At H.E.'s request, went up to Government House for a talk. [Colville] is very concerned about a reported decision of H.M.G. to wind up the Secretary of State's service on 1 May this year. If they offer any reasonable terms at all to the individuals concerned, they will certainly opt for the Home service. Others, who cannot be placed, will hesitate to stay on without any British

[1] 10 February 1947.   [2] 13 February 1947.

guarantee. Therefore, (*a*) H.M.G.'s power to resume the administration, centrally or locally (under Sect. 93) would be fatally weakened; (*b*) the immense value of I.C.S. experience will be lost to the new Government during the transitional and early stages.[1]

The next day, 17 February, was a day filled by rumours crowding in from Delhi:

> Sardar Vallabhbhai Patel's interview with Associated Press of America. Gandhi's reported secret and urgent letter to Jawaharlal Nehru, Liaqat Ali Khan's declaration at Aligarh University—all show that a new crisis is approaching. . . .
> Meanwhile I read with amusement that Vallabhbhai Patel has refused to interfere in the Madras crisis—this presumably means that Mr. Prakasam (Congress Prime Minister) will be sacrificed. This is due to his enemy at Delhi, Mr. Rajagopalachari[2]—the powerful Congress figure in Madras politics. But it is not more than a local and personal row. Prakasam is supposed to be on good terms with Gandhi, so the old man (who is *not* on good terms with Patel) may save him yet.[3]

This last, however, was a minor complication compared to the great issues which were now to come to a head. The Interim Government was falling to pieces. It was generally believed that Liaqat Ali Khan, the Finance Minister, had refused to divulge his Budget plans to his Congress colleagues. Nehru had addressed formal complaints to the Viceroy and had been informed (or so it was said) that he should await an early statement by the British Government. Meanwhile, Liaqat Ali Khan had declared that only the establishment of Pakistan as an independent Indian State would satisfy Moslem aspirations.

In this situation I looked forward with eagerness to the interview which Liaqat Ali Khan had arranged for me to have with Jinnah. This took place on the evening of 17 February, the most critical day. We had left Bombay at eight in the morning, reaching Karachi in the early afternoon.

We drove out to Bahawalpur House, Malir, about eight or nine

---

[1] 16 February 1947.
[2] Chakravarti Rajagopalachari, later Governor-General.
[3] 17 February 1947.

miles from Karachi, where Jinnah and his sister Fatimah lived in a pleasant villa:

> Its approaches are jealously guarded by armed sentries, and the whole compound is surrounded by barbed wire. We were received by one of the secretaries, and after our credentials had been established and a short wait at the secretarial bungalow (we were a little before time) we were introduced into the main house. Mr. J. and his sister received us very courteously and gave us tea. . . .
> J. is a man of striking appearance—thin, almost emaciated, with long bony fingers and a strangely shrunken, skull-like head. His voice is low and very beautiful, under wonderful control. The orator, indeed the actor, are clearly a great part of the man.
> Miss J.—with long, white hair and beautifully modelled face—is almost a replica of her brother.[1]

After tea, Miss Jinnah and John Wyndham withdrew and our talk began:

> After some graceful enquiries about Mr. Churchill, Sir John Anderson, Mr. Eden and Mr. Butler, Mr. J. plunged into his speech. This was clearly one which had been delivered before, and was to be considered as a whole. Although much in it was well known to me, any attempt to shorten this preliminary exposition and come to the immediate position was courteously, but firmly, repulsed. It was clear that any anxiety on my part to save his time and spare his health would be resented, not welcomed. . . . J. is obviously a man of frail and nervous type. Work and worry have taken a great deal out of him. He complained at tea of the strenuous exertions of the last year—the long discussions and wrangles with the Cabinet Mission; the move to Simla; the journey to London.[1]

Jinnah at that time was an ageing man, but he clearly had considerable reserves of power, and I felt that the strong will could master the weak body. I was particularly struck by the style and skilful arrangement of his arguments:

> The 'set' speech was admirably delivered—the theme well thought out and the phraseology at once precise and forceful. He

[1] 17 February 1947.

must have been a first-class advocate. One of his methods—no doubt more used in a public meeting, but still not neglected in a private talk—is to lead the listener along a path of a balanced and impartial exposition and then suddenly confront him with the stark conclusion.[1]

Broadly speaking, this was his position:

> A united India, if it is also to be a democratic India, is an impossibility. At different times, by Hindus, Mussulman (he always says Mussulman, not Moslem, Mohammedan, or Muslim) and British, India has been brought into a temporary unity by force. Such a unity has only been made possible by autocracy—benevolent or otherwise. It never has been, and never can be, based upon a real unity of the people. The differences are too great and too deep. They override economic or social divergencies. They are endemic. India is a continent—or sub-continent—not a nation. She can never be a nation.[1]

I ventured to interpose the question 'Why, then, did you accept the Cabinet plan?' He replied that he only did so under the greatest pressure and at considerable risk to his own authority:

> After all, you cannot argue for ever. We argued for weeks and months. Whether there can be a united India is a matter of argument or opinion. Finally I agreed to test it in practice.[1]

He went on to point out the safeguards inherent in the Cabinet plan if it had been followed honestly:

> First, the grouping system; second, the right of the groups to frame their own constitution; third, the circumscribed nature of the subjects reserved for the centre—defence, foreign relations, communications; fourth, the arrangement by which no additional powers could be granted to the centre save by a majority of Hindus and Moslems voting separately in each group; fifth, the temporary and experimental nature of the plan—ten years only, with the full right of review and secession after that.[1]

For all these reasons he had unreservedly accepted the plan put forward by the Cabinet Mission, both the short-term and the long-

[1] 17 February 1947.

term plan, including the creation of an Interim Government and Constituent Assembly. He then went on to expound point by point, with relentless logic and quotation, what he called the bad faith of Congress:

> They had never, at any point in the tortuous history of the affair till today, honestly and without reservation, accepted the plan. They still had not accepted it. But, by great skill in manœuvre and propaganda and by the vacillation and weakness of H.M.G., they had reached the position in which he and his friends were being put in the wrong. It is true that on 29 July he withdrew formally his acceptance—but that was only to protect his own position, since neither Congress, nor the Sikhs, nor the scheduled classes, nor the Princes had accepted. In spite of his protests, the elections were held—Governments were formed; the Interim Government was formed, the whole situation was allowed to develop in a manner quite regardless of the plan itself.[1]

Jinnah was clearly bitter about the treatment which he had received, and especially over the Viceroy's change of position on the formation of a Government and his willingness to overlook the reservations of Congress. (Incidentally, to some extent this confirmed Wavell's own expressions of regret in his last talk with me.)

> Even now in their most recent declaration, the reservations regarding the Sikhs, the references to the right of a province or even part of a province to opt out (before the elections) and various other points, Congress had evaded and twisted the plan.[1]

The situation had therefore changed since the time when he accepted, in all sincerity, the British Government's proposal:

> Reluctantly, believing the fundamental realities to make a united India impossible, he yet accepted for the sake of peace. But Congress never changed or wavered. Their purpose was a united India, to be achieved either rapidly or in stages, in which the Caste Hindus would impose their will and their rule.[1]

Jinnah declared that the British Government could only, in logic and fairness, reach the same conclusion.

[1] 17 February 1947.

While he was speaking, it became clear to me that his policy was now to sit tight and wait:

> If—by threat of withdrawing from the interim and from the provincial Governments—Congress are able to force H.M.G. to drive the Moslems out of the Interim Government and to allow the Assembly to proceed, the League will boycott the whole affair and bide its time. The die will be cast. Nothing can then prevent civil war in India, and chaos and destruction and rivers of blood.[1]

Meanwhile I asked my host what in his view the British Government ought to do. He replied without hesitation:

> H.M.G. are in a very strong legal and moral position. They are still in a stronger physical position than they imagine. They should say to India and to the world, 'We have tried; we have tried almost more than human patience allows or goodwill requires. We asked you to frame a plan. After months of talk you failed. We then framed our own plan. We believed and hoped that you had accepted it honestly. It is clear that you have not, so that plan has failed.'[1]

'Yes,' I said, 'but what next?' Before coming to this he described t he growing weakness of the British and the things we had allowed Congress to do under our eyes:

> First, they were forming themselves into a military organisation. They were using the disloyal officers of the I.N.A. and dismissing or degrading loyal officers. Secondly, they were using all their power in Congress provinces to set up a complete stranglehold on the administrative machine. Thirdly, they were— apparently encouraged by us—allowing a sort of *de facto* independence to come into being. The two provisos of the Cabinet plan—(*a*) the reference to the British Parliament, (*b*) the satisfactory treaty between Britain and India—were being ignored or treated as obsolete. Fourthly, as at Bihar (where he alleges the massacres were organised by the high personalities of Congress) a reign of terror was being threatened.[1]

[1] 17 February 1947.

This, however, did not answer my question. I therefore pressed him for his frank advice as to what the British Government now should or could do. His reply was clear and definite:

1. We could announce that, on a certain date, we could leave India. We had tried to hand over to a well-constituted successor. We had failed. We would go.
2. We could announce that, as all other plans had failed, we would maintain our rule. All advance to independence would cease—for, say, ten years.
3. We could do as we are doing now—let things drift on, till (when our power to intervene had gone but our responsibility remained) the clash would come and India be drenched in blood.

Of these, (1) and (2) he thought only theoretical plans. Neither could be adopted in practice. (3) . . . seemed probable but would be terrible in its effect. It would undo our whole work—of 150 years and more—and bring us material injury and the moral reprobation of the world. The blood of millions of poor, harmless, helpless Indians would be on our head.[1]

There was, however, a fourth course, and it must be done quickly and firmly:

We should announce that the Cabinet plan had failed, since nobody had really accepted it. We should state the facts calmly but relentlessly, sparing no one.

We should ask, however, Sections A, B and C to meet, form a Constituent Assembly for each, and work out a suitable constitution for each. These would then become three separate organisations, independent of each other. They should then be asked to meet freely and decide what arrangements they would negotiate—by treaty, as between sovereign States—for communications, trading, etc., just as Norway and Sweden might do.

Failing the willingness of any one of the sections to follow this course, we should allow [the other] sections to meet and work out their constitution as suggested. For a recalcitrant section, we should work it out ourselves.

Treaties would be freely negotiated between these sovereign

[1] 17 February 1947.

States with themselves and with us. There could be no doubt which sections would wish to range themselves with us.[1]

The sections, or groups, were of course those set out in the plan of the Cabinet Mission. Jinnah had every right to regard it as the one that held the field in spite of the steady drift away from it. His last observation was the nearest he came to suggesting that the Moslem provinces would wish to range themselves in close connection with the Commonwealth and if possible negotiate a definite treaty of alliance with Britain.

With these final words Jinnah brought the interview abruptly to an end. There was nothing more to be said. With a few courtesies and messages of goodwill to his friends in Britain he took me into the garden, where I said goodbye to him and his sister.

> Mr. J. has evidently immense talents. A subtle and clear reasoner and an admirable expositor of his case, he is also (not by any means too common a combination) a man of fundamental sincerity and force of character. Given his underlying assumptions to be true and based on an accurate assessment of the realities, as apart from the dialectics, of the situation, all else follows. If a free and democratic Indian nation is an impossibility, then either there must be the return to autocracy or separation. If, on the other hand, Mr. Jinnah is living in the past; has exaggerated the fundamental differences of Mussulman and Hindu; has not observed the growth of more lasting and deeper divisions, destined perhaps to be more important—such as economic stresses and the like; underestimates the centripetal forces, and the hope that may be felt in a scheme, where the emphasis on state rights is (at the start) so great and on federal powers so slender; if the modern forces, material and spiritual, sweeping through the East are destined to overwhelm and render obsolete these divisions now so formidable, and bridge these gaps, now yawning so wide; then, indeed, the safer and wiser course is to proceed resolutely with a policy of Indian independence and Congress government, even at the risks involved. [But] only those should venture to make this great decision who can draw upon a profound knowledge of Indian affairs or wide experience of Indian life and character.[1]

[1] 17 February 1947.

On the following afternoon I went to the opening of the new Assembly:

> A very interesting performance, rather like a charade imitation of H. of C. Nowhere was the division of the two nations more marked—the Congress Hindus, in their *dhotis* and Gandhi caps, and the Moslems, ranging from European dress and fez, to Baluchistan tribal dress.[1]

The Speaker, after his election, did most of the talking, often answering members' debating points:

> He did not regard the speeches being addressed to him as a mere formality.[1]

This no doubt was the tradition of our early Parliaments when the Speaker used often to deliver long orations and was regarded to some extent as the leader of the House.

In the evening Sheikh Ghulam Hussain Hidayatallan, the Prime Minister, came to call:

> An old and experienced politician, who when Sind was part of Bombay presidency had sat in the Executive Councils of successive governors and resigned from them at appropriate moments.[1]

He seemed to have a pretty good grasp of the political situation and was well acquainted with the leaders of all sides:

> He told me that Mr. Jinnah in old days (when he was a Congress politician) used to reproach him (Ghulam Hussain) for being 'an English stooge'. But he had always held the view that Mussulmen could not have it both ways. They could not at once insult the British and appeal to them for support. Now even Mr. Jinnah could not carry the League with him with any further concessions.[1]

The Prime Minister thought that Jinnah had taken a big risk in agreeing to the Cabinet Mission's plan. This move had proved tactically successful, since Congress had relied upon the League to refuse.

> Now there was no way out. Mussulmen would *not* accept caste Hindu discrimination. They would not exchange masters—and

[1] 18 February 1947.

for the worse. There would be civil war in India, unless we were strong and imposed a settlement.[1]

Nor, in his view, should H.M.G. yield to Congress threats of leaving the Government, either at the centre or in the provinces. He felt that they would not do so in a hurry and gave a somewhat cynical reason for his confidence:

> They had free houses, free servants, free rent, light, heating and Rs.30,000 furniture allowance—and a reputation for simple living. They would not abandon all this. And if they did, someone else would be willing.[1]

His message to Churchill and his English friends was 'Do not be bluffed by Congress':

> All the time the Moslem leader smoked an excellent cigar and drank one whisky and soda after another from H.E.'s stores. In any case old and rather decrepit, it was with difficulty that . . . I helped him down the long passages to his car. He gave me one final dig in the ribs and [a] portentous wink, observing 'There are two nations in India. Those that drink whisky and those that don't.' On this rather cryptic observation, he stumbled and was lifted into the car and left. All the time he wore his astrakhan cap. A fine man.[1]

On 20 February we finally left Karachi. We reached Cairo at 5.30 and went to the British Embassy 'where we saw the news of Attlee's announcement and Wavell's fall. A dramatic end to the story!'

So it was true. The Government had decided to 'quit India' and given a fixed date for their departure. On 20 February, the Prime Minister read a declaration in the House of Commons on behalf of the Government, announcing 'their definite intention to take the necessary steps to effect the transference of power into Indian hands by a date not later than June 1948'. He went on to explain that if the Cabinet Mission's plan proved a failure and a constitution had not been worked out by a fully representative Constituent Assembly before that date, the Government would have to consider whether its powers should be handed over as a whole to some form of Central

[1] 18 February 1947.

Government, or whether in some areas they should transfer their powers to Provincial Governments. They would act in whatever way seemed most reasonable and in the best interests of the Indian people. With regard to the Indian States, the doctrine of paramountcy would end with the transfer of power. In the interval, negotiations could take place between the central power and the Indian States regarding the future. Much had to be settled and much was left uncertain. One thing was determined–the rule of the British Raj would end in June 1948. At the same time, Wavell was to be succeeded as Viceroy by Admiral Lord Louis Mountbatten.

When I reached home a day or two later, I found Churchill and his colleagues engaged in a series of anxious discussions. By far the most well-informed and experienced among us was Sir John Anderson. Although he sat in the House of Commons as an Independent, he had accepted Churchill's invitation to join our deliberations and speak from time to time from our Front Bench. On this occasion, his wide knowledge and the immense reputation which he had earned in India, as well as at home, as an administrator of the first order and as a man of outstanding physical and moral courage, gave him a pre-eminence both in counsel and in debate. Owing to the abolition of the University seats, this was the last Parliament of which he would be a Member. Meanwhile he held an important and even dominant position in the House on the questions with which he was most familiar.

I had got to know John Anderson during the war when I was an Under-Secretary at the Ministry of Supply and often had to attend committees over which he presided. Then I learned to admire his patience, wisdom and firmness. During my years in the Mediterranean I did not see much of him. But after the war I began to form a close friendship with him, which ripened into intimacy and lasted until his death in 1958.

The Government's action had certainly brought the issue to a head. In the debate in the House of Lords, which took place before that in the Commons, Lord Templewood, formerly Sir Samuel Hoare, who had been responsible for the 1935 reforms, described the Government's policy as 'unconditional surrender at the expense of many to whom we have given special undertakings'. Lord

Halifax, whose intimate knowledge of the Indian politicians and statesmen gave him special authority, seemed doubtful and hesitant. 'I have the gravest doubt,' he said, 'about this early fixing of the date in June 1948 ... no one who has ever worked in India can think of these problems ... without a feeling in his heart very much more poignant and painful than mere anxiety. But while it is easy to say: "This is wrong", it is not easy to say what is right.'[1] After expounding his misgivings at length, he ended, however, with a conclusion which, if unexpected, had a considerable effect. Although hedged about with double negatives, it was a declaration which, coming from him, must have given comfort to the Government:

> With such knowledge as I have I am not prepared to say that, whatever else may be right or wrong, this step must on all counts certainly be judged to be wrong. I am not prepared to say that, for the truth is that for India today there is no solution that is not fraught with the gravest danger. And the conclusion that I reach ... is that I am not prepared to condemn what His Majesty's Government are doing unless I can honestly and confidently recommend a better solution.[1]

Many wavering or hostile peers were influenced by Halifax's attitude.[2]

In the House of Commons, the debate did not take place until 5 and 6 March. It was of a very high order. Cripps presented the case with his usual clarity. There were only two alternatives. The first was to stay in India for another ten or fifteen years, hoping in that time to create a situation where we could ultimately give independence to an All-India Government. This was impossible for three reasons. First, because the Secretary of State's Services had been allowed to run down and even temporary recruitment had been abandoned; secondly, because we had not the military forces available; and thirdly, because it placed an intolerable burden on Britain. Why should we have to face all these difficulties because the Indians could not make up their minds? We should warn them

> that there was a limit of time during which we were prepared to maintain our responsibility while awaiting their agreement.[3]

[1] *Hansard*, House of Lords, 26 February 1947.
[2] The Earl of Birkenhead, *The Life of Lord Halifax* (London, 1965), p. 592.
[3] *Hansard*, 5 March 1947.

The only other alternative, therefore, was to fix a definite term to our authority. Surely the most effective way of making the Indians come to some agreement among themselves, either for a unitary system or for an amicable partition, was to bring the pressure of the time-limit to bear.

Anderson, who followed in a most impressive speech, objected strongly to the fixed date. He rejected altogether, or put the responsibility for it upon the Government, the argument based on the weakness in the Secretary of State's Services and on the military position. But he put much greater stress upon the series of events by which the Cabinet plan had been twisted and distorted. He felt that the fixed date would have the opposite to the desired effect and would induce all the parties concerned to be all the more obstinate in negotiation. This was especially true unless there had been some prior decision as to the Government to which we were to hand over power. Was there to be one or two—a united or a partitioned India?

As the debate proceeded, this began to emerge as the main issue. Assuming that we had to go because we had not the power to stay, and taking the situation as it was at this moment, the argument was nicely balanced. It was only upon this—a comparatively narrow question—that the House was formally asked to decide. The Conservatives had put down a reasoned amendment against the declaration, 'which, by fixing an arbitrary date, prejudices the possibility of working out a suitable constitutional plan either for a united or a divided India, which ignores obligations expressed to minorities . . .'. This was defeated by an overwhelming majority.

Nevertheless, many other questions were naturally raised by various speakers, including Anderson, for there were many unanswered questions. There was deep anxiety lest we betray those groups to whom we had given specific pledges, such as the Indian States, the 'depressed classes', the tribal areas and other minorities whom we had undertaken to protect. What, finally, would be the position with regard to defence? Yet there remained the supreme question which even Anderson could not answer. What was the alternative, now that we had been driven or lapsed into a position which we could no longer hold? Could we afford, in the Prime

Minister's words, 'to drift on'? Would it not be better now to accept this course, hazardous and inglorious though it might be?

Aware of this difficulty, Churchill, on the second day, in a speech of wide compass, devoted himself primarily to an account of the actions taken by preceding Governments, including the Coalition Government and the Caretaker Government, which he defended. He argued that the course taken in recent months had been one of continual shift. The Government had now thrown over even the plan of the Cabinet Mission. He made this prophecy:

> The Government, by their 14 months' time limit, have put an end to all prospect of Indian unity.[1]

But what might be the conditions in which we should leave? Gandhi, of course, in the famous 'Quit India' statement, had been willing to face this. He had said, after the Cripps war-time mission:

> Leave India in God's hands, in modern parlance, to anarchy; and that anarchy may lead to internecine warfare for a time, or to unrestricted dacoities. From these a true India will arise in place of the false one we see.[1]

This, declared Churchill, seemed to him indistinguishable from the policy which the Government were determined to pursue. He ended with a sombre peroration:

> It is with deep grief I watch the clattering down of the British Empire, with all its glories and all the services it has rendered to mankind. I am sure that in the hour of our victory, now not so long ago, we had the power, or could have had the power, to make a solution of our difficulties which would have been honourable and lasting. Many have defended Britain against her foes. None can defend her against herself.[1]

Yet whatever might be said of the handling of matters in the last eighteen months, there was much to be said for the Prime Minister's argument when he came to wind up the debate with his usual imperturbability. He declared that we could not go back, nor could we remain as we were. Britain, after all that she had done for India, could do nothing more:

[1] *Hansard*, 6 March 1947.

K

We believe that we have done a great work in India. We believe that the time has come when Indians must shoulder their responsibility. We must help them. We cannot take this burden to ourselves.[1]

If the Government's decision came as a great shock to public opinion in Britain and throughout the Commonwealth, to the Indian politicians and public the new policy seemed hardly credible. While the Press and politicians covered the British Government with praise for their determination to go by a fixed date, there was an undercurrent of scepticism. Was it perhaps some trick, some ingenious device, by which after the Indian politicians had been thoroughly discredited the British might resume their old authority?

Wavell's first act after he received the news of his supersession was of characteristic generosity. He saw both Nehru and Liaqat Ali Khan and urged on them the need for immediate co-operation, expatiating on the greatness of their opportunity. But by the time of the new Viceroy's arrival on 23 March little progress had been made. Lord Mountbatten acted with remarkable rapidity and decision. His almost daily conferences with both Gandhi and Jinnah were proof of the sense of urgency which had been introduced into the internal squabbles of Indian politicians by the British Government's announcement and by the forcible character of this young and vigorous Viceroy. Nevertheless, it soon became clear that those who prophesied that all chance of a united India was now lost were right. Nehru himself made an admission of the inevitability of partition on 18 April at a conference at Gwalior, and seemed to accept that this must involve the partition both of the Punjab and Bengal. The claim of the Moslem leaders to Pakistan was thus rapidly admitted. But a grave difficulty still faced them—what should be the limits of each State? Congress declared that communities that did not wish to join Pakistan should be allowed to remain in India. This, of course, raised at once the future of the Sikhs and Hindus in the Punjab, the problem of Assam and perhaps even that of the North-West Frontier Province, as well, of course, of Bengal.

Meanwhile the situation in the Punjab and in the north-west

[1] *Hansard,* 6 March 1947.

grew steadily worse. Lord Mountbatten's courage in his visit with Lady Mountbatten to Peshawar at one of the most critical moments of the rioting won universal admiration. Such was the perseverance and determination of the new Viceroy, ably supported by Lord Ismay, that by the third week in May a plan had been agreed in principle. It was disclosed in confidence to Churchill and one or two of his most intimate colleagues by Attlee and the Viceroy, who had returned for a few days to London. Following their explanations, Churchill called together the full Shadow Cabinet and as a result, with no doubt much sorrow but without the smallest ambivalence or equivocation, wrote the following letter to Attlee to express the willingness of the Opposition to facilitate the progress of the plan:

21 May, 1947

My dear Prime Minister,
    I have now had an opportunity of consulting my colleagues upon the terms of a possible settlement in India which you and the Viceroy put before us last night.
    As a result I am in a position to assure you that if those terms are made good, so that there is an effective acceptance of Dominion status for the several parts of a divided India, the Conservative Party will agree to facilitate the passage this Session of the legislation necessary to confer Dominion status upon such several parts of India.

Believe me,
Yours sincerely,
Winston S. Churchill

He must have sent it with a heavy heart, for he knew well that it was the end of all our hopes and that the independence of a partitioned India would be secured only at a very heavy price. How heavy, no one knew or could foresee. Attlee replied as follows:

21 May, 1947

My dear Churchill,
    I am much obliged to you for your letter indicating the attitude you and your colleagues would be prepared to adopt in the event of the settlement described to you by the Viceroy being accepted and of legislation being required this Session.

Yours sincerely
C. R. Attlee

Accordingly, when the Prime Minister rose on 3 June to announce the new constitutional plan, he knew that he would receive the support of the Opposition. The basic features were comparatively simple. The Indian sub-continent would be divided into two parts—India and Pakistan. The broad outlines of partition were agreed. The main difficulties arose concerning the provinces of Punjab and Bengal. The future of these provinces would therefore rest with representatives in the Legislative Assemblies. The representatives of the Moslem districts and the others would meet and vote separately for or against partition of the province. A simple majority in each section would be accepted as decisive. If the vote were for partition, a boundary commission would be set up to determine the precise frontier. In Sind and British Baluchistan there would be a referendum as to whether to join the existing Constituent Assembly or form a separate one. The same was to apply to the North-West Frontier Province. The Sylhet district of Assam, predominantly Moslem, would similarly vote whether to adhere to Assam or East Bengal.

Attlee made it clear that the British Government had no intention of trying to suggest, still less to impose, a constitution, even in outline. It would be for the Indians to make their own. With regard to the Indian States, paramountcy would disappear on the transfer of power and the States' destiny would thereafter be in their own hands. The most important new feature, resulting from this rapid agreement achieved by the efforts of Lord Mountbatten, was that the Government were now willing to introduce legislation immediately, in order to anticipate the original date of June 1948. An Act of Parliament would transfer power to the successor States on a Dominion status basis, but this would not prejudice the right of the Constituent Assemblies to decide in due course whether or not to remain in the British Commonwealth.

The Second Reading of the India Independence Bill was an historic occasion. The Prime Minister spoke with his usual clarity, explaining in some detail the various clauses of the Bill. He hoped that the severance of India into two parts would not endure, and that in any case there would be close co-operation between the two new Dominions. He dwelt on the unique character of the Commonwealth and recalled a happy phrase of the Prime Minister of New Zealand 'that the Commonwealth represented independence with something added, not independence with something taken away'.

Churchill was unable to attend through illness, and I was commissioned to speak on behalf of the Opposition. On the general question there was really little to be said. But I thought it right in speaking officially for my party to pay a tribute to the work of those who had served India so well in the past:

> Never, in the long course of history, has an alien nation given so much of its best. Service in India became a family tradition and affection for India a legacy from father to son. Nor should we think only of those who rose to great distinction. To humble members of these services, administrative and technical, to the collector, the commissioner, the health officer, the famine officer, the police, the judiciary, to all these, both British and Indian people owe an immeasurable debt. By the achievement of this period of our rule in India, the British stand justified. Much will be left in the material sense—railways, dams, irrigation schemes, health services and the like—but perhaps the greatest contribution which the British genius has made has been the sense of equal justice, incorruptible and unchangeable, carried out equally for Hindu and for Moslem, for the poor as for the rich, the humble as for the exalted. This has set a standard of equity unrivalled in the history of the world.[1]

The Bill received the Royal Assent on 18 July and accordingly became effective on 15 August. The King, no longer Emperor, sent a message of goodwill to the new Dominions. The price to be paid proved indeed heavy, for riots broke out of a particularly violent and bloody kind in Lahore and Calcutta. In the Punjab the Sikhs were determined on a separation from Pakistan, but they were faced with a bitter choice; when the Boundary Commission reported, allocating Lahore to Pakistan, there was a violent reaction from the Sikh population. There then began the tragic tale of mass murder and arson lasting for many weeks and even months. No one knows to this day the total of casualties involved. It was accompanied by the long streams of refugees across the borders. By 1948

[1] *Hansard*, 10 July 1947.

it was believed that some five and a half million Moslems had crossed into Western Punjab, now part of Pakistan. On the other hand, although this reign of terror dominated certain parts of India, the new system gradually began to take shape. One ulcer remained, and remains to this day, to poison the relations of India and Pakistan—the struggle over the future of Kashmir. This province, of which the ruler was Hindu but the population almost over-whelmingly Moslem, was allocated to India. This decision raised strong opposition in Pakistan and led to something in the nature of a civil war, eventually halted on armistice lines which still remain unchanged. The question was brought to the United Nations in the beginning of 1948. In spite of the efforts of the Security Council and various United Nations commissions appointed to find a solution; in spite of the sincere efforts of British friends to bring the matter to some harmonious end; in spite of long negotiations between Nehru and the successive Prime Ministers of Pakistan, the dispute remains unresolved. It was, in 1965, to lead to the outbreak of war between the two countries.

Although in these years I had no further personal involvement with either India or Pakistan, it may be convenient briefly to record some subsequent events.

In Pakistan, Jinnah, who became the first Governor-General, died in September 1948. He had been the great popular leader of the Moslem League. It was largely due to his influence over the mass of his followers that Pakistan came into being. His death removed a source of stability. Had he lived, Pakistan might have been spared many of its subsequent troubles. Liaqat Ali Khan, the first Prime Minister, was assassinated in October 1951. Perhaps no greater loss was ever suffered by a newly independent nation than by the death under a fanatic's pistol of this essentially wise, generous and moderate-minded man. In India, by a similar outrage, Gandhi was shot in January 1948. His death was a grievous blow to his countrymen and a shock to all the world. Fortunately Nehru remained to govern India till his death in 1964.

It was an encouragement to us all that both Prime Ministers attended the Commonwealth Conference of 1948. Even when India became a Republic in 1950, to be followed six years later by

Pakistan, both were ready to recognise the British monarch as head of the Commonwealth. The general opinion in Britain accepted the view that the Commonwealth, hitherto joined together on a monarchical basis, could and must continue and develop in its new form.

The same pressure of events which brought about the final independence of India led in these years to similar changes throughout the whole area. In none of these was I directly concerned, but I certainly accepted them as a part of an irresistible movement.

At the end of 1946 Attlee announced that Burma was to obtain full self-government by the quickest and most convenient process. There were the usual problems of internal disturbances and of minority tribes or groups. Nevertheless, by the end of 1947 the Royal Assent had been given to an Act to provide for the independence of Burma, which came into effect on 4 January 1948. In accordance with the decision of the new Burmese Government, Burma did not apply for admission to the Commonwealth.

In Ceylon, after a new Constitution granted in 1946, reserving only certain powers—defence and external affairs—to the Governor-General, movement was equally rapid. The new Constitution became operative in September 1947, but by November of the same year the British Parliament passed a Bill giving Ceylon full and unrestricted powers of legislation in all matters. Ceylon, therefore, became an independent Dominion on 4 February 1948 and still remains a member of the Commonwealth.

Plans for constitutional changes in Malaya began to be discussed in the spring of 1946. By the beginning of February 1948 the nine Malay States and two settlements (Penang and Malacca), covering all the area formerly under British rule except Singapore, were formed into the Federation of Malaya, which was to become independent in 1957. Although the new Federation had to face a grim period of disorder through Communist terrorism in a large area, by the assistance of British military forces and the close co-operation between these and the new Government order was gradually restored after a long and painful struggle.

In the Caribbean, where already important constitutional advances had been made, the process was extended in 1949 by a new Constitution for Trinidad, with virtual power to the elected majority. The first negotiations were begun for the West Indies Federation which later, after a short initial experiment, was found in effect to be impracticable. Throughout the whole area the principle of independence and self-government was steadily accepted.

In Central Africa, the same forces were at work. Apart from the question of Federation, the discussions for which were adjourned in the autumn of 1951, almost in the last weeks of the Labour Government, substantial advance was made in both Northern Rhodesia and Nyasaland by the appointment of Africans as unofficial members of the Executive Council and by their direct representation on the Legislative Council.

In West Africa, a new Constitution was approved by the British Government for the Gold Coast, involving virtual independence but leaving ultimate responsibility to the Governor in an emergency. The agitation led by Kwame Nkrumah for 'Dominion status now' led to a state of emergency in the spring of 1950, and when elections were held in 1951 the Convention People's Party, led by Nkrumah, was successful. This territory, therefore, soon to be called Ghana, was approaching formal independence at the period when the Labour Government fell.

Similar developments were taking place in Gambia and Sierra Leone. In Nigeria, a new Constitution came into force in January 1947 by which the elected members became a majority of the Legislative Council. Through the following years until the summer of 1951, frequent conferences were held and committees were at work to plan the next step. The Federation, with its three Regional Assemblies, was promulgated in June of that year; elections were held and a Central Legislature, composed of members elected from the regional legislatures, came into being.

In Kenya, there was already by 1948 an elected majority on the Legislative Council, although the officially appointed members, together with the European representatives, still outnumbered the Africans. If in the peculiar circumstances of Kenya the change was not so rapid, it had begun and was to prove irresistible.

The advance towards self-government also began in Uganda and Mauritius. In Malta, a new Constitution was promulgated in 1947 which provided for internal self-government, excluding only matters of strategic importance.

It will be seen that following the example of India, Burma and Ceylon, the 'wind of change' soon began to blow rapidly through the whole Colonial Empire. The course, therefore, was already set by the time the Conservative Party came into power in 1951. When I became Prime Minister in 1957, advances towards independence had been made on almost every front. If some of the last stages proved especially difficult and perilous, this was perhaps inevitable. Certainly, the most experienced of our Colonial administrators were convinced that nothing would be gained by delay.

One melancholy addition should be added to the record, for completeness. On 18 April 1949 Eire left the Commonwealth. But, as could only happen with Irish affairs, the effect has been almost negligible. The relations between Britain and Eire go on unchanged, with growing rather than diminished respect and affection between the two peoples.

I have not sought in this chapter to do more than describe in some detail those events with which I had some personal connection. But it is right to record how rapid was the movement towards independence in these years, 1945–51, set in motion as a result of pre-war decisions, but greatly accelerated by the war and its consequences. It is often forgotten in controversies about later changes how far we had travelled in the immediate post-war years. The 'wind of change' did not sound the 'bugle of retreat'[1] under my Premiership as a sudden and discordant note. A more friendly critic has declared it to have been 'the reveille to realism and the challenge to meet new problems with initiative and imagination'.[2]

[1] Lord Salisbury in the *Daily Express*, 12 October 1965.
[2] Wheeler-Bennett, *A Wreath to Clio*, p. 59.

CHAPTER X

The Conservative Revival

THE two-party system is essentially English. For more than three hundred years, with some interruptions, it has dominated our political life. We have exported it elsewhere— to Scotland, Ireland and Wales, where it has never been endemic, and older loyalties and fragmentations still survive. In the United States it continues after nearly two centuries, in spite of its growing unreality in terms of political content.

The two great parties may be said to have first taken shape in the Civil War. In spite of their internal divergences of opinion and varying shades of doctrine, Cavaliers and Roundheads represented two distinct approaches to political and religious questions in which can be traced their successors—Tories and Whigs. From the Restoration until the death of Queen Anne, even in an age of unlimited patronage and a limited franchise, General Elections broadly reflected the changing moods of national feeling, especially in the counties. Accordingly, great fluctuations of fortune were suffered or enjoyed by Whigs and Tories, and the tone and temper of successive Parliaments were subject to violent alterations. But with the coming of the Hanoverians, following the ignominious failure of Bolingbroke and Harley in 1714, came also the long Whig predominance. The Tory Party remained divided between convinced Jacobites and the grumbling country gentlemen who connected Whiggery with war and a high land-tax. Throughout the first half of the eighteenth century politics were to turn on the manœuvres of the various sections of Whigs grouped round their individual chieftains, who only occasionally accepted the leadership of an outstanding genius like Chatham. With the accession of George III, the 'King's friends' came into being, controlling nearly 150 votes in the House of Commons and forming an almost separate party. The inglorious end of the American war led to the collapse of the King's power, and the true party system revived. Although the younger Pitt was nominally a Whig, he was in fact the creator of a new Tory Party, which enabled him and his successors to wage the long struggle against Napoleon, and even to maintain their position for fifteen years after his final defeat.

During this long Tory predominance the Whig Party, like the Tory Party, had been divided into factions—followers of Burke or Fox, those who accepted the war and those who were pacifists or sympathisers with Napoleon. After the passing of the first Reform Bill in 1832 the Tory Party suffered a crushing defeat. The triumphant Whig majority seemed destined to hold power for a generation. Yet Peel was able to restore the fortunes of his party within a few years to a point when a discredited Whig Government could only be induced to retain office by their romantic consideration for the feelings of a young Queen. By 1841 Peel's triumph was complete.

Peel was in a sense the first of modern Conservatives. He fully understood that after a serious débâcle a party can only be rebuilt by the character of its leadership, by good organisation, and—to use the modern jargon—a new 'image', involving a revaluation and restatement of policy. The leadership Peel provided himself. His only possible rival, the Duke of Wellington, was ready enough to forgo his claims. The new organisation, as readers of *Coningsby* will remember, was based upon the famous slogan: 'Register, register.' More than a hundred years later this was one of Lord Woolton's main demands upon the constituencies:

> It is necessary to have a marked register; and there is nothing more laborious—or more important—in political organization than the preparation of this register.[1]

Of course in the old sense it meant that Conservative supporters must be induced to get their names placed upon the voting list. In modern times it means careful canvassing in the intervals between elections, so that when the test comes supporters can be cajoled or transported to the poll with smooth efficiency.

[1] The Earl of Woolton, *Memoirs* (London, 1959), p. 341.

In creating a new 'image' for the party, Peel depended upon his own personality as a representative of the second generation of the new commercial class now rising to power. He relied equally on an alteration of the name of the party to Conservative. He thus hoped to escape from the embarrassing tradition of Eldonian Toryism.

Peel dealt with policy by the publication in 1834 of the famous Tamworth Manifesto, perhaps the earliest and most important of such political declarations. By all these measures he tried to bring the party out of the odium of being governed by aged, stupid and reactionary forces, and to put itself forward as the instrument of ordered progress. While the young Disraeli may have jeered at this manœuvre in his famous description of the new Conservatism as 'Tory men and Whig measures', it proved remarkably effective.

It is true that twelve years later Peel destroyed the very instrument which he had created by his sudden abandonment of the protectionist principles on which he had just been re-elected—by the repeal of the Corn Laws. The consequent collapse of the Tory party in 1846 was not due to a mere swing of the pendulum towards the Whigs; it was one of those occasions when a party destroys itself. As a result, the Conservatives, with two brief exceptions when they suffered under all the difficulties and often humiliations of minority Governments, did not recover a true parliamentary majority until Disraeli's great triumph of 1874. The shattering of the Tories by the acceptance of free trade in 1846 led to a collapse similar to that which followed the death of Queen Anne in 1714.

Thus for nearly thirty years the Whig Party, in its various forms, held the field. Once more rivalries developed between the various groups and personalities, with Russells always to the fore. Often no single party held a clear majority and Whig Governments depended on a coalition of Whigs, Liberals, Radicals, and the Irish brigade— a position to which Asquith had to submit after the election of 1910 when the great Liberal majority of 1906 faded away. In the middle years of the nineteenth century the situation was complicated by the fact that nobody was more conservative in the general sense of the word than Palmerston. His ten years' control of Parliament and his wide popularity made Disraeli's task almost impossible. Palmerston certainly knew that the secret of politics was to appeal to middle and moderate opinion.

The Whig Party showed throughout the last century considerable skill in adapting itself to the gradual revolution which it had promoted. The Reform Bill of 1832 had not in fact, as was threatened, destroyed the authority and political strength of the nobility and landed gentry. Even the disappearance of the pocket boroughs had left many constituencies under the influence, if not absolute control, of powerful landowners, in the small boroughs as well as the counties. The Act of 1867 made no substantial difference. But the industrial revolution and the rise of a large middle and upper middle class made it necessary for the Whigs gradually to make some concessions to the Liberals and Radicals. Yet it is noticeable how even in Gladstone's administrations peers predominated over commoners. It is said that a Whig grandee in the middle of the century once remarked that no man ought to sit in a Cabinet as one of Her Majesty's confidential advisers who did not possess a park with deer in it. But the rearguard action was on the whole cleverly conducted. It was only after Palmerston's death that the final merging of the Whigs with the Liberals and Peelites was to take place.

During all this period, with reduced party attachments, the House of Commons itself increased in importance. The debates were on a high level; the divisions uncertain. Owing to the fluidity between the various groups, the Whips were never sure how a particular vote might go. Although divisions were rare, they were often decided for or against a Government by small and unpredictable margins. This indeed was the great period of Parliamentary debate, when the orators were not merely compelled to listen to or deliver speeches with a foregone conclusion, but felt that they might sway the issue. It was the time when arguments and speeches, delivered with that prolixity which the Victorians seemed not only to endure but to enjoy, could persuade waverers and decide the fate of Governments.

After 1874 began the alternation of organised parties with outstanding leaders fighting spectacular duels, and presiding over political machines of steadily increasing efficiency outside Parliament.

It is true that in 1886 the Home Rule issue led to the secession from the Liberal Party of the Liberal Unionists, drawn from both the Whig and the Radical wings, led by Lord Hartington and Joseph Chamberlain respectively. But this was not as fatal a blow to the Liberals as the abandonment of his party's policy by Peel. Although it led to a Conservative reign of twenty years, by 1906 a Liberal Government was returned by the largest majority which any Government was to enjoy until after the General Election of 1931.

The election of 1906 has often and rightly been regarded as one of the greatest blows to the Conservative Party in its history. Yet it is remarkable that within four years, at the two elections of 1910, the Conservative and Liberal parties were equal in the House of Commons. Moreover, the skilful management of the party by Arthur Balfour between 1903 and 1905, so often derided by ignorant historians, served the main purpose which he had in mind. Unlike Peel he was not moved by economic dogma. If in his determination to preserve unity he shed both his protectionist and free-trade Ministers, he preserved his party intact. His great rival Asquith was to see the historic Liberal Party shattered and almost destroyed within ten years of Balfour's ignominious electoral defeat.

The historic continuity of parties is perhaps somewhat shadowy, since policies change and shift. Yet the main themes endure, and men and women are led to adhere to one or other of the two parties by an attitude of mind which is characteristic of successive generations. Continental fashion, based upon the physical shape of the legislative chambers, has introduced the term 'Right' and 'Left', which suits the variety of groups and factions. The rectangular shape of the House of Commons and the practical fact that in every decision the ultimate choice lies between 'Aye' or 'No' has made us favour a two-party structure. Of course, the normal system is subject to the occasional pressures brought about by such unusual strains as Peel and Gladstone were to impose upon their parties and which followed the fall of Asquith.

The Tory and Conservative Party, like the Whig and Liberal, has pursued varying and often conflicting aims. There have been times of reaction or mere immobility and stagnation. But in each successive period great leaders have brought fresh and invigorating thought to renew its vitality. Disraeli, with a more disciplined genius than Bolingbroke's and with an imagination that Peel altogether lacked, restored and re-educated his party. Lord Randolph Churchill, in a dramatic interlude, short and tragically curtailed, made a similar contribution in imitation of the great master. Joseph Chamberlain, Radical reformer and Imperialist, brought with him, in spite of many tribulations, a new fervour and a new appeal, which spread to every class of the population. Moreover, in successive Parliaments there have been reformist groups and progressive thinkers. Conservatism has never become a temple for the preservation and worship of obsolescent doctrines. Indeed, it might sometimes be reproached for being too pragmatic and even opportunist. It has certainly maintained its elasticity, its life and strength, through many failures and disappointments. Few of the great Whig writers and theorists in the first half of the nineteenth century could have believed that the Whig and even the Liberal Party were fated to disappear, or that a hundred years later and after the granting of universal franchise, including women as well as men, Conservative Governments would obtain an increasing measure of power at three successive elections.

A party of the Left tends to gain adherents from newly-enfranchised classes or from radically-minded youth, but must necessarily lose from time to time to the Right. So it proved with the Whigs. As Liberal and Radical pressures grew, a number of the Whigs began to slip over into the Tory ranks. Had it not been for the Irish question, the process would no doubt have been slower. But perhaps it is not unfair to say that many were not sorry to take the opportunity in 1886 to be rid of the dangerous tendencies which they felt more and more dominant in the Liberal Party and escape from the tortuous, yet compelling, pressures of Gladstone's genius. The Liberals, in their turn, succeeded in gaining support from the movements of the Left which were coming into being at the turn of the century. When the Labour Party was founded, as a wholly new political organisation, upon a strange combination of Marxist theory and trade union tradition, the Liberals were able to accept and even patronise their new allies, just as the great Roman legions would welcome the support of slingers and bowmen as skirmishers and auxiliaries.

In the Parliament of 1906 there were some 30 in this new group. Sometimes they were elected as Labour, sometimes as 'Lib-Lab.', in seats where arrangement had been made to prevent a triangular contest. Some, like John Burns, were even brought into the Government. Thus up to the First War the new Labour Party was regarded with neither jealousy nor alarm by the powerful Liberal machine. In 1914 the small Labour Party was split between supporters and opponents of war. To the first coalition in 1915 Asquith had no difficulty or qualms about admitting Labour representatives such as Arthur Henderson and William Brace. Then came the fall of Asquith in 1916 and the forming of the second coalition, under Lloyd George. The Liberal Party was irreparably split—not on policy but on the much more galling issue of personality. It never recovered its unity or its power. Asquithians and Lloyd Georgeites, in spite of certain temporary *rapprochements* between the wars, were never really reconciled. A row between political opponents seldom leaves much bitterness. But an internal feud, like a family quarrel, can be the most lasting and the most deadly. Although Asquith and Lloyd George and their respective families and followers came to-gether occasionally on what might be called a 'wedding and funeral basis', the rift was never mended.

The premature break-up of the Liberal Party prevented what might have been a more natural development involving the com-bination of the Labour with the Liberal and Radical forces in a new party of the Left. It allowed the party which MacDonald and Snowden had founded to seize the vacant position. Thus in the election of 1922, when Lloyd George's coalition fell, 142 Labour Members were returned to the House of Commons. A year later Labour was able to form a Government, although a minority Government. From that date, sometimes in opposition, sometimes in office, the Labour Party became, like the Whig Party of old and the Liberal and Radical Party later, one of the two great parties in the State. It is true that it suffered, in 1924 and again in 1931, grave electoral set-backs. But so firmly based was its wide trade union and working-class appeal, as well as its attraction for those intellectuals who, in the nineteenth century, would have followed Bright and Cobden or Morley and Dilke, that it supplanted the Liberals. It easily consolidated the authority which it had won, partly by good management and partly by good fortune. The old Liberal Party, in a country which is not attracted by a fragmentation of parties and forces, began rapidly to decline. For the nation instinctively feels that multiplicity of parties must lead to the hideous alternatives of a series of weak administrations formed by intrigue and sustained by interest rather than by principle, or the collapse of the Parliamentary system and the rise of some form of dictatorship. Thus the Liberals, although able to secure between 3 and 11 per cent of the votes at various elections, have declined from a party into a group. This is not due to any lack of skill and enthusiasm. It is inherent in the situation. There have been many attempts to form centre parties and coalitions in our history. Except for short periods, they have always failed. Two great parties, under whatever names, will continue to hold the field and, with fluctuating fortunes, to contend for the mastery.

It was with such considerations in mind that I pondered long and deeply over the state of the Conservative Party after the election of 1945. During the late summer and autumn, such time as I could spare from my business was devoted to preparations for an early by-election. Certainly, if Bromley was typical of the general state of the party throughout the country, the heavy defeat which we had suffered was not surprising. Compared with the high membership of experienced organisers and committee men and women to whom we were accustomed in Stockton before the war, the Bromley Association was almost non-existent. There was a popular chairman, and an elderly agent. There was little else. This, of course, was largely due to the war, for nowhere can the devotion to war service of every kind have been more general. But it was also due to pre-war notions of what was needed in political activities. Canvassing street by street seemed not merely novel but somewhat distasteful. Ward committees were unknown. As a result, the large and almost automatic majority which my predecessor had enjoyed in previous elections fell in 1945 to a dangerously low figure. None of this was the fault of the people concerned. They had ambled along easily in security. In pre-war days they considered the seat so safe as not to require any large or active membership. If Bromley was at all typical, it was clear that the Labour Party, with their trade union organisers and their carefully built-up propaganda, in the last two years of the war, had been supported by a machine infinitely superior to our own.

After my re-election, I began to consider the whole problem more profoundly. There were those who said that Labour would be 'in for a generation'; the Conservative Party was 'out for good'. My knowledge of political history made me sceptical about these facile prophecies. I reviewed the past and took comfort for the future. Nevertheless, active steps were needed.

First, there was the question of leadership. In 1846 the party had been left without a leader. Balfour, after the defeat of 1906, had lost not merely the greater part of his Parliamentary support, but even his own seat. The Tariff Reform controversy had confused and almost split the party; and although Balfour was able to maintain himself until after the two elections of 1910, the intrigues against him finally forced his resignation, in November 1911. With Churchill the situation was far different. He was the undoubted and undisputed head of the party. He had led the country to victory out of the jaws of defeat. He was a supreme national and international figure. Yet at the end of the war the people, who felt a deep sense of gratitude to him, would have done anything for him except return him to power as a Tory Prime Minister. They would have acclaimed him as a duke; they would have contributed to build him another Blenheim. But in the post-war mood they did not want him, and still less his political friends. It was clear to an unbiased observer that it was not Churchill who had brought the Conservative Party so low. On the contrary it was the recent history of the party, with its pre-war record of unemployment and its failure to preserve peace. These memories had fatally, although unfairly, impaired Churchill's chances of electoral success.

The question of leadership, therefore, did not arise. It is true that as the years passed there were murmurings both in the Parliamentary Party and among his colleagues. There were even meetings of ex-Ministers to voice their complaints to the Chief Whip.[1] Sometimes the 1922 Committee, the most influential body of Private Members in the House of Commons, became restive. Sometimes there was the feeling that the leader of the Opposition devoted too much of his time to writing history and travelling about the world making speeches of international importance, and too little attention to home politics. All this, of course, arose mainly from the frustrations of our apparent failure to make any progress in the House of Commons or in the country. These murmurings were serious in 1947, but were quieted without much difficulty. Early in 1949, after our failure to win a by-election in South Hammersmith of which we had high hopes, they were heard again. But after the great successes in the spring in local elections, both for the boroughs throughout the country and for the London County Council, which were the first fruits of Woolton's practical work, they were silenced for good.

In any case, such intrigues were foolish as well as unworthy. Any attempt to remove a man whom the whole nation knew to be the greatest Englishman of this or perhaps of any time would have been deeply resented by the country and proved fatal to the party's hopes. Moreover, it would have certainly failed. Anyone who knew Churchill intimately must have realised that he was a man impossible to frighten and equally difficult to dislodge. He knew well that all the cards were in his hands. Any aspiring Brutus would have received short shrift from the public.

Next in importance to the leadership was its name. I felt strongly that just as Peel had strengthened the reputation of his party by the change from Tory to Conservative, so the time was now ripe for a similar stroke. There was certainly no purpose in changing the name unless at the same time a new policy could be launched, adapted to modern needs. I therefore began an agitation on both issues which I pursued with some vigour. The hard work which I had done before the war in promoting the policies contained in *The Middle Way* now began to seem suddenly fruitful.[2] The old

[1] James Stuart, *Within the Fringe* (London, 1967), p. 145.

[2] Harold Macmillan, *The Middle Way* (London, 1938); reissued, with *The Middle Way: 20 Years After* (1966).

ideas sprang once more into life. I preached them in my constituency and in many parts of the country. I hoped that a new name and a new policy would attract the moderate or wavering section of the public. The policy, at any rate, had already proved successful in Bromley. For although the Labour vote had remained uncomfortably high, the Liberal vote dropped disastrously—the same candidate who had polled over 12,000 at the General Election polling less than half that number six months later, in a total vote which was remarkably high.

Accordingly, in the summer of 1946, I began assiduously to develop this theme, by speeches at Conservative gatherings great and small, and by articles in a number of popular newspapers. A widespread practice had grown up of Conservative fêtes or rallies on Saturday afternoons during the summer months. Although these were chiefly intended to attract a wide range of visitors of all parties and ages and of both sexes, providing them with the enjoyment of a varied range of amusements and in the hope of securing substantial additions to the local funds, it was also usual to interrupt the proceedings by a political speech. These gatherings afforded an opportunity, if wisely selected and prudently used, for promoting my ideas. On these occasions ex-Ministers were naturally in considerable demand. So far as the immediate audience went, it was important to realise that the speech was an unwelcome interruption and essentially a tribute to custom or propriety. It was something the audience had to swallow. On the same principle that children are given a dose of medicine between generous provision of lollipops, so the orator was fitted in between more alluring items, such as the Dagenham Girl Pipers or a motor-bicycle display. Nevertheless, if the text were circulated to the Press before the meeting took place, it could be sure, if it had any news value, of wide circulation in the Sunday newspapers.

I chose the summer of 1946 to launch my plan, partly by speeches in my own constituency, partly by articles, but above all at two large Conservative rallies, one at Hatfield and the other at Chatsworth. It seemed to me that these would be suitable places in which to inaugurate my campaign, since the first was essentially a Tory, the second a Whig and later Liberal Unionist stronghold. I was not unduly serious about this affair or very hopeful of its immediate success. My purpose was by calling attention to the name of the party—which I knew would be 'news'—to emphasise the need for a thorough 're-thinking' of policy. Only a genuine process of modernisation and democratisation would enable us to face the problems of the day, and to seek the support of the electorate in due course with any hope of success. Since 1886 the Conservatives had only obtained power by a coalition with the Liberal Unionists. Nor was it until just before the First War that the two groups were finally merged. The Liberal Unionists had brought with them not merely Whigs, anxious about the future, but a new, vigorous, lively group of Radicals and progressives. Now, once more, we needed a party of union, a party which could comprise all that was common to those who rejected Socialism but wanted progress.

At Hatfield, in a speech that caused some stir, I declared that within a few years there would be a strong reaction against the Socialist Government and its ways:

> When the reaction comes we must not fail. We must be ready; we must be armed with the spiritual weapons of unity and faith. The new democratic party—for that is what it will be—must be prepared for its high task. We must cling to all the sound traditions of the past—all that is good and noble.
>
> At the same time, we must have a fierce and passionate faith in the future. But instead of arrogance and malice, we must foster humility and charity. For, united in war, the British people are sadly divided in peace.
>
> The watchword of the democratic party will be unity, and unity will command self-sacrifice in every class and rank and calling. It will seek to create in Britain, not economic slavery in a Socialist State, but true economic and political freedom in a mutually responsible and tolerant democratic society.

This left purposely vague what this democratic party was to be. Was it a new name or a new description? Urgent questions were asked of the officials of the Conservative Party, and the gossip-writers and the cartoonists soon got to work. In the fortnight between the Hatfield and Chatsworth meetings, where I intended to pursue the argument, the newspapers' offices buzzed with the

RECHRISTENING OF BLIMP—*Cartoon by Low*

conflicting accounts of what my ideas really were. One of the happiest results was a glorious cartoon by Low illustrating the 'Re-Christening of Blimp'.

By the time the Chatsworth meeting took place the political reporters and commentators were on the alert. I repeated the same sentiments, and with the same lack of precision. I wanted a new policy, or at any rate a policy re-thought to fit modern conditions; I wanted to rally all classes to a constructive and progressive programme, forgetting the divisions of the past. After all, a great gulf stood between us and our predecessors. Years of war had changed the aspect of the whole world and confronted us with new and vast problems. Surely some of the old prejudice could be forgotten too?

> The great dividing-line is between those who believe in the prime Socialist dogma—the nationalisation of all the means of production, distribution and exchange—all, mark you, not selected and suitable undertakings, but all—and all those who see in such a development the grim nightmare of a Totalitarian State.

Against these crude dogmas I felt the great body of our citizens

> wished to see a solution of modern problems which would secure both freedom and order. Such a solution would be based on the principle of balance, of moderation, of the middle way.

I went on to say that in that great army stood first and foremost the powerful Conservative Party; with them were already ranged the National Liberals.[1] On that fundamental issue would also be found the official Liberals, for whom at the last election two and a quarter million votes had been cast. In addition, many who had voted Socialist were now beginning to doubt. Surely men and women of moderate opinion could on this fundamental issue be rallied to our cause. But they must not feel that the Tory or Conservative Party demanded a forced or reluctant conversion. They wanted free allies. It should be a new union, and it might well be that its new inward spirit should be given the outward and visible sign of a new name.

A wide and often animated discussion of these matters did nothing but good. It called attention to a much larger issue than the

[1] This section of Liberals had ranged themselves with the Conservatives since the General Election of 1931.

name of the party—that of its principles and its policy. My modest intervention achieved my main purpose. In the years that were to follow, a new Conservative Party was to be created, spiritually attuned to the life of the post-war world and the new society.

In the summer of 1946 Lord Woolton accepted Churchill's pressing invitation to become chairman of the party. Woolton had never been a Conservative. He had always been an Independent with a Liberal background and tradition. He has himself described how he only joined the Conservative Party on receiving the news of its overwhelming disaster in the election of 1945. No more suitable choice could have been made for this post. Woolton was not only a great organiser, but he was also the best salesman that I have ever known. His wisdom, charm, generosity and genuine kindness made him admired by all and loved by his friends. In addition his name was a household word. As Minister of Food throughout the most difficult years of the war, he had managed in an almost miraculous way to keep the people contented on the barest rations on which they had ever been—till then—asked to live. I think it was because, unlike many men in high positions, and certainly most bureaucrats, he made people feel that he really cared about them, There was hardly a housewife in the whole country who, whether or not she approved the recipe for 'Woolton pie', had not got in her mind a happy image of a beneficent old gentleman who would certainly have given her anything he had. In addition, in his wife. Maud, we gained a priceless asset, for she was loved wherever she went—and she went everywhere.

Woolton agreed with me about the name of the party, and often discussed it with me. He knew well that the word 'Conservative' seemed somehow unattractive to the mass of the modern electorate, and especially to those who had looked forward through the bitter years of the war to a new and exciting world:

> Large numbers of Conservatives were trying to find a new name for the party because 'conserving' seemed to be out of joint with this new world that was demanding adventure and expansion and a rejection of the economic restraints of the pre-war life of this country. . . .[1]

[1] Woolton, p. 334.

He would have preferred to call the party the 'Union Party':

> That, indeed, is its proper title, representing unity of the Empire, the essential unity between the Crown, the Government, and the people, and embracing the idea that is certainly true of this country, that we dislike class conflict almost as much as we dislike either the vague internationalism of the political senti-mentalist or the foreign creeds of Marxian Socialism or Russian Communism. We are very like a family—indulging in times of security in much diversity of opinion; in times of pressure, or emergency, or of danger, quickly and strongly united.[1]

Nevertheless, he took the view that a party could only afford to change its name at a period of success, not at a moment of failure; through strength, and not at a time of weakness. (Unfortunately, when that time comes, there are always many more pressing prob-lems.) When we came to the autumn conference of the party it was clear that this was the general view, and he accepted it. But he tried to deprive our opponents of the advantage of their name by always calling them 'Socialists' and not 'Labour'.

Woolton's inspired management of the party machine was one, if not the principal, cause of our ultimate success. He was able with supreme skill to control everything himself and yet give the impression that he left everybody alone to carry out the responsi-bilities which he had placed upon their shoulders. He realised, moreover, that a political party, like a religious or charitable in-stitution, consists almost entirely of voluntary workers. When he became chairman he was surprised and even shocked at the loose and confused structure which he had inherited—a large number of independent or semi-independent groups and no well-thought-out method of co-ordination. The system had grown up bit by bit. His first instinct was to scrap the whole thing and start again. The National Union of Conservative and Unionist Associations had been largely built up by Randolph Churchill as a rival to the power of the leaders and the Whips, then armed with complete and un-challenged authority. It had now become a loyal and vital part of the whole. Together with similar semi-independent bodies grouped round the centre it performed two functions. It encouraged the

[1] Ibid.

enthusiasm and interest of individuals, without which any voluntary organisation collapses, and prevented any section or individual obtaining undue power. In any case, Woolton believed that he could make the system work in practice:

> The truth was that whilst it seemed, on paper, almost ridiculous to call this an organization, what mattered was not machinery, but people, and like so many other British institutions—which highly intelligent foreigners fail to understand—this organization at the Central Office had in fact grown up around a lot of very hard-working and faithful members of the Party, and, by its decentralization, was fulfilling the primary function of any good political organization by its work in the constituencies.[1]

Apart from general problems of organisation, one of the most pressing matters was that of the selection of candidates. More than twenty years before I had been struck by a passage in a speech by Baldwin. It was at a party meeting after his defeat at the General Election of 1923. He told us that we had learned our lesson and could have learned it no other way. We must take it to heart and apply it. He remarked upon the appeal which the Labour Party made to the young, and the opportunities which it offered. He went on:

> Now there has always existed in our party a desire to choose a rich man as candidate. But if you must have a candidate who can water his constituency with £1,000 a year you are going to have a choice of about half per cent of the population, and if you are going to fight a party that has the choice of the whole population, you will never beat them in this world, and, more than that, you will never deserve to beat them.[2]

Unfortunately, neither Baldwin nor his colleagues took any steps towards reform. Many of us had long resented the system by which certain seats, generally the safest, often fell into the hands of men who were of little use to the Government as back-benchers and still less as potential Ministers. If not openly for sale, they not infrequently fell into the hands of twentieth-century nabobs. I remember being told by a friend of mine, who had rather unluckily lost his seat in 1929, that he had applied for a constituency where

[1] Woolton, p. 333.   [2] G. M. Young, *Stanley Baldwin* (London, 1952), p. 74.

there was a very large Conservative majority. He was gratified to find that his name was among the first six of the many aspirants. He was duly summoned to attend, and he and his competitors were hospitably received by the chairman of the association. He had expected that each would in turn be asked to address the members of the association, at a meeting at which at least three or four hundred would be present. He had duly prepared himself for the ordeal. To his surprise it appeared that no such procedure was intended. The chairman explained that he thought that a number of speeches of this kind would be rather a bore and wholly unnecessary. He then placed upon a table a top hat. 'Now, gentlemen,' he explained, 'if each of you will write on a piece of paper what will be the amount of the annual subscription which you would be prepared to make and how much you would contribute to the election expenses on each occasion, and place it in this hat, I think this matter might rapidly be settled in a very agreeable way. You will then, I trust, be my guests at dinner.' And so the choice was made. My friend was not successful, but the dinner was first-class.

As part of the reforms which were introduced under Woolton's chairmanship, this question was firmly dealt with. It was one of many subjects referred to a committee over which David Maxwell Fyfe presided. The report was unanimous and decisive. In future there were to be no financial barriers of any kind to candidates; the amount a candidate might subscribe to supplement funds was restricted to £25 a year; a Member of Parliament could give up to £50 a year. All election expenses, which previously fell largely, if not entirely, upon the candidate, must be met out of constituency funds.

> The change was revolutionary and, in my view, did more than any single factor to save the Conservative Party. It raised alarm as well as enthusiasm. Treasurers who had relied considerably for their income on their wealthy Members of Parliament wanted to know where they were going to get enough money to pay for all that I was demanding. The reply was simple— from the rank and file of the Party; people respect the things for which they pay. We had taken the vital step; the Conservative Party had determined to rely for its subsistence on its own local

members; it had become at least as broad-based as the Socialist Party—and there was work for everyone to do. Here was Tory democracy in action. The way was clear for men and women of ability to seek election to Westminster.[1]

The results were twofold: the first entirely healthy, the second perhaps a little more doubtful. The effect of throwing all the financial burden upon the constituency was in every way salutary. Although it created some alarm among constituency chairmen, it forced them no longer to look outside for assistance, but rather to aim at being self-supporting, and later to accept the duty of providing their quota towards the central funds. But there was one aspect of the reform which was not so satisfactory. By the endorsement of the full independence of the constituency organisation in the adoption of candidates, the Central Office and the leaders of the party virtually abandoned any control over their selection. There was a nominal power of veto which rapidly became obsolete, except perhaps in some very special cases. There followed, as Maxwell Fyfe himself has pointed out, a tendency for local associations to use their freedom without sufficient thought to the interests of the party as a whole. This was especially the case in the safe seats:

> . . . . and far too many of them were obscure local citizens with obscure local interests, incapable—and indeed downright reluctant—to think on a national or international scale.[2]

He added a further criticism:

> What made the situation particularly annoying was that many excellent candidates, who would have made first-class Members and probably Ministers, were left to fight utterly hopeless seats not once, but two and even in some cases three times, while the safe seats went to men of far lower calibre. This was to cost the party dear.[2]

Nevertheless, the reform was essential at the time, and in spite of some drawbacks has proved generally beneficial. The complete freedom of choice given to the constituencies was an inevitable consequence of the new and heavy responsibilities which Woolton placed upon them with good humour, but bland insistence.

[1] Woolton, p. 346.   [2] The Earl of Kilmuir, *Memoirs: Political Adventure*, p. 158.

By the same insinuating methods he succeeded in introducing a new plan to improve the standing and remuneration of the party agents. This reform threw considerable expense both upon the local organisations and the central funds, since it included the institution of a proper pension scheme. But it was an essential part of the re-construction of the party machine. He also gave generous encourage-ment to the growth of the 'Young Conservatives', who began rapidly to expand in numbers and efficiency until they became probably the strongest youth movement in Europe.

Woolton's next move was in the sphere of local government. He realised that owing to our opponents having long decided to treat this as a party affair, we must, however reluctantly, conform. Although in many ways regrettable, this decision was inevitable and politically sound. For the selection of candidates and the fighting of local elections played an invaluable role in building up the strength of the Conservative associations. Up to now we had not faced this issue, leaving the Socialists to be opposed by 'Indepen-dents' or 'Ratepayers' associations' or similar bodies. Together with the decision to contest local elections on a party basis went the creation of a local government organisation at headquarters and an increased interest in the party as a whole in local problems. It was also an opportunity for attacking centralisation. 'Town hall, not Whitehall' was a typical Woolton slogan. He also insisted that the first day of each party conference should be devoted to local govern-ment discussions and debates.

All these reforms, of course, cost money. In addition to those activities directly under Woolton's control, he had to provide for those which were under Butler's management—the revived Research Department which Neville Chamberlain had begun in 1929, but which had disappeared during the war. It was now greatly enlarged in scope and functions. There was also the Conservative Political Centre, founded at the end of May 1945 on Butler's initiative, which acted independently of the Central Office with its own publications, and in a sense played the role of a Conservative Fabian Society. Both these grew steadily in authority under Butler's imaginative leadership. They were outside the control of the Central Office and separately housed. In Woolton's own words they were 'altogether independent except when the bills came in'. For all these various efforts, as well as for the general work of the party, centrally and locally, large sums had to be raised. The new chairman had placed upon the local associations almost alarming responsibilities involving in most cases at least doubling or trebling their existing income. Woolton therefore launched a national appeal for funds. Here again he showed his remarkable knowledge of human nature. He toyed with the idea of asking for some modest amount, but decided that the higher the target the more likely he was to hit it. So the £1 million fund was launched and the total reached.

I took little part in these developments, although since Woolton and I were neighbours in Sussex I often used to have a chance of discussing them with him. The only point that I tried to press upon him was based upon my own experience, especially in Stockton. Elections, we used to argue, were won not in the public halls and at meetings large and small; they were won in the street. They were also generally won or lost before the election took place. My wife, who became both expert and indefatigable in this work, knew and was known in almost every house in Stockton, more especially in the poorer quarters. She was respected by all and loved by many. I remembered that at the beginning of our adventure in the North of England more than twenty years before, we had found that coming as strangers this was the only way to make ourselves known and to gain adherents. It was equally important to enlist a band of enthusiastic supporters, who would go out into the streets week after week and be regarded by the people not merely as supporters of a political party but as friends. Of course, many other Members in those years adopted similar plans, and gradually the system began to expand and be refined. The committee members in each ward knew and were known by every member of the street or streets appointed to their care. Woolton was soon persuaded that

the battle was going to be one not of public platforms and large halls and cheering crowds and processions, but the hard and dreary round of door-to-door canvassing by people who knew what they were talking about. . . .[1]

[1] Woolton, p. 361.

This technique, which he subsequently called 'Operation Door-Knocker', became a fundamental part of the new Conservative approach to the electors.

Moreover, he fully understood how important it was that canvassers should be well informed and intelligent. Stupid and ignorant canvassers could do an enormous amount of harm. It therefore became essential that all so employed, especially the 'Young Conservatives', should be well supplied with arguments, not merely from the pamphlets which they were distributing, but from real study. This was achieved by the Conservative Political Centre, the so-called 'two-way movement of ideas', the summer schools, the weekend schools, and the lectures and study groups. The social activities of party organisations, both for the young and the middle-aged, must continue as an attraction and a relaxation as well as a means of raising money. But Woolton rightly regarded them as a means to an end. The missionaries of a party, like those of a church, must be well informed as well as enthusiastic.

With an undisputed leadership, with future candidates likely to be more widely and democratically selected, with a party organisation gradually arising from the ruins of the past to a strength unsurpassed in its long history, there remained the creation of a new 'image'. This must depend upon the formulation and popularisation of new policies, based indeed on old principles but adapted to new and changing conditions.

There were many who were in grave doubt as to whether these tactics were correct. They believed that we should win back power partly through the normal swing of the pendulum and partly as a result of the mistakes and misfortunes of our opponents while in office. These views found advocates among experienced politicians as well as among the more old-fashioned Members, strongly represented in the safe seats and still in the full vigour of their incapacity. Churchill, while favouring the propounding of new ideas, as shown by the Zürich and Fulton speeches, feared that the elaboration of too detailed proposals might be merely to give a 'hostage to fortune'.[1] This has indeed always been a hazard for parties in opposition. If

[1] J. D. Hoffman, *The Conservative Party in Opposition, 1945–51* (London, 1964), p. 110 and *passim*.

their policies are sensible and moderate, it is not impossible that they may be filched by the Government of the day. After all, the clothes of Tory bathers can as well be stolen as those of Whigs.

There was general agreement that what were called the principles of Conservatism should be restated and fortified. Yet some thought that we should rest content with their famous exposition in Disraeli's Crystal Palace speech of 1872, when he laid down that the Tory Party had three great objects: 'To maintain our institutions, to uphold the Empire, and to elevate the condition of the people.' These were admirable on a broad basis, the last being especially impressive at the time. But they were really insufficient for the situation more than seventy years later. Nevertheless, apart from general principles, a distinction could be drawn between a policy and a programme. A detailed programme always has disadvantages; it should at any rate be reserved for the election manifesto. But such a programme should not be framed out of the blue. It should follow naturally from policy statements, approved by the leader and confirmed by the party conferences in the years between elections. Such declarations should try to cover ground somewhere between principles and programme. But they should be sufficiently precise to make a real impact. I was determined to do what I could towards this end. It might well be that when the election came we should use very similar arguments to those deployed in the past. But they must be put forward by a party which had acquired, by its actions and restatements of policies in the meantime, a reputation for prescience as well as moderation and for being in touch with the needs and moods of the age. This we had notably lacked in 1945. Above all, the party must reconcile itself to the need for a mixed economy and for a synthesis of free enterprise and collectivism. In other words, publicly and privately, I continued to promote the theme of *The Middle Way*.

Such a restatement of policy was likely to find strong support among the younger members of the party, especially by Quintin Hogg, Peter Thorneycroft, and others who had collaborated in the Tory Reform Group during the war. By our candidates it would be especially welcomed. But it would be wrong to suppose that those who adhered to traditional concepts, particularly on foreign or Imperial issues, were hostile to new ideas on economic and social questions. Indeed, for the policies which I advocated during these years I gained much support from friends whose orthodox Toryism no one could suspect. I received, for instance, a remarkable letter from Lord Cranborne[1] in the spring of 1946 which admirably expressed this view:

So many Conservatives tend to be negative. They are agin the Socialists. That is not enough nowadays. The greatest danger today is the apathy of the rank and file of the Conservative Party, an apathy which comes from a spirit of discouragement and defeatism. They see Socialism being riveted on them every day that passes, and they don't see what is to be done about it. The only alternative to this is an alternative progressive policy. That is where men like you can help. Personally, I see our future in a spreading of capitalism. The fault of the Capitalist system seems to me to be not that there are too many capitalists but too few. We want to have more people owning their own houses, farming their own farms, sharing in the control of the industries in which they work. I know that it is very easy to state this general principle, and far more difficult to give it practical application. But I believe that it is the line of progress that we should study and advocate.

The discussion of the party conference at Blackpool in October 1946 showed the general demand for a restatement of Conservative policy, particularly on industrial questions. Accordingly, a committee was set up to produce a considered document. Of this Butler acted as chairman. Oliver Stanley, Oliver Lyttelton, David Maxwell Fyfe and I represented the Front Bench. We were assisted by Derick Heathcoat Amory, David Eccles, Sir Peter Bennett and Colonel James Hutchison from the back-benches. The secretaries were David Clarke, Reginald Maudling and Michael Fraser. Together we constituted a powerful and representative group. We met frequently and, apart from our work on the committee, we made visits to the industrial areas and held talks with leading Conservative industrialists and trade unionists. My field was the North-

[1] Later 5th Marquess of Salisbury.

L

East of England, including Newcastle and Leeds. Others went to Liverpool, Manchester, Cardiff and so forth. I recall with admiration the skill with which Butler presided over our discussions and steered us through many difficulties. There were some amongst us whose minds were naturally more cautious than others, but the interplay of argument was always stimulating. We were fortified by some of our number who had long industrial experience.

After the document was drafted, it was sent to Churchill. I was surprised at the attention he gave, not merely, as one might expect, to the drafting but to the substance. With some amendments, his general approval was given and the document was published in May 1947. Although, naturally, many of its proposals seem rather dated now and many proved impossible to put into legislative form, there is no doubt that the publication of this document was a landmark in the history of the party. Some supported it with enthusiasm and some opposed it as 'Radical' and 'semi-Socialist'; others believed that it could never be implemented. But it was generally regarded as both courageous and politically wise. While reasserting the need for freedom and private enterprise at a time when regulation and nationalisation were being vigorously pursued by the Labour Government, it nevertheless presented a coherent picture of the roles of capitalism and collectivism in a mixed economy. With other similar documents published in the following year, it proclaimed the theme which inspired the thirteen years of Conservative government which followed the final overthrow of the Socialists in 1951.

The 'Industrial Charter,' as it was called, proved our determination to maintain full employment, to sustain and improve the social services, and to continue the strategic control of the economy in the hands of the Government, while preserving wherever possible the tactical function of private enterprise. Our purpose was 'to reconcile the need for central direction with the encouragement of individual effort'. We also accepted as irreversible the nationalisation of coal, the railways, and the Bank of England, and the impossibility of unscrambling these scrambled eggs. The final section comprised the so-called 'Workers' Charter', of which the general object was 'to humanise, not nationalise'; to create security and status for industrial workers with continuity of employment and defined contractual rights.

The principles laid down in this document guided our policies in the future Conservative Governments. Many of the detailed proposals have been translated into law. Monopolies have been dealt with, at least to some degree; price maintenance has been abolished with rare exceptions; many of the provisions for improving the status of the workers have been given legislative effect. Nevertheless the importance of declarations of this kind, especially from parties in Opposition, lies not so much in the detailed proposals as in their general tone and temper.

The reaction of the metropolitan Press was not unexpected. The *Daily Mail* and the *Daily Telegraph* were enthusiastic, *The Times* ambivalent. The *News Chronicle* was critical, finding the proposals 'too obviously prompted by the desire to attract the Liberal vote'.[1] The *Daily Express* and the *Evening Standard*, after an uncertain start, became increasingly hostile, acting no doubt under Lord Beaverbrook's directions. As usual, the provincial papers were much more intelligent in their criticisms; on the whole they were favourable. Among the weekly journals, the *Spectator* hit the mark. It found that the Charter removed 'the last excuse for labelling the Conservative Party as at present constituted as reactionary'. The *New Statesman and Nation*, *Reynolds' News* and *Tribune* were of course hostile. The last prophesied that 'before the year is out the Butler Charter will split the Tory Party as it has not been divided for half a century'.[1] As the days passed, Lord Beaverbrook's attack became more and more vicious, and he was joined by some of the more obscure papers of the Right.

In the House of Commons a number of Conservative Members were critical and alarmed. The leader of this school was Sir Waldron Smithers, who fondly believed himself to be a good Tory, but in fact held opinions on economic and social matters indistinguishable from those of the Manchester *laissez-faire* school in the middle of the nineteenth century. The point to which they most objected was the acceptance of the nationalisation of coal and railway transport as irreversible. But even before the party conference in October,

---

[1] Hoffman, pp. 152–3.

the attack began to waver. Lord Beaverbrook's papers continued to be hostile, sometimes in leading articles and, more effectively, in the gossip columns. 'Crossbencher' in the *Sunday Express* was particularly virulent. Broadly, those elements in the party which followed consciously or unconsciously the Whig or the older Liberal tradition were opposed to the new Conservatism. The true Tories accepted it with growing enthusiasm.

Inside the party and in academic and intellectual circles, Butler managed affairs with extraordinary skill. Backed by the highly gifted members of the Research Department, he had been largely responsible for the development of the new policy. He defended it with equal knowledge and subtlety. A great part of the burden of public speaking in favour of the charter and of counter-attacking its opponents, in whatever quarter, fell on my shoulders.[1] I was only too happy to undertake this task because it seemed to me that the policy and character of the party were now almost miraculously developing on the lines that I had preached during those sterile years between the wars. To this end I spoke at meetings all over the country and wrote a number of articles in the Press. This was all the easier for me because it had been my consistent theme in earlier months. For instance, in the previous autumn I had declared our intention to put forward a new industrial and economic policy in the light of modern conditions:

> Whether it is to be called a new policy or not, I do not know. It is certainly in the true tradition and philosophy of Conservatism at its best. The broad division between the Opposition and the Government is now beginning to appear in a precise form. The Socialist Government talks about planning, but it is more and more apparent that they do not understand, and certainly do not apply, its principles. They confuse the roles of the State and the individual. By attempting too much, they risk achieving too little. . . . [Our policy] is based upon the theme of co-operation between Government and industry. It insists on each playing its proper part. It will require a new sense of partnership between ownership, management and labour. The distribution of property is the basis of democracy, not its concentration in fewer and

[1] Hoffman, p. 157.

fewer hands—least of all centralised ownership by a semi-totalitarian State. It is by the separation, not the confusion, of functions that we shall find our way through the many dangers which threaten us.[1]

> Socialism leads inevitably to Totalitarianism. German Socialism led to Nazism. Russian Socialism led to Communism.
> The British tradition, to be found equally in Toryism and Radicalism, rejects the inevitability of the class war and insists upon the essential unity of the nation.[2]

I had also insisted on the need for a new relationship between capital and labour:

> The problem of industry is only partly economic; it is largely moral and psychological. The cure is to be found in a new code—if you like, a new charter—by which capital, management and labour shall work as a team, in healthy and genuine co-operation for a common purpose.
> In peace, no less than in war, a house divided against itself cannot stand.[2]

With regard to nationalisation, I had continued to follow the line of *The Middle Way*:

> Nationalisation of industry does not solve the human problem. A great State monopoly is no better—in some ways it is worse—than private monopoly. We are against monopoly—public or private.
> That is not to say that there is no place for the State in industry. Of course there is. But with a few exceptions, when special conditions prevail, that place is at the centre, not the circumference. The Government must settle the broad strategy of policy.[3]

Accordingly I declared:

> We believe that the State exists to serve the people; not the people to serve the State. We want to level up, not level down.

[1] Speech at Epsom, 23 November 1946.
[2] Speech at Truro, 9 April 1947.
[3] Speech at Wandsworth Town Hall, 24 April 1947.

We do not want to abolish property, but to make it more widely distributed.

We believe in real democracy, political and economic. In every country it is becoming more and more apparent that Socialism and democracy cannot live together. One means tyranny, benevolent or otherwise. The other means the cultivation of Freedom and Progress.[1]

After the publication of the Charter, partly as a result of my prewar reputation and partly in answer to my many public speeches, the attacks of the Press began to be centred upon me. In spite of my affection for Lord Beaverbrook, I was forced to reply:

The *Daily Herald* complains that the Industrial Charter is not really Conservative policy. So do the *Daily Express* and the *Evening Standard*, the twin voices of Lord Beaverbrook. Now Lord Beaverbrook is a man of great qualities, public and private. As a Minister in time of war he rendered incomparable service to the nation. But his judgement has not always been right on political questions. . . . He accuses me of having seduced the Conservative Party into a progressive statement of policy. I would gladly accept the blame for this, if it were blame. But in fact there has been no seduction. The Industrial Charter is merely a restatement in the light of modern conditions of the fundamental and lasting principles of our Party.

Finally, among the critics we have Sir Herbert Williams and Sir Waldron Smithers. With them are associated other gentlemen for whom time does not merely stand still but, if anything, runs backwards.

So all the forces of reaction in the country, the *Daily Herald*, Lord Beaverbrook, Sir Waldron Smithers & Co., are united in saying that this Industrial Charter is not Tory policy. What they really mean, all of them, is that they wish it were not Tory policy. Fortunately, their wishes cannot be granted. In any case, important as our critics may be, I prefer to rest upon the tradition of Disraeli, fortified by the high authority of Churchill.[2]

These objections I summarised in a phrase which was widely repeated:

[1] Speech at Wandsworth Town Hall, 24 April 1947.
[2] Speech at Church House, Westminster, 14 June 1947.

The Socialists are afraid of it; Lord Beaverbrook dislikes it; and the Liberals say it is too liberal to be fair. What more could one want? Was ever a child born under such a lucky star?

There was one comment which gave me special pleasure. It was a criticism by 'Crossbencher' which seemed in fact a compliment:

This report is a triumph for Mr. Harold Macmillan. [He] once wrote a political treatise called *The Middle Way*. This is the second edition.[1]

So the battle raged inside and outside the party. But every day that passed it became more and more apparent that the tactics of our opponents would fail. When we came to the conference in October, Woolton with his usual sagacity made it clear that there was to be no attempt by the leaders to enforce the Charter upon an unwilling or doubtful body of delegates. Churchill had given his general blessing; the conference had every right to discuss and come to its own conclusion.

I had long experience of Conservative conferences before the war, and in those days the main body of the delegates were definitely representative of the diehard rather than the progressive wing of the party. They were accustomed to view with distrust and alarm any concepts outside the established orthodoxy of the day, more especially if they were put forward by the more youthful section. It was largely due to Woolton's reforms that in the conference of 1947 and in those of succeeding years the delegates represented either a moderate or a definitely progressive point of view. Hence, when the question of the Industrial Charter came to be debated, they were not content with a mere acceptance of these new ideas as a general guide or a contribution to the subject. They called for a more precise endorsement. By a series of amendments to the original motion for which Peter Thorneycroft, supported by Ian Orr-Ewing, was mainly responsible, a far more definite formula was approved. The conference was not satisfied with merely welcoming the Charter as a basis for discussion, but accepted it 'as a clear statement of the general principles of Conservative economic policy.' A further amendment, by Maudling, amounted to full approval. The Young

[1] *Sunday Express*, 15 May 1947.

Conservatives were especially enthusiastic. Thus, as a result of our three months' campaign, the opponents, who at one time seemed likely, with the help of the Beaverbrook Press and the rallying of similarly reactionary forces, to constitute at least a formidable minority, were reduced to one or two dissident voices.

In his own speech to the conference, Churchill, while still unwilling to enter into details, gave firm support to the new Conservatism which always appealed to him sentimentally, since it seemed to be a return at the end of his long and colourful life to the Tory democracy of which his father, Lord Randolph, had been the pioneer. This endorsement completed the struggle for the Charter with all its implications for the future of Conservatism.

The success of the Charter and its virtually unanimous acceptance by the party marked an important step in Butler's career. During the war he had gained high regard among all parties for his success in devising and carrying through Parliament an Education Act which marked an important advance in the development of national education. He had shown his diplomatic qualities by the skill with which he negotiated at least a temporary settlement of the problem of the Church schools, Roman Catholic and Anglican. His work in guiding the unfolding of the new Conservatism placed him in the first rank of the party's leaders.

If the Charter marked an important and even revolutionary stage in the development of Conservative thought, it was not without its attractions to moderate Labour and Liberal opinion, at least among the rank and file. In Churchill's own words:

> It is a broad statement of policy to which all who are opposed to the spread of rigid Socialism can now rally.

In the course of the continuing campaign I continued unblushingly to appeal for Liberal aid. Perhaps the most dramatic setting in which I was able to argue on these lines was at a gathering at Hawarden Castle in September 1947. This meeting was presided over by Charles Gladstone, Mr. Gladstone's grandson and Squire of Hawarden. It seemed indeed strange that such a gathering should be held in these hallowed surroundings. There may have still been some who could recall the thousands of Liberal pilgrims who used to assemble in the famous park to pay homage to the Grand Old Man and to listen to his splendid rhetoric. This holy soil of Liberalism was now, at Charles Gladstone's own suggestion, made available to support what in his opinion was the only effective body capable of fighting Socialism. Charles Gladstone had been a housemaster at Eton and a personal friend, since my son had been in his house. He had made his position clear in a letter to *The Times* which was simple, straightforward and convincing.

I stayed with him on the Friday night until the Sunday afternoon. It was indeed an extraordinary experience for me actually to be living in this historic place of which I had heard so much in my childhood from John Morley and others of my father's friends. My host assured me that the great man's library had remained untouched since his death. He had given away his theological collection, which was extensive and valuable, and many other books, but those which remained and the study in which he lived and worked had been unchanged for some fifty years. I noticed with curiosity, and almost incredulity, that among the busts that ornamented the room was one of Disraeli. This seemed to me so strange that I questioned Charles Gladstone about it. He assured me that it had always been there with those of Pitt and other famous men. I wondered why Gladstone had had this representation of a man whom, if he had been capable of so un-Christian a feeling, he must almost have hated. Was it to warn him against the dangers and temptations of the evil one? Or did he stick pins into it as a magical device? The mystery remains unsolved.

In his speech, Charles Gladstone made it clear that he had never identified himself with any political party or taken any part in politics. He was a Liberal by tradition and by conviction. He was one who looked for the greatest possible measure of freedom for every human being in all stations of life:

> People asked, 'What would Mr. Gladstone think of things today and what would he think of the Liberal Party?' That was a matter for speculation, but I would ask in counter what would Lord Salisbury think of the Conservative Party today? What would Mr. Disraeli think? They might suggest that the Conservatives had stolen a great deal of the old Liberal thunder. I

believe that to be the truth. I believe that the Conservative Party represents all that was best in the old Conservative Party, the old Liberal Party, and a great deal of all that was best in the old Labour Party before it was infected by the intellectual theorists.

Naturally I followed this lead. I reminded them that over a year ago, at similar gatherings, I had put forward a plea for the re-alignment of political forces in the country. In every nation in the civilised world there were two powerful and opposing themes: on the one hand, the various forms of the Socialist creed; on the other, the broad democratic ideal.

Here, at Hawarden Castle, from one of the sacred places of Liberal principle and tradition, I ask this question. What divides— at this moment—the Liberal and Conservative parties? What separates them? Nothing—except the memories of the past. Each has made great contributions to the political and social progress of the nation. Each seeks to find a solution of modern problems which will secure both freedom and order. Each seeks a balance between individual rights and the claims of the com-munity. Each recognises that social justice requires us to secure for every individual a firm basis below which he and his family must not be allowed to fall. Each equally demands, as well as security for the worker, increased opportunity, combined with real incentive and enhanced status. Each, moreover, condemns with equal vigour the grave mishandling, by the present Socialist Government, of our internal and external economy.[1]

I have often thought about that meeting held in the garden of that famous house with the old ruined castle on the hill looking down upon us. It was one of the oldest parts of Britain, with Roman Chester nearby and long traditions of conflict and struggle between contending forces through the generations. Some thought that his grandson had perhaps been disloyal to the great man's memory. Many more applauded his courage and sincerity.

Certainly, Mr. Gladstone's personality seemed to pervade the whole place—house, garden, and park—the latter still boasting many fine oaks which had escaped or not been ripe for his axe. But, above all, when I went to Communion Service early the next day there

---

[1] Speech at Hawarden Castle, 6 September 1947.

was a living proof that his influence and the strength of his faith still remained. For the little country church was crowded with worshippers.

After the 'Industrial Charter', further policy documents were compiled and published under Butler's guidance. The next landmark was *The Right Road for Britain*. It was the work of a committee of which Eden took the chair and Butler, Salisbury, Woolton, Maxwell Fyfe and I were members. I took a lively interest in this and did my best to press forward on a progressive and imaginative line, circulating a number of papers to my colleagues and sometimes appealing to Churchill for his support. This document was largely derived from the policy statements which had gone before. But there were new and important sections on foreign affairs and on the social services. This was the last of the series, and when the final manifesto was published for the General Election of 1950 under the title *This is the Road*, it was little more than a condensed version of the longer statement.

These activities in effect crowned Woolton's work of reorganisation. The choice of candidates; central and local finance; independence of local associations; the improvement in the position of agents; the entry into local government politics; the new devices for propaganda by every means: all these would not have succeeded in re-establishing the confidence of the people as a whole in the Conservative Party had it not been for the remodelling and restatement of our policies. We had to convince the great post-war electorate that we accepted the need for full employment and the Welfare State; that we accepted equally the need for central planning and even, in time of scarcity, physical controls. We had to devise and publicise a position in between the old Liberalism and the new Socialism. I was conscious, of course, that many of the Right wing of the Labour Party were working on a similar synthesis. Morrison, for instance, had long realised that the Labour Party could not otherwise obtain and still less maintain political power. Equally, it was essential for us, apart from any detailed plans or proposals, to present this new picture of modern Conservatism. Nor were we doing more than following in the footsteps of the greatest of our predecessors. We, too, had to 'educate our party'.

All this was a source of great satisfaction and even some little pride to me. For the leaders of my party and its members as a whole had now broadly accepted the policies for which I had so vainly striven in the past.

The need to expound the new policies made heavy demands upon Conservative Members, especially former Ministers. Almost every weekend was occupied by a speech in some part of the country, often involving long and tedious journeys. These, together with my work in the House of Commons and in the European Movement, as well as the managing of my own business, made life pretty strenuous. However, these were happy years. My children were married, grandchildren were beginning to appear, and our life at home and among our friends was gay and stimulating. But we were all glad when the time of the General Election approached.

On 10 January 1950 Attlee announced the dissolution of Parliament, with polling day on 23 February. We were prepared and hopeful. Nevertheless, we realised that we had a formidable undertaking in front of us. The Government had a majority in the House of Commons of 166 over the Conservatives and 136 over all parties combined. To overcome so great a superiority in a single election and to obtain a working majority for ourselves would be difficult and almost unprecedented.

Every General Election appears to those engaged in it as candidates to be of outstanding, if not unique, importance. All are said to be turning-points in history. In fact, with few exceptions, they are rather tame affairs. In this, the first real test of the post-war electors—the election of 1945 had been fought under unusual conditions—Woolton rightly determined to avoid personalities and keep the argument upon the high level of conflicting principles and policies. Although those accustomed to the old knockabout methods found the campaign 'decorous' and even 'sedate', the high poll (at 84 per cent) showed that the lack of rowdyism and excitement was due not to the apathy of the electors but rather to a serious approach to their responsibilities. Nevertheless, we did not escape some irrelevancies. The Labour Government, in their policy document *Labour Believes in Britain*, had announced plans for the nationalisation of sugar, cement, meat distribution, cold storage and the chemical industry. Not unnaturally, the managers or proprietors of these undertakings had carried on a vigorous campaign through the winter by posters, newspaper advertisements and other methods to resist these threats. This roused the indignation of Morrison, who seemed gravely shocked by the unhelpful attitude of those who were about to be expropriated: 'Cet animal est très méchant; quand on l'attaque, il se défend.' Accordingly he declared that all the costs of these sinister activities would be charged against the permitted expenses of Conservative candidates. Woolton wisely advised firms to stop their advertising from the moment of the dissolution until after polling day. But Lord Simon, an ex-Lord Chancellor, and David Maxwell Fyfe, an ex-Law Officer, disputed the soundness of Morrison's law. However, it all proved a trumpery affair. Although it caused considerable excitement among politicians the public was unmoved.

Churchill conducted a powerful campaign with remarkable energy. As usual he attacked his opponents with gusto. Although Morrison, on whom the burden of reply chiefly fell, clearly enjoyed the contest and bore no rancour, Cripps reverted to his pre-war form with personal jibes at Churchill for his age. With sly humour, Churchill riposted by issuing a formal denial of reports that he had died.

There were the usual political broadcasts by the leading figures. But Woolton wisely selected for one of the three allotted to us Dr. Charles Hill,[1] known to millions of listeners as 'The Radio Doctor', who was standing as a 'Liberal and Conservative' candidate. It was undoubtedly the most effective in the campaign. For Dr. Hill it proved the preface to a distinguished and successful political career.

The Liberals, after great wrangles between the different sections of the party and against much pressure from local associations, which in many cases would have preferred agreements with us, finally put up 475 candidates. This was a disappointment after all our efforts to woo them. But since they polled only 9.1 per cent of the electorate and only 9 were elected (319 forfeited their deposits), there can be no doubt that a large number of Liberals did in fact vote for Conservative candidates.

[1] Later Lord Hill of Luton.

Since my own position in Bromley was reasonably secure, I devoted many days to speeches in different parts of the country. One of the advantages of not having reached the front rank is that one's speeches are seldom given national publicity at a General Election, when there are so many more distinguished competitors. This allows one to make more or less the same speech with the necessary adaptations. These were in the main devoted to expounding the policies which I had worked so hard to promote. My own election address was simple enough:

A sound political policy must be firmly based. It must rest upon a spiritual as well as a material foundation. Men and women have both duties and rights. They owe a duty to God and to their neighbours (or, to use a modern phrase, the State). These are their responsibilities. They also have a duty to themselves and their families. These are their rights.

The excessive individualism of the *laissez-faire* age underemphasised man's duty to his neighbour, and exaggerated the rights of the individual man and family.

The Socialist (or Collectivist) doctrine similarly neglects the rights of the individual and inflates the rights of the State.

Both of these extremes are wrong, being based on a materialist philosophy and without moral foundation. One leads to anarchy; the other to slavery.

The right course is *The Middle Way*, to combine Progress with Freedom.

I wrote these words in my address to you four years ago. I see no reason to change them.

Two pages followed, in elaboration of this theme.

I found that in general this moderate line was acceptable to audiences, with, of course, a suitable sprinkling of jokes and wisecracks, chiefly directed against the extremists on the Labour side. Indeed, Bevan and Shinwell, for all their charm and sincerity, proved a real blessing. Englishmen do not much like a man who stigmatises as 'vermin' his opponents, who after all constitute about half the nation; or one who declares that he does not care 'two hoots' for any but his own supporters. Indeed, one of the interesting features of the 1950 election was the movement of both parties towards the centre. Of the 100 Communist candidates all but three lost their deposits; and the extreme Left-wing Labour members who had been expelled from the party, such as D. N. Pritt, John Platts-Mills, Leslie Solley, and Konni Zilliacus, failed altogether.

The campaign ran its course without any particular stunts. Emotion was to be reserved for a thrilling finish. For some reason, only some 260 seats' returns came in before the early hours of the next morning, and little could be deduced from these except by the real experts. The declaration of the result in Bromley took place on the afternoon of 24 February. During our count, other results were coming in all the time, and it soon became clear that it would be a neck-and-neck race. Bromley had now been divided into two, Beckenham and Penge being constituted a separate constituency. The electorate, therefore, was reduced to some 50,000 voters. My own majority of 10,688 was more than satisfactory. When we went along after the declaration to the offices of the association, we found a crowd of people watching the returns with breathless excitement. At three o'clock the gap had narrowed to fifteen; at four it was six; at a quarter to five, one; at about five o'clock the parties were equal. The ding-dong contest continued until the Labour Party began to draw away, and by eight o'clock it was certain that there would be a Labour majority. The final figures gave the Conservatives and their allies, the National Liberals, 297 votes in the new House of Commons and Labour 315. There were nine Liberals returned. Thus the Government majority was reduced to only seventeen over the Conservatives and National Liberals and six over all parties combined. Since on any issue of confidence the nine official Liberals would certainly support the Government, there was a clear, but not what was in those days regarded as a working, majority.

Taken over the whole electorate, the swing to the Conservatives was 3 per cent. Those who regarded democracy as merely the raw material for psephologists naturally felt that this was a disappointing result after all our efforts. But statistics are often misleading. In Middlesex and the Home Counties generally, the swing was between 7 and 8 per cent; in London it was over 5 per cent. Naturally, in the strongly-held Labour constituencies—the coal-fields and the older industrial areas—the swing was non-existent or less than the average. The national percentage, therefore, did not really represent the true result either factually or psychologically. It was patent that there had been a great change of mood and temper since 1945. Then 'Labour' had swept the country and was confident of retaining power for a generation or more. The Tories were a beaten army and almost a rabble. Now, after nearly five years of Socialism, the Government had been returned by only a minimal majority. It is true that in the redistribution of seats we gained some twenty-five by the abolition of the old Labour pocket boroughs, which the movement of population had left almost deserted. On the other hand, the university seats had been abolished, involving the loss of two outstanding personalities, Sir John Anderson and Sir Alan Herbert. But, whatever the figures, it was clear that the tide had turned.

The General Election of 1950 was universally regarded as the prelude to another round. Attlee properly declared that 'the King's Government must be carried on'. But the question on everyone's lips was 'for how long?'[1]

[1] Earl of Kilmuir, p. 170.

CHAPTER XI

Decline and Fall of Labour

THE new Parliament lasted longer than many superficial observers thought probable. It was opened on 6 March 1950 and dissolved on 5 October 1951 – a period of nineteen months. The interval between the two General Elections was therefore greater than the tenuous nature of the Parliamentary majority on which the Government depended seemed likely to allow. The reasons for this were twofold. In the first place, great political parties, like championship boxers, need a respite after one fight before they can re-enter the ring, partly to recoup their strength and partly to collect sufficient financial backers for another contest. Secondly, great changes had taken place in the organisation and solidity of Parliamentary parties. In the nineteenth century no minority Government or one depending on a slender majority could continue in office for any length of time except with the goodwill of their opponents. But the more recent development of the party system had resulted in a much tighter control. The fluidity which had characterised former periods had now become frozen into the strict mould of party loyalties. The independent Members on the Left had almost disappeared; on the Right they were becoming less numerous and influential. Even the dissidents and the discontented could easily be brought into the lobby like patient sheep when the fate of the Government was involved. The 'whipping' on both sides was efficient and merciless. Time after time the hopes of the Opposition were to be disappointed. Nor was it possible to see, at any rate in the opening months, any chance of forcing another election.

Against that event there was a good deal of talk among Conservatives of trying to secure not merely a Liberal abstention but a definite Liberal alliance. For this we must find a suitable basis:

> There is a great deal to be said, in principle, for an experiment in Proportional Representation, limited to the big cities. It could do no harm and might do good. How else are the great Socialist 'blocs' to be eaten into? It seems absurd that an immense and dangerous change like steel nationalisation should be made effective by a majority of six. A capital levy, of any extent, could be carried in the same way.[1]

Nothing came of these ideas, although Churchill seemed to favour them. Meanwhile, the Liberals in the House of Commons almost always voted for the Government; or, on those issues on which it was impossible for them to do so, gave the Government Whips sufficient notice of their intention to avoid any danger or mishap. On other occasions they found it easier to divide their small numbers into two or even three groups, some voting for the Government, some against, and some abstaining. Their sole purpose seemed to be to prevent an early defeat of the Government.

All these uncertainties led to a high degree of tension throughout the Parliament. However strong our feelings had been from 1945 to 1950, we were then in so hopeless a minority that there was no element of surprise in the steady march of overwhelming majorities against us. Now there was always the hope of a lucky division turning in our favour. Yet even in the spring of 1951, when the Government was seriously shaken by the loss of some leading Ministers and the resignation of others, the Labour Party stood together:

> We are to put a motion forward next Tuesday on the raw material situation. This will not be a vote of censure; yet, if it were carried, I think the Government would fall. It has been carefully framed to make it very difficult for Bevan, Wilson, Freeman, etc., to vote against it.[2]

But in vain was the snare laid:

> It seemed hardly possible that Bevan, Wilson & Co. would vote *against* this motion, as it was couched almost in their own words. However, Bevan announced (in a few words only and reserving his right to speak later on the whole subject) that he would vote for the Government.[3]

[1] 5 October 1950.   [2] 25 April 1951.   [3] 1 May 1951.

Already by the autumn of 1950 I had sensed the growing grip of the party machines and the Whips' office. When I was called upon to wind up the debate on the Address, on which there was to be another of these tense divisions, I observed that although we prided ourselves on 'government by discussion', we must frankly admit that there were very few occasions when discussion seemed to influence votes. Accordingly, 'for the purposes of influencing a Division a doctor may be more important than an orator'.[1] I went on to remark that although independence seemed to be disappearing from Parliament, there was a growing number of electors who owed no party allegiance. While we were forcing ourselves into an increasingly rigid mould, we were really the creatures of those independent men and women who decided the result of elections, the fate of politicians, and the fortunes of Governments and parties: 'We are anchored to our political destiny by the floating vote.'[1]

As each vital debate arose, the newspapers speculated on the results, unconscious of the fact that there could be little doubt except by the chance of illness or unavoidable absence affecting one side more than the other. In February 1951 I had been taken ill and therefore missed the greater part of an exciting week. Churchill had made a strong attack on the steel nationalisation proposals. But when the division came,

> The Government (after all the newspaper speculation as to the possible effect of influenza) won by 10 votes; seven Liberals voted with us. The figures were 308 to 298. Every vote (except mine) was accounted for. These are really extraordinary figures— such as no one remembers—and indicate the growing strain on all sides. Every more or less ordinary division in the committee stage of a second-rate bill is working out at 450–500 Members present. On these 3-line Whip occasions there are, of course, no ordinary pairs. Only the dying are paired nowadays![2]

The next day the majority fell to eight; another Government supporter had fallen ill and I had returned. But the Government clung on.

> Of course, some may die; but unless those with uncertain seats choose to die, it's no good. There is said to be one dying

---

[1] *Hansard*, 7 November 1950.   [2] 9 February 1951.

now; but with a majority of 20,000, it makes a farce of it. Moreover, those who are older and presumably most likely to collapse under the strain, generally have the safest seats.[1]

On 1 March 1951, in an all-night sitting on the Service Bill, the Left wing of the Socialist Party made a serious attack on one of the clauses:

> The 'comrades' kept up a running fight till the early hours, including some pretty wounding references to former speeches of Socialist Ministers. After Clause 6 had been disposed of, we had an amendment in Clause 7 which we pressed to a division, and voted 84–82 (down by 2 votes).[2]

When we came to Clause 12 I got up and opposed it, although we had put no motion to that effect on the order paper. I hoped that some of the Government supporters, expecting no more divisions, would have slipped away.

> This manœuvre was not altogether successful, but did result in a tie: 82–82. Naturally, the Chairman of Committees gave his casting vote for the Government.
> And 'so to bed'.

The next day we beat the Government on a Private Member's motion by four votes.

> Since this was a very important subject—shortage of raw materials—and the President of the Board of Trade (Harold Wilson) chose to deliver a great speech, the defeat was a blow.[3]

But it was not mortal.

In the middle of March 1951, on my return to England from a short visit to Scandinavia, I found the House in an extraordinary condition. It was

> completely out of control, like an unruly class under a weak French master. Everyone freely insults each other and combines in insulting the Speaker. I have never seen anything like it before. Each day, after Questions, there are long wrangles on questions

[1] 9 February 1951.   [2] 1 March 1951.   [3] 2 March 1951.

of procedure or privilege. . . . The Government have persuaded the Speaker to intervene in the selection of standing committees. These, and other petty internal disputes, are argued with passionate violence.[1]

By this time all kinds of injuries were being inflicted on our country from many parts of the world. Yet with so narrow a majority, a spirit of partisanship and conflict prevailed:

> We have no power, no credit, no authority abroad. But we can quarrel like fun at home. Coming back (after only a week's absence) into this atmosphere is like entering a madhouse.[1]

So it went on day after day:

> I do not remember quite such a sense of strain between the parties since the old days of the General Strike and the Trades Dispute Bill. To add to the confusion, the Speaker is clearly breaking up. He has always regarded a late sitting as a sort of personal affront. [As a result] his rulings are attacked and argued about, and he allows general talk about them to go on, for sometimes half an hour at a time. Late at night, he alternates between weak appeals and weaker threats.[1]

There followed abstruse arguments about the use of 'prayers' – that is motions to rescind a particular Order in Council – which at that time could be moved after the normal time for the House to adjourn and go on more or less indefinitely through the night. In despair at the success of our tactics, Wilson

> announced that if the Tories insist on 'prayers', he will stop all trade negotiations which might require new 'orders'.[2]

This was a curious blunder, of which Churchill made effective use in the grand style. So the wrangling went on. I was responsible for a phrase which achieved some notoriety:

> 'This kind (that is the Government) goeth not out save by Prayer and Fasting.' The nation has for some time been doing the fasting. Now it is for the House of Commons to try the prayers.[2]

[1] 12–17 March 1951.   [2] 20 March 1951.

In June 1951 we had a sitting of nearly twenty-two hours, lasting from Thursday afternoon until after noon on Friday:

The Government majority was between 8 and 20 (mostly about 10) all through. Churchill stuck it out, much to the delight of the party, and voted in every division.[1]

In July,

We beat the Government by a majority of 3 on Committee stage of the Forestry Bill. Not a great victory, but a mild irritant to them, which will mean that they will put out 3-line Whips for every day and all day till the end of the session.[2]

The public were not, I think, much impressed by all these scenes, and in some ways they proved to our disadvantage. But in the circumstances they were inevitable. The intensity of political warfare grew steadily as the Parliament proceeded. Churchill, who remained at heart a boy, loved the opportunity for a rough and tumble. But perhaps, in view of the approaching election, he also wished to demonstrate his strength and vitality in spite of his seventy-six years:

Conscious that many people feel that he is too old to form a Government and that this will probably be used as a cry against him at the election, he has used these days to give a demonstration of energy and vitality. He has voted in every division; made a series of brilliant little speeches; shown all his qualities of humour and sarcasm; and crowned all by a remarkable breakfast (at 7.30 a.m.) of eggs, bacon, sausages and coffee, followed by a large whisky and soda and a huge cigar. This latter feat commanded general admiration. He has been praised every day for all this by Lord Beaverbrook's newspapers; he has driven in and out of Palace Yard among groups of admiring and cheering sightseers, and altogether nothing remains except for Colonist II[3] to win the Ascot Gold Cup this afternoon.[4]

If for these nineteen months the House of Commons was amusing and often exciting, I fear that our behaviour did not add much to the dignity of Parliament. In the earlier Parliamentary periods this

[1] 6–8 June 1951. [2] 16 July 1951.
[3] Churchill had started racing, and this proved a very successful horse.
[4] 16 July 1951.

would perhaps not have been regarded as unusual. But the growth of the power of the executive during the war had produced a feeling that to harass a Government by Parliamentary methods was somehow not playing the game. However, it was a pastime which Churchill thoroughly enjoyed.

Throughout all these Parliamentary scenes Attlee retained his characteristic self-control, sometimes amounting almost to nonchalance. In the course of these months not only was he himself attacked by illness, but he suffered the loss of two of his most important and most loyal colleagues—Bevin and Cripps.

Herbert Morrison, who had proved a successful, almost triumphant, leader of the House of Commons and a tower of strength to the Government both in Parliament and outside, succeeded Bevin as Foreign Minister. In this role he was less happily cast. His speeches, admirably attuned to raising party enthusiasm in a crowded House, and his talent for political propaganda and organisation were quite unsuited to the more difficult, because less manageable, problems with which he was soon to be confronted. I never felt that he was at ease in the Foreign Office. He was out of his depth, and seemed conscious of his inability to grasp the fundamentals of the issues or to suit his style of oratory to his new position:

> A long and rather boring foreign affairs debate. Herbert Morrison read out the same *tour d'horizon* sort of speech which the F.O. boys used to write for Ernest Bevin. But at least E.B. used to interpolate here and there some gruff and idiomatic phrases of his own (much to the alarm of the young men in the box).[1]

Morrison was, however, quick to grasp the internal political opportunities in any foreign situation. When the Persian and Egyptian troubles began, he tried hard to entice Churchill into an attitude which he could denounce as 'warmongering'.

But Morrison certainly did not seek the Foreign Secretaryship. Indeed, his appointment was scarcely fair to him, and his unimpressive performance in what he himself calls 'the most onerous peace-time job in government'[2] was no doubt one of the reasons

[1] 25 July 1951.   [2] Morrison, *An Autobiography*, p. 273.

why he failed to obtain the leadership of the Labour Party after Attlee's retirement. This was a bitter blow, for he had every reason to regard himself as the great organiser of the victory of 1945, and the natural heir and successor to Attlee.

Cripps was followed by Hugh Gaitskell, who proved an admirable choice. Although his speeches tended to be something in the nature of economic essays, yet his manner was conciliatory and he soon won the respect of the House as a whole. I watched his progress with growing interest. When he came to his Budget, which was in general both sensible and honourable, he gained for the first time a national reputation:

> Gaitskell, the new Chancellor of the Exchequer, was a pupil of Dr. Dalton. He has imitated his rather pedantic style, tedious exposition of the obvious, weak gestures, and irritating smile. But if he is Daltonesque in manner, he is Crippsian in matter. The speech was a success; having all the elements which make a speech successful today. . . .
> The broadcast was even better.[1]

Undeterred by his exiguous majority and growing pressures, internal and external, and the loss of his most notable and loyal colleagues, Attlee nevertheless held on with courage and determination. He had indeed to face new and unexpected perils. These arose overseas, but in each case had immediate and dangerous reactions upon the home scene. The British economy, already over-stretched, was subjected to additional strains which were to threaten a serious crisis, or even collapse, by the autumn of 1951. He was confronted in turn by the outbreak of the Korean War, the seizure of British oil installations in Persia, and the anti-British developments in Egypt. Of these, the second was after years of negotiations satisfactorily adjusted; the third contained in it the seeds of many future troubles. But the first, the Korean War, had immediate and profound repercussions on both the economy and the Labour Party.

After the final defeat of Japan in the Second World War, the occupying forces of Russia and America had met in Korea and halted

[1] 10 April 1951.

on the line of the 38th Parallel. In April 1946 a conference was held between the representatives of the two powers, which failed to reach agreement on the question of reunifying Korea. After a further year's delay the delegates reassembled. Once again, no solution could be found. The United States thereupon put the matter before the United Nations, and a commission of that body was appointed to supervise elections for a constituent assembly. The U.N. Commission duly arrived in South Korea in January 1948, but its members were not allowed to go north of the dividing-line. Nevertheless, elections were held in the South, and a suitable proportion of seats were reserved for the North Koreans should they be ready to attend. The invitation was, however, refused, and a 'People's Republic', with all that this sinister appellation had come to imply, was set up in the North. Both the Russians and the Americans agreed to withdraw their armed forces. By the end of 1948 the Russians claimed to have completed their evacuation. They had, however, left behind them in North Korea a Russian-trained and equipped North Korean army of some 125,000 men. Six months later the United States completed their own withdrawal, leaving a constabulary of 50,000 South Koreans to preserve peace and order. Throughout the rest of the year border clashes were frequent, and by the end of 1949 units of Koreans trained by Chinese Communists were beginning to re-enter North Korea. There followed an uneasy peace, watched with some alarm by the Americans, but not generally regarded as likely to prove a serious danger. On 25 June 1950, however, the North Koreans launched a strong attack across the 38th Parallel. At the request of the United States the Security Council met immediately. This body was in the happy situation of being boycotted by the Soviet Government, on the ground that China was still represented by the exiled Government of Chiang Kai-shek in Formosa. In the absence, therefore, of a Russian veto it was possible to obtain a unanimous vote demanding the withdrawal of the North Koreans and calling on the assistance of all member nations. Two days later President Truman announced that United States air and sea forces would be sent to help the South Koreans in defending their territory. On 2 July the Americans committed ground forces in addition. Within a few days forty-eight States agreed to give some kind of support—armed, economic or medical. By the end of the year fourteen nations had actually sent some military contribution. Britain first undertook to send naval and air units, and soon promised an army contingent. In accordance with a recommendation of the Security Council, the nomination of a Commander-in-Chief of all the U.N. forces rested with the American Government, and General Douglas MacArthur, the hero of the Japanese war, was appointed to the post.

Attlee had no hesitation in meeting what he regarded as a direct challenge by a Communist-controlled power: 'This is naked aggression and it must be checked.' His speech included the words 'I am certain that there will be no disagreement, after our bitter experiences in the past 35 years, that the salvation of all is dependent on prompt and effective measures to arrest aggression wherever it may occur.'[1]

The House supported the Government's decision without dissent. Nor did the Ministers fail to point out that the Communist attack was only one manifestation of Communist pressure. We ourselves were faced with a similar threat in Malaya. Although some Labour Members were critical about sending troops to this distant scene of war in view of all our other commitments, yet Parliament and the nation rallied to the need for action. Indeed, there was a moment when many of us thought that the consequential effects, both as regards defence and rearmament and on the economy, would be so serious that there might well have to be a new Coalition before we were through. It was for this reason that the Government's decision in September to go ahead with the last stages of steel nationalisation, and force this party measure through an emasculated House of Lords, was so bitterly resented by the Conservatives. From that moment our debates continued with unabated animosity, and all hopes of a concentrated national effort to meet the new emergency were inevitably doomed.

The first British troops, small in number but representative of the national determination, arrived at the end of August and were soon expanded into a Commonwealth division, which fought with skill and courage throughout the campaign. By the middle of

[1] *Hansard*, 27 June 1950.

September the United Nations forces had reached the 38th Parallel and had ejected the invading troops. But the Americans then determined to make a drive across this line to the Chinese frontier. Accordingly, on 9 October, U.N. forces crossed the 38th Parallel. Throughout October the battle swayed to and fro. A massive and impressive counter-attack by Chinese 'volunteers' forced the U.N. troops back to their first positions and even beyond. There was considerable alarm at the strength and ferocity of the Chinese and North Korean armies and their effective handling. By November the issue was still in doubt:

> It seems today as if MacArthur's optimism was misplaced, for the papers tell us of a great N. Korean counter-attack, in which anything between 100,000 and 200,000 Chinese may be involved—in other words, the American war with China has begun. It may, of course, be that the Russo-Chinese plan is to involve the Americans and their allies as deeply as they can in this Far Eastern adventure, and then turn the heat on somewhere else. It is said that Iraq is repudiating her treaty with Britain. This may be followed by Persia becoming troublesome. The Russians might then be tempted to start a drive in the Middle East, where the prize is really great—[the] oil supply in the Old World.
>
> Meanwhile, with typically British escapism, the House of Commons is thoroughly enjoying itself discussing whether the Festival of Britain amusement park should or should not be open on Sunday afternoons.[1]

At this juncture, a reported observation by the President resulted in acute alarm in the House of Commons:

> It appears that President Truman, in his usual Press Conference, was asked about the atom bomb. He said 'it is under consideration'. (This was afterwards explained to mean that it, like everything else, was always under consideration.) One would have thought that Parliamentarians would have taken this well-worn phrase (or cliché) as a synonym for doing nothing. However, it seems to have thrown the Labour Party into something like

[1] 27–28 November 1950.

panic. A circular letter to the Government soon obtained over 100 protesting signatures.[1]

Finally, at the end of a day unlike anything since Munich, Attlee announced his intention to leave immediately for Washington:

> This decision, announced in the Commons, caused the same hysterical reaction as when Chamberlain made his famous flight.[1]

Meanwhile, the vast Chinese armies were pouring in and no one seemed to know whether the Anglo-American troops would be able to form and hold a defensive line:

> What is to me almost more alarming is the 'wishful thinking' of our people. No one seems to understand the close alliance between Communist China and Communist Russia. I am very sceptical indeed of the idea that China can be detached by kindness.[1]

A more serious objection to Britain being deeply committed in the Far Eastern war was a military one:

> Our weakness (that is, of the Free World as a whole) is so marked, that it is surely very risky to get involved more and more deeply in this part of the world front.[1]

Some feared a new Russian move in Europe. Others felt that MacArthur had acted foolishly, and probably beyond his instructions, in venturing beyond the 38th Parallel and carrying the war up to the Chinese border. This was expressed with force, if not with propriety, by Shinwell, now Minister of Defence, who delivered a violent criticism of MacArthur in a weekend speech:

> It seems that Shinwell's extraordinary attack on MacArthur has done him and his party a good deal of harm at home, but has *not* been widely reported in the American press. In these circumstances, it hardly seems wise to advertise his 'gaffe' any further by a motion of censure. Moreover, the truth is that Shinwell was probably right in saying that MacArthur went beyond his instructions. The real gravamen of the charge is, however, . . . for having no clearly stated directives and no effective consultation and control such as the Combined Chiefs of Staff had in the war.[2]

The retreat continued and very little news reached us from Washington of the progress of Attlee's talks with Truman. It was

[1] 30 November 1950.   [2] 6 December 1950.

clear, however, that there was a serious rift between the two Governments. What should the next step be? Should it be appeasement or war? Should we offer China a seat in the United Nations as a reward for aggression? Or would it be better to pour in all possible additional forces and re-establish the old frontier, having achieved a full victory? At this time Churchill and others were anxious about 'the prospect of being "bogged down" in the East while we are so weak in the West'.[1] For myself, I felt sceptical about a Russian attack in the West which must involve the formidable reply of atomic war.

> Is not the greater danger that of Europe being gradually driven in on herself, as first the Far East and then Middle East are overrun or so dominated by fear of the Communist powers that all our influence disappears?[1]

Conservative Members were anxious, and their distress showed itself at various unofficial meetings. With some of my colleagues I thought that we were in danger of putting too much emphasis on the strategic advantages of disengagement in the East:

> We have not sufficiently emphasised the moral issue—the unprovoked aggression—and so forth. Nor have we given strong enough warnings against an Eastern 'Munich'. Whatever might be the technical advantages of not 'getting bogged down' (as the phrase goes) in Korea, I am sure that a moral defeat would mean the end of the white man's position in the East and that the moral collapse might easily spread to the West.
>
> If Indo-China goes, Siam follows. Then Malaya falls. Hong Kong is of course indefensible in such circumstances. Burma goes next, and Communism may easily seize India. Europe's supremacy in the world largely depends on her position in Africa and Asia.[2]

Attlee returned from the United States and reported to the House on 14 December

> in a good speech, displaying considerable courage. It was clear that it was not to the taste of his party. I was much struck by the large number who are at heart appeasers or defeatists. These

[1] 11 December 1950.   [2] 13 December 1950.

include the old Radical chapel-going pacifists on the one hand (respectable if rather dour types) and the intellectual Communists and fellow-travellers on the other.[1]

As a result of many discussions with his colleagues, Churchill followed with an admirable survey of the broad situation, holding the balance exactly right between what was required in the East and in the West. He concluded with an appeal to the Government to drop the steel nationalisation at least during this critical period. This was naturally the signal for the coming together of the divided Socialists.

> If the object of a speech is to divide the other side or exploit divisions which are showing themselves, it was not adroit. But I think it will encourage many of our supporters in the country, who are perhaps beginning to feel that we are giving almost too much support to the Government, without the slightest thanks or gratitude in return.[1]

Incidentally, Shinwell's outburst, although unusual, seemed almost justified, for Bevin, who was now growing very feeble, made the curious revelation

> that General MacArthur received his instructions not from any UNO staff organisation, or from any Anglo-American staff organisation, but from the American Chiefs of Staff. We had made representations about our views as to advancing beyond the 'waist', but they had not been accepted.[1]

In the New Year another powerful offensive was launched by the Chinese which was held with difficulty. Then followed a number of peace proposals, floated by mysterious agents, in America and Europe, which were swallowed at their face value in the usual quarters. They seemed to me mainly intended to drive a wedge between the Americans and their allies.

> The news from Korea continues both bad and obscure. It looks as though the plan was now to retreat to the Pusan bridgehead, to which we were driven back at the beginning of the

[1] 14 December 1950.

campaign. Meanwhile a new 'peace' or rather 'cease-fire' proposal has been framed at U.N. and will be put to the Chinese. It proposes direct negotiation with the Chinese Government both about Korea and about Formosa and other Far Eastern problems.[1]

The Indian Government, inspired by Nehru, were bringing great pressure on the Americans for conciliation—an attitude strangely different from that which they took to the problem of Kashmir. Finally, and reluctantly, the Americans agreed to a U.N. proposal for a 'cease-fire'. On the night of 17 January I dined with Woolton at a party at which Bob Menzies (Prime Minister of Australia), Sidney Holland (Prime Minister of New Zealand), Eden, Maxwell Fyfe, and Lyttelton were present:

> While we were at dinner the news came through of the Chinese refusal to consider the 'cease-fire' offer which UNO had proposed, largely at the suggestion of the British Commonwealth. There was a general sense of relief, for a conference might have proved very dangerous for the Anglo-American alliance.
> There was also a general agreement that we should now concentrate on the campaign and try to hold some part of Korea.[2]

The line was soon successfully stabilised. But somewhat alarming accounts reached us about MacArthur. A recent visitor, for instance, told me:

> The General seems to live in a more and more fantastic atmosphere of royal pomp, surrounded by obsequious 'yes-men'. His political and military plans are not revealed to anyone—least of all to Washington.[2]

By the spring of the year, it was clear that

> MacArthur is domineering, but at least knows what he wants—which is to engage and defeat Communist China as soon as possible (like Churchill with Bolshevist Russia in 1920). Truman vacillates; Marshall is said to be senile and ineffective. The British Government, weak and divided, exercise little or no influence on events.[3]

[1] 12 January 1951.   [2] 17 January 1951.   [3] 7 April 1951.

All this was in sad contrast to the position which we had enjoyed during the Second World War, with the Churchill–Roosevelt combination served by a closely-knit military staff. However, within a day or two firm decisions were reached, and on 11 April the President took the risk of dismissing MacArthur and replacing him by General Ridgway. There were to be no more 'adventures'. We were to concentrate on holding and consolidating the line of the 38th Parallel.

Towards the end of June an unexpected move was made by Jakob Malik, the Soviet Government's representative at the United Nations, who

> delivered a very curious broadcast. Most of it consisted of the familiar denunciation of American Imperialism, the Atlantic Pact, etc., etc. But there is a suggestion of an armistice in Korea, based on both sides observing the 38th Parallel. The Sunday Press is full of this; but it seems to be a little too much like the old Hitler game. It will be interesting to see the reaction of the American administration.[1]

On 29 June an offer of armistice terms was made by General Ridgway. It was accepted 'in principle', and the discussions began on 10 July. The talks proved tortuous and were protracted for several months. The Chinese were cleverer at this game and succeeded at one time in putting the American generals in the position of a

> defeated body of men offering unconditional surrender! That is what American (and indeed all) generals can do unless they are provided with 'political advisers'.[2]

Finally, on 27 November, the Armistice Commission which had been set up agreed on a cease-fire line, but owing to interminable arguments about the interchange of prisoners, fighting continued in a desultory manner.

Nevertheless, it was clear that the war was in effect over, and although many months and even years were to pass before a formal peace was accepted, on 14 July 1953 for practical purposes the Korean War was at an end.

[1] 29 June 1951.   [2] 5 August 1951.

This great struggle had important reactions upon Anglo-American relations; it quickened the pace of European rearmament, including—however reluctantly—German participation. It was to have similar repercussions on British defence policy, with drastic effects upon our financial and economic difficulties, involving in their turn important political consequences.

The first impact of the Korean War was naturally upon the defence programme for 1950. This had already been found unsatisfactory by Churchill when the White Paper was published in March. He had complained that with all our commitments in Europe and overseas, we were in the position of not being able to send even two brigades to any part of the world at short notice. The whole question now became urgent. Within a few months Bevin was reluctantly forced to accept a project of German rearmament, which he had characterised as 'mere folly' when pressed by Churchill in earlier debates. After some deliberation, the Government began to make definite proposals to add to our own military capacity. At the end of July they announced an additional £100 millions for defence expenditure, mainly for the purpose of expanding Fighter Command. Although some ground forces were to be sent to Korea, the Minister of Defence emphasised the prior claims both of Hong Kong and Malaya. At the same time, the release of Regulars from the forces was suspended, and there was a limited recall of reserves.

Churchill was not impressed by the scale or timing of these proposals and kept pressing for a secret session to allow frank and uninhibited discussion of our difficulties. Although Attlee did not favour this plan, Churchill persisted. On 27 July he moved to 'spy strangers'. Such a motion, if carried, has the effect of ejecting all save Members and officers of the House. The motion was defeated by only one vote. When the debate followed, Churchill's speech was sombre but impressive. He was particularly concerned about the dangerous inferiority of the defensive power of Western Europe in conventional forces. Russia had at least 80 divisions available, Western Europe had 12; Russia had 25 or 30 armoured divisions, we had two. The main, if not the only, defence of Europe rested on the 180 American heavy bombers in East Anglia. Yet they could be used only at the frightful cost of letting loose atomic war. Our

M

chief effort should be to protect these bombers at all costs. What had we done? We had sold 100 jet planes to Argentina and 110 to Egypt, whose Government, in defiance of their treaty obligations, was now denying the Canal to British ships on the ground that cargoes might be destined for Israel.

A similar appeal for an increased contribution by Britain was made by the United States Government. Whether yielding to their influence or to Churchill's demands, the Government at last announced an important, almost spectacular, development of their policy of rearmament. There would be a three years' defence programme on a much enlarged scale. £3,400 millions would be spent over these years. Defence expenditure would now rise from 8 to 10 per cent of the national income. Naturally there would be serious repercussions. The balance of payments would be endangered, since imports must rise and exports be reduced. To meet the situation the Government appealed for a new sense of urgency and a corresponding increase in production.

A few days after Parliament adjourned, Churchill and some of his colleagues were together at Strasbourg. He told us that he had asked for a talk with the Prime Minister, who had received him courteously but seemed uncertain and baffled by the difficulties and dangers:

> [Churchill] was much depressed by his interview the other day with Attlee. It seems that to scrape together 3,000 men and their equipment for Korea will take two months! Even their anti-aircraft guns can only be obtained by taking some of those now in Lincolnshire defending the American 'atomic' bombers.[1]

However, the Government did what they could. At the end of August increases in Service pay were announced, and the period of conscription was lengthened from eighteen months to two years. This was indeed a courageous step, in view of the traditional attitude of the Socialists to National Service.

When Parliament reassembled after only a month's holiday, another important debate took place. It was clear that no amendment could be moved to the Government's motion, for we supported

[1] 6 August 1950.

the three main proposals: more pay for Regulars, two years' National Service, and a vague but substantial rearmament programme. There was to be a three-day debate. Since the announcement made by the Prime Minister on the defence side was more definite and stronger than we had expected, a great part of the discussion turned upon the economic consequences.

The Prime Minister opened the debate in his usual manner – precise, cold, correct – but with a certain dignity. *The Times* likes this sort of thing because it reminds them of Chamberlain. The weakness is the utter lack of leadership. 'We have done all that is expected of us'; 'We are doing all that our allies have asked'; 'We are doing as much as anyone else'; 'We were asked by the Americans to do so-and-so, and we responded.' It is rather an uninspiring attitude for the Prime Minister of Great Britain. Sometimes when one shuts one's eyes, one believes oneself back in 1937–39. The responsible Socialists – sound and trusted men – are put up to make the same sort of speeches which respectable Conservatives used to make. Whiteley follows Margesson.[1]

The Government now proposed to raise the sum to £3,600 millions in three years. This would be spent on the establishment of six to ten Regular divisions, of which one armoured and one infantry division would be based at home. The two armoured divisions now in Germany would be made up to strength and a third added. There would be the equivalent of twelve Territorial divisions by next year. Our air strength would be substantially increased by an expansion of the jet fighters, and the new Canberra bomber would be improved. All this amounted to a considerable programme, and there was little for us to criticise except the lack of foresight in allowing our weakness to remain uncorrected for so long. Churchill accordingly welcomed the new plans. There was one arresting passage in his speech on the respective functions of a Government and Opposition:

Both Governments and Oppositions have responsibilities to discharge, but they are of a different order. The Government, with their whole control over our executive power, have the

[1] 12 September 1950. William Whiteley was the Government Chief Whip, as David Margesson had been before the war.

burden and the duty—and we can all see that it is a very heavy one—to make sure that the safety of the country is provided for; the shape, formation and direction of policy is in their hands alone.

The responsibilities of the Opposition are limited to aiding the Government in the measures which we agree are required for national safety, and also to criticising and correcting, so far as they can, any errors and shortcomings which may be apparent, but the Opposition are not responsible for proposing integrated and complicated measures of policy.[1]

He went on:

In voting for what the Government propose, which we are going to do on this occasion, we in no way limit our right and duty to comment with the fullest freedom upon their policy and the course of events.[1]

I felt at the time that this would become almost a *locus classicus* on the constitutional relations of parties in power and parties out of office.

When the Labour Party Conference took place in the autumn, there seemed a good deal of confusion as to how the problem of rising prices, costs, and wages was to be met. In perhaps rather a cynical mood I recorded my feelings:

The only thing clear was the plan to 'soak the rich' to pay for rearmament. Even Morrison had to accept this. Cripps was away—in his clinic. He is said by some to be ill, by others to be mad. Since he has always been both, I expect him to return and resume his post as Chancellor of the Exchequer.[2]

Early in the next year, on 29 January 1951, Attlee, with real political courage, announced an extended defence programme which was ill received by many of his supporters, the critics on this occasion not being confined to the extreme Left. With characteristic bluntness he declared that new and painful sacrifices would be needed. New taxes would be required; savings in social services must be made; civil expenditure must be cut back or postponed. When a few days later we were told that the total now proposed

---

[1] *Hansard,* 12 September 1950.   [2] 5 October 1950.

had been raised to £4,700 millions in three years, exclusive of stockpiling and capital investment, it was clear that the economic situation must become serious, and without firm handling might prove disastrous. But we could not withhold our admiration for the skill by which he had succeeded in getting so extended a plan accepted by his Ministers and his party. The fact that there had now been three versions within six months, each increasing in size and expense, marked at any rate a sense of the Government's growing efforts to measure up to the level of events.

All this time there had been almost open talk in London about a possible Russian reaction to the opportunity offered by the Korean War. Many, however, thought such fears exaggerated. After a party at an important embassy I recorded the discussion:

> The chief talk is now openly about whether the Russians will attack Yugoslavia this summer. The Ambassador tells me that the Yugoslavs now think this less certain than they thought some months ago. The Korean affair has made the Russians think a bit. They did not expect any American reaction. There are others who say that Scandinavia may be 'cleaned up' first. It is a strange world—or rather dual world—in which we live. With one half of our minds we do our daily business; make plans for next year and so forth. With the other we discuss (privately and unreported) the approaching end of the civilised world. All the same, I believe it will somehow survive.[1]

With the Conservative Party giving general support to the Government's defence programme, the interest began to pass from the military to the financial and economic problems. How was this new burden to be paid for? What would be the effect on our economy? The American loan had been spent; the country was already heavily taxed, partly to meet our debts, partly to sustain our post-war commitments, and partly to meet the ever-growing demands of the Welfare State. We had already been driven to one devaluation; we seemed now to face the prospects of another. We all, therefore, awaited with anxiety the introduction of the new Budget and its implications. It was to be the first, and last, Budget of the new Chancellor of the Exchequer, Hugh Gaitskell.

[1] 31 January 1951.

A period of comparative stability in wages and prices had already come to an end. The nationalised industries—coal and railways—led the way in increases both of prices and wages, each laying the blame on the other. Although a system of price controls was still operating in principle, it was admitted even by Ministers that a further rise of prices was inevitable. The food subsidies amounted to £400 millions a year, and it was a firm decision of the Government not to allow any increase in that figure, which had been fixed by Cripps. Any rise, therefore, in the cost of wheat or meat must be reflected in a price to the consumer.

It was this deteriorating situation, now to be further worsened by the bill for rearmament, which Gaitskell had to face. Believing, no doubt, that consumption would be diminished or at least controlled both by rising prices and physical shortages, he proposed only modest increases in taxation. These included 6d. on the standard rate of income tax, an increase of the profits tax on distributed profits from 30 to 50 per cent, 4d. a gallon more on petrol, a higher entertainments tax, and increases on the purchase tax on cars, wirelesses, and domestic gas and electrical equipment. All this seemed reasonable in the circumstances, and although the Opposition had detailed criticisms which led to the usual protracted debates on the Finance Bill, particularly on clauses restricting overseas investment, the real interest lay in Aneurin Bevan's position. Gaitskell, supported by Attlee and the Government as a whole, was determined to impose a curb upon the growing expenditure under the National Health Service. Bevan had boldly declared that he would never be a member of a Government which imposed any charge upon those who used the Service. Since in the Budget speech Gaitskell announced legislation to secure that the patient should pay half the cost of spectacles and half the cost of dentures— hitherto supplied without charge—the human drama which so often lies hidden between drab statistics soon began to excite a growing interest in all political circles. The Prime Minister was in hospital, and the nature of his illness made it desirable that he should be spared worry. It was difficult to imagine anything more likely to interfere with his treatment than a visit from Aneurin Bevan and Harold Wilson. Poor Attlee had to endure this trial the day before the Budget. But he seems to have met the ordeal with his usual phlegm. Yet he must have felt deeply the loss of Cripps. Gaitskell certainly followed Cripps's strict theories, and invited the same sense of duty and sacrifice amongst all classes to which Cripps had appealed. It was evident that Cripps would have introduced these or similar limitations in social expenditure. Even in the Health Service, then and now the Sacred Cow of Socialism, his authority with the Left of the party was so great that Bevan's revolt would have carried little weight or might never have taken place. Bevan was a genial, impulsive and not wholly unworldly revolutionary. But Cripps, with his odour of sanctity and his fine record of violent agitation, was the 'sea-green incorruptible'—the Robespierre, not the Danton. To this pre-eminence in his party Gaitskell could not yet aspire, although his courage and determination never failed.

After a week of speculation, Aneurin Bevan's resignation as Minister of Labour was announced on 23 April. The interchange of letters was in a new style, which has now, alas, become fashionable —'My dear Clem', 'My dear Nye'. These informalities have been much imitated since. But in this case they scarcely concealed the hearty dislike between the correspondents. Moreover, it was clear from Attlee's somewhat testy reply that he felt that Bevan had extended the area of dispute 'a long way beyond the specific matter to which, as I understood, you had taken objection'. For Bevan had stated his opposition not merely to the charges on false teeth and spectacles, but to many other features of the Budget. He complained that the new burdens were unfairly distributed between the different social classes. He argued that the scale of military expenditure was unattainable. He protested against the Chancellor of the Exchequer's intention to rely on a rise in prices to control consumption, without regard to the industrial dislocation and discontent which would inevitably follow. Finally, he declared that the Budget marked the beginning of the destruction of the social services in which Labour had taken a special pride. Bevan made his personal statement the same afternoon.

I have heard many such statements, from Eden, Cranborne (Salisbury), Duff Cooper, Sam Hoare, and so on. Eden was so careful to spare his colleague that it was obscure to many people just what was his quarrel with Chamberlain. Cranborne was restrained, but severe. Duff Cooper was truculent, but in classical language. Sam Hoare almost burst into tears. Bevan's 'apologia' was certainly novel in manner, if not in matter. It was a violent castigation of his colleagues, delivered with incredible asperity, not to say malice. Up to a certain point it was well done; but he lost the House at the end. Members were shocked by his explanation of why he agreed to the 1s. contribution towards prescriptions and the 25,000 cut in house-building last year. He had only agreed because he knew these measures were impracticable and could not in fact be carried out. He outmanœuvred— not to say 'double-crossed'—his colleagues.[1]

There was much speculation about Bevan's future. Many Members felt that he had 'done for himself'.

I am not sure. He said things which a large majority of the Socialist Party like to have their leaders say. His anti-Americanism is really a popular line. The attack on the Budget was liked by many of them. The Socialists are very angry at his 'disloyalty'— which threatens their own seats. . . . But really they agree with his sentiments. 'Why not a capital levy?'[1]

Attlee survived the immediate storm, but nobody believed that the Parliament could now run much beyond the autumn.

Wilson, President of the Board of Trade, has also resigned and will presumably speak tomorrow. It is said that Freeman (who is Under-Secretary at the Ministry of Supply) is resigning. This will make it awkward for Strauss, who is still shivering on the brink. I predict that both he and Strachey will [hesitate] when it comes to the point.[1]

The next day the Press was violently critical of Bevan. Their sensitive reporters and leader-writers appeared to be shocked by his cynical disloyalty. I still felt that he might become both formidable and dangerous. His speech was not directed to the election of 1951 or 1952, but he was looking further ahead. The next afternoon

[1] 23 April 1951.

Harold Wilson made his statement. He had resigned from the Board of Trade in sympathy with Bevan:

> It was more in the classical style–modest and mournful. The House and the Labour Party liked it. No more resignations at present, except Freeman. After Wilson came the debate on the Teeth and Spectacles Bill. All quiet so far.[1]

My feeling about Bevan's strength in the Labour movement was to be justified within a few months by the tone of the Labour Party Conference at Scarborough:

> The news came through during the afternoon that in the election to the Socialist executive Bevan tops the list by an immense majority. Shinwell is thrown off, after 15 years' service, and replaced by Mrs. Castle, a Bevanite.[2]

To the Conservatives such a result was not unwelcome–at least in the short term:

> If it is clear that 'Bevanism' is in the ascendant, a lot of Liberal and middle-class votes may cross over to us.[2]

Meanwhile the Parliamentary Labour Party had rallied round the Prime Minister and his Chancellor of the Exchequer. Dalton, always ready for the fray, described the attacks on Gaitskell as 'vicious, untrue, and unworthy'. But resignation, sickness and death had gravely weakened the strength and prestige of the Government. In 1945 the leading Ministers had been largely drawn from Churchill's war colleagues. Now a new generation, commanding less national support, was succeeding. But undoubtedly these trials– economic, financial and finally political–were largely the consequences of the protracted Korean War. To these tribulations came on 2 May the sudden decision of the Government of Iran to 'nationalise' the wells, installations, and refinery which were the property of the Anglo-Iranian Oil Company.

Within a few days of this declaration, the necessary legislation was passed through the Iranian Parliament. Although this came as a sudden blow to Parliament and the public, there had been many

---

[1] 24 April 1951.   [2] 2 October 1951.

signs of impending trouble. The agreement between the Anglo-Iranian Oil Company and the Government of Iran dated from 1933 and provided for rising payments as the tonnage of oil and the dividends paid by the company increased. Cripps's dividend limitation, therefore, not unnaturally seemed to the Iranians a trick by which they were being deprived of money due to them. The British Government was a large shareholder; it was in addition exacting large sums in taxation from the Company; and now by preventing the rate of dividend from being raised, it was depriving Iran of her fair share by a subterfuge. Eden had warned Cripps of this danger, as indeed had the directors of the company. But Cripps had been unmoved by these arguments.[1] The company was a British-registered concern. It was therefore bound to conform to the system of 'voluntary' limitation, whatever might be the result.

The company had offered to negotiate a new agreement based upon a fifty-fifty division of profits. Since the Prime Minister, General Razmara, was a responsible and reasonable politician, there seemed every hope of a settlement. Unhappily Razmara was assassinated on 7 March. A few weeks later Dr. Mossadeq, who had long been a fervent advocate of 'nationalising' the oil industry and was chairman of the oil commission, succeeded to the Premiership and insisted on immediate action. Morrison records his indignation:

> It was a shocking example of modern diplomacy, or lack of diplomacy, of which the subsequent nationalising of the Suez Canal in defiance of treaties was another.[2]

But the position had its ludicrous aspects of which the Iranians were well aware. The British Government accepted the 'principle' of nationalisation. Since it was the basis of their own political creed they could hardly do less, although they had not up to now regarded it as a convenient item for export. They demanded compensation; but obviously any fair price would be on a scale far beyond the means of Iran to provide. They next proposed arbitration in accordance with the 1933 agreement between the company and the Iranian

---

[1] The Earl of Avon, *The Eden Memoirs: Full Circle* (London, 1960), p. 193.
[2] Lord Morrison, *An Autobiography*, p. 282.

Government. When this was rejected, the British Government submitted the dispute to the International Court.

At this stage the Americans were certainly unhelpful. Perhaps the oil interests were jealous; perhaps the politicians were not sorry to see Socialist Britain hoist with her own petard.

> I do not like the news from Persia; still less the rather unfriendly American attitude. Acheson (Secretary of State) appeals to Britain and to Persia to keep calm! As if we were two Balkan countries being lectured in 1911 by Sir Edward Grey![1]

Meanwhile Dr. Mossadeq raved and ranted like a lunatic. It seemed almost impossible for the British people with their sense of the ludicrous to take him seriously when he made perpetual appearances in pyjamas and gave interviews from his bed. Nevertheless, the situation showed no improvement. Early in June the company sent a mission to Teheran with the offer to pay £10 millions down and £3 millions a month pending the settlement of the dispute, and proposing that the Iranian assets should be invested in a national oil company which would grant their use to a new operating company in which the Iranians would be represented on the board. Certainly, if such a proposal had been made several years before it would have been acceptable.

In a visit to Abadan and Teheran and to the oilfields in 1947, I had felt doubtful of the wisdom of the company's attempt to preserve an exclusive control of an undertaking so vital to Iran. Lord Cadman's successors did not seem to know how to handle so proud and subtle a people. Admirable in the field, the company was less ably represented in the capital. Yet Teheran, not Abadan, was the key to the problem.

It was difficult to estimate how far the Iranians were moved by genuine emotion—a wave of patriotic feeling led by the almost fanatical Mossadeq—and how far they were enjoying more sinister encouragement:

> Rougetel (formerly British Ambassador in Teheran—during the 1947 crisis—and now in Brussels) told me last Saturday that the Russians were really behind the whole thing, and used the

[1] 17 May 1951.

so-called Persian patriots or nationalists as much as the 'Tudeh' or Left-wing party.[1]

By 20 June we heard that the Iranians had refused the company's counter-offer. The crisis seemed to have arrived. Morrison's instinct, although not then known to us, was for drastic action:

> My own view was that there was much to be said in favour of sharp and forceful action. The Cabinet was, however, left in little doubt that mounting an effective attacking force would take a lot of time and might therefore be a failure. In the end we had to abandon any military project, with the exception that we would have used force if British nationals had been attacked.[2]

In other words, the British Government would use at least a show of force to cover a safe retreat for our nationals, but not to protect our property.

> In drawing this distinction between life and property, they are of course altogether overlooking the effects on British prestige in the Middle East and the probable developments in Persia. It may well be that the whole Persian economy will collapse. But in that case, a Russian-controlled Communist Government will take over Persia, and a huge new gain made by expanding Russian Communism. There is really no middle course to be followed in this affair. We might have taken a very generous line and offered to give them the whole concern—in that event, we could almost certainly have got an arrangement to manage it for the Persians on an *agency* basis. The profits would have been considerable, if not quite so large. The oil would have physically remained in our hands in peace—and in war. Alternatively, we could have landed troops to protect our property. This would have led—not to war—but to partition. The Russians would have held the north and we the south of Persia, divided by the great mountain range.[3]

As the days of decision now seemed to be approaching, the Opposition asked for a debate. Although our back-benchers were incensed and would have liked to recommend or even demand the immediate despatch of troops, Churchill was unwilling to commit

[1] 5 June 1951.
[2] Morrison, *An Autobiography*, p. 282.   [3] 20 June 1951.

himself to the details of any military operation about which he was quite ignorant:

> He is also very conscious that Morrison and Co. are just waiting to fix the 'warmonger' accusation upon him.[1]

Somewhat unexpectedly, the Foreign Secretary refused to open the debate:

> I think he hoped, by lying back, that some at least of the Conservative speakers would be led into some incautious phrase, which he could then pounce upon and denounce as 'warmongering'. But he reckoned without the immense skill and experience of Eden (who opened faultlessly) and the discipline of the others.[2]

The first speech from the Labour back-benchers was delivered by the Member for Doncaster, Ray Gunter:[3]

> I have never heard him open his mouth in debate before; but he made an admirably robust and patriotic speech, contemptuous of the Persians (among whom he had apparently lived at one time) and so imperialistic as to be almost 'jingo'. This rather surprised and clearly mortified Morrison and his friends.[2]

When Morrison came to reply it was clear why he had not spoken before; for he had nothing to say. He emphasised the distinction between the defence of 'life and limb' and the protection of 'property'. The plan now was to appeal to the Hague Court and hope that when it came to the point the Iranians would not be so foolish as to destroy their only source of revenue. His speech was ill received by a somewhat baffled House.

On 27 June, after Questions, Churchill asked the Prime Minister if he would receive him and some of his friends for a private talk. This was at once agreed. It certainly was wise to give a feeling of co-operation between the parties over so serious an issue, and it would also provide us with some information. Churchill, in reporting his discussion, made it clear that there was some hope of a settlement and of great international pressure being brought to

---

[1] 20 June 1951.
[2] 21 June 1951. [3] Later Minister of Labour 1964–68.

obtain it. The tanker position was satisfactory, nearly all the owners having agreed to a boycott. Although our Government was still uncertain how to play the hand, it seemed that the whole affair might be very protracted and that sufficient internal pressures might develop to force the Iranians to be more reasonable. When he came to the 1922 Committee, Churchill

> spoke with great moderation and caution about Persia. It is clear that he thinks there may be a change for the better and that it would be foolish for the Tory Party to 'stick its neck' out. This was not to the taste of some of his audience.[1]

But he prudently remained in a very cautious mood.

> The latest move [is] the announcement that (contrary to their first decision) Dr. Mossadeq and the Persian Government are willing to 'discuss' the oil crisis with Averell Harriman, President Truman's 'adviser'. This certainly supports Churchill's waiting policy.[2]

Harriman arrived in Teheran to be greeted by Communist riots. Although he declared that he was not a 'mediator', it was clear that he had in fact assumed this role. His intervention assisted the Conservative leaders in their difficulty, for further discussion had to be postponed. In any debate it would not be easy to balance on the nice edge between 'warmongering' and 'appeasement'.

> What is becoming more and more clear is that the balance of parties—with Socialists and Tories watching each other all the time—is not conducive to the public interest. No one dares to do anything but wait for 'something to turn up'. Micawberism is universal.[3]

Meanwhile we awaited news of Harriman's mission.

> The Persians seem now to have got themselves into the advantageous position of being bribed by the Russians individually and by the Americans collectively. They sit quietly in the middle, watching the bids go up and up.[4]

The Harriman mission failed. When he came to London it was

---

[1] 28 June 1951.   [2] 10–12 July 1951.
[3] 16 July 1951.   [4] 17 July 1951.

to urge Ministers to resume negotiations in Teheran. A debate was now inevitable. Since I had been asked to 'wind up' for the Opposition, I spent the previous day at Chartwell going over Churchill's speech. With his usual skill he had prepared a great deal of material which would stand whatever might happen in the next twenty-four hours. But he was continually distracted by one of his new hobbies — an indoor aquarium with tanks of tropical fish, minute but very lovely. He was quite fascinated by their delicate beauty. On this occasion he gave me an inscribed copy of Volume IV of his war history, *The Hinge of Fate*. It was really amazing to realise the amount of work of which this extraordinary man was capable, in spite of his age. Since the war, with its appalling strain, he had fought two General Elections and was about to fight a third; by the Fulton speech he had been the inspiration of the Western rally against Russian aggression; he had launched the European Movement; and he had completed four volumes of his book.

Before the debate took place, Morrison had delivered a violent harangue to the Durham miners accusing the Tories of wanting war. But his opening speech in the House was long and dreary. As Churchill observed, it would be really better if the Foreign Office were to write his speeches for the Durham miners and he were to write his own speeches for the House of Commons.

Churchill replied in one of his most devastating and polished efforts. (It was much improved on the version he had completed on Sunday.) He was in tremendous form and under a mass of chaff and invective covered the only weakness of his position — that is, the brake which he has put during the last six weeks on the more ardent Tory spirits. He thus established a complete ascendancy over the party and indeed over the House. His opening passage about the changed position of Britain since the war and the loss of prestige, etc., in the world, which could however be to some extent rebuilt with American partnership, was very fine. Also his account of the functions of an Opposition (based on a dictum of Lord Lansdowne). They might caution against, but they should be very chary of demanding particular military operations. This was the task of Government.[1]

[1] 30 July 1951.

When my turn came I protested against the imputations and insinuations that one party, which after all represented at least half the nation, was seeking or would thoughtlessly risk the dangers and sufferings of war. It certainly seemed

> a new twist in the laborious and distorted presentation of the history of the years before the Second World War with which we are so familiar.[1]

It was surely our duty to sustain the courage of our people; we ought to disdain to exploit their fears.

Attlee ended up with

> that pawky imitation of Baldwin which he does so well. He is expert at lowering the temperature and generally reducing the whole thing to a pleasant Sunday afternoon at [a] boys' club. He sat down at 9.57 without answering any question.[2]

When he resumed his seat, I called out 'What about the evacuation of Abadan?' The Prime Minister made the strange reply that there might have to be a withdrawal from the oil wells and from some part of Abadan, 'but our intention is not to evacuate entirely'.[3]

> There was some applause and some silence from the Government benches; hearty applause from ours. The clock struck. The debate was over. This is certainly an odd and haphazard sort of country.[2]

The next stage in this complicated story was a mission led by Dick Stokes, Lord Privy Seal, which arrived in Teheran at the beginning of August. Once again the negotiations failed. Once again the British Government accepted the 'principle of nationalisation', a foolish and indeed fatal phrase, which was bound to cause an infinity of trouble. Throughout the early days of August little news came through except that the Iranian Government seemed to be anxious for a settlement, although Dr. Mossadeq clearly feared the assassin's knife or pistol if he were to weaken. The Iranian Government now claimed that under the law the only matters that could be discussed were compensation, the employment of foreign experts, and the sale of oil to former customers.

---

[1] *Hansard*, 30 July 1951.   [2] 30 July 1951.   [3] *Hansard*, 30 July 1951.

Meanwhile, with the news from Korea and Iran equally bad and the economic situation deteriorating, the Parliament seemed unlikely to last much longer:

> Pre-election fever is growing in intensity. The press on both sides is beginning to clamour for an early election. Attlee is lying low, like Brer Rabbit, and sayin' nuffin'. Anyway, he has got lumbago.[1]

However, on 19 September the evening papers on their own responsibility—or perhaps as the result of a leak, for the Cabinet had sat in the morning—announced 25 October as polling day. At 9.15 the same evening the Prime Minister confirmed these rumours in a short broadcast message. The dissolution would be 5 October and polling day 25 October.

It was at this juncture that we heard the news that Mossadeq had ordered all the British employees of the company to leave Teheran by 4 October, the date Parliament was to meet, to pass a vote of sympathy with the King after his serious operation. Mossadeq certainly seemed to have a sense of humour.

The time for words and argument had now passed. Faced with the latest Iranian demand, some action must be taken. Although the British Government decided to submit the whole dispute to the Security Council, they were forced to accept meanwhile the expulsion of the British managers and employees, and the evacuation both of the oilfield and of Abadan. The retreat took place in the most humiliating manner imaginable.

> The Persians refuse to allow the British cruiser to come alongside the pier (which is British property) so that the last 350-odd British employees may go aboard. These men and women will not even be taken out in the launches belonging to the cruiser. They will be ferried out by Persian launches, 30 at a time, in the presence of an immense crowd of Persians, Indians, etc., employees of the company. It is difficult to conceive any procedure more calculated to destroy the last vestige of British prestige.[2]

So ended the first stage of this long dispute. It was not finally

---

[1] 18 September 1951.   [2] 2 October 1951.

to be settled until nearly three years later—three years of serious damage to Britain's balance of payments and growing economic chaos in Iran. After the change of government in the United States at the beginning of 1953, when it became clear that the new Republican administration was not prepared to underwrite the Iranian economy, Mossadeq's prestige began to wane. Although his tenacious grip on power was sufficient to drive the Shah into a temporary exile in August 1953, he was arrested by the army before the month was out, and his successors negotiated an agreement with the British oil interests, in which the Americans were closely involved.

Together with the struggle in Iran, our difficulties with Egypt now came to a head. Ten days before the election the Egyptian Government denounced our treaties, and serious rioting took place with considerable losses to British property. These were accompanied by the usual false reports of so-called British atrocities. This event was the culmination of several years' pressure. The Israel–Egypt armistice in 1949 had brought an uneasy truce into the area. But it was clear that the policy of the Wafd party and of the Egyptian patriots was to hasten our evacuation both of Egypt and of the Sudan. In November 1950 a unilateral announcement had been made by the Egyptian Government of their intention to denounce the treaty of 1936 which was the governing instrument under which our rights in the Nile Valley had been regulated, together with the Condominium of 1899, establishing dual control of the Sudan. Bevin had replied by saying that Britain would abide by the 1936 treaty until changed by mutual consent. As regards the Sudan, it must decide its own future. This was followed by the suspension of arms to Egypt on our side and considerable interference by the Egyptians with our shipping in the Suez Canal on the ground that cargoes might be destined for Israel. All tankers on their way to Haifa had been stopped.

Through the spring and summer of 1951 diplomatic notes were exchanged, without effect, and the Egyptians continued their provocation:

> The Egyptian Government . . . has now started to stop our ships at sea. This, and still more the nonchalant attitude of the

Foreign Secretary [Morrison], infuriated the Tories and even some of the Socialists (especially the Jews).[1]

At the beginning of October decrees were passed in Cairo providing for the denunciation of the treaties, and rioting began. The British Government replied by inviting Egypt to participate in an Allied Middle Eastern Command with the United States, France and Turkey as our partners. We also proposed that any British troops in excess of an allocation to be agreed by this new Command should be withdrawn. This offer was contemptuously refused.

The final decision to denounce the treaties was, therefore, the culmination of many months of argument and threats. It was one more of the serious troubles which crowded upon the Labour Government in their last period of office. It was in this atmosphere of increasing difficulties at home, with a dangerously threatening economic crisis accentuated by the events in Iran and Egypt, that the stage was set for another trial of strength between the two great parties.

In making this decision to seek a new election, many of Attlee's colleagues felt at the time that the timing from the point of view of the Labour Party was ill chosen. Yet Attlee was undoubtedly right. The problems at home and abroad could no longer be effectively dealt with in a Parliament so nicely balanced. He may have hoped that on the two effective cries of full employment and the maintenance of peace the Labour Party might return fortified to meet so many dangers. He may have been riding for a fall and sought a welcome release from office, which he had now sustained through six years of war and six years of peace. Whatever his motives, the die was cast.

[1] 10–12 July 1951.

CHAPTER XII

General Election, 1951

I T was one of our recreations during the First War to study that
admirable, if sometimes recondite, volume *Field Service Regula-*
tions.[1] This rich quarry seldom failed to produce a nugget of pure
gold. One that sticks in my head is the following: 'Disembarkation
is carried out in a similar manner to embarkation.' The same thing
might be said about the General Election of 1951 in its relation to
that of 1950. The manifestos published by each party were much
the same. A good deal of time had been spent in preparing ours; but,
in effect, *Britain Strong and Free* was little more than a new edition of
This is the Road, in itself mainly a condensed version of *The Right
Road for Britain*. Similarly, the Labour document followed familiar
lines. The same was true of much of the arguments in the broadcasts
and on the hustings. The Labour Party stood broadly on their
maintenance of full employment and their introduction, in a new
and spectacular form, of the 'Welfare State'. The Conservatives
replied by criticism of the stagnation of the economy and the
restrictive controls which everywhere hampered enterprise, and
the miserably low standard of living, especially in terms of rations.
The new contest was thus regarded as merely a repetition of the
former struggle. With all the divergences of view, there was one
point at any rate upon which all Members of the previous House of
Commons were agreed. Everyone was glad to see the end of a
frustrating and frustrated Parliament.

There were, however, some important differences from the last
contest. The Liberal candidates had fallen from 475 to a mere 109.
The effect of this proved favourable to the Conservatives, since
when no Liberal stood the Liberal vote either abstained or was
divided in the proportion of three to two in favour of the Conserva-

[1] *Winds of Change*, p. 63.

tives.[1] In addition, while the 1950 election had taken place at a not unfavourable moment in the fortunes of the British economy, by October 1951 a new financial crisis was reaching a critical stage. A few days before the dissolution Gaitskell had announced an unprecedented fall in the gold and dollar reserves in the third quarter of the year of about $600 million. The other new feature in this election was the Labour claim that if the Conservatives, and more especially Churchill, were returned to power the country would be likely to be plunged into war. Thus, if 1900 was the 'Khaki' Election, and 1918 the 'Coupon' Election, the election of 1951 will certainly be known in history as the 'Warmongering' Election.

One question had been raised by the Conservative Party to the forefront of domestic issues. This was the famous pledge to build 300,000 houses a year. This banner had been firmly nailed to our mast at the Conservative Conference of 1950 at Blackpool. The delegates met in a mood of enthusiasm, excited by the great recovery of the previous election and straining at the leash for a new effort. They attended the hall with commendable fervour and listened quietly and attentively. But on the housing question it was

> quite obvious that here is something about which everyone feels quite passionately. The delegates reflect not political but human feelings in their demand for a target of at least 300,000 homes a year. They were really determined as well as excited.[2]

Contemptuous of the miserable performance of the Labour Government, the hall was clearly bent on raising the bid, whatever the platform might say. Lord Woolton handled this situation with consummate skill. Indeed, but for his deft intervention we might have been committed to a figure quite out of our power to achieve. When Churchill came to speak at the final meeting he accepted the 300,000, although he referred to it not as a minimum but as a target. The night before he spoke the housing pundits and economics experts tried to get him to disavow this pledge. But he wisely refused. Incidentally, at this conference he made a memorable speech with a fine piece of acting. In 1950 we almost achieved

[1] D. E. Butler, *The British General Election of 1951* (London, 1952), p. 242.
[2] 13 October 1950.

victory. The next trial of strength could not be long delayed. He appealed for

'One more heave to get them out'. The gesture (as it should do) preceded the words, and was finely done. First a long swinging motion of the arms from the shoulder—long strokes forwards and backwards; then a wonderful hunching of the great shoulders, like a giant Sisyphus. It brought down the house.[1]

The Conservatives approached the election full of confidence. It was true that in the sixteen by-elections which had taken place during these two years no seat had changed hands. Nevertheless, there had been a marked swing against Labour; and even accepting the normal view that by-elections can be deceptive, we were encouraged by these figures. Similarly, the Gallup Poll had moved steadily in our favour; although it was probable that as the election approached the margin would narrow, there was every hope of obtaining a good working majority.

On 20 September Churchill invited some of his leading colleagues to lunch. It had already been decided to cancel the party conference at Scarborough. The policy paper already prepared could stand with slight amendment. He would himself compose a short declaration, which proved to be a little masterpiece. He persuaded me to return for dinner.

Somebody had sent him some caviare which put him in a good temper. He has finished Volume V of the War History completely. It is passed for press. Vol. VI (the final volume) is in type and practically ready. (Lord Ismay and his team—Col. Deakin, etc.—could see it through to publication if necessary.) But Volume VI must not be published till *after* the Presidential election of 1952, since it deals very frankly with C.'s disagreement with Truman about Russia at the end of the war. This immense task (a million and a quarter words) has taken much of his strength.[2]

He was very conscious

of the difficulties which would face any Conservative administration, both at home and abroad. He could not add to his own reputation; he could only hazard it.[2]

[1] 14 October 1950.   [2] 20 September 1951.

The general view was that the decision to dissolve so suddenly had been Attlee's own, and this was confirmed by a talk that I had with Gwilym Lloyd George the following day:

> He told me that he had heard (on really good authority) that Attlee's decision to dissolve was quite suddenly taken, and that neither Morrison nor Gaitskell were consulted, even by telephone. (They are in U.S.A.) At the rising of Parliament, all Ministers, except Dalton, were against holding it now. But Bevan has, in effect, blackmailed Attlee by threatening to withdraw his support unless the Parliament were dissolved. According to L.G. there is much despondency in the Socialist ranks. Nevertheless, wherever I have been, I am impressed by the class solidarity of the Labour vote. They grouse, and tell the Gallup Poll man that they will never vote Socialist again – but when the election comes, they vote the party ticket.[1]

When we met on 22 September Churchill read us some preliminary drafts of his manifesto. He also raised an important question of policy:

> He felt concern about the Stock Exchange boom and the general feeling which might be created, and exploited, by the Socialists that the Conservative party was that of business and profits and dividends. Something must be done (from the political point of view) to counter this. Could a plan be devised which would be politically advantageous and at the same time economically sound? What about a restoration, in a modified form, of the Excess Profits Tax during this rearmament period?[2]

There was a long discussion on this but, rather surprisingly, everyone seemed to agree with his proposal. A committee was formed, of which Anderson, Butler and I were members, to produce a draft.

On the day of the dissolution I had a curious conversation with Brendan Bracken who, although not standing himself, seemed to be in the very thick of things:

> According to his account, Churchill intends to stay a year or 18 months as P.M. (not more) in the event of a victory at the

[1] 21 September 1951.　　[2] 22 September 1951.

polls. (Incidentally, B.B. is quite confident about victory.) 'Eden will go to Foreign Office; Butler to the Exchequer; Lyttelton to Production.' What would I like? The service departments will be under-secretaries in effect, as in war.[1]

One idea would be to have a permanent chairman of the Chiefs of Staff Committee—an American plan which we subsequently adopted. In this case I could be Minister of Defence unless Churchill took this post himself. Alternatively, there was the Leadership of the Commons. With Eden at the Foreign Office it would be impossible for him to act as Leader. Would I like this? And so this strange conversation continued. Another major point was mentioned. Churchill was anxious that Maxwell Fyfe, who had an undeniable claim to become Lord Chancellor, should be Home Secretary. (And so it was ultimately arranged.) Churchill had also set his heart on getting Cys Asquith as Lord Chancellor, chiefly because he wished his last administration to hold both an Asquith and a Lloyd George. Unhappily the former found his health too frail.

Before starting on my campaign I went to Chartwell at Churchill's request to discuss his broadcast. I had sent him a minute with a few thoughts. We went through it together. I felt it would turn out well, and so it did:

> In his moderation and vigour, in his clarity and technical adroitness in delivery, Mr. Churchill gave the best Conservative broadcast of the election, perhaps the best broadcast for any party. It was thought by many to have been his finest personal effort since the war.[2]

As before, I made a number of speeches in different parts of the country outside my own constituency. My theme was simple, and since I was still in the fortunate position of not being often reported it could bear constant repetition:

> At this, as at all elections, a great number of matters are raised, on many varied topics. These are often important in themselves. But they are not decisive in the great march and drama of history. Today, there is really only one issue. Is it to be Socialism, in its

---

[1] 4 October 1951.   [2] Butler, pp. 66–67.

various forms and degrees, moderate or extreme, hard or soft, red or pink? Or is it to be Freedom and Order, with a fair balance between the rights and the duties of each individual man and woman? Is it to be another period of the Socialist Government, with all that this implies at Home and Abroad? Or is it to be a new Government? Is it to be 'the mixture as before'? Or is it to be a New Deal?

As the election proceeded, it became clear that the lead with which we started might well be eroded during the course of the campaign. This was caused by the wide circulation of a large number of untrue statements, partly contained in speeches and partly spread by rumour. We were to cut the social services, which for some strange reason the Socialists now believed only started in 1945 instead of being the result of generations of effort by Conservative and Liberal statesmen for over a century; we would abolish rent control; we would destroy family allowances; we would cut teachers' salaries; we would reduce old-age pensions; we would increase National Service from two years to three. All these falsehoods had a wide and dangerous circulation. At every meeting I tried to deal with these llegations in detail. I added, in a more comprehensive rebuttal:

> Against all this flood of falsehood, put up the barrier of memory. When you hear the new lies, remember the old. And, once more, take comfort in all this. Falsehood is not the sword of the strong man, exulting in his strength, it is the crutch of the lame and crippled man, conscious of his weakness.

But the most formidable storm of all, which had begun only as a moderate breeze some months before, now blew up into a hurricane of misrepresentation.

The events in Iran naturally gave an impetus to the 'warmongering' campaign. When, in spite of Attlee's assurance that it was intended to keep a footing in Abadan, total evacuation took place, it was natural that Churchill should attack this breach of the Government's undertaking. Morrison replied by asking whether the Conservative view was that the country should have gone to war. Although Churchill countered by stating that this was a matter where the responsibility and power rested solely with the Government, there was little doubt that the controversy was being sustained to further the general attack upon Conservative bellicosity. I tried to answer this with a speech which for once was widely reported:

> The Socialists asked us 'Would you have gone to war in Persia?' It is a ridiculous question like 'Have you stopped beating your wife?' It is made still more ridiculous by the revelation that as late as September 22nd they turned down a new offer for discussions. They concealed this.

This revelation was based upon an article in the *Manchester Guardian* which had given the full facts of the somewhat startling refusal of the Government to continue the talks at a critical moment. Nevertheless, in spite of the expectation that the Government would be severely handicapped by a serious international set-back, in fact the turn of events favoured the Labour Party in their general campaign.[1]

The accusation against Churchill was not only wounding but singularly foolish. Had the country listened to him in the vital pre-war years, what he termed 'the unnecessary war' might have been avoided. Yet the fact that he was known as a great war leader somehow or other, by a curious confusion of thought, led many people to be persuaded that he would welcome another opportunity of displaying his special qualities. In his final speech at Plymouth he did his best to refute these attacks:

> This is a cruel and ungrateful accusation. It is the opposite of the truth. If I remain in public life at this juncture it is because... I believe that I may be able to make an important contribution to the prevention of a third world war. . . . I pray indeed that I may have this opportunity. It is the last prize I seek to win.

The effect of propaganda, like that of advertising, grows with repetition. It began in the early summer and continued with ever-increasing force. In May Dalton had declared:

> If we get Churchill and the Tory Party back at the next election we shall be at war with Russia within twelve months.

Although most of the other Labour leaders managed to create the same impression less crudely, by innuendo rather than by direct

[1] Butler, p. 118.

assertion, in almost every speech the suggestion was spread in one form or another. In the constituencies an attempt was made by the canvassers to create something like panic. A typical slogan was: 'Vote Tory and reach for a rifle, Vote Labour and reach old age.' Yet the most effective instrument in this campaign of calumny was wielded by the *Daily Mirror*, with its immense popular circulation:

> The essential argument was symbolised by the ambiguous and suggestive phrase 'Whose finger on the trigger?' which the *Daily Mirror* had coined in the late summer and which it repeated in its first editorial on the election, saying that this posed the supreme issue at stake.[1]

The next phase has been fully described by the historian of the election:

> The *Daily Mirror* did not return to this theme until October 15th; on that day it began a special election feature devoting its second page to election letters from its readers; the first of these was prominently headlined, 'The Finger on That Trigger Must Not Itch'. On October 18th it carried a front-page story based on a Paris despatch printed in the New York weekly, *The Nation*, to the effect that Mr. Churchill would deliver a 'peace ultimatum' to Stalin. On October 19th it elaborated the story, again on the front page, under the headline 'What DID Mr. Churchill say in Paris?' while a back page editorial headed 'Ultimatum Talk', while admitting that 'evidence was lacking', gave a warning against putting 'pressure' on Russia and demanded an explanation from Mr. Churchill. The Conservative Central Office issued a statement by Mr. Churchill describing the Paris report as 'completely false', and on October 20th the *Daily Mirror* published this in an almost identical position to its first story under the headline 'I didn't say it, says Churchill'. On the same day its election letters on the second page were grouped under the two headings 'When Labour's Finger Guards the Trigger' and 'Who's Churchill Leading Now?' On October 23rd the election letters were given pride of place in a spread across the two centre pages, and those which posed the war issue were again accorded prominence under the headline 'Whose Finger on the Trigger?' Then on the eve of the election the *Daily Mirror* let itself go.

[1] Ibid., p. 121.

'Whose Finger on the Trigger?' became a front-page banner headline above photographs of intending Labour voters, 'a cross-section of Britain's workers'. Finally, on polling day itself, the *Daily Mirror*'s front page was devoted to a sensational spread on the same theme which led Mr. Churchill to issue a writ for libel against the newspaper.[1]

Unfortunately, a writ for libel was of no immediate avail. Even the settlement of the case seven months later, when the *Daily Mirror* made a handsome apology and paid Churchill's costs and substantial damages, which he devoted to a suitable charity, passed almost without a ripple. The damage was done; the front page on polling day must have swayed hundreds of thousands, perhaps even millions, of votes.

When the ballot papers came to be counted on the night of polling day, it soon became clear that the most we could hope for would be a very small majority. Indeed, when counting ceased in the early hours of 26 October, we had only gained 11 seats. Nevertheless, the pattern was encouraging. Almost everywhere Labour majorities were reduced and Conservative ones increased. Although the average swing over the whole country was only 1·1 per cent, in nine-tenths of the constituencies it ranged from 1 per cent to 4 per cent.[2] In the end we achieved a net gain of 23 seats and Labour suffered a net loss of 20. Since the Liberals were now reduced to 6 and making allowance for 2 Irish Nationals and 1 Irish Labour, we had a majority of 26 over Labour and 17 over all parties combined. It was enough but only just enough. My own conclusions were as follows:

It is now possible to form a view of what has happened at this election. The nation is evenly divided—almost exactly even. For if allowance is made for unopposed returns, the votes cast on either side are just about the same. The Liberal party has practically disappeared in the House of Commons. But whereas last time they polled over 2 million votes in the country, this time (since they had only 100-odd candidates) the Liberals have had only the choice of abstention, voting Conservative, or voting Socialist in 500-odd constituencies. As far as one can see, north of the River

---

[1] Butler, pp. 133–4.   [2] Ibid., p. 242.

Trent they have gone 2 Conservatives to 1 Socialist. This is very marked in Scotland, and in places like Durham or North Yorkshire which have suffered under the Socialist tyranny. By this means both Middlesbrough [West] and Darlington were won by us. In the Midlands, the Liberal vote has either abstained, or gone fifty-fifty or even worse. This explains Lincoln, Birmingham, Nottingham, etc. The Liberals of this area have too much of the Civil War radical and Roundhead tradition to give a Cavalier vote....

So the result is, once again, a moral stalemate. This follows a long innings by a Government which has made a tremendous number of mistakes; has had egregious failures in administration; and has been thrown about, like a rudderless ship in a storm, from crisis to crisis. At first sight, therefore, one can only form the most gloomy forebodings about the future. What will happen, after 3 or 4 years of Tory Government, with the inevitable mistakes and failures? Moreover, what will happen with so many almost insoluble problems crowding on us, at home and abroad? Will there be a terrible reaction at the next election, and another 200 majority for Labour, with Bevan this time (not Attlee) at the head?

Against this, is the remarkable fact that our seats have been very steady. We have not lost one. Even seats which we held by 30 or 40 votes have improved. The truth is that the Socialists have fought the election (very astutely) not on Socialism but on Fear. Fear of unemployment; fear of reduced wages; fear of reduced social benefits; fear of war. These four fears have been brilliantly, if unscrupulously, exploited. If, before the next election, none of these fears have proved reasonable, we may be able to force the Opposition to fight on Socialism. Then we can win.[1]

In my own constituency the figures were satisfactory. My majority had now risen from 10,688 to 12,125. Since there was no Liberal candidate, it was clear that the great majority of Liberals had either abstained or voted for me.

The result of the election was undoubtedly a disappointment to the Conservative Party. We had been confident, judging by the Gallup Poll and from other indications, of obtaining a majority of at least fifty and perhaps more. The swing against us at the end was partly no doubt caused by the normal rally of estranged Labour

[1] 28 October 1951.

voters to their own Government. But it was largely the result of the
bitter onslaught against Churchill on the 'warmongering' issue.
'A third Labour Government or a third world war' had proved a
devastating slogan. One of the ablest of the Labour campaigners
was certainly right in claiming that by making the issue of war and
peace a dominant one they had limited the success of the Conservative
Party. However, apart from his understandable anger against the
Daily Mirror, Churchill bore no rancour. As usual, he passed from
the conclusion of one event to face the next.

Attlee resigned at five o'clock on the evening of 26 October.
Within two hours it was announced that Churchill had accepted the
King's commission. The process of Cabinet-making now began.

Churchill certainly adopted an unusual scheme for this purpose.
According to the six o'clock news on 27 October, nine Ministers
had been appointed. Whether this was to be the whole or part of the
Cabinet nobody seemed to know. There was much confusion as to
whether the 'Nine Bright Shiners' were to stand alone, or whether
this Government was to be sold to the public on the instalment plan
like so many other modern commodities. It proved afterwards that
Churchill thought it would be 'a splendid idea; it kept up the public
interest; a series of bulletins showed a developing action, and so
forth'. But, in fact, it was an error. More serious was that he had
decided to become himself Minister of Defence. It was really not
possible for him at his age to undertake this dual role. Within a very
few months he reached this conclusion, and Field-Marshal Alexander
was appointed in his place. The decision that Eden should be both
Foreign Secretary and lead the House of Commons was equally
unwise. Even under war conditions it had proved an almost impossible strain for him. Now, with a tiny majority, it would be quite
unworkable. This, too, had to be altered, and Harry Crookshank,
who in the second batch of appointments had been made Minister of
Health, had to give up this post to become Lord Privy Seal and lead
the House of Commons—a task which he performed with outstanding success.

In the course of the day Lord Woolton rang up and I congratu-
lated him on the success of his organisation; but he seemed rather
moody. He was unhappy about the Ministry of Defence. As for

myself, he said of course I should be offered a post in the Cabinet, but he found this procedure as puzzling as I did. The first batch of Ministers had already been sworn in, and the public and Press were confused. Two choices somewhat surprised the political world as well as the public. Everyone knew that Oliver Lyttelton had worked hard to fit himself for the conduct of financial and economic affairs. He was one of the few of us who had a practical knowledge of commerce and industry. It was generally thought that he would become Chancellor of the Exchequer. But Churchill preferred Butler, and by this appointment made him in effect the third person in the political hierarchy. Next to himself and Eden, Butler held the leading post. However, Lyttelton proved an admirable Colonial Secretary. Another appointment which was to many surprising, but in fact prudent, was that of David Maxwell Fyfe to be Home Secretary:

> Fyfe's appointment is a good one. He will be a better Home Secretary than Minister of Labour. His speeches and writings thoroughly frightened the unions, and in spite of Churchill's denials during the campaign, made them alarmed and caused them to rally all their forces. He will be a good Home Secretary. . . . Monckton's appointment [as Minister of Labour] is unexpected, but good. He has a more subtle and a more flexible mind than Fyfe. He should do very well.[1]

On the morning of 28 October I received a message summoning me to Chartwell.

> On arrival, at 3 p.m., I found [Churchill] in a most pleasant, and rather tearful mood. He asked me to 'build the houses for the people'. What an assignment![2]

I was rather taken aback by this proposal. I knew nothing whatever about the housing problem except that we had pledged ourselves to an enormously high figure, generally regarded by the experts as unattainable. I asked what was the present housing 'set-up'. He said he had not an idea, but the 'boys' would know.

So the boys (Sir Edward Bridges, Head of the Civil Service, and Sir Norman Brook, Secretary to the Cabinet) were sent for—

27 October 1951.   [2] 28 October 1951.

also some whisky. It seems that there is much confusion in all this business. Broadly speaking, the old Ministry of Town and Country Planning retain these functions, but is now called Ministry of Local Government and Planning. All the functions of supervising Local Government in general remain with it. It also has to administer the ill-fated Town and Country Planning Act. It is also responsible for Housing. But the actual agent which controls all building, whether for Housing or other purposes, is the Ministry of Works. (This also does the work of the old Office of Works.) The building priorities or allocations are made by the Cabinet. It was at once clear that the Ministry must be rechristened, in order to pin the Housing flag firmly to the masthead.[1]

Of course, the Minister would be in the Cabinet and the Minister of Works would not. Churchill went on to say that to build 300,000 houses, which we were pledged to do, was a great adventure. If I did not want it I could have the Board of Trade. But that was a mere matter of routine.

We then discussed who should be Minister of Works, and I wondered whether Lord Swinton could be persuaded to take such a post, although after so long an experience in the Cabinet it would not be easy. (Later he accepted the Duchy of Lancaster, and in that capacity was of invaluable help to me because raw materials, including steel, came under his control.) Who should be my Parliamentary Secretary? I proposed Ernest Marples. Yes, he would accept Marples. He knew a great deal about housing and indeed about many other things. He was a clever man. At the end of this conversation Churchill solemnly said to me:

'It is a gamble—[it will] make or mar your political career. But every humble home will bless your name, if you succeed.' More tears. I said I would think about it.[1]

My wife had driven me over and was walking in the garden with Mrs. Churchill. I joined her and asked for her advice, which from a long experience I knew to be generally sound. She was in no doubt at all that I ought to accept. I had always agreed to do anything that I had been asked by Churchill, and it had up to now succeeded. When I went to Algiers nobody could have thought that the

[1] 28 October 1951.

Churchill arrives at No. 10 for the first Cabinet of the new Government, October 1951

The Press during the 'warmongering' election, October 1951

appointment would turn out as it did. It had for the first time earned me real status in the political world. She also reminded me of my experience at the Ministry of Supply and the many friends with whom I had kept up from those days. Surely we could build the houses in the same way that we built the tanks and the guns.

So I went back to the P.M.'s room and told him that I would do as he wished.[1] Much goodwill and many blessings followed. Being now, as it were, readmitted to the official family, I was made to stay. It was fun to join again in the old scenes which reminded me of the war-time Churchill. Children, friends, Ministers, private secretaries, typists, all in a great flurry but all thoroughly enjoying the return to the centre of the stage. I was reminded of the signal that went round the Fleet in 1939 – 'Winston is back'.

Meanwhile,

the usual . . . 'va et vient'. Lord Leathers arrives. He is to be Secretary of State for co-ordination of Transport, Fuel and Power. But where is Sir John Anderson? He is to be a viscount and co-ordinate Raw Materials, Supply, etc. Has he been told this? No, not yet. Let's ring him up. So this is done. Meanwhile Clem Davies has come and gone. Will he be Minister of Education? He would love this, but what about the Liberal party? He will try to persuade them, but Megan L. George and Lord Samuel will resist. He leaves for the meeting. (We hear later – on the wireless – that the Liberals will not play.) Then much talk about junior offices. Harry [Crookshank] and Patrick Buchan-Hepburn (who have arrived) are very strong on this. Churchill hardly knows the names – except that Eccles must have a job. And then Ralph Assheton. [Then there are other posts to be filled] not in the Cabinet, like Postmaster-General, Minister for National Insurance, etc. But what about the Service ministers? . . . And then the Speaker? Shall it be W. S. Morrison or Hopkins Morris – both good men? And so on.[2]

Out of all this confusion some kind of a plan did at last emerge. In these long discussions, which continued during the afternoon and

[1] 'The first list . . . did not include the name of Harold Macmillan. . . . Macmillan eventually went to what was regarded as a backwater, the Ministry of Housing.' The Earl of Kilmuir, *Memoirs: Political Adventure*, p. 191.

[2] 28 October 1951.

N

evening, it was clear that whatever the future had in store for us, at any rate

> we are certainly buying this business at the bottom of the market. There is a financial crisis, a foreign crisis, a defence crisis. Everything is in a state of muddle and confusion. It is 1940, without bombing and casualties—but without also the sense of national unity. Can this be somehow created? All these—and many other—questions are posed, discussed, turned away from, returned to from 3 to 7.[1]

At last my wife and I left for home. When I got back I began to realise what a burden I had undertaken. I knew that Churchill was grateful to me and would back me; but I had not any real clue of how to set about the job. This exciting day ended on a lighter note. The telephone was ringing from Chartwell and from No. 10 for me urgently. I expected some new turn of the wheel. But it was only that James Stuart, Dorothy's brother-in-law, who was believed to be in Scotland, had disappeared.

> But he is wanted, to be Secretary of State for Scotland. Nobody can say the Tories stand about waiting for office. It is a job to get hold of them![1]

Two days later, on 30 October, with a number of other Ministers, I kissed hands on my appointment. I thought the King looked worn but somewhat better than I expected after his recent illness. Alas, it was to prove only an illusory convalescence.

[1] 28 October 1951.

PART THREE

Office Again

1951–1955

CHAPTER XIII

Building the Houses

B EFORE the winter was out a deep pall of grief was cast over the people of Britain and the Commonwealth. The troubled but glorious reign of King George VI came suddenly to an end.

Although the King was attacked by a serious illness in the spring of 1951, he seemed to make a good recovery. Even after the operation which he underwent in September, he rallied sufficiently to attend to his public duties. Indeed, a Commonwealth tour was announced for the following year. He performed the formal act of the dissolution of Parliament on 5 October, and although he was still known to be weak, he was able to carry through the ordinary business of a Council. His recuperation progressed normally in the early months of the winter, and so marked was his progress that Sunday 2 December was appointed a day of national thanksgiving for the King's recovery.

Meanwhile Princess Elizabeth, accompanied by the Duke of Edinburgh, carried out a most successful tour of Canada and the United States, which the King celebrated on 4 December by appointing both his daughter and son-in-law to the Privy Council. He spent Christmas at Sandringham with his family and was able to deliver the usual Christmas message, although, unknown to the public, the strain had been relieved by a previous recording, phrase by phrase, as his strength allowed. At the end of January he returned to London and attended a theatre accompanied by the Queen. On 31 January the King went to London Airport to bid farewell to Princess Elizabeth and the Duke, who were setting out on the first stage of a journey which was to take them to East Africa, Australia, and New Zealand. Nearly all his subjects must have seen, either in the Press or on the television, a picture of him, hatless and wind-blown, waving goodbye.[1]

The King then returned to Sandringham and all seemed well. It was therefore a terrible shock when on the morning of 6 February my private secretary interrupted me while I was receiving a deputation to say that an emergency Cabinet had been summoned for 11 a.m.:

> He whispered to me, 'The King is dead. No . . . announcement yet.' As I walked from the Ministry to Downing Street, I was told that the news was now public.[2]

When we met, the Prime Minister told us the sad story in a few simple and moving words. The King had been at Sandringham apparently in normal health. He had gone out for a day's hare-shooting and seemed happy and relaxed. After dinner he had gone to bed at his usual hour and fallen peacefully asleep. Early in the morning his heart had stopped beating.[1] The suddenness and unexpectedness seemed to add to the bitterness of the blow. The Cabinet sat for a few minutes in silent sorrow. Yet business had to be done. The Lord Chancellor and the Speaker, who had been specially asked to attend, were consulted as to the procedure, and the Lord President was asked to deal with the immediate question of the Accession Council.

> The last time that a monarch was proclaimed *in absentia* was on the death of Queen Anne, under rather more perilous circumstances than today, so far as the succession is concerned.[2]

In spite of the absence of the new Queen, it was decided to hold the Council at 5 p.m. at St. James's Palace and the summonses were immediately sent out in accordance with tradition. Each House of Parliament, when it met at 2.30, was to be adjourned until 7 p.m., when Members would start taking the oath of allegiance.

I could not help thinking, while this was being discussed, of those unhappy twelve months, from the end of 1935 to the end of 1936, when I, like many others, had sworn the oath of allegiance as

---

[1] John W. Wheeler-Bennett, *King George VI: His Life and Reign* (London, 1958), pp. 800 ff.

[2] 6 February 1952.

a Member of Parliament, to three monarchs–King George V, King Edward VIII, and to the King who had just died. Although I had not known the King intimately, I recalled those splendid days in North Africa when he had reviewed his soldiers, sailors and airmen, and above all the historic arrival at Malta on the bridge of the cruiser.[1] Nor could I forget the kindness and sympathy which he and the Queen had shown to me. On my visits home I had always been summoned to an audience, or to an informal tea and talk. I remembered too the extraordinary grasp of detail; the inherited royal memory; and the combination of simplicity and dignity.

The Cabinet was naturally concerned about the safe return of Princess Elizabeth, now Queen. Many felt that the dangers of an air journey were by no means negligible. Nevertheless, it was agreed that she would wish to come back as rapidly as possible and had probably by now already started. In the afternoon a further question arose as to the proclamation. The old form had included a reference to 'the Crown Imperial', which it was felt might now cause difficulties in the new situation of the Commonwealth. The real meaning of this phrase had been largely forgotten or obscured. The Crown Imperial, originally meant of course, that a King who claimed this title owed no fealty to an Emperor or any other superior. However, perhaps only historians and antiquarians would be aware of its origin and others would misunderstand its significance. It was therefore decided to omit these words and to introduce into the recital of titles the expression 'Head of the Commonwealth'. The Accession Council had always consisted of 'the Lords Spiritual and Temporal, members of the Privy Council, and other Principal Gentlemen of Quality, with the Lord Mayor, Aldermen and Citizens of London'. It was now agreed to add 'representatives of other members of the Commonwealth'.

At 5 p.m. we assembled at St. James's Palace, entering by Ambassadors Court. The meeting of the Council took place in the large room upstairs–and very fine it is. Lord Woolton (as Lord President) presided. There was a very large assembly of Peers, Ministers, ex-Ministers, Privy Councillors, High Commissioners,

[1] *The Blast of War*, pp. 349–50.

etc. The Lord Mayor and the Aldermen were present in their robes—all others in morning clothes.[1]

The Lord President read the draft declaration proclaiming Queen Elizabeth II. I am not sure how far we were aware at that time of the difficulties that might be raised in Scotland, where many regarded the new Queen as the second of England but the first of Scotland.

> Various other draft orders were read, including instructions to the Lord Mayor, to the Secretary of State, etc., for proclaiming the Queen, firing guns, sending 'circular letters' (presumably to Lords-Lieutenant), etc. After this, we all signed the great parchment scrolls, which were laid out for the purpose.[1]

We now heard that the Queen was expected back the next evening, and it was agreed that she should be received by a small group including the leaders of the Labour and Liberal parties. That night Churchill gave a broadcast message to the people:

> It was the best piece of prose I have heard or read from him. Some phrases will live long such as 'during these last months, the King walked with Death as if Death were a companion, an acquaintance whom he recognised and did not fear. In the end, Death came as a friend.' His references to the Queen Mother and Queen Mary were very fine. The last sentence was memorable. 'I, whose youth was passed in the august, unchallenged, and tranquil glare of the Victorian Era, may well feel a thrill in invoking once more the prayer and anthem "God Save the Queen".'[2]

On 8 February I went with other Privy Councillors and notables to St. James's Palace. We assembled in the old Levee Room. Punctually on the stroke of ten the ceremony began by the Lord President nominating a small number including Churchill and Attlee 'to wait upon Her Majesty'.

> The Queen's entrance; the low bows of her Councillors; the firm yet charming voice in which she pronounced her allocution and went through the various ceremonious forms of the ritual

[1] 6 February 1952.   [2] 7 February 1952.

(including the oath to maintain the Scottish Church) produced a profound impression on us all.[1]

Of course, the effect would have been much more brilliant had we all been in full dress like the Earl Marshal, the High Steward of Westminster (Lord Halifax), and one or two others, including the officers of the Household Cavalry and the Brigade of Guards. In contrast our dark coats and striped trousers presented rather a scruffy appearance.

The lying-in-state and the funeral have often been described. I never shall forget the moving scene of the Queen Mother in her deep mourning, who had come with the Queen to Westminster Hall at a moment when I happened myself to be present with my wife and children.

King George was sincerely mourned by all his subjects and by countless men and women in every walk of life throughout the world. All had understood how unwillingly he had succeeded to the grievous burden of monarchy in the most trying conditions, and how anxious had been the years of his reign. Perhaps the best tribute to his memory was paid by the Queen herself at the un-veiling of his memorial nearly four years later:

> It was this unassuming humanity, this respect for the 'home-spun dignity of man', which enabled my father to preserve in a changing world that affection and respect for the Crown by which our free Commonwealth of Nations is united.[2]

Nor did she claim too much in the simple but true statement at the end of her speech:

> He shirked no task, however difficult, and to the end he never faltered in his duty to his peoples.[3]

I was appointed Minister of Housing at the end of October 1951, and held this office for exactly three years. They proved in many ways the happiest and the most rewarding of my time as a Minister. If I missed the excitements of the Mediterranean campaign, my work was almost as difficult and inspiring as that of 'arming the

---

[1] 8 February 1952.
[2] Quoted in Wheeler-Bennett, p. 804.   [3] Ibid., p. 805.

8

TIDES OF FORTUNE

nation'. The obstacles with which we had to contend were in many ways different from those which faced us from 1940 to 1942, but almost equally baffling. I was soon to be grateful for the lessons which I had learned from my former chiefs, especially Beaverbrook. Success would certainly require some unorthodox methods, and we should have to fight hard—especially against those inveterate 'planners' who, arguing with irrefutable logic from false premises, arrived irresistibly at wrong conclusions. As in the old Ministry of Supply, improvisation and a certain ruthlessness would be necessary. Of course, there would be risks; but there would also be rewards. Departments which deal with large questions of general policy can seldom hope for definite fruits or proved results. Here, at least in the housing field, there would be a simple test—the figures of houses and flats actually completed.

The Conservative Party had certainly given hostages to fortune. Whatever the refinements about 'targets', the country expected 300,000 houses a year. Since the figures were published at monthly intervals, here was a scoreboard on which the eyes of all the critics, friendly and hostile, would be continually riveted. There could be no evasion by indefinite excuses about the economic climate or the difficulties of labour and materials. The relentless figures would tell their own tale.

Yet his advisers had persuaded even so determined a man as Aneurin Bevan that 200,000 was the absolute maximum at which it would be reasonable to aim. In fact, since 1948, there had been a short-fall even in this modest total. Moreover, this target had been fixed in a period of comparative economic calm. The first half of 1951 had not yet reflected the distracting pressures upon the economy which resulted from the ambitious rearmament programme to which Attlee and his colleagues had committed the nation. Indeed, as Churchill was soon to admit, owing to its enormous size, both in terms of money and in physical resources, the programme proved beyond our capacity to achieve in the time proposed. Moreover, while the devaluation of 1949 had given some temporary advantage to our exports against the rising production of Japan and Germany, now reviving from the destruction of war, yet this only softened the blow. Soon British internal prices began to rise substantially.

Rearmament was in addition claiming the services of many of those very industries, especially engineering, which were the main source of exports. As the year progressed, these troubles had begun to grow, and by the time the election came we were drifting before another economic storm.

This then would be the first obstacle; for if the classical methods were to be applied, the Treasury would certainly demand the cutting of imports, a rise in the Bank Rate, and a reduction of the so-called 'capital investment programme'. Indeed, it was more than likely that we would be limited to finishing the houses that had been started upon the much more modest level of the late Government's plans. There would be powerful resistance to new starts and an expanding programme. As a result, I was destined during the first months and even years to wage a continual battle with the Treasury for my fair share, or rather for more than my fair share, of the resources which the experts told us would be available. In this conflict I learned particularly to admire Butler's technique. Faced with the need for immediate restrictions, which he imposed over a wide field of consumer goods, and even extended to many capital projects, he always kept in mind the need for a positive as well as a negative policy. Even in the chill refrigerating chambers of Great George Street, he somehow preserved his warm expansionist heart.

If the financial hurdle could be overcome, or evaded, my next problem lay in the administrative instrument available for the job to be done. The Ministry to which I succeeded had been, until lately, part of the overloaded Ministry of Health; and when given an independent existence, it had been rechristened the Ministry of Local Government and Planning. It was staffed in the main by officials who had dealt with local government affairs, and was, therefore, a department concerned with guidance, advice, supervision, sometimes even warning and reproof, but never with positive action. It operated by circular and memorandum, seldom by personal contacts. Moreover, since it had no direct powers, it did not, like the Ministry of Supply, place orders with the contractors, large or small, whether in the private or the public sphere of housing. 1,500 or more local housing authorities in England and Wales were responsible for licensing 'private enterprise' houses and for ordering and programming 'council' houses. But there was no urgency or drive; no production organisation, central or local; no progress officers; no machinery for identifying and breaking 'bottlenecks'. The Ministry was in no sense a 'Production Department'—yet somehow or other, in spite of its constitution and the rules of White-hall, it had to be turned into an active and vibrant machine. I had given it a new name—the Ministry of Housing; I must breathe into it a new spirit.

Next came the vital questions of policy. During the years of the Labour Government, building for sale by private enterprise had been greatly reduced, hampered by insufficient licences and over-abundant regulations. Building societies had practically ceased to function. The building industry, which had been under rigid control during six years of war and six years of Socialism, had lost all elasticity. It had accustomed itself to operating in the discouraging and enervating atmosphere of a siege economy. Our materials—steel, alleged to be essential for the building of flats and even buildings of several storeys, timber, almost entirely imported, cement and above all bricks—were, to use the familiar jargon, 'in short supply'. There was also the need to prevent the old houses from falling into disrepair or even ruin. If this problem was to be dealt with we must make at least some impact on the question of rents, millions of which were still controlled, some at pre-1914 levels. Closely con-nected was the scandalous condition of the slums. Except where the Blitz had done a work which, however tragic, was often salutary, slum clearance had been virtually abandoned for many years. Yet how could we destroy houses in which people could at least find shelter, however bad the conditions, until we could show some encouraging results from the new houses springing up around them?

Finally, there was a strange piece of legislation called 'The Town and Country Planning Act'. I had paid no attention to this measure while it was passing through Parliament in 1947. Nor can I claim that I—or indeed any of my advisers—ever fully understood it. But it involved a fiscal instrument known as the 'development charge', the result of which, if not perhaps the purpose, was to hold up all development.

These, and some related difficulties, including the needs of the New Towns and the 'blitzed cities', were the main questions which were to occupy my time and effort for three years. As before, when I had been concerned with war supply, I could think—and even dream —of little else. In Opposition or on the back-benches a Member is properly interested in a whole range of subjects covering a wide field of policy. But when serving in a Ministry of this kind, so absorbing and so vital to the success of the Government as a whole, it was essential to concentrate the whole of my thoughts and actions upon the forcing of a narrow, although heavily defended, position. In some departments, of course, where the pressure is less, a Minister can carry out all his departmental duties and yet have ample time for the general questions which come before a Cabinet. Thus he can properly perform the duties that are inherent in the concept of the collective responsibility of Ministers. I am now conscious that in many spheres I was unable to deploy and defend my ideas with unimpeded vigour. In one field—that is, the general financial and economic problems—I played my part to the full. That was because a solution was essential to my own work. For on the policies pursued depended our success or failure to redeem the housing pledge. But to other questions—defence, foreign affairs, and above all, European unity, to which I had devoted so much labour under Churchill's inspiration while in Opposition—I could now give only occasional attention. In later years this laches has been a most grievous burden on my conscience. This was perhaps excusable. For the fierce and almost frantic pursuit of the housing target filled my mind and that of those who worked with me almost to the exclusion of everything not directly related to the achievement of our purpose. Day in, day out, we worked at the Ministry, in the regions, and, above all, in the corridors of Whitehall. Debates and questions in Parliament were an irritating, sometimes galling, distraction. But we knew that success would bring its own defence. The first months were sometimes disheartening. Yet when the results began to show themselves, there was a wonderful sense of accomplishment and exhilaration. These feelings were shared by our officials at the Ministry, who became increasingly imbued with a spirit of urgency and enthusiasm. There was, in addition, the sporting instinct of our friends, who watched the figures with growing excitement, and sometimes, perhaps, with almost a punter's interest. For the monthly completions were the subject of many friendly wagers.

During the election the full gravity of the economic situation had not unnaturally been minimised by Ministers and was unknown to the Opposition leaders. But the true situation was immediately set before Churchill by the Treasury in a minute which revealed that we were 'heading for early bankruptcy' unless immediate remedies were employed. As soon as Parliament met, he revealed this fact and added that he had sent a copy of the memorandum to Attlee, in order that he might know the Government's starting-point.

As regards overseas payments, the crisis was worse than the situation in 1947 or even in 1949. Although during the first half of 1951 the figures had been relatively encouraging, by the end of the year the deficit would be of the order of £500 to £600 million. Nor were future prospects any better. Although Butler had at once taken emergency action by ordering a cut of £360 million in imports and had raised the Bank Rate to 2½ per cent, it was clear by the opening days of 1952 that even more vigorous remedies would be required. Government expenditure, especially on capital account, was to be drastically reduced; at the same time Churchill had to agree that there must be some recasting of the rearmament pro-gramme, since it would not be possible to spend the £1,250 million set aside for the current year by the former Government. He ob-served that Bevan 'by accident, perhaps not from the best of motives, happened to be right'. Yet this measure would not result in any real saving, since the expenditure was to be postponed rather than cancelled.

Ministers laboured throughout these first weeks and months to wrestle with the problem. The Prime Minister had succeeded in adjourning Parliament from early in December to the last days of January. But this interval, with the exception of a few days round Christmas, was filled by continual discussions between groups of Ministers and ministerial committees. By the end of January it had become clear that the first emergency methods had not been able to reverse the position overnight. The drain on the reserves continued even more intensely, and it seemed that still greater sacrifices must be made, since it was believed that by the middle of 1952 the reserves would be down to £500 million, the level at which devaluation had become necessary in 1949. Accordingly a further cut in imports of £150 million was announced on 29 January and yet another of £100 million in March. The Bank Rate was increased to 4 per cent.

Since we were still living in the war economy of tight control and Government purchasing, it was possible to make import savings by decree. The pound was not convertible, and we were able to exercise discrimination in licensing imports without infringing our obligations. Accordingly, tobacco imports were cut; stockpiles were drawn upon; and the meat ration, since when we took office there was hardly more than three weeks' supply in stock, was reduced from 1s. 5d. to 1s. 2d. a week. Woolton characteristically tried to compensate for this by an increase in the bacon ration: but the meat ration was not restored until six months later. Since the demand, or rather the claims, for steel appeared to exceed the supply by something of the order of a million tons a year, a system of allocation was introduced. General building was not to exceed in 1952 the level achieved in 1951. Investment programmes in railways, fuel, power, and even sewerage and water were to be reduced. Nor was any likely alleviation for our difficulties to be found in non-dollar purchases. Not only was there a dollar shortage, but a shortage of all currencies. In Butler's own words, 'all foreign currencies' had become 'hard'.

Meanwhile we must try to develop Commonwealth and Sterling Area resources, reduce still further military expenditure overseas, and exercise restraint in respect of wages and the general standard of living. Although such a programme was not encouraging for a new Government which had been elected on a policy of expansion, it was no doubt necessary. It might indeed have been better if, instead of taking two or three bites at the poisoned cherry, we had made all the cuts within the first week. One bold decision was reached. The instalment of the interest and sinking fund of the

American and Canadian loans was duly paid, although this meant a further loss to the reserves. Many of us began to ask ourselves whether Great Britain could ever become a going concern again if she continued to carry the whole burden of operating a banking as well as a trading system, and shoulder all the obligations of sterling as an international currency.

After one of these meetings I wrote glumly in my diary:

> A most gloomy affair. The 'balance of payments' position grows daily worse. More cuts are to be made in imports, and we must in addition draw heavily on stockpiles. Foreign travel is to be cut to £25 allowance.[1]

Churchill had meanwhile gone to Washington, and some final decisions awaited his return. The Budget was to be brought forward, and it was hoped that by the middle of March we should have finished the painful task of restriction.

I had at this time an enlightening discussion with Gaitskell:

> Since we shared the closed compartment of a Pullman (and were alone) we talked freely and agreeably. He feels rather more hopeful about the second half of the year than he has said in public (for he wants to help on this side). But he believes that (a) the terms of trade are moving a little more favourably; (b) Butler's measures should help to stop flight of capital; (c) American buying is beginning and will increase.
>
> But he fears that these crises in the sterling–dollar situation are endemic. Things will improve, and then perhaps another crisis in 18 months. Our problem is how to get a large enough reserve of gold and dollars to stand the pressure. If the Americans were to raise the price of gold it would be the easiest way out. But (a) they would hardly do this during a boom in U.S. It is a measure reserved for a slump; (b) there is a danger that it might lead to a popular outcry against buying gold at all.[2]

I carried away pleasant memories of that talk:

> Gaitskell [is] essentially a moderate by temperament as well as conviction. He is able, and agreeable.[2]

[1] 22 January 1952.   [2] 2 February 1952.

As I came to see more of him in subsequent years, this impression of his charm and integrity was continually strengthened.

Just before the Budget was introduced, a new problem presented itself:

> In spite of all our efforts to save imports, cut internal expenditure and generally do all the right things at home, we are going to be ruined by our customers in our capacity as bankers. The drain on sterling cannot be stopped unless something drastic is done about this.[1]

The question of the sterling balances, which had to be met in many cases by 'unrequited exports', was a complicated one. In some parts of the Sterling Area the huge sums which we owed represented the cost of defending their populations and territory in war. To many of us this burden seemed not only onerous but unfair. A new plan was devised to block or fund (at nominal interest) all sterling balances up to 90 per cent for 'foreigners' and 80 per cent for the independent Sterling Area members. The rest would be convertible, but at no fixed rate. A market in transferable sterling and a free gold market would be opened in London, and our remaining reserves would be used to support the rate.

This scheme, which was somewhat hurriedly thrust at Ministers by the Treasury, has since been the subject of much discussion by economists and historians. It seemed to me then that it had serious disadvantages. The Commonwealth Finance Ministers had met in London and only just left for home. Would it not seem very panicky and indeed almost frivolous to tear up the whole of the arrangements upon which they had recently agreed and to substitute a completely new project? Nevertheless, I felt that although the timing was bad and dangerous, in essence the plan might perhaps be right. Many years have now passed, and the concept of fixed exchanges has been widely accepted throughout the world, as well as an extended machinery for freeing world trade as far as possible. The situation is therefore very different from that which faced us early in 1952. But at that time strong arguments were deployed in favour of what came to be known as the 'floating rate'. Naturally some

[1] 29 February 1952.

Ministers felt that we had received too little notice of so sudden and so drastic a proposal. Yet it was discussed fully and without prejudice at many meetings.

> The Treasury ought to have warned us for the last four weeks that the 'cuts' would not do the trick so long as the leakage (through our banking customers) was allowed to go on. All their estimates [have] been proved wrong. It is not worth while making all these tiresome and unpopular cuts, if the leakage keeps going on through the Commonwealth, etc. We might do better to wind up the Sterling Area (except for U.K. and the Colonies) altogether.[1]

In the end we adopted the policy of relying on the series of defensive measures already agreed and postponing the larger question until there could at least be some proper negotiation.

> It is very likely that we shall come to this in April or May. But that would be after . . . consultation and discussion; not as a panic matter, amounting to default (or 90 per cent and 80 per cent default).[1]

Yet I was left uneasy:

> . . . if this plan was right, it was right in November. Really, it was right in 1945! For the whole basis of the plan is that it is impossible to carry on a central banking business as large as that of the Bank of England with such slender reserves. To have nearly £3,000 millions 'at call' and to have none of the huge debt by the Bank to its customers funded, is an impossible position. (This has been the basis of Churchill's long and instinctive feeling that the 'sterling balances' must be dealt with.) The position has been, to some extent, dealt with by the release agreements. This at least regulated the calls made by customers.[2]

Agreements were now reached, controlling the rate at which the balances could be drawn down. These were an alleviation, if not a cure. Moreover, the debts were not all relics of the war. The Australian position had been built up suddenly by high wool prices. The money had been paid into the pool, and we could scarcely

---

[1] 29 February 1952.   [2] 1 March 1952.

object to their drawing heavily on their account. The chief anxiety was now caused by a continuance of the loss of dollars in January and February:

> But the cuts which we made in imports (since contracts have *not* been repudiated) have scarcely had time to become effective, and the Commonwealth cuts have hardly started.[1]

So we soldiered on, relying on orthodox policies.

When the Budget came it proved sensible and was well received. There was a considerable surplus 'above the line',[2] but Butler rightly proposed no substantial increases or decreases in taxation. The expenditure on food subsidies was to be reduced from the £410 million fixed by Cripps to £250 million. But family allowances were correspondingly increased, as were war-disability and other pensions. The standard rate of income tax was unchanged, but alterations in the children's allowance, in earned-income tax relief and in the rates at the lowest taxable level conferred considerable benefit to the mass of the wage-earning population. It was thus a 'neutral' Budget.

Throughout all these discussions, whether in the Cabinet or in Cabinet committees, I had naturally to think chiefly of my own housing needs. But I was equally anxious to find some method of moving to an expansionist policy, an approach with which I think Butler sympathised. Sometimes the magnitude of the problem oppressed me, for each new Treasury assessment seemed more depressing than the last. According to one of these 'ruin stared us in the face':

> ... we are in for a pretty rough time. If we escape collapse over the 'balance of payments', it will only be to plunge into a degree

---

[1] 1 March 1952.

[2] By tradition the national accounts of Britain have been kept for centuries on a cash basis; that is to say the Budget of the year dealt with 'Cash In' and 'Cash Out'. No difference was made between payments on Capital Account and payments on Revenue Account. The Dalton Budgets of 1946 and 1947 initiated a new system, which has remained in force. Cash payments and cash revenue are accounted for above the line. Capital investments are placed below the line, as are any receipts on Capital Accounts.

of unemployment which the people (after years of over-full employment) will regard as intolerable and will be told has been deliberately organised by the Tories.[1]

We all knew that the critical months for sterling would be July to September. Meanwhile, there was a great swing back against us politically in the local elections in April:

> The party is stunned by the set-back in the County Council elections and looks forward with much apprehension to the Borough elections in May. . . . Prices rise, unemployment grows, Lancashire is in something like collapse, food gets less and more expensive, and the 'cuts' are rigorously opposed and exploited by the Socialists. At the same time, the balance of payments problem, though slightly eased, is by no means solved.[2]

At the same time the overseas situation was overcast:

> American aid is almost completely cut off, and they are doing all they can to force down the prices of rubber and tin. There is no hope of any short-term solution of the Persian question, and an immense loss to the balance of payments follows.[2]

The position in Egypt was equally disturbing.

It was now agreed that there should be a meeting in November 1952 attended by Commonwealth Prime Ministers, and that every effort should be made to prepare a constructive plan. In spite of my other preoccupation, I felt I must make some contribution. I therefore prepared two papers, the first of which was circulated during the third week in June and the second at the beginning of July. If the re-reading of old speeches is an unrewarding exercise, the perusal of old memoranda years after they were written is an even more melancholy experience. Some of the problems have been resolved, or at any rate certain definite courses of action have been accepted; others still remain with us. But the internal and external conditions have changed; and what might have then been practicable methods of approach have now, nearly twenty years later, passed

[1] 29 March 1952.   [2] 8–10 April 1952.

into the limbo of history. Nevertheless, there may still be some interest in these discussions which then seemed to us so urgent and vital.

The Treasury view was presented with admirable clarity. Urgent remedies were still needed, in addition to those already implemented. Above all, an increase of our exports to non-sterling markets of some 20 per cent was essential. This must fall largely upon the metal-using industries, and would be met partly at the expense of defence and partly by further restricting the social programme. As a policy, this certainly had the merit of simplicity. But I doubted whether it was either sound or practicable. Could it produce any lasting solution? The Treasury themselves admitted that there was 'no "hump" but a continuing mountain range of difficulties'. Surely their solution was just a continuation of the Cripps–Gaitskell policies. In any case nobody believed that exports to non-sterling markets could be increased by 20 per cent – certainly, the Board of Trade did not. If this could not be done, 'then the prospect before us is not gentle decline but catastrophe'.

I felt that a far more dynamic and positive approach was necessary, an approach, moreover, that took into account the fact that our problems stemmed from a permanent change in Britain's economic position relative to the rest of the world and could not be solved by short-term improvisation. I suggested that our aims should be to increase home production – particularly of food, coal, other minerals and any machine-tools or consumer goods being imported from the dollar area; to reduce still further, as a systematic and continuing policy, our imports from the dollar area and other areas with which we were in deficit, and, where necessary, to substitute for them imports from the Sterling Area; to develop in the Sterling Area alternative supplies of the food and raw materials we needed and were currently obtaining from non-sterling sources; to make the best, from the point of view of our capital and consumer goods industries, of the new markets created by the adoption of the foregoing policies; and to continue to promote the maximum exports to non-sterling areas consistent with these policies.

The opponents of these ideas naturally maintained that they involved the danger of setting up an artificial system of exchanging high-priced goods in a new form of autarchy. Much stress had been laid upon this by some of my colleagues. But I pointed out that although American protectionism suffered from this defect in its early stages, the increasing size of the market and the corresponding opportunities for mass production completely altered the picture over a period of time. Might not the same be done in the Sterling Area? Furthermore, in spite of high sterling prices, the shortage of dollars in the non-dollar world was working in our favour. Of course there would be a temporary increase in the balance of payments problem. We should meet it by the reduction of all dollar or non-sterling imports that were not absolutely essential, even if we had to accept temporary cuts in our social programme. But these must result from an act of declared policy and not as a result of administrative failure.

Yet this was only one aspect of the policy. Could we not now take the lead in Europe? If reciprocal trade and currency arrangements could be made with European countries, by the creation of something like a merger, or at any rate a close co-operation between European currencies and sterling, could we not take the first steps to build a vast new market, in which we could develop our strength and assert our independence?

The West European countries were in much the same position with respect to the dollar world that we were in ourselves. Many of their economists and industrialists had already been thinking of insulating their economies from the dollar on lines similar to those I was advocating. Uncertain of British policy they were tending to the idea of making the Schuman Plan Community a more or less exclusive trading area, an eventuality which would only increase our own problems. The difficulties in their way, however, are at least as great as those which we should encounter if we tried to restore the Sterling Area by our own unaided efforts. There was reason to believe, therefore, that they would be greatly attracted by the prospect of becoming in some way associated with us and our plans for restoring our economic strength.

There remained, of course, the problem of Canada with its dollar currency. Yet the preferential system would at least give Canadians some certainty that any of our dollars available would be spent in

Canada rather than the United States, and as our strength grew so would our purchasing power in Canada increase.

I maintained that a great error would be made in trying to limit investment, either at home or in the Commonwealth. In the long run, or even in the shorter run, we must try to get out of the debtor position and re-establish our old position, when we were a creditor nation. The balance of payments in any particular year was not so important as the fundamental situation. In spite of many subsequent alarms this analysis has proved true. I have always felt instinctively that herein lies the real test of a nation's strength. The lack of short-term liquidity may be troublesome and embarrassing. But the absolute assets of a country, like those of a business enterprise, and its power to earn, must be the final test. So it has proved.

> Perhaps the best evidence for the post-war record is to be found, not in the trend for the current balance or the basic balance but in the transition from debtor to creditor status. At the end of the war the United Kingdom was a debtor (possibly a heavy debtor) on international account (short-term and long-term combined); within less than twenty years it had become a creditor with a net surplus of assets which at the end of 1964 exceeded £2,300 million.[1]

The Treasury countered by appealing to the views of the City and the Bank of England. To this I was tempted, perhaps improperly, to make the disrespectful reply that, while the authority of the City, and particularly of the Bank of England, must always be great, yet the most tender critic of the financial and economic policies proposed by successive Governors could scarcely maintain that the Bank had always given wise advice to the Government of the day. I cited various examples, such as Lord Cunliffe's estimate of the capacity of Germany to pay reparations; the advice of Mr. Montagu Norman given to the Chancellor of the Exchequer of the day to return to gold at a parity of $4.86 to the pound; the long deflationary policy which had caused a wave of emotional ill-feeling among the working classes against the capitalist class that was still not yet expended; the

---

[1] A. R. Conan, *Westminster Bank Review*, August 1967, p. 11.

events of 1931, and the apparent concession to American banking opinion of the standards of the unemployed; finally, the ill-advised return to convertibility in 1947. All these raised at least doubts in many minds. All sensible people respected the authority of 'the world of Banking and Finance', but one did not therefore have to subscribe to the dogma of City infallibility. The Chancellor of the Exchequer, having a great sense of humour, *was* amused.

During all these months there were fierce attacks on my housing plans, which I had with difficulty contained. But I did not abandon, even under new threats, my broad theme. Convertibility and non-discrimination should be the culminating point in a national design. They certainly should not be risked at a moment of weakness. Everything was now to be staked on the November conference of Commonwealth Prime Ministers. We would not get out of our difficulties by freezing sterling; we could only get out of them by developing at home, and in the Sterling Area, our maximum strength and expanding energy. If we had meanwhile to cut imports further, I would accept this—even timber imports—so long as I was still allowed to find some method of obtaining results by ingenuity of design. But any further demands upon the people must be, and be seen to be, a plan of conserving our strength of action; of crouching before the bold leap forward to our destiny. Whatever sacrifices might be asked of the consumer, we must aim at expansion rather than restriction of production, agricultural as well as industrial. Nor were my hopes altogether illusory. The extraordinary achievements of agriculture and its major contribution towards the balance of payments in recent years are the result of capital investment, high skill, and technical and scientific progress. We have not protected or given guaranteed prices to a declining and inefficient industry. On the contrary, we have built up by these means the most highly capitalised, the best equipped and the most efficient agricultural structure in the world. A great part, if not the whole, of productive industry has achieved similar results.

At one moment I began to despair and to wonder whether all this effort was worth while. The Commonwealth and European plans, both then within our grasp, seemed to me worthy and not impracticable. But it would perhaps be better to stick to my own last and cobble away at that. Although many of my colleagues expressed sympathy, I felt often disappointed, even bitter:

> I have been reading the reports of the officials. . . . They are not encouraging. 'They murmured as they took their fees, there is no cure for this disease'. Perhaps it would be better to give up the struggle and ask to become the 49th State. But then, what would happen to the officials? The Americans would not take them on.[1]

Nor did the debates on the economic situation in the House of Commons do very much to help. In one of these Bevan made the most effective speech but, as so often, it was unconstructive. In the course of it he made a fierce onslaught on Gaitskell, which for once roused Attlee. On the following day, when the House met.

> we had an incident without parallel. Attlee got up after Questions to make a 'personal' statement. (This procedure is usually to defend oneself, not to attack somebody else.) He said that Bevan had disclosed Cabinet secrets and broken the tradition which bound colleagues on this. (This was in connection with the beginning of the rearmament plan during the Labour Government.) Bevan was not in the House, but Ellis Smith (Labour) . . . asked if notice had been given to him by Attlee. The reply was 'Yes'—but it seems that either by accident or design the letter did not reach him. Bevan will make a statement tomorrow.[2]

Bevan had a very full House for his defence:

> It was admirably done. He dwelt at some length on the strongest part of his case, viz. Attlee's fatuity and incompetence in not making sure that his letter to Bevan was delivered before he spoke yesterday. Merely to give a note, at 1.30, to the messenger on the door was an incredibly casual method.
> On the substance of Attlee's complaint, Bevan was not on such strong ground. But his reference to what happened in 1931 (after the collapse of MacDonald's Government) was very agile.[3]

But these exchanges between a divided Opposition, although an amusing distraction, did not provide a solution to our own diffi-

[1] 27 July 1952.   [2] 31 July 1952.   [3] 1 August 1952.

culties. In this, as well as helping me in my own housing work, one of my most stalwart supporters was Swinton. His long experience, his acute mind, his admirably concise and effective method of presenting his views, were deeply impressive. We both felt that many of the experts did not think enough in terms of realities. They seemed insufficiently concerned with the creation of real wealth, and too much with the fluctuations of bank balances and reserves, which often reflected artificial and even superficial movements.

The date of the Commonwealth Conference was now approaching, but no large purpose or central plan seemed yet to have emerged. When we had the final discussions towards the end of November, I feared that there was a new slide towards the Treasury and the Bank of England point of view. I therefore restated my position as clearly as possible:

1. No convertibility into a fixed exchange. 'If you [are] to be free, you must float.'
2. Convertibility must be sustained on its own merits – that is, it must represent real conditions of stability, due to genuinely improved production in the non-dollar world.
3. Quantitative restriction, etc., cannot be removed till it is safe; in danger, we must be free to reimpose, unilaterally, the protective measures we need.[1]

This seemed to meet with the approval of my colleagues, and there were at least some points on which we were determined not to yield.

When the Conference met, agreement was reached on general objectives, but so far as any public statement was concerned they were either vague or seemingly unobtainable. The curbing of inflation, the raising of the standard of living, the extension of trade —all these were sound enough, but little more than expressions of hope. Naturally some of the Commonwealth members would have liked full convertibility of their currencies into dollars, whatever the result on sterling. But, broadly, they were helpful and understanding. If the Conference did not achieve very much in detail, it made a good general impression. It was certainly a notable triumph

[1] 24 November 1952.

for Butler. The 'collective approach' avoided the main pitfalls and seemed at least to make some forward steps on the uphill, winding road.

So ended 1952 – an anxious, difficult, and often distracting year of argument and controversy. Yet it was a year of at least limited progress. In 1953, partly as the result of our short-term measures, partly from a growing sense of confidence in Britain's determination, partly perhaps arising from those mysterious ebbs and flows that still seem to dominate these rapidly changing economic currents, the improvement became marked and the tensions were accordingly relaxed.

Throughout all this period the Prime Minister maintained remarkable vitality. There was hardly a Cabinet, however serious the situation, without some gem. For instance, after two hours on a long and difficult issue, the only relief came when a Minister said 'I have tried to put the case fairly.' 'A very dangerous thing to do,' growled Churchill. On another occasion he was concerned at the cost of keeping a criminal lunatic in Broadmoor, which had arisen from a verdict of 'guilty but insane' on a young footman. He had already made the reflection that it was encouraging to note that even in these degenerate days there were still houses where it was possible to shoot a brace of butlers. He was now pressing the Home Secretary as to the cost of keeping this unhappy man in detention. 'What could you do it for?' he asked. 'A monkey a year?' I reflected that it must have been many years since this expression had been used at the Cabinet table.

In the course of another rather dreary session we were given an account of some disturbances in Bechuanaland arising out of the decision regarding Seretse Khama. After the story had been told and the Minister had informed us of what he proposed to say, Churchill summed up the situation as follows:

> Indeed a terrible position. An angry mob, armed with staves and stones, inflamed by alcohol, and inspired by Liberal principles![1]

On another occasion he was puzzled, or affected to be, by an argu-

[1] 10 June 1952.

ment about the difference between short- and long-term interest rates. 'I recall, as a boy, entering into a transaction with a Mr. Attenborough about my gold watch. I do not recall any such pedantic distinctions.'

At a later date, in connection with the Korean War, the Dean of Canterbury, known as the 'Red Dean', had been making foolish accusations about 'germ' warfare. His allegations had caused wide-spread indignation at home and overseas. The very word Canterbury clothed him with a spurious authority, but he could not be removed:

> 'At home, he does not matter. In the East, they would surely say "they are afraid of this holy Fakir, so they wish to silence him". Of course, these ecclesiastics would be better employed in preparing us for a better world and even in facilitating our safe arrival there!—but we can do nothing against the Dean.'[1]

The first months of 1953 brought us growing relief. Although nothing very substantial had emerged, either from the Common-wealth Conference or from the talks which Butler held in Washington in March, the economic climate was steadily improving. Meanwhile, we had succeeded in two important objectives. The admission of Japan to GATT[2] was postponed, and we were also able to avoid any definite move towards convertibility.

> There is really no sense in a convertible sterling in existing conditions. We might suffer as badly as in 1947.[3]

On 13 April we were told the main outlines of Butler's Budget:

> Its main theme is, I think, right. A fillip to industry. Here, he proposes to restore 20 per cent (half the original) initial allowances for new plant; he will bring E.P.L. [excess profits levy] to an end on a fixed date; he will cut all purchase tax (at whatever rate) by a quarter; he will take 6d. off the income tax. This, of course, will be called a 'Capitalist' Budget. But then we believe in Capitalism as the best instrument for the prosperity of the people. As a sop, a few minor income-tax adjustments and sugar to be 'off the ration'. (This has been done by buying a million tons of surplus Cuban sugar at a very good price.) A good Budget.[4]

[1] 10 July 1952.   [2] General Agreement on Tariffs and Trade.
[3] 10 March 1953.   [4] 13 April 1953.

I had pressed for the abolition of excess profits levy because I thought this would encourage the manufacturers of bricks and cement to invest in new plant. But the allowances were equally important. The Budget undoubtedly marked an improved position, and demonstrated the increasing strength of the economy.

Churchill was correspondingly elated. The story went round that when he was rather impudently asked by a Member in the smoking-room how long he proposed to remain as Prime Minister, he replied with a twinkle, 'Till the pub closes.' A variant of this ran, 'I shall certainly stand at the next election – probably as a Conservative.'

The so-called 'collective approach' went on, the purpose of which was, so far as I could ever understand, to create a situation in which the whole Sterling Area would be able to accept convertibility. I still pressed my alternative policies – the Commonwealth and Europe – in which some of my colleagues and I believed so earnestly but which had always been ridiculed by the experts. All the same, every month things got better:

> For the moment, the Government are in a favourable position – the balance of payments [deficit] reduced, taxation reduced, full employment maintained.[1]

The new fear which began to haunt financial commentators was that of an American slump, with its serious impact upon Britain and Europe. The end of the Korean War had, of course, considerable effects on the American economy, and by the autumn many economists, including the leader-writers of the *Manchester Guardian* and the *Economist*, seemed to regard at least a minor recession as inevitable. In these circumstances, since our reserves would be necessarily affected, there was some discussion as to the precise effect of the waiver clause in the American loan agreement. This phrase was obscure, and although we had not invoked it in our worst difficulties and had no intention of doing so, it seemed to some that any doubt should be removed. I remember Churchill once asking me at dinner, 'What does a waiver mean? Does it just mean I won't pay?' Oliver Lyttelton declared that Americans thought it meant 'Britannia waives the rules' – but this seemed a little unfair.

[1] 6 May 1953.

By the end of the year we felt on reasonably firm ground, although it was clear that there was little hope of any further help from America:

1. They will *not* lower their tariffs.
2. They will *not* simplify their tariff procedure.
3. They will *not*, through I.M.F. or in any other way, put up a fund to back sterling and thus assist us to go for convertibility.

So the great Treasury dream is over! We had better get back to Tariffs and to the Commonwealth–Europe plan.[1]

The frantic days of meetings and discussions in a situation of crisis were succeeded throughout 1954 by a period of comparative calm. Nobody could explain how this had happened, and some of the critics seemed rather mortified. From my narrow point of view as Minister of Housing it was all very satisfactory in the short term, although perhaps dangerous in the long. The Budget of 1954 was described by Butler as a 'carry-on' Budget. It neither stimulated purchasing power nor reduced it. *The Times* and the *Economist* took the view that the recent results were gratifying, but only due to favourable world conditions. These might not continue. However, for a time at least, they did. Thus, by one of those strange processes, inexplicable but common, the whole scene had changed. The economic crisis which we had inherited in 1951 seemed pretty well to have faded out by the end of 1954. What perhaps we had failed to realise is that it was not merely an epidemic attack, but that there were endemic weaknesses and dangers which might recur. Yet we actually reached a point by the spring of 1955 in which, for ordinary purposes, convertibility between non-resident holders of sterling was achieved in practice. The financial pressures, which at the beginning of my period of office had made my task in housing almost impossible, had gradually disappeared, until the Treasury no longer fought much of a battle about my expenditure. By now, in any case, they regarded it as a hopeless effort; for they knew I had the support of the Prime Minister and my colleagues in putting the housing programme high in the scale of political necessities. They also knew that I would fight my corner toughly and, if neces-

[1] 29 December 1953.

sary, back my demands by resignation. So long as the great scare lasted I was always in trouble. But when, like the Snark, the crisis slowly and silently vanished away, my departmental anxieties on this account faded too.

Perhaps the most urgent task which faced me when I was appointed to the Ministry of Housing was that of creating an efficient organisation, both at the centre and throughout the country, to get the houses built. It soon became clear that we would need something nearer to the war-time model if we were to look for any success. The Permanent Secretary, Sir Thomas Sheepshanks, was a charming and cultivated man with a background of scholarship and the Church—he was the son of a bishop—and with agreeable manners. He had a wide knowledge of the Civil Service and a deep respect for its conventions. He was well liked by the local authorities and their organised bodies. But he knew nothing of the problems of industry or of production. There were two Deputy Secretaries—Sir John Wrigley, whose knowledge and experience of local governments were unique, but who was approaching retiring age—and Dame Evelyn Sharp, exceptionally able and gifted, with a strong personality. I felt that from the first I should find in her a useful ally and that she would not object to the unconventional methods that we might adopt. But clearly there must be somebody to play the role of director-general, as in the war-time production Ministries. To achieve this presented two problems. First, to select the man and persuade him to serve; secondly, to introduce him into the existing system. After talks with some of my old war-time friends, such as Sir Graham Cunningham and Sir William Rootes, I decided to try to get Sir Percy Mills. I had known him well when he was Machine-Tool Controller,[1] and had kept in touch with him since. He was an administrator of proved character and success. He had served the Government for six years during the war and for three or four more years in Germany as chief economic adviser. He was therefore well accustomed to Whitehall, where he had many friends. But he had now returned to his old position in industry. Would I be able to induce his colleagues to make another sacrifice and release

[1] *The Blast of War*, p. 95.

him for at least another year? When Sir Percy came to see me, he was as usual modest about his capacities, but frank about the difficulties. He would be willing to come, but it would not be easy to arrange. 'Perhaps I had better go and see the chairman myself and try to persuade him to release you.' 'I don't think that would be any good,' said Sir Percy. 'He has never heard of you.' 'Well, who has he heard of?' 'Only Churchill. Churchill is his hero, his God.'

Acting upon this advice I managed to see the Prime Minister the next evening. I had prepared the text of a letter which he must write to the chairman, asking for Sir Percy's services. He was rather gruff about this, but finally I persuaded him that this was the only way I could build the houses. 'All right,' he said, 'I'll send the letter. Get it typed and I'll sign it.' 'No, Prime Minister, you will have to write it in your own hand. It cannot be typewritten.' This was a grievous burden to Churchill, who dealt always in dictated letters and minutes. 'I shall do nothing of the kind. This is an imposition.' 'Well, Prime Minister, I am afraid if you do not we shall not build the 300,000 houses.' 'What is to be done with the letter, if I do write it?' 'It will be framed in glass to show both sides and kept as a treasure. It will also be necessary to have a signed photograph of yourself.' 'I don't send signed photographs, except to very few people—never to those I don't know.' 'Well, Prime Minister, this man is more important than many of the others whom you do know. He is the man who will decide. I only want two men to help me. You have given me Marples, who is an exceptionally brilliant engineer and organiser. If we get Sir Percy, who is a first-class executive, I believe we can do the job.'

After some further discussion I won my point. Armed with these credentials, I paid a visit to the Midlands. I came, I saw, and, by presenting my gifts, I conquered.

There was naturally some trouble about this appointment, both in Whitehall and in the House of Commons. In Whitehall, it was explained to me at some length that we had moved a long way from the war and that there was no real place now for people like Sir Percy Mills. Moreover, was he to be executive or advisory? How would he rank with the Permanent Secretary and the various

Six houses built in seven weeks: the opening ceremony, March 1952

departmental chiefs, in our Ministry and outside? What precisely were his functions?

> I am having trouble with the civil servants about Percy Mills. They want him to be advisory; I want him to be executive. Things are much changed since I was in office before. The 'Trade Union' of officials is back in power. The Treasury planners are supreme. Ministers are treated very politely, but with firmness, as temporary nuisances.[1]

Even Sir Edward Bridges, an old school-friend and the most unprejudiced of men, seemed perturbed. Finally, a long paper was composed, with all kinds of conditions and qualifications, and brought to me. I said it would be quite agreeable to me, but in fact all this argument was unnecessary. I would regard the conditions like those which appear on the back of a debenture. 'Nobody ever looks at them unless the interest is in default. In any case, Sir Percy, who is a man of the utmost tact as well as drive, will soon win not merely the confidence but the affection of those with whom I have asked him to work.' And so it was to prove. In the House of Commons there were some objections to Sir Percy's appointment, which was officially announced on 28 November. Bevan could not resist a jibe at 'dollar a year men'. But the Press was favourable.

Within a few days of my own appointment I decided to see the representatives of the builders' unions. Sir Richard Coppock and Sir Luke Fawcett, the trade union leaders, came to see me at my request at the House of Commons. They were very friendly and pleasant:

> I told them that I knew little or nothing about the problem. They were much amused by this. 'The last Ministers knew everything. It was no good trying to talk to them. They talked to us.' This referred to Bevan and Dalton. The union leaders support the Labour Party. But they have very little affection for the political leaders.[2]

I then saw the leaders of building employers, including Richard Costain, who was to prove enthusiastic and helpful.

The next step was to set up a small ministerial council after the

[1] 19–24 November 1951.   [2] 5–9 November 1951.

o

pattern of the war-time Ministry of Supply. This soon began to operate effectively, although some regarded it as a dangerous innovation. It reduced the number of written minutes and reached rapid conclusions. But even with improved organisation we needed help. We were dependent on other departments, particularly the Ministry of Works. By the middle of November I had agreed with the Minister, David Eccles, and with Lord Swinton, who was looking after raw materials, upon a machinery to manage the whole building programme for the benefit of all departments:

> This is the only way to see that house-building, repairs, factory building, schools, etc., are regarded as a whole and carried through with mutual goodwill and common sense.[1]

We accordingly asked the Scottish Office to join us. As a result a Building Committee of the Cabinet was authorised. This gave us the help of the Cabinet Secretariat, with an excellent secretary in the shape of Freddie Bishop. He afterwards became principal private secretary first to Eden and then to myself at No. 10. He was a man of exceptional brilliance, and flexible as well as loyal. This gave us an efficient mechanism at the centre.

It soon became clear, however, that since we had really no direct control of the house-building programme, we must set up a strong regional organisation. With our new machinery, we could get our hands upon materials so far as stocks and finance would allow. We could improve and simplify the methods and design of house-building, and devise all sorts of schemes for saving time, money and labour. But we could not operate effectively unless we could create in each region a working team to watch and control the detailed programmes and restore something of the spirit of war-time enthusiasm. This would mean a widespread effort. We must set up Regional Housing Boards. We must also be tireless in visits to the local authorities. We must take housing out of politics. We must create a public opinion in support of what we were soon to call 'The Housing Crusade'.

By the very first day of January 1952 we discussed our detailed plans.

[1] 15 November 1951.

Sir P. Mills is very anxious to set up Regional Housing Production Boards, with Ministry of Labour and Ministry of Works officials and representatives of labour and builders. This frightens the department; but I have decided in favour of Sir Percy's plan.[1]

These were early days, and doubts and hesitations were to be expected:

The department still worries about Percy Mills, though what we should do without him, I shudder to think. He approaches every problem with realism and precision; his suggestions are at once bold and ingenious; and he has a quiet persistence which enables him to get his way. Since he is both quiet and courteous, they cannot complain that he is the 'vulgar businessman'. Yet they are suspicious, particularly of the speed with which he works. The Secretary (Sir T. Sheepshanks) expressed very fairly and frankly his anxiety in a long talk. I think I was able to persuade him that the system not only would work but must be made to work.[2]

The Treasury had for a long time been trying to bring to an end the regional system, which was a war-time creation and justified not only by the needs for production but by the difficulties of communication. They were certainly not attracted by 'The Great Housing Crusade' which I launched at Nottingham at the end of January. Even worse was the concept that we should add to the officials on the boards representatives of the builders and of the building unions. However, we carried out our plan.

In announcing the creation of the boards, each of which had an independent chairman—usually an industrialist of note—I made clear what their task would be:

They will try to cut out red tape and simplify procedure; to help to solve the production problems which are thrown up from time to time and from area to area as the programme develops; to break bottlenecks; to overcome shortages; to deal rapidly with all the difficulties which will inevitably arise, and which are inseparable from the determination to move forward

[1] 1–4 January 1952.   [2] 8 January 1952.

at a steadily growing pace. I trust they will also help to build up that enthusiasm, that moral urge, without which no great task can be successfully attacked and effectively completed.[1]

Thus, with our joint ministerial meetings in Whitehall, we achieved a pretty complete system of co-operation, both locally and centrally.

By 14 February Mills was able to launch the first Regional Housing Board at Bristol. This was followed by similar bodies throughout the country, and although we continued to have a good deal of trouble from some of the higher civil servants who were behaving in a petty and old-maidish way, we gradually overcame their opposition.

Throughout March the Boards were being formed:

> The Housing machine is getting into shape. The Regional Boards are being formed. . . . Mills is displaying imagination and determination.[2]

By the middle of March, although the Permanent Secretary was still doubtful of all these new and unorthodox methods,

> all the other civil servants (including Sir John Wrigley and Dame Evelyn Sharp) are working with enthusiasm and seem to be learning gradually how little they know about production or business management. I really think they are beginning to enjoy the sort of modified 'Beaverbrookism' which, with the help of Marples (my Parliamentary Secretary) and Mills, I am trying both to preach and to practise.[3]

It was soon necessary to increase the authority of the Boards. The more we ran into difficulties with shortages and bottlenecks, the more vital was the need to deal with them on the spot. Yet even as late as April 1953, when their usefulness was fully proved, I had to make a formal come-back to a further attack by the Treasury:

> Most of the day-to-day work on housing is done in the regional offices. To disturb them at this moment, just when we are within sight of the target, would be fatal.

The Housing programme still largely depends on the local

---

[1] Speech at Albert Hall, Nottingham, 22 January 1952.
[2] 4 March 1952.   [3] 13–14 March 1952.

authorities; and their extraordinary success . . . is due to the work of the regional staff. Sometimes we need to quicken the pace; sometimes we need to slow it. This cannot be done by letters. It needs the most discreet handling; many authorities, after all, are politically opposed to us.

We are hoping for 300,000 houses this year. But it is going to be touch-and-go on the materials. We are having to urge on authorities every possible economy in the use of bricks; we may have to do this with other materials. The authorities don't like it; but as a result of persuasion by the regional staff most of them are co-operating. Unless we can get the economies, we shan't get the houses. We can only get them by constant following up. Letters are worse than useless.

I added that if my colleagues had become indifferent to the number of houses which were built each year,

> Maybe we will then be able to fold up all our regional offices. But when that time comes, I hope to fold up too.

The challenge was not taken up.

It soon became necessary to remould all the rest of the department on similar lines to the Housing section, and although there was considerable resistance we got our way. From time to time the Permanent Secretary complained that all my proposals and methods were what he called 'unconstitutional':

> The Secretary (and only the Secretary) can advise the Minister. He must consult Sir Edward Bridges, the head of the Civil Service. So the Bishop consults the Archbishop! What a lark![1]

By the end of 1952 all our internal difficulties had been largely overcome, and the chief trouble was to arrange the organisation of the work when we lost Mills, a prospect which we all faced with dismay. Although the housing returns were now beginning to show results, I felt anxious as to how we would manage. The flow of orders, coupled with the fact that we had not yet broken down seriously on materials, was now at last creating confidence in the building industry, both among employers and men. Although

[1] 1 March 1952.

performance was uneven, productivity was rising. Nevertheless, complaints still continued:

> I have amused myself by composing a reply to a quite ridicolous letter which I have received, signed by the Chancellor of the Exchequer, but obviously written by one . . . of the Treasury [officials]. He complains that the Building industry is employing more men. But he does not say that productivity has increased by a much larger percentage—nearly double.[1]

On 8 December Mills had to leave us:

> Sir Percy Mills came to see me in the afternoon to say 'good-bye'. He has completed his year of service. This was a melancholy occasion and it will make things much more difficult. But I am very lucky to have had him, and he has given us a good start. Meanwhile, 1953 will be a year of struggle and difficulty. Bricks and cement will be the chief headaches. 'It will be a damned close-run thing' like Waterloo. But I think we shall get through if we work hard now.[2]

By this time we had all learned a great deal. I kept, of course, closely in touch with Mills, and his advice was always freely available. It was from the high opinion I had formed of his previous work and from my recent experience of what he had achieved in this vital year that when I came to recommend a Cabinet in 1957 I invited him to join us. Our friendship has remained and grown stronger year by year. I do not at all blame some of the officers of the Ministry for being worried by the new and turbulent spirit which we had introduced. It so happened that none of them had been engaged in war production or production Ministries. But they were intelligent people, and soon began to enjoy this novel experience. Indeed, when at the end of 1955—I was then Foreign Secretary—I wrote to Sheepshanks on his retirement, I received from him a most charming letter in which he referred with pleasure to our work together. 'Your period,' he wrote, 'really was a great time for the office. . . . I shall always retain happy memories of the time I worked for you.' This I am sure was genuine, for although our methods may have seemed strange, he and his colleagues were

[1] 10 September 1952.   [2] 8 December 1952.

able and patriotic men, inspired by high ideals and fine traditions.

The housing problem which confronted us in 1951 was partly the legacy of the nineteenth century, during which, in spite of a high rate of building, a rapidly growing population resulted in deplorably crowded conditions in the old cities, leading to the creation of slums and semi-slums. It was aggravated by the system of rent control which had come into being in the First War and which, without having been wholly relaxed, had been reimposed in the Second. Thus a great many houses whose life might have been prolonged by seasonable repairs were continually falling below standard. Moreover, it cannot be denied that a great deal of 'jerry-building' took place which, coupled with rent control, left us with a great stock of houses gradually becoming beyond repair. During the Second World War building had virtually ceased for six years; and since in these years approximately one house in every three had been either destroyed or damaged, sometimes superficially, sometimes severely, by German bombs, the immense task of repair and clearance had interfered with new building. So far as we could tell from the first returns of the 1951 census, the excess of households over dwellings was something of the order of 1 million. Moreover, of the 13 million existing separate dwellings, over 2 million were shared by two or more families. The rate of construction since the war had fluctuated; only once, in 1948, had it exceeded 200,000.

'Work, food and homes', in Churchill's famous phrase, were the main demands of the people as a whole after the war. He was able in the course of his last administration to claim that the first had been provided in full; as regards the second, rationing was finally brought to an end in 1954; and substantial progress was made towards the third of these reasonable requirements.

It is difficult now to realise the atmosphere of stringency and even defeatism in which we still lived six years after the end of the war. Nor was it possible in the circumstances to sweep away at one blow all the hampering regulations which seemed justified by the estimated shortages of labour and materials and the immensity of the unsatisfied demand. No house of any kind could be built without a licence issued by a local authority. No local authority could build council houses or allow private houses to be built, whether for rent or sale, except within the allocations made to it yearly by the Minister. The size and cost of such houses were rigidly controlled. At the same time, local authorities had been instructed not to issue more than one licence in every ten for private building. This rule had subsequently been modified to one in five, although the regulation was still permissive, not obligatory. On 19 November 1951 I put forward a plan to raise this to one in two, making at the same time administrative arrangements to continue the control of the maximum size and the conditions of resale to ensure that the houses went to people genuinely in need of a home. Secondly, I proposed to allow the sale of municipal houses subject to appropriate safeguards. On such houses the subsidy would naturally cease to be payable. Thirdly, I intended to encourage the building of smaller houses by local authorities. Happily, under Dalton's administration, plans had already been prepared which, while establishing minimum standards for living-rooms and bedrooms, could effect a substantial reduction in overall size, with consequential savings in labour and materials. I made it clear to the Cabinet that none of these proposals could increase the total number of houses built in 1952, except perhaps in so far as the wider facilities for building houses under licence could bring smaller builders back rapidly into house-building. I did, however, feel sure that these changes, together with the new energy I hoped to instil into the housing authorities and the building industry, would increase the numbers in 1953 and subsequent years.

These proposals were approved by the Cabinet and announced on 27 November.

A storm of supplementaries followed my announcement; but I think the Opposition were really rather stunned. Attlee and Morrison both rose to supplementaries, which is unusual.[1]

A vote of censure was immediately tabled, but I noticed that only two of the three proposals were condemned. Dalton was wise enough to see that the third, that is, the design of the smaller house,

[1] 27 November 1951.

was in accordance with his own ideas. Altogether, when the debate took place it proved rather a flop:

> Dalton began, with a speech in very moderate tone. I followed. . . . Dalton was very scornful of the phrase 'comparable housing need'. What could it mean? (This was as between applications for [privately built] houses . . . and [council] houses. . . .) In answering, I was able to say that the words were [taken from] the text of the last Government's formula. Curiously enough, Bevan (who followed me) fell into the same trap (about another paragraph). I let him work himself up into a great show of indignation about another phrase. What could these enigmatic words signify? They were a trap, a swindle, etc. I then got up and said 'I am afraid I must ask you to explain their meaning. Once again I have been guilty of plagiarism. They are your words, taken from your circular of 1948.' He never recovered, and the rest of his speech rambled badly. What a lesson to 'verify your references'.[1]

As in later years, the Labour Party seemed confused as to whether they wished to oppose all houses for private ownership or whether they only wished to oppose any extension on the grounds that this would be at the cost of building new council houses. On the second point I was able to show from previous experience that it was not likely that private enterprise could take up more than one in four of the permitted allocation. Therefore, if we got only 200,000 houses in 1952, the number of council houses would still be as great as any year previously achieved. But of course I confidently hoped that there would be a substantial increase in council houses, as well as to be able to meet the need of the private house-owner. The same objections were raised against the sale of council houses. We were all still bemused by the theory of a rigid capital investment programme and a mathematical formula based on labour and resources believed to be available. No one seemed to pay any regard to the possibility of rapidly attracting the small builders and filling up small vacant plots in a village or town not suitable for large-scale development. Nor did anyone realise how full order-books and a sense of confidence could raise productivity or how ingenuity could find substitutes for scarce materials. But, apart from these objections,

[1] 4 December 1951.

the Socialists then—and perhaps even now—disliked the idea of widespread house-ownership.

Devout practising Socialists really believe they can manage everybody else's affairs better than the people themselves can. They believe that sincerely, and they believe that it is necessary for their purpose to concentrate property. Curiously enough, this view has been held by many sections and institutions in our country during our long history. At one time it was the Church; at another the King; then the feudal barons; at another, the great Whig landlords; and then the great industrial magnates. Like so many of their predecessors, Socialists only approve of property if they control it. They only support landlordism, if they can be the universal landlord. In the same way, they disapprove of tied cottages—unless, of course, they belong to the nationalised industries. . . .[1]

Our purpose was different.

We wish to see the widest possible distribution of property. We think that, of all forms of property suitable for such distribution, house property is one of the best.[1]

Of course we recognised that for many years the majority of families would want houses to rent. But we meant to see that they had a chance to own their own home. I had discovered that during the previous Government a poster had been issued by the National Savings Committee to support the savings campaign, of which I had obtained a copy.

It depicted a man leaning over a gate and looking longingly at a cottage in a garden, and the caption was 'A bit of land of his own'. But that was too dangerous. It might be held by the thoughtless or the ill-instructed to imply that the Government of the day was urging people to save in order to own property. This was rank heresy and might lead to schism. So Lord Silkin went quickly to work, the inquisitors were put upon the job, the poster was withdrawn, and the artist was no doubt duly reprimanded and perhaps liquidated.[1]

On the whole, therefore, this first clash ended to our advantage.

[1] *Hansard*, 4 December 1951.

Meanwhile the Press was friendly, including the *Daily Mirror*, and the public were for the moment prepared to wait.

The next difficulty was that which necessarily followed the raising of the Bank Rate. There immediately began a wrangle regarding the interest to be charged on local loans. Since interest rates were likely to continue to rise, it was a matter of great importance to my housing programme. For if they were increased, housing subsidies must be raised correspondingly, even to maintain the present scale of building. I argued throughout that the object of raising the Bank Rate was to stop people doing unnecessary things. If, therefore, the Government wished to stop more houses they had only to say so. As I told my colleagues, it was quite easy to do this; but to try to encourage local authorities and individuals to build more and then raise interest rates seemed merely perverse. Fortunately the normal review of subsidies was soon due. Their structure was extremely complicated, to meet different needs. Eventually I was able, before the end of February 1952, to announce that there would be an increase in housing subsidies in order to allow the local authorities to meet the higher interest. The standard annual subsidy was raised from £22 to £35 12s. per house, the Exchequer as before contributing three-quarters and the rates one-quarter. This settlement, which caused me a great effort to achieve, may have been theoretically indefensible but it was certainly practical. It was strongly attacked in *The Times*, and this had some effect on a number of our Conservative supporters. The *Economist* took the same view. Apart from the need for houses, it never seemed to occur to these critics that the question of subsidies and of rent control could only be dealt with as a whole. So long as the latter could not be touched, the former must remain. The time had not yet come to deal with the problem of rents. The houses must go up before the rents.

The necessary legislation went through its normal course comparatively calmly and was finished before the end of July. I felt that Bevan, with whom I had always been on very good personal terms, was enjoying the battle and that his blows, though formidable, were not intended to leave any lasting wound. The sittings in the Standing Committees upstairs, as in all Bills at this time, required somewhat delicate management:

As we have only a majority of one, and not enough to move the closure, this had had to be done by kindness.[1]

Nevertheless, I learned much from the arguments in the course of these discussions both in Whitehall and in the House of Commons. Quite apart from the size of the programme, there was still much to be done about methods of achieving it. We must soon begin to

> think out some of the next forward moves which will now be possible, based on an expanding programme. The most important of these are (i) to reduce the swollen river of 'subsidised' house-building and increase the trickle of 'private' building; (ii) to deal with 'rents', and therefore 'repairs'; (iii) to get rid of 'development charge'.
>
> All these objectives are interwoven and together could be presented as a complete and coherent plan.[2]

By the middle of December 1951, in co-operation with the Minister of Works and the Secretary of State for Scotland, I was ready to argue the case for an expanded programme. I asked for definite authority to build new houses with the necessary services—sewage, electricity, gas, etc.—at the rate of 300,000 a year. This figure must be reached by stages. I wanted authority for at least 800,000 in the first three years. Only if this was agreed could the Minister of Works plan the necessary materials and fitments with confidence and success. The shortage of steel and timber might make it necessary to make adjustments and devise new methods. In addition, the proposed arbitrary cut in the amount which the Minister of Works could license for repairs was unworkable and foolish. He must use his own judgement, in accordance with local conditions.

> I ask for authority to get away from all this annual planning and this grandmotherly control by the Treasury. I want to build 800,000 houses during the next three years. I should expect to do 230,000 in 1952; 265,000 in 1953; 300,000 in 1954. If I can get this authority, the Minister of Works and I can plan together the necessary supply of building materials. By reducing

[1] 30 May 1952.   [2] 25 July 1952.

flats; by having more two-bedroomed houses; by having smaller houses, we can get this 300,000 with a remarkably small increase of steel. We shall have difficulties and bottlenecks. But the Treasury don't want us even to try.[1]

Looking back, I can see how anxious the Chancellor of the Exchequer must have been about my activities and how loyally he and his colleagues fought their battle. The precise conception of the annual capital investment programme was of course of great value to them, but it did not suit me. When Churchill talked to me about this privately, he thought I was being rather obstinate. Was I not satisfied? After all, my demands had not been turned down. There would be further discussion and enquiry.

I replied 'No. Another committee means another month. I have already wasted two months getting started. I must begin to reorganise the builders and above all the makers of building materials. I [must] ask the Cabinet to accept a formal approval of my broad plan.'[2]

At the next meeting everything seemed to go perfectly. I explained all the points on which I wanted approval and there was no comeback.

So we have thrown the 'double-six' and are started on our Housing snakes and ladders.[2]

But I was too sanguine. As the great economic storm grew in violence, I was all but swept off my feet. How I blessed the Conservative Conference of 1950 and the famous target, soon regarded as a pledge. This was my sheet-anchor, by which I could ride out the gale.

In the early months of 1952 the battle was renewed, fortunately on a more restricted front. Our housing was in theory secure; but there was still a fight about water, not indeed primarily for housing but for industrial needs. During the lull I reflected upon the dangers of having announced an expansionist housing programme in a restrictionist atmosphere. So different was the intellectual climate from that since prevalent that not only the denizens of Whitehall but

[1] 15 December 1951.   [2] 28 December 1951.

the professional economists, who wrote extensively in the serious news-papers and journals, were deeply shocked by my intransigence. On the other hand I took comfort from reflecting on the character of such men:

> They hate action and risk. That is why they have become dons and civil servants. They worship security, the Mammon of today, and more destructive of the power, wealth, and strength of England than any of the false gods which we have worshipped from time to time. But the public as a whole is sympathetic and the 'popular' press specially so. . . . I think we have created the idea that we are at least trying to do something about Housing.[1]

By the end of March I was still waiting for the counter-attack. Meanwhile I felt we were making progress:

> The Housing policy is developing. We have reached much more flexibility and a greater measure of freedom. We have over half a million houses 'on order'—instead of less than 200,000. Will the materials and labour be there? Labour, certainly; materials, for the moment—but next year will be very difficult. Sir Percy Mills, with his quiet but inflexible will, has really moulded the whole Ministry to our purpose. I could have done nothing without him.[2]

It was not until the end of June that the so-called capital investment programme for 1953 came under discussion. It struck me as a rather academic exercise. The real point, of course, was still how to reduce imports. It was proposed that licences for the import of 85,000 standards of timber should be withheld. The Treasury calculated that this would save some £5.5 million. But it would also lead to a reduction of 30,000 houses. Meanwhile Marples had work-ed hard at a design of a house which required practically no timber, using cement as a substitute. I christened it 'The Boneless Wonder'. However, even if this succeeded, it could scarcely affect the 1953 programme, since the houses for completion in the greater part of that year must have been already started.

After much argument a new plan was put forward, demanding the stabilisation of the 1953 housing programme at 230,000. This, of course, was quite unacceptable to me. I was able to point

<hr>

[1] 27 January 1952.   [2] 29 March 1952.

out that I had already received authority to build at approximately the following rates: 230,000 for 1952, 260,000 for 1953, and 300,000 for 1954. There were now half a million houses in the programme, one quarter of a million under construction and the rest either under contract or in unused instalments issued to the local authorities. Even if I issued no further allocations, there would still be at the beginning of next year over 360,000 houses in the announced programme. There was no way of stopping or slowing it down except either by refusing tenders or licences in respect of allocations already made, or by failing to produce the actual materials. The first would have to be announced, with all its political and industrial consequences. The second would postpone the crisis, but only to accentuate it.

Of course 1954 was another matter. If the Government now decided to abandon the objective of 300,000, we then could slow down the rate of instalments and allocations. I pointed out that I could do little at this stage to alter the cost or design of houses already under construction. But the smaller design was now coming into use, and the so-called 'People's House' would cover at least two-thirds of the 1953 programme. This, although it did not make a great saving in timber, saved in fact 10 per cent in structural materials. We were designing the timberless house, but it could not yet be fed into the programme.

But what seemed to me the fundamental mistake of the yearly capital investment system was its lack of reality. Although for convenience and for the purpose of political propaganda a calendar year was a useful measure, it had but a slender relation to a production programme. This should be a continuous and steady process. The building industry had bitter memories. The mistakes of booms and slumps at short notice had been made before. They must not be made again.

Fortunately for my argument there was a published report of a Working Party on building, set up by the last Government under the most respectable auspices. They had stated emphatically:

Unfortunately the building industry, more perhaps than any other, has in the past suffered on account of recurrent failure to implement announced programmes. If building is to be looked on as a tap which can be turned on and off for economic reasons, then efficiency cannot be expected.

My plea, therefore, was to make no change for 1953, although I would do everything possible to save both in money and materials. No decision need yet be made for 1954.

The argument continued, but it was becoming more and more unreal. Several of the experts called in never abandoned their briefs; some even read them like a breviary. Nobody could actually estimate accurately the output of the building industry.

> The planners say (with a sort of Olympian certainty) £1,600 m. If the whole claims of all departments are admitted in full, there is a 10 per cent difference. If on the slightly lower scale of their revised claims, a 5 per cent difference. So why go on arguing about this completely theoretical point?[1]

When we looked like reaching an agreement on timber and steel, the question of cement arose. 1·9 million tons had been set aside for export.

> 'But can we push up cement production? After all, cement is indigenous. It's only Thames mud and chalk.' 'But that will require capital investment.' And so it goes on.[1]

I found it difficult to think that anyone could take all this quite seriously.

> If any one really believed all this absurd stuff, he could only end where its inventor, Cripps, ended—in a Swiss clinic.[1]

These strictures were of course too harsh, but they represented our mood at the time.

Meanwhile, day after day, and in various forms, the discussion continued with occasional intermissions for other equally urgent problems. It was still difficult to make people understand that the 1953 programme was arranged and contracted for; that no change in design could become effective until the latter part of 1953;

[1] 11 July 1952.

and above all that the slightest hint of any cut would wreck confidence and diminish output. I was still sceptical of the argument in terms of a money ceiling. The balance of payments was another thing. But I could keep going at full speed with an additional cut of £4½ million on timber imports at present prices. Prices were still falling, and by 1954 I was confident that we could build the 300,000 houses, either with low-price timber, if this situation continued, or with 'The Boneless Wonder'. Marples and Mills gave me splendid support in these anxious days. By the end of the summer, chiefly by mutual exhaustion, we won our point. We owed much to Churchill's sympathy and quick grasp of the fundamental questions at issue. The target of 260,000 houses for 1953 was retained on the understanding that within that target every effort should be made to save both Labour and imported materials.

The housing figures were good, and by the time the Conservative Party conference took place in the autumn it looked as if we should get at least 230,000 houses for 1952, since completions showed a rise of 22 per cent, houses under construction of nearly 20 per cent and the new starts of some 30 per cent. At this conference both Marples and I were well received, and I paid a special tribute to Eccles and the Ministry of Works. But I knew the pitfalls ahead:

> It really is rather comic, after all the years of conflict and unpopularity! But it will not last. It is all right to put up the houses. But the next job is to put up the rents![1]

About this time there arose a new storm as a by-product of the capital investment dogma, beginning as a little cloud and ending in a violent tempest. This was the question of the 'blitzed cities'. I had some warning of this, since towards the end of September 1952 I paid a visit to Plymouth. I visited all the housing sites and went through the usual mayoral ceremonies. But the real business of the day lay in a conference with the reconstruction committee. Plymouth had suffered grievously from enemy bombardment, but under Lord Astor's leadership admirable preparations had been made for the rebuilding of the city when the time should come. Some progress

[1] 10 October 1952.

had been made, but those concerned were now anxious to press ahead. I could give them no comforting news, for I knew that the proposed allocation for all the eighteen blitzed cities was wholly inadequate.

> This 'Capital Investment Programme' is really intolerable. It is especially silly in a place like Plymouth, where there are no armament or export factories—or indeed any factories—to build. Plymouth's factory is the Royal Naval Dockyard. So—if I lose my battle with the Treasury—a lot of people will be unemployed at Plymouth, including (after the next election) the Hon. J. J. Astor.[1]

This awkward problem began to exercise Members of all parties when the House met, and some decision had to be reached and announced, for it was becoming known that the sum available was likely to be severely reduced. How severely even the critics did not fully realise.

The position was simple. Since 1949 successive Ministers had been given an investment allocation, apart from any question of housing, to enable some reconstruction to take place. The actual value of work done in the last three years had been £2·3 million in 1949 and 1950 and £3·5 million in 1951. The allocation of course merely meant that licences were given. The Government provided no money except for some special grants to meet loan charges for land purchased but unused. Construction was almost entirely financed by private developers, and consisted mainly of offices and shops. If the 1953 figure were cut to £2·5 million it left a negligible amount for new work, since the completion of works in progress would take at least £2 million in the coming year. A bitter row would develop when this proposal was made known. From the political point of view there were 68 Parliamentary seats involved, of which 28 were held by Government supporters. Up to now the steel shortage had been a convenient excuse, but since everyone had begun to hear of the success in the last year of substituting reinforced concrete and in some cases load-bearing walls for steel, it was obvious that this cock would not fight much longer. To a

[1] 24 September 1952. Mr. Astor was Conservative M.P. for Plymouth (Sutton).

considerable extent specialised labour was required for the shops and offices, and there was likely to be little interference with ordinary building. Indeed, if sufficient was not available, men would drift out of the building industry or go on the dole.

I proposed that there should be an authorisation for new work of a further £2 million in 1953, that is, a total programme for the year of £4·5 million. Where a project should be and when it should start should be settled by the Minister of Works through the machinery of the Regional Building Committee. This would prevent interference with priority building for defence, industry, housing or schools. Nor should we forget that in nearly every case the developers were spending their money without subvention, subsidy or assistance. If we put them off for too long we might put them off altogether.

I was in the habit, somewhat irreverently, of giving jaunty headings to my memoranda, often taken from *Alice in Wonderland*. In this case I used two quotations, both of which I thought relevant:

> It's 'Tommy this, an' Tommy that,' an'
> 'chuck 'im out, the brute';
> But it's 'Saviour of 'is country', when
> the guns begin to shoot![1]

Of course, we must first concentrate, as we are doing, all available building labour on those parts of our cities which have suffered most. . . .[2]

I think it was these that did the trick.

In March 1953 a short debate took place which gave me an opportunity of explaining the purpose of the capital investment programme, then scarcely known to the general public. I tried to take a middle way between complete freedom, for which we were not ready, and too rigid a system. I had always maintained that

> economic planning is a vital need of our present structure of society, divided, as it is, into two sectors, one publicly controlled and financed, and, therefore, only capable of being controlled by direct planning, and the other privately controlled and financed

[1] Rudyard Kipling.
[2] Speech by Churchill at Central Hall, Westminster, 15 March 1945.

and capable of control by other, possibly more old-fashioned processes.[1]

I had to make it clear that in the case of the blitzed cities, since the capital investment programme included all work that was done on private or public account, it had nothing to do with the method of payment. The test was the availability of labour and materials. But the estimate could never be absolutely accurate. It dealt with global amounts throughout the whole island, although we all knew that labour was not mobile and even physical assets could only be carried for great distances at high cost. Moreover, the estimated total productivity of the building industry in any one year was the result of a series of abstruse calculations which could only give a general guide. There was a margin of error. The method was practical and wise so long as it was not pedantically used. Allowance should also be made for the increase of productivity year by year. In any case it was not so much the allocation which mattered but the work actually completed. Here the figures were hopeful. In 1952 we had completed £4·6 million worth,

> which was certainly higher than a meticulous application of the investment programme by my Department might have suggested. One of the beauties of these things is that no one can add up the figure until the end of the year. . . . At the same time, we have built more houses in these cities and the rest of the country than either we or anybody else thought possible. . . .[1]

We would feed in the new licences after local examination of each city and town and the particular conditions operating in each. I felt sure that this was the wise and flexible method.

This debate was short and on the whole non-partisan. It was of interest because it lifted the curtain on some of the mysteries in which the system of central planning control was still shrouded. At any rate we had no more trouble with the blitzed cities. This problem, which had once threatened to become a grave political issue, died of inanition, but of course without any particular expression of gratitude to the Government.

The expanding housing programme being now secured against

[1] *Hansard*, 2 March 1953.

erosion, we felt under an obligation to do our best to reduce by every possible means the burden on the Exchequer. This could best be done, on the financial side, by increasing the trickle of private building to augment or even to some extent replace the rising river of subsidised houses. Accordingly, in August 1952, permission was given to the local authorities to ignore the ratio where they wished to issue additional licences. This was the best way to keep in check the growth of the subsidies, which was under constant attack. There was indeed much confusion on this question because these subsidies were of a contractual character. It would be a gross breach of faith to repudiate arrangements already made. The best hope was to obtain a greater proportion of the expanding programme from the unsubsidised houses. In December 1952 I made a further statement, in effect suspending the need for licences for private builders for houses of not more than 1,000 square feet. Private builders could also erect up to twelve houses at a time on their own account. The local authorities were instructed to issue licences automatically to both classes of applicants. Naturally there was considerable debate in the House about these modest moves to freedom, which were lauded as progressive or denounced as reactionary according to the predilections of the orator. Most people, however, regarded them as evidence of the improving building situation. About the same time the limit for unlicensed repairs was raised to £500 for private work and to £2,000 for industrial and agricultural purposes. We were thus going forward by stages. (I thought of General Giraud's 'politique de perroquet—progressivement'.)[1]

Since all these steps required the approval of my colleagues, I thought it wise at the same time to obtain a clear reaffirmation for the 300,000 target to be reached at least by 1954, and to warn them of the grievous news that the figure might be reached earlier. The weather had been good in 1952, and favourable to building. Indeed, by the end of the year there were 240,000 houses built as against 195,000 for 1951. We were therefore pretty confident of the success of our broad operation. At the same time the steering of the two separate streams was bound to be a difficult operation. It

[1] *The Blast of War*, p. 293.

was not of course capable of the precise management which some people seemed to think easy.

But there was a more serious obstacle than the licensing arrangements which had now to be faced. It arose from the provisions of the Town and Country Planning Act of 1947. To tackle this immensely complicated question, which had been somewhat academic from my point of view in the first months, now became urgent. For it was only by grasping the nettle of the development charge and obtaining the repeal or amendment of the financial provisions of the Act that real progress could be made in the private sector.

If this part of my inheritance from the previous administration was tiresome and distracting, it is only fair to pay tribute to two more profitable legacies.

The Labour Government had shown real imagination in launching the New Towns. The Conservative Party had only given a somewhat grudging and lukewarm welcome to this policy. But time has shown that with all their inherent difficulties the New Towns were to prove a wise and even profitable venture. There were many teething troubles, especially in those days of restricted resources. Nevertheless, as soon as I came into office I determined to give all possible assistance to their progress, and to rely upon them for at least a modest contribution to the total housing effort. The chairmen and members of these boards were in general eminently suited to their task. In some cases changes of personnel became desirable. But all worked with conspicuous enthusiasm under conditions which must have been in those early days discouraging and even frustrating.

The New Towns depended for success on creating a balanced community. They needed new industries with their employment capacity; new housing; new schools; new shopping centres; new churches and general amenities. To provide them all at approximately the same time was no easy task. Moreover, the problem arose of preventing the New Towns becoming a sort of convenient dump to receive the overflow of the most crowded cities, particularly of London, without regard to other considerations. The character of the new population was important, in order to create real communities, capable of enjoying a true civic life. Naturally the problems presented varied greatly between the different localities.

Where a New Town enjoyed the advantage of an old village or township round which to build, the progress of the new community was easier. For this reason, and partly because of the great skill and knowledge of its chairman, Sir Thomas Bennett, Crawley proved successful from the start. This was equally true of Stevenage and similar places. Others, such as Basildon, which were constructed round an almost non-existent core, presented serious difficulties. The development of Harlow was at first equally troublesome. I was fortunate in being able to persuade General Sir Humfrey Gale—an old friend of Algiers days and one of the finest administrative officers who ever served the Army—to take the chairmanship of the former and Dick Costain of the latter. Perhaps the most acute problem in nearly all the New Towns was that of providing sufficient schools. Naturally by far the largest part of their populations consisted of young people with children. It became therefore vital to provide schools on a scale which would have been inappropriate to a community with more normal age-groups. Yet if the proportion of children was at first unduly large, it was hard to foresee how the situation would develop as the years went on. Another more simple and very human difficulty, the shortage of old people, threw exceptional burdens upon the young married groups. I was much struck when I heard of a complaint of the shortage of 'aunties' and 'grannies' which made the arrangements for baby-sitting almost impossible. This was the result of a community of pioneers.

My immediate predecessor, Hugh Dalton, had devoted much energy and enthusiasm to the project of the New Towns, which we owe to his initiative and drive. We did everything possible to promote their growth and well-being. This was a valuable inheritance for me.

Another legacy of a similar character which I found on taking office, proved almost equally useful. A Bill had been drafted with the title of the 'Town Development Bill'. I soon recognised that this would be an important asset in developing my programme. Its purpose was simple. It was to secure that large cities wishing to provide for their surplus population could do so by orderly and friendly arrangements with neighbouring authorities. Small towns or urban districts, which were, for this purpose, to be known as 'receiving authorities', would be assisted to develop their own areas, with the help of the 'exporting' authorities and some Government grants. This measure, by providing the necessary accommodation for the staffs involved, has certainly facilitated many valuable overspill schemes and made a contribution to the movement of industry and offices out of the great cities. I was determined, in spite of some opposition, to press on immediately with this Bill. When it was introduced, I paid full tribute to its true parents, and the paternity was duly acknowledged by Dalton. Even Bevan, although criticising the Bill as 'petty', seemed to be more anxious to annoy his old colleague than to attack me. By a strange inconsistency,

> he approved of the clause which I thought he might oppose—that giving power to local authorities to sell [the] freehold of land in their estates, subject to ministerial approval.[1]

Naturally some Members, who represented the areas which were likely to be 'receiving authorities', were not altogether enthusiastic. But they accepted the situation with a good grace.

The origins of the Town and Country Planning Act of 1947 went back to the days of the National Government, starting with the famous Uthwatt Report and the 1944 White Paper. The Bill was founded on the Report, and followed it closely. Although the Labour Government of the day bore the responsibility for its final form, the broad scheme undoubtedly arose from a joint and non-party effort. As Churchill observed, 'We were all in it together.' Unhappily I was now in it up to the neck.

The Act consisted of two parts. In the first were embodied the wide planning provisions which we had no desire to change—indeed, they were essential in our small island with its large population. Their principles had been long established by the legislation of successive Liberal and Conservative Governments. They were now buttressed by the new Act, itself the outcome of a Coalition initiative.

[1] 25 February 1952.

It had strengthened and made effective powers which, for one reason or another, had failed adequately to deal with a situation of growing complexity. Its main objects were to co-ordinate planning throughout the country by the preparation of comprehensive development plans, in the light of which day-to-day development should be considered; to extend the power of public bodies to acquire and develop land for planning purposes, and to this end the scope and scale of Government grants to local authorities were enlarged; and to bring all development, with very few exceptions, under control by making it subject to planning permission from the local planning authority or from the central Government. The aim of all this was to secure that land should be put to the best use in the interest of the whole community. Thus building on good agricultural land or land containing good minerals could be prevented. The outward sprawl of towns could be restrained. Ribbon development could be stopped. New housing could be more effectively planned. While land must often yield to industrial or housing development, agricultural values and amenities should, wherever possible, be preserved. In addition, certain buildings of special historical and architectural interest could be protected from development. These were the admirable concepts against which neither I nor any members of the Conservative Party had any complaint. How far we could succeed in these objectives might be disputed. But certainly no Minister or Government could quarrel with these aims or fail to do their best to operate powers placed in their hands by the Act. The local planning authorities were equally doing their best in the same spirit. All this was common ground between the parties.

It was only in considering the second part of the Act – the financial provisions – that I found myself, by the spring of 1952, in real difficulty. There were two aspects of the financial arrangements which were of special importance. Under the first, a fund of £300 million had been provided – notionally at least – as compensation for owners who considered, and could show, that the value of their development rights had been depreciated by the Act. The truth was that the Government were under a statutory obligation to pay out the whole of this sum in the middle of 1953 to recompense admitted claims. The second, and from my point of view far more objectionable feature, was that there had been imposed a charge, known as a development charge, to be paid by those who received planning permission for any purpose. This was supposed to represent the increased value of their land resulting from the permission to develop. Both these financial provisions I wished to repeal. But it was the second, in particular, which, being deeply resented by the public and regarded as at once an incomprehensible scheme and an odious imposition, had clearly become an almost fatal bar to the increase of private development, especially in housing. It was therefore from a practical standpoint that I was anxious to repeal this part of the Act, while retaining the planning sections undisturbed.

At the beginning of July 1952 I put before my colleagues a plan to repeal both the global distribution of £300 million and the development charge. After much discussion and the consideration of many alternative proposals, I succeeded in obtaining approval by the middle of November.

In theory, the 1947 plan may have been excellent; but in practice it had failed to work. Perhaps this was because it tried to deal at the same time with two quite separate issues—planning and taxation. Many people felt, and still feel, that there should be a tax on 'betterment', that is the so-called 'unearned increment' that an owner of land may obtain by the efforts of the community rather than from his own. This concept goes back to Henry George and, in a more modified form, to Lloyd George. It has recently been reintroduced into our fiscal system. Whatever may be the arguments for this as a tax, it was, in my view, a mistake to turn a Planning Act into an engine of taxation. Above all, it was fatal to link it with a tax on development.

In any case, as an instrument of taxation, the 1947 system was blunt and blundering. It made no attempt to deal with a great part of betterment, which often accrued to properties under existing use. Nor was it possible to assess its incidence with the precision which taxation requires if it is to be equitable and acceptable. Professional valuers no doubt did their best; but the assessments for development charge were never scientific and were bound to become more and more inaccurate as a free market in land disappeared into history. The Central Land Board was partly an agent of the Inland Revenue and partly a planning authority. In the first it duplicated work which could be better done elsewhere. The second was its only true function.

As the Act had become operative, and especially after my measures which seemed to foreshadow a renewal of private building, the opposition to the development charge grew in strength and bitterness. The House of Commons had already debated this question, on a private motion, and scarcely any supporters were found for the charge or tax, even from the Opposition benches. There were already many cases of incomprehensible decisions as to the amount of charge leviable. It seemed clear that since there was no true principle of assessment, it had become a matter of bargaining between the tax-gatherer and the victim. The assessments certainly varied in an extraordinary way from place to place and case to case; and agreement between the taxpayer and the Board appeared to be reached by methods more suitable to an oriental bazaar than to the traditions of the British revenue system.

This tax was in theory supposed to compensate the Treasury for having purchased for the global sum of £300 million all the development or planning rights of all land. But while one set of people were to get compensation—whether adequate or inadequate—the payment was to fall on that very class on which we had to depend for the development of our housing programme and our industrial extensions. On the housing developers, great or small, it was an intolerable burden. Nor would there be any sense in merely reducing the tax, as was strongly urged in our preliminary discussions. Either the tax must be removed altogether or it would remain, of unknown quantity, hanging over all development, and presenting a serious handicap to our purpose of increasing at the maximum possible speed the rate of private and unsubsidised house-building.

I had some difficulty in persuading the Treasury, some of whose officials suffered in an acute form from the old radical anti-landlord complex, that I was not merely wanting to put money into the pockets of the owners of land. It was equally difficult to persuade some of the great landowners in my party that I was not depriving them of a benefit. For under the 1947 scheme the landowner would obtain, if he made a claim—and practically all large or well-advised landlords had done so—a proportion of the £300 million lump sum of compensation, whether he had any plans for developing his land or not. Claims covered not merely land already developed or ripe for development, but the whole island from John o' Groats to Land's End. Moreover, in many instances, the owner had no intention of ever developing the land for which he made a claim. Nevertheless, because he was debarred from doing so, he was entitled to collect a substantial sum of money which would be an agreeable windfall, but to which he seemed to have no real right in equity or common sense. There were many such cases. At a time when we were so embarrassed and seeking economies in so many directions, to pay out £300 million in the summer of 1953, whether the claimant had suffered injury or not, seemed to me contradictory and even absurd.

The whole scheme of the £300 million was unsatisfactory, apart from the immediate burden on our finances. There had been no reason to suppose that the totality of admitted claims would add up to this sum. In fact the total so far had come to about £350 million. But some owners, especially small owners, had probably not claimed since it was generally supposed that the fund would never pay more than two or three shillings in the pound. In any case, it was an arbitrary figure and not the sum of agreed claims to be paid out once and for all. Secondly, the development charge, although in a sense a balancing feature, was in fact nothing but a tax. Nor was there any reason to suppose that the totality of the charges would recoup the Government for the £300 million. In theory, when planning permission was given, there was an increase in the value of the land. But the increase was a fixed asset which might or might not be realised later. The charge had to be paid in cash. Even if the charge could be passed on by the developer, it could only fall on the purchaser. It was thus a tax on houses.

The real weakness of the scheme was that those who showed effort and enterprise, that is the developers or their customers, had to pay what seemed to them a totally unfair addition to their expenditure, whereas a large number of landowners, who had suffered no practical damage, would receive sums in respect of the theoretical development value of land which they had no intention of selling for that purpose or developing themselves. In other words, the 1947 scheme gave benefits to the idle and injured the active.

On 1 December 1952 I moved the Second Reading of the Bill, the purpose of which was first to abolish liability to development charge in respect of future schemes of development, while retaining the need for planning consent in any development or change of use, and secondly, to suspend the payment of the £300 million fund, for which new provisions would be made. This was a comparatively short Bill, for its objects were simple, but the complications involved were wide-reaching and inevitable. These were set out as a White Paper and would be a subject for further legislation. We had to unwind arrangements already made; we had to deal with claims already admitted but separately assigned or sold; we had to provide long and intricate measures to tie up all the ends and to make provision for many uncertain points.

I could not refrain from recalling Macaulay's story of the criminal who was given the choice of reading Guiccardini's history of Florence, a long and ponderous work, or being sent to the galleys. He chose the history; but the first volume was too much for him. He changed his mind and opted for the oar. I had felt something of the same despair when I tried to cut my way through the tangled jungle of the financial provisions of the 1947 Town and Country Planning Act.

The Labour Party, with few exceptions, made little attempt to defend the development charge at the time, nor have they since attempted to revive it. They have recently decided to tax betterment, not development. Whether this will prove successful and free from troublesome repercussions remains to be proved. But certainly, as a tax on betterment, the 1947 scheme must have failed.

. . . I do not think that the main purpose of the 1947 Act was to tax betterment. If it were, it was a very bad way of doing it. Owners who sold their land for development have on occasion kept all the betterment, passing the whole cost on to the developer —in spite of the fact that the developer had to pay the charge—

and, moreover, the Acts made no attempt to secure the betterment which accrues to existing use, houses with vacant possession
and shops and offices with [their] . . . values enhanced for that
same reason.[1]

It was no doubt important to deal with the financial aspect of planning. But it seemed unnecessary to buy all development rights,
however remote, over the whole of Great Britain in order to provide
compensation for immediate and limited cases.

> I am reminded of Charles Lamb's Chinaman who burnt down
> his house to get roast pork, and who, each time he wanted a fresh
> meal of this delicious animal, built up his house and burnt it
> down again, pig and all.[1]

Although it was not possible to pass the Bill through all its
stages and obtain the Royal Assent until 20 May 1953, we had
taken the precaution to enact that the development charge should
come to an end immediately on the introduction of the Bill. Therefore, for those who were prepared to speculate on the chances of the
Bill becoming law, development charge in effect ended on 1 December 1952.

Thus the process of removing the administrative and legislative obstacles to unsubsidised house-building was effectively
accomplished by the end of 1952, after twelve months of effort.

The second Town and Country Planning Bill, which was consequential on the first, dealt with arrangements for paying compensation. Our purpose throughout was to maintain all the benefits
of the planning provisions of the 1947 Act without the evil effects
of the £300 million pay-out or the development charge. After all,
the object of planning

> is not to stop development; it is to promote it in the right places
> and at the right time. So we got rid of development charge—it
> passed unlamented—and, as for compensation, we decided not
> to pay it all out in haste lest we repented at leisure. We undertook
> to provide a system of pay-as-you-go, and here it is.[2]

I had hoped that to transform a scheme for paying a lot of claims
all at once into one for paying them only when the occasion arose

---

[1] *Hansard*, 1 December 1952.   [2] Ibid., 15 March 1954.

would be a fairly straightforward undertaking. But it proved a difficult matter to cover all the different cases which might arise. Since 1 July 1948, for the first time in the history of land ownership in our country, the development value of land and the land itself, which had always been inseparable, had become divided. The development value had theoretically been acquired by the State, and the individual retained merely the claims on the £300 million fund. Thus the claims had become a separate entity, a form of property which could be sold and assigned or left by will apart from the land itself. Many of the complications of this Bill arose as a result of trying to disentangle what had happened over the last few years. We had an obligation

> towards those claim holders who have already suffered injury; claim holders who have paid development charge; claim holders who have sold their land, sometimes voluntarily, sometimes under compulsion, for something less than its full value on the expectation of this payment; claim holders, also, who have already been refused permission to develop their land.[1]

Not everyone who had paid a development charge would be repaid, but only those who held a claim or who had paid a high price for land without taking over the claim and had since paid the charge.

My speech was, according to Disraeli's famous advice in such a predicament, long and obscure. But it served its purpose.

Further progress was slow, and by Whitsun we had only reached clause 43 out of 72 clauses and 8 schedules. But as so often happens, good relations with the Opposition leaders, together with the salutary effects of boredom, enabled us to finish the committee stage by 2 June. Unhappily, the Bill had not been very well drafted, and I had to table twenty pages of amendments on the report stage, following discussion with my advisers and amicable talks with the Opposition. The Third Reading was finally passed on 13 July 1954. Even then the Bill did not receive the Royal Assent until November. For I had to secure in the House of Lords some special concessions for cases of real hardship in connection with

[1] *Hansard*, 15 March 1954.

compulsory purchase. These partly arose out of a case which became notorious – that of Mr. Pilgrim.

Early one morning I was rung up in my flat by the duty clerk at
No. 10. 'The Prime Minister would like you to come immediately.
It is very urgent.' When I got there, I was ushered upstairs and
found Churchill in bed, finishing a substantial breakfast, soon to be
followed by the inevitable cigar. He was wearing the famous Chinese
dressing-gown, and his favourite budgerigar was perched on his
head. The bed was strewn with newspapers. But there was no
benevolence in his manner. Indeed, he was in a fierce and angry
mood; and poured out a flood of accusation and reproach. 'Why
have you done this man to death – you and your minions? Have you
not read the papers – the *Daily Mirror*? Have you not heard of
Pilgrim's suicide? You are responsible for Pilgrim's death. How
are you going to make atonement?' For the moment I wondered
whether the Prime Minister had suddenly gone mad. Pilgrim;
death; atonement – what could it all mean? However, when I had
read the papers – and more accurately when I got to my office – I
was able to ascertain the facts about this sad affair.

In 1950 Pilgrim had bought half an acre of land, next to his own
house, in Romford. He had paid £400 – too high a price in view of
the 1947 Act. He apparently did not wish to use it for building,
but to retain it as an amenity. But had building been allowed, a
development charge would have been payable. Had a public
authority bought it they would only have paid existing use value.
Unfortunately no claim had been made by the previous owner, and
in 1952 it was too late. This unhappy man had in effect paid for
development value but was not getting it or any benefit in lieu. Of
course all this arose from the fatal separation between development
value and land. Still, if it had remained undeveloped, perhaps all
would have been well. But the land was subsequently acquired by
the local borough for housing purposes. The existing use value was
declared to be £65, and the borough could not in law pay more.
Unfortunately, Mr. Pilgrim had borrowed the money for his
purchase, and the prospective loss so preyed on his mind that he
committed suicide. Had he or the previous owner made a claim,
he would in due course under the 1947 Act have been paid £335.

Floods added to the Ministry of Housing's problems: Lynmouth was devastated on the night of 16 August 1952, and the East Coast in February 1953

But, unhappily, no claim had been made. Even under my Bill now going through Parliament he would have gained no benefit. For we had decided that it would be impossible to deal with cases where a claim ought to have been made but had been neglected.

Although I stuck to the principle of only dealing with admitted claims, I was ready to see some discretionary power included for hard cases so long as it would not imperil the general scheme. In Mr. Pilgrim's case, the local authority would have been willing to pay the sum involved if they had been empowered to do so. Suitable amendments were devised to cover such cases by *ex gratia* payments, as a concession though not as a right.

Churchill's anger was characteristic. He could not bear anything that seemed unfair, especially when humble folk were the victims. Unhappily, in this complicated question there were many inequalities for which it was almost impossible to provide. But, in a sense, poor Mr. Pilgrim's death may have been a benefit to others. Churchill, although persistent, was at last brought to believe that I had not been the cause of this man's martyrdom.

When the Bill was finally through the House of Commons, I received a most generous letter from Dame Evelyn Sharp, the Deputy Secretary:

> We never could have done it if you hadn't been the Minister. If I may say so your handling of the Bill has been the most brilliant thing I have ever seen. You have brought it through without a scratch, and I do not know anyone else who could have done it.
>
> I have been very distressed that we added to your difficulties by the atrocious first drafting; and most grateful to you for your patience over this added and unnecessary burden.

She rightly warned me that some further amendment would be necessary to deal with inequalities arising in the case of compulsory purchase. But I knew it was impossible to undo the 1947 Act all at once. Meanwhile, our main purpose—the removing of obstacles to private development—was satisfactorily achieved.

Now a new Land Board has come into being, including, among other duties, that of tax-collecting. At least no one has ventured to revive development charge. Certainly I was glad to escape at last

P

from this tangle. In one form or another, it had occupied my time and that of some of the ablest members of my department for a space of nearly two years.

All through these two years there was a continuous struggle to secure the necessary materials for private houses, council houses, schools and other essential work, including repairs of all kinds. The shortage could be relieved partly by popularising the design for the smaller houses and partly by raising the proportion of two-bedroom houses, which were in great demand. But in the main we had to concentrate upon economy in the use of materials and increases in their supply. By some means or other we must extract more than a pint out of the statistician's pint pot.

The first difficulty was steel. Here I was indeed fortunate to have the assistance of Lord Swinton. At our very first meeting he decided that we must have a proper system of allocation. This took some weeks to arrange, and it meanwhile became apparent that, at least on paper, there would be a deficit of about 1 million tons. Swinton, however, was a very experienced administrator and, believing that the returns of stocks were bound to be understated, he had little hesitation in distributing more paper licences than there was steel to meet. This policy proved successful, and a great alleviation at a time of our greatest need. My contribution was to reduce the number of blocks of flats and to set about an immediate investigation as to the use of load-bearing walls. The new Building Committee played a great part in persuading architects and builders to substitute reinforced concrete for sectional steel. In the course of 1952 we brought about a useful and indeed permanent change in construction methods. Naturally there soon began to be a shortage of the necessary bars, which the steelmakers were not very keen to produce. By February 1952 we had introduced a new price schedule to encourage their manufacture. Also, in the name of the Building Committee, I made an appeal to the great steel-users to economise. My old friend, Lord Alexander, was now Minister of Defence. His actual powers over the Service Ministries, great users of steel, were at that time shadowy, and even his long experience seemed unable to plumb 'the depths of concealment to which the quartermaster type of man could stoop to protect his stores'.[1] Nevertheless, armed with his authority, I had some success. Although the steel problem worried us throughout 1952, the propaganda for the new methods was highly successful. By the end of the year steel shortages became much less noticeable and could generally be dealt with by the regional officers.

Timber presented equal difficulty. Unfortunately, owing to the depletion during the war of home-grown supplies, ripe and often unripe, practically all soft wood had to be imported. Here again we could do something by new designs and by encouraging the use of hard woods, either home-grown or imported from the Sterling Area, at least in privately built houses. Although heavy cuts were made in our supplies, we just managed to get through, and in the end it was not necessary to make much use of the 'Boneless Wonder'. Undoubtedly the decision to abolish the war-time Timber Control and return the buying to private merchants gave good results. By the end of 1953, with the greater amount of imports allowed, our problem was in effect resolved.

Bricks proved a serious trouble all through, for as the programme expanded the demand grew at a prodigious rate. Moreover, the cost of moving bricks over long distances was heavy and in some cases impracticable. We were able, however, to bring a larger number of the smaller brickyards back into production and to induce the large organisations, like the London Brick Company, to put on additional shifts. Here I was able to help them by persuading the Minister of Labour to produce the extra labour, largely Italian. The Services also made their economies. The most difficult to handle were the great independent barons of the nationalised industries. The British Electricity Authority, for instance, like the Pharaohs of old, erected vast monuments of brick construction for their power stations. It seemed impossible to induce them to adopt reinforced concrete in its place. I used to watch with a breaking heart those millions of bricks being, as I thought, misused. The crisis was reached at the end of 1952, and after a meeting of the principal regional officers we issued a new appeal for saving to all departments, as well as a request that orders should be placed well

[1] 29 March 1952.

ahead. Far too many constructors seemed to think they could draw on bricks as in pre-war days from an accumulated stock. During the Christmas holiday I signed 1,500 letters to mayors of boroughs and chairmen of urban district councils, appealing to them for their help in saving, especially by design. Many bricks were still being wasted in unnecessary additions or embellishments to a housing scheme. At the turn of the year I decided that we should import a certain number of bricks from Belgium. The Treasury agreed, and this reinforcement, although small in comparison to the total demand, helped to avoid a serious breakdown.

Cement, which was the fourth vital material, worried us from the beginning, and naturally as the new methods came into use more cement was required. But cement too could be saved. Here we were unlucky in the large demands which followed the floods at the beginning of 1953, as well as those of the Air Ministry, although after a personal appeal they undertook to help in every way they could. Fortunately the great radar installations were coming to an end by the end of 1953. But this alleviation was more than equalled by a vast outpouring of cement into the ground for the use of the American bombers. Nevertheless, by one means or another, we struggled through. Cement production, which could be increased without too great delays, rose steadily.

Throughout 1954 materials caused us only minor difficulties or dislocations.

Meanwhile, by the middle of 1953, the general programme was making real headway. The figures were improving month by month. Indeed, we were beginning to think in terms of stabilising the housing programme and turning our attention to the long-neglected need for slum-clearance. The visible success, although gratifying to our own supporters, was not altogether to the taste of the Opposition. We were widely accused of having neglected other forms of building in order to concentrate on houses. For this reason a debate was staged on 1 July 1953 on school-building. The Minister of Education, Miss Florence Horsbrugh, had been cruelly attacked on this issue. But she was able to give a detailed and convincing reply. In winding up the discussion I observed that it seemed that the real purpose of the attack had been to use the question of schools to belittle the housing record of the Government:

> It is, of course, very annoying and very distressing to the Opposition, whose leaders declared categorically to the nation that it was impossible to build more than 200,000 houses in a year. It is still more annoying to find that 240,000 houses were built under the first year of 'Tory misrule'.[1]

I went on to say:

> It must be still more irritating to see the figures rising month by month. I do not know what the final figure for 1953 will be, but if it should be a good one well on the target, a bull's-eye, or even an inner, will there be loud and prolonged applause from the party opposite?[1]

I could not understand why the Opposition were so niggling and jealous. It was not I, nor my Parliamentary Secretary, nor even my department who had done the job. It was the master builders, the craftsmen and the labourers in the building industry, helped by the local authorities, whether Conservative- or Socialist-controlled, and the developers, large and small, who had joined in the spirit of the 'Housing Crusade'. Bevan had accused me of having stepped up house-building by cutting down schools, factories, and power stations. 'When the Labour Party was in office there was a balanced housing programme.'[1] This allegation was, however, to be answered by facts and figures.

I then turned to the figures. Before the debate everyone had been anxiously awaiting the result of a by-election at Abingdon.

> I had therefore prepared two speeches—one rather subdued in tone, the other a triumphant vindication of our policy. . . . The Abingdon result did not come out (as we had hoped) by one o'clock. But it was on the tape at 2.15—and a smashing victory. In spite of the intervention of a Liberal candidate, and in spite of the stupidity of the returning officer (which gave no time for the postal votes to come back) our majority rose by nearly a thousand. This is a very significant result for it was thought to be a gravely 'deteriorating' seat. . . .[2]

[1] *Hansard*, 1 July 1953.   [2] 1 July 1953.

One little trick amused the House:

> After a passage about school-building and housing, I said 'Now what are the figures? You have heard them, but I will repeat them.' Then I picked up a great volume of statistics—called *Monthly Statistical Summary*, and well known to Members— adjusted my glasses, and said 'Here they are. Neave 22,986, Castle . . .' (These were the figures of the Abingdon by-election.) There was a great roar. Even the ranks of Tuscany were in fits of laughter.[1]

But the relevant figures were equally good. Taking the test of work done, which in my view was the real one, our record for school-building could not be disputed. Both in 1952 and in 1953 it was far above that achieved in the lean years of the previous Government. This was true of primary schools, secondary schools, educational buildings, including technical colleges and all the rest. Allowing for changes in money values the average for the years before our return to power had been £34·5 million. In 1952 the figure was £50 million. In 1953 it would be £54 million. So much for work done.

> 'Ah,' they say, 'but what about work started?' They all say that. Mr. Morgan Phillips said it, so they have to say it. It is 'His Master's Voice'. He says, 'Don't bother about the work done; just think of all that we started.' Of course, the Socialists do start a lot of things. They are wonderful starters. There were more hares started under Socialist rule than ever before in history. But none of them will ever get killed. Everything is begun and nothing is finished. They say, 'Finish it? That is just a dull, pedestrian, unimaginative job; leave that to the Tories.'[2]

For the factories it was the same story. In spite of the housing drive, the figure of factory building had risen year by year from £102 million in 1950 to £118 million in 1952; and that in spite of the steel shortage. In the blitzed cities we had completed this year £5·5 million worth of work, as against £2·3 million in 1950 and £3·5 million in 1951.

The old controversy about planning had been raised, and I took the opportunity to repeat my position:

[1] 1 July 1953.   [2] *Hansard*, 1 July 1953.

I am not unfamiliar with the word 'planning'. I was a planner when it was a far less respectable occupation than it has now become. To me planning has always meant a broad policy, a general programme . . . a strategic and not [a] tactical operation. The potential output of an industry in terms of money is a good and useful guide, but we must not fall into the trap of thinking that because it is convenient to measure output—whether of men or materials—in terms of money, those men and materials can be moved about from place to place and project to project with the same ease that money can be passed from one Vote to another.[1]

What we therefore had to do was to use all the contractors, large and small, carefully chosen and adapted to their particular jobs. They could not be switched about like pawns in a game. The human material in the building industry was not just a solid mass. There were firms and men suitable for house-building who could not be employed in skilled engineering or heavy construction work. There were small firms who could join in the housing drive in our towns and villages without impinging on the labour required for large-scale factory building. That confidence had been restored throughout the industry was proved by the fact that the period taken for completions in both house-building and school-building had steadily diminished. Productivity had continually increased. If, on the other hand, one took the test of school places, it was clear that the educational programme had not suffered. School places provided had already risen by nearly 100 per cent. Moreover, owing to better designs due to the co-operation of all Ministries concerned, we were now getting more school places for the same amount of money. In other words, over the whole programme of houses, schools, factories, clearance of old houses and the beginning of the attack on slum areas, including slum schools, we could claim that our programme, by the adaptation of a famous phrase, 'has been increased, is increasing, and ought to increase further still'.

This was a successful day for us, with a good majority—33. One or two of my Labour friends did not vote, for they thought the attack foolish and insincere.

[1] *Hansard*, 1 July 1953.

The next day the Press was favourable. But the papers also carried the news which I had put out officially the night before—that I must go to hospital within a few days for an operation. I entered St. Thomas's on the 6th at about 8 p.m., after a Cabinet which had met at 5.30. In the course of it Oliver Lyttelton, noticing that I was looking a little strained, passed me a piece of paper:

'Have you seen this epitaph?

> Here lies Dr. Dalton
> Filled with gloom:
> He can't betray
> The secrets of the tomb.'

This is cruel, but good. How strange that episode was. That a man should—as Chancellor of the Exchequer—give away Budget secrets would hardly do in Trollope (in spite of Phineas Finn). That he should do so in real life, and then go back into a Cabinet, is incredible.[1]

I was only out of action for a fortnight. For some months I had suffered acute pain from gall-stones. Indeed, I scarcely knew how to get through my last speech. But the operation was wholly successful owing to the care of my excellent doctor (Sir John Richardson) and the skill of the two surgeons who attended me (Mr. Boggon and Mr. Nevin). Within a few days I was receiving visitors and papers from the office. On the morning of 28 July I was able to leave hospital to attend a Cabinet. Meanwhile I had received, not yet for publication, figures for houses completed in the first six months of 1953. They totalled over 145,000; so we were clearly well on the way.

Progress continued and private enterprise building, so long restricted, began to expand substantially. By the time the Conservative Conference took place, in October, it seemed almost certain that the 300,000 target would be reached in two years and not in three. At any rate I was able to claim that we had completed in eight months of 1953 more houses than had been built under the previous Government in the whole of 1951. The speech was an

[1] 6 July 1953.

'... 299,998, 299,999 ...' —*Cartoon by Vicky*

easy one to make since things were going pretty well, and the audience was responsive. Nevertheless I have always found it difficult, speaking after a number of resolutions and at the end of a long morning or afternoon, to catch the attention of the delegates from the start. I therefore made it a practice to open with some unexpected observation. This time my speech began as follows:

> ... I read in the newspapers a few weeks ago that Mr. Attlee had returned from a holiday in Yugoslavia with a pair of antique flint-lock pistols and a fiddle with one string. Just the thing one would suppose for a Labour Party Conference! Even though I am faced with the task of replying to, I think, 44 resolutions on two vast subjects, I have not thought it necessary to have recourse to such desperate remedies.[1]

For the rest I based myself on the earlier debates in the House of Commons, fortified by the growing figures improving month by month.

A month later:

> I have just got the October Housing figures—over 30,000—a post-war record. The 300,000 should be 'in the bag' now. ... The Treasury statisticians are beginning to get very alarmed![2]

On 1 December I was able to announce that we had now reached our target:

> ... from 1 November 1952 to 31 October 1953 we had built 301,000 houses. Therefore we had done the job in the second full year of the Government's administration. This was received with great applause by Government supporters, and made a good note to end on—especially as Churchill came in for the end of the speech.[3]

December produced 29,000. So in the calendar year 1953, the figures reached 318,000-odd. Already in the summer I had realised that we should be accused of building too many houses! Indeed, we could easily have achieved 350,000 in the following year had we taken no steps to control the swelling river. We therefore decided to

---

[1] Speech at Margate conference, 9 October 1953.
[2] 15 November 1953.   [3] 1 December 1953.

leave private enterprise to go ahead as rapidly as possible and indeed
to encourage it by every possible means. We could thus make some
saving both to the Treasury and the local authorities. Of course it
was important to keep the council houses at a high figure, but it
was clear that the time had come when we should be thinking of
stabilising the programme and switching some of the effort of the
subsidised building to slum-clearance and an attack on overcrowding.

The work of our Ministry was not confined to housing and allied
problems. Our functions extended to almost any difficulty or
disaster in which local authorities were involved. One of these
occurred in the summer of 1952, when, after three very dry
months, in early August thunderstorms followed one another, day
after day. In the night of 16 August 1952 nine inches of rain were
said to have fallen on Exmoor, producing terrible floods. As soon as
I heard the news by the wireless I arranged for our own engineers
to go to the spot. I then set out to see for myself. The chief sufferer
was the small seaside resort of Lynmouth. One or two other villages
had also been affected.

> The urban district consists of two separate towns, each of
> about 1,000 inhabitants—one, Lynton, on the hill; the other,
> Lynmouth, on the shore. The damage was to Lynmouth, and
> caused by the tremendous flood forcing the river out of its bed,
> so that what was the High Street is now the river. The immense
> quantity of boulders (said to be 40,000 tons) destroyed the
> bridges. The problems of reconstruction are very considerable;
> the major cost will be on roads and bridges.[1]

I met all the local councillors, representatives of the county council
and the heads of the military and police and of the voluntary services
at a conference in the little Town Hall.

> Everyone talked at once . . . there was much goodwill but
> not much order. A great deal of splendid rescue work had been
> done since Friday night (when the disaster happened). It is
> mainly now (so far as the human side of the problem goes) a

[1] 19 August 1952.

matter of getting a proper steering committee and one person to act as head and give orders.[1]

Naturally there were demands for immediate promises of Government grants for reconstruction.

> I told them I would consider this with the Ministers concerned, but persuaded them to concentrate on getting immediate work done before arguing as to exactly who is to pay. Anyway, in addition to grant-aided services (like roads), there is need for generous response to the fund to be raised by the Lord-Lieutenant. Finally, some kind of orderly operation . . . was agreed and I have no doubt things will begin to improve.[1]

It was important to look after the people who had been evacuated without destroying the economic life of the seaside resort. I got them to agree, therefore, not to take over the remaining hotels, but to leave them open to encourage visitors and maintain employment in the little community.

> The chief danger now is (a) at Lynmouth of the [high] tide early in September; (b) in the villages of collapse of buildings, etc. (a) is quite serious. It will need hard work between now and then to build up a sea wall which can keep out the sea if there should be a strong westerly wind with the next tide.[1]

Naturally the Press, the newsreels and the B.B.C. were full of the sufferings of North Devon and especially of Lynmouth. Apart from the Relief Fund we were able to arrange satisfactory grants for the work of restoration. Altogether, by the end of the month, £300,000 had been subscribed and parcels of clothing and other necessities were sent on a generous scale.

But in the following year an even graver and more widespread disaster took place. On the last night of January 1953 there were floods on the East Coast from the Orkneys to Kent on a scale hardly ever experienced in Britain. The disaster caused havoc of different kinds and degrees. It was said to be the result of a strong north-east gale coinciding with the time of spring tides. Others believed that it was caused by what is called a 'sea surge', alleged to have risen to a

[1] 19 August 1952.

height of eleven feet or more, combining with the gale and the high tide. Little was known of these surges except that some authorities believed that it was just such a combination of tide, wind and surge which many thousands of years before swept away the last of the chalk ridge binding Britain with the Continent and thus turned Britain into an island – for good or ill.

On that Saturday night my wife and I got back late from an entertainment in Bromley. The wind and the rain were terrific, and we had difficulty in keeping the car on the road. On the next day – Sunday – I was rung up by my officials as well as by the Press and told the news. It was clear that a great calamity had taken place. Naturally, Churchill was on the telephone most of the Sunday afternoon and evening, 'but came to a stop soon after midnight'.[1] I thought I should take the lead and consequently summoned a conference next morning of all departments concerned. We got a proper procedure going and a committee of officials under Sir Frank Newsam (Permanent Secretary of the Home Office), as well as a committee of Ministers under the Home Secretary. I thus succeeded in voting myself out of the chair, and no better choice could have been made to deal with so great an emergency than the senior Secretary of State. Maxwell Fyfe carried out his task with extreme devotion and efficiency. A Lord Mayor's Fund was soon opened and reached £5 million by the end of the year – the largest sum ever raised by such an appeal. The Government undertook to give pound for pound, but of course the raising of money was the least of difficulties.

The chief problem is still about evacuees. We do not think that they amount to a very large number; but there are more than can be handled either in rest centres or by private hospitality without *some* payment. Dame Evelyn and the other Ministries have worked out a scheme for a 'billeting' allowance. The Treasury . . . are rather doubtful. Yet we *must* have a definite statement by tomorrow (Friday). This is 'Budget day' in every working-class household. Unless we can make an announcement these people will drift back from private houses and crowd, perhaps overwhelm, the centres. It is really remarkable how kindly

[1] 2 February 1953.

neighbours have been. In Whitstable about 6,000 people are homeless. Yet only 50 are in the 'rest centres'. All the rest have found a home in Kentish towns and villages.[1]

One of the criticisms soon to be made by the Opposition was that we had reduced the sums available for sea defences during recent years. It is true that there had been some cut in the money spent to prevent erosion.

But a cliff may crumble away, without letting in the sea![2]

Indeed, it was the old sea-walls, some of them dating from medieval times, which had been overwhelmed.

I was fortunately soon able to make an announcement about billeting, the main points of which were repeated by the B.B.C.:

We shall pay 10s. 6d. a head lodging allowance for each adult; 5s. for each child. I am sure this will help enormously and probably save us money on . . . halls, emergency hospitals, etc., in the long run.[3]

There were, however, other problems still remaining to be solved, especially in connection with the Lord Mayor's Fund.

There will be a demand for compensation as of right, not by charity. This will have to be resisted, for the sums involved would be large; the principle of insurance would be endangered; and there would, in the end, be public indignation against [companies and] corporations receiving 'compensation' from H.M.G. in respect of risks against which they could have insured.[4]

I had been criticised for declaring it to be an untenable proposition that all losses of every kind should be met by the Government, without regard to whether people had insured or ought to have insured, and taking no account of need or hardship. The temptation was too great to be resisted, and the Opposition tabled a hostile motion. However, when it came to be debated on 23 March, James Chuter Ede—who spoke as a former Home Secretary— realised that he had tried to press the point too hard.

[1] 5 February 1953.   [2] 2 February 1953.
[3] 6 February 1953.   [4] 19 February 1953.

Fortunately for them they had realised this in time so . . . Chuter Ede, who opened, 'roared like any sucking dove'. David [Maxwell] Fyfe made a masterly exposition of what H.M.G. had done, was doing, and intended to do. This virtually finished the debate.[1]

Maxwell Fyfe gained in reputation both by his handling of the problems caused by the floods and by his speeches in Parliament.

The most important thing, however, was to see that the old sea-walls were restored. By the end of February there was still some danger, of which hourly warnings were given. Nevertheless the temporary work was satisfactory and no more trouble occurred.

It was difficult to assess the total cost to the country of this great disaster, but the Home Secretary estimated it at between £40 million and £50 million, excluding the cost of permanent repairs or improvements of the sea defences. Between 150,000 and 175,000 acres had been flooded with salt water, and although two-thirds of this area would not be seriously affected, the rest might be lost to agriculture for many years. Although 25,000 houses had been flooded, only some 400 were destroyed. As for further measures, we decided to set up a committee under Lord Waverley to consider the whole problem. No wiser choice could have been made. It was perhaps somewhat surprising to realise that so large an acreage both of agricultural and built-over land was below the high-water level, and the fact that we had lived comfortably enough under these conditions, with the exception of two similar disasters in Roman and in medieval times, did not abate the immediate sense of danger. Nevertheless, with their traditional phlegm, the British people soon began to forget about it. We spent a great deal of money in one way or another, but of course full protection against some future recurrence could only be provided at an astronomical cost.

During this period I made a tour of the whole area by light aeroplane and it was certainly an extraordinary sight to see the extent of the damage. As usual the nearer you were to the front line of disaster, the more cheerful and friendly the people seemed. Apart from the human suffering and the loss of material assets, I

[1] 23 March 1953.

naturally deplored the tons of bricks and cement which had to be poured into reconstruction or defence works.

After the floods came the flies, for like the plagues of Egypt all these troubles seemed to fall upon my unhappy head. In the summer of this year the seaside resorts of the South Coast were attacked by vast hordes of flies, apparently impossible to reduce or control. I paid visits to some of these towns—Brighton and Eastbourne—with learned professors as well as more speculative and enterprising manufacturers of ingenious remedies. Some wished to poison the flies with a spray calculated to be fatal to them although harmless to visitors, including bathers; some wished to crush the seaweed, by which they seemed to be brought, by specially designed engines already available in various commercial arsenals; other devices, all worthy of the White Knight, were suggested. On these visits I was always hospitably entertained, and there was a general feeling that the Minister had done his best. Fortunately, like so many other troubles, the flies in due course disappeared.

During all these months I had been considering the most intricate and politically dangerous of the problems connected with housing. In July 1952, a report of the Sanitary Inspectors' Association had pointed out that the annual wastage of houses was equal to and perhaps even exceeded the new accommodation likely to be made available. This was due partly to the deterioration into slums of some of the older houses, but even more to the lack of repairs. This in turn arose from the system of rent control.

On 9 July 1952, at our little Ministerial Council, we had our first talk on rents. While I felt that only when they saw that the new houses were going up in large numbers would people accept any approach to this prickly subject; on the other hand, since to formulate legislation and carry it through would take us anything up to eighteen months or two years, we had better begin to think about it. Politically, we had to remember that to raise the rents of nearly two-thirds of the total houses, affecting anything between 16 and 20 million people, was not exactly an easy operation. The attitude of the general public towards rents had changed as the result of two wars:

One of the embarrassing legacies of war is the change in the pattern of spending. Since necessities, like food, are short and many luxuries, like music-halls and cinemas, impossible in the black-out, with clothing, dancing, travel, holidays, etc., rationed or impracticable, all the inflationary wages of the people are spent on the few available luxuries or pleasures. Roughly these are tobacco, alcohol–and (for the war) books. (Now television, cinemas, dancing, etc., are taking the place of books.) But it is hard to get back the idea that the first thing on which the family income should be spent is living accommodation.[1]

By the middle of September, at the request of my colleagues, I put forward the outlines of a plan.

I argued that rent restriction and new housing were closely inter-locked. The former could only be dealt with, at any rate politically, in the climate of success in the latter. There were nine million houses occupied at artificially low rents of between 6s. and 8s. a week as against the economic rent of an ordinary new house which would be at least 30s. a week. Even making the fullest allowance for the difference in the standards of accommodation provided, this large pool of houses at frozen rents was a deterrent to unsubsidised build-ing and to house-owning. Some of these houses were falling out of use; many more out of repair. Some of course were not worth repair –their proper fate was demolition. For this purpose the pre-war campaign for slum-clearance must be resumed. To this end, the solution which we ultimately adopted was a differential rate of subsidy, giving local authorities an incentive to concentrate upon slum-clearance. The New Towns were naturally given the full rate, for they made a contribution to rehousing, and at the same time enjoyed no old houses by which rents could be averaged. The bulk of this stock of rent-controlled houses could continue to provide good homes for many years if properly maintained. However un-popular increases of rent might be, it was reasonable for owners to receive and tenants to pay increased rents for the purpose of maintaining their houses in the proper state of repair. Rents could equitably be raised on the understanding that no increase should be payable unless the houses were put in a good condition by their

[1] 27 September 1952.

owners. In the long term it might be possible to base rents on valuation for rating, but this would have to wait, since, as a result of a flaw in the Local Government Act of 1948, a new valuation had got to be undertaken. The 1948 Act had proved unworkable, since the formula to be employed revealed, when tests were made, ridiculously unfair results as between different classes of houses. I should have to introduce a measure to postpone the Act from coming into effect and to provide for a new valuation on a basis which the Inland Revenue officers could operate.

The postponement Bill was passed with little difficulty by December 1952. The following year—on 8 May 1953—we had to introduce a new Bill to take the place of the provisions which had broken down. The valuations were to be undertaken by the Inland Revenue, as under the previous Act, but using a new formula. It was impossible to foretell when the work could be finished. But at any rate when it was done the system would be equitable as between individuals and between areas. It would clearly have been a reactionary step to return responsibility for valuation to the local authorities. Since so much depended, in the way of distributing grants from the central Government, upon a uniform system of valuation, we must wait until the Inland Revenue officers could finish their task. This Bill also, although more closely debated, passed into law within three months.

Meanwhile, if the new valuation should not be ready in time, we must content ourselves with the old pre-war valuations with the necessary additions of new property, if we were to use them as a method of dealing with increases of rent. By working hard during the Christmas vacation I was able to put forward a comprehensive plan to the Cabinet by the last week in January 1953. It was

set out in four Cabinet papers—three main papers and one cursory note. All these I have written myself (with . . . help and comments from the department) and all are based on the paper which I wrote on Boxing Day. They are now all in proof and I was able to deal with this and return them to the Cabinet printers over the weekend.[1]

[1] 24 January 1953.

As usual, I prefaced my covering note with quotations. They ran as follows:

Grant that we may both perceive and know what things we ought to do, and also have grace and power faithfully to fulfil the same.

Quem deus vult perdere, prius dementat. . . .

The first was meant as an encouragement, the second as a warning.

The papers, which were long, dealt with the whole question of houses, old and new, including rents, repairs and slum-clearance, as well as valuations for rating. My proposals for a new Valuation Bill were accepted without demur, since they were clearly necessary whatever might be the decision as to their use as a basis for increasing rents and promoting repairs. Owing to great pressure of other business, it was not until the middle of April that the Cabinet was able to hold a full discussion on the larger issues. In the intervening months we were able to re-examine many difficulties and devise many refinements. I had also persuaded Churchill to allow a small committee to examine my proposals and draft Bills which were already beginning to take shape.

Meanwhile I had been attacked by the first symptoms of the malady for which I had ultimately to go into hospital. I had to get the Valuation Bill and two other minor Bills through Parliament. These could have been left in the able hands of Marples. But I was determined to last out until my main project had either been accepted or turned down. Recurring bouts of pain, from which I suffered from time to time, made this difficult, but with the help and against the protests of my doctor I succeeded.

Churchill now began to take an interest in this affair.

P.M. rang up and asked for some housing 'dope' for a speech he is to make next week in Scotland. He seemed very excited about 'Housing Subsidies' and 'millions of houses falling down because the landlords cannot do the repairs'. I told him to read the papers which I had circulated. . . . He seemed much relieved that I was better and would be at next week's Cabinets.[1]

[1] 9 April 1953.

The next day I dictated some notes which I hoped would serve his purpose. He had to make a major speech in Scotland.

> I warned him *not* on any account to talk about *rents* (except in the most general terms) . . . until the Local Elections are over. Nothing is worse, in politics, than to expose a flank prematurely.[1]

Unfortunately, the news had begun to leak to the Press that we were about to grasp this nettle.

On 16 April a long discussion took place.

> The P.M. asked me to explain it in two sentences. I replied, 'I'm afraid that's not possible. I will do it in ten minutes.' I had prepared a text—every word and all the figures, and provided them with charts and tables.[2]

I had meanwhile sent instructions to the appropriate officers of my department to ensure that the necessary flow of bricks, cement, tiles and the like should be concentrated upon completions and to prevent too many starts in this year which might have a disturbing effect upon the future. It would soon be more important to concentrate upon repairs and conversions than merely to score more runs in the field of new houses.

Butler, who was already apprised of all the details, supported me nobly, and so did Churchill. As a result a general approval was given to my proposals. Churchill spoke to me at some length the same evening. He believed that legislation to amend the Rent Restriction Acts must be so designed as to bring no financial benefits to landlords. It must be clear that the Government had one purpose only, to increase the number of habitable houses. He had seen that the Labour Party, in a recent pamphlet, had admitted that the controlled rents of some houses did not provide sufficient income to maintain the property in good repair, and that tenants would benefit by amendment of the Acts, enabling a part of the rent to be spent on maintenance and improvement. There might therefore be a political opportunity in the coming session to pass legislation which could fairly be described as designed to increase the stock of habitable houses.

The idea now was to publish a White Paper on our plans early in

[1] 10 April 1953.   [1] 16 April 1953.

November just before the debate on the Address. This would cover the whole plan. The Second Reading of the Bill would be taken before Christmas. At the end of July I told my colleagues

> that if ever the 'White Paper' (which will be circulated—in first draft—to the Cabinet tomorrow) is actually published, we must 'see it through'. In other words, if this plan is launched, there can be no dissolution this autumn—or indeed for two years.[1]

By this time the local authorities had become enthusiastic about new housing and were beginning almost to outrun my targets, having regard to the availability of materials and the heavy charge upon the Revenue of the subsidies. I was all the more anxious to persuade them as soon as possible to switch a part of their efforts to conversions and improvements of old houses and to a renewed attack on the slums.

By the end of August, when the House had adjourned for the holiday, we were in good shape. The Rating and Valuation Bill had become law. I had completed the third or fourth draft of the White Paper. Apart from the second Town and Country Planning Act on which we were engaged, I could concentrate upon Repairs and Rents. All these plans, however, were to some extent complicated by Churchill's illness in the summer of 1953 and the uncertainty about his future. The White Paper was again discussed in September and October with the special problems of Scotland in mind. Here James Stuart, Secretary of State, whom I had consulted on the whole plan for many months, was especially helpful. One or two Ministers asked why the rent could only be raised if the landlord could show that he had actually spent the money on repairs. Why could not the condition of the house be the sole criterion? The answer to this was simple. The state of the house could not be the only test because we knew of thousands of cases where the landlord had done nothing for years and the tenant in despair had done the repairs himself or at his own cost.

Finally, on 5 October, the Cabinet agreed both to the text of the White Paper and to the draft Bill. I repeated my opinion that if we published this politically dangerous proposal to raise rents over so

[1] 28 July 1953.

large a proportion of the population, we must go through with it. It was strange that so much hung upon this point, which I felt necessary to emphasise, for it was clear that this would mean no election until 1955 and had considerable bearings on the question of Churchill's ability or determination to remain in office so long. Nevertheless, I thought it my duty to repeat this warning; if we introduced a Bill, however fair and reasonable it might be, there must be a chance of the plans at least beginning to work out in a way which would command general approval.

The White Paper, under the title of *Houses—The Next Step*, was published on 3 November. The new policy had its place in the Queen's Speech, and Churchill referred to it in general terms when opening the debate. Morrison followed, and in the course of it complained of the popular version of *Houses—The Next Step* which we had called *Operation Rescue*. He declared that this was a gross misuse of the Government machine, making it an instrument of party propaganda.

> Later when Bevan repeated it in a more offensive form, I was armed with some of the Socialist Government's own productions— far more propagandist and better illustrated than my humble effort! As I pointed out, 'The Budget and You' in 1949 even had a strip cartoon.[1]

I began by stating that in 1939 it had been estimated that only 6 per cent of the population were living in unfit or overcrowded houses, although there was much to be done for their improvement and the clearance of slums. At that time the stock of houses, although of varying quality, was almost equal to the number of separate families. Now, however, in spite of all that had been done, there were still large numbers waiting on the housing list year after year. The reason was twofold. First, the higher standard of living had brought about a general demand for a better standard of housing; secondly, apart from any growth in the population, there was a marked difference in its composition. There were more single people; more old people; and more young married couples wanting a home of their own.

[1] 5 November 1953.

I turned next to the question of the existing houses and their general state of repair. There were the two million or more held by the local authorities. These bodies could be relied upon to maintain the condition of their property. They were also empowered to raise rents as they thought fit, and they were doing so. We estimated that, taking Great Britain as a whole, of the 13·5 million individual dwellings, about 6 million had been built during the last thirty-five years. On the whole they were in a good state. But we had 7·5 million built before 1914. Half of these were a hundred years, and a quarter from sixty-five to a hundred years old.

> Altogether, 5 million of these were built while Queen Victoria was still on the Throne and many before the . . . Public Health Act of 1875 was put on the Statute Book. That Act, the House will remember, and the Artisans' Dwelling Act, were the . . . contributions of the Tory Party under the greatest of its leaders, Benjamin Disraeli. It is a strange thought that the progressive opinion of the day, especially the intellectual opinion of the day, scoffed at these measures because they conflicted with the fashionable *laissez-faire* doctrines which were then current.[1]

If there had been no Second War, and if slum-clearance had gone on at the rate reached by 1938, many of these houses would long ago have been demolished. But for the moment we had to face the facts as they were. Even if we were to build 300,000 houses a year, it would take a long time to replace these older houses. They were meanwhile an asset which we must preserve, and we must try to tackle the question of the old houses with the same vigour which we had put into the provision of the new houses. It was a highly complex problem incapable of a simple and single solution.

> We must, therefore, have a comprehensive plan for repairs, maintenance, improvement, conversion, demolition and replacement.[1]

For convenience we had divided the houses into four main groups. First there were the best—the houses essentially sound, which could be kept in good condition if the income coming in was sufficient for this purpose. At the other end of the scale were the

[1] *Hansard*, 4 November 1953.

slum houses which we must pull down and replace as soon as possible. But if we were realists, we must face the fact that they could not all be pulled down and rebuilt within the next few years.

> Some must remain in use—a sad fact, but a true fact. The people cannot be put out into the street. The Government feel that so long as some of these houses must remain in use something must be done to give them first-aid and make life a little better for those who are condemned to live in them.[1]

Thirdly, between these extremes, there was an intermediate class which we called 'dilapidated'—in a bad state, but nevertheless worth repairing. Some of these could not be made fit by the owner at any reasonable expense. Others the owners could deal with voluntarily or compulsorily. Fourthly, there was a class of houses which could give many years of good service if improved.

> The tenants want bathrooms, hot water, better cooking arrangements, and so forth, and many houses which are soundly constructed can be brought up to this standard at far less cost— certainly, in far less time—than it takes to build new houses altogether.[1]

This class included houses too big for present-day needs, which could be converted into good flats.

This exposition of the problem led naturally to the measures proposed. For this purpose some account was necessary of the remarkable history of rent control. Some rents had been controlled since 1914 and still remained at that level, plus the 40 per cent increase allowed in 1920. Others came out of control between the wars and went back into control at the outbreak of the Second War. Some escaped control because of the value of the house or the character of the tenancy. The effect had been that many rents bore no relation to the cost of keeping the houses in current repair. They also bore no relation to each other. After the most careful sampling in a number of towns, we had found extraordinary variations. Houses of the same rateable value, of the same type, in the same street, with the same amenities, varied from 7s. to 17s. 6d. in their rent. A special committee had been set up to consider what would

[1] *Hansard*, 4 November 1953.

be the cost of maintenance today compared to pre-war. They concluded the cost to be about trebled. The local authorities, of course, were able to put up their rents. We proposed to leave them that responsibility without interference. What were we to do about this vast number of privately owned houses?

One idea was to relate the rent to the assessable values of the houses as valued for rating. Lord Silkin had put forward this plan as a long-term solution; but owing to the failure of the 1948 Act it would be some time before a new valuation would be ready. Meanwhile the house repairs must be done or the houses would continue to deteriorate. We therefore proposed to allow what we called a 'repairs increase' in rents. Our object was to increase the income of a house with strict regard to present rents, devised to operate as fairly as possible, and at the same time to ensure that no rent should rise as the result of the repairs increase beyond a certain maximum percentage. We had also to make sure that any increase in rent was actually spent in repairs and did not merely add to the retained income of the landlord. To achieve this the method we had adopted was to allow increases of twice that part of the assessment for rates, which was normally known as the 'repairs allowance', with the proviso that no rent should be increased to more than twice the gross value. Therefore, if the rent was already as high or higher, it would not be affected. It had been suggested that under this plan the rents of 5 to 6 million houses would rise between 4s. 7d. and 5s. 5d. a week. That, of course, was not correct, as was shown by the statistics which I published in the White Paper. For instance, in the case of 4 million houses rated at £15 a year, the maximum to which the rent could rise was 11s. 6d. If it was already at that figure there would be no increase; if it was 10s. 6d. it would rise by 1s.; 9s. 6d. by 2s., and so on. Only if it was 6s. 11d. would it rise by the full 4s. 7d. This safeguard became known as the 'stopper'.

There were vitally important provisions by which the house would have to be in a good state of repair and the landlord if required would have to produce a certificate that the repairs had been done within the last three years. This was to prevent an increase of rent where the tenant and not the landlord had done the work. With these explanations, it was at any rate not difficult to persuade the

House that given the extraordinary variety of rents, arising from the various systems of control, a flat percentage increase such as had been adopted between the wars would be grossly unfair.

I then turned to the other extreme—the slums or semi-slums. Here it was not possible to give altogether reliable figures. When the Second War began there were 140,000 houses scheduled for demolition. All or nearly all of these were still inhabited. By now the slum houses were probably two or even three times that number. Some experts estimated the total at half a million. It was a terrifying picture. I now proposed with the help of Government grants to induce the local authorities to set about this task at full speed. Materials were coming along, and I felt sure that with the same energy as was being put into the building of new houses, slum-clearance would begin again. But with the best will in the world, in some cities it would take ten, perhaps twenty, years to clear the whole mass away. What then was to happen to these people while waiting for their turn?

> Something must be done; we cannot just leave them there in houses which are getting worse and worse while their hopes are getting lower and lower. It really is a great human problem and a great challenge to any Christian nation.[1]

We proposed, therefore, that the local authorities should acquire these houses at the site value only, as they had a right to do. They would be responsible for the care of the people until new accommodation could be made available. Meanwhile they would do what they could for these houses.

> They will patch and mend them; they will clean and furbish, so that they will at least become rather better places to live in. They will not be good; they never can be good; but the people will know that something is being done for them, that they are not forgotten, and that their turn is coming.[1]

I recognised that this was a hard task to put upon the local authorities. They were proud of their properties; they would not like becoming slum landlords. Yet I felt sure they would recognise that they

[1] *Hansard*, 4 November 1953.

would be trustees in the true sense of the word and that this new duty would be a work worthy of their past traditions. Such an experiment had already begun in the city of Birmingham. Indeed, it was to their initiative that I owed the idea of extending the plan over the whole country.

These then were the two extremes—the houses which landlords could be expected to keep in good condition either with no repairs increase or with an increase appropriate to each house where the present rent was too low on the one hand, and the slum houses on the other. In between there was the category which we had called 'dilapidated', houses in a bad state but which could be put right. Landlords had a statutory obligation to see that their houses were sound and fit for human habitation. If a landlord failed in this duty, the local authorities had the right to do it for him and recoup the cost out of the rent. This Bill would strengthen their powers, and I should expect them to make good use of their enlarged authority.

Finally, there was the question of houses capable of being improved or converted:

> We all know of the large number of houses, built especially in the first expansion of the great towns, which are sound structurally, well built technically, and often designed for those our reactionary ancestors called the middle class, now called, I believe, the middle income groups. The trouble about those is that they were built for another age. They lack modern amenities, and they are often too large for single family occupation.[1]

It was a happy feature of a progressive society that the luxuries of one age became the necessities of the next. These changes took place so rapidly that it was difficult for younger people to realise how quickly they had come about. One of the most agreeable if not the most dramatic change in the way of living in my lifetime had been the bath. After some description of the bath in my childhood and in my youth—generally a round tin affair, with hot water heated on a gas ring—I passed to the question as to how we were to deal by conversion and improvement with these houses, the structure of which was sound and good. The Bill would include proposals

[1] *Hansard*, 4 November 1953.

for assisting local authorities and owners or developers by the appropriate grants to undertake this task.

This comprehensive design was thus fairly launched. When we came to the Second Reading, the Opposition were in a difficulty. Morrison was handicapped in that Bevan, with whom he was on the worst terms, had already declared that the only remedy was for the local authorities to take over all the houses in the whole country, presumably raising the rents much above the figure which my Bill contemplated. Morrison was shrewd enough to see that the proposal to load the local authorities with the ownership and management of 7 million houses was quite impracticable.

Bevan's most effective point, however, had been the argument that the additional rent would hardly be a sufficient inducement to the landlords. Here again the Opposition fell into some confusion. Marples who introduced the Second Reading was quick to point out that at a recent by-election the Bill had been denounced as 'a rich harvest for the landlord'. Now Bevan had said it would be of no more use to them than 'a mouldy old turnip'. Churchill urged me to make much of this in my speeches in the country. 'They must declare,' he said, 'on which line of attack they propose to rely. Following the rules of the Turf, they must state which horse was the pacemaker and which was being ridden to win.'

When Parliament met in January 1954, it soon became clear that this long and complicated Bill, with over forty clauses and five schedules, would take some time to get through.

> Now we have only to sit patiently through another $7\frac{1}{2}$ hours of talk, while Aneurin Bevan (by the media of new clauses) develops his great ideas of Housing reform. These he will try to pin on the reluctant Attlee, Morrison and Co. He is trying to force the Labour Party to accept his principle of public—or at least municipal—ownership of all houses now owned by landlords.[1]

All this was rather fun for us, although disturbing for the more moderate Labour Members.

I had been concerned that so small a proportion—only 6 per cent—of the unsubsidised, privately built houses were being devoted to

[1] 11 March 1954.

letting. I was anxious to see whether we could not bring back into the market developers who could provide such accommodation. We therefore introduced an amendment on the Report stage, freeing from rent control all new building of houses and flats and all new conversions of existing houses for letting purposes. The opposition to this was considerable. But I felt that it was another move to freedom.

> This is not a question of jumping the queue . . . this is a question of people being allowed and encouraged to get into the right queue, not forced, as many people of better means are today . . . to sponge upon their neighbours by living in subsidised houses.[1]

In the Third Reading debate, I reverted to Bevan's proposal that all housing should be nationally or municipally owned. Whether this was to involve the extermination of the owner-occupier seemed obscure, but I assumed that these, like kulaks, would be allowed to survive at least in the early stages of the revolution. Even so, it was a formidable picture of the future under Socialism. Although the Opposition divided against the Third Reading, there was by this time little heat in the controversy. At any rate we could claim that we had shown some courage in dealing with a problem from which others had run away.

After a number of amendments, drafting and otherwise, in the House of Lords, the Act received the Royal Assent on 30 July 1954, just two years after our first discussion in the Ministry on the problems of rent, rent control and repairs.

It now became necessary to popularise and explain the Repairs and Rent scheme. The usual methods of publicity by the Press and the wireless were not so freely available in those days; but we brought them into our service as far as possible. In addition we arranged a practical demonstration of the various methods of conversion and improvement. Ernest Marples, with great ingenuity, devised an exhibition in Holles Street, just off Oxford Street. Here were some hundred-year-old terraced houses, already condemned as slum property, but essentially well built and easily convertible into

[1] *Hansard*, 13 April 1954.

decent flats. One house was left in its old-fashioned, decayed form, without bathroom or proper kitchen. Two others were converted at a cost of under £800 each into modern flats. Marples had taken a great deal of pains to get the 'décor' correct. In fact I had to warn him that he had been so successful in collecting quaint pieces of furniture and china and other Victoriana, including stuffed birds, that some people might think the unconverted flat in this style more attractive than the converted ones with their modernistic furnishings.

Looking back upon all this I am sure that what we did for the conversion of the 'dilapidated' houses, for slum clearance, and the mending and patching of slums which could not yet be destroyed, met with substantial success. It certainly set people thinking upon new lines, and much useful work was done in subsequent years. On rent control Bevan's original criticism was probably right. The rise in permitted rents may have proved insufficient in many cases to enable the landlords to make the necessary repairs. Nevertheless our plan broke the ice of rigid rent control. Nobody had dared attack this thorny problem, and quite a lot was achieved under our scheme. But it was left to my successors at the Ministry to make the next move.

Work had meanwhile continued on the general question of subsidies. At the end of July 1954 the Cabinet accepted the idea of a differential subsidy to encourage slum clearance. We were now hoping to get 150,000 unsubsidised houses in 1956, and this must mean some curtailment of the council houses, or at least some switch of council work from what were called 'general needs' to slum clearance.

The Repairs and Rent Act, embodying 'Operation Rescue', was the last of our many plans to reach fruition. I had indeed prepared in the spring of 1954 a note upon the great collection of skeletons which I had found in my ministerial cupboard in the winter of 1951. Some of these had been decently disposed of within the last two years; others were on their way to the burial ground; but many remained. I therefore circulated a paper setting out the matters which I felt should be dealt with, although probably not until the next

Parliament. The first concerned the reform, or at any rate the re-organisation, of local government. The second was the question of the financial relations between the central and local governments. The third was that of rating and the need to bring to an end the derating of industry. This scheme, bold and effective nearly thirty years before, had served its purpose. Fourth, the equalisation grant needed amending. Fifth, still further steps should be taken to deal with housing subsidies by progressive concentration of slum-clearance and overcrowding, and to provide larger inducements for house ownership. Finally, the tiresome question of requisitioned houses—a relic of war conditions, which chiefly affected London—must be dealt with and properties either purchased or returned to their owners. I called this summary 'Operation Round-Up'. Since my term of office was soon to come to an end, all these problems remained for a future Minister.

The party conference was held at Blackpool in October 1954, and the recent Bill was both discussed and criticised. I naturally reminded the audience that four years ago in the same hall the delegates had made their memorable demand for an ambitious attack on the housing problem. Some would remember the scene when Lord Woolton stopped the bidding, if I dared use the expression, at 300,000. 'He might have made it guineas. We could have managed that all right.' After praising all those concerned, especially my Parliamentary Secretary, Marples, and Eccles, the Minister of Works, I told them that some 350,000 houses would be built in 1954. We had now turned our attack to another, less popular front. Yet in human terms what we were now trying to do was even more vital. It was for the party to explain and defend the new measures. All this seemed acceptable to the audience.

In October 1954 Churchill reorganised his administration and asked me to become Minister of Defence. I had now been three years at the Ministry of Housing and I was ready for a change. Much as I disliked leaving a fascinating post, I felt that Churchill's decision was right. At any rate we had enjoyed ourselves and could feel a modest sense of satisfaction. In the first year the services of Percy Mills had been invaluable; indeed, without him we could have achieved little. Even after he had given up his full-time appointment, he was always ready to help with his advice. He attended many of our conferences during the next two years, and there was no step which Marples and I took without consulting him and getting the advantage of his experience and judgement. In Marples I had a colleague of outstanding loyalty and devotion. He was, moreover, a man of infinite resources, great ingenuity, and untiring energy. I was glad, indeed, at a later date to be able to recommend him for a Cabinet post. Of the civil servants Sir Thomas Sheepshanks, after a somewhat bewildered start, began to get the general idea of what we were trying to do. Although often disapproving of our methods, he finally took a fatherly interest in our success. The pillar of the Ministry was Dame Evelyn Sharp. She was without exception the ablest woman I have ever known; she was also one of the most charming. All through the ranks of the Ministry and among the regional officers there grew up during these years a sense of comradeship and even enthusiasm. The same was true of Eccles and the Ministry of Works. With the Scottish Office we worked in close association, and the quiet efficiency of James Stuart made our task easy.

Thus, on 18 October 1954, three of the happiest years of my life came to an end. I was indeed fortunate both in the appointed task and in my fellow-labourers. When I thought back to the scene at Chartwell where it had all begun, I felt sincerely grateful to Churchill, who, in peace as in war, had given me my chance.

The Queen opens the exhibition in Holles Street devised by Ernest Marples to show how decayed houses could be converted into decent flats

Pierre Mendès-France and John Foster Dulles

CHAPTER XIV

Europe in Travail

WHEN the new Government took office in the autumn of
1951, it found itself confronted with a number of grave
problems. During its last year Attlee's administration had
struggled through increasing pressures on every front. The economy
was in the throes of one of those recurrent crises, which, whether by
ill luck or ill management, seem to become especially acute whenever Socialist Ministers are in power. At the same time the external
situation, both in Europe and throughout the world, was confused
and menacing. As a result, the next three years, from 1951 to 1954,
were to prove a period of baffling and complicated diplomacy, in
which the British Government was naturally expected to play a
leading role.

The return of Churchill to power was hailed throughout Europe
and America as likely to mark a wholly new approach towards the
question of European unity. His great prestige, unrivalled since the
days of Marlborough, and the energy with which he had thrown
himself into the founding and promotion of the European Movement, not unnaturally served to raise widespread hopes. Now at last,
after so many hesitations, Britain might be expected to give a
definite lead. If what followed was to prove a sad disillusionment—
almost a betrayal—it is right to recall some of the difficulties, internal
and external, with which Churchill was confronted.

Not merely was the British Cabinet facing something like
economic collapse at home and relying upon so slender a Parliamentary majority that its survival seemed in question; there was also
an ambivalence, if not a division, within its ranks on the European
question. Moreover, by the last months of 1951, the situation had
developed in a way which left less freedom of manœuvre than would
have been possible a year or two before.

The European Movement, founded as an unofficial organisation in December 1947, had led to the establishment of an official body, the Council of Europe, with its two organs–the Council of Ministers and the Consultative Assembly. Largely through Churchill's pressure, Western Germany had been admitted to full membership. On the economic side, the Schuman Plan for coal and steel had been devised and accepted by six nations–France, Italy, West Germany, and the Benelux countries. In spite of the efforts of the Conservative Party in Opposition, this plan had reached fruition without Britain being associated with its formulation. In its final form, therefore, it was cast in that highly organised supranational mould, including the whole constitutional paraphernalia of sovereignty, which was so distasteful to British opinion of all parties. Many of us believed that, had we associated ourselves with the drafting of the scheme from the beginning, the countries concerned might have been led to agree to a more acceptable because less rigidly bureaucratic and legalist approach. Nevertheless, there was nothing now to be done, except to reaffirm our determination to associate ourselves as closely as possible with the new community and to take steps to appoint an observer to the meetings of the new body. On this there was no difficulty; and it was rapidly agreed that a suitable message should be conveyed to a meeting of the Council of Europe in November 1951.

Owing to the temperamental divergences of opinion among Ministers, the precise terms of this statement were the result of a compromise in the Cabinet. Some of us would have liked it warmer; others, no doubt, would have preferred it to be more tepid. But by this time it was not so much the question of the Schuman Plan as that of the European Army which held the field. After much negotiation, by the end of the summer of 1951 the Pleven Plan had developed into what came to be known as the European Defence Community, and its broad terms had been agreed among the nations concerned. It was clear that to such an organisation, which retained all the supranational features of the Pleven Plan, Britain could not give her formal adherence. We could become associates but not members. This decision, taken by the Labour Government in the last months of its existence, was accepted by its successors. Nevertheless, it was with great heart-burnings that those of us who had taken so deep an interest in the European Movement began to see us excluded from yet another vital aspect of the life of Europe. The Schuman Plan—if it should ever come effectively into being—must be accepted. That defence should fall exclusively into the hands of the six nations would be a further blow. Even more dangerous developments might follow.

In the first weeks of the new Government an unhappy misunderstanding was caused by the apparent contradiction between a statement which Maxwell Fyfe was authorised to make on behalf of the Cabinet at Strasbourg in November 1951 and the answers to questions which Eden as Foreign Secretary gave at a Press conference in Rome a few hours later. Fyfe's words had been approved and were as follows:

> ... I cannot promise full and unconditional participation but I can assure you of our determination that no genuine method shall fail for lack of thorough examination which one gives to the needs of trusted friends.... There is no refusal on the part of Britain....[1]

This was naturally thought warm and forthcoming, even if somewhat vague. Eden contented himself with repeating a declaration already made by Herbert Morrison two months before, announcing Britain's wish to establish 'the closest possible association at all stages of its development' with the European continental community. Unhappily, in answer to questions, he made it clear that the word 'association' did not imply that British units and formations would be part of the European Army, but that there might be some other form of association. These rather frigid sentiments seemed to many unhelpful or even contemptuous. It is hardly the method of describing the armies of Marlborough, Wellington, Haig or Eisenhower fighting in the decisive battles of the world. These two statements, coming so close together, have led to much controversy, then and since. But this incident, although it caused a considerable flurry at the time at Strasbourg and grave concern among the supporters of the European Movement, had no decisive importance. It was, however, symptomatic of the different approaches of British Ministers to the problem, and it seemed to underline the ambivalence of the new administration. Some of us, led by Churchill, had

---

[1] Earl of Kilmuir, *Memoirs*, p. 187.

been protagonists of the European Movement and were keen supporters of Strasbourg. Eden, Salisbury and others were believed to be tepid Europeans, more convinced of the difficulties than of the advantages. These sceptics asked how the great problem could be resolved of the association of the British Commonwealth and Colonial Empire—still for the most part largely under our control—with Europe upon lines of any new constitution or any supranational authority. Here indeed lay the core of the difficulty. But others of us felt that, so great was the desire for some solution, we should, by seizing the initiative, be able to achieve an acceptable compromise. I myself believed, and with good reason, that the power of the French federalists was exaggerated. After all, the French are the most insular people in the world, as has recently been shown. Most Frenchmen were not much concerned with creating a new constitution for Europe. Their immediate anxiety was how to reconcile the rearmament of Germany with the security of France. Surely we could meet this difficulty without the elaborate and almost unworkable machinery contemplated by the framers of the European Defence Community.

From the individual point of view, a sad distinction between Opposition and Government is the narrowing of the panorama that stretches before one's eyes. In Opposition the whole field is open—foreign and Commonwealth affairs, economic and social questions—and all in general terms. But when one becomes a Minister, especially a Minister in such an office as Housing, it is very difficult not to find one's outlook circumscribed rather than widened. Of course, Cabinet papers, Foreign Office telegrams and other relevant memoranda covering the whole range are circulated to every Cabinet Minister. Their volume is, however, overwhelming and their style generally designed to repel rather than attract readers. In Cabinets, in spite of the nominal equality and constitutional collectivity of decision, there are, in fact, degrees of power and authority, as in every other human institution. There are the 'big boys'—the Prime Minister, the Foreign Secretary, the Chancellor of the Exchequer—who, with perhaps one or two men of special weight and experience, constitute, in effect, a governing group. By long tradition, foreign affairs fall under the guidance of the Foreign Secretary and the Prime Minister. Their colleagues, especially those who may be said to have been taken off classical studies in order to specialise on the modern side—and the Minister of Housing is very much one of these—are expected to get on with their own work and listen silently, or at the most with occasional interrogatory observations, to the discussions dominated by their superiors. It is true that Churchill enjoyed Cabinet meetings—indeed, in the last phase they constituted the most important part of his work. He therefore liked to stimulate discussion and often to prolong it. But it was apparent to the less important Ministers that their leading colleagues were often impatient and anxious to proceed with business rather than indulge in desultory reflections on the matters, great and small, for which they sought a decision. If the Headmaster was discursive, the senior boys were impatient. Of course, when supreme issues arise every Minister has a right and a duty to express his view and support it if necessary by resignation. But many questions do not erupt in any special crisis or demand a drastic and immediate decision. The problems drag on from day to day and from meeting to meeting; and if one is engrossed in one's own work, it is very hard to do more than keep up with what is happening in larger affairs. Moreover, it is hard to fight a war on two fronts, as history has proved. My immediate battle was with the Treasury. For this I needed an active alliance with No. 10 and at least the benevolent neutrality of the Foreign Office.

Naturally I did my best to keep in touch with European issues, in which I had taken such an interest and had played a certain part. Whenever possible, I discussed them with those of my colleagues who had been specially active at Strasbourg, such as David Maxwell Fyfe, as well as with Duncan Sandys and David Eccles, who unhappily were not in the Cabinet although members of the administration. To Eden I would make occasional appeals both written and spoken. I was always treated with his characteristic courtesy and charm. But the Foreign Secretary was often abroad, and even in discussion he was so well informed and convincing upon any particular point that it was difficult to raise and defend more general concepts.

In the discussions that we had at the end of November and the beginning of December 1951, Eden and those who agreed with him

were able to make a strong case. Why should we now interfere with
E.D.C.? The discussions were complete on the military side, and it
only remained to press on with the political negotiations—first for the
six Governments to agree on the creation of the European Defence
Community, and secondly for ratification of the treaty by the Parliaments concerned. Except for actually joining it, we should now do
everything we could to make E.D.C. succeed. If the French politicians were hesitating, we should urge them to go ahead on the
course they had planned. While I could not argue against the view
that the coal and steel and the defence structures, as now devised,
were unacceptable to us, I frankly hoped and believed that they
would break down. If they were successful, it might be a short-term
advantage, especially if it facilitated immediate German rearmament. But the long-term future would be grim indeed. There would
be a European Community, from which we should be excluded,
and which would effectively control Europe. This was the historic
struggle in which we had been engaged first against Louis XIV,
then against Napoleon, and twice in our lifetime against Germany.
Germany was weak now; in the long run she would be stronger than
France, and so we might be bringing about in twenty years' time
that domination of Europe by Germany to prevent which we had
made such terrible sacrifices twice within a single generation. It
should, therefore, be our hope that the Schuman Plan and—more
important—E.D.C. would fail. If we could not kill the latter openly,
we need not strive officiously to keep it alive. When E.D.C. was
dead and buried, we should then be in a position to take the
initiative in organising an alternative system. I was convinced that
if we stated our terms they would be accepted. The whole of Europe
was waiting for a lead, and they could not understand why it did not
come from a new administration led by Churchill.

Some of my colleagues in the Cabinet shared this view, but it was
dismissed by the majority as unrealistic, and as disregarding the
immediate danger—the growing Russian pressure. From this point
of view, the only vital thing was the early organisation of the forces
in NATO, including a German contribution. I was myself somewhat
sceptical of this argument. It was not, I felt, the twenty or even thirty
divisions we might eventually muster which would deter the 120

Soviet divisions from further aggression. It was the overwhelming preponderance of atomic power.

Throughout these years until the final solution at the end of 1954, the French were torn by conflicting doubts. In spite of Russia's threatening aspect both in the West and in the East, was Russia really the enemy most to be feared? Would it not be wise to revert to the older French tradition which had operated through the whole of the Third Republic and which had at least forced Germany to fight a war on two fronts? Would it not be better to try to make terms with Russia, to keep Germany neutral and unarmed, and thus maintain French security? If, however, the weight of argument was to fall in favour of accepting Russia as the main danger, then it would no doubt be right to support German rearmament but prudent to tie it up with as many conditions and safeguards as possible. Hence arose the plan for the European Army under strict supranational authority, political and military, and organised on a basis which would minimise the danger of large German formations under German control. Even so, the French were continually trying to find additional methods to prevent the Germans, once they had become rearmed, evading the obligations of, or even seceding from, the new European community. They were soon to seek British and American assistance to this end.

This was the French dilemma. The Germans were torn equally between fear and hope. Dr. Adenauer's position was not yet fully established. Although agreements were being negotiated, to be signed in Bonn in May 1952, by which West Germany could become an ally instead of an occupied country, yet Adenauer was attacked by many patriotic Germans on the ground that if West Germany associated herself completely with her Western allies, any hope of Russia agreeing to the reunification of Germany would be lost for ever. Russia, in her turn, exploited this situation, and during the spring of 1952 began to put forward proposals for a meeting to discuss the question of German reunification. Eden played off this intervention with considerable skill by immediately raising the question of a United Nations Commission to arrange the conditions of German elections.

All these considerations and conflicting motives were continually at work during these fateful years in Germany as well as in France. The negotiations for an urgent solution were destined to last for nearly three years. Throughout this period Churchill gave no sign. The official Foreign Office doctrine prevailed: wait for E.D.C.

Many of my friends in the European Movement who were not in office soon began to express to me their alarm at the way things were moving. Dr. Joseph Retinger, one of the founders, called upon me in January 1952 in a state of considerable emotion. 'Why,' he demanded, 'does not England announce her terms?' The pressure for federalism was not so great as we imagined. The Germans still disliked the French. The French were still suspicious of the Germans. Britain must take the lead. Instead of telling European countries what we could not do, we ought to tell them in straightforward language what we would do.

Early in 1952 I was much distressed by a memorandum compiled in the Foreign Office on European integration, which was given a wide circulation. It seemed to me to be based upon a complete misapprehension of the reality and strength of the movement for European unity. It indeed treated the whole of these efforts with a certain amount of levity and contempt. I compiled for my own interest a reply, and after consultation with David Maxwell Fyfe I decided that the prudent course was not to circulate it as a Cabinet paper but to send it direct to Eden. For this he thanked me and undertook to study it carefully. He found my views 'stimulating'—ominous cliché!

I had been shocked by the Foreign Office opinion that complete union of the Schuman Plan countries would not be harmful in the short term to the United Kingdom, and would only ultimately be dangerous if Germany emerged as the predominant partner and used her position to our disadvantage in the economic and political field. There might also be some danger that a Third Force would come into being which would be neutral in the case of a world conflict. This was a degree of myopia which a mole might envy. But the argument which most concerned me was the claim that, owing to her position as a world power, Britain could not join a movement for integration; she could only associate herself with it in a friendly fashion. This was essentially a reversion to the isolation of Fox and of Chamberlain. In addition, it seemed to duck the whole question. We could not, of course, join a federation which would limit our membership of the Commonwealth or our association with the United States. But federation was not the only form of constitutional association between states. There could be a confederation, based on continuous consultation between Governments; a Consultative Assembly could be used to create a European public opinion; European currencies could be linked individually or collectively to sterling; a European preferential area could be created, inter-locking with our own system of Imperial Preference; and specialised but not supranational authorities could be set up for such matters as defence and heavy industry. We could certainly participate in a European Army, composed of national units of at least divisional strength, in which the joint command would be responsible, as in the NATO concept, to the different national Governments. The French, already fighting a war of first-class magnitude in Indo-China and with enormous commitments in North Africa, would certainly not commit their whole forces to the European Army. We could make similar reservations. If we did nothing, the French, German and Italian federal system—'Little Europe'—might, in spite of all French hesitations, come into being—but without Britain. It would be encouraged by the United States, and in the long run it would represent both an economic and political danger to Britain and even to the Commonwealth.

It was true that the three Governments seemed to have decided *en principe* for such a federation; but this would be reluctantly accepted by the Dutch and the Belgians. Nor was I at all sure that the French Parliament would in the end agree. If it could be per-suaded to do so, it would only be in default of any alternative. But if we did all we could to persuade the French and other Governments to accept E.D.C., we should be creating that very grouping from which even the Foreign Office paper foresaw ultimate dangers.

Surely we ought now to announce the broad outlines of the kind of European union which we should be prepared to join? It would then be for the Continental nations to choose between such a union and a closely-knit federation without Britain. Such a stroke might well succeed. If it failed, then and then only should we consider our new association with the Continental federation in order to influence its policies and mitigate its dangers.

However, neither the Foreign Secretary nor the Government as a whole found my views sufficiently 'stimulating' to lead to the action I desired. They decided on a different policy, and our official line soon became clear. We would bring all possible pressure upon the French to join E.D.C. and we would even consider various kinds of declarations and guarantees to prevent the treachery of one member of the European community against another – in other words, the secession of Germany.

In February 1952 the Council of NATO, meeting in Lisbon, approved plans for the proposed establishment of E.D.C., but since the treaty was not yet ratified this was little more than a formal figure in the long diplomatic quadrille.

Meanwhile, having regard to the launching of the Coal and Steel Community, and in anticipation of the European Defence Community being agreed by all the Governments and ratified by all the Parliaments, Eden put a series of proposals to the Committee of Ministers of the Council of Europe during March. They were immediately named the Eden Plan. Their purpose was stated to be the strengthening rather than the weakening of the Strasbourg structure by arranging that the institutions, both of the Coal and Steel Community and of the Defence Community, and of any other such specialised bodies, should be organised in connection with the Council of Europe. This aroused much anxiety on the part of many of my friends, for it appeared much more likely that the institutions of the Six would absorb the Council, and that the rest of the countries – Britain, Sweden, Norway, Denmark, as well as Greece and Turkey – would soon have little purpose or influence.

It seemed to me that this was not the time to remodel the Council of Europe. The Coal and Steel Community was not due to be set up until six months after its ratification by all six countries. The Defence Community was still a long way off and there would be plenty of time to deal with the question if and when it arose. I feared that if the Defence Community came into being without us, there would ultimately be a Europe dominated by Germany. The only forum where we could bring our influence to bear would be the Council of Europe. Therefore I saw no sense in letting the Council become an institution of the Six. Moreover there was the wider question of our whole attitude to the problems of Europe and European unity. This seemed an opportunity for an imaginative and bold initiative by H.M.G.

I consulted some of my intimate friends such as David Eccles and Duncan Sandys who, although not members of the Cabinet, could exercise considerable influence. Duncan Sandys, who was most helpful to me behind the scenes, said that Churchill seemed somewhat dazed and unable to realise the degree of disillusionment throughout Europe. Everyone had hoped that the new Government would set a new tone. But nothing new had emerged, from either side of Downing Street.

On 10 March 1952 I lunched at the French Embassy with my old friend Massigli, and got the strong impression that even if the French Government lasted (which seemed unlikely), it was doubtful whether the French would finally accept the Defence Community without some closer association of Britain with the organisation. I recorded my thoughts:

> What folly there has been during the vital and formative years ! The absurd constitution-making of Schuman and Monnet on the one side; the isolationism of Bevin and the Foreign Office on the other, have brought this about.[1]

How strange all this seems after a decade of de Gaulle in power. How still more strange and more tragic it may appear when the next turn of the wheel takes place in France.

When the Cabinet met on 13 March 1952 to discuss my views on Europe, I received loyal support from David Maxwell Fyfe. But it was clear that Eden, although not himself present owing to illness, would gain the almost unanimous support of his colleagues. The discussion was of some value and might perhaps have some useful effect at a later stage. On the more restricted issue, Eden's proposals for the reorganisation of Strasbourg were formally agreed. I asked for my dissent to be noted in the minutes. Churchill, not unkindly,

[1] 10 March 1952.

observed that this was not necessary. My views would be on record. Altogether it was an unpleasant experience. I still did not know what to do. During the next few days I seriously contemplated resigning from the Government. My resignation would have been a blow–but by no means so powerful a blow as at a later stage, when I had proved myself a successful Housing Minister. In the Cabinet itself I should have had little support, except from Maxwell Fyfe, the Home Secretary, who felt deeply and was even more committed than I.

But what of Churchill? He was giving no lead on these general issues. He was prepared to await the outcome of E.D.C. Could we appear more orthodox and devout than the founder of the Crusade? Above all, I (like Maxwell Fyfe) was devoted to Churchill. I had for him not merely reverence but love. What could I do–within a few months of the formation of the Government–except follow my leader's advice and imitate his patience? Of course, only historians can really be certain of one's motives. But, so far as I can analyse my own without their aid, I think the dominating reason for my decision to remain was affection for and loyalty to Churchill.

In any case, apart from these general considerations, it was difficult to find a precise point on which to base a break. It is easy to resign in opposition to a clear and positive policy. It is more difficult to do so on the ground that the Government of which one is a member is following a course which is negative and obscure. I therefore decided to compose a further minute to Churchill, re-stating my views on this whole matter, and then to wait. But I did not feel that I was making any progress. I was unhappy, all the more since my friends outside the Government were pressing me to take a lead. At the same time I had plenty of troubles of my own. I was fighting the Treasury for money and trying to create some kind of organisation which could build the houses. It seemed rather quixotic to carry on a battle with the Foreign Office on this par-ticular issue to the final conclusion. In point of fact, although the Eden Plan was adopted by the British Cabinet and by the Council of Ministers at Strasbourg and confirmed by the Consultative Assembly at the end of September 1952, the whole question was soon to become academic, for the breakdown of E.D.C. robbed it of its relevance.

Meanwhile, French hesitations continued. The full story of these negotiations is admirably set out in the appropriate chapters of Eden's *Full Circle*.[1] In the course of 1952 two decisions of importance were at last reached. On 26 May the German Treaty was signed in Bonn between France, America, Britain and West Germany. It ended the occupation statute, and subject to certain important reservations regarding Allied rights, which were necessary in view of the division of Germany and the status of Berlin, restored to the West German republic full control of their internal affairs and their foreign policy. On the next day the European Defence Community Treaty, with its related protocols, was signed in Paris. At the same time reciprocal guarantees were entered into between NATO and E.D.C. Eden was accordingly able, with considerable satisfaction, to inform the House of Commons of this complex series of treaties and declarations. He claimed that they must be treated as a whole and that they marked a considerable step forward in the search for security. The House of Commons was satisfied; France was not.

I recorded my feelings at the time:

> The E.D.C. and the German agreements and the whole complex of undertakings and guarantees have been successfully negotiated—a great triumph for Eden. But I do not think they will be ratified by the French or German parliaments. Will this be a disaster, or does it give Britain another chance?[2]

During the next two years, while the fate of E.D.C. was in the balance, Eden acted with scrupulous loyalty to his Continental colleagues. He felt that since we had been unable to join the European Defence Community in the form suggested, we had no right to make alternative proposals. If we were to do so we should be regarded as wreckers, and the ultimate failure of the Ministers of the six countries to sign or the Parliaments to ratify would be held against us. British perfidy would have brought about the failure of European unity. The only thing, he argued, which we could honourably do was to support E.D.C. When the new structure came into being we could then find how we could best work with it.

---

[1] The Earl of Avon, *Full Circle*, chaps. iii, vii.   [2] 30 May 1952.

Everyone for the moment seemed to be dragging their feet. It was therefore in the long-term interest of Europe for Britain to accept any proposal that could command Continental support. But from the wider point of view I myself was full of apprehensions. I still believed that if this new Community came into being, with its own Defence Minister, Assembly and closely integrated armies, the future of Europe would turn out to be a Europe without Britain. We had already, through our own fault, been shut out of the Coal and Steel Community. If we were to find ourselves excluded from European defence, it would mean a Europe of six countries, excluding only the periphery—Scandinavia, Britain, Greece—a Europe self-sufficient and inward-looking, perhaps for a short period creating some degree of general confidence, but likely to prove a barrier to a true renaissance of Western Europe, and unable to offer a rallying point for Central and Eastern Europe if and when the Soviet grip came to be relaxed. I therefore watched the complicated and often tortuous game being played between France, Germany and America with a certain detached cynicism. Once I had made up my mind not to resign over this issue, I could play the role of spectator. If, as I hoped, E.D.C. were to break down, then there would be a new opportunity and Britain might have another, if perhaps a last, chance.

The estimates of what would be France's ultimate decision varied enormously. Lord Layton, whom I saw in June 1952, felt that the major French preoccupation would be to delay, if not to prevent, German reunification. If therefore the Germans ratified, he thought the French would do the same.[1]

Later in the year I had a talk with Massigli:

> He is very worried about the position in France regarding E.D.C. He thinks it now very doubtful whether the Assembly will ratify (or ought to ratify). French are only just beginning to realise (with a shock) what is involved in 'Federation'. Far better had they followed our original plan for 'Confederation'. Moreover, with the French army so much committed in Asia, will not Germany soon regain the old leadership? I asked whether he had spoken to Eden on all this. He replied, he could not speak so

[1] 22 June 1952.

confidentially to a Foreign Secretary (or sometimes, so critically of his own Government) as he could to an old friend 'off the record'. . . . The Bill would no doubt go first to the Assembly (for what we would call a second reading debate) and then to the Foreign Affairs Committee. In this Committee it could be delayed (if necessary) so as to allow of a fresh negotiation on certain points. Meanwhile, the obvious and growing hesitations of the French have made many Germans feel that they ought to ratify without more ado ! If it is bad for France (it is argued) it must be good for Germany !¹

I kept receiving grave warnings on wider issues from my friends in the European Movement, and particularly from those in ELEC (European League for Economic Co-operation). Beddington-Behrens, a faithful friend, told me of the other developments that were taking place on the economic front. If these succeeded, there would be a European economic community on the same lines as that for the coal and steel industries, and once more Britain would be excluded. This would be a serious, perhaps a mortal, blow.

Similarly, alarms reached me from other sources, especially from our Conservative Members at Strasbourg. My son-in-law, Julian Amery, kept me continually informed. Lady Rhys Williams, who combined a remarkable knowledge of technical economics with an almost prophetic power of grasping the long-term implications of large questions, sent me a memorandum in January 1953 which foretold future developments with remarkable accuracy. Britain, in her view, had only three possible courses. She could attempt to remain a world power in her own right, influencing the conduct of other countries as far as possible—the policy we had pursued through the centuries. Or she could adopt a policy of isolationism and independence, concentrating her strength entirely upon her own defence and advantage, and abandoning all attempt at a position as a world power—in other words become another Sweden. Thirdly, she could become, in effect, another state of the United States. (A fourth alternative, to make a separate alliance with Russia, seemed hardly worth discussing.) If we chose the first alternative, said Lady

¹ 31 October 1952.

Rhys Williams, the only method of remaining a world power was to go in with Europe:

> Britain cannot possibly remain a world power upon the present basis. The Commonwealth is non-existent, except as a Coronation pageant; the Middle East and the Moslem world are filled with anti-British nationalism, Africa is smouldering into flame, India may go Communist at any time, and Europe is about to settle down into a completely anti-British mould, the main hope of whose statesmen will be to pillage British trade, while claiming her contribution to the defence of their own frontiers against Russia.
>
> To continue upon the present line (i.e. to stand back from Europe and try to force France to embrace Germany) is to court utter disaster.
>
> . . . If Britain stays out of Europe, and allows this development to occur, she is abdicating all possibility of remaining a world power. It is only by dominating Europe now that she can continue to appear sufficiently strong to command the respect of the rest of the world, including the Dominions, and before long, the Colonies too. The Sterling area can disappear overnight if Britain ceases to be a world power on a recognisable scale, and much if not all of our overseas trade can disappear at the same time.

If decisions were taken immediately, some sort of European union could be achieved on our own terms:

> [Britain] will have the full approval of America, and will, indeed, be America's saviour inasmuch as she succeeds in holding West Germany to the Western side. She can build up a great new sphere of influence, not only in Europe, but in the world as a whole. Far from shedding her Empire, she will hold it to her because she will be strong enough to act as a magnet, which is not the case today. The outlook *could* be fair. Russia could be intimidated; Germany might be tamed; the Christian civilisation of Europe might be revived and re-developed. Solvency and even riches might be attained. A partnership with Africa might be built up. Democracy and freedom might be sustained over a part, at least, of the earth's surface.

She argued further that while there were certainly risks in going into Europe, the advantages were immense and the dangers of any other course as great. The prospects of Britain in isolation were equally alarming when looked into carefully. It would be impossible to maintain a favourable balance of trade or of payments on the basis of 'Little England'. Yet this idea was undoubtedly attracting certain people–the old isolationists and defeatists. A complicated federal structure of Europe on the lines dear to the French constitution-builders was nonsense, but a concrete proposal would now be acceptable, both as regards an economic structure and as regards defence. Europe must be confederal, developing a loyalty to the conception of Europe, but rejecting, as we still had time to do, the extreme federal systems. This would never in effect be accepted by France on the political level, even if swallowed–*faute de mieux*–in certain fields of defence and economics.

This document was certainly remarkable in its prescience.

At this time the American line was simple. In the initial stages we were told that Washington was anxious for us to join E.D.C., in spite of all the obvious objections. But Eden told us that General Eisenhower, who was at that time Supreme Allied Commander, did not consider that this was necessary. 'Association' could be equally effective militarily. At the same time the Americans brought great pressure on all the six countries concerned to ratify E.D.C. It was in this connection that, on 14 December 1953, Dulles used his menacing phrase, suggesting that if France did not accept E.D.C., America would have to make 'an agonising reappraisal' of her position. It is somewhat ironical to recall the hysterical reaction in France to the threat that the Americans might leave Europe. Almost anything must be done to prevent so dire an event. This was of course before the success of NATO had generated the hope that Russia's expansion across Europe had been halted. It was also before the return to power of General de Gaulle.

As the months passed, the hesitations and uncertainties continued. A series of proposals were made to assist the French: a declaration of support by Britain and America; a treaty between Britain and E.D.C.; and other similar guarantees. Still the French hesitated.

In March 1953 I circulated a further paper, questioning our

desire to see a Six-Power federal Europe 'with a common army, a common coal and steel industry, and eventually ending with a common currency, monetary policy and free trade area'. Whether such a federal state would ultimately be controlled by Germany or not, it could not be to our interest either as an island or as an imperial power. Naturally the French would like to put the burden of the breakdown of E.D.C. upon Britain, but every new concession that we put forward was only met by another demand. I suggested, therefore, that we should put no further pressure on the French and hold out no further inducements. If E.D.C. broke down, that would be our opportunity. Eventually Eden assured me that we should make no further concessions to the French and he was not proposing to do so. If the Germans ratified, no doubt this would have a great effect in France. He repeated that he still held the view that E.D.C. was the quickest method of obtaining a German contribution to defence.

On 11 May 1953, Churchill delivered a speech on the possibility of some accommodation with Russia which made a dramatic impact on world opinion. Some thought that this speech, although prepared with much wider purposes in view and following concepts and ideas on which he had long been brooding, did much to discourage the French from taking the plunge into a tightly-knit 'Little European' system.

The Germans ratified E.D.C. in the Bundestag on 19 March 1953, followed by a ratification by the Bundesrat in December of the same year; but France still delayed. She was turning more and more to the possibility of a direct agreement with Russia rather than face the future dangers of German rearmament.

After the turn of the year, in spite of earlier decisions to let matters take their course, Eden was authorised to make still further and more attractive proposals to induce the French to ratify. By March 1954 we were offering almost everything but marriage. This was followed in April by a treaty between Britain and E.D.C. subject to French ratification, a British armoured division would be placed within a European army corps.

In October 1953 Schuman had assured me that E.D.C. offered much the best method of containing Germany and would certainly be ratified; but reports from France during 1954 continued to cast doubt on the possibility of carrying the plan through the French Assembly. The British Ambassador in Paris also held this view.

Adenauer, whom I saw during a visit to Bonn in June 1954, believed that if E.D.C. were not ratified, a most serious situation would arise in Germany. This was my first conversation with the German Chancellor since the days of the Hague Conference. I had gone to Germany at the invitation of the German Government to discuss housing problems. After a dinner in my honour he took me aside for a talk. He delivered a long and fascinating discourse, covering not merely the immediate problems but the whole history of the German peoples from Roman times until the present day. I found this monologue deeply interesting, at any rate on hearing it for the first time. During the next nine years I was destined to listen to it on every occasion when we met.

The Russians were now using Churchill's proposal for a Four-Power meeting with some effect. It was intended to prevent the implementation of E.D.C. and above all the rearming of Germany and the admission of West Germany into NATO. Very properly, Eden insisted that some pledge of Russian good faith should be demanded, for instance the signature of the Austrian Treaty, which had been hanging fire for so long.

More than two years after the signature of the E.D.C. treaty in Paris, fresh efforts were made by Mendès-France to obtain from the other five countries concessions which were discriminatory against Germany, and clearly not acceptable.

A conference held in Brussels on 29 August 1954 to consider Mendès-France's new proposals ended in failure. The French Prime Minister continued to undermine the genuine enthusiasm of the European-minded Frenchmen without really satisfying the French 'patriots'. Accordingly, it was no surprise when, on 30 August, news came of the final decision of the French Assembly. Ratification was defeated by 319 votes to 264, 43 Deputies abstaining. It was noticeable that Mendès-France refused to make ratification a 'question of confidence', and took a somewhat detached line in his own speech. He spoke more as a referee than as an advocate.

It is curious how (after all the speculation and estimates over the last two years) my original view has been confirmed. I looked up again my Cabinet paper on the subject in February 1952, when I foretold that it would not pass. I still think that it's a good result for us. 'Federation' of Europe means 'Germanisation' of Europe. 'Confederation' (if we play our cards properly) should be British leadership of Europe. However, at this particular moment, I have no desire to get drawn into too much controversy with the F.O.

... Reading between the lines, it would seem that a great deal of the French opposition to E.D.C. was not nationalism but defeatism. Herriot's speech was pure Pétainism. It was the combination of patriots and neutralists which was fatal to E.D.C.[1]

A day or two later, although unwilling to circulate a Cabinet paper of my own, I felt

that *we* ought to take the lead, and not just follow meekly in the American track. Anyway, the Americans must surely by now realise how wrong they have been about E.D.C. (and our F.O. also). France has resented the American pressure, almost amounting to blackmail and sometimes bribery. This has been one of the main troubles all through. I don't think we ought now to allow our annoyance with the French to warp our judgement. There ought to be a *European* as well as an *Atlantic* policy.[2]

In any case, the final breakdown of a policy which had held the field for so long placed a great responsibility upon the British Government.

During this long and bitterly disappointing negotiation, covering a period of nearly three years, Eden showed a high degree of diplomatic skill. He also proved a most courteous and understanding colleague. I often felt that I sent him too many proposals and made too many interventions in the Cabinet. But he never showed irritation or vexation. I have many letters and memoranda from him dealing with the points that I had raised, all in friendly terms. My affection for him was deepened during this period, for he was a most loyal friend. Nevertheless, I felt that I could not make him understand the depth and scope of my anxieties. He was always looking

[1] 3 September 1954.   [2] 4 September 1954.

for a solution of the short-term problem—the rearmament of Germany and her admission to NATO. My eyes, rightly or wrongly, were fixed upon a more distant future—the organisation of Europe in the second half of the century, and the place which Britain and the Commonwealth should hold in a great design.

I now conceived the idea that the rearmament of Germany and her admission to NATO could be made more acceptable to French opinion and more palatable to the British Labour Party by the incorporation in NATO of an existing European alliance. Accordingly, towards the end of August 1954, I raised the question as to whether Germany could not now adhere to the Brussels Treaty,[1] of which she was not a member. The Brussels Treaty, negotiated by Bevin in 1948 between France, Britain and the Benelux countries, continued to subsist within NATO. We might find a solution along these lines. Of course it could be objected that the Brussels Treaty did not contain the supranational element which was so dear to the federalists and to which, for some reason, Dulles appeared to attach decisive importance. He was soon to develop this argument with his usual ponderous prolixity. I discussed the matter with Julian Amery, and with his help I prepared a paper which I sent to Eden.

My paper, by suggesting a European box inside the Atlantic box, was really based on Churchill's 1950 plan at Strasbourg. I was accordingly gratified when, in the course of a talk on 8 September 1954, Eden accepted the idea of using the Brussels Pact as the way out. He had already asked me to send a copy of my paper to Churchill. Eden also decided to undertake a diplomatic Odyssey, in order to sell this idea to our friends and allies. In the course of the next few weeks he was to visit five capitals. He has given a vivid description of this difficult and—on the whole—successful undertaking.[2] With his charm and powers of persuasion, his journey proved a turning-point, although Dulles did his best to throw a spanner in the works. Dulles could never resist the opportunity for an air journey. Accordingly, he announced his intention of flying to Bonn and then to London. He added what Eden calls 'a long rigmarole of criticism of the Brussels Treaty because it is not

[1] See above, p. 132.
[2] The Earl of Avon, *Full Circle*, pp. 151–8.

supranational'.[1] Dulles's intervention was most unfortunate, and might have done great harm. Adenauer, however, stood firm, as I judged from my talk some weeks before that he would be likely to do. He stated that the United Kingdom had done all that was possible, and that he had no criticisms, but only admiration. Adenauer, with some faults, never lost his head and was capable of supreme common sense. When Eden returned, the Cabinet had little difficulty in accepting the Brussels Treaty solution.

However, as the negotiations proceeded, the French began to raise their terms. A Nine-Power conference was summoned to meet in London, consisting of the five Brussels Treaty powers (France, Britain and the Benelux countries), Italy and West Germany; the U.S.A. and Canada. The Conference all but broke down on the French demands for further and more discriminating measures to control German rearmament. This was the great fear that haunted them, and Mendès-France continually declared that he would not obtain the support of the Assembly unless their anxieties were met.

> Anthony feels it necessary to give a new pledge to Europe—as indeed we have often discussed together but for which formal Cabinet approval has never been asked. We must undertake to keep four divisions (or their equivalent) and tactical air force under SACEUR's command and on the Continent of Europe. If we offer this (he feels) we may get agreement at the Nine-Power conference. If not, the whole Western alliance may collapse and U.S. revert to 'peripheral defence' or (worse still) 'Fortress America'.[2]

This was indeed a formidable—and as was soon to prove—an onerous obligation. Up till now, our occupation costs had fallen on Germany. With a new and independent West German republic, they would be payable by us. Moreover, since the Brussels Treaty powers were to be the only authority who could relieve us, by a majority vote, from our undertaking, and since the Brussels Treaty had another 44 years to run, the charge would fall on two more generations of our countrymen.

Nevertheless, the stake was—or seemed to be—high indeed.

[1] The Earl of Avon, p. 158.   [2] 27 September 1954.

Accordingly, on 28 September the Cabinet took their historic decision. After still further attempts by the French to exact still more advantages, the Agreement providing for the inauguration of Western European Union was signed in Paris on 23 October 1954.

Whether we were wise or not to enter into so binding an undertaking, it is difficult even now to say. Certainly the provisos regarding any future strain upon sterling were badly drawn, and gave us only the right to discuss the problem with our partners without any power to make our own decision. During subsequent years this has proved a perpetual source of anxiety and difficulty. Nor have the recurrent arguments about maintenance costs done much to improve Anglo-German relations. Nevertheless, in view of the chaotic situation in Europe at the time, the threats emanating from the American Secretary of State, and the fears about Russian intentions, this decision can no doubt be justified. But it is to be deplored that a commitment so contrary to British traditions—that is, a permanent stationing of large bodies of troops on Continental territory—should have been entered into without any corresponding arrangements or understandings as to the future development of Europe, political and economic. It has certainly been a bitter pill for us to swallow when, in later years, we are repelled by the French Government which was almost a suppliant for our guarantees against their fears of a revived Germany. That we have adhered to our undertakings in completely changed circumstances is forgotten, as is our succour of France after her tragic collapse in 1940. If it has now happily been possible for the French to forget the injuries which they suffered at Germany's hands, for the benefits which they have received from Britain it seems impossible for them to extend any sincere forgiveness.

CHAPTER XV

The Great Commoner

C HURCHILL formed his third and last Government at the end
of October 1951, just a month before his seventy-seventh
birthday. In spite of the strains and stresses of his long and
dramatic life, culminating in six years of the most terrible war in
history, this extraordinary man seemed to retain all the exuberance
and much of the resilience of youth. He even remained something
of an *enfant terrible*. Only very few had known of the slight stroke
which he suffered in the summer of 1949, from which he had made
an apparently complete recovery. In any case, he had subsequently
fought two General Elections, and had published two further
volumes of his history of the Second World War—the two remaining were to appear during his last Premiership. Nevertheless,
one could not but admire his courage in taking up the task again
at his advanced age when, in Harry Crookshank's vivid phrase,
there were skeletons not hidden in the cupboards but dangling like
candelabra throughout Whitehall. The foreign, defence, economic,
food and fuel situations were all bad, some desperate. Moreover,
Churchill knew that he could not add to his reputation. He could
only hazard it.

Had it been possible he would no doubt have reverted to the
small War Cabinet system which had served him so well. But this
would not have been tolerated in peace. However, the Cabinet
was small by later standards, being limited to sixteen. Nearly all
were old friends and comrades from the years of the war, like Oliver
Lyttelton, James Stuart—his Chief Whip—and to a lesser extent
myself. Butler and Maxwell Fyfe were equally close colleagues. The
only new member of the Cabinet, who could be said to represent
the youth of the party, was Peter Thorneycroft. If these faces brought
no sense of novelty into our councils, they were his familiars, with

many of whom he had worked and striven through the darkest days.

He also introduced or restored the plan of grouping departments through a system of 'overlords'. The Ministry of Defence already had some authority over the Service Departments, at least in theory. Now Lord Leathers was put in charge of Shipping and Transport, as well as Fuel and Power. Agriculture and Food were entrusted to Lord Woolton, as Lord President of the Council. The Ministers immediately responsible for all these departments were not in the Cabinet, but were supposed to act under the superior guidance of their chiefs. There was much to be said for this if it should really result in a pyramid, with a clearly defined point of decision—though even in defence the full implementation of such a plan was ten years away. But where there was no statutory basis, even of the slenderest kind, the new structure began to break down, for two reasons: first, because the position of an overlord, armed with little but an office and a private secretary, soon becomes shadowy and indeterminate; secondly, because however loyal to their nominal chiefs, the subordinate Ministers begin to feel overriding obligations to their separate departments. Moreover, since the Ministers were in the House of Commons, and the House was already jealous of a Cabinet in which the peers had so large a part, this contrivance, however valuable in principle, became unworkable in practice.[1]

At this time Churchill was supremely happy. He was back in No. 10; he was surrounded by his old intimates; and he faced a situation as perilous in its own way as that with which he had been confronted ten years before. I well remember the first Cabinet. After the congratulations were over, he passed immediately to business—at home and abroad. He himself gave us a review of the defence situation, with which he was much dissatisfied. He asked the Foreign Secretary, Eden, to describe to us the difficulties of the Middle East and elsewhere. He was followed by Butler as

[1] Sir John Anderson was invited by Churchill to act as overlord of the Treasury, the Board of Trade, and the Ministry of Supply, but declined, regarding the system as inappropriate in peace-time. See Sir John W. Wheeler-Bennett, *John Anderson, Viscount Waverley* (London, 1962), p. 352.

Chancellor of the Exchequer, who had indeed a sorry story to tell. After these preliminaries, action must be taken without delay. The work of the defence review Churchill undertook to complete himself before his projected visit to Washington. The rest was to be carried on by the Ministers concerned, aided by various Cabinet Committees. In this heavy programme the Prime Minister outstripped his colleagues. For he succeeded in completing the defence review before the end of the year.

Although occasionally at Cabinets Churchill indulged in long monologues, occupying the greater part of the session, I was soon to discover that this was not necessarily a sign of the weakness of age. When he took up a great deal of time himself it often indicated that he was undecided as to the course he should recommend, or that he wished to postpone a discussion on some other item on the agenda. Sometimes it meant that his mind was really occupied by graver matters on which he was brooding.

In general, he regarded Cabinet meetings as an important instrument in the formation of policy and the creation of a sense of loyalty between Ministers. He liked and encouraged argument and discussion. He did not at all resent contrary points of view being put forward, however forcibly. 'Fight your own corner,' he used to say to departmental Ministers. Nor would he allow younger Ministers to be overborne by the authority of those of superior rank or experience. He enjoyed Cabinet meetings, and held a much larger number of Cabinets—twenty-two in the first two months—than his predecessors. He was not a good chairman, as Attlee was, if one regards the object merely to get through the agenda as rapidly as may be with some kind of decision on the record. Nor did he regard a Cabinet as a board of a company where the various executive directors should try to accomplish their own business with as little trouble as possible, scarcely sharing in the discussion of the problems of their colleagues. He certainly did not regard a Prime Minister as the chairman of such a board, which so often becomes little more than a formal method of registering decisions already taken. He treated the Cabinet as a deliberative body. No doubt some busy Ministers found his method dilatory and tiresome. I felt that Eden, who was often overwhelmed by anxious and difficult problems requiring immediate decisions, suffered under this deliberate and sometimes rambling procedure. For myself, since, with the exception of the issues which directly concerned me, I took little part in discussion, I thoroughly enjoyed all these Cabinets. Apart from the question of European unity and the large economic issues upon which the success of my housing plans depended, I generally tried to keep in the background. I was thus able to watch his methods with admiration and delight, only merging into dismay when my own items on the agenda were consequently delayed from week to week.

Churchill had been brought up in an older period when the luncheon hour was a quarter to two, or at the soonest half past one. Apart from any private arrangements, no doubt fixed for an earlier hour, most Cabinet Ministers seem nowadays to commit themselves to a variety of luncheon engagements of a more or less public character. As the hour of one o'clock approached, a certain restlessness developed among Ministers as they began to calculate the time it would take them to get to the Connaught Rooms, the Savoy Hotel or the Dorchester. By ten minutes past one some began silently to leave; but if the Prime Minister was in full flood he took little notice of this. Sometimes I have known by the end of the session scarcely a moiety remaining. Although he was always careful to ensure that no vital decision should be taken at such a time, he was by no means disconcerted. For he was either testing the opinion of the remaining Ministers, or just amusing himself, or, not uncommonly, giving us the first rehearsal of a speech which he was about to deliver to a larger audience.

When the flat racing season began there were, I remember, certain days when Churchill appeared clothed in a peculiar kind of black alpaca jacket, such as clerks used to wear in offices. If one peered under the table, one could see a pair of sponge-bag trousers below the Prime Minister's chair. This meant that he was going racing, and that the Cabinet would almost certainly end at ten or five minutes to one, in order to give him time to put on a suitable top garment and reach the course either by car or train. On one such occasion I had hurried to Victoria Station, for I was due to address a meeting of local government accountants, assembled in

Brighton. As I passed along the platform I saw Churchill already ensconced in a Pullman carriage with some intimate friends. He saw me; and with his usual courtesy asked me to join and share his company and his luncheon. But I thought he would prefer to be with his own party and therefore declined. 'Where are you going to, my dear?' he cried. 'I am going to Brighton.' 'Oh! Racing I suppose.' 'No, Prime Minister, I am going to a meeting of accountants.' 'Turf accountants, I trust? That should be jolly.' Alas, my afternoon was not to be as agreeable as his.

If Cabinet meetings were sometimes long and tedious, and if Churchill often took up too much of the time himself, yet there was hardly a word that dropped from him, whether of playful humour or historical reflection or pregnant thought for the future, that was not memorable.

At the time of the Coronation, in which he took the deepest interest, the question of uniform for Cabinet Ministers arose. Few of us had the appropriate dress, and the cost of purchasing a new one was almost prohibitive. The first decision was that we could go in evening clothes, with black knee-breeches and silk stockings. But this was later reversed. Churchill had learned that uniforms could be obtained from Moss Bros or similar shops. There was no reason why a second-hand uniform would not do, and the effect would be much more impressive if we were properly attired. He recalled his father's disgust when, after his resignation as Chancellor of the Exchequer, he had tried to sell his Chancellor's robe to his successor. Goschen would not buy—'the first case in history', protested Lord Randolph Churchill, 'where a Jew has refused to buy old clothes'. Next arose the question of the procession. According to tradition, not only the Army Council but the Board of Admiralty (as well as the Air Council) should ride. But the Sea Lords, it seemed, were nervous of equitation. The First Lord protested that it took eighteen months to train a horse. 'You mean,' retorted the Prime Minister, 'it takes eighteen months to train an admiral.'

From time to time there was desultory talk about the House of Lords. Churchill was on the whole against meddling with it. 'What does it matter that the peers do not come? They are like the Home Guard—ready in case of danger.'

Even after his serious illness in 1953 his buoyancy and humour were soon restored. For instance, there were protracted arguments about the place of meeting of the proposed Four-Power conference, in which the Russians proved singularly intractable and obstinate. Finally they suggested Berlin. Churchill observed: 'This is one of the occasions where the more sensible of the parties gives way.' At about the same time he produced an unusual variant on the phrase 'That has been settled': 'Oh, you mean that you have reached a point where you can't carry the argument any further.' Similarly, when a question of a minor Bill had arisen, which had caused us great difficulty and—with our slender majority—seemed likely to risk a defeat on the second reading, Churchill was firm about the wisdom of concession. 'If one is to be hanged,' he said, 'it should be for a capital offence.' He went on to observe: 'It is never necessary to commit suicide, especially when you may live to regret it.' Or, reverting to the memories of his youth: 'Sometimes it needs more courage to decline to jump a fence in face of a large field, than to go for it and break your neck.' At a time when Foster Dulles, the American Secretary of State, was being particularly difficult over the defence problem of Europe, he remarked: 'Mr. Dulles makes a speech every day; has a press conference every other day; and preaches on Sundays. All this tends to rob his utterances of real significance.'

Later, when speaking to me of my own political experiences, he reminded me of all the ups and downs. 'Politics are full of uncertainties. It is not a flat race, it's a steeplechase.'

There were, of course, many graver sayings, more especially when he was thinking of the fears which haunted the world. At that time the East–West split seemed far more immediately menacing than it does now. He pondered deeply about Germany and the two wars. 'The past should be forgiven, even though it cannot be forgotten. In any case, it need not be the pattern of the future.' This was a typical reflection. Again: 'The terrible fact is that the Soviet Government fears our friendship more than it fears our enmity.' An unexpectedly subtle thought.

Perhaps one of his most masterly and moving performances was his exposition of the nuclear problem to the Conference of Commonwealth

Prime Ministers, held in the Cabinet Room in almost the last months of his Premiership. It was a wonderful effort, ending on a buoyant note. In speaking of the deterrent, now in Russian as well as in Western hands, he drew some comfort from this balance. 'Hope may prove the child of Fear, and Safety the twin brother of Destruction.'

Readers of the minutes contained in the appendices of his volumes of war memoirs will not be surprised to learn that Churchill showed remarkable interest in a vast variety of matters, great and small. He retained to the last an almost schoolboy delight in searching out strange and recondite pieces of information with which he often confounded less informed civil servants or Ministers. He was particularly sensitive on matters which affected the public, such as the rise in transport and railway fares, or indeed anything that directly affected ordinary people. It has been urged in criticism of his methods that he was too ready to avoid industrial strife at any cost and used the charm and skill of the Minister of Labour, Walter Monckton, to stave off immediate difficulties by timely concessions. On the other hand, it may well be argued that with the critical state of financial affairs, and in view of the slender majority by which we governed, any extensive or prolonged industrial dispute might have proved disastrous.

He took an interest in almost every aspect of affairs at home, ranging from the way in which ordinary people had to live to the minutest breach of individual liberty by bureaucratic interference of which he might read in a popular newspaper. It was his practice to send a motor-car to Fleet Street each night to collect the first editions of all the London papers, which he would read with avidity. This enabled him to get ahead of the news for the next day. He would see something in the paper—an attack on a Minister or an alleged administrative scandal. He would then dictate a minute which the unhappy Minister received in the early hours of the next morning, probably before he had read the papers and on a subject about which he had heard nothing. On one occasion I was the victim of one of these rebukes. I have already told the story of poor Mr. Pilgrim and Churchill's reaction.[1]

One of his main concerns on returning to office was to deal with

[1] See above, p. 428.

the dreadfully low basis of food to which the country had been condemned. Churchill was worried and angry when he learned that the public as a whole were living on even worse rations than during the war. His programme—at both elections, 1950 and 1951—had been 'Work, Homes and Food'. As to the first, there was full employment. As to the second, he trusted me to do the job and backed me loyally. As to the third, he was determined to get his way. Since he complained that he found figures and weights somewhat confusing, he asked Gwilym Lloyd George, Minister of Food, to reproduce in a model the actual amount of rations allowed to each individual. This exhibit duly appeared on a large tin dish—a painted piece of meat, a little heap of sugar and the rest. The Prime Minister looked at it with some satisfaction.

'Not a bad meal,' he said. 'Not a bad meal.'

'But these,' cried the Minister, 'are not rations for a meal or for a day. They are for a week.'

'A week!' was the outraged reply. 'Then the people are starving. It must be remedied.'

And remedied it was. For many Cabinets following this incident we had lengthy dissertations on the productivity of pigs. If meat could not be rapidly imported or the supplies of cattle and sheep improved beyond the relatively slow processes with which nature had endowed them for regeneration, there was the homely pig, an animal easy to rear, naturally gay, gratifyingly prolific. It could bring comfort to the humblest home as pork or bacon. In either form it was equally welcome and equally prized. There must be a pig 'drive'—as in war-time—and pigs must supply the sad interval before beef and mutton could be restored to their proper place in the working man's home. In spite of the experts, Churchill persisted. It was largely through his obstinate efforts that food rationing was finally brought to an end in July 1954.

As remarkable as his fertile mind and powers of expression was his insistence on hard work. I have never known a man more industrious than he. His devotion to duty remained undiminished even in old age and when infirmity must have made his labours onerous and painful. Come what may, the great machine rolled forward. His appetite for work, which was immense at the beginning of the Government, had hardly dwindled at the end, although he certainly became slower and less decisive. At his best—in the early years—he could preside over a great agenda and cope with large quantities of business in an unflurried way. Sometimes he was perverse and delayed business, but there was usually a reason behind it. Above all, he projected a style and polish to the business of governing, maintaining a fastidious dislike of officialese and jargon of all kinds. He always gave his colleagues a sense of partaking in large affairs. In his view, to be in a British Cabinet was a privilege—perhaps the highest privilege that could fall to any subject. There was in those days a panache—even more, a real distinction—in the conduct of the nation's affairs.

Because he knew that I was interested in style, he often used to send for me to assist, with criticism or ideas, his own orations, whether in the House or on the platform. Although I knew, from old days, the meticulous care which he gave to the composition of any written or spoken words, I marvelled at his extraordinary application. Nothing was too much trouble. Every sentence was written and rewritten; every quotation was checked; every phrase weighed in the balance. It was indeed a moving spectacle to watch this old man, approaching his eightieth year, taking such infinite pains. The House of Commons was conscious of this and correspondingly flattered. Members on all sides knew that, whatever criticisms might be brought against Parliament or doubts cast on its position in modern times, Churchill regarded it as the centre and source of power, and treated it with a combination of affection and respect.

Although not Leader of the House—he had entrusted this task to the skilful hands of Harry Crookshank—Churchill took an almost passionate interest in the life of Parliament. Brought up in the House of Commons, he regarded it as the central pivot of all political action. He believed, and with some justice, that success or failure in the House, even with the more restricted reports of modern newspapers, gradually seeped through the Members to the constituency parties, and thence to the country as a whole. He attended the House regularly; although he was disinclined to sit through long debates, he was meticulous in his appearances in the smoking-room. This was of special importance, since so many of his Ministers were peers and others seemed unwilling to make themselves easily available to their fellow Members. On this account, because he was a real House of Commons man, he always had the sympathy of the back-benchers.

Churchill's mastery of the House of Commons remained as great as ever, although, as in the case of every great artist, there was not a flat level of competence. There were triumphs, and failures. He could strike many different notes. On occasions, with violent, devastating, but purely partisan attacks on Socialism and the Socialists, he would rouse the Opposition to something like fury and our own side to corresponding enthusiasm. At other times he would strike a national note and revive the old feelings of unity which had carried the country through the horrors of war. A typical instance of the latter was at the very beginning of the Government, when he made a long-awaited speech upon defence. It had been supposed that he would enter into a detailed dissertation on the weaknesses and deficiencies which he found upon entering office. He did no such thing:

> Either by design or by mistake, the debate ended in a great demonstration of national unity. C. praised the Socialists for conscription, for the atomic decision (including the American atomic bombers in E. Anglia), for the efforts at rearmament, etc. Although he indicated the serious position of the air service, he did not press any charge of neglect. Shinwell tore up his speech; C. got up, tears in his eyes, and praised Shinwell as a patriot. All this left the Tories rather dazed. But what a strange end to a warmongering election! Perhaps this was partly C.'s purpose. Also, no doubt, to lay the foundations of a national position when he goes to Washington.[1]

For within a few weeks of taking office, he determined on a strong effort to re-establish the old relationship with the American Government.

His rare failures nearly always resulted from his falling into a partisan wrangle on a high issue. The Socialists were quite happy to enjoy his knockabout performances on one of the normal subjects of controversy between the parties. But they were distressed if he included in a statement on great international affairs a bitter attack

[1] 6 December 1951.

R

on their leaders. Such an occasion arose in a debate on the question of the H-bomb in March 1954. In that month the United States exploded a hydrogen bomb, an event which caused widespread excitement and alarm. Actually, the Americans had made a successful experiment in November 1952, followed by the Russians in August 1953. But these had created no great stir. Now much detailed information was released about the dimensions and character of the experiment which brought home to the public the hideous reality of nuclear warfare. For the first time a lot of particulars were given about 'fall-out' and its terrible effect on this and future generations. Apart from the appalling nature of the weapon, if used in war, everyone seemed to believe that the experiments themselves would fatally poison the atmosphere, and contaminate the populations of the world. This was the beginning of a controversy which was not finally settled until nine years later, when the Test-Ban Treaty was agreed between Russia, the United States and Britain.

Churchill made a statement to Parliament on 30 March 1954 in which he rejected the suggestion that Britain should attempt to dissuade the United States from testing the weapon which was 'the greatest deterrent' against the outbreak of another major war. After he had spoken there was rather a confused scene. But it had become clear that at any rate the more rabid spirits in the Labour Party thought they were on a good thing. There seemed a good hope that the old 'warmonger' slogan could be revived. But the more responsible leaders did not show their hand. Some of the Press began to run a virulent campaign against Churchill, alleging that we had sunk to the position of a satellite without any power to influence American policy. The *Daily Mirror*, not unnaturally, took the lead with immense headings similar to the old election ones: 'Churchill Confesses', 'Churchill Powerless to deal with U.S.A.' and the like. The *Daily Herald* was equally violent; a wave of panic seemed about to seize the country.

A debate took place on 5 April; and after a moderate speech by Attlee which, in strange contrast to the flow of excited questions the week before, commanded general approval and respect, the House and the Press expected that Churchill would follow a similar tone— perhaps a little more realistic and better phrased but on the same note. But he began by referring to the agreement he had made with Roosevelt in 1943 and its abandonment by the Socialist Government during their term of office. In other words, he claimed that he had retained for Britain a veto on the use of the atomic or any other bomb developed by the Americans, and that this had been wantonly thrown away. This unexpected accusation infuriated the Opposition, puzzled the Government back-benchers and led to a long and angry scene. Attlee made some effective interruptions, and Churchill, thrown off balance, muddled his case in answering. After about twenty minutes of storm and cries of 'Resign', 'Dirty', and all the rest, he was able to finish his speech, the latter part of which was couched in the tone generally expected. But coming after the previous portion the peroration was ineffective and fell flat.

It was the greatest failure—on the surface at least—since Churchill's speech on the abdication of King Edward VIII.[1]

After this debate I went into the Prime Minister's room. He knew that his performance was a failure, but he was absolutely game. He insisted on going into the smoking-room, and sat chatting to the 'boys' until nearly midnight. He was not going to slink off to bed. Indeed, the defeat was not complete. If he had suffered a tactical set-back, he had won a strategic victory. There would be no more attack of 'Whose finger on the trigger?' Our reply would be 'Who gave away the veto?' or 'We had our finger on the safety catch. Who took it off?' There was no real harm done; there was perhaps some gain. Perhaps the saddest part about this incident was that it revealed to the House and the public how old he had now become.

In thinking over this scene, of no great importance but of some interest in judging of Churchill's Parliamentary powers, I recorded my view:

Churchill's failure was due to two things. First, the contrast between the general 'non-partisan' character of the debate and the damaging revelation was too harshly made and was inartistically led up to. Secondly, his power of recovery has gone. His hearing

[1] 6 April 1954.

is bad; he was rather staggered by the noise; he was temporarily 'knocked off his perch'. All he could do was to force his way through the delivery of his prepared text. Of course . . . his method of speaking (with every word prepared) has this inherent danger. But . . . a few years ago he would have been able to readjust himself to the situation.[1]

Arthur Balfour, whose remarkable mental agility made him one of the most nimble of all debaters, once criticised Churchill by suggesting that although his batteries might be very powerful they were not very mobile. A sudden attack or swift retort therefore sometimes left him at a loss. He had nothing like the quickness of wit characteristic of Lloyd George.[2] Yet Churchill learned during these years a new power of repartee, apparently extempore, though in set speeches he relied always upon the written text. In those days he used to answer questions four days a week. (The Prime Minister's question days have since been reduced to two.) A Parliamentary question must appear printed on the Order Paper a day or two before it can be asked. The first answer, therefore, has been care-fully prepared by civil servants and approved by the Minister con-cerned. In modern practice, however, the original question is often merely a peg on which the Member who has asked it, or others, can hang what are called supplementary questions for which no notice is required. There is, therefore, a great art in speculating what these 'supplementaries' are likely to be, and being ready beforehand with suitable replies, which should, if possible, be short, witty, and decisive. One evening I found Churchill at work at the Cabinet table, apparently absorbed in his task. 'What are you doing, Prime Minister?' I asked. 'Oh, Parliamentary questions. Preparing improvisations! Very hard work!'

During the early months of Churchill's administration, the state of the economy and the financial position were of dominant im-

[1] 6 April 1954.
[2] I remember an example of this in my first Parliament. A Tory Member was jeering at the Liberal Party for being broken into so many disparate sections—Asquithians, Lloyd Georgeites, National Liberals, Liberal Nationalists, and all the rest. 'In the Liberal Party,' he declared, 'there are many mansions.' Lloyd George, who was lolling in his seat and apparently scarcely listening, immediately flashed back: 'Yes. And in the Tory Party there are many *flats*.'

portance. We seemed to be in one of those crises when something like national bankruptcy was threatened, or at least so the Treasury experts told us. Attlee, at any rate, had believed them.

This situation brought Butler at once to the centre of the stage. I had not expected this appointment, nor did the majority of my colleagues. It was the general opinion among us that Oliver Lyttelton would become Chancellor of the Exchequer. But for whatever reason, although Lyttelton was one of Churchill's oldest and most trusted friends, a boon companion of old days, the choice fell on Butler. Before the war I did not know Butler at all, and certainly was out of sympathy with his views. For he was Under-Secretary at the Foreign Office in the most ignoble period of our history since the days of Charles II and the Treaty of Dover. Nor had I seen anything of him in the war; for most of the time I was either immersed in the work of my department or serving overseas. But in the years of opposition I got to know him well and worked closely with him. I formed a high regard for him and a sincere admiration for his gifts. His conduct of our policy research was on lines very agreeable to me, since they followed my own ideas of the inter-war period. I was surprised but not concerned at Churchill's decision. My contests with Oliver would perhaps have been more jovial and more boisterous. But that was all.

Throughout the long economic discussions, in which I took a considerable part, Churchill presided with marked skill and close attention. He extended his full sympathy and confidence to Butler, on whom lay so onerous a burden. Nevertheless, he was not easily taken in by the jargon and verbiage of Treasury memoranda. He had not forgotten the way in which he had been misled by the Treasury and the Bank of England in 1925, when he approved the fatal return to gold and the over-valuation of sterling, with all their dreadful consequences. Although he was somewhat at sea in the more recondite theories of currency, especially the various plans that poured out from the Treasury on convertibility either at a fixed or floating level, he brought great common sense to bear on their practical application. Sometimes he showed surprising knowledge of the changing way of life and the new aspirations of ordinary folk. 'Hire-purchase' was then, and has remained, a favourite target for deflationists. Churchill protested that 'no self-respecting suitor today dare approach the young lady of his choice without the promise of at least a washing machine'.

His long experience had taught him the public dislike of petti-fogging changes and minor annoyances. For instance, if there were cuts to be made, they should not be doled out one by one, but saved up and brought out all in one fell swoop. The public reaction in the long run would be much less severe. Nothing was more to be de-plored than a series of irritations. Nor was he ever induced to accept the extreme demands of the restrictionists. He was instinctively an expansionist both in private and public affairs. But at the same time he showed great flexibility under the pressure of discussion.

He disliked these first eighteen months of economic distress and hardship because his humanity was pained at any form of cut or the imposition of any additional burden upon the people. He was correspondingly encouraged as the position gradually improved.

From my point of view, at any rate, I could always rely on the Prime Minister supporting my housing programme. I certainly never canvassed his support. Yet in the battles which I had with the Treasury and with others of my colleagues on housing matters, I felt that Churchill was always on my side. For he knew as well as I that whatever else might emerge which could throw lustre on the administration or bring political advantage, the one easily measur-able and easily ascertainable success would be the progress of the housing campaign.

But it was upon Imperial and foreign affairs that Churchill mainly concentrated his efforts, and in the last years of his life in office it was to them that he directed the full strength of his powerful and imaginative mind. Towards the end there were, not unnaturally, signs of fatigue and perhaps some failure of balanced judgement. Nevertheless, when his purpose was once formed he held to it with obstinate resolution.

The relations between a Prime Minister and a Foreign Secretary are never easy. In the nineteenth century they were the source of many wrangles and some political disasters. Sometimes a strong Foreign Secretary, like Palmerston, reduced his leader almost to physical collapse. A weak Prime Minister, like Lord Aberdeen, allowed his country to drift into war by vacillation and lack of authority. Lord Rosebery, who was Foreign Secretary when he became Prime Minister, had wished to combine both offices; but having been dissuaded from this course he found little difficulty in keeping a close control over Lord Kimberley. Lord Salisbury, during the greater part of his reign of nearly twenty years, solved the difficulty by holding both offices. Asquith and Edward Grey had an easy and harmonious relationship, with deep loyalty on both sides. Lloyd George, although he had treated Balfour with respect, undoubtedly dominated Lord Curzon and sometimes reduced him to a lachrymose despair.

MacDonald, who during his first administration had, like Salisbury, combined the two posts, had certainly gained a great reputation at the Foreign Office, but had lost his grasp of internal affairs. Under the more easy-going Baldwin there had been little difficulty. Later Attlee was equally ready to give Bevin his head. But Neville Chamberlain had taken so dominating a control as to drive Eden to resignation. I therefore watched, always with interest, but sometimes with apprehension, the development of the relations between Churchill and Eden. Churchill had for many years treated Eden as his natural successor. If not his son, he was certainly his heir. He would sometimes tease him, sometimes pet him, occasionally thwart him. Many of these open discussions in the Cabinet without preliminary consultation were clearly not always to Eden's liking. But the Prime Minister, unless it suited him to think otherwise, took the view that the Cabinet was entitled to a full and frank debate on all the details of foreign policy.

Most of us realised the fearfully heavy burden which lay upon Eden during these years. First there was the baffling problem of the Korean cease-fire and the interminable negotiations before the armistice was finally signed—a period of some twenty months. Then there was the Berlin Conference, which ran from 25 January to 19 February 1954, and finally broke down because of Russian intransigence. There was the war in Indo-China, followed by the Geneva Conference, brought to a successful conclusion by Eden in July 1954, almost single-handed, in spite of the elephantine obstinacy of Dulles. There was the long struggle to reach an agreement on the problem of Trieste. Here the negotiations dragged on for almost three years before they were finally concluded. In addition, there were three and a half years, from October 1951 until March 1955, before the most complicated negotiations with Iran and with the Americans led to a final settlement of the oil dispute which had arisen from Mossadeq's seizure of the refinery at Abadan and the properties and concessions of the Anglo-Iranian Oil Company.

In all these matters I took little or no share, and watched their developments as best I could as they were reported from time to time at various Cabinets. With occasional interventions, generally wise and helpful, Churchill left the conduct of these tangled questions, any one of which would have been sufficient to occupy a Victorian Foreign Secretary for years, in Eden's hands. That he surmounted them all is a tribute not only to his skill but also to his rare patience and persistence. There were, however, two subjects, which ran like a thread all through these years, upon which the Prime Minister took himself a leading part. The first of these was Egypt. The second was Russia.

On 28 March 1947, under the terms of an agreement made by Bevin, as Foreign Secretary, with the Egyptian Government, the last British troops had left the well-known Kasr-el-Nil barracks in Cairo. The agreement accepted the principle that the remaining British forces, which had been in Egypt for sixty years or more, should be withdrawn. It was no doubt inevitable; but nevertheless it was a sad moment. It was unhappily followed by no real goodwill. The Egyptian nationalists immediately raised the question of the Sudan, over which the Egyptian King claimed sovereignty, while the British administrators favoured self-determination for the Sudanese. This was to poison our relations for the next decade. Furthermore, the problem of the defence of the Suez Canal was not really settled, but was left to depend on the 1936 Treaty of Alliance with Egypt.

In October 1951, a few weeks before our return to office, Nahas Pasha, the Egyptian Prime Minister, had denounced the 1936 Anglo-Egyptian Treaty, which still had five years to run. Since there was no provision in the treaty allowing for such an action, this was a flagrant example of that disregard for contractual obligations which Eden rightly regarded as the main cause of the deterioration in international relations. Meanwhile there had been serious rioting in Cairo, coupled with attacks on British subjects and property. King Farouk was not popular and indeed was rapidly becoming contemptible. Though no doubt he would have favoured moderation, he was unable to make effective any policy of his own.

There followed three difficult and unhappy years which culminated in the signing on 19 October 1954 of an agreement covering the defence of the Canal and the maintenance of our Suez Canal base. Eden has described in detail the course of these tortuous events.[1] During this period there took place the riots of January 1952, with the burning of Shepheard's Hotel and the Turf Club and the destruction of banks, shops and business premises, while a number of British subjects were murdered in cold blood. Under threats of British military retaliation, the King dismissed Nahas's Government and appointed a more moderate figure. The Americans, as usual, were all the time pressing us to come to terms, especially over the Egyptian claim to sovereignty over the Sudan. Churchill, like all his party, was deeply concerned about our obligations to the Sudanese. But he was equally anxious over the problem of the defence of Suez, and wanted American co-operation to set up some kind of joint command in the Middle East in which America and our allies would share.

General Neguib's military coup in the summer of 1952, followed by the King's abdication, led to the establishment of a dictatorship which still continues. As so often happens, the first revolutionary figure was soon to be overthrown by one of his subordinates. Yet in some respects the question of the sovereignty of the Sudan, in which the King's personal pride had been involved, was eased by the revolution. By February 1953 an agreement on the future of the Sudan was signed, which provided for a transitional period of self-government, leading to the time when the Sudan should have a free choice between absolute independence and some form of union with Egypt.

[1] The Earl of Avon, *Full Circle*, chap. x.

R2

For the next period, the problem of the Canal Zone held the field. When during Eden's absence Churchill found himself in the spring of 1953 temporarily in charge of the Foreign Office, he pressed forward with vigour the beginning of the talks. But their progress was slow and spasmodic. In May 1953, for instance, they were broken off:

> In Egypt, there is to be an interval for a fortnight. No doubt the Egyptians (who already rely on the American Ambassador, Caffery) . . . are hoping to get something out of Dulles, who is due to arrive in a day or two. . . . Dulles is sure to make a 'gaffe' if it is possible to do so. The battle as to who is to control the Republican party is only just beginning. General Eisenhower seems, at present, to be more a referee than a leader. Perhaps he will assert himself later on.[1]

Nor were things much improved by the strange episode of President Eisenhower presenting a revolver as a gift to General Neguib. Nevertheless, Churchill, who was by now preoccupied with the question of relations with Russia, was prepared to let the situation develop and to concentrate upon a settlement of the Canal base on any terms which would give us both a reasonable period of tenure and the right of re-entry. But the Egyptian Government continued to stall or ask for more concessions, and by the end of 1953 Churchill was again toying with the idea that the British and Americans should establish a joint base in Egypt as representatives of NATO. The Egyptian Treaty now seemed likely to go through in a form which would involve considerable loss of prestige and dangerous political effects at home. But what was the alternative? To sit indefinitely on the Canal with 80,000 troops and at huge expense? Certain members of the party, led by Charles Waterhouse and Ralph Assheton, with the active support of Fitzroy Maclean and Julian Amery, were totally opposed to a British withdrawal from the Canal. Yet even they realised that we could not keep so large a body of troops there indefinitely. A plan was put forward for leaving a brigade without a treaty; but that seemed to involve the worst of both worlds. I recorded my thoughts at the time:

> If we get a treaty on the present proposals—we shall carry the

[1] 6 May 1953.

party, but with 20 or 30 voting against. This might mean that Eden's position would be gravely compromised. . . . Swinton was very clear that the Treaty was right. We ought not to worry when we have done right. . . .

If we don't get a treaty, we shall have to put into effect a plan of voluntary concentration and partial or complete evacuation.[1]

At the end of the year it seemed that an impasse had been reached and that we were approaching the final breach. The Americans were very unwilling to commit themselves to help in any way. They were even extremely reluctant to bring pressure to bear by refusing to advance to Egypt substantial sums of money at this juncture. Once again Churchill, although disposed to force the issue by fixing a date on which our offer should lapse, was not anxious to press his point against Eden's advice. He was still concentrating on Russian plans. He was therefore willing to allow Eden to play the hand in Egypt, although from time to time exercising a restraining authority.

By the beginning of 1954 little progress had been made.

The reasons are: (i) the Neguib regime is afraid of an attempted *coup d'état* by the Moslem Brotherhood. It must therefore keep up its xenophobia. (ii) Caffery, the American ambassador, continues to give them aid and comfort. (iii) [The Labour left-wingers] have told them that H.M.G. will have to give in. Caffery's behaviour is really too bad, because it is not what the President or even the State Department really intend.[2]

Later in the month it seemed that the 'Committee of Revolution', having liquidated the Wafd and the Moslem Brotherhood, were now becoming conscious that they relied only on the army. But Neguib's regime was drawing to its close. On 25 February Nasser appeared to have seized power effectively. However, the struggle was by no means over. Neguib made a comeback which enabled him to exercise a degree of authority for some months to come, and only after a remarkable alternation of ups and downs, when now Neguib, now Nasser, seemed to be triumphant, was the fight for power resolved. Neguib's ultimate fate was obscure; but Nasser, with a resilience

[1] 20 December 1953.　　[2] 1 January 1954.

unusual in Middle Eastern politics, has succeeded in maintaining himself through all the vicissitudes of fortune.

The weakness of our position all through was twofold. In the first place, the 1936 treaty was due to end in 1956—only a few years ahead. Secondly, the military strain on Britain was becoming almost intolerable. With our commitments all over the world, there was scarcely a reserve division available, and Churchill knew as well as anyone the impossibility of keeping large forces immobilised indefinitely in Egypt.

Since the prolonged negotiations seemed unlikely to be fruitful— they had been suspended from March till July—and the situation in the Sudan, where we had only one battalion, was becoming steadily worse, Eden then produced a plan by which, so long as we had the right of re-entry in case of war, we agreed to put the base under British or Anglo-American civilian contractors.

By this time Churchill had satisfied himself that the military arguments were overwhelming. In the first place, the right wing of NATO now rested on Turkey and even on Pakistan. Secondly, in an atomic war, whether by A- or H-bomb, it would be difficult to see how we could reopen the base, and indeed its value was doubtful. Meanwhile, the army was wasting away on the Suez Canal at the cost of £50 million a year. There was nothing to do; there was no training; men were being killed by sporadic raids; and there were no amenities. He now therefore declared that he was prepared to defend the new proposals on purely military grounds, whether in or out of office. The Minister of Defence and the Chiefs of Staff were satisfied that an agreement of some kind must be reached, and by the end of July the terms were finally arranged, largely through the skill of Anthony Head, the Secretary of State for War, who carried out the final arrangements. These covered the organisation and servicing of the base in peace-time, and its facilities when it was necessary to put it on a war footing. In that event our rights would include the use of Egyptian ports. We were also to enjoy landing and overflying facilities for the R.A.F. after our forces had been completely withdrawn. Equally important, it was decided that both parties would uphold the 1888 convention guaranteeing freedom of navigation of the Canal.

All through this long controversy we had been thinking largely in terms of the Russian aggression in the East and in the West and of the possibility of general war. Hence the Americans, with fluctuating enthusiasm, joined with us in an attempt to organise a Middle Eastern defence system in which Egypt should play her part. But this idea the Egyptians never formally accepted, and the plan lapsed. In spite of his temperamental resistance to what seemed to be retreat and abandonment of long-held positions, Churchill, once he had made up his mind, gave Eden generous support. At a time when his own future was uncertain, Churchill could certainly have made trouble by stimulating the dissident group in the Conservative Party. These opponents of any treaty were reckoned in something of the order of forty. But he would never stoop to such tactics. Indeed, it was his stout defence of the treaty, both in private and in public, which swayed the waverers.

Nevertheless, the whole of this long dispute was painful in the extreme. We could not of course then foresee that Nasser, once he had finally obtained supreme control, would turn to expansionist aims in the hope of creating a great Arab empire, or would move so rapidly towards increasing covert and open threats against Israel, while preparing to repudiate with complete cynicism Egypt's international obligations with respect to the Canal. Perhaps the major argument which swayed Churchill in the end was the fact that the treaty was so soon to expire, coupled with the new adventure on which he was so passionately launched to bring about some solution of the fatal rivalry between the two great power-blocs of the world. He knew that so long as this state of tension was unrelieved there would be little hope of preserving order and peace and a respect for rights of others among the nations of the world.

The development of Churchill's thought during the long-drawn-out Egyptian crisis was fascinating to watch. It illustrated the two sides of his character—the nostalgic memories and pride in our great Imperial system, and the imaginative effort by which, even at his great age, he could grasp the realities and try to attune British policy to the conditions of a new era. Just as he naturally shrank from the

disappearance of the British Raj in India, so he could scarcely bring
himself to agree to the abandonment of the Nile Valley, which we
had held for so long, for all its strategic and political implications,
and which we had only a few years before defended with such valour
and at so high a cost. At the same time he fully realised the implications of the changed balance of power in the world.

His mind, for all its remarkable range, tended to concentrate
upon a single major problem. Here indeed lay his greatness and his
strength. Before the war, when he was among the first to realise the
dangers which Hitler's policies presented, he would brush aside the
problems presented by Franco or Mussolini as minor, or at any
rate to be considered only in relation to the German menace.
Similarly, partly perhaps because of his inability, in the peculiar
circumstances of Europe's slow and tortured approach to the problem of its own defence, to make any serious contribution to the
problem of European unity, to which he had devoted so much effort
while in Opposition, he now began to brood increasingly upon the
question of Russia. It was he who, by the Fulton speech in 1946,
had pointed to Russia as the new danger to mankind. There had
followed the rallying of the Western peoples under the aegis of the
NATO pact. If the conventional military arrangements were still
doubtful and ineffective, peace had nevertheless been secured by
the overwhelming strength of America's atomic power.

From occasional conversations with the Prime Minister and
his intimate friends, I realised that he had now abandoned or postponed any effort to realise his European conception. He was impatient with the French and did not seem to understand their
hesitations. Of course this attitude encouraged all those who were
sceptical of the European Movement, some of whom did not
greatly regret

C.'s strange unwillingness to defend the ideas and ideals which
he did so much to promote. I suspect that they regard his change
of front as pure opportunism. Europe has served his purpose
while he was in opposition; now he need not worry. This is not, I
believe, the truth. His mind is now much more obsessed with the
practical need of getting some genuine defences into being and

with keeping the Americans in the ring. For him, these are the first things which we must pursue first.[1]

In the early months of his administration, his efforts were mainly directed to the organisation of adequate defences and to keeping America up to the mark. But the explosion of the American hydrogen bomb, and the possibility that they might even try to force the issue before Russia acquired similar strength, a course which appeared to be recommended by some of their military advisers, caused him grave anxiety. One Sunday early in 1953 when I was staying with him at Chequers, I found him in a sombre mood, brooding on all these matters. He was waiting impatiently for President Eisenhower's reply to an invitation to a meeting:

> But he (and everyone else) had forgotten that it was Washington's birthday, and that for two or three days at this anniversary everything stops in the U.S.[2]

For Churchill, business never stopped.

As it became clear that the Russians had obtained by their own skill or by treachery the full nuclear secrets, Churchill began to worry more and more over the dire prospect that seemed to be opening up before the world. The whole concept of atomic or nuclear warfare filled him with horror. Apart from his sensitiveness to the vile charges of warmongering which were brought against him from time to time, his humanity and kindness as well as his vivid imagination made all this hideous prospect an almost permanent burden upon him and oppressed his mind. He had spent many years of his political isolation in trying to prevent the Second World War by giving due warning against it. If he had shared in some of the glamour and glory of honourable warfare (indeed, he must have taken part in more war campaigns than almost any man in history), these after all belonged to a period when, heavy as were the casualties and severe the suffering, warfare had been conducted on what might be called decent and respectable lines. This mass destruction was to him an appalling nightmare.

A few days after this talk came the death of Stalin on 5 March:

[1] 18 February 1952.　　[2] 22 February 1953.

Stalin's death is today officially announced by the Kremlin. All through yesterday the strangest bulletins, with an extraordinary wealth of detail, both as to the illness and its treatment, were published to Russia and to the world. It appeared as if all the doctors were heavily insuring themselves against accusation of incompetence and treachery.[1]

There was not yet any indication as to where power would reside, whether in an individual or in a committee. Would it be Molotov, Malenkov, Beria or another? Within a day or two we were told of

the succession of Malenkov to the position of Augustus, with Beria (the secret police) as Caesar. Molotov is Foreign Minister, but seems no longer of the Imperial family.[2]

The fall of Beria in July—to be followed by his execution—was believed to be on the whole an advantage. About this time Marshal Tito arrived for a visit to London, and Churchill gave a great dinner for him at No. 10, to which I was invited. I had known Tito in the war, and he had not forgotten me. In the course of a short conversation, he told me that the struggle for supremacy in the Kremlin was by no means over—indeed it had scarcely begun.

If the mere death of Stalin did not necessarily portend a significant change in Soviet policy, it opened up new possibilities. Churchill cautiously remarked: 'The most dangerous moment for evil Governments is when they begin to reform.'[3] Unhappily, the first symptoms were not encouraging, for the Russians shot down a British bomber in the Berlin Corridor, which led to a sharp exchange of angry Notes, but the fact that the Chinese, presumably with Russian consent, were taking a more favourable attitude towards the compulsory repatriation of prisoners in Korea was encouraging. There were signs of what was called the Russian 'peace drive'.

At that time I myself was sceptical:

I cannot but remember the fable of the Sun and the Wind. The fake Sun of a new geniality may (unless we are very careful) do more to hinder and even stop rearmament than the icy blasts of the last few years.[4]

[1] 6 March 1953.   [2] 7 March 1953.   [3] 14 April 1953.   [4] 4 April 1953.

Nevertheless, there were clearly

> some [benefits] to be got from the present internal position in Russia. We might even get [a formal] end of the Korean war. But we have no guarantee that this will not mean renewed pressure in Indo-China and Malaya.[1]

It was clear how Churchill's mind was moving when he told us that he thought Eisenhower's response to the apparent Russian thaw seemed unduly freezing. The State Department clearly wanted to restate in detail the conditions for a real détente if not a formal peace. In Korea, back to the Yalu river; free elections in a united Korea under U.N. supervision; a peace treaty in Austria; free elections in satellite countries; a united Germany; disarmament; and perhaps the imaginative Baruch plan for international control and inspection of atomic production. Churchill felt that though these things were right in principle,

> to state them so baldly (not to say crudely) might be thought by world public opinion as rather a negative act at this moment. It would seem as if a sudden frost had nipped spring in the bud— even if it were no real spring.[2]

At the same time, the Prime Minister was pleased to have re-established a friendly contact with the President and to be able to discuss frankly with him the developing situation.

About this time—the spring of 1953—the Press had begun to attack Churchill's lack of 'grasp' and incapacity to produce any coherent policy on economic or political matters. But any question of his retirement was soon out of the question: for, on 6 April, the announcement was made of Eden's serious condition and the need for an operation. This was to lead to difficult and complicated surgery, and early in June he had to go to Boston for further treatment. Churchill at this time seemed to me to be working under great pressure. Owing to Eden's absence he had temporarily taken charge of the Foreign Office. Undeterred by the mass of routine work, he was full of his own thoughts and struggling to express them. He had already welcomed the speech which Eisenhower had

[1] 4 April 1953.   [2] 14 April 1953.

delivered on 16 April, the first since the death of Stalin, appealing to the new leaders of Russia to turn the tide of history and come to terms with the West. The President stuck to his declaration that some specific act, such as signing the Austrian Treaty, would be a pledge of peaceful intention, more convincing than printed Notes or public speeches. Yet his general tone was what Churchill wished, and he acclaimed it generously. The Russians' reply to Eisenhower in a long Note, which was clear and rational, was unusually free from abuse.

The stage was therefore set for Churchill to deliver one of the most important and dramatic of the many great speeches which he made to the House of Commons in his long career.

In opening a general debate on foreign affairs, he dealt at length with the relations between the Free World and the Communist powers. He accepted the view that Russian policy might in part be explained by fear, especially fear of a revived Germany. But the formation of NATO and the strength of the Western world in conventional as well as unconventional weapons had halted any further Russian aggression. It might be necessary now to try to remove Russian anxieties. This could perhaps be done by a defence pact with both Germany and Russia guaranteeing each against attack by the other, on the lines of the old Locarno Treaty. At any rate, this was a time for searching out whether there was a change of mind, as well as a change of masters, inside Russia. Perhaps a small private conference at the highest level might be productive. It should not be 'overhung by a ponderous or rigid agenda'. Even if no definite agreement could be reached, something might be done among those gathered together to see whether there was not a better purpose in the future than to tear the human race in pieces.

This famous speech was received almost with awe by the House and by the country:

> Churchill made a 'great' speech yesterday on Foreign Affairs. 'Great' as a Parliamentary performance; 'great' as the effort of a 78-year-old Prime Minister taking on the additional job of Foreign Secretary; and 'great' as in the sequence of the pre-war,

war, and post-war speeches which have profoundly affected public opinion in the world.[1]

As a result of his determination to deal with the larger issue, Churchill was in favour of immediate accommodation in the Far East. He assumed that the Korean armistice would go through and swept aside American and Chinese hair-splitting as of no importance.

> But the highlight of Churchill's speech was the offer of a Three-Power talk (or so it amounted to) on the old Roosevelt, Stalin, Churchill model. This excites the enthusiastic support of the Opposition, the less vociferous approval of the Conservatives, the interest and sympathy of all Europe and the Commonwealth but, of course, the alarm of Washington.[1]

It so happened that the day after the speech I attended a party at which the American Ambassador and one or two of his staff were present. It was clear to me that the juniors had listened to Churchill's speech with alarm and almost indignation, but 'the Ambassador thought it "great stuff" and was in almost complete agreement.'[1]

There was, of course, a danger that this, together with other questions, would make a breach in the Anglo-American efforts, and I must admit that I shared some of these apprehensions. As I learned some months later, the Foreign Secretary also had his anxieties. What concerned him was whether the policy of sustained pressure on Russia and the building up of strength in Europe had yet gone far enough to permit of such an attempt at a détente. Timing was everything. Churchill certainly had not consulted the Cabinet as a whole before he made his speech. Yet since he was at the time Foreign Secretary as well as Prime Minister, there could be no strong objection taken, although some members of the Cabinet were not slow to contrast the time given to comparatively small points in our long meetings with the omission of so huge an issue from prior discussion. Nevertheless, Churchill was determined to move forward. He believed, and continued to believe, that the supreme moment had come. He regarded his efforts to prevent a third world war as the final service he might give to the nation and

[1] 12 May 1953.

to the world. Nor was there any question of 'appeasement', as some people tried to read into his words. This was neither implicit nor explicit in his speech. He wished to move from strength, which the West undoubtedly had, not from weakness, as had been our mistake in the fatal days before the Second World War.

Much at this time depended on the meeting which he hoped to arrange with Eisenhower, and great was his delight when on 21 May he was able to inform the House that President Eisenhower had expressed a wish for a personal meeting with the French Prime Minister and himself to discuss these great affairs. The place would be Bermuda—British territory—and the date the middle of June. This would allow for the views of the Commonwealth Prime Ministers to be available, since they would all be assembled for the Coronation on 2 June.

Even the sudden decision of Syngman Rhee to liberate 20,000–30,000 prisoners of war did not seem to threaten a renewal of the war in Korea. These men were North Koreans, alleged to be anti-Communist, and the Allies had demanded for them the right to choose whether to stay in South Korea or to return home. For two years there had been argument about this single point; when Syngman Rhee took the matter into his own hands, there was great indignation among the Chinese and North Koreans and some general alarm. I did not myself think it would make much difference:

> If the Russians and Chinese want to stop fighting, they won't bother about the prisoners. Indeed, to make this incident a reason for breaking off the truce negotiations is really to play into Syngman Rhee's hands and do what he wants—for he wants to go on with the war![1]

This proved to be the case, and everything now seemed set fair for the Bermuda meeting for which Churchill had worked so hard. Unhappily, owing to the fact that the French Government had fallen and that there was no new Government yet in being, a further postponement until the end of June seemed likely. This failure to construct a Government in France, as well as a violent

[1] 18 June 1953.

swing to the Left in Italy, leaving De Gasperi's coalition only just in the majority, was disconcerting:

> It looks as if Europe was breaking up under Malenkov's sunshine. Stalin's icy blasts kept it together.[1]

It was now

> solemnly announced that the Russians are to demobilise an army of 120,000 the existence of which they have always denied.[1]

At this moment, with hopes set so high and all the world agog, came the tragic news of Churchill's sudden illness. The bulletin issued from Chartwell, on 27 June, was as follows:

> The Prime Minister has had no respite for a long time from his very arduous duties and is in need of a complete rest. We have therefore advised him to abandon his journey to Bermuda and to lighten his duties for at least a month.

In fact he had, four days before, suffered another stroke.

[1] 14 June 1953.

CHAPTER XVI

Churchill the Peacemaker

O N Monday 29 June, the whole national Press was filled with the news of Churchill's illness:

> By issuing the communiqué on Saturday, it was *in* all the Sunday papers, but did not altogether dominate them. The news was thus broken to the people in two stages. On Sunday, the emphasis was on the 'temporary' postponement of the Bermuda Conference. This, in view of the apparent deadlock in Korea, would not have surprised the public in any case. On Monday, the chief interest was in the P.M.'s actual condition. The news was still rather scant, but the impression given was that he was completely 'fagged' out and must rest.[1]

The Cabinet had been summoned for 12 noon. In the absence of the Prime Minister and the Foreign Secretary, Butler presided. Lord Salisbury was in his usual place on the left of the Prime Minister's seat. It soon became clear to us that these two men, with great courage and devotion, had taken upon themselves the burden of decision at this critical moment. Butler gave us a short account of the visit which he and Salisbury had paid to Chartwell on the Friday, where they had found Churchill in poor health, but very gallant. He revealed to us what we had only surmised – the nature of his illness. It was a terrible shock to us all. Although the story was told simply and discreetly, many of us were in tears or found it difficult to restrain them. The arrangements for business were discussed and the statements to be made in the House agreed. It was left obscure who was to 'run' the Foreign Office. Lord Salisbury was to 'help'; but this plan immediately broke down under pressure from the House of Commons.

[1] 29 June 1953.

On the next day I went after Parliamentary questions for a talk with Harry Crookshank—my best, oldest and staunchest friend. He told me how the Salisbury arrangement has broken down. The pressure from Attlee and the House as a whole was too great to be resisted—somebody must be in charge of Foreign Affairs. So after some telephoning to Chartwell, this was arranged. Lord Salisbury is appointed 'Acting Foreign Secretary'. (There are precedents for this both in Lord Balfour's and Lord Curzon's time.)[1]

Harry Crookshank seemed concerned about the fact that I too was shortly to go into hospital. He felt that the effect of three of the Cabinet being *hors de combat* simultaneously would not be encouraging. Later in the afternoon I saw Butler on some departmental matter and he urged me to postpone my own treatment. Dr. Richardson, however, whom I saw the same night, was quite firm: 'No more delay, or I might become very ill. We had left it too long already.'[1] It was therefore agreed that I should go to St. Thomas's on the evening of 6 July.

On 2 July I had been summoned to Chartwell and arrived before dinner.

When I went into the sitting room, only Lord Moran was there. He told me that he was very satisfied—more than satisfied—at the progress made. But he feared I might be rather shocked at P.M.'s appearance, although he was much better in the last two days.[2]

My first impressions were of astonishment that a man who had suffered such a calamity could show such gaiety and courage. During dinner, and until he went to bed, just after 11 p.m., his talk seemed much the same as usual. The atmosphere was not oppressive, but almost lively. Early in the dinner he said to me:

'You know, I have had a stroke. Did you know it was the second? I had one in 1949, and fought two elections after that.' He then described how he had gone from Strasbourg to Lord Beaverbrook's villa in the South of France and had had a seizure after bathing. He said his arm was almost restored and his leg

[1] 30 June 1953.   [2] 2 July 1953.

much better. There were certainly times, at and after the dinner, when I thought he was putting on an act—but it was a jolly brave one, anyhow.[1]

Many times in the evening I was nearer to tears than he, for never had I more admired his extraordinary strength of will. Our talk covered a wide range:

> We discussed the possibility of a Dissolution; death and Dr. Johnson's fear of it; Buddhism and Christianity; Pol Roger—a wine, a woman and a horse; and many other topics.[1]

But he soon turned to Germany and Europe:

> He had read my papers and was grateful. His mind was not fully made up. He felt that now time was getting on and we must await the German elections, and the French decision on E.D.C. But he did not despair. He hoped the Americans would agree to talk with the Russians.[1]

He knew of course that Eden would not be fit to take up duty until the autumn, but he was awaiting his return in August with impatience.

After Churchill had gone to bed I learned the full story of this terrible week:

> The attack was at the Gasperi dinner—on Tuesday June 23rd. It was slight and the P.M. was got off to bed. Lord Moran could not be got till the next morning. [Churchill] got to the Cabinet room without too much difficulty and got through the Cabinet meeting without disclosing what had happened. (I certainly noticed nothing beyond the fact that he was very white. He spoke little, but quite distinctly. I remember that he called to me 'Harold, you might draw the blind down a little, will you?' I also noticed that he did not talk very much.)[1]

After the Cabinet, Churchill was still anxious to go to the House and answer questions, but he was dissuaded from doing so. The next day he left for Chartwell.

> He got much worse—the clot seemed to grow and his arm and leg movements got worse. It seems, therefore, not to have been a

[1] 2 July 1953.

sudden and incapacitating paralytic stroke, but something which began fairly gently and grew steadily worse.[1]

On Friday, Butler and Salisbury had gone to Chartwell and it was decided to issue the announcement on Saturday at 3 p.m. However, on the Saturday his condition deteriorated and the end seemed near.

> Then he rallied—and has been getting steadily better since Monday or Tuesday. On Monday he was telephoning and so on. Today I could see his state—a sick but a very gay man.[1]

Butler and Salisbury took a heavy responsibility in agreeing to what was undoubtedly the wish of the Prime Minister and the members of his family that the medical bulletin should be issued in a comparatively hopeful form. However, I felt that they were fully justified. It was only fair that Churchill should have a few weeks to make up his mind.

> He has two courses. He can go on till October and then hand on to Eden. Or he can go on till October—and then, if he is all right—go on 'till the pub closes'. It is clear that the old man has this in mind. Out of chivalry to Eden and in repayment of all that he owes him, he must not hand over now to Butler, unless he feels in conscience unable to serve the Queen efficiently in the essential work of the First Minister. To do this it is not necessary to walk or make speeches—I mean, for a few weeks.[1]

Churchill had spoken to me about my own operation and strongly urged me to have it immediately. He felt that he could hold out at any rate for the present.

Before going to hospital I attended a Cabinet at which the situation was reviewed and we all felt more hopeful. The Prime Minister was telephoning as freely as ever and seeing friends and reading papers. It was agreed that Salisbury should go to Washington to attend as a deputy for Eden a conference of American, French and British Foreign Secretaries and try to keep alive the idea of a Four-Power conference. This would at least maintain some impetus and prevent Churchill's initiative from collapsing. Although talks 'at the highest level' were not acceptable to the United States or France,

[1] 2 July 1953.

a conference of the Foreign Secretaries of the four countries—the
U.S.S.R., the United States, the United Kingdom and France—
was proposed for the autumn. This at any rate was a good result.
Nevertheless, the communiqué at the end of the conference seemed
to strike

> a very *jejune* note, obviously written by the Americans, and full
> of omissions. It's a long way from the Churchill idea of a talk
> between heads of states, with no fuss and no agenda.[1]

While I was in hospital I had many visitors, among them Field-
Marshal Alexander, who seemed to think that Churchill would
certainly carry on until the autumn, when he would make way for
Eden. I was not so sure of this.

> If, when the time comes, he feels completely restored to health,
> he may well decide to go on. It is clear that these 'strokes' or
> 'seizures' are of a very mild kind. It is remarkable that he should
> have had the first in 1949 without any apparent effect on his
> mind or body. It may well be that he will recover as well from
> this one. A great deal will depend on his will and how much he
> wants to go on. Again, I think this depends on whether he can
> see any opening in the foreign situation, which he could hope to
> explore and exploit.[2]

Churchill's improving health was confirmed by Swinton who also
came to see me in hospital. According to him the Prime Minister's
mind had never really weakened. His minutes and memoranda
had never been more lively or more powerful. Massigli, who was
another visitor, talked chiefly about the unlikelihood of the French
Assembly ratifying E.D.C. so long as there was any chance of
talks with Russia. The Russians were rabid against the Americans,
whom they believed to be determined on war. How far this fear was
genuine and how far a piece of propaganda, it was hard to tell. We
both agreed that it would be difficult to get Eisenhower to a conference except perhaps for a signing ceremony. On 24 July I was
able to leave hospital and go home to Sussex.

I was concerned at the rumours that the Cabinet were somehow
trying to go back on the line of Churchill's great speech:

[1] 16 July 1953.   [2] 19 July 1953.

Anyway, Churchill was in full charge and the policy was agreed. What had happened was that Churchill was the only man who might have cajoled, threatened, or even forced the Americans to do what he wanted. His illness had made this impossible, and he fully recognised this.[1]

The Labour Party naturally tried to make out that Churchill's policy was being thrown over:

> Of course, the attempt to drive a wedge between Churchill and the rest of the Government is absurd. Once he was unable to go to Bermuda, there was no chance of anything more than was (with great skill and perseverance by Salisbury) obtained at Washington. Nevertheless, it has helped the Socialists a lot in the House and the country. Fortunately, Eden is out of all this. The amusing result is that it will certainly encourage Churchill to go on. For the 'warmonger' who nearly lost us the last Election, is now the 'peacemaker' who may win us the next![2]

To the general public, it seemed an unreal suggestion that Lord Salisbury had lost a Cold War battle that Churchill had nearly won; for clearly if the Russians wanted to be reasonable, there would be no difficulty in making a start at the meeting of Foreign Secretaries. In any case, Salisbury made it clear that Churchill considered that we had obtained the best possible results from the Washington talks, which in no way closed the door to his wider plan.

Meanwhile,

> Beaverbrook continues his vicious attacks on Salisbury (acting Foreign Secretary). Salisbury stays the weekend with Churchill at Chequers. Then Churchill goes to stay (so it is stated) with Beaverbrook in the South of France! It's a strange and unpredictable world—the life of the great![3]

But the Socialists were beginning to realise their danger:

> They have now elevated Churchill into the 'angel of Peace'—they have beatified, if not sanctified, him. What if he recovers after all—or worse still, dissolves on the cry 'peace with Russia'?[4]

[1] 24 July 1953.   [2] 31 July 1953.
[3] 2 August 1953.   [4] 31 July 1953.

However, Parliament was now to be adjourned, and there was likely to be an opportunity for reflection.

The next fourteen months, until the reconstruction of the Government in October 1954, were dominated by the twin questions of Russia and of Churchill's ability and desire to remain as Prime Minister. These were closely interlocked. Fully occupied with my own affairs and the pressing need to introduce fresh and complicated legislation, I had only occasional glimpses at Cabinets and in private discussions of the development of this high drama. Some of my own plans, such as the Bill to increase rents, must clearly be affected by any decision as to the date of dissolution. But in the first few months the chief doubt was whether Churchill could last long enough to hold the fort until Eden's return.

At the beginning of August I had a long talk with Eden. He had just returned from New York and was about to leave for his Mediterranean holiday. Although the shock of this third operation must have been great, he seemed, except for some loss of weight, to be restored to his old self—quiet, courteous and charming. I too felt the advantage of having got rid of the infection which had been poisoning my body.

The problem of Churchill's recovery was still unresolved. Eden told me that he had made considerable progress in recent weeks, but

> he still drags the left leg; the arm is not right yet; the mouth is down on one side, and he sometimes—though by no means always—speaks thickly. He could not make a public appearance at present; he might do a broadcast; but this would be risky.[1]

Eden was naturally anxious to avoid any charge of intrigue; consequently, after seeing one or two colleagues, he was leaving immediately for the South of France and then for a yachting trip. He would not return until October. Harry Crookshank, who was Leader of the House, expressed his anxieties both to Eden and to myself.

> ... if the Session had not mercifully ended, and the smell of Blackpool or the Highlands been in the nostrils of Members,

[1] 4 August 1953.

we could not have gone on. In the last few weeks, with a new crisis in foreign affairs every day, and no P.M. or F.S., the position was becoming intolerable.[1]

Everything, of course, depended on the Prime Minister's appearing at the Party Conference in October.

In the middle of August, while most of us were on our summer holidays, there was a typical example of the Prime Minister's remarkable powers of recovery and his great mental agility. A great row had broken out as a result of the publication on 8 August, after Parliament had risen, of the declaration by the Sixteen Powers about the obligations they had undertaken to incur if the Chinese or the North Koreans were to break the recently negotiated armistice. Since no mention had been made of this by either Butler or Salisbury at the time of the armistice, the Government were accused of bad faith.

> *The Times* has attacked the Government in a portentously solemn (and silly) leader. . . .[2]

This was followed by similar Labour protests. This had to me a somewhat comical aspect, for the implication was that

> Battling Butler and Salisbury the Sadist, who are believed to have St. Winston the Peacemaker in duress, must be deposed from their brief and inglorious tenure of self-appointed power.[2]

Then suddenly Churchill appeared in Downing Street:

> . . . (like Tiberius returning from Capri) he dictates a devastating and typically Churchillian reply; recalls the Socialist record and the debate of February 1952 (I remember it all, for I wound up for the Government with a 'whose finger on the trigger' jibe, which brought me the deepest roar of cheering I have ever got in the House of Commons). . . . After this terrific broadside, which all the Press including the *Chronicle* accept as overwhelming —except *The Times* which ignores it altogether—the old P.M. is more firmly seated than ever, and while his colleagues are having a brief holiday, chooses this moment to reassert his authority and his pre-eminence in political wisdom and courage. The splendid phrases of the 'statement from No. 10 Downing Street' made the 'F.O. spokesman's' stuff seem very thin.[2]

[1] 4 August 1953.   [2] 16 August 1953.

After this I had no further doubt that the Prime Minister intended to remain in office, not merely to preserve the ultimate leadership for Eden, but to carry out the plan on which he had set his heart with all the vigour that his marvellous courage could rally.

He presided over a Cabinet on 18 August, the first which he had attended since the end of June. There was a large crowd in Downing Street and a sense of delight at the knowledge that Churchill was back. He was looking remarkably well, much better than when I had last seen him. He was, of course, sitting down, and we did not see him stand or walk; but 'he was in tremendous form, full of quips and epigrams. There was a long and difficult agenda, but he did not seem to tire at all. Whatever the differing views might be about the future, no one could withhold a sense of amazement and admiration.

Meanwhile, a dreary interchange of Notes between the Soviet and the Allied Governments on the subject of the reunification of Germany and the Austrian Peace Treaty was in full swing. The official announcement of the Russian explosion of the H-bomb was made on 20 August, but, since this news was already expected, it made little impact on opinion except to underline the terrible dangers into which the world was drifting. A few days later the Russians refused to attend a conference on the Austrian Treaty.

During this melancholy exercise Salisbury showed me many of his draft replies for circulation to the Allies, and I assisted him to the best of my ability. It seemed to me that our answers ought always to be as simple as possible. 'Nothing could be worse than (in Bedell Smith's phrase) trying "to conduct the conference by correspondence".'[1] The trouble was that the Americans, no doubt under Dulles's direction, seemed always to prefer long, argumentative and often querulous ripostes.

While all this was going on, I had a talk with the American Ambassador, Winthrop Aldrich, with whom I began to form a friendship which ripened into real intimacy. He told me

that the President was so devoted to Churchill that he was much distressed, first by his condition, secondly by the apparent drifting

[1] 18 August 1953.

apart of Anglo-American policy. He thought that the May 11th speech, with all its merits, was a mistake. . . .[1]

The Ambassador went on to say that Eisenhower was embarrassed by Churchill's attempt to revive, by personal correspondence, the old Churchill–Roosevelt relationship. I said that of course F.D.R., like Churchill, was an artist and a politician, and Eisenhower was neither. I agreed, however, that this informal correspondence between the Prime Minister and the President should be reserved for exceptional occasions. Like everything else, if it became common, it lost its value. But I insisted that

> the American administration must recognise that, whether they liked the speech of May 11th or not, it was a world event of great importance. Nothing could put us or our policy back into the pre-May stagnation. Churchill had broken up the ice. It was on the move. We must learn to steer among icebergs.[1]

Nevertheless, the Prime Minister was of course unable, at any rate at this stage, to carry out his full work with his old vigour. There was much discussion about the idea that Eden should become Deputy Prime Minister—a post, incidentally, which really does not exist in our constitution. Nor was it easy to see what would be the position of a Foreign Secretary with Churchill and Eden on top of him. I argued strongly against this plan with any of my colleagues who were discussing it.

There was another Cabinet on 25 August in which the Prime Minister once again appeared in great form:

> He talked well and wittily, but not too much; handled the business well; had a kind word for everybody.[2]

From my point of view I was strongly in favour of avoiding a dissolution, in order that I might carry out my housing legislation during the following year. I especially did not wish to drop my Rent Bill; but it was difficult to see how Parliament could be dissolved two to three months after everybody's rent had gone up. I remembered the 1929 election, when all rating valuations had risen a week or two before the poll.

[1] 19 August 1953.   [2] 25 August 1953.

Throughout August there was much public interest in the visits of Ministers and others to Chequers, and the Press was full of speculation as to Churchill's intentions. I myself felt that this was somewhat exaggerated. I thought that he was probably bored and wanted to see and talk to as many people as possible for his own distraction.

On 31 August I was summoned to Chequers.

> I had not seen him since I dined with him at Chartwell, about a week after the attack—except, of course, at the two Cabinet meetings. But in the open, and moving, is a more severe test. His recovery has certainly been remarkable. He walks pretty well, although he still drags the left leg slightly. The arm seems recovered; the face shows no or little sign. The speech is as clear as before. . . . On the other hand, if you happen to look towards him when he is off guard, he looks—as he is—a very old man.[1]

Although we did not go to bed until after midnight, the talk was only desultory. All sorts of possible plans for a reconstruction of the Government were discussed, chiefly based upon the desire of some of the older Ministers to retire, which would involve abandoning the 'overlord' system.

On the next day we had a further talk alone in which a great number of possibilities were canvassed quite frankly. He was in a particularly charming mood—thoughtful and sympathetic. As a result of a lot of soliloquy, cross-questioning, and normal discussion, my impressions were clear:

> (a) The P.M. intends to remain P.M. as long as he can 'face' the Party Conference and the House of Commons. 'Face' means, of course, meet the physical strain. He is what he calls 'bad on his pins' still—but this is improving. If he maintains the progress he has made since I last saw him, he thinks he can do it.
>
> (b) His purpose is not merely (or so he protests and no doubt persuades himself) to prolong his tenure of office. He thinks he can contribute something—perhaps something vital—in the next six months or so to the world situation.
>
> (This means he wants to go on till May 1954, when the Queen returns from her visit to Australia, etc.)[2]

[1] 31 August 1953.   [2] 1 September 1953.

Eden could remain as Foreign Secretary or become Deputy Prime Minister, as he preferred. I said that, of course, this was out of my sphere, but that I did not honestly feel that Eden becoming Deputy Prime Minister was a good plan. It would make the position of the Foreign Secretary almost impossible.

We talked in some detail about my own job, which I was anxious to complete; but I made it clear that I could not carry my Bills and get the Royal Assent before May 1954.

> 'That will do very well,' he murmured. Evidently May 1954 is the date he is all the time working to. He will stay till May 1954—till the Queen returns.
>
> Then, of course, he will see—and if his health stands it—the next date will be the autumn of 1954 or the spring of 1955.[1]

We had an interesting discussion about France, Germany, E.D.C., etc. He did not believe E.D.C. would be signed, and was thinking out an alternative. In a sense, everything turned on the Germans.

> 'The only thing the Russians fear is a re-armed Germany.' 'Yes,' I said, 'everyone keeps saying that. But does it not follow that it's the only card we have to play?' He agreed.[1]

We then spoke about Eisenhower.

> I tried to give him the picture of E. as I had known him and to make the P.M. realise that E. would never willingly go to a 'high-level' meeting. He would not trust himself. He likes to work through the staff, in the orthodox way. Although I was a Minister of Cabinet rank, I always dealt with the Chief of Staff, General Bedell Smith, in Algiers and seldom direct with Ike. Men had their different ways of working. This was his way, and I thought it a prudent one.[1]

Churchill agreed to all this.

> 'But I might go and have a talk with Malenkov myself. I would go to Russia. I would willingly go to Russia.'[1]

It was for me a memorable and touching occasion. He treated

[1] 1 September 1953.

S

me with almost paternal kindness. Yet it was sad; for although painted in vivid and splendid colours, it was a sunset scene.

Churchill's plans for the coming weeks were certainly good publicity:

> He goes to York, for the Leger. After the race, he goes in the royal train to Balmoral. And there is every hope that the Queen's horse may win ! If so, Lord Melbourne must be there !¹

Eden returned from his holiday at the beginning of October and attended a full Cabinet on the third, when all Ministers were present. After the Prime Minister had welcomed him on his return to duty, we turned to business, of which there was plenty—Egypt, Trieste, Housing and many other questions. I made it clear that if we were to go ahead with my plans, we should not risk a dissolution for at least eighteen months.

The next important event was the Margate Conference. Both Eden and Butler made admirable speeches and had a tremendous welcome, but amid all the orations and amusements of the conference the excitement was concentrated on the Saturday afternoon. How would Churchill come through his ordeal?

> The answer was really magnificent. He spoke for 50 minutes, in the best Churchillian vein. The asides and impromptus were as good as ever. His voice seemed sometimes a little weak, and once or twice flagged. But this happens to everybody in the course of a long speech.²

Altogether, the old man had triumphed once more by sheer persistence; and the public, in and out of the conference hall, shared almost ecstatically in his triumph.

Another test came at the opening of Parliament, when the Prime Minister spoke in the Debate on the Address:

> [His] performance on November 3rd was really remarkable. It was the first speech he had made in the House of Commons since May 11th. He was far more confident than at Margate. Indeed, he was complete master of himself and of the House. It seems incredible that this man was struck down by a second

---

¹ 1 September 1953.   ² 11 October 1953.

stroke at the end of June. I would not have believed it possible at any time during the summer or even in the early autumn.[1]

Meanwhile, there was little to be done regarding Russia except to try to make sure that our replies to the harsh, argumentative or sometimes offensive Russian communications took a more friendly form. At the beginning of November, in eighteen pages of 'dismal and turgid smog', the Russians proposed a series of impossible conditions for the solution of the German problem. In a sense, this confirmed Churchill's instinct that an interchange of written documents would lead nowhere. If any progress were to be made, it should be by personal meetings without agenda.

Churchill was now looking forward to the Bermuda Conference, which was fixed to take place between 4 and 8 December and was to be attended by the President and the French Prime Minister. He left for Bermuda in fine form, delighted with the great ovation which he had received from all sides of the House on the day before he left. 'This was to wish him luck for Bermuda. It was a kindly, and typically British gesture.'[2] The journey, on which Eden accompanied him, involved a long flight and a tiring meeting, as well as a speech at a dinner given by the Speaker of the Bermudian House of Assembly.

Fortunately, the atmosphere had been much improved by a further Russian Note which was published on 27 November. In this latest communication the Soviet Government accepted the proposal for a Four-Power conference which the Western Powers had been making throughout the summer and autumn, and suggested Berlin as a suitable place. No date was proposed. In order to save face, the Russians added that they would raise at the conference the question of calling a Five-Power conference, to include China. This last point had hitherto been resisted by the Allies, but was acceptable in its new form. It is strange now to reflect how soon the Soviet and Chinese Governments were to fall out.

The chief outcome of the Bermuda Conference was to accept the Russian proposal and to suggest 4 January as the date of the meeting. In other respects it achieved little. Two other pieces of

[1] 5 November 1953.   [2] 1 December 1953.

good news were published at the same time—the final settlement of the Trieste problem and the agreement to resume diplomatic relations between Britain and Iran. These agreements constituted considerable triumphs for the Foreign Secretary. On Boxing Day a Russian reply was received about the date, and the Berlin Conference was now definitely fixed for 25 January 1954. Although this was to be a conference of Foreign Ministers and not of Prime Ministers or Heads of State, Churchill felt much encouraged by this more favourable development.

The Russian motives were not easy to fathom.

> I never could understand why they did not accept the earlier suggestions for a Four-Power conference. If their idea is to hold up E.D.C. and German rearmament, why did not they agree before, instead of sending a series of argumentative replies—about China, etc.? Julian Amery has had some talk with the Russian chargé d'affaires, who tried to make out that the Russians really want a settlement both on Germany and on the atomic problem. It seems to me that the weakness of the position of the Western powers lies in the E.D.C. question being still unresolved. It should be pretty easy for Russia to drive a wedge between France and the other two Western Governments on this issue. The Russians will try this obvious game.[1]

It was now generally assumed that Churchill's resignation would take place when the Queen returned from her long Commonwealth tour in mid-May. But I myself felt that he would not abandon his hope of fruitful negotiations with Russia. Even if the Berlin Conference were to fail, he would press on with his own plans. Dining with him on 29 December, I tried some probing. It was clear that he would not undertake another General Election. In spite of the precedent of Palmerston, this would be impossible at the age of eighty-one. Nor would he

> risk another defeat—so he will resign before a dissolution. But he will go on as long as he can, always having a date ahead, which (when reached) can be extended for a new reason. Last autumn, he had to stay for Eden's return. Now he must stay to get him through the Egyptian trouble. Then it is the Queen's

[1] 27 December 1953.

return. By next summer, another reason will be found. But it is at once so rusé and so naïve, that it is very engaging! Of course, I am no fair judge, for he does not worry me. With his mind on Russia, and the whole world, he leaves me alone so long as the result is good—which it is. But it must be difficult for Eden. . . .[1]

Our main weakness, at this time at any rate, did not lie in the conduct of foreign affairs. Every Foreign Secretary must accept a great measure of interest, or even interference, from the Prime Minister of the day. It was in the conduct of economic and home affairs that the trouble lay. We had a number of very able Ministers; but with the physical disabilities from which Churchill still suffered and the fact that the most powerful second figure was the Foreign Secretary, we felt that in home affairs we were drifting without the formulation of any fixed plan—without a new theme or a new faith. We had almost completed the job of restoration and recovery. We now seemed to need a new programme. This mood was perhaps unduly pessimistic. The next two General Elections were to prove that the confidence of the people in the Conservative Party was not lessened but rather enhanced. One of the difficulties was in the Cabinet itself. There were too many elderly Ministers, and new blood was required. The younger members of the party were as usual anxious to be given a chance. But this must all await the Prime Minister's decision about his own future.

The Berlin Conference opened on 25 January, and has been fully described by Eden.[2] Molotov was in his most negative mood, and by 18 February it was clear that there was complete deadlock on every European question. There was no settlement for Germany and no hope of any Austrian treaty. Nevertheless, with the problem of European defence and German rearmament still unsettled, I felt that

the truculence of Molotov is much less dangerous than a show of moderation. The neutralist forces in France and Italy have been correspondingly weakened. M. Bidault's reputation has grown. . . .[3]

[1] 29 December 1953.
[2] The Earl of Avon, *Full Circle*, pp. 53 ff.   [3] 20 February 1954.

If Berlin ended in utter failure as regards Western questions, on the Eastern side there was more hope of progress. It was agreed to hold a conference in April of five powers, including China, to discuss Korea and Indo-China. This represented a concession by Dulles and a success for Eden. The conference duly met at Geneva in April and lasted till July. Once again Eden demonstrated his remarkable powers of negotiation, and an agreement was reached which he has summed up as follows:

> The result was not completely satisfactory, but we had stopped an eight-year war and reduced international tension at a point of instant danger to world peace. This achievement was well worth while. All now depended on the spirit in which the agreements were carried out.[1]

Eden was the central figure at Geneva, and Churchill and the Cabinet gave him full support throughout these long and tortuous discussions. The fact that they were in progress, and that they depended for their success on Eden's personal direction, made it all the more clear that there could be no question of a change of Government, at least during the summer of 1954.

During these months I saw Churchill from time to time. On one such occasion, when we dined alone, he was in his most genial mood. He talked a good deal about the future but was uncertain of his own plans. He was still brooding about the atomic and hydrogen bombs and the terrible destructive power that seemed to menace the future of mankind. During the long absences of the Foreign Secretary and the protracted discussions at Geneva, Churchill began to think more and more about finding some method of persuading the Americans to agree to 'high-level' discussions with the Soviet leaders. Anxious to make some progress, he decided at the beginning of June to make another visit to Eisenhower, whether alone or accompanied by Eden. His colleagues were considerably alarmed at the idea of his going off on his own accompanied only by Lord Cherwell (who was not now in the Cabinet) on a mission which would almost certainly be misunderstood or misrepresented. If the Geneva Conference was over, Eden should go too. If it was not

[1] The Earl of Avon, *Full Circle*, p. 142.

over, Churchill's visit should be postponed. The real trouble, of course, was Eisenhower's determination to avoid talks with Churchill alone. He would insist on having Dulles at his side; for this reason it seemed important that Eden should accompany the Prime Minister.

In the middle of June, after a dinner in honour of the Austrian Chancellor, Dr. Raab, the Prime Minister took me into the Cabinet Room.

> He had intended to resign in July. But how could he go to negotiate with the President with the sense of only having a few weeks more of power. It would deprive him of authority. Yet we were perhaps coming at last to a climax. After talking with the President, he might be able (with the President's approval) to see Malenkov. All this would take time. So he would prefer to wait for the changeover till the end of September.[1]

On thinking this over I thought I ought to be perfectly frank with Churchill. It seemed to me that the end of September was the worst possible moment for a changeover. I therefore wrote him the following letter on 18 June:

> Private and Confidential.
>
> Dear Prime Minister,
>
> I have thought a great deal about the matter which you mentioned to me after dinner on Wednesday. It was indeed kind of you to take me into your confidence. I appreciate this very much.
>
> But I must tell you, frankly, that in my view, if a new administration is to be formed this year, it would be a great advantage for Ministers to be installed in their new offices before and not after the summer holidays. Indeed, I think this is really essential. Otherwise we shall waste two or three very precious months.
>
> Of course, there may be developments in the international sphere which would override these considerations. You and Anthony must judge these.
>
> I need hardly say that I am not in the least concerned with my own position. But if someone is to take on my job, the sooner he can start the better. And this applies all round. Once more, I must tell you how much I appreciate serving you, and the support and confidence which you have shown me.

[1] 16 June 1954.

There was nothing more that I could do.

> My duty is done, for I am sure that to delay any further might fatally compromise our chances of winning again. We shall have enough difficulties as it is.[1]

I received a curt acknowledgement from the Prime Minister, but I did not expect more. On the assumption that he really meant to retire at this time I am sure my advice was good.

Although the Geneva Conference was not concluded, a meeting in Washington was arranged, and Eden was able to go, in spite of his other preoccupations.

> The travellers have left—amid the plaudits of the Press and the people. Churchill enjoys it all; and to a more limited extent, I think Eden gets help and strength from popular admiration. Certainly, after his speeches [in Parliament] at the beginning and at the end of Wednesday's debate (June 23rd) his position in the country is higher than it has ever been. He had the support of both sides of the House and this was generously given.[2]

Unhappily, it was clear that Dulles was still unfriendly and that a rift was beginning to develop between our two countries. Differences on the Far East were spreading into other fields. For this reason we all felt that the visit was wise and timely.

> One of the difficulties is the weakness and amateurishness of the American administration. Eisenhower is a generous and noble figure. But he is not a strong character. . . . The Republicans have put up a poor show against McCarthy. Eisenhower has treated the problem as Charles II treated Titus Oates—let the plague run its course. (But a lot of innocent victims are sacrificed meantime.)[2]

A more sinister meeting was taking place at the same time in Delhi between Nehru and Chou En-lai. Even if agreement was reached at Geneva, it would clearly be necessary to organise some kind of defensive system in the Far East, similar to that provided by NATO in the West.

[1] 18 June 1954.   [2] 25 June 1954.

Although the meeting in Washington was outwardly successful, it achieved little positive result. The President was always glad to meet an old friend. But he had a hearty dislike of these or any other conferences. He preferred to keep in the background until some final decision had to be taken, for or against a definite project. Preparatory and detailed discussions on possible lines of approach should be entrusted to the staff. The principals should reserve themselves for approving the conclusions. The Prime Minister, on the other hand, thoroughly enjoyed these affairs. He always liked staying at the White House and was delighted with his personal reception and the deference with which he was treated. But he was obsessed by his hopes of going down to history not only as the greatest War Minister but as the greatest peacemaker in the world. He was therefore thinking only of Russia; all the other problems which worried the Foreign Ministers of many countries hardly mattered to him. He was working against time, for he knew that he must soon make a definite decision about his own future. He had told Eden early in June that he meant to retire at the end of July.[1] He had changed his mind in view of his visit to America, but was talking freely in terms of September as the date, although the Chief Whip seemed now to think that he would stay until the end of the year. In any case, he knew that if he, an old man, was to play the role of the saviour of mankind from the horrors of nuclear war, he could scarcely avoid seeming, in his father's phrase, 'an old man in a hurry'.

Eden had little hopes of much fruitful business with the Russians at this time. Although willing to go along with Churchill up to a point, in his heart he preferred the policy of first building up our strength. This seemed to him all the more important because we had not yet succeeded in solving the problem of European defence. The prolonged debates on E.D.C. were still continuing, and no agreement had yet been reached on German rearmament. He had had to tear himself away from the Geneva discussions in order to go to Washington. With the Geneva Conference suspended in rather unpromising circumstances, it was no wonder that the Foreign Secretary was more concerned with the immediate problems which

[1] 5 June 1954.

lay ahead than with the dreams and ambitions of the Prime Minister. Perhaps the only gain to be obtained from the Washington Conference was the possibility of some agreement with Dulles about South-East Asia.

It was not surprising that under these circumstances the talks were more fruitful in the exposition of various ideas than in any definite conclusions.

The two British principals returned by boat. In the course of the voyage, against Eden's wishes and advice, Churchill dispatched a rather fulsome message to Molotov, suggesting a personal meeting between himself and Malenkov and his colleagues. The telegram made it quite clear that the Americans were not committed. Any meeting could only be on a Two-Power basis, at least to start with; but it might develop into a Three-Power or even a Four-Power affair. The question of time and place would have to be settled. It was also made clear that Churchill's purpose was to find out the Russian feelings unofficially before sending any official invitation or proposal. Eden's instinct was against such a message, but he finally agreed to it on the boat. It was therefore sent to London for dispatch. Molotov's reply was cordial; but it seemed that the Russian Presidium was almost as confused as the British Cabinet was soon to be.

> There was one paragraph [in the Russian answer] which ran as follows:
> 'We feel that such a personal contact may serve to [sic] carrying out a broader meeting on the highest level, if it [presumably the meeting] is accepted for all the parties which are interested in easing the international tension and in strengthening peace.'
> This phrase might be interpreted to mean America, or Red China, or both.[1]

Owing to some confusion on the ship and to the position not being fully understood in London, the important telegram was sent off without the Cabinet being consulted or informed. It was natural therefore that a good deal of trouble followed. The first doubt arose about President Eisenhower. It seemed somewhat

[1] 6 July 1954.

disingenuous on Churchill's part to send this message to the
Russians a few days after leaving his American host without informing or consulting him. Churchill, however, took the view, and
with some justification, that he had made his intentions clear while
he was in Washington.

> When they had discussed it, Dulles had said 'You are to be a
> go-between?' 'No,' replied Churchill. 'For I know on which side I
> stand. I will be a reconnoitring patrol.' Anyway, Eisenhower
> always said 'You have a perfect right to act alone.' Churchill
> accepts, according to his own account, that his will be a 'solitary
> pilgrimage'. But if he fails, there is no great loss. . . . If he
> succeeds, the peace of the world will be saved. Anyway, he is
> 'expendable'.[1]

In spite of the strong doubts of some of the members of the Cabinet, I felt myself that there was nothing to be done except to accept
the situation. I also felt that the British people would applaud this or
any other gesture which might lead to some 'relaxation of tension'.
Owing to the apparent intransigence of Dulles, and the antics of
Senator Joseph McCarthy and the rest of the anti-Communist
extremists, even moderate opinion in Britain was becoming more
and more anti-American. In any case there was nothing to be done
except to inform the President in full as to what had happened and to
wait for his reply. When Eisenhower's answer came it was generous
and honourable in tone and temper; but he clearly refused to
take any responsibility for this sudden move. He was naturally
surprised and somewhat hurt by the invitation having been sent
only a day or two after Churchill had left Washington. ' "You have
certainly not let the grass grow under your feet, etc." '[2]

Churchill was himself beginning to have second thoughts about
his proposed pilgrimage to Moscow. Why not Stockholm or Vienna
or even Berne? All he wanted to do was to begin his Apostolic
mission. A Two-Power conference must lead to a Three- or Four-
Power one including France; he would suggest that the Russians
should make a striking gesture of good faith—they would sign
the Austrian Treaty and Eisenhower would come to London to

[1] Ibid.   [2] 8 July 1954.

sign although not to negotiate; and so his dream would come true. All this was moving but rather sad; for we knew in our hearts that much as we loved and admired our great leader, his life had now passed far beyond the great climacteric. His mind was as fine as ever, for short periods; his character as strong as in his prime. But he was not capable of any prolonged or detailed negotiation. Indeed, unless we were careful such a confrontation might have a tragic ending.

The disquiet of some of the members of the Cabinet looked at one time likely to lead to a serious collision. I did my best to act as a mediator, and my strongest arguments were that we could not appear to oppose the substance of Churchill's desire for a top-level meeting, still less to give in to American pressure. It was really a matter of procedure. What we had to do was to try to gain time by declaring that no meeting was possible until the end of the Geneva Conference, and then try to divert it to a neutral state. Churchill was soon to accept this position; and Eden, now back at Geneva, had a talk with Molotov of which the Cabinet were informed.

> [Eden] broke to him that Churchill would not want to go to Moscow. What about Berne, after a happy finish to Geneva? There must be a good finish to Geneva. M. did not seem unduly put out, although he said they would prefer somewhere in the Soviet Union.[1]

Eden also mentioned the possibility of London as well as Berne. If it was in London the President might come after all!

On 20 July the news came of the successful termination of the Geneva Conference. The result seemed

> far more satisfactory than one could have hoped. Laos and Cambodia are given a chance to live a separate non-Communist life. Vietnam is partitioned—the French leave Hanoi and the north— rather a tragic event for the great Catholic community. But they could not have held on, and a retreat or evacuation is better than a massacre. The south (including all Cochin-China) remains—free. But there is a general expectation that at the elections which are to be held in two years' time the south will vote 'nationalist' or

[1] 13 July 1954.

'communist', unless some local figure can be built up on the other side. The Americans will 'respect' the agreement, though standing aloof from the struggle to get it—all this fell on Eden. He must have worked with extraordinary patience and skill. Although there are already some rumours of 'Munich' (foolish, because there is no parallel at all) yet I think Eden's prestige and authority will be much increased.[1]

A few days before the news was received, Churchill sent for me and we had a long talk about the situation. He seemed not to resent my letter about his proposed date of resignation. With characteristic agility he turned the situation to his advantage. 'If Geneva succeeds,' he cried, 'the Russian visit will be made easier. If it fails, it becomes all the more necessary.'

> P.M. was very nice and took quite well some pretty tough things which I said (whenever I got a chance!), e.g. that he treated his Cabinet very badly, like Lloyd George and Chamberlain; that he should inform us of the date of his resignation; that it should be *before* the Party Conference in October. The only way that I can find to treat him is in a half-bantering way, with a good deal of chaff.[2]

Fortunately the position was eased by the Russians themselves. On 24 July Eden rang me to say that

> A completely new situation has been created by an identical note to China, U.K., France, and U.S. suggesting a meeting of all European powers. This (embarrassing as it may be to answer) is obviously to wreck E.D.C. (and ultimately NATO). But it makes a completely new problem . . . and (by a strange paradox) may serve at least to unite the British Cabinet.[3]

And so it was to prove. The first task now must be to answer the Russian Note. This generally took between five and six weeks, while various Allied countries were consulted and texts and drafts were interchanged.

The Russian Note was both tendentious and disingenuous. It was clearly wise to delay any reply, at least until after the French Assembly had debated E.D.C. But a new embarrassment was soon to

---

[1] 20 July 1954.   [2] 16 July 1954.   [3] 24 July 1954.

arise. On 1 August I heard that a reply had come from Molotov which was

> not unfriendly to the idea of the personal visit, without waiting for the Three-Power reply to the last Russian note. Nothing was said of place—only time.[1]

It was difficult to avoid the suspicion that they hoped by these tactics to prevent E.D.C. and any effective European military organisation, including German rearmament, and even as a consequence to bring about the fall of Adenauer and his foreign policy. After some discussion, Churchill replied that Molotov's message did not fit in with the plan which he had in mind. He felt that the new Russian Note

> obviously superseded for the time being the small informal meeting . . . which might have been the prelude to a Three- or Four-Power meeting at top level.[2]

To this Molotov answered that he did not see any reason for considering that the two were incompatible, pointing out that Churchill had suggested in July an unofficial meeting without any kind of agenda. Churchill, taking his Cabinet into full confidence, proposed to answer in some such words as these:

> It was not my intention to convey that I had changed in any way from my original project. But your unexpected revival of your Berlin proposals created a new situation, since it would not have been possible to have a large and formal international conference at the same time as the unofficial Two-Power top-level meeting which I proposed. . . . The British, American, and French Governments whom you addressed officially are now preparing their replies. . . . These will no doubt be dispatched in the course of this month. Let us therefore wait until we know what is going to happen about this and then re-examine my project in the light of events.[2]

Harmony, at least among his colleagues, was thus restored. When, in September, the three powers replied to the Russian Note, it was to refuse to attend a conference unless Russia would agree to

---

[1] 1 August 1954.   [2] 2 August 1954.

sign the Austrian Treaty and to allow free elections throughout Germany.

Early in August, the American Ambassador asked to see me, seemingly more anxious to obtain news than to give it. I told him that Churchill's policy had the support of the country and that whatever rumours he might have heard about Cabinet disagreement, they were on procedure rather than on substance. At the same time the Ambassador repeated an amusing comment of Herbert Morrison, answering a criticism of Attlee and Bevan for paying visits to Moscow and Peking, as they had recently done. Morrison replied, 'Well, one has to run jolly fast to keep to the left of Churchill nowadays.'

On my return from a short holiday, I got a message inviting me to Chartwell. Churchill was in a relaxed and amiable mood. In the course of luncheon, which lasted until nearly 4 p.m., after a certain amount of desultory discussion about Soviet policy, E.D.C., NATO, Adenauer's position, the French confusion, and the like, we got to the real point. He had now made up his mind not to resign in September as had been the original plan. He reminded me that I had protested against this as being too late to allow for a successful Government to be formed before the end of the year. He therefore made it clear that he proposed to stay as long as he could. He produced in favour of this plan a number of arguments:

First, he (and he alone in the world) might be able to steer through the complications of Foreign Policy and international problems. He had a unique position. He could talk to anybody, on either side of the Iron Curtain, either by personal message or face to face. Having now fully recovered his health, he could not abandon [his] commission. . . . Secondly, a 'fag-end' government, formed at the end of a Parliament, could never succeed. Such brilliant figures as Lord Rosebery and Arthur Balfour had been swept away, in spite of their talents and their charm, when they had to succeed to Gladstone and Salisbury. It would be much better for Eden if he (Churchill) were to go on till the Election. Or, perhaps, it might be wise to let Eden become P.M. just *before* the Election. That could be decided later. Thirdly, he was P.M. and nothing could drive him out of his office, so long as he could form and control a Government and have the confidence of the House. This continual chatter in the lobbies and the press about his resignation was intolerable. It arose, of course, from his illness last year. But he was now recovered. Naturally, like any man of nearly 80, who had had *two* strokes, he might die at any moment. But he could not undertake to die at any particular moment! Meanwhile, he did not propose to resign.[1]

Naturally, all this did not pour out in a single flood of rhetoric. There were pauses, questions and silent broodings, and I had to make appropriate remarks at intervals in order to encourage him to tell the whole story. When he pressed me for my opinion, I thought it right to give it sincerely and truthfully. I said

that (i) there was no reason to suppose that the foreign problems were temporary or passing; (ii) that there were arguments the other way about the 'fag-end' administration. We needed a new impetus and a new theme. Anthony Eden might give us these. It was impossible for him. (iii) Since he had repeatedly told everybody that he proposed to resign this autumn, it was he who was responsible for this widespread (even general) assumption. He had said farewell to the Women's Party Conference at the Albert Hall this summer. But much more important, he had many times in the last few months told Anthony that he was on the point of 'handing over'. First he had told him the Queen's return, that is May; then he had said, July; finally, in a letter, written on June 11th (which I had seen), he had categorically told Eden that he would resign the Premiership in September. Anyway, what had he now said to Eden?[1]

Churchill naturally did not much like this, but as always treated what I said calmly and courteously. I had once observed to him that I could speak to him more frankly than some of his colleagues. He had long treated Eden as an eldest son, and even if Eden were to break down in health, there were many senior to me. In the case of great estates, the eldest son can never speak to his father about the wisdom of handing over property; a younger son who has nothing to gain is the person who should undertake the task,

[1] 24 August 1954.

however disagreeable. It was in such a spirit that I had always spoken to him, and he had accepted this as a fair point.

I now asked again—what had he said to Eden and what was this new plan? It proved to be that Eden should become Deputy Prime Minister, Leader of the House, and responsible for the 'home front'. He would speak in the country; he would take control of the party machine; he would 'plan' the programme for the next election. He would be, as it were, to use an analogy of commerce, the managing director, while Churchill remained as chairman. If only Eden would agree to this, all would be plain sailing. I replied frankly that I thought this decision would be a severe shock to Eden and that he would be much more likely to wish to stay at the Foreign Office. At any rate, I urged him not to let things drift but to bring them to a head. We really must settle, and within a few weeks, what was to be done and how we were to plan our work. To this Churchill agreed and undertook to send Eden a letter in these terms.

But it was not only the question of the Premiership which must be settled. The Government had ceased to function with full efficiency; many of the Ministers were unsuited to their posts; no one co-ordinated policy; Cabinets were becoming long and wearisome, as well as too frequent. The Parliamentary Party, already discontented, might soon break up into groups and cabals; the whole party machine was losing grip. All this was due to the continual uncertainty, discussed openly in the Press, as to Churchill's intentions.

It was at this time that the Prime Minister, approaching eighty, and uncertain both of his own future and of the Government's, gave a demonstration of his courage and panache which is among my most treasured memories. I was passing through London and he invited me to luncheon at Downing Street, but since the household was on holiday we went to Buck's Club.

The great car, flying the Standard of the Warden of the Cinque Ports; the bows and smiles to the crowd; the hat and cigar, and stick—superb showman. As we drove along a gaping St. James's Street to the Club in Clifford Street, he was recognised and cheered.

The luncheon—which was chosen with a great deal of care and

detailed criticism of this or that dish or wine—was not a bad one
for a man of 80. A dozen oysters; cream soup; chicken pie;
vanilla and strawberry ice. Moselle and brandy washed this down.
I'm afraid I could not manage the soup or the ice-cream.[1]

There were two or three important but highly confidential subjects about which he wished to consult me. Since he had not got his
hearing-aid, this presented some difficulties. It was hardly possible
to discuss any of the points intelligently without doing so in what
amounted to a general meeting of the members. Butler joined us
after luncheon, and things got a bit easier when one or two members, including Bob Laycock, who were old friends of Churchill,
tried to keep the field from pressing too near the Master. By the
time we came to leave, a large crowd had collected outside in Clifford
Street.

> The departure—with P.M., Chancellor of the Ex., and Minis-
> ter of Housing in the car together—was a superb affair. 'I think I
> may still be not all on the debit side,' he chuckled. It was almost
> as if he had put the whole thing on for our benefit.[1]

Churchill now began to discuss various plans for a reconstruction
of the Government under his leadership with Eden (when he was
available), with Butler, and sometimes with me. For most of
September, and indeed most of October, Eden was taken up, not by
consideration of his or Churchill's immediate future, but by visits
and negotiations in the leading capitals of Europe to establish the
Western European Union following the French rejection of E.D.C.

Churchill told me that if Eden would accept the position of
Deputy Premier, I could go to the Foreign Office. Alternatively,
if Eden preferred to keep the Foreign Office, I could look after the
'home front', including economic affairs—an impossible suggestion,
since no Chancellor of the Exchequer could agree to surrender his
traditional responsibility.

It seemed that we had better try to face the Conservative Conference and the meeting of Parliament without change. Perhaps
Churchill might decide to resign after his eightieth birthday celebrations on 30 November.

[1] 14 September 1954.

A little later Lord Woolton informed me that

> There has been a careful survey of the position by the most experienced agents—each area working as a team. The result of this exercise confirms the Gallup poll, etc. An Election now, under the present Government, would lead to a disaster electorally. The margin might not be large (like 1945) but it would be decisive. A further examination confirms the view that nothing can avoid this result next year, except a complete change in the structure of the Government and a new P.M.[1]

I asked him whether he proposed to send this appreciation to the Prime Minister. He said yes; but with his usual sagacity he was against forcing the issue. That might lead to a long and bitter split in the party, which would be worse than losing an election.

There now began to be talk about the idea that I should go to the Ministry of Defence. Since Eden seemed to assume that I would be glad to take the post,

> I explained that I thought this a bad idea. (i) There was nothing to do, the whole programme having just been fixed—a day or two ago—for next three years. (ii) the public would think either that Lord Alexander had made a mess of it, and that I was being sent to clean it up; or (iii) that we had more or less given up hope of peace and were desperately preparing for war— or both! If A.E. wants to stay at F.O. (which of course is his right and on which he should not be pressed or influenced by anything except what he feels best) then I had better be Minister without Portfolio or something of the kind.[2]

Eden's European preoccupations prevented any decisions being taken for the present; but since Churchill was apt to discuss all these matters very freely, many rumours continued to circulate as the date for the Party Conference approached.

It was now the general view of the leading members of the Cabinet that, quite apart from Churchill's own decision as to his future, there should be a large reconstruction of the Government amounting almost to a new administration. After the Cabinet of 1 October, Churchill asked me whether I shared this opinion, I said

22 September 1954.   2 24 September 1954.

I did, whereupon he discussed with me a number of schemes all turning on Eden's acceptance of the position of Deputy Prime Minister and Leader of the House. He outlined the main appointments, which he had in mind. Crookshank, now Leader of the House, was to go to the Home Office. I was to be Foreign Secretary. My only question was whether Eden agreed. I added that I thought the Prime Minister should realise how distressing this constant change of plan had been to Eden. Churchill replied that

> he must try to persuade him. It was clear that [Churchill] is absolutely determined to go on and is not willing to contemplate any definite retirement date.[1]

I certainly felt that this prolonged internal crisis in the Government must be resolved, or we should all get on each other's nerves. Accordingly, on 2 October, I composed a letter to the Prime Minister in the following terms:

> I am grateful to you for taking me into your confidence yesterday. May I do the same?
> I can quite see that there are difficulties about making more sweeping changes in the Government at this moment. But I feel that the most important thing now is Anthony's position. This is vital.
> After all that has happened, I hope you will find it possible to come to a clear and definite arrangement with him about the date of the hand-over.
> He must know this, and have a fair run on his own before the Election. Otherwise I fear we may lose him now, as well as the Election, when it comes.

After the Cabinet on 5 October, Churchill kept me back:

> What did I mean by the last sentence in my letter 'We may lose Anthony and also the Election'? I said that I thought he was thoroughly fed up and would require a clear understanding about the future.[2]

However, Churchill did not seem in any way annoyed. He observed that the date might be sooner rather than later; but he did not wish

---

[1] 1 October 1954.   [2] 5 October 1954.

to bind himself. I answered that I thought nothing mattered except a clear plan. Otherwise there would be continued confusion, inflamed by perpetual rumours in the party and in the Press. Churchill agreed

> that the reconstruction must be settled and announced *next* week—before Parliament met. [He] was very friendly, and rather thoughtful—almost wistful.[1]

I found myself more and more anxious to get something settled.

> It's particularly tiresome to be forced to act as a sort of mediator between Churchill and Eden. I am very fond of them both. If we can get everything settled without a permanent quarrel, it will be a miracle. But it's really very important, for the Party and the country—as well as for our old friendships.[1]

The Party Conference that year was held at Blackpool, and went off pretty well. The Prime Minister spoke for over an hour, and although stumbling occasionally over words, recovered himself with excellent asides and impromptus. The day after we got back I was summoned to Chartwell, where I found Churchill alone. He was in a radiant mood. Everything had been settled in accordance with his wishes. He

> remains P.M. without any commitment, written or verbal, as to date. Eden stays at F.O.; Rab, naturally and properly, at Exchequer. Fyfe replaces Simonds as Lord Chancellor—and a few other changes. I am to be asked to 'supplant' Harry Crookshank as Lord Privy Seal and Leader of the House. He is to be Home Secretary. (As he is my oldest friend, this is pretty difficult.)[2]

I explained to him my difficulty about Crookshank, and Churchill promised to discuss this further with the Chief Whip. Now that the changes had been decided, he was anxious to carry them out quickly.

The next day (11 October) Churchill rang me up and asked me to see Crookshank myself. I said that I would do so, but everything must depend on his willingness to make the change. I would do nothing to supplant so old a friend. Crookshank was quite clear as

[1] 5 October 1954.   [2] 10 October 1954.

to his views. He thought Churchill ought to go, but he could not be 'plus royaliste que le roi' or rather 'que le prince de Galles'. But he did not want to be Home Secretary, nor did he advise me to take on the leadership of the House.

> No one, except the Prime Minister or Deputy Prime Minister of the day, could exercise the leadership of the House in the Victorian sense. It could not be done by him or by me, if we were only fourth or fifth in the hierarchy. So it was better to run it as he had done, as adjutant (as it were) not as Commanding Officer. I said at once that this settled it.[1]

I accordingly telephoned to Churchill, who was still at Chartwell, and said that I could not possibly agree to take Crookshank's place. I would take Defence if he offered it to me. I understood that Eden would like this, as it would give him some help on the NATO and Brussels Treaty work. It would leave Crookshank in a job which he had carried out with conspicuous success. Churchill seemed somewhat put out, but I comforted myself with the thought that he usually recovered quickly.

In addition to all our other preoccupations, September and October were harassing months on the industrial front. There was a dock strike, a newspaper strike, and a threatened railway strike. All these Monckton handled with his usual calm efficiency. But it meant a lot of Cabinet meetings and Cabinet Committees to settle our policy.

The Prime Minister seemed content with the new arrangements:

> Everything is settled, at last. (Of course, it may be unsettled in another hour or two.) [Crookshank] will remain Leader of House and Privy Seal. I will go to Defence. Monckton agrees to stay, at least through the winter. So Lloyd George can be Home Secretary and Minister for Wales. (Very good.) David Maxwell Fyfe to be Lord Chancellor. Eccles to Education . . . Sandys to Ministry of Housing. Selwyn Lloyd to Supply.[2]

I was anxious about the future of Ernest Marples, my admirable Parliamentary Secretary at Housing. He was to go as a Parliamentary Secretary to the Minister of Pensions. Since the Pensions

[1] 11 October 1954.   [2] 12 October 1954.

Bill was to be the main piece of legislation for the coming session, this would be a useful experience.

On 18 October the full list of the new Ministers was published. The inference was generally drawn by the Press and the public that, with such a wide reconstruction of the Government, Churchill's retirement was not likely to come as soon as had been popularly believed.

Meanwhile, the retirement of Lord Simonds and Lord Alexander from the Cabinet deprived us of two most agreeable colleagues. Since Lord Simonds had no political experience and was originally appointed Lord Chancellor by Churchill, because he wished to keep Maxwell Fyfe in the House of Commons, the change was fully justified. The Field-Marshal was not sorry to go, and when he handed over to me seemed relieved by the prospect of escaping from all the complications of a political world in which he was not at ease. The main loss, and it was a serious one, was that of Oliver Lyttelton. He was determined to return to business life, where he had already made an important mark before the war. Nevertheless, his departure was a great grief to me. He was one of my oldest friends from school days. I had watched him at work through all the troubles and vicissitudes of war, as well as during the anxious years of so-called peace. Able, witty and intensely loyal, Lyttelton was a man of marked strength of character who particularly shone at moments of difficulty or crisis. Fortunately my friendship with him was to remain unchanged through all the succeeding years.

That the general public seemed satisfied with the new administration was shown by a by-election at Aldershot, caused by Lyttelton's elevation to the peerage, where there was no change in the percentage of votes cast.

> The two parties seem to remain as they were, neither advancing nor in retreat. It is a curious situation. Even [the Labour Party's] attempt to exploit the Old Age Pension grievance doesn't seem very successful.[1]

In the West Derby division of Liverpool, Maxwell Fyfe's seat, we did even better. The result was

[1] 30 October 1954.

a great triumph for the Government, and a corresponding set-back for the Opposition. They have tried cost of living; they have tried abolition of food subsidies; they have tried rents; they have tried pensions—none of them has proved winners.[1]

Here the Conservative majority had risen from 1,707 to 2,508 on a much reduced poll,

in spite of the new housing estates, which were supposed to be so dangerous. (Perhaps they are going to be a bit grateful for their houses after all!) There is no doubt that it's a great blow to the Socialists, who hoped to win the seat.[1]

In home politics some particular question is always blowing up and tends to assume a disproportionate importance. At this time there was much agitation about the need for increased old-age pensions. Although the Minister, Osbert Peake, was fully in command of the situation, it was not easy to get a complete scheme ready for immediate legislation. The Prime Minister took a special interest in this and was unceasing in his effort to bring matters to a head. After much pressure, the proposals were finally ready by 1 December. I remember one incident during the discussions. The Minister had talked a great deal about the retiring age. Should it remain at sixty-five or should it be advanced to sixty-seven? 'Not compulsory, I suppose?' asked Churchill. 'Well, no man is really fit for work after sixty-seven or sixty-eight,' was the reply. The Prime Minister's face at this was a masterpiece of acting.

Although I was now fully occupied with trying to find my way through the maze of defence problems, Churchill still continued to consult me about his own future. I was now also to see him actually at work other than in the Cabinet. For he presided at meetings of the Defence Committee, and with his unrivalled knowledge and authority took a leading part in all defence discussions. This was to prove a new experience for me, and I fear confirmed my opinion of his failing powers. When I was Minister of Housing I had no difficulty, for he was not interested in the details of my problems and gave me full and loyal support in all that I wanted to do. But now

[1] 19 November 1954.

I saw him at much closer quarters and was saddened by signs of increasing fatigue.

On 1 November he asked me to dine with him alone to discuss the future. By now I was well accustomed to speak or write to him frankly, and I did so again on this occasion. I tried to impress upon him the fact that since the Parliament ought not—according to the normal convention—to go beyond the end of 1955, a General Election must be held in that year. Since he was not prepared, as I understood, to lead the party in any other Parliament, it was essential that his successor should have a free choice as to the date. This was only fair, as the selection of the date might prove of vital importance. In fact, General Elections could only take place in the spring or autumn. For my part I preferred the spring, and in any case Eden should have the chance to choose. This would mean that he must take office in the first months of 1955. Although Churchill at first felt that he could have gone on until the early autumn, I was very insistent on the propriety of leaving the choice of date to the new Prime Minister. In my view the spring was by far the best.

> We should introduce and pass the Pensions Bill in December and January. Then (as soon as the Commonwealth Premiers have left—about February 10th) Churchill should resign; Eden should form a Government . . . and dissolve.[1]

The General Election should be held as soon as possible, and we would have the advantages of strategic initiative and tactical surprise, coupled with the excitement and interest in the change-over. There would be no 'lame-duck' months for Eden; the Pensions Bill would be passed, and any benefits to be expected from the Budget would lie ahead. 'Anticipation,' I claimed, 'in politics as in love, is better than satisfaction.' Churchill seemed attracted by these ideas, which were in effect carried out, but with the difference that the Budget was to be introduced before the actual change of leadership.

Before the end of the month, however, the Press began to take a hand:

> There is a lot of talk in the papers about an early dissolution. The Beaverbrook press is urging Churchill to lead the party in

[1] 1 November 1954.

another Election! Meanwhile, administration gets more and more difficult.[1]

Parliament was opened on 30 November. This had been arranged to coincide with Churchill's eightieth birthday, and it was naturally a wonderful opportunity for expressing the deep affection and admiration of Parliament and the nation.

Just before Christmas there was a meeting of leading Ministers under Churchill's chairmanship, nominally to discuss the date of the General Election. It was rather a painful occasion, since it was impossible to evade the question as to who would lead the party. There now followed a period of indecision and uncertainty in the old man's mind. He seemed unable to reach any decisions. Those who had the deepest affection and respect for him felt equally disinclined to face or postpone this vital issue.

So the year ended; in rather a grim mood, for the foreign scene was still troubled. The Russians had made a further attempt, on 13 November, to prevent the ratification of the Western European Union by proposing a conference of all European countries. The British formal reply, on 29 November, insisted that no talks could be undertaken until after W.E.U. was established. On 9 December the Russians threatened a great increase in armaments in the face of what they called 'emergent German militarism'. The high hopes which had followed the death of Stalin and inspired Churchill's speech of May 1953 seemed to have been temporarily, if not finally, frustrated. Although the South-East Asia Collective Defence Treaty had been signed at Manila in September between the United States, Britain, France, Australia, New Zealand, Pakistan, Thailand and the Philippines, India and Ceylon would not share in this effort. In the Far East the Chinese Communists threatened to attack Chiang Kai-shek's Nationalists in the off-shore islands, Tachen, Matsu and Quemoy, and President Eisenhower thought it necessary to make a formal declaration that Formosa and the nearby Pescadores islands would be defended against any Communist attack. Both in the West, therefore, and the East, the tensions seemed to be mounting. Never had Churchill's unique authority been more needed; but I

[1] 22 November 1954.

could not hide from myself the knowledge that now, as for many months past, he would be incapable of conducting any serious discussion or negotiation with these tough and cynical opponents. He could appeal to sentiment and to the crying needs of humanity; but it still seemed that such an appeal would fall on deaf ears. For the moment the strengthening of our own forces remained the essential preliminary.

At home we were threatened with a railway strike, and in the early days of January the necessary preparations had to be made for the emergency—a Council at Sandringham, the Proclamation and the meeting of Parliament. In my new capacity I had to decide whether to cancel leave for the troops. Fortunately I took a gamble; for after hours of discussion and debate the railway strike was settled at midnight on 6 January by granting an increase of 6s. a week to the lowest-paid railwaymen. This concession was naturally attacked by *The Times*, the *Economist* and the *Manchester Guardian,* who were deeply shocked at what seemed a very bad precedent. There was, however, a good case for these men being allowed to share in the growing prosperity of the nation. What was really disturbing was the feeling that we were being blackmailed during the negotiations. At the same time I did not feel that all the blame was on the one side.

> Compared to the old railway General Managers (Sir James Milne and Co.) the Transport Commission is a very unwieldy and bureaucratic affair. Negotiations drag on for months and months, and things are not improved by so many members of the Commission being ex-trade union leaders—poachers turned gamekeeper.[1]

The economy as a whole was now beginning to fall under considerable pressure, and certain measures would soon become necessary to impose some restraints. This was an example of the application in a mild form of 'Stop and Go'; and since Butler took the necessary steps in time, the result proved good and any serious crisis was avoided. I did not fail to take note of this lesson.

On 7 January I went to see Churchill at his request. I had to

[1] 7 January 1955.

discuss a number of defence problems in which he took a special interest. All through lunch he was very charming. One of the private secretaries made a remark about somebody being popular in his department. Churchill at once replied: 'That means that he gives his subordinates little to do, lets them go early and defends them in all the muddles they make. Give me a man who is unpopular in the service.' He began now to talk about the General Election, and I felt he was trailing his coat, hoping to be contradicted. In any case, since Eden was leaving at the end of February for the Manila Conference and then going on to India, Pakistan and Turkey, there now could be no change of Government until the end of March.

On the following day Lord and Lady Moran came to lunch with me among other guests at Birch Grove House. Moran began to speak about Churchill's health and capacity for work. I thought it right to be frank, and told him that my affection and loyalty to the Prime Minister made me hope that he would stick to his plan of handing over when Eden returned. If he repeated this conversation, it could hardly have been any news to Churchill. For this was the advice which I had given consistently for a considerable period, both orally and in writing.

Yet every visit to Churchill was still a delight. I remember, for instance, being summoned early one morning at about this time by an urgent message. He was in bed with the little green budgerigar sitting on his head. The cage was on his bed, a cigar in his hand, and a whisky and soda was by his side, from which the little bird took sips from time to time. The bird then began to fly about the room, perching sometimes on my shoulder, sometimes on the Prime Minister's head, while all the time Gibbonesque sentences were rolling from the maestro's mouth about the Bomb—the most terrible and destructive engine of mass warfare yet known to mankind. From time to time the bird said a few words in a husky kind of voice like an American actress, and sipped a little whisky. A bizarre but memorable scene.

As the weeks of January went by, the foreign situation did not improve. Towards the end of the month Chou En-lai declared his determination to 'liberate' Formosa. Eisenhower immediately asked the authority of Congress to use the armed forces of the United States to secure and protect Formosa and the Pescadores, and both Houses passed resolutions authorising the President to act. Naturally, in addition to our general concern, the special dangers of Hong Kong were always in our minds. We might hope for United States help; but we knew from bitter experience how indefensible the military position really was. It was indeed fortunate that the Commonwealth Conference began at the end of the month, when the line which the Foreign Secretary was taking was agreed by all concerned. The only encouraging signs appeared to be in Moscow, for it was clear that the Russians did not want a war in the Far East which it might not be possible to limit.

Indeed, both Moscow and London are working (somewhat paradoxically) on the same lines and trying to restrain their friends.[1]

The United States Government decided to help the Chinese Nationalist forces to evacuate the island of Tachen, one of those in dispute. This left Quemoy and Matsu, of no great military significance but of considerable psychological value. These were to continue to present a worrying problem for many years. Although we did not altogether agree with the President's determination, his reply to our suggestion that these also should be evacuated and a stand made only in Formosa and the Pescadores was certainly a powerful, well-argued and persuasive document.

His reasons are (1) that Formosa, if Nationalist morale is destroyed, may fall out of their hands—a useless instrument of defence—if the Chinese attack and internally Chiang collapses. (2) The whole of S.E. Asia will be affected by any more Chinese and Communist advances. (3) It would be a Munich—but even Hitler at Munich promised not to have any more aggression. He did not, in fact, keep his promise. But the Chinese absolutely refuse to make any such promise.[1]

One encouraging aspect of this crisis was that Nehru was friendly and helpful throughout. The British people as a whole neither understood the issue nor seemed unduly alarmed. No doubt the

[1] 31 January 1955.   [2] 22 February 1955.

presence of the Commonwealth Prime Ministers was a steadying influence. This was the last such conference over which Churchill was to preside. If it was his swan-song, it certainly struck a high and noble note.

Early in February dramatic news came to us from Russia:

> The great excitement of the week has been the fall of Malenkov. This typically Russian affair has been staged with the usual melodramatic effects. Malenkov has fallen. But why was he not shot? Because he is brother-in-law to Khrushchev? What weakness! What deviation into bourgeois sentimentality! Well, perhaps he *will* be shot—later on. At present he has been made Minister of Fuel and Power!
>
> But what's it all about?
>
> Malenkov admitted his guilt. He has neglected agriculture. But he had nothing to do with agriculture. That was Khrushchev's job, who now succeeds to the job of boss. It's all very odd.[1]

At the time I did not sufficiently understand the true implications of these changes and the way in which they were brought about. Nor did it ever cross my mind that I was destined to have close contacts with Khrushchev in a few years' time. The significance of course was that the ability to change the leadership without bloodshed marked the end of the Stalin regime. Although Khrushchev, like Stalin, by becoming Secretary of the Party controlled the whole mechanism (Bulganin as Prime Minister had little real authority), he neither wished nor was able to follow the brutal methods of Stalin in dealing with his enemies or rivals.

At this time the work of the Ministry of Defence brought me into frequent contact with Churchill. I felt that he was definitely reconciled to his retirement and consequently, both at Cabinet meetings and in private discussion, he was in a relaxed and even merry mood. There were of course occasional relapses—for instance, during the financial measures which Butler had to take to deal with a slightly overheated economy. Although these were of modest proportions—an increase of 1 per cent in the Bank Rate and some changes in hire-purchase—the Prime Minister persuaded himself

[1] 11 February 1955.

that 'in view of the financial crisis he cannot leave the sinking ship !'[1]

But when I saw him at Chartwell on 26 February, he was in a very mellow mood, charming and paternal. He was anxious to support the Budget as Prime Minister, and I told him that this could easily be arranged by its introduction before the end of March.

[The Prime Minister] said he had in mind April 5th as the day he would tender his resignation. There should be one day's interval to preserve the reality of the Royal prerogative—this he thought very important.[2]

The rest of our discussion was about the speeches which we were to make in the forthcoming debate on defence.

Before the end of this debate, he was stung into an interruption:

He got up and began to tell us about the inner story of his desire to have a top-level meeting with the Russians. I sat next to him on the bench, trembling with anxiety as to what he might say. . . . He began with his talk with Eisenhower; the President's reluctance; and then his own illness—'I was struck down—paralysed.' He 'stroked' his left arm, side and leg with a most moving gesture. The House sat in absolute silence. Then he told the story of [last] summer. How would it end, I thought? All this is 'off the cuff'. . . . Shall we get on to [the difficulties at home]? No; he had slid successfully past these traps. It was Russian intransigence and campaign against E.D.C. which had made him wait. Now we must wait till after the London—Paris agreements have been ratified.[3]

This was one of the most tense scenes which I have witnessed in the House of Commons. If Churchill showed some of the weaknesses of old age, he had not lost the courage of his prime and had added to it something even more effective—the deep sincerity of a man who, knowing his days of power were now numbered, longed to make his final contribution to the safety and happiness of the world.

There now began a strange and unexpected complication in the shape of a newspaper strike, the effect of which was that so far as the ordinary public were concerned a semi-darkness descended upon all those who depended upon the metropolitan Press. On 26 March

[1] 25 February 1955.   [2] 26 February 1955.   [3] 2 March 1955.

all the London weekday and Sunday papers, together with their Manchester and Glasgow editions, were brought to a halt. This dispute was not to be settled until 21 April. During the whole period, therefore, of Churchill's final resignation and the change-over of Government, there was no chance for the public to read the full tributes to his wonderful achievements which would otherwise have been available to them. Every newspaper in the world was publishing the story of Churchill's amazing career and unique services. It seemed a cruel misfortune to befall a man who was not only our greatest states-man but also one of our most distinguished authors and journalists.

On 4 April the Prime Minister gave a dinner party—an historic occasion at which the Queen was present. Since only a few of his Cabinet colleagues were among the guests, I felt much honoured by an invitation.

> Now that he has really decided to go, we are all miserable !
> Happily, we shall forget the last few months (which have been very trying and nerve-racking, especially for Eden) and we shall only remember the greatness and grandeur of this unique man.[1]

After dinner the Prime Minister, in defiance of all precedent, made a speech in proposing the health of the Queen.

Churchill showed me the text of his speech before it was delivered and gave me a copy afterwards. It ran as follows:

> I have the honour of proposing a toast which I used to enjoy drinking during the years when I was a cavalry subaltern in the reign of Your Majesty's great-great grandmother, Queen Victoria. Having served in office or in Parliament under the five sovereigns who have reigned since those days, I felt, with these credentials, that in asking Your Majesty's gracious permission to propose this toast I should not be leading to the creation of a precedent which would often cause inconvenience.
>
> Madam, I should like to express the deep and lively sense of gratitude which we and all your peoples feel to you and to H.R.H. the Duke of Edinburgh for all the help and inspiration we receive in our daily lives, and which spreads with ever growing strength throughout the British realm and the Commonwealth and Empire.

[1] 4 April 1955.

Never have we needed it more than in the anxious and darkling age through which we are passing and through which we hope to help the world to pass.

Never have the august duties which fall upon the British monarchy been discharged with more devotion than in the brilliant opening of Your Majesty's reign. We thank God for the gift he has bestowed upon us, and vow ourselves anew to the sacred cause and wise and kindly way of life of which Your Majesty is the young, gleaming champion.

The Queen, in reply, said that she too wished to do something which few of her predecessors had had an opportunity of doing, and that was to propose the health of her Prime Minister.

This historic occasion was a fitting end to a unique career.

At the last Cabinet meeting the Prime Minister's goodbye was warm and affectionate. He seemed to be quite undisturbed by any of the recent difficulties. Eden answered on behalf of us all. We then trooped upstairs for the photograph to be taken, as is customary, in the big drawing room.

On the same night, 5 April, Churchill had his audience with the Queen, and at noon on 6 April Eden was sent for. When the House met, Attlee made a charming and witty speech with a generous tribute to the greatest Englishman in our history. In congratulating Eden he referred to the well-known story of Melbourne, who, when hesitating to accept the Premiership, was encouraged to do so in the following words:

Why, damn it all, such a position was never held by any Greek or Roman, and if it only lasts three months it will be worth while to have been Prime Minister of England.

In spite of all the excitement over a new Government and a probable General Election, life somehow seemed very flat after Churchill left. Although the last period had been trying and often painful, the memory of this was immediately washed away. When the death of a loved parent or friend comes at last, the final years or months of weakness or suffering or decay are all forgotten, and one's mind goes back at once to the great days, the high qualities, and the splendid character of the man we have lost. So it was with Churchill.

T

We think of him in his prime, not in his decline. Although he was to live on for many more years, this day— 5 April 1955 –marked the end of his political life. All the little trivialities and troubles passed into oblivion. We remembered only the strength and splendour of the man. We remembered, too, the infinite occasions of his grace and charm, the wonderful compensating smile or words of encouragement after long and tedious arguments. We recalled also the supreme days of his career– 1940 to 1945. If we now turned to our new tasks, it was with a sense of duty rather than a sense of exultation, for we knew that we should never see his like again.

There are some critics who declare that Churchill's last decade in politics was a failure, and added little to his reputation. Others go further and say that he should have retired altogether before the election in 1945, at the crest of the wave. The answer to this somewhat morose judgement is simple. It would have been quite out of keeping with Churchill's character to have abandoned his position at the end of the war without a fight. It would have been still more unnatural for him to have retired after an electoral defeat. He was a born fighter, endowed with unrivalled courage and tenacity. Moreover, these ten years were by no means barren. In some respects they were as fruitful as any in his life. There was the Fulton speech in 1946 which led to the aligning of the Western and democratic countries against the advancing menace of Russian aggression. There was the foundation of the European Movement which has led to the recovery of Europe; and if his full plans have not been realised, this does not detract from the breadth and originality of his vision. No Minister out of office has ever had such an effect on foreign policy. At the same time, his conduct of the Opposition gave new life and impetus to the Conservative Party. With the memory of his father among the most impelling motives of his life, he threw his weight in support of the development of progressive Conservatism.

In the four years of his last administration, he brought the country a high degree of economic recovery from the low level to which it had declined by the end of 1951. His favourite slogan, 'Work, Food, Homes', represented a genuine belief that these were the chief needs of the people. His promises were carried out to the letter.

Full employment was maintained without undue inflation; the system of rationing which had lasted all through the Labour Governments was swept away; and houses were built upon a scale which even the most friendly critics believed unattainable. At the same time, he supported his Foreign Minister in many baffling and complicated negotiations, some of which brought to a final close many difficult problems and all of which tended towards general pacification. His last service was to have the vision to realise that the Soviet monolith would itself begin to undergo changes inseparable from growth and the lapse of time. Although he was not able to see his dreams fulfilled, he nevertheless set the Western statesmen on a path which they have subsequently pursued. Not merely 'peaceful co-existence' but something like a genuine détente has been brought about by those who followed in the trail which he had blazed.

CHAPTER XVII

The Nuclear Shadow

MY period at the Ministry of Defence, from October 1954 to April 1955, was somewhat frustrating. From my knowledge of Churchill's intentions I knew that it was unlikely that I should be in the same post for more than a few months. I was reminded of my position in the summer of 1945 when I had been Secretary of State for Air in the so-called 'Caretaker' Government. Nevertheless, there was plenty to do.

I was soon to realise how greatly different was the Ministry of Defence from the Ministry of Housing.

> This new Ministry of mine is a queer kind of affair. I have no power; yet I am responsible for everything—especially if it goes wrong. The P.M. is always busy about defence affairs—on Wednesday the defence committee sat under his chairmanship for nearly six hours. (It's true that it could all have been done in 20 minutes.) When I ask for a small meeting with the Service Ministers, about 40 or 50 people turn up![1]

The fundamental flaw of the Ministry was soon clear to me. In any case, within a fortnight I had a visit from Lord Montgomery, whose conversation was as usual refreshing and stimulating.

> He, of course, has spotted the real weakness of our defence set-up. The Minister has no power and the Chiefs of Staff need a professional head. But all this could not be altered without legislation. I must do my best with the instrument I have.[2]

The title of Minister of Defence had been assumed by Churchill in May 1940; but he was a Minister without a Ministry. He was content with the small group of 'planners' who operated under Lord Ismay. In war, a Prime Minister can take the leading role in

[1] 29 October 1954.   [2] 8 November 1954.

strategic and sometimes even in tactical decisions. At any rate, with his unrivalled experience and in the desperate situation in which the country found itself, Churchill had little difficulty in carrying out his task through the professional chiefs of the three Services. The First Sea Lord, the C.I.G.S. and the Chief of Air Staff met him almost daily, and the vital decisions were taken by a body in which the ministerial heads of the Service departments played only a minor role. Again, the Prime Minister devoted himself largely, though by no means exclusively, to the needs of war. Many important aspects of the home front were controlled by committees under the Lord President or other Ministers.

When the war ended, a more normal system was revived. At the same time, a Ministry of Defence was set up by Act of Parliament. A. V. Alexander—afterwards Lord Alexander ('the one that runs the Co-ops, not the one that wins the battles', as Churchill mischievously observed)—was appointed to the post and a department on the usual pattern was set up to support him. Nevertheless, the constitutional responsibility of the three Service Ministers, whether statutory or traditional, remained unchanged. Both under Alexander and under his successors there was no clear frontier drawn between the powers of the Minister of Defence and those of the First Lord and the Secretaries of State. It was not clear whether they were equal or subordinate. Each certainly claimed that, with their separate accounting officers responsible to Parliament and their duties laid down by statute, they had full independence. The Minister of Defence was 'a co-ordinator, not a master'.

Nor was the peace-time position of the Prime Minister altogether clear. The Defence Committee, the only Cabinet Committee of which Parliament and the public were at this period officially informed, had no fixed membership or functions. Churchill, of course, took a personal, almost passionate, interest in the major problems. But at such meetings, which the Service Ministers normally attended each accompanied by his Chief of Staff, the position of the Minister of Defence became somewhat ambiguous. In the normal course of discussion, the Prime Minister as chairman naturally turned to the Service Ministers or to the admirals, generals and air marshals concerned for comment or advice. Thus, while authority nominally resided in the Minister of Defence, unless this post was combined with the Premiership effective power still remained with the Service Ministers and their professional advisers. In later years, when I became Prime Minister, I was determined to remedy the inherent weakness of the system. I made many tentative approaches, always to come up against strong and sometimes emotional resistance. It was not until almost the end of my term as Prime Minister that I was able with the help of Peter Thorneycroft and Lord Mountbatten to bring about a reorganisation of the whole structure by which a real unity of the Services could be created, at any rate at the top.

Meanwhile, I had to operate with the instrument available. The Permanent Secretary of the Ministry, Sir Harold Parker, was an experienced administrator who seemed aware of the difficulties and anomalies. The Deputy Secretary, Sir Richard Powell, was a man of exceptional ability who subsequently rose to the highest posts in the Civil Service and after his retirement made his mark in finance and industry. The chief military adviser, General Brownjohn, was a universal favourite and a skilled negotiator. But it was something of a shock to move from the Ministry of Housing, where, subject to the need to avoid or evade the Treasury watchdog, we were in full control of our affairs. I was now to find myself enjoying only vague and indeterminate powers. Above me was a Prime Minister who probably knew more of the theory and practice of war than any living man; below me and nominally under my guidance were three powerful Service departments with their long and cherished traditions and fortified by the victorious outcome of the greatest war in history. In addition, there were several other Ministries concerned. The most important was the Ministry of Supply, which was responsible for most of the vital armaments on which defence depended. There was also the Home Office, with which we had to deal on Civil Defence, and the Ministry of Labour on the use of manpower and the period of service. I found my chief support in our Scientific Adviser, Sir Frederick Brundrett, who combined immense knowledge with a quiet sense of humour. I remember a discussion towards the end of November on the question of the replacement of a particular and vital weapon. Discussion about this had lasted for four years; it would be at least five or six years before this replacement could be ready. Since no one seemed to have any very clear idea of what it was for, after a very long and well-attended meeting we decided to recommend against it altogether. Sir Frederick came up to me afterwards full of congratulations and observed that it was almost the first decision he had known to be taken during his service in the Ministry.

The immediate task before me, however, lay rather in the diplomatic than in the technical field. It is difficult even now to recall the mood of those years. The breakdown of the old war alliance and the Russian threat had concentrated professional as well as amateur thought upon the need for organisation in defence of the West and the acceptance that any major war would inevitably be preceded or accompanied by a nuclear duel between the Great Powers on both sides. Hence the importance of a rapid solution of the problem of the European contribution to NATO, only recently resolved by Eden's efforts and still awaiting formal ratification. Hence, too, the urgent need for German rearmament. Equally important was the need to ensure that the restored and buoyant economy of Germany should bear its fair share of the cost of defence.

Accordingly, three days after my appointment, I was instructed to leave for Paris to attend meetings in connection with NATO. In this organisation the Foreign Ministers were the chief representatives of each nation and formed its governing committee. But Ministers of Defence were expected to attend and allowed to play a modest part.

It was my first experience of the new diplomacy. On arriving in Paris with Sir Harold Parker and my private secretary, I went immediately to the Embassy over which Sir Gladwyn Jebb presided with a remarkable combination of hospitality and skill. I found Eden there, and was able to congratulate him on the Garter which he had been awarded the day previously by the Queen. This was a well-deserved tribute to the efforts he had made to save European unity in these agonising conflicts over defence. Everything had now been settled except the future of the Saar.[1] On this the French

---

[1] Since the defeat of Germany, France had had overall responsibility for the Saar, though an agreement signed in 1950 between France and the Saar had given legislative,

naturally saw the chance of driving a hard bargain. But if this difficulty could be overcome, only the formal signing of letters, declarations, protocols, resolutions and treaties would be necessary.

> As usual, there is an immense documentation—but it need not trouble me! Or anyone else, now, if the Saar is settled. That's the question. Lunched at L'Hôtel Matignon—a party given by Mendès-France. A lot of old friends were there—Massigli, Parodi (head of Quai d'Orsay), Margerie (Directeur Politique). I was next to M. Bech (Luxembourg)—a great character.[1]

Everyone seemed in a state of considerable agitation, and our host, Mendès-France, was very late, having just held a protracted meeting of his colleagues:

> According to reports, leaked purposely or inadvertently, the Cabinet is taking a very stiff line. If the French cannot get satisfaction over the Saar, they will bring down the whole fabric of Western European Union, the Germans in NATO, and all the rest. It's hard to say how much of all this is serious and how much is bluff.[1]

This was not my first experience of the methods of French diplomacy, nor was it my last. There seemed to be little difference between Algiers and Paris.

We then went to the formal meeting of the NATO assembly at the Palais de Chaillot. The hour announced was nominally 3.15, and by four o'clock it began to get going. These new international gatherings struck me as very curious affairs. But no doubt the Congresses of Vienna and Versailles were not altogether dissimilar, at any rate in the numbers of people who drifted like moths to the international candle. The first session was one of the Nine Powers[2] and was held in a comparatively small room; only about a hundred people were present. The necessary formal resolutions were passed and a number of documents signed. We then went off to a much larger hall:

---

administrative and juridical autonomy to the Saarlanders pending final settlement in a peace treaty. The Saar mines were managed by France, and there was an economic union of the two countries.

[1] 22 October 1954.   [2] See above, p. 482.

Here 14 Foreign Secretaries were assembled round a sort of rectangular stadium. There were 14 Defence Ministers and about 300–400 other people—experts and advisers, as well as the Secretariat of NATO, with Pug Ismay,[1] beaming and genial as ever. Mr. Stephanopoulos is president of NATO for the year. Since he seemed deaf, blind and terribly nervous, this tended to lengthen the proceedings.[2]

There were the usual adjournments for resolutions to be framed and the communiqué prepared. But all was plain sailing, and in spite of the *longueurs* and the almost intolerable heat, it was an impressive ceremony made all the more dramatic by the presence of Dr. Adenauer and the Germans as observers, although not yet as members, and by the backstage negotiations on agreements, proposals and counter-proposals by those concerned and those not directly concerned about the Saar.

Eden thought it better not to intervene at this stage, although Dulles seemed anxious to take a hand. But since Mendès-France and Adenauer are both dining at the British Embassy, it was thought something might be done after dinner.[2]

All this was rather a new world to me after recent years confined to houses, rents and repairs. But I had seen something of the same atmosphere at Strasbourg—with the difference that Strasbourg was a gathering of amateurs without power. Here professionals were making decisions which might affect the future of the world. On the next day, it appeared

that quite a lot *did* happen after dinner at the British Embassy. The French Prime Minister and the German Chancellor were left in the library after dinner alone. 'Experts' were available in various other rooms. Neither Dulles nor Eden took any part. When the conference broke up at about 2 a.m. it was clear that great progress had been made.[3]

As a result of all this activity,

The Germans and the French came to terms over the Saar and

[1] General Lord Ismay, Secretary-General of NATO, 1952–57.
[2] 22 October 1954.   [3] 23 October 1954.

the full series of agreements were signed at the Quai d'Orsay; the NATO agreement at the Palais de Chaillot.[1]

This was a proud moment for Britain. The federal solution of European unity, of which E.D.C. was the supreme example, was dead, the confederal concept represented by Western European Union was very much alive. Out of this maze of confusion Britain had guided Europe.

At this time nuclear power had to be accepted as the main, and indeed in the present state of NATO's organisation the only, effective deterrent against aggression by the Soviet Government. Apart from the immediate consequences of this strategic concept, many urgent questions had to be resolved. It was, of course, the purpose of NATO to raise as rapidly as possible large armies mainly armed with conventional weapons. But since the necessary agreements had only recently been signed, and the process of German rearmament would take some time to achieve, little more could be done than to organise as effectively as possible a sub-structure for supply, a system of command, and the best tactical plan that could be evolved for such ground troops and air forces as were in being to resist any attack. But everyone knew in their hearts that it was upon the nuclear power of the United States, supported by that of Britain as it developed, that such resistance must depend. In this field there was still a serious lack of co-ordination between Britain and America, and even duplication of effort. In the interests of security— or perhaps of commerce—Congress had, in August 1946, passed the McMahon Act, thus depriving us of the full knowledge of American nuclear development which we had enjoyed under the agreement made between Churchill and Roosevelt during the war. I was able at a much later stage to remove this impediment. Moreover, no arrangements had yet been made to specify which enemy targets, especially those most important to the United Kingdom, would be dealt with immediately by American bombers.

But there now arose an even more intricate and embarrassing question: by whose authority and by what machinery would the

[1] 24 October 1954. The Saar agreement, highly favourable to the French, included provision for a referendum on the proposed Saar Statute. It was held in October 1955 and resulted in overwhelming rejection of the Statute.

nuclear power be used? If it was to be an effective deterrent, its credibility must above all be sustained. The Soviet Government must be certain that its use would be rapid as well as effective. There was a further complication:

> I fear that the public will be rather alarmed to discover that we really cannot fight any war *except* a nuclear war. It is quite impossible to arm our forces with *two* sets of weapons—conventional and unconventional. The Air Force and, in course of time, the Army will be largely equipped with nuclear weapons of one sort and another. This means that if the Russians attacked . . . with conventional weapons only, in the first instance, we should be forced into the position of *starting* the nuclear war, with all that is implied—including the counter-attack on U.K. From a purely military point of view, there is no way out. We should be utterly crushed in a conventional war. But, politically, it is full of danger, at home and abroad, and may lead to a fresh outburst of defeatism or neutralism.[1]

Much debate was destined to revolve round the directive which was to be settled in Paris at the NATO meeting in the middle of December. I was anxious that we should get some discussions with the Americans and the Canadians before this took place; but the time proved too short to make much progress. The difficulty of any directive was that it seemed calculated to tell officers what they were not to do except in real war, without informing them how they were to recognise war. Perhaps it was like the elephant—difficult to define, but you knew it when you saw it. A further problem arose. The Supreme Allied Commander, Europe (SACEUR), whoever he might be, was only in charge of those forces allocated to his command. This altogether excluded the American Strategic Air Force. I described this difficulty as follows:

> 1. Where their Strategic Air Force is to start from Great Britain they can only do it with our consent. (I don't know what arrangements they have with other countries like Spain.)
> 2. Where they start off on their own they need not ask anyone but themselves. However, they have indicated that they will not act without some consultation with their leading Allies.

[1] 25 November 1954.

When I got to Paris, a meeting was arranged in the morning of 16 December at the Embassy with Dulles and his team and with 'Mike' Pearson, Canadian Minister for External Affairs. Eden was in charge and mine was in the main a silent role. The NATO committee had produced a paper requiring that plans should be prepared on the basis of using atomic and thermonuclear weapons in the case of a Russian attack. This had caused much talk in the Press and in the Parliaments of the NATO countries. Doubts and anxieties had been increased as a result of a lecture recently given by Field-Marshal Lord Montgomery, who had emphasised the weakness of our situation in conventional arms. As a result of our talks in London, we had prepared our own formula for the directive. The Americans had ready a different one, which suited us better and was safer politically than our draft. Planning on a nuclear basis was agreed, but the right of Governments to make the final decisions as to the use of such plans was reaffirmed.

This did not deal with the problem of a sudden all-out attack—the so-called 'bolt from the blue'—nor was it possible to do so. In such a case our reply must be immediate, almost automatic. This would in effect depend almost entirely upon the United States. However, the formula seemed to suit us politically, and we accordingly went along to the conference at the Élysée Palace, where Mendès-France agreed to our proposal. On the military issues all was plain sailing. But the French Prime Minister raised once more the question of the Saar:

> On this he put up a really brilliant piece of cross-examination (there was no other word for it) first of Dulles and then—to a lesser degree—of Eden. The Americans [had given the French]—at different times and by different mouths—very complete assurances both for the period before the Peace Treaty (whenever that may be) and for the Peace Treaty itself. We had done (through Bevin) something of the same [kind], although Marshall and Acheson were more precise.[1]

Both Eden and Dulles regretted that their predecessors had gone so far, and this Mendès-France knew.

[1] 16 December 1954.

THE NUCLEAR SHADOW 569

He was well documented (better than we were) and pushed his points quietly, but relentlessly. It was a perfect performance, and both Americans and British were very embarrassed.[1]

This was good debating, but not perhaps very good diplomacy, for it annoyed both Dulles and Eden.

The next day the NATO meeting took place in the morning. The scene was much the same as before—nominally three Ministers from each country and the secretariat; in fact several hundreds present in the great hall. In the restricted meetings, the supporters are supposed to be cut down to two or three per country, nevertheless there seemed to be a large number who had stayed to join the throng. The business had been well prepared, and there was no difficulty in getting agreement to the various items.

In the afternoon we all made speeches from three o'clock onwards. I had been informed that I had to say something on the contributions to be made by Britain. I ventured to put forward one point which had struck me as a new recruit:

It's *not* now a short, sharp, or intensified effort that we have to make. It's a long, grim, and determined struggle. It's not just an all-out sprint—it's a kind of marathon race upon which we are engaged, and we need therefore every weapon in our collective armoury—economic, political, psychological, as well as the technical instruments of modern warfare. Indeed, in this contest of wills, it will be the moral and spiritual qualities which will count, as well as the material.

I went on to say that in my opinion it was wrong to argue that

these new weapons, revolutionary as they are, have lessened the chances of peace. On the contrary, I believe they have enormously increased them by adding so greatly to the power of the deterrent.

As regards my own country, I had to emphasise our contribution both to the deterrent and conventional forces and to call attention to the fact that

[1] 16 December 1954.

the U.K. has recently entered into fresh and unprecedented commitments by the London and Paris Agreements. Alone of the NATO Powers, our island people have made a binding contract with the continent covering 50 years – two whole generations.

All this would mean additional burdens in foreign currency, and the maintenance of our economy on a sound basis was therefore as important a contribution as any other. This speech seemed well enough received.

On the following day, 18 December, there was a luncheon at the Hôtel Matignon, followed by a lengthy talk between Mendès-France, Dulles and Eden.

> The first subject was the Saar. Mendès-France bargained for a very long time about the letter of support he was to get from the American Government for the period *up* to the Peace Treaty. He got what he wanted, by dropping his claim for the second period. But the Peace Treaty . . . seems like the Greek Kalends.[1]

When I got home, our first task was to consider what deductions were to be drawn from the accepted strategic concept. In view of the difficulties about the new 'generations' of aircraft and other weapons, two decisions were soon taken. The Anti-Aircraft Command would be abolished. There was no role that it could play at the present time with conventional artillery. The Auxiliary Air Squadrons would have to be reduced, owing to the complexity of modern military aircraft. Both these decisions were announced in the debate on the Address, and were well received by the Press. The Prime Minister had already told Attlee, who entirely approved, about the abolition of Anti-Aircraft Command. But there was also now a new horror which for the first time came to the general attention of those in Whitehall and began to leak through to the Press. This was connected with the question of 'fall-out', not merely if these terrible weapons were used in war, but to a minor and not negligible degree in H-bomb tests. Early in December I had to tell the Cabinet that the main facts were available to departments and could not long be concealed from the public. A new system of Civil Defence would

[1] 18 December 1954

have to be developed, to be much more mobile and more highly trained. We should try to agree with the Americans upon a fresh presentation. Although some progress was made during the next few weeks, this matter was left to be formally presented in the Defence White Paper and discussed in the defence debate.

Almost at the end of my time at the Ministry one final point arose on the use of nuclear weapons. There was now being added to the vast power of the atomic bombs, whether launched by the Strategic Air Force or Tactical Air Force or later to be delivered by rockets, a whole range of smaller and more precise nuclear weapons. During March 1955, Eisenhower and Dulles had publicly advanced the thesis that a clear distinction could be drawn between the large thermonuclear bombs upon the one hand and these smaller weapons upon the other. We had been invited to take suitable opportunities to emphasise the technical and moral justification for the use of 'tactical' nuclear arms. Our Chiefs of Staff were clearly of an opinion that there was no purpose in this, nor was it even true that the smaller explosions produced no fall-out. The suggestion which Dulles had made that these could be used in the framework of conventional armaments and only against 'military targets' would lead merely to the old and sterile argument as to what was meant by this expression.

Eden and I proposed a firm line in opposition to the American argument. In our view, even if it were possible scientifically and militarily to draw the suggested distinction between small and large nuclear weapons, there were grave objections to doing so. The possession by the West of a stock of nuclear weapons of all kinds and the ability to deliver them was the most important factor in achieving our aim of preventing war. An attempt to divide them into those which were small and therefore morally justifiable and those which were large and therefore immoral would inevitably reduce their deterrent value as a whole. It would be fatal to give the impression that so long as no hydrogen bomb was dropped on Allied territory, none would be used against Russia, or that the only likely victims of nuclear weapons in a new global war would be the armed forces and not the civilian populations or centres of government and industry. Moreover, for the deterrent to achieve its maximum effect, the

Russians must be left in no doubt that the use against the West of any of their nuclear weapons would immediately bring upon them retaliation from the whole Allied armoury. The proposed distinction was impossible—no dividing line could be drawn. If it were possible it would be dangerous, for it reduced the only value that lay in the horrible engines produced from the arsenals of modern science. Although this discussion was to continue in a desultory form, our arguments were conclusive.

Apart from these grave problems, which formed the principle cause of concern to all those connected with defence, I had begun to realise the almost equal significance of the 'Cold War', especially when directed against our colonial possessions.

The paradoxical effect of the emerging balance of nuclear power was, it seemed to me, that the risk of a major war would continue to recede as its character grew more devastating, but the corollary was that the 'Cold War' would continue for a long time at its current tempo and perhaps indeed be intensified. I felt that during the next few years our Colonial Empire in its varying stages of development would probably be a vital 'Cold War' battleground. If we were defeated there, much of our effort in Western Europe would be wasted. Trouble in the Colonial Empire might be inspired by the Communists. Alternatively they might exploit unrest which stemmed from other sources, such as nationalism or even tribalism.

To meet this threat the first essential was good intelligence.

> No one is wholly responsible—it's partly Defence, partly Colonial Office, partly Foreign Office. There's no central anti-Communist organisation with any drive in it. 'Cold War' alarms me more than 'Hot war'. For we are not really winning it, and the Russians have a central position . . . and a well-directed effort, with strong representation (through the Communist party) in every country.[1]

We had been taken by surprise both in Malaya and Kenya. We must be forewarned if we were to be forearmed. Although I knew that there would be the usual departmental resistance, I felt that with so broad-minded a Colonial Secretary as Alan Lennox-Boyd it

[1] 30 November 1954.

ought to be possible to make progress in this field. I asked for authority to have these questions examined by a small committee of Ministers. My idea was to form a committee with Lord Swinton, whose great experience on these matters was universally respected, as chairman, and that I should try to persuade General Templer to act as director of the operation. I felt that only by entrusting the enquiry and the duty of making recommendations to a single man could we hope to succeed. The Cabinet quickly agreed, and by 17 January I was able to offer the task of reporting on colonial security and intelligence to this distinguished officer. He accepted at once. I had not met General Templer before and was deeply impressed:

> He is certainly a remarkable figure—a bundle of nerves yet a strong character; very sure yet modest.[1]

His directive was quickly agreed, and it was arranged that he should make his full report by 1 May. In view of the nature of the work, we were anxious to avoid a public announcement, but by the middle of March the newspapers had got hold of the fact that the General was working for us. A statement had therefore to be put out in as innocuous a form as possible. Although my change of post was to bring to an end this official association with the General, I was fortunately able to see much of him when he became C.I.G.S. He belongs to a small but select body of men of first-class brains, imbued with a passionate devotion to the Crown, the fighting Services, and the nation.

One of our main ambitious was then, as it has been since, to reduce our military commitments abroad and build up a strategic force at home. But with the undertaking to keep large forces in Germany, together with the new dangers in the Far East, it was difficult to see from where the relief could come. The Hong Kong garrison could scarcely be run down, nor could we withdraw prematurely from Malaya. The Far Eastern conflict had to be handled with special delicacy for two reasons. America's relations with the Chinese Nationalists were a source of continual anxiety to us. In addition, we had to be specially considerate of the anxiety of Australia and New Zealand dating from the Singapore disaster

---

[1] 17 January 1955.

of 1942. The recent signing of the SEATO pact had increased rather than reduced our obligations. The approaching conference of Commonwealth Prime Ministers was to afford an opportunity for frank discussion of all these difficulties.

One of the main reasons why Churchill had agreed to the Egyptian Treaty was his desire to release the troops who were immobilised in that area. Yet even these could not be withdrawn too swiftly without affecting the morale of the civilian contractors, who had undertaken the care of the installations of our base. At the same time it was accepted that in the case of such a disaster as a third world conflict, there could be no question of slowly building up large forces at Cairo or Alexandria as in the last war. A brigade flown rapidly to the Gulf would be of much greater value.

We had at this period large forces under arms. It seems strange now to recall that in 1954 over 800,000 men were serving in the Navy, Army and Air Force, of whom some 300,000 were National Servicemen. These were backed by reserve and auxiliary forces of over 600,000. The two years' National Service remained in force, although this method of maintaining distant garrisons was becoming more and more expensive. We could not yet see much likelihood of filling our needs, even if these were substantially reduced by voluntary enlistment. In addition, the problems of Civil Defence had to be faced and resolved in the light of the new nuclear danger. Finally, the weapons and armaments, conventional and unconventional, of all three forces had to be provided and the necessary plans had to be made for the new forms of weapons—guided missiles and the like. All this had to be done within a limit which the Chancellor of the Exchequer had set at £1,525 million for 1955–56, without allowing for the costs of British forces in Germany, which it was still hoped to recover in whole or in part.

One useful agreement during my term of office was in hand for the future of the Simonstown base. This package deal, which would enable us both to use the base in time of war and to sell a considerable quantity of major arms to South Africa, raised some doubts in the Admiralty. But Lord Swinton, in whose judgement I had great confidence, strongly supported it. Although there were certain political dangers, from the Right as 'another surrender' and from the Left as an immoral compact with the 'reactionary' South Africans, this solution stood the test for more than thirteen years until it was wantonly jeopardised by our Labour successors.

My part in the 1955 Commonwealth Conference on these great issues was naturally small, although on 2 February I had to open a session with an exposé of the broad strategic results of the thermonuclear weapons in the Hot War and in the Cold War. A draft of the Defence White Paper was by now available and was given privately to our Commonwealth colleagues. But fortunately for me, the main responsibility fell on the Prime Minister, who carried out his task in a masterly manner—a wonderful performance for his age. It was at this conference that our decisions to manufacture the thermonuclear or hydrogen bomb were first announced. Much of our subsequent discussion turned on the new and revolutionary concepts in Commonwealth defence which this decision entailed.

It was quite impossible for me before the publication of the new White Paper to do more than concentrate upon the main issues requiring immediate decisions. I was able to settle its general character early in January; and the major question that then remained was how to deal with the aircraft programme. On the bomber side we were in a good position; but the fighters were in a sad state of confusion. The simplest method appeared to be to come out with a frank statement of the facts and to do this in a separate document to be published in addition to the normal Defence White Paper. Our predecessors had ordered two types of fighter aircraft—the Hunters and the Swifts. Marks 1, 2, and 3 of the latter had proved failures, and there was nothing to be done but announce their rejection. We had little real faith in Marks 4 and 6, but further tests were being made. Marks 5 and 7 might perhaps be good enough for certain specialised roles. Both these types were put into production in 1950–51 almost from the drawing-board. While this policy had proved successful before the war with the comparatively simple aeroplanes of the day—the Spitfire and the like—this step, although no doubt justified by the situation at the time of the Korean War, had proved only partially successful. Painful as the decision was, we must abandon the Swift and put our faith in the Hunter, which was already proving a successful aeroplane of the most modern type. This aircraft White Paper was approved by the Prime Minister in February, and on the whole the Press was not unduly critical. Some of their correspondents no doubt felt cheated and wanted a dramatic scandal. But the Opposition were naturally not anxious to press the issue too hard, since the original decisions had rested with the Labour Government. At the same time as the Swift decisions were announced, we arranged to go ahead with 'Blue Sky', the first air-to-air missile. All this was an unhappy introduction to what has proved for successive Governments one of the most baffling of the many problems in the production of modern weapons. We must now accept that there must be failures as well as successes, disappointments as well as realised hopes. This has been true even in the United States with their immense resources. The more advanced and the more sophisticated these engines of war become, the greater the risks. Moreover, the long period between the beginning of research and development and ultimate production makes all estimates of costs almost worthless.

Overwhelmed with the difficulty of making our own weapons, some of which were of doubtful value, I had now to ask the Cabinet to purchase from the United States a ground-to-ground missile known as 'Corporal'. This was a guided missile with an atomic warhead. Its range was up to seventy-five miles. It was therefore known as a tactical weapon. The purpose of adopting this American invention was twofold: to promote co-operation with the Americans in weapons research, and to avoid overloading our own programme. We ordered eight sets of ground equipment and eleven missiles, to cost £9½ million over a period of three years. So far as we could then foresee, this was the only way of ensuring that our troops could obtain atomic artillery support before 1965. It was clear that we could hardly leave our forces in Germany without such additions to their armoury, when they were available to American and probably to German units.

In spite of all these varied activities, my chief effort was directed to drafting and securing the approval of the Prime Minister and the Cabinet to the main Defence White Paper. Naturally, public attention was largely concentrated on the momentous announcement of the Government's decision to produce the hydrogen bomb. By publishing this paper a few days after that on aircraft we succeeded in separating minor, although important, issues from these tremendous decisions, which in spite of all criticisms have so far been maintained by all succeeding administrations.

For me, perhaps the most absorbing experience was working with Churchill in connection with the two-day debate on defence in February 1955. The normal practice is for the Minister of Defence to speak first and defend the White Paper, which is presented to Parliament in his name. Churchill wished to reverse this procedure.

He was very apologetic for speaking first on Tuesday. He felt he must do so. It might be his last big speech; and since he had taken the burden of responsibility on himself about the hydrogen bomb, he should open the debate. He also did not feel up to sitting through the debate and intervening later on.[1]

In the belief that I should be opening, I had prepared my speech and sent him the draft. He had read it and liked it very much.

He had read every word of it—he repeated this several times and seemed to regard it as a great feat.[1]

He wished me to begin the second day, but I felt that this would not do. The Minister of Supply should do this, dealing with the aircraft difficulties, and I should wind up. Churchill then showed me his speech, in which there were some splendid passages but one fatal flaw:

Almost at the beginning, he throws doubt on the practicability of *any* disarmament plan because enough of the plutonium stuff can be . . . hidden away from inspectors to blow up most of the world.[1]

I told him that if he put this point with all its implications and its news value at the beginning, no one would listen to the rest of his speech. Moreover, he must not in his last Parliamentary oration seem to destroy the main hope of the world—disarmament. He agreed to this at once; but when I saw the draft the next day it still

[1] 26 February 1955.

contained this very defeatist passage on the impossibility of any form of disarmament in the nuclear field. I accordingly wrote a minute and with the help of his private secretaries the amendments were finally made. On the morning of the debate I was summoned at 9 a.m. and the whole speech was gone through at length, with all the usual accompaniments which made such sessions quaint and memorable.

Churchill's speech, the last major oration which he was to deliver in the House of Commons, made a deep impression. Largely devoted to the story of the atomic and hydrogen bomb, it was noble in tone and temper. He moved his audience with the depth of his conviction. While admitting that there was no defence against nuclear weapons, he believed that it was our duty, and the duty of the free world, to maintain them as the major deterrent against a third world war. Thus, in due course, the deterrent might well prove the road to disarmament.

There were two fine passages which are well worth recalling, the first early in the speech and the second in the peroration:

> What ought we to do? Which way shall we turn to save our lives and the future of the world? It does not matter so much to old people; they are going soon anyway, but I find it poignant to look at youth in all its activity and ardour and, most of all, to watch little children playing their merry games, and wonder what would lie before them if God wearied of mankind.[1]

These were his final words:

> ... there is time and hope if we combine patience and courage. All deterrents will improve and gain authority during the next ten years. By that time, the deterrent may well reach its acme and reap its final reward. The day may dawn when fair play, love for one's fellow men, respect for justice and freedom, will enable tormented generations to march forth serene and triumphant from the hideous epoch in which we have to dwell. Meanwhile, never flinch, never weary, never despair.[1]

The Opposition amendment had carefully refrained from questioning the Government's decision to manufacture the hydrogen

[1] *Hansard*, 1 March 1955.

bomb. Indeed, a few weeks before the publication of the Defence White Paper, Attlee had told his followers that it was essential for the defence of Britain. Shinwell, who opened the debate after the Prime Minister, was thus in some difficulty, for the Opposition amendment took broadly the line that while they censured our methods they agreed with our policy.

The debate which followed was well conducted on both sides:

> Healey (the [Labour] right-wing foreign affairs specialist) got terribly tangled up trying to be too clever and played straight into the hands of Bevan. Martin Lindsay, Conservative, fell into the same trap—we ought to state clearly what things an aggressor could not do without starting nuclear war. He did not seem to realise that this would lead to giving him everything else on a plate.[1]

I was impressed by the clarity with which this dilemma emerged in our discussion. It was indeed important not to tie ourselves up with over-elaborate formulae and directives to our commanders.

On the second day, after an attempt by John Strachey to bring all the Labour Party together under a single umbrella, to which Selwyn Lloyd replied with remarkable skill, the feature of the debate was Bevan's intervention:

> I thought it the ablest I have heard him make. He attacked Churchill violently. He had one good and telling phrase: 'The magnificence of his language serves to conceal the mediocrity of his thought' (a fair hit). All this preliminary tactical exercise—great praise for Strachey and Shinwell, with great attack on Tories—succeeded rather too well. For (as soon appeared) it was not [its] real purpose.[2]

Bevan soon stung Churchill into an interruption of deep personal interest, but not wholly relevant to the argument, which was now developing, on the use of nuclear weapons.[3] After this digression, which Bevan had not expected, the inherent interest and tense character of which made it difficult to pick up the thread of his own speech, he very skilfully began to reveal his real purpose:

> He associated himself with Shinwell in the point about 'should we use nuclear warfare if they didn't?' What did paragraph

[1] 1 March 1955.   [2] 2 March 1955.   [3] See above, p. 555.

22 of the White Paper mean about defending ourselves with nuclear against Russian conventional superiority? He had supported the bomb as a deterrent. He would support its use if the enemy began it. But this was something he and his friends could not support. If the Labour motion really meant this, he and his friends must abstain. Would Attlee give his interpretation? Would he answer this question? On his answer must depend their decision.[1]

I had some difficulty in preventing Churchill from giving the answer himself, a course which would have been greatly to Attlee's relief and enabled him to keep his party together. However, I was able to prevent the Prime Minister from saying more than 'My right hon. Friend the Minister of Defence will refer to this point tonight when he winds up the debate.'

'Why not now,' cried the loyal Attleeites, hoping to be helpful. I got up and said I thought it would be more courteous on my part to wait until Mr. Attlee had spoken. So Bevan resumed his speech.[1]

It was now obvious that the debate, intended by Attlee to demonstrate the unity of the party, would end up in a shattering display of disunity and confusion. But he did his best and did not answer the questions raised by Bevan. The Shadow Cabinet had apparently met during the evening but had failed to reach agreement. He therefore contented himself with saying nothing at all, certainly nothing appropriate to a vote of censure.

When Attlee sat down, the Speaker called on me. So I made a gesture of rising, but as slowly as possible,

so as to give time to Bevan to get up, which he did. Peremptorily, and offensively (seeing that he was parading so openly this quarrel inside the party), he asked Attlee to reply categorically to his question. He shuffled and hedged: 'I was speaking in general terms.' Bevan, with a sarcastic gesture, threw up his hands.[1]

Although the House, or at least the Opposition, were somewhat excited, it was not difficult to make the point that it was impossible for any Government to tie themselves down to precise answers to

[1] 2 March 1955.

hypothetical questions as to the exact circumstances in which this or that weapon would or would not be used.

It is important, of course, that the aggressor should know what he may not do, but I think that it is equally important that he should not be told too invitingly what he may do.[1]

This last debate was an enthralling experience, with a full House during all the major speeches and with many dramatic incidents. Churchill seemed to dominate the scene from start to finish. It was a memorable and worthy end to his incomparable career.

I was in many ways sorry to leave the Ministry of Defence when the new Government was formed. Much as I looked forward to going to the Foreign Office—a formidable task—I had become keen upon the work and was beginning to understand some of the fundamental problems. I felt that my time had been too short to do anything very effective and yet too long to avoid all responsibility. Some important decisions were taken, but many problems, alas, remained. It was, at any rate, a satisfaction to meet again many of my old friends with whom I had such agreeable contacts during the war. Although ten years had passed, some of those now at the heads of their professions were men that I had known and admired in comparatively junior posts. At any rate, it is always a joy to be working with and for the fighting Services.

[1] *Hansard*, 2 March 1955.

CHAPTER XVIII

The First Summit

'No two men have ever changed guard more smoothly.' These are the words which Churchill used to describe his resignation and Eden's summons to succeed him.[1] However, as will have been seen, just as intricate drill movements can only be perfected by quite a lot of heavy work on the barrack square, so the final relief of the political sentries was preceded by nearly two years' manœuvring.

Eden accepted the Queen's Commission and kissed hands on his appointment as Prime Minister on 6 April. On the following day I became Foreign Secretary. Eden had certainly wished to give the Foreign Office to Lord Salisbury, and was quite frank to me about his preference. However, he decided that to place the Foreign Secretary in the House of Lords would throw too heavy a burden on the Prime Minister, since the House of Commons would insist on more than an Under-Secretary to handle Foreign Office debates. He had witnessed after his own resignation in 1938 the unhappy results when Lord Halifax had become Foreign Secretary in the Lords and the chief weight of representing him in the Commons had fallen on Mr. Chamberlain as Prime Minister. In Eden's own words, he would have had to be 'principal Foreign Office spokesman in the House of Commons, a heavy additional load on any Prime Minister'. Although this hesitation suited me, since the Foreign Office was the summit of my ambitions, Eden proved to be mistaken. When subsequently I recommended Lord Home as Foreign Secretary, there was a mild flutter of excitement in the House of Commons and some ineffectual protests from the Opposition. But by almost universal admission the plan proved very successful. In order to avoid the dangers which Eden foresaw, I appointed

[1] The Earl of Avon, *Full Circle*, p. 265.

Edward Heath as Lord Privy Seal, to be the Secretary of State's principal coadjutor and to represent him in the Lower House.

I could now look forward to a few weeks of fascinating work and, if we were to win the election and I showed reasonable efficiency, to four or five years in this great post. After that the time would come for retirement and rest. Such were my thoughts when I was appointed; like so many prognostications for one's own future they proved to be inaccurate in almost every particular.

Eden rightly made few changes in the administration beyond those which necessarily flowed from Churchill's resignation and his own succession. Selwyn Lloyd took my post as Minister of Defence. Since he had been a Minister of State at the Foreign Office and had subsequently been Minister of Supply, he had already considerable experience. Reginald Maudling, one of the Treasury Ministers, succeeded him as Minister of Supply. Lord Home became Commonwealth Secretary in place of Lord Swinton. I deeply regretted the loss of the latter, and Eden would have been wise to have included him, at least in a sinecure post, for he was one of the ablest, most versatile and most loyal of colleagues.

The immediate need was to fix the date of the election. Nearly all the Ministers whom Eden consulted were for holding it as early as possible. We should gain nothing by six months' delay and might lose the advantage of the initiative and the freshness of a new leader. Accordingly, on 15 April, the Prime Minister announced that Parliament would be dissolved on 6 May, with polling day on 26 May. Although it was difficult to form any estimate of the prospects, it was clear that once again the issue would be nicely balanced.

> No one can tell how this election will turn out. If there is no marked swing either way, we may just pull it off, with the help of the seats we gain by redistribution. But there are bound to be *some* losses, and we can't afford many.[1]

The political situation was calm, with no great emotion on either side. The electorate would have to weigh the results of four years of Conservative administration against the promises and past

[1] 6 May 1955.

performances of Socialism. The main feature of the Budget had been a reduction of 6*d*. in income tax. It was therefore liable to be attacked as 'a rich man's Budget'. But the successful negotiations with the Indian Government which led to a reduction of their import duties on British cotton of more than 50 per cent was good news; in addition, the removal of the purchase tax on cotton goods was likely to please both producers and consumers.

I soon came to the conclusion that the most important contribution I could make to meeting the anxieties of the nation was with regard to the dangers of a third, and no doubt nuclear, war. Almost a year before, the Government had accepted a resolution welcoming

> an immediate initiative by Her Majesty's Government to bring about a meeting between the Prime Minister and the heads of the Administrations of the United States of America and the Union of Soviet Socialist Republics for the purpose of considering anew the problem of the reduction and control of armaments and of devising positive policies and means for removing from all the peoples of the world the fear which now oppresses them.

Nothing had yet been done, but there seemed to be some hope of arranging a Four-Power conference in which these subjects could be discussed. I realised, however, that in the fantastic atmosphere of party politics an immense distinction was going to be drawn between 'top-level' and 'not quite top-level' talks. Foreign Secretaries, it seemed, were regarded as very small beer in these high controversies. 'Top-level' meant Heads of Government or Heads of State. This, of course, was a legacy of Churchill's famous speech of 11 May 1953. In the atmosphere of an election the difference might prove vital. Naturally Sir Ivone Kirkpatrick, the Head of the Foreign Office, with his clear, if sometimes acid, approach, was quick to point out that

> the issues at stake, Germany, disarmament, the Far East, nuclear warfare, etc., are highly complicated issues. They cannot be settled over the coffee cups. Our experiences of so-called top-level meetings are not encouraging.

He also reminded me that the most satisfactory and substantial progress up to date had been made by old-fashioned methods of diplomacy and not by the method of top-level meetings.

But he fully agreed that it would be naïve to suppose that an attempt to develop this case,

> however skilfully and pertinaciously conducted, would cure the British people of its faith in negotiations at the summit.

He was not, however, unduly concerned lest any announcement by the Prime Minister should upset the President. 'I do not think,' he minuted me, 'that he would be excessively annoyed, since the Americans are adjusted to the idea that even the best of friends must embarrass one another for electoral reasons.'

I therefore began to try to work out a plan which might prove acceptable to our allies. At my first appearance as Foreign Secretary in the House of Commons on 25 April, I was able to answer a question in which this hope was raised. After referring to the imminent ratification of the Paris Agreements, I declared my intention at the forthcoming NATO conference on 9 May to discuss with the French and American Foreign Ministers and with the German Chancellor the question of a Four-Power conference. I added that we would be glad to take part in talks at any level, whether Heads of Government or Foreign Ministers.

We were now about to be launched into the General Election, and we must work quickly if we were to work effectively from the political point of view. Accordingly I had a talk with Winthrop Aldrich, the American Ambassador in London, on 27 April and told him of our view on a meeting of Heads of Government. He did not seem surprised or alarmed, although he was doubtful about Eisenhower's public response. It was not, however, until we got to Paris that I could make much progress.

Before leaving, I went to see Churchill, who was back from his holiday in Sicily and living temporarily at the Hyde Park Hotel. Now, and until my final retirement from politics, I made it a regular practice to inform my old chief of what was happening and gain the advantage of his unrivalled experience. On this occasion he seemed in good form and full of interest in the new developments. Among other things, he was pleased with a *mot* about Sir Hartley

Shawcross, formerly Attorney-General in the Labour Government but now making more and more Centre and 'Right-wing' speeches. 'Churchill calls him "Sir Shortly Floor-cross"! (There is a Trollopian ring about this.)'[1] He was certainly in a position to recognise the symptoms from his own experience.

I next discussed with Eden a plan which I had been turning over in my mind for some days. I had already tried it on some of the newspaper correspondents in a cautious way. Top-level talks had, in my view, been wrongly conceived.

> Churchill had (or gave) the impression that we wanted something like the Casablanca, Cairo, Quebec, or Yalta Conferences.
>
> Here in an atmosphere of fervid rush and hurry, vast decisions were reached in a few crowded days. This may have been right among allies, in dealing with war. (It was a failure and a disaster at Yalta, which was chiefly about post-war problems.) Eden naturally opposed this very unbusinesslike and hurried procedure, as unsuitable to peace conditions. It has also been expected that great and almost final decisions would be reached at a 'top-level' conference with Russia.[2]

If no such decisions were reached, the public would be correspondingly disappointed and disillusioned.

> But why not think of a 'top-level' meeting as the 'beginning', not the end? Lines of fruitful approach would be discussed and then handed on to Foreign Secretaries and experts to explore further. A second conference might succeed the first. Some decision (or settlements) of a limited kind might be reached, as the starting point for more work and study.[2]

I had now to promote the concept of a prolonged period of negotiation, perhaps over years and even generations, rather than a single meeting which would almost certainly fail. Accordingly, I drafted a telegram for Eden to send to Eisenhower outlining this plan. I also sent a copy to Dulles, together with suggestions to Roger Makins, our Ambassador in Washington, about handling it in a way that might attract them both. I ended the day with a visit to Chartwell. Churchill was in good form and even merry.

[1] 30 April 1955.   [2] 5 May 1955.

He made one sly dig at Anthony: 'How much more attractive a top-level meeting seems when one has reached the top !'[1]

The President's reply was not altogether discouraging. While he was surprised that we had gone so far as to present our ideas as a definite proposal, Eisenhower quite understood the importance of this project to us in present circumstances and was disposed to be helpful. But he also had to consider his own public opinion. He agreed that all the Foreign Ministers, who would soon be meeting in Vienna to conclude the Austrian Peace Treaty, might discuss the matter and report to their Governments what subjects should be raised at the summit, in order to discover whether there was likely to be a general willingness to set honourably and honestly about the task of finding some solutions. Makins, in reporting his discussion with Dulles, was hopeful that our proposal might be accepted, but we must give it a little time. If the four Foreign Ministers could get together first, a subsequent higher-level meeting would not be excluded. It was clear from this that my best chance was to win over Dulles. Before leaving for Paris I had a further talk with Winthrop Aldrich, who gave me a useful sketch of Dulles's character and some suggestions as to how he might best be handled.

On 7 May I left for Paris with my two Private Secretaries, Anthony Rumbold and Andrew Stark, both men of high quality. My first task was to call upon Dulles at the American Embassy. I found him surrounded with a great number of advisers, including Winthrop Aldrich, and the American Ambassador in Paris, Douglas Dillon.

He received me very courteously and after a word or two, suggested that I might like to talk with him alone. I said yes. Our talk lasted about three-quarters of an hour. During the last half of it, Aldrich was present—and very helpful. We had a good preliminary interchange of reminiscences, messages from the President, Bob Murphy and others and all seemed very pleasant. I found Dulles much more gracious than I had expected. He sometimes seems to be rather dreamy—as if he were thinking

[1] 5 May 1955.

about something else. Then he does not look at you—or else 'through' you. But he has a pleasant smile and chuckle.[1]

I unfolded my plan, taking care to put it forward as something entirely new and altogether different from that proposed two years before by Churchill.

> I did not believe that a meeting of Heads of Government should be regarded as the *end* of a negotiation, but the beginning. I envisaged one or two meetings of the four Foreign Secretaries to make preliminary arrangements and discuss the main lines on which the problems should be approached. Then the meetings of Heads of Government—to last a few days (not more than a week) —then more meetings—perhaps in different groups so as to include different powers, according as to whether the East or West was under discussion (Germany or Indo-China).[1]

I added that I felt that we were entering into a period when a whole series of such meetings at different levels might be required; gradual progress might thus be made towards easing some of the world's difficulties. Eden and I were very anxious that this plan should be considered on its merits; it would, of course, help us in our election, but it was not just an election stunt.

> It responded to a deep feeling in the hearts of our people (and we believed of other European peoples) and in addition was a practical approach to the problem before us.[1]

Dulles took all this very well,

> doodling incessantly (for he is almost as great a doodler as Attlee) —and occasionally asking a question. . . . He quite understood my idea. It was not to be another meeting like the war meetings— Casablanca, Cairo, Teheran, Yalta. It was to be a new procedure altogether, and should be so presented.[1]

After this talk the experts of both sides were summoned. Our officials had been trying meanwhile to 'sell' the idea to their American counterparts. On returning to the British Embassy I telephoned to Eden at his request and told him in guarded terms that I thought we were making progress.

[1] 7 May 1955.

President Eisenhower

The formal signing of the Austrian Peace Treaty, 15 May 1955

At this time the problems of the West were not causing the French as much concern as the position in the Far East. The same evening, in a meeting at the Hôtel Matignon, there were long and rather painful discussions upon the whole problem of Vietnam, where the non-Communist forces in the south were divided between pro- and anti-French factions, with American aid concentrated on the section least favourable to the French. But at this stage there was little I could do except listen to the views expressed by Dulles, M. Edgar Faure, the French Prime Minister, and M. Antoine Pinay, the French Foreign Minister. This sort of meeting of Ministers of different countries with their accompanying teams of supporters struck me as a slightly ridiculous method of negotiation, but it had become the recognised technique for international discussions. I always thought it extremely difficult to carry on any useful conversations in so large a company. In any case this meeting, like many others, proved inconclusive. Both the French and the Americans were trying to bluff each other. Our chief interest was to maintain the settlement recently reached at Geneva and to protect our interests in Malaya.

On the same day there was a great dinner at the British Embassy of all the Foreign Ministers of the countries who were to form the new Western European Union—that is, the old Brussels Pact powers plus West Germany and Italy. I was asked to preside, and we succeeded in eating an admirable dinner and finishing all the business by 11.30 p.m. This brought me many compliments on the speed with which our work had been concluded.

But my immediate task still lay before me, and when I went round on Sunday morning, 8 May, to see Dulles, he told me that

> He had been thinking about my proposal. Without com- mitting himself even to recommend it to the President, he had been struck with my idea. When he had discussed our telegram with the President before leaving Washington on Friday, he had not really understood our plan. He wondered whether his staff and mine could prepare a draft telegram which he could submit to the President, setting out the idea. [They] certainly could.[1]

[1] 8 May 1955.

u

I next called upon Adenauer, who delivered an interesting and impressive dissertation upon the history of the Russian Revolution, its excesses, its uncertainties and its weaknesses. He was not willing to be accused of disloyalty to NATO, an organisation to which Germany was to be formally elected on the following day, but he believed some progress could be made without endangering larger interests. He asserted—and in this he showed considerable foresight —that the Russians were chiefly afraid of being dragged into war by the Chinese. I did not, at this stage, do more than discuss in general terms the matter which was foremost in my mind.

While awaiting the President's reply, we met on 9 May for the formal plenary session of NATO.

> This was really a solemn and moving scene. Apart from for-
> malities, the only business was the admission of Germany. After a
> preliminary oration in rather bad French from the Chairman (M.
> Stephanopoulos), each representative of the 14 Powers made a
> short speech of welcome to the newcomer—the latest-joined
> member of our club. We sit in alphabetical order round the table
> (or rather oblong). I spoke last but one, Mr. Dulles (U.S.)
> coming after me.
> This ceremony, with all the speeches, films, television, radio
> and all the rest, took up most of the morning.[1]

I felt proud to be present on such an historic occasion. Nevertheless, I was soon to find that when one matter is settled another immediately crops up. In spite of the agreement which Adenauer had made with Pinay about the Saar, the French were trying to reopen the question. However, in the afternoon, at a restricted session of NATO, there was a useful debate about the wider political problems. By arrangement with Dulles I explained my plan for a Four-Power meeting, but in general terms, and equally applicable to one of Heads of Government or of Foreign Ministers. Before dinner Dulles and I met Pinay and explained the position. The President had now moved, under Dulles's advice, almost to full acceptance of our plan. We therefore gave Pinay the text of a proposed invitation to the Russians which had already been agreed with the Americans.[2] It included a suggestion for a meeting of Heads of Government after

[1] 9 May 1955.   [2] Reproduced below as Appendix Two.

a preliminary meeting of Foreign Ministers. Although the proposal was limited to a preliminary discussion of the problems and agreement on the methods to be followed 'in exploring solutions', our main purpose was secured. Whatever the formula, no meeting of Heads of Government would be able to avoid the realities of the issues involved. Dulles tried to make out that the President was undecided, but it was clear that the matter was, in fact, settled.

The next day I had a meeting alone with Dulles at the Palais Chaillot.

> Before Pinay came in, [Dulles] asked me whether I would think it would do if the Vice-President came instead of the President. Thinking this was a joke, I told him of the famous music-hall joke. 'Poor Mrs. Jones, what a terrible thing has happened to her !' 'What has happened to her?' 'Why ! haven't you heard?' 'No, I haven't heard.' 'Why, she had two fine sons. One of them went down in the *Titanic*, the other became Vice-President of the United States. Neither of them was ever heard of again.'
>
> Harold Caccia told me that while I made this reply, Foster Dulles put on a look of Queen Victoria saying 'We are not amused.' (It seems that the President made this proposal quite seriously !)
>
> However, when the story was over, he laughed outright (rare for him) and said 'I guess poor Nixon wouldn't like that.' So it was dropped. The President will come. So we have brought off the first *grand coup*. (There remains Austria, and the Saar.) Pinay came along, and we settled the final text, method of delivery, and time of publication of the invitation.[1]

On 10 May I returned to London and found myself involved in a television appearance as part of the election campaign. This ordeal was quite new to me and my performance was weak and jejune. I had to give a talk of a few minutes to be followed by a film which, although rather childish, was not perhaps altogether ineffective. But it was a disappointment that I could not announce the invitation to Russia, since the release had been fixed for midnight. When the news was published on the following day, both the British and French Press were enthusiastic.

[1] 10 May 1955.

Immediately after the broadcast I returned to Paris. Although the final meeting of the NATO Council in the morning was merely to settle the communiqué, there was a difficult session of the Western European Union in the afternoon which lasted for four and three-quarter hours. Since I was acting as chairman, I found it an exhausting experience.

After immense efforts we got an agreement on all the points outstanding between the French and the Germans on the Saar Statute. It was a tough job, and I was very anxious at some moments. Pinay fought hard (but quite fairly) for his clients, the present Government of the Saar (which is pro-French). Part of the compromise was suggested by me—that I should see the Saar Prime Minister tomorrow—whether to get his agreement or to inform him of the agreement reached was left rather vague.[1]

I was able to carry out this duty in a laborious but successful discussion, and so this matter was finally disposed of.

But the labours of 11 May were not concluded. At 10 p.m. I went together with my advisers to another meeting on Vietnam.

M. Faure behaved reasonably; so did Foster Dulles. But, oh, how long! At midnight it was clear that an agreement had been reached, if only someone would put it into words. This I finally did—on one sheet of paper—and it was accepted as a fair summary.[1]

The election campaign was now in full swing. I was somewhat anxious as to my absence. Although I knew my own constituency was safe, I had undertaken a number of engagements to speak in different parts of the country. However, I had perhaps been able to give more important help by the arrangement for the top-level meeting than by any speeches that I could have delivered, however eloquent.

Before I could return to England there was another task which, if it could be successfully accomplished, would add something to the prestige of the Government. It was the completion of the long negotiations for the Austrian Treaty.

I knew nothing of the background of the prolonged struggle over

[1] 11 May 1955.

the negotiations for an Austrian treaty except a few references which had occasionally been made at various Cabinet meetings. The story was simple, but the motives that lay behind the long delay were obscure. As a result of protracted negotiations from 1947 to 1950 between the Four Powers, Britain, the United States, France and the Soviet Union, the main lines of the treaty were agreed; indeed, only five articles of relatively small importance remained in dispute. For whatever reason, the Soviet Government evidently decided that they did not wish to conclude the compact. During the next four years they put forward a number of irrelevant pretexts for obstructing any further negotiations. Then, at the Berlin Conference of 1954, a year before I took office, the three Western Foreign Ministers told Mr. Molotov that they would accept the Soviet text of the five articles in dispute if only he would bring the affair to a conclusion. Somewhat taken aback by this, Molotov stalled, putting forward new conditions and refusing to fix any firm date for the evacuation of the occupying forces from Austria. However, in March 1955, the Soviet Government began separate discussions with the Austrian Ambassador in Moscow. This was followed by a visit in April of an Austrian delegation headed by the Chancellor and including the Vice-Chancellor and Foreign Minister. During these talks, the Russians offered to sign an Austrian State Treaty without delay. They even agreed that the occupation forces of the Four Powers should be withdrawn not later than 31 December 1955.

A long and dreary argument about the so-called German assets was to be brought to an end by a final payment of $150 million, in return for which the assets would be returned to their Austrian owners. The Russians also undertook to restore to the Austrians the Danube Shipping Company, against cash payment, and their oil undertakings against payment of crude oil spread over ten years. Finally, they were ready to discuss the 'normalisation' of Austro-Russian trade and even the return of Austrian prisoners still held in Russia for war crimes. In return, the Austrians—or so we believed—renewed the proposals originally made at the Berlin Conference a year before and undertook to adopt permanent neutrality, perhaps on the Swiss model. In addition, they would do what was possible to obtain international support for this declaration and would welcome an international guarantee of the inviolability and integrity of Austrian territory. Following this, the Russians suggested to the three Western Governments a conference of the four Foreign Ministers for the purpose of concluding and signing a formal treaty. The Western Powers naturally agreed, but proposed that some preparatory work should be put in hand by the four ambassadors, who should meet for this purpose, with Austrian participation, on 2 May.

The Soviet Government, with their usual calm effrontery, immediately censured the Western Powers for delaying tactics. After a policy of procrastination which had lasted a good eight years, they now complained about ten days' delay. They even indulged in extensive propaganda in condemnation of our action in proposing an Ambassadors' Conference prior to the meeting of Foreign Ministers. In fact there was a practical and necessary job to be done. It was important to get an agreed text ready for signature when the Ministers arrived or, at least, to leave as few loopholes as possible. Although the text would probably follow that virtually agreed many years before, owing to the lapse of time nearly one hundred formal amendments would be necessary in the draft. Moreover, it appeared that, as a result of the Austro-Russian talks, some articles would have to be deleted. We did not anticipate much difficulty over all this, but we were entitled to insist upon a proper procedure.

A much more urgent question remained open, for which it had been necessary for me to get the formal consent of the Cabinet towards the end of April. Roughly, there were two aspects of the problem. Should we recognise an Austrian declaration of neutrality on the Swiss model? Secondly, should we participate in a Four-Power guarantee? On the first, the obvious purpose of the Soviets was to obstruct the rearmament of Western Germany under the Paris Agreement by presenting a neutral Austria as a useful pattern for Germany to follow if she hoped to obtain reunification. 'Accept neutrality,' the Russians were preaching to the Germans, 'and you may obtain the priceless gift of military evacuation, and thus—and thus only—can East and West Germany be reunited.' But, whatever the motives, the new Russian position was wholly acceptable to the Austrian people and it was clear that they were ready to pay this price for a treaty.

The Chiefs of Staff were consulted and produced an admirably drafted but somewhat inconclusive assessment of the military and strategic interests involved. They finally informed us that 'a neutral Austria, debarred from joining NATO or from giving transit to NATO forces, was acceptable only provided that its neutrality was made really effective and was guaranteed'. This masterly statement of the obvious did not inform us how the neutrality was to be effective or how it could be adequately guaranteed. Nevertheless, it was clear that on this first question there could be no doubt of our willingness to accept a neutral Austria. The only other matter that arose in this connection was whether Russia was ready to allow Austria to become a member of the United Nations or join other economic organisations in Europe. There would no doubt be other difficulties, but we must do our best to obtain the maximum freedom for the Austrian state.

But participation in a Four-Power guarantee of Austria's integrity and neutrality raised more serious anxieties. Under the draft treaty the Austrian armed forces were to be strictly limited, leaving Austria defenceless against external aggression. There was thus no real analogy with Switzerland—or even Sweden. I explained to the Cabinet that if the Western Powers refused to participate, there was a danger of separate Austro-Russian bilateral agreements which would give Russia alone the right of intervention. On the other hand, we had poignant memories of the Belgian guarantee. However, I felt that it would be best, in order to avoid leaving the field entirely to the Russians, to enter into some kind of a commitment, provided the American and French Governments were ready to do the same. This could vary from a collective guarantee, only operative if all the guarantors agreed that it should come into effect, to a series of individual guarantees which could be either binding on the guarantor or permissive. I also made it clear that, before any definite commitment, Parliament would have to be consulted and asked to ratify the undertaking, and the Commonwealth Governments would have to be kept closely informed at all stages.

Meanwhile it had been reported to us that Molotov, at a party given to the Austrians in Moscow, had taken great pains to bring the British, American and French representatives into the picture. He and Bulganin were both saying that the five countries all ought to settle this treaty rapidly. 'We have taken ten years so far; let us not waste another ten years.'

Armed with full authority, but with the vaguest ideas as to what were the implications of this new Russian attitude, I set off from Paris for Vienna on 13 May, leaving electoral troubles behind me and looking forward to a new and even exciting adventure. There were still some points of disagreement in the ambassadorial discussions. But when the Russians heard that Dulles refused to come to Vienna unless they yielded on two articles, they immediately gave in.

It was only possible to speculate on the reason for the change of Russian policy towards Austria. It had certainly been rapid. Only a year before the Russians had justified their retention of troops in Hungary on the grounds that it lay on their line of communication. If Austria was to be abandoned, what about Hungary? Moreover, there was something slightly comical about the sudden elevation of neutrality on the Swiss model into a political principle—not only of practical value but of high ideal importance. During the war neutrality had always been denounced by Russia as a proof of 'pro-fascist cowardice and an avenue to profiteering'. Now, suddenly, it became an idyllic freedom from military entanglements. To add to the paradox, Swiss neutrality was not recognised by either Russia or America.

It is still difficult to assess the real motive which actuated the Soviet Government. Many of us flattered ourselves, at the time, that this marked a change of heart in the post-Stalin period, and was a good augury for summit negotiations. To some extent this was true; but it now seems more likely that the Austrian Treaty was used as part of the game of 'power politics' which followed Stalin's death. Khrushchev, in order to fulfil his personal ambitions, had to play his hand carefully. First, he had to concentrate on the destruction of Beria. For this purpose he collaborated with Malenkov among the younger men and Molotov among the old guard.

Malenkov's premiership lasted from 1953 to the early part of 1955, when he was ousted. Khrushchev then turned against Molotov, who had been his partner up to now. Molotov was a sincere revolutionary of the old type and temperamentally against negotiation with the Western Powers. He opposed a *détente* and was a traditional supporter of orthodox Communist policies. Similarly, he disliked any reconciliation with Tito. No doubt to his disgust, a State visit to Yugoslavia was actually announced the day before the signing of the Austrian Treaty. Molotov went to Vienna in his capacity of Foreign Minister; but he was not included among the notabilities who were to go to Belgrade. This team consisted of Khrushchev, Bulganin, Mikoyan and Shepilov. All this was intended to weaken Molotov, and led to his ultimate fall.[1] How far the decision to accept the Austrian Treaty was reached in Moscow on its merits and how far merely as part of the rivalry between the heirs of Stalin, one cannot say. It so happened that Molotov represented a stern puritanical Communist line; good Communists must not be contaminated by contact with the West. Khrushchev, therefore, having disposed of Beria and Malenkov, made this inflexibility of Molotov a source of reproach. Had Molotov stood for a forward and flexible policy, would Khrushchev have attacked him as a heretic? No one can say. But it was fortunate that in this case the victor in the struggle, in the course of these personal rivalries, found himself committed to a policy which has proved of advantage both to Russia and the Western world. In any case, even making full allowance for the cynical character of Communist politics, I am persuaded that the path which it suited Khrushchev to follow on the way to power was one which was agreeable to his temperament and intelligence.

I took with me to Vienna Harold Caccia, Deputy Under-Secretary at the Foreign Office. He was particularly well received by the Austrians since he had been a popular High Commissioner in Vienna for four years. William Hayter, British Ambassador in Moscow, met us in Vienna and gave us an interesting account of the sudden change of attitude of the Russians and his view of their motives. Although their ultimate purposes remained unchanged, he

[1] See Robert Conquest, *Power and Policy in the USSR*. (London, 1961), *passim*.

felt that they genuinely wanted and needed a period of reduced tension in the short term.

The weather was perfect, with bright sun but not too hot. The people were in a very gay mood, looking forward with delight to the prospect of the end of the occupation after ten years. The British had only a token force of one battalion, but the Americans had 20,000 troops and the Russians double or treble that number.

On the morning of 14 May I went with the British Ambassador, Sir Geoffrey Wallinger, to call upon the Austrian Chancellor, Dr. Julius Raab. The Foreign Minister, Dr. Leopold Figl, was present. They were housed in Maria Theresa's old palace—a lovely building.

> Both were in a state of barely suppressed excitement. Could it really be true that the Russians (with their 40,000–60,000 troops in this small country) could perhaps be gone before the autumn?[1]

After a general talk,

> We were shown round the lovely rooms of this palace, including [that in which] the Peace Treaty of Vienna was actually signed. This is the room with the five doors, specially built so that the Tsar and the Emperor of Austria and three kings could enter the room simultaneously—a splendid solution to the problem of precedence.[1]

There followed a meeting at the American Embassy at which Dulles, Pinay and I discussed the proposed procedure. We also had to decide our line for the after-dinner talks with Molotov. It was now agreed that we should propose the end of July or beginning of August for the Four-Power top-level meeting. Lausanne or Geneva would suit us equally well.

We left the Embassy at 4.30 for the formal meeting.

> A lovely sunny day; the streets fully of happy people; cheers and hand-waving as our car passes, with the Union Jack. Great crowds outside the Allied Control building. They cheered, clapped and waved, as I got out. I stood on the steps, bowed, waved, etc., as the photographers clicked their cameras and the radio [reporters] did their stuff.[1]

[1] 14 May 1955.

Dulles proposed that Molotov should take the chair, and this was agreed. The business of settling the final text of the Treaty was soon over. Then, rather unexpectedly, Molotov began to read an elaborate *exposé* about the Moscow agreement between Russia and Austria, insisting on having the first five paragraphs read in all languages. He then produced and read out a draft declaration for the Four Powers to sign on the neutrality of Austria. We naturally protested that we had not got the text of either statement. In addition, the Treaty had to be approved by the Austrian Government and Parliament before there could be any question of a Four-Power guarantee. After some discussion Molotov dropped the whole matter and the session closed.

> Molotov was some distance from me, and I could not observe him closely. He seemed to me smaller than I had supposed and older (we are all older!). He is grey, not black any more; a very pale pasty face; a large forehead; closely cut grey hair. He wore a very respectable black suit—and looked rather like a head gardener in his Sunday clothes.[1]

Molotov has been described by Churchill in *The Gathering Storm* as a man of outstanding ability and cold-blooded ruthlessness. However this may be, he certainly presided over our meeting with scrupulous correctness, without waste of time and with the expertise of a professional chairman. That night, after dinner at the American Embassy, where we were all gathered, he was in a pleasant mood and disposed to that rather heavy joking which is the Russian manner of being relaxed. During the period of talking and drinking before dinner he made his first reference to the British General Election, a subject to which he reverted during the rest of the evening at frequent intervals. There were the usual toasts and the conversation, although slow because of the translations, was easy. After dinner the main discussion was on the proposed Four-Power meeting.

> Dulles explained *le plan Macmillan* and the idea of the Heads of Government giving an impulse to a continued process of negotiation through the Foreign Secretaries and other suitable agencies.

[1] Ibid.

Molotov was very insistent on the Heads meeting and did not seem to like the meeting of Foreign Secretaries *before* the Heads. Dulles explained that it should all be *one* meeting, with Foreign Ministers perhaps arriving a day or two before to fix final arrangements. Molotov hoped there would be no agenda. Dulles agreed. The meeting was really intended to leave agenda behind for further work. Both agreed that public opinion in all our countries should not be led to expect a spectacular success, but rather the inauguration of a new system of patient pursuit of a peaceful solution. Molotov repeated several times 'new impulse'.[1]

All this was satisfactory to me because it was the plan which I had persuaded the Americans to accept.

Molotov was anxious as to the place of the meeting. He would like it to be Vienna—as a symbol of neutrality. But Dulles made it quite clear that the President would not come to an occupied country. In any case, I reminded Molotov that there would be another chance of a talk at the end of June at the United Nations anniversary meeting in San Francisco. We managed also to persuade him to drop the idea of the Austrian declaration of neutrality and the Four-Power undertaking to respect it; this should be referred to the Ambassadors for further consideration. I had the feeling that Molotov realised the difficulties involved, both for Britain and America, in anything like the old Belgian guarantee.

The following day, 15 May, the formal signature of the Treaty took place in a large saloon on the first floor of the Belvedere. This magnificent palace and garden were the present of the Emperor to Prince Eugène, just as Blenheim was Queen Anne's gift to Marlborough. We all agreed to make short speeches, but Molotov could not resist a long piece of propaganda. After the signing, which was an impressive and historic occasion,

> we all went repeatedly on to the balcony facing the gardens. The immense crowd greeted all the Foreign Ministers (at their various appearances) with wild applause. I thought Molotov got most applause ! Perhaps because they will be so glad when the Russians —all 60,000 of them—finally go away. Or it may have been that

[1] 14 May 1955.

the Communist Party had organised a special *claque* to cheer for him. Anyway, it was all very emotional.

A lot of champagne was drunk *inside* the Belvedere, and the crowd was intoxicated with joy in the gardens *outside*.[1]

There followed an immense luncheon with a vast number of people in the royal palace, in the old wing once occupied by Maria Theresa. It began at 2 p.m. and ended at four.

Pinay and I (not Dulles or Molotov!) then went to the Te Deum, which was beautifully sung before all the civil and ecclesiastical notables, in the Cathedral Church of St. Stephen.[1]

After a short interval we all had to start off again, in evening clothes, for a dinner at the Schönbrunn Palace at 7 p.m.

This was in a splendid hall, again with lovely gold plates (we had much of this at the luncheon) and lovely china—belonging, I suppose, to the Imperial House. The flowers were wonderful also. (This is a specially good time for Vienna—the lilacs are all out in the city streets, gardens, and much other blossom as well.) The toasts were short. We each gave one in turn.[1]

There followed a reception, with over 2,000 guests, in the ballroom of the Schönbrunn Palace. Among the guests were

the Cardinal, and the Archbishop and other ecclesiastics . . . in full splendour. Molotov was introduced to them, but seemed rather embarrassed.[1]

Before leaving for London I went, at Molotov's request, to call upon him at the villa which he occupied and spent a pleasant afternoon with him, the discussion covering a wide range. Among other things he talked of music (he was a cousin of Scriabin the composer) and about the deep interest he took in the music lessons of his little great-niece or granddaughter. He certainly showed, that afternoon, a softer side of his character. His great round head was impressive and his heavy black moustache framed curiously dreamy eyes. On the one side he seemed just an efficient operator; on another, something of a philosopher.

The conclusion of the Austrian Treaty marked an important step

[1] 15 May 1955.

in the pacification of Europe. There remained, of course, the need for ratification by the Austrian Parliament and by all the countries concerned. The only outstanding point was, in fact, settled at San Francisco on 20 June, when the four of us agreed that if the Austrian Parliament required us to implement the commitment to make a declaration on neutrality, we should all use the same text.

To complete the story, on 29 June I moved the Second Reading of the Austrian State Treaty Bill in the House of Commons.

> Why we had to have a Bill at all was obscure to me, and (by the time I had finished speaking from my brief) was equally obscure to the House ! However, we got all stages by 5.30 p.m. ![1]

On 27 July—all the countries having ratified the Treaty—it came into effect. In accordance with our agreement, all foreign troops were withdrawn by the end of October. The Austrian neutrality did not preclude Austria from joining international organisations of a non-military character. Moreover, since she was bound to defend her neutrality, it allowed Austria to raise her own army. Before the end of the year Austria was admitted to membership of the United Nations. Altogether, this episode was an agreeable interlude in our relations with Russia, and held out some hope for the future. Combined with the agreement for the summit meeting, it certainly made a useful contribution to our electoral prospects.

It was now high time to get back to England and take some part in the election. On the day of my return, 17 May, I was cast in a minor role in another television performance. It was a curious and not altogether satisfactory experiment. Ten newspaper editors asked questions and five Ministers sat in a row like schoolboys to answer them. My colleagues were Eden, Butler, Monckton and Macleod. It was said to have been reasonably successful, but it must have seemed very amateurish. In those days television was only beginning to influence political controversy. We had all been brought up to the routine of schoolroom or open-air meetings in the constituency or larger gatherings in public halls. We had later begun to learn something of the art of the radio. But none of us had acquired at this time

[1] 29 June 1955.

any expertise in television. Moreover, our questioners were still respectful and even reverent. I was later to get some experience of more novel and less courteous methods; but I cannot claim ever to have mastered this art which now appears an essential qualification for an ambitious politician.

On the same evening I had a talk with Lord Woolton, who told me that things were going reasonably well but that the Liberal intervention had been so planned as to lose us fifteen seats or more. On the next day, according to the Gallup polls, a small swing in our favour seemed likely. But the result was still uncertain.

> It is strange to feel on how little turns one's personal life. I may be back at St. Martin's Street in a week—or at the Foreign Office for several years (unless I make a fool of myself!). No one seems to know what is happening. There has never been a 'quieter' election—a little too quiet for my taste.[1]

Two days before the poll the expected bombshell from the *Daily Mirror* burst.

> It is just a very scurrilous attack on Tories and Toryism. I doubt if it will do much harm. But, of course, it has a huge circulation. The chief idea is to say that the Tories are bound to get in, so 'vote Labour' and keep their majority small.[2]

I had devoted this day to a tour in Yorkshire, speaking in Pudsey, Bradford and Keighley, as well as at Shipley. I ended up at Halifax, where my son Maurice was contesting a seat held by Labour.

> The hall was packed—I should think 1,500—and Maurice was speaking (very well, I thought) when I arrived. I spoke for three-quarters of an hour and had a tremendous reception. Then we had questions—which everybody enjoyed very much, because [Maurice and I] parcelled them out between us and it was a good 'turn'.[2]

I had left the conduct of the campaign in Bromley almost entirely in the practised hands of my wife. On polling day we toured the constituency as usual and went later to the Savoy to see the results coming through. As so often, the first to be announced was Salford

---

[1] 22 May 1955.   [2] 24 May 1955.

West–a Tory swing of well over 2,000 votes. By midnight, although there were very few seats gained, it was clear that we should win: no landslide but a slight swing to us, or away from the Socialists.

> At 1 a.m. I went to Conservative Central Office. When I got into Lord Woolton's room, where the results were coming out and being analysed, Halifax came through. Maurice *in* by 1,500. I was so excited that I dashed back to the Savoy, where I found Dorothy, almost in tears, the centre of congratulations from all sides. It is really splendid–so good that he has *won* a seat, and all on his own.[1]

At Bromley, where the result was not announced till 27 May, the figures were satisfactory, my majority being up by just over 1,000. Over the whole country we had improved our majority from seventeen in the old House to sixty in the new. We had gained 49·7 per cent of all the votes cast against Labour's 46·4 per cent. Eden had given us a splendid lead–he never put a foot wrong during the whole campaign.

Although we were now to be plagued by a railway strike in which the ASLEF men all came out while the N.U.R. stayed in, this was perhaps the best time to have it. It began immediately after the election and lasted seventeen days. The Government were quite right not to be forced into any more concessions, but considerable harm was done to the economy, some of which was only revealed as the months went by.

> A heavy importation of coal will be necessary. This will mean $60m. or $70m. on the exchange. On the other hand, the fact that (*a*) industrial and general life could stand up to at least a four-fifths stoppage of trains without collapse; (*b*) that the men got virtually nothing more than they could have had at the beginning, may have a deflationary effect and do something to stop the see-saw of wages and prices which has begun to show itself in the last year or two.[2]

However, with the election safely over, I could leave these questions to my colleagues and resume my work at the Foreign Office with some sense of security.

[1] 26 May 1955.   [2] 15 June 1955.

The formal Russian reply to our proposal for a summit meeting actually reached us on polling day, but their intentions had already become known. After some argument as to the place of meeting, by the middle of June the Soviet Government agreed to our suggestion that the Heads of State should meet in Geneva on 18 July.

Much energy was now directed to secret discussions as to the various plans to be put forward at the conference on the main questions – Russia, Germany and disarmament. The so-called 'Eden Plan' for a small demilitarised zone to separate the Eastern and Western forces was debated at great length, both in our own camp and with our allies, with all kinds of variations and permutations. Although nominally the agreed purpose of the summit meeting was to 'identify' the problems and form and prepare an agenda for further negotiations, the condition by which we persuaded the President to come was now by silent consent put upon one side, since it was tacitly assumed that the substance, as well as the form, would be a matter for open debate.

I arrived in New York on 16 June with a substantial body of advisers and on the same day Dulles and his team came to visit us. We were staying at a house on the West River, some twenty minutes from New York, which was comfortable and old-fashioned and infinitely more agreeable than an apartment in the city.

> We soon settled down to the usual procedure – each principal, like a boxer, with his seconds or trainers crowded behind him. After luncheon, to which the French came (including M. Pinay, Foreign Minister, Couve de Murville, M. Hoppenot, etc.), the game changed, as it were, to three-handed cribbage.[1]

The subjects ranged over Gaza and the Israel problem, nuclear warfare, how to handle Adenauer, and what concessions we might ultimately offer the Russians as a price for German reunification. All this seemed to go very smoothly and was finished in a short session. In the afternoon, the conference which the French arranged chiefly covered procedure and content.

> It was slow batting (not as good as a run a minute) but very safe play. Stumps were drawn for the day about 5 p.m.[1]

[1] 16 June 1955.

The next day a further meeting of the same Ministers and teams, amounting to some twenty or thirty people, in the so-called 'Presidential Suite' of the Waldorf-Astoria Hotel, took up three hours of heavy going before lunch. The Foreign Office had now fallen into the American habit of writing what were called 'position' papers. But the fault of the system was that both we and the State Department seemed to concentrate more on discussing what it was we wanted than considering how we were to achieve our objectives. The new word 'identification' now became the favourite piece of jargon. It soon came to be believed that if a problem could be defined, it could in due course be resolved. In the evening Chancellor Adenauer, with Herbert Blankenhorn, his principal adviser, joined the party. He gave us his ideas, which seemed sensible enough.

(1) He wants some further 'disarmament' move by the Western powers for propaganda purposes. (He is on dangerous ground here; but then he does not understand the nuclear problem.) (2) He is absolutely determined that Germany should stay in NATO. (3) The Americans and Canadians must stay in Europe. (4) But he believes the position in Russia to be such that they want a *détente* and might be got to give up East Germany in exchange for some security in Europe.[1]

Behind this apparent concentration upon the problems of Western Europe lay more urgent and in many ways more alarming dangers in the Middle and Far East. As the weeks proceeded, it became more and more apparent that these anxieties were more real than those in Western Europe, where at least a form of military and political stability had been reached.

This short trip to New York gave me an opportunity of making my first visit to the extraordinary United Nations building, a vast glass edifice filled with people throwing stones at each other. I called upon Dag Hammarskjöld, whose chief anxiety seemed certainly to be China and not Russia. But judging from what Dulles had told me, there was not likely to be any development in the Far East at present. Dulles was pretty cagey in what he said to me, with occasional bursts of remarkable revelation. On the China problem

[1] 17 June 1955.

generally, I felt that he would like to be flexible if he were not the prisoner of a public opinion which had been largely formed by his own party.

Before leaving for San Francisco, where we were to go for the tenth anniversary of the founding of the United Nations, I had a talk with Adenauer, who called to see me. We dismissed all the hordes of advisers, only Blankenhorn and Caccia remaining.

> [Adenauer] developed in detail the theme on which he had lightly touched earlier. . . . He has his own plan for 'disengagement' in Europe—not at all unlike (though more drastic and more ambitious) the plan which (among others) we discussed. . . . It has great advantages . . . since it does not distinguish between the countries of origin. . . .
>
> Adenauer's plan is . . . a demilitarised zone in the middle, where no forces or installations would be allowed. Then on each side . . . another . . . where certain weapons and forces [were] allowed, but not others. Then still another . . . with less restriction.
>
> The general idea would be (1) equality of forces in Europe; (2) disengagement; (3) control of types of armaments allowed *within* the controlled areas.[1]

On 19 June we flew to San Francisco, where I hoped to have a chance of meeting my old friend Eisenhower. But to our mutual disappointment no opportunity was practicable without upsetting the many Heads of Government as well as Foreign Ministers who had assembled for this ceremonial occasion. However, on the morning after his arrival he 'called me up' at my hotel about 8 a.m. and the following conversation occurred:

President: Hallo, Harold. How are you?
H.M.: I'm fine.
President: I'm fine too. It's fine to hear your voice. How are you getting on?
H.M.: I'm getting on fine.
President: I'm going to try to see you today after my show. There will be an interval.
H.M.: That's fine.

[1] 17 June 1955.

President: How are you getting on with Foster?

H.M.: I'm getting on fine.

President: Foster's a bit sticky at first, but he has a heart of gold when you know him. You have got to get to know Foster. He's all right when you get to know him. He told me that I couldn't see you because of the others.

H.M.: I only just wanted to hear your voice again. I couldn't leave America without that.

President: That's right. That's what I told Foster. I didn't want to see you as British Secretary. I wanted to see you as my political adviser.

H.M.: That's fine.

President: How's Anthony?

H.M.: He's fine.

President: That's fine. Tell Anthony I'm going to get to Geneva on Sunday morning. I figure to get there early. I want a good talk with Anthony that day.

H.M.: That's just what Anthony would like.

President: Then there's another thing. I want to have a friend of mine around, Jimmy Gault.[1]

H.M.: Of course.

President: It will mean a lot to us if you have got Jimmy Gault over there.

H.M.: Jimmy's in the City now.

President: God, is he a stockbroker? I thought he was in shipping.

H.M.: I hope so, that's much better.

President: All right, I'll see you after the show.[2]

This interchange, though not profound, was at least relaxed.

No doubt because of the geographical factor, everyone in San Francisco seemed to be much more concerned about the Far East than anything else. If no progress was made with conciliation, it was feared that an attack on the 'off-shore islands' (Matsu and Quemoy) might precipitate a crisis. This continued to be an acute anxiety for a long time.

In the evening we all went to the great Opera House where the formal meeting of the United Nations took place. The audience

---

[1] Brigadier Sir James Gault had served as military assistant to General Eisenhower both during the war and later in SHAPE.

[2] 20 June 1955.

must have numbered between three and four thousand. President Eisenhower, whom I had not seen for four years, did not look much older but seemed rather strained. His speech was well composed and well delivered. After it was over there was an adjournment, and we all went to a reception, where the heads of delegations were greeted by the President of the United States. He went round the circle, saying a word to each. I stood next to Molotov, and while waiting interchanged a little light banter. When the President came to me he wrung my hands warmly and said some nice words, referring to our talk on the telephone; protocol did not allow more.

In the evening there took place in the famous Union Club of San Francisco a dinner party at which, having been elected an honorary member, I acted as host. Dulles, Molotov, Pinay and I dined together alone, with only interpreters, in a private room which I had secured. It was a somewhat strange gathering in so respectable, indeed so conservative, an atmosphere. After dinner we moved to another room where we were joined by our advisers, limited to three each.

> This conversation, to which we had all looked forward and for which I had travelled all these many miles, proved a failure—or at least a comparative failure. Molotov was in rather a mischievous mood; he accepted, more or less, all the procedural plans which were presented to him for the July meeting. Then he asked that the whole matter should be discussed between the three ambassadors and the State Department at Washington. This infuriated M. Pinay, who lost his temper. Altogether, the four hours' talk . . . was rather a flop. While the world outside thought that we were settling the fate of the world, we fenced round the merest trifles.[1]

Only two points of any importance were settled; first, that we should not make long propaganda speeches to each other at the summit meeting (an agreement which was destined to be broken), and second, that we should issue a joint Press communiqué each day (which was scrupulously honoured). Dulles explained that the President would not dine or give dinners at Geneva.

[1] Ibid.

This is very foolish, but is a 'hang-over' from the political odium which has been built up against Yalta, etc. Anthony will, of course, want to entertain, and I reserved all his entertaining rights![1]

On the following day, after delivering my ceremonial speech, I had a further talk with Dulles. It was clear that the American administration was more worried about the Far East than about the West.

[They] do not really know what to do about China. They know, in their hearts, that their policy has no future—except the risk of disaster. They have not the courage to take over Formosa themselves. That would be 'Colonialism'. So they have to support a cruel and corrupt administration, which may 'double-cross' them and come to terms with the Communists at any minute. They cannot 'get off the hook' themselves, and they resent anyone trying to help them. But I must say that Foster Dulles does not himself show any resentment—at least, not to me. He seems to want comfort.[2]

Before leaving San Francisco I motored out at Molotov's request to the villa which he had rented. It was about forty-five minutes by car from the centre of the city—a typical 'tycoon' residence,

with large cool rooms, fake furniture, swimming pool, etc. Rent $4,000 for ten days. A garden—a fence—plenty of room for all the Russians.[2]

Harold Caccia and Anthony Rumbold were with me; he had two of his people. The talk lasted an hour, in a pleasant enough way, but chiefly fencing, with occasional little thrusts on either side into the realities. Each time I saw Molotov I was struck by the strange duality of his character. In spite of his reputation for a hard, negative, brutal attitude, when one saw him alone there appeared an unexpected attractiveness and even softness. I felt that the Russians wanted a *détente*, that they were really frightened by the American bases in Europe, and that they would like to reduce the expenditure and effort on armaments.

[1] 20 June 1955.   [2] 21 June 1955.

But will they pay the price? Anyway, will they pay *any* price for something that does not really achieve their purpose?

[Our proposals do] not really give them what they want—which is the break-up of NATO *and* the withdrawal of the Americans.[1]

On the next day General Carlos Romulo, a great little speaker from the Philippines, succeeded in torpedoing by ridicule as well as by oratory Molotov's ambitious plan for a peace declaration about which he had been making much propaganda. When Molotov came to speak it was a disappointing performance, at any rate for the outside world. He took nearly an hour, having 'borrowed' the time allotted to the satellite delegations. It was simply

> a repetition of everything he and his propaganda machine always say. He put a great deal of weight on his proposals for disarmament. But it took us nowhere. He merely took out the old cards, turned them face upwards, and gave *no* indication at all as to which (if any) he would discard.[2]

After the conclusion of the San Francisco celebrations I left Los Angeles by the Scandinavian airline on a route over the top of the world which had only just been started. I landed at Copenhagen and from there went to Oslo where the Queen was making a State visit to Norway. It was the custom for the Foreign Secretary to be in attendance, and these few days were indeed a happy interlude. On the last night the Queen gave a memorable dinner to the King of Norway and his court on board the Royal yacht. I was invited to return with her by sea.

The stage was now set for the summit meeting. Innumerable plans and variation of plans were discussed between the Western leaders. At any rate we had travelled a long way from the original conception of a meeting the sole purpose of which was to 'identify' various problems rather than make some effort towards their solution.

Eden was already clear in his mind that there should be three ingredients in our collective proposal. In addition to a demilitarised strip, which might be defined according to agreed conditions, there

[1] 21 June 1955.   [2] 22 June 1955.

should be a plan for the limitation of armaments within specified areas of Europe. This would imply an agreed ceiling and—if possible—a common system of control, for any form of disarmament or limitation demands both control and inspection. The third part of Eden's plan was a European security pact to be supported partly by action and partly by assurances. The action would be covered largely by the first two proposals.

However, although our British colleagues were satisfied, it was still necessary to convince the Americans, who were obstinate in their determination to stand firmly by the terms of the formal invitation to the summit meeting. I did not feel this could be resolved except by the Prime Minister and the President themselves; nevertheless I felt certain that the actual pressure of events and the conduct of the discussions would solve some of our difficulties for us. For instance, there was no objection to the discussion of a large number of different types of solution to a problem, so long as they were introduced 'by way of illustration', and there was no implied commitment to any one or the other. This was a typical example of Dulles's strange method of thought. I, of course, maintained that after the illustrations had been freely interchanged it would be necessary for the Heads of Government to produce some definite text for the Foreign Secretaries to work on; for instance, a study of how to achieve a unified Germany without adversely affecting the security of the Soviet Union.

Although it was understood that the main subjects for discussion would be the problems of Germany, disarmament, and the relations between Russia and the Western Powers, the dangers of the Far East were always in the background. In many of our private talks they formed the chief topics for consideration and debate between the Western Governments.

Soon after my appointment as Foreign Secretary, there had been some suggestion of a guarantee of Formosa by the 'interested powers' if the Chinese Nationalists would agree to evacuate the off-shore islands. I shrank from recommending so onerous an obligation. It seemed wiser to propose that the matter should be raised at any Four-Power meeting which might be arranged. Meanwhile the position had been slightly improved by Dulles's response to Chou En-lai's willingness, expressed at the Bandung Afro-Asian Conference in April, to negotiate with the United States. Although Dulles's first reaction was frigid, nevertheless, at a much advertised Press conference on 26 April, he appeared to have modified his position. We did our best to get some negotiations started. Indeed, one of my main arguments in persuading Dulles to agree to summit talks was that Chou En-lai would be unlikely to force the issue while the summit was in prospect. Dulles had agreed that we needed time for the purpose of bringing pressure upon Chiang and the Chinese Nationalists to evacuate the islands. In his talks with me in May he emphasised this reason for welcoming the summit.

There then began a complicated period in which Krishna Menon, leader of the Indian delegation to the United Nations, got into the act in a big way, by a series of prolonged discussions with Chou En-lai. Although Chou En-lai seemed willing to enter into negotiations, and the United States not altogether hostile, the main problem was to define the basis for any useful talks. Menon's intervention was at once useful and confusing. It upset the Secretary-General of the United Nations and met with little response from Washington. Nor did Menon's personality attract Dulles.

> He dislikes Krishna Menon, who has interfered with the U.N. approach. So (according to Hammarskjöld) nothing more will be done, while the Chinese await the result of Menon's diplomacy. Judging from what Foster Dulles has said about China, there is not likely to be any real development at present. The Americans could not understand Menon's plan, and didn't like it, as far as they did understand it. I have a feeling that Dulles would like to change his approach to the Chinese problem, but is just waiting for public opinion in the U.S. to allow him to do so.[1]

I had a talk on 20 June with 'Mike' Pearson, who expressed the fear that the Chinese might suppose—if there were no response—that the American opinion was hardening. In this case they might precipitate a crisis by an attack on the off-shore islands.

Dulles, although by his very method of conversation and approach difficult to fathom, now spoke far more frankly than I had yet known him to do.

[1] 17 June 1955.

He really began to 'let his hair down' about the Far East. He doesn't know what to do. He really wants to get Chiang off the [off-shore] islands, but he can't do it. He sent Robertson[1] and Admiral Radford[2] to do it—some weeks ago—but they failed. He then started a long account of his early experience with *émigrés* (at the Paris Conference in 1918) and [how] they always let you down.[3]

In the end he reverted to what had essentially been the Menon plan. This meant a series of piecemeal talks settling minor causes of dispute.

By the end of June I felt that the American administration had become more flexible towards the problem of the Far East, and that the greatest danger was some ill-judged move by the Chinese Communists which would immediately involve retaliation. As the summit conference proceeded, we were to find that the Far East situation, though not formally discussed, was generally felt to be more dangerous than that in Europe.

After a day or two in Paris, where we had further talks, the Prime Minister and I reached Geneva on Sunday, 17 July.

The conditions at Geneva were agreeable. It was hot—but not too hot—and the villas in which the great men were housed were comfortable and cool. Eden and Eisenhower and Dulles each had their separate house which had been loaned them by distinguished citizens of Geneva. M. Faure, the French Prime Minister, and all the French occupied a villa not far from the President's, and the Russians had a large establishment a little further out of the city. I, being of inferior rank, stayed in an hotel—the famous Beau Rivage, where most of our Foreign Office advisers were also housed. There was something reassuring about the solid and ornate Edwardian decoration.

Eden had brought with him Sir Norman Brook, the head of the Cabinet Secretariat, and I had with me Sir Ivone Kirkpatrick, the head of the Foreign Office, in addition to my private secretaries. Fortunately, we had been allowed to bring our wives, and, although there was little amusement for them, it was pleasant enough as a change from the pressure of London. In addition to Clarissa Eden

---

[1] Walter S. Robertson, Assistant Secretary of State for Far Eastern Affairs.
[2] Admiral Arthur Radford, Chairman of the U.S. Joint Chiefs of Staff.
[3] 20 June 1955.

and Dorothy, there were Madame Faure and one or two other Frenchwomen who could make up agreeable parties. But the Americans and the Russians were strictly masculine.

This summit meeting had caused intense excitement and aroused wide hopes in every country. It was the first gathering of its kind since the end of the war and the fatal division of the world into the Communist and the free nations. It met in an atmosphere, hardly remembered now, which the first revelations of the power of nuclear weapons had spread: a degree of alarm, and even terror, which only the passage of time has softened. That President Eisenhower—the General who had led the Allied armies to victory—should come himself to this meeting was welcomed as a hopeful sign. It was known in what deep respect he had been held by the leading Russian commanders. If there was no single man to speak for the Soviet Government with the authority of Stalin, it was hoped that, in the milder regime of something like a Cabinet system, an atmosphere of conciliation might arise. Large crowds, therefore, and a mass of photographers and television operators attended every gathering, official and unofficial. By the historic lake with its background of noble mountains, entertained by the authorities of the oldest democracy in the world—here there might be hope of progress. If the Swiss Federation had resolved the problem of old national hatreds, could not their example be copied by the great nations themselves?

On the Sunday morning—the day before the conference opened—there was a small meeting in the President's villa. He seemed in happy mood and took me for a little walk alone before we began our talks; however, he spoke about our old associates rather than our present difficulties.

The conference took place in the library of his villa. Eden and I; Faure and Pinay; President and Dulles; and about two advisers each (we had Kirkpatrick and Norman Brook). The President's speech—or rather a summary of it—was passed round. No one seemed to have any particular view about it, except to ask that the passage about the 'satellites' and 'tyranny' might be modified. This was done.[1]

[1] 17 July 1955.

The French Prime Minister, Faure, then gave a long *exposé* of his ideas. While he did not seem to demur on the question of Germany, he was more interested—whether for internal or external reasons was not clear—about making some progress over disarmament.

> He had prepared an elaborate plan by which an international body should be set up to which we shall all pay the sums we are going to save by disarmament. The money will then be re-distributed to help 'backward areas'. He claims that this obligation to pay is the only real sanction to make sure that the disarmament really takes place. Neither the Americans nor the British seemed very keen about it.[1]

Fortunately we had no Treasury representatives with us; so we gave a polite if insincere assent to these ideas.

Eisenhower then put forward the outline of his plan, though without detail since it was still necessary to conform to the American theory that we did not put forward 'plans' but only 'illustrative suggestions'. With translations for Pinay's benefit, since Faure spoke or at least understood English, this took up the whole morning.

> We all lunched with the President—a disgusting meal, of large meat slices, hacked out . . . and served . . . with marmalade and jam. The French were appalled.[1]

The conference began at 10.15 next morning, the road to the conference hall—the old League of Nations building—being packed with sightseers and lined with police. The room in which we met filled me with horror the moment we entered it. The protagonists were sitting at tables drawn up in a rectangle; the space between them was about the size of a small boxing ring. But this arena was itself surrounded by rows of benches and seats which were provided, presumably, for the advisers but seemed to be occupied by a crowd of interested onlookers. The walls were decorated with vast, somewhat confused, frescoes depicting the End of the World, or the Battle of the Titans, or the Rape of the Sabines, or a mixture of all three. I could conceive of no arrangement less likely to lead to

[1] 17 July 1955.

intimate or useful negotiations. The whole formal part of the conference was bound to degenerate into a series of set orations. It was only when the Heads of Government or Foreign Ministers met in a small room outside in a restricted meeting that any serious discussion could take place.

The Russians were represented by Bulganin, Molotov and Khrushchev, Bulganin being apparently in charge. Formal speeches took up the whole day. Bulganin was friendly in manner, but stiff in matter. Eisenhower said some pleasant things, and proposed that the Foreign Ministers should meet the next morning to recommend an agenda. The Heads of Government would meet in the afternoon. All the speeches were to be published.

When the Foreign Ministers met the next morning, Pinay presided and asked me to speak.

> I said that I had read attentively all the speeches of yesterday, copies of which had been distributed. I had observed that there were some subjects which every speaker had included in his list, others which had been referred to by some of the speakers but not by all. I thought it would be sensible to deal first with those topics which everyone had included. These were:
> Reunification of Germany
> European security
> Disarmament
> Development of contacts between East and West.[1]

Molotov, who spoke next, added that there were other topics, such as the Far East, world trade, and the end of the Cold War, which ought not to be forgotten. Dulles then observed that, in that case, satellites and the question of international Communism should have a place.

> At one time, I thought we should have a long and inconclusive discussion about the agenda. But half-way through the second round, Molotov accepted my proposal.[1]

The Heads of Government met in the afternoon. I recorded my impressions as follows:

[1] 19 July 1955.

FIRST ROUND

Anthony Eden: What about safeguards?

Bulganin: We are strong; we do not want safeguards. Abolish NATO.

President: I assure you NATO is for peace.

Faure: We must unite Germany.

SECOND ROUND

Anthony Eden: You say you do not want safeguards. Why do you propose a European pact?

Bulganin: Abolish NATO. No more to say about Germany.

President: I have said my piece.

Anthony Eden (interrupting): The question of Germany is not exhausted. We must think about it.

Bulganin: Let's get on to the question of European security.

Faure: All right. But the two questions are interlocked.

Then we all went away.[1]

All this took about three hours.

Never having attended anything of this kind before, except the Vienna meeting, I felt somewhat concerned at the great waste of time; but Kirkpatrick assured me that this was the usual form. Moreover, arguments about the agenda were sometimes of real significance and not merely superficial. For instance, as Eden reminded me, at the Potsdam Conference the agenda had been drawn up with the Italian Peace Treaty and the Austrian Peace Treaty as the first two items.

> For two years thereafter the Russians had refused to discuss Austria until the Italian Treaty had been concluded.[2]

These interminable speeches would have been unbearably fatiguing had there not been frequent intervals when we all went off to drink together at the admirable buffet. Everybody was very cheerful, and there was a great deal of affability and friendliness displayed.

On the first evening the Russians came to dinner at the Prime Minister's villa. It was a purely Anglo-Russian affair, and we had told them that we wanted to talk business, which they had accepted, seemingly with alacrity.

[1] 19 July 1955.   [2] The Earl of Avon, *Full Circle*, p. 305.

Bulganin looks like a Radical-Socialist Mayor of a French industrial town. He might be *un bon papa*. He affects a jolly, friendly, but not undignified style. He is fat, about 60, and is a good figurehead. All his observations at the formal meetings have been read from a text. At dinner, and afterwards, he talked pretty freely.[1]

Eden conducted the whole affair with great brilliance, exerting all his charm, both during and after dinner. My impressions, made at the time, were as follows:

(*a*) They are very relaxed, after the removal of the tyrant, Stalin. (They said, with glee, that since 1953 they worked a normal day, instead of all night!) (*b*) They do not want another Stalin—a bloody and uncertain tyrant. (*c*) Khrushchev is the boss, but *not* another Stalin. He controls the party and thus, in a country where there is no Parliament, he controls the Government. (*d*) They are unable to accept the reunification of Germany in NATO, and will fight it as long as they can. This is partly because their public would be horrified. After all, the Germans treated them terribly and they hate them. (*e*) They do not fear war; they do not really believe that the Americans are going to attack them. (*f*) They are anxious about China. They told us so. They (like us) wish that Quemoy and Matsu could sink beneath the sea. (*g*) They may fear—in the long run—that China will be a danger to them on their eastern flank. I think they might prefer a weak nationalist or capitalist China, which they could plunder, to a Communist China, which they have to assist. (*h*) They do not want the conference to fail. They will play for a draw.[1]

Eden made a gallant attempt to get the Russians to agree to some compromise which would at least keep the question of reunification alive. I thought they were impressed by his fairness.

It would be tedious to describe the details of this famous conference. Eden has given an admirable account, and the State Department was soon to publish the official story. Moreover, those speeches which were not officially published were, in fact, leaked to the Press.

On 20 July Eden and I went to breakfast with the President and Dulles at the unconscionable hour of 8.30 a.m. Eisenhower was

[1] 19 July 1955.

determined to get something that could be called a success or at any
rate to avoid a failure. After a rather inconclusive meeting with the
Foreign Ministers, the Heads of Government did at last agree to
disagree.

> But it was also agreed to give to the Foreign Ministers the task
> of writing a directive for themselves tomorrow morning, to be
> 'shown up' in the afternoon to the Heads.[1]

When the full conference met in the afternoon of 21 July, Bulganin
was in the chair and began with a long speech of his own. Although
the subject was nominally disarmament, in reality he discussed the
question of European security, NATO and all the rest. He even
produced the text of a new European treaty to be entered into
between the NATO and Warsaw Pact powers. He then changed to a
new theme nearer the subject of debate. But since his plan really
included the immediate abolition of all nuclear weapons without any
effective system of control, it was not a valuable contribution.

> Eisenhower spoke next—a very moving, though not very
> coherent address. He proposed to throw open everything, on
> both sides of the Iron Curtain, to full inspection by anyone.[2]

Clearly the President attached great importance to this dramatic
proposal, which was destined to be rejected by the Russians after
their return to Moscow. He thought that by providing facilities for
mutual aerial inspection a real advance could be made towards a
sense of genuine security. Eden then made another modest but
practical suggestion:

> Why not inspection, first 100 miles, then 200 miles, then still
> further—with the present line as the centre?[2]

Thinking of the realities which lay behind all this diplomatic screen,
I passed a note to Kirkpatrick:

> 'To abolish the nuclear now would spread terror throughout
> Europe.'[2]

For I was beginning to reflect more and more upon the strange fact
that peace was being preserved, not endangered, by nuclear power.

[1] 20 July 1955.   [2] 21 July 1955.

Geneva, July 1955
Molotov, Bulganin, Khrushchev, Zhukov, Faure, Macmillan, Eden, Dulles

The first summit, Geneva, 17 July 1955

'The protagonists were sitting at tables drawn up in a rectangle; the space between them was about the size of a small boxing ring . . .The walls were decorated with vast, somewhat confused, frescoes depicting the End of the World, or the Battle of the Titans, or the Rape of the Sabines, or a mixture of all three. I could conceive of no arrangement less likely to lead to intimate or useful negotiations.'

This paradox was to confuse and invalidate much of the subsequent arguments about disarmament.

On the following day, 22 July, we met for breakfast at Eden's villa.

> Dulles came and ate boiled eggs one after another . . . we tried to get him to talk. . . . But he ate and talked so slowly that we got little out of him which we did not know before.[1]

In fact the Foreign Secretaries, when they met alone in the morning as directed, made some progress.

> The text of the directive on European Security is agreed. The text on Germany is agreed, except for the point about Eastern and Western Governments of Germany having a 'right' to participate. This Adenauer can never accept.[1]

But it all took a long time. Indeed, when the hour had passed 1 p.m., Pinay, whose first experience this was of Russian stonewalling tactics, was very disturbed. Molotov teasingly proposed that we should meet again at 2.30. This prospect was almost too much for him and he suggested 3.30 instead.

> I admitted that I was going to lunch with the French, and was looking forward to it; but I thought perhaps 3 p.m. might do. Molotov said 'Mr. Macmillan always makes compromises—and good ones. Let it be 3 p.m.' So it was agreed.[1]

The French luncheon was certainly superb. There was a relaxed and happy atmosphere. Clarissa, Dorothy and Madame Faure were the ladies. The French had not forgotten their experience and put on a long series of exquisite courses, with wines of equal distinction. It was a demonstration of the refinement of the Old World against the barbarism of the New, whether in the East or in the West.

This was a painful day with little to show. What with the meetings of the Foreign Secretaries and the Heads of Government we did not finish till 8.15 p.m. The British delegation then attended a Russian dinner given in their honour. The atmosphere was relaxed and easy. The Russians, who are very hospitable, enjoy parties and

[1] 22 July 1955.

x

we had all the usual delicacies followed by toasts, sentimental speeches about the last war, about comradeship, about future co-operation, combined with a great deal of chaff. I felt more and more that Bulganin, although nominally the head, was of minor importance and that Molotov was already a sick man.

> Khrushchev is the mystery. How can this fat, vulgar man, with his pig eyes and ceaseless flow of talk, really be the head—the aspirant Tsar—of all these millions of people and this vast country?[1]

Also present was Marshal Zhukov, a regular soldier who might well have served either in the old Russian or in the British army. It was at this dinner that Eden invited Bulganin and Khrushchev to come to England the following spring, a proposal which they accepted with apparently genuine pleasure.

My impressions were as follows:

> 1. They do not want war. So long as nuclear weapons exist, they know it to be impossible. Of course, they would dearly like to get the weaker powers to abandon nuclear weapons.
> 2. They are not very keen on their Chinese connection. It is a convenience now to have such an ally; but it is drawing very heavily upon their resources, both industrial and military. Moreover, they look ahead and wonder whether China may not be a danger.
> 3. Although they brag about the agricultural situation, they are alarmed about it.
> 4. They hate and fear the Germans. They will do everything to stop German unification, so long as NATO exists.[1]

The work of the conference was now in a sense complete. The best that could be done was to agree upon the directive for the meeting of Foreign Ministers later in the year. At the end of a very long day an agreement was at last reached in the form I had originally proposed, linking European security and German re-unification under a single heading. What was perhaps equally important was the approval of an acceptable form of words on the disarmament directive. The final arguments were carried on at a

[1] 22 July 1955.

restricted meeting. The Russians were disposed to contest almost every word of the text, and there were some anxious moments when the President seemed to have been put into a position from which he could not retreat. But by five o'clock we had accomplished all that was possible. It only remained to hold the formal plenary meeting in the large hall, which was fixed for 6.30. M. Faure was in the chair and called on Eden, whose speech was short and in exactly the right tone. Bulganin followed, with a long boorish speech, restating all the position which they had taken up on the first day and from which they had been gradually forced. No doubt it was partly intended for home consumption and partly due to mere peevishness. The President was very angry but only allowed himself one sentence of rebuke and then delivered a noble little address.

Thus ended the conference after six days of hard work, both at the table and behind the scenes. The President and Dulles went straight to the airfield, and we made our farewells to the French and returned for dinner. We were to have one further meeting with the Russians at their request. Here our discussion was almost entirely on the problems of Indo-China, on which the Russians seemed to be taking a very reasonable view.

> Bulganin then began to talk about his visit to England. Khrushchev broke in and seemed quite delighted with the prospect. It was agreed that they would 'discuss it with their colleagues' in Moscow. They hoped to be ready for an announcement to be made in the House of Commons on Wednesday.
>
> They then raised the question of other visits—military missions, naval visits, etc. It is obvious that Marshal Zhukov wants a trip of his own ![1]

Eden next made an appeal to them on the question of prisoners of war, of whom there were believed to be a very large number, both German and Italian, still in the Soviet Union, but the Russians vigorously protested their denial.

> Khrushchev told a long story to prove that he had tried to get one particular Italian sent back some years ago—but he was dead, at Irkutsk in Siberia.

[1] 23 July 1955.

If what they said is true (which none of us believe) then hundreds of thousands of these poor people must be dead. Eden handled this very well, I thought. He went on just long enough to wound them, and perhaps alarm them (since they seem to want to be loved), but not long enough to be discourteous or inappropriate to a visit of this kind.[1]

What, if anything, had the conference achieved? Speaking to reporters on his return to England, the Prime Minister said:

I think we were wise in not trying to get down to too much detail. We really tried to achieve three things: to agree upon the nature of the problems we have to solve; to chart the course; and to try in private discussion to reduce the sense of mistrust. I think it is true to say we succeeded in all three more than I anticipated.[2]

Others were more sceptical and felt there was no real gain except for general amiability, in contrast to previous conferences. When it came to the debate in Parliament Eden elaborated his first statement in a clear and well-argued speech. Morrison, who followed, was fair and even generous. Perhaps the announcement of the visit of Bulganin and Khrushchev added something to what would otherwise have been a very pedestrian discussion. I had to wind up and found it hard to say much, although the House was sympathetic. As I told them:

... a Foreign Secretary is always caught by a cruel dilemma— hovering between the cliché and the indiscretion. He is either dull or dangerous.[3]

In reflecting on Geneva, a strange, and to me novel, experience, I felt some encouragement, largely because of the strong impression left in my mind that all the great nations who were in the nuclear game now accepted that modern war, that is nuclear war, was quite impossible and could only lead to mutual destruction.

It is important that other nations, like China, should know it too. 'Peace,' say all the leader-writers, etc., 'is now assured because everyone knows that there can be no victor in war today.'

[1] 23 July 1955.
[2] *Annual Register, 1955,* p. 45.   [3] 27 July 1955.

Then after a few intervening paragraphs, they go on to say 'Ban the nuclear bomb.' But is this syllogism really sound? Is the deduction correct? If we abolish the nuclear bomb (which has abolished war) shall we not bring back war? This is a danger, even if we succeeded in a water-tight system of control, inspection and all the rest, which is impossible.[1]

The Russians seemed to me to be persuaded of this fact. What perhaps they did not realise any more than we did was that the danger of the virtual abolition of war between the Great Powers, owing to their nuclear strength, might lead to the encouragement of minor conflicts between smaller nations who had no such inhibitions. My experience at Geneva supported me in the efforts I was subsequently to make as Prime Minister towards a *détente* with Russia. But I did not then fully realise how serious was the effect of the breakdown of any Concert of Great Powers or how dangerous this would prove to be as the great Empires gradually withered away, to be succeeded by a general Balkanisation of the areas within which they had once been able to preserve peace and order.

Soon after our return, I made a pilgrimage to Chartwell where I found Churchill alone.

He was very grateful for the small attentions which I have been able to show him. Montague Browne (formerly one of his Private Secretaries and now back in the Foreign Office) goes to see him two or three days a week. He helps him with his immense correspondence and also brings a selection of foreign telegrams for him to see.[2]

He was much interested in Geneva but, after some discussion, it became clear that he preferred to revive old memories.

I was able to get him to talk about the First War, Gallipoli, Lloyd George and so on. He said that of all the offices he had held, the Admiralty (other than the Premiership) was the one he enjoyed most. But, alas, its glamour had gone. Nuclear warfare and the Ministry of Defence had extinguished the old brilliance of that office. He thought Asquith ill advised, and but for his

[1] 25 July 1955.   [2] 5 August 1955.

friends he could have maintained himself [in 1916]. But, with all his merits, he could not run a war. His mind was too set.[1]

On their way home from Geneva the Russian leaders thought it necessary to spend several days in East Germany, pledging their loyal support. This was followed on 8 September by a visit by Adenauer to Moscow. He was able to conclude an agreement for the return of nearly 10,000 so-called 'war criminals' (the only German prisoners of war the Russians admitted to be still holding), together with any other Germans who might be found in Soviet territory. The price that the Chancellor was forced to pay was the establishment of diplomatic relations. There were many who felt this was a considerable diplomatic victory for the Soviet. But I did not share their concern. 'At least it will stop the Germans rebuking us (as they are apt to do) for our weakness towards the Russians !'[2]

A few days after Adenauer left, the Soviet Union signed a treaty with the East German Government, ostensibly according them the same sovereignty as was enjoyed by the Federal Republic. The Western Governments, in response to a request from Adenauer, countered at the end of September by a statement that they regarded the Federal Republic as the sole legal representative of Germany. They added that they considered existing frontiers as provisional until a peace treaty could be negotiated. Whether this was an altogether wise move or not may be disputed; but it formed part of a number of diplomatic manœuvres on both sides in anticipation of the meeting of Foreign Ministers at Geneva.

At home, while the public was prepared to await the outcome of the autumn conference on European questions, they began to be deeply concerned about disarmament. The apparently comprehensive Russian proposals had made an impact on public opinion. Yet we knew that the Russians themselves recognised the difficulty of any system of inspection and control, by which alone the abolition of nuclear weapons or indeed any effective limitation of armaments, could be enforced. I myself felt that at the forthcoming session of the Disarmament Subcommittee in the United Nations we must insist on a full discussion of this vital matter. If it should become clear

[1] 5 August 1955.   [2] 17 September 1955.

that no efficient system could be devised, and if the Russians agreed that we were all afflicted by the same difficulty, then we should at least have widened the areas of agreement between us. Meanwhile we must not delude ourselves. We must not be led away into a false disarmament based upon mere 'declarations of intent' without any effective system of control. The public certainly expected some positive action, and this was a political problem which we must face. In spite of pressure from many quarters I continued to maintain that we should concentrate upon forcing the Disarmament Subcommittee of the United Nations to make an effective study of the realities—that is, inspection and control. Without these, a convention to abolish nuclear weapons might be a positive threat to peace, since it would weaken the deterrent to war and produce a dangerous competition in the clandestine production of nuclear arms.

Animated, if often ignorant, debates on the disarmament question were to continue for many years without any positive result. Among the principals the discussions were mainly fencing, although used by both sides as propaganda. It was not till long afterwards that agreement was reached for the banning of nuclear tests. Even then, President Kennedy and I had regretfully to accept the limitation of the treaty to those tests which could be readily checked by scientists in any part of the world—that is, atmospheric tests. We were unable to include the abolition of underground tests owing to the refusal of the Russians to accept any system of inspection, however limited, upon Russian soil.

The state of our own development of the nuclear weapon was at this time a matter of some concern. We were not yet ready for our own tests. An agreement to abolish tests would therefore be embarrassing to us; but this would not be an overriding consideration if a genuine and enforceable system could be devised. I also felt that we should be ready to discuss the reduction of conventional forces to any agreed figures, and should be prepared to put into force such a limitation forthwith. In addition, we might propose that the nuclear powers should immediately undertake not to use unconventional weapons, of whatever kind, against any country, unless aggressively attacked. But we should not allow ourselves to be pushed even by popular pressure into the acceptance of proposals which we sincerely believed to be both ineffective and dangerous. I was still chiefly worried about the fallacy in which we seemed likely to be caught: 'Nuclear warfare has made war impossible. Therefore abolish nuclear warfare.'

CHAPTER XIX

Seeds of Strife

O N 25 September I went to New York for the meeting of the United Nations, attendance at which had become an obligation upon all Foreign Ministers. Although it was difficult to make any very valuable contribution to the formal debates, these gatherings afforded a useful opportunity for informal discussions.

On my arrival I was met by our admirable representative, Sir Pierson Dixon, who had served with me in Algiers. He told me

of President Eisenhower's attack of coronary thrombosis, which took place in the early hours of Saturday morning at Denver.[1]

This sad news created a universal wave of sympathy and sorrow. Even among the usual crowd of photographers and Press men,

there seemed to be a sense of strange quiet—almost of reverent hush. The whole of America is gripped with anxiety.[1]

When I saw Dulles the next day he told me that he hoped, and believed, that the President would make a speedy recovery. Meanwhile we went on with our work, and a series of meetings was arranged with the Americans and the French.

These went off very well, the ground having been admirably prepared by the official working party. I managed to get agreement about the only question in serious dispute—the British idea of the demilitarised zone.[2]

There was also an opportunity for the discussion of other questions at a dinner given by Dulles to the Foreign Ministers—including, of course, Molotov. So far as the arrangements for Geneva were concerned, everything was readily agreed. But there were more difficult matters which we felt bound to raise.

[1] 25 September 1955.   [2] 27 September 1955.

While at Geneva, Eden and Eisenhower had discussed the Far East at length, the former maintaining that the commitment to the islands of Quemoy and Matsu was a source not of strength but of weakness. The President had accepted this diagnosis. He recognised his heavy responsibility and was resolved to restrain Chiang. But he was unwilling to do more than try to persuade him to regard these positions as outposts rather than as strongholds, thus diminishing the loss of prestige if they were finally captured. The Russian leaders had not disguised from us in our private talks the drain on their resources which the Chinese connection involved and their concern about the future. All we could do at Geneva was to counsel patience; but the Russians fully recognised the threat to world peace which the Far Eastern crisis presented.

In the course of September agreement was reached between the Americans and Chinese regarding the exchange of their nationals in one another's territory. By the time, therefore, of our talks with Molotov in New York, the situation, although still a source of anxiety, seemed no longer as tense as hitherto. Indeed, when we met in Geneva at the end of October Molotov only raised in a somewhat perfunctory manner the question of Communist shipping detained by the Nationalist authorities in Formosa. By now our chief concern was to persuade the Americans to take a more tolerant view of the question of British trade with Communist China. This was always a delicate issue in our relations with Washington. Although we felt strongly that the list of prohibited exports was far too wide, in view of the much greater difficulties arising elsewhere we agreed to postpone a final decision until the end of the year. In the course, therefore, of a few months the Far Eastern dangers, though they were later to become accentuated, had for the moment faded into the background. All anxieties, other than those of the great European issues, were now concentrated upon the growing confusion in the Middle East and the alarming signs of Russian intervention.

As Minister of Defence I had been obliged to stress the importance of some agreed Anglo-American policy, if only to secure help to the friendly Governments of Iraq and Iran. In February 1955 Turkey and Iraq had signed a mutual defence pact in Baghdad to which, on

4 April, Great Britain adhered. The adhesion of Pakistan to the Baghdad Pact announced in July was an important gain, and even Dulles was now prepared to tell the Iraqis that America would agree to join, as full members, if a Palestine settlement could be reached. But all attempts to consolidate stability in the Middle East were bedevilled by the Arab–Israel conflict.

In the Nile valley the story of 1955 was one of unilateral and unrequited British gestures. We evacuated the Sudan; we made preparations to leave the Canal zone; we agreed to a new arrangement for the release of sterling to the Egyptian Government, and we also undertook to provide arms on a limited scale. We had, unhappily, in the agreement of 1954 made no provision for Egypt's lifting the blockade against Israel. In May, alarmed by Egyptian propaganda and intransigence and fearing an Egyptian attack, Moshe Sharett, the Israeli Prime Minister, had asked the United States for a guarantee. Dulles, unwilling to guarantee frontiers which the Arabs wholly repudiated, would only consider such a measure if an understanding could be reached between Israel and the Arab world.

A plan was now put forward confidentially by Dulles for the settlement of the Arab–Israeli dispute which became a subject of much anxious discussion. It was to provide for the establishment of a sovereign Arab right-of-way across the Negev without impairing the Israeli sovereign right-of-way to Eilat on the Red Sea. The idea was that Israel should cede two small triangles in the extreme south of the Negev, a few miles north of Eilat, one to Egypt with its base on the Egypt–Israel frontier, the other to Jordan with its base on the Jordan–Israel frontier. The points of the two triangles would meet on the Israeli road from Beersheba to Eilat; and at this junction, which might need mixed or international supervision, a road from Egypt to Jordan under complete Arab control would pass over (or under) the road to Eilat, which would remain under complete Israeli control. It was believed that this combination of diplomacy and engineering would be a novel, but perhaps decisive, feature in the settlement proposed. This plan, fantastic as it appeared, was Dulles's pet idea. Like the White Knight, he claimed it proudly as his own invention.

Dulles's scheme was adversely reported on by both the American and British Ambassadors in Cairo and little progress seemed possible. Although in the middle of June there was some improvement in the situation at Gaza, where border incidents had been continuous, a rumour reached us that the Egyptians were likely to turn now to the Russians.

During the Debate on the Address all that I could do was to reiterate the British Government's determination to keep some equilibrium in arms delivery and to stand by the Tripartite Declaration.[1]

Meanwhile I kept urging Dulles to join the Baghdad Pact and finance the supply of British Centurion tanks to Nuri es-Said's Government in Iraq.

> We had been left with the Turco-Iraqi pact, which the Americans started, and then ran out of. Could he help us with Nuri Pasha in two ways: (*a*) promising to join the Turco-Iraqi pact *after* [his ideas for an Israel–Egypt settlement] had been launched; (*b*) by buying Centurion tanks from us – by off-shore purchase – to give to the Iraqis ?[2]

At the summit conference, Eden and I had done our best to persuade the President to join in a gift to Iraq of British Centurion tanks. The President agreed that if we would give ten, the United States would give seventy or more to be provided from our stocks by 'off-shore purchase' – a most satisfactory arrangement.

In this baffling atmosphere, where, apart from the Israeli problems, the relations between the Arab States themselves were changing with the rapidity of colours in a kaleidoscope, there was one minor satisfaction. The Saudis had been interfering by propaganda and money with our position in the Aden Protectorate. I had persuaded the Cabinet to send substantial reinforcements and this led to an immediate restoration of order. Sir Ivone Kirkpatrick did not fail to point out the moral both to me and the Prime Minister, 'Stay strong in Aden and the Gulf.'

Although Iraq, under the sagacious leadership of the royal family and of Nuri Pasha, seemed a reasonably solid element in a fluid

---

[1] See above, p. 149.   [2] 14 July 1955.

situation, Nasser was already beginning to stir up the Arab countries by the violence of his propaganda. Any sign of moderation was denounced and the more stable Governments of the Arab countries had begun to show their alarm at the pressure to which they were being subjected. Syria, Saudi Arabia and Jordan were all coming more and more under Nasser's influence, and the usual mixture of bribery and terrorism, so common in Middle Eastern politics, was playing its part. Although the Syrians had assured Nuri Pasha that the Egypt–Syria pact was directed against Israel and not against Iraq, subsequent events were to prove how justified were the anxieties of our Iraqi friends.

After we returned from the summit meeting long and complicated messages flowed between London and Washington regarding the United States' willingness to adhere to the Baghdad Pact, and to follow a path on which they had themselves launched us. Dulles continued to take the line that this would only be possible if and when a Palestine settlement had been reached and fortified by an American guarantee. He therefore proposed, on 19 August, to publish his plan for a settlement, but in a more generalised and less specific form.

> Dulles has now proposed (*a*) to make his statement in quite general terms; (*b*) to make it on 25 or 26 August. This has caused No. 10 to flap. However, Sir Ivone appeared quite calm on the telephone.[1]

I was in favour of the Americans going ahead, because in the form in which it was now to be made I did not think there would be any serious Arab reaction. Moreover,

> we get ten Centurion tanks for Iraq, with the promise of more to come. . . . Any speech made in America after this date will be much worse—because electioneering will soon begin and blatant wooing of the Jewish vote.[1]

Also we had now a clear promise that if the Arab–Israel tension could be reduced, America would join the Baghdad Pact. This would be a prize for which something could well be risked.

[1] 19 August 1955.

I was now beginning to understand something of Dulles's strange and complex character. With all his faults—his agonisingly slow speech, his unwillingness to look you straight in the face, his deviousness of method—there was something engaging about him if you could once penetrate the surface. His rare smile had great charm. Although I had only seen him in action for a few months, I could understand both the admiration and the distrust in which he was held by many of his own countrymen. He had been an ardent student of foreign affairs for many years and had worked for various American administrations both in Paris and elsewhere. But his almost encyclopaedic knowledge seemed to result in a small end-product. With an impressive frame and speaking often with an outward appearance of authority, he was in fact hesitant and un-certain. But a natural vacillation was covered with fine words and a succession of ingenious plans. Our difficulty was that Eisenhower was completely under his influence; except on very rare occasions of supreme importance it was no good appealing to the President over the head of the Secretary of State. Kirkpatrick, with his usual humour and shrewdness, was well aware of what was happening. He wrote to me in the course of the disputes as to the publication of the Dulles plan:

> There is something in Mr. Dulles which particularly irritates the Prime Minister. So you will not be surprised to hear that he is more than annoyed at Mr. Dulles's latest antics.
> But my impression is that he has blown off steam and will not wish to provoke an open row with the Americans.
> The draft statement is really not too bad and I am sure that our best course is to make the best of it.[1]

Actually, when the announcement and our supporting statement was published, its reception in Iraq was good, although the other Arab States hesitated, awaiting a lead from Egypt. Unfortunately, almost at the same time there were dangerous incidents in Gaza, and on 4 September an Israeli attack was launched. As I had to explain to the Italian Foreign Minister, Gaetano Martino, who visited me about this time, the flare-up in Gaza had stolen the limelight

[1] 20 August 1955.

from Dulles's proposals. However, no country had yet denounced them. In the middle of September the Israeli Ambassador, M. Eliahu Elath, a pleasant and sincere man, called to see me.

On instructions, he asked certain questions (which I knew he would ask) and I gave certain replies (which he expected me to give). After that, we had a most helpful talk about the situation.[1]

The arming of Egypt, partly with our help, had worried Israel, but the Ambassador fully accepted that we had done our best in concert with the French and Americans to keep a fair balance in our supplies to the various contending countries. Naturally he complained that if a guarantee to Israel had to await a final settlement, this in effect gave the Arabs a power of veto. On the other hand, I had to point out that it was difficult to guarantee frontiers which nobody had agreed. If the new plan were successful, the situation would be changed.

But the Egyptians were unyielding. They still demanded at least the Southern Negev and declared that the system of corridors would not prove satisfactory. Nevertheless, even they did not altogether reject the American scheme. Then came a piece of news which marked an alarming development.

On 22 September we heard of an important arms deal between Egypt and Russia on a scale which would seriously alter the balance of power in the Middle East. It was clear that notwithstanding all the benefits which we had unilaterally conferred upon Egypt, we had won no gratitude. Nasser had now realised that with a little pressure he could induce both the West and the Soviets to bid up each other's price. The actual deal, to be carried out through the medium of Czechoslovakia, was for a hundred MIGs, a hundred tanks, some submarines, and the assistance of Russian technicians for a 'limited period'. All the countries of the Middle East had hitherto relied on the Western powers. While there had been many arguments about details, it had been generally accepted that deliveries should be on an equitable basis. Now there had entered a new and sinister element into this already complicated tangle of confusion. Was this the beginning of a definite decision by the

[1] 15 September 1955.

Kremlin to enter in a big way into Middle Eastern politics? Was this a move of the new Russian imperialism? Were we back at something like the situation which successive British Governments had faced at recurring intervals in the second half of the nineteenth century?

The Prime Minister and I met immediately and sent urgent telegrams to Washington. I also registered a complaint with the new Egyptian Ambassador, M. Samy Aboul Fetouh, who could only murmur somewhat insincerely that the deal was not yet completed. When I saw Dulles in New York he

> told me that he had spoken strongly to Molotov about it and told him that the President and he both took a most serious view of it. Molotov tried to pass it off as a purely commercial transaction, but Dulles would not have that. We talked all round the question, and what we might do to bring pressure on Nasser, either by stick or carrot, or a combination of both treatments.[1]

Alas, neither was to prove effective. On 27 September Nasser formally announced the completion of the deal, and the fat was now publicly in the fire. It was in this atmosphere that the four Foreign Ministers met after dinner the same evening in New York. The conference took its usual form:

> ... four armchairs for the protagonists, in the middle of the room, with all the seconds, trainers, etc., ranged behind.[2]

After referring to arrangements for Geneva and some matters regarding election of new members to the United Nations, Dulles asked whether there were any other questions to be raised. I opened up the problem of Palestine. It was surely in the interests of all the Great Powers to keep things quiet in this area while we were trying to negotiate larger issues. Here in Palestine there was a situation at once tense and delicate between Egypt and Israel. We had tried to keep a balance in their armaments and to prevent an arms race as far as possible. I had heard rumours of a large sale by Russia of arms to Egypt. If so, this would have a grave effect throughout the Middle East.

[1] 26 September 1955.   [2] 27 September 1955.

Molotov replied on rather different lines from what he had said to Dulles. He said he knew little about the matter, but would enquire. He agreed that tension should be kept low.[1]

But how could a balance be maintained? Perhaps, he suggested, through an interchange of information? Meanwhile he seemed rather embarrassed and even furtive.

This sudden incursion of the Russians into a field from which hitherto they had kept studiously aloof was a source of deep anxiety. By agreement with me, Dulles undertook to send a personal protest in writing to Nasser, as well as through the American Ambassador in Cairo. Nevertheless, Molotov's offer to exchange information about arms contracts raised an important question of policy. Eden was inclined to accept this at its face value and hoped to bring the Russians into some agreed policy for keeping the arms of the different countries in the Middle East on a basis of reasonable equality. Although there were obvious attractions in this idea, there were also dangers. Hitherto, Russian policy had been to leave the Middle East alone. Was it prudent to invite them in?

At a dinner given by the Russians I was able to press Molotov a little as to what he meant by exchange of views. My conclusion was

> that the Russians will not be cajoled out of this new move by Eden or anyone else. They are approaching Syria, Saudi-Arabia, Libya and other countries. It is really the opening of a new offensive in the Middle East, while Europe is 'contained' by the Geneva spirit, and the Far East has become temporarily stabilised. Nor does this cost them anything. The weapons they will distribute will be obsolete or obsolescent, and will soon be replaced in any case.[2]

Nor was I much comforted by M. Mohamed Fawzi, the Egyptian Foreign Minister, who called to see me at his own request. He was a skilful diplomat of the old school, smooth and insinuating. He called the arms episode 'a most regrettable matter'. Nevertheless the situation was still 'flexible'. I could only express my amazement at this arms agreement, which seemed quite contrary to the whole

[1] 27 September 1955.   [2] 29 September 1955.

spirit of the previous year's Anglo-Egyptian Treaty and full of dangers for the future.

Eden was now very anxious to send a personal appeal to Bulganin; but I was frankly concerned about his proposed wording which seemed to me dangerously wide. Fawzi had made it clear to me that Egypt would not be satisfied with the corridor arrangements in Dulles's proposal and was now demanding not merely the southern portion but the whole of the Negev. Behind his suppleness there was a hard and even challenging note which made me suspect that he was sure of Soviet support. My own feeling was that any personal message to Bulganin would not be effective and that our right course was to support Iran and other States who would join us in the Baghdad Pact. Above all we must make a new effort to persuade the Americans, who were still dallying, to take the plunge. I had gone to Washington, and the telegraphic interchange with London continued merrily. I disliked the last paragraph of Eden's draft.

> He cannot make an offer on behalf of the Americans (who disagree sharply) and the French (who have not been asked) to sit round the table with the Russians and discuss our arms programme to Middle Eastern countries.[1]

Immediately on my return to England I heard that the Prime Minister had held up his telegram to Bulganin for the Cabinet to decide. This was a considerable moral victory, for I felt myself drifting into the position in which Eden had himself been forced by previous Prime Ministers. Messages of this kind must be agreed by the Foreign Secretary of the day and any divergencies must be submitted to the Cabinet. However, since my points had been effectively met in the revised draft, I was satisfied. The telegram was accordingly sent off on 4 October. This little controversy had its comical side, because after all the excitement and the pleas for urgent action in London it was discovered later that in any case neither Bulganin nor Khrushchev was in Moscow and that our Ambassador there would have no opportunity of seeing them before 10 October.

[1] 2 October 1955.

Our broad policy, however, was beginning to take shape.

I want to get Persia into the Baghdad Pact; to give *all* we can to Iraq and get U.S. to do the same. I want to declare for the immediate independence of the Sudan (Nasser will not relish this), and get Americans to reduce economic aid to Egypt and transfer it to Iraq.[1]

It was also vital to get our tanks off to Iraq as soon as possible and press the Americans to follow suit. The Geneva spirit was all very well, but if it merely produced a certain amount of relaxation in the West and fresh Russian aggression in the Middle East, it was a poor result for all our efforts.

Bulganin's reply when it came was not very encouraging. He asserted that there was no reason for anxiety about Egypt's decision to purchase arms from Czechoslovakia. Egypt had received arms from many countries already and one could understand her desire to ensure her defence and safeguard her independence. Nor were there any political conditions attached—it was a purely commercial transaction. In any event, the best method of reducing tension would be a general agreement on disarmament in accordance with the Russian proposals. The only comfort I could take was the formal adherence of Iran to the Baghdad Pact on the same day (11 October) that we received this somewhat disingenuous answer from Moscow.

In the midst of all these alarms and excursions I had to fit in a visit to the Conservative conference at Bournemouth and to deliver a speech on 7 October. I took the opportunity to set out our objectives in the forthcoming meeting of Foreign Ministers.

Whether we succeed or not depends upon the answer given to a very simple question: why does the Soviet Government object to the establishment of a united Germany under a system of free elections? Now, of course, I quite understand that after the terrible sufferings of war and the terrible injuries inflicted upon Russia by the Nazi armies that the Russian people and Government should have determined that this should never be allowed to happen again, and that the soil of holy Russia should never again be defiled by an invader. So it was perhaps natural to use

[1] 4 October 1955.

the countries which their armies had occupied after the war as a
kind of protective screen. That was at least understandable, and
if we are to make progress, you know, we must try to understand them. But if this is the difficulty I am sure it can be overcome. I am sure we can formulate plans which the world will
feel – and I hope the Russian Government will feel – would give full
protection to Russia against any threat which might come from a
reunited Germany, whether such a Germany chooses to join
NATO or whether it prefers to remain neutral.

These are the security proposals which the Western Heads of
Government sketched out last May and which we shall present
in greater detail in a few weeks. We are prepared to add to a legal
pact actual military dispositions and arrangements, arrangements
for mutual inspection or control to serve the same purpose, that
is to underwrite the words of a pact by the deeds of military
understanding. If these proposals do not, as they are stated
or will be stated, fully satisfy and meet the Russian requirements, why then, we say, let them suggest amendments and we
will certainly consider them in the spirit of wishing to reach
agreement.

Meanwhile I could not disguise from myself the dangers which
lay ahead. The more accommodating attitude, at any rate on the
surface, which the Russians had shown at Geneva and our willingness to accept it at its face value might well lead some other Governments to weaken the solidarity of the anti-Russian front. We had
passed from a war of position to a war of movement. Though the
prizes might be higher, the conduct of foreign policy was more
tricky.

If Russia had now decided to side with the Arabs against Israel
and if their offers of arms were not limited to Egypt, it would be
difficult to hold the loyalty of other parts of the Arab world. Then
our oil interests, and some thought our survival as a Great Power,
would be at stake. What had we to counter this? We could try to
convince the Arabs of the danger of Communism. Russia would
not give help without some return, and the price to be paid would
be disagreeable, especially to the more conservative States. Our only
effective measure seemed to be the creation of an Arab bloc led by
Iraq. But this of course might involve the hostility of other Arab

powers and would be geographically difficult if both Egypt and Syria were ill disposed or fell under Communist Governments. We were soon to meet the Russians at Geneva. We must make a fresh effort to point out to them the dangers which they were creating, whether as part of a definite policy of aggression or without full realisation of the implications.

Everything was now set for the Geneva meeting. Meanwhile a new and irritating problem arose which required immediate attention. Saudi Arabia was now demanding the Buraimi oasis, to which they had no real claim but which was vital to our oil interests. An arbitration tribunal had been agreed and had begun its work in September. But owing to the conduct of the Saudi member and the widespread attempts at bribery, the British representative withdrew and the arbitration broke down. Our only course was to support the local ruler, whose rights we accepted, and to occupy the area by force. In all the circumstances I thought it wiser not to consult the United States or even the old Commonwealth territories about our decision. This operation was successfully carried out on the morning of 16 October and the House of Commons duly informed. Attlee loyally supported the Government's action, and when I told Dulles in Geneva what had happened, he did not seem unduly disturbed, although a day or two later he complained that the State Department was upset because they had had no prior warning. I explained that this was due to anxiety to avoid involving him in any accusation of complicity, and with this explanation he appeared satisfied. The charge of bribery was fully justified, for when we occupied the area a Saudi police detachment was found in possession of sums of money far in excess of their requirements, and of documents amply confirming our charges. The Gulf rulers were of course completely in accord with our action, which enhanced their own security.

A similar difficulty arose later in the year in this area, where we acted resolutely and to our ultimate advantage. The Imam of Oman, who exercised a local authority under the suzerainty of the Sultan of Muscat and Oman, had begun, with Saudi financial and political backing, to assert his complete independence. He even ventured to send ambassadors to Cairo and elsewhere. Eden agreed with me that this must be stopped and that we must give full assistance to the rightful sovereign who enjoyed a historic claim to our protection. Over this action many difficulties subsequently arose, but the final result was one which proved altogether to our advantage.

Before leaving for Geneva I had a further talk with Dulles in Paris about the Middle East. He agreed to push on with more tanks to Iraq and send military and political observers to the Baghdad meeting; but he still shrank from full American membership. He pleaded the necessity for any formal treaty to secure a two-thirds majority in the Senate; but admitted that the difficulty might be avoided by a 'Congressional resolution' in favour of America joining the Pact. America would give no guarantee to Israel but would agree to a restatement of the Tripartite Declaration of 1950. This brought us to a discussion of developments in Syria, which now seemed to be moving into the Moscow–Cairo axis. He was anxious that Syria should not be allowed to go Communist, and seemed ready for some counter-action.

We next talked of Egypt, and decided to try to get the Aswan Dam for a Western group, by some means or other. He read me a telegram giving an account of a meeting in Washington between the [World] Bank and the State Department, and asked if we would join. I said 'Of course we will'. . . .[1]

During the next few weeks the question of Germany and European security and that of the Middle East seemed inextricably intertwined. It was our duty to concentrate primarily on the task which we had been set by the Heads of Government at the Geneva meeting earlier in the summer. As far as this was concerned, the problem still remained. How was it possible to reassure Russia against the dangers of a reunited Germany? This was discussed between the three Western Foreign Ministers in Paris and at a wider meeting of NATO on 25 October. Was there some new security pact or some new guarantee that we could offer? Dr. Halvard Lange, the Norwegian Foreign Minister and an old friend from Strasbourg days, came to see me at his own request. He was pessimistic about the prospects, believing that the Russians would never surrender East Germany.

[1] 26 October 1955.

He added that this applied *even if Germany offered neutrality*. This was interesting, since the Norwegians are well informed and have good judgement. He is probably right.[1]

In this mood, and oppressed by many conflicting anxieties, we arrived at Geneva on 26 October. Sir Ivone Kirkpatrick and other Foreign Office experts came with me, and John Wyndham took good care of all our material needs. We occupied a small but agreeable villa which was more comfortable than the hotel. Once more our meetings had been arranged to take place in the same gloomy surroundings. Pinay was in the chair and, after some procedural matters had been agreed, began on Item I, German reunification and European security. After a few remarks he formally tabled the Anglo–American–French plan. There then followed a comical piece of manœuvring.

Molotov moved that we do adjourn till tomorrow, so as to *start* Item I tomorrow. We agreed. Then, Pinay being a bit slow off the mark in closing the session, Molotov raised a point of order. He said that since we had not *begun* the debate on Item I (which was untrue), no document could be laid on the table or published. We argued about this, till 7.30 p.m.! Of course, though no one mentioned it, Molotov's real purpose was to prevent our document being published. All the Press of the world had been summoned to various Press conferences to hear it expounded.[2]

The second meeting began at four o'clock on the following day (28 October) and lasted till 7.15 p.m. I began with a short explanation of our plan, and ended by reading out the full document. Molotov followed with an uncompromising speech.

At the end of his prepared oration, he tried to reply to some of my points extempore. It was very poor.
Foster Dulles replied, extempore, [and] quite admirably. His points were well taken and well argued. He was quite short. Pinay (who had been to Paris and back) read out a speech composed [for him], in a clear voice.[3]

[1] 26 October 1955.   [2] 27 October 1955.   [3] 28 October 1955.

That was all for the day, and no sign of progress could be discerned, even by the most optimistic. On 29 October the third meeting took place at three o'clock. Molotov was in the chair and 'passed', as we expected. Once more I tried to clarify the issue as we saw it:

> Our position is that Germany should be free—as of right. This is the right of any nation ten years after war. If, when free, she joins the Warsaw Pact, it is rather we who need additional guarantees. If she is neutral, there is no additional risk to Russia over the present position, where three-quarters of Germany by population and two-thirds by area is already in NATO. But to compensate Russia for the Eastern zone *also* joining NATO (if Russia is willing to liberate it), we offer this Treaty of Assurance.[1]

I thought Molotov older and less confident than he had been at the former Geneva meeting or at Vienna. He seemed rather shaken when I reminded him that it was the Russians who had armed 100,000 men, with tanks, etc., in Eastern Germany, while in West Germany not a single soldier had yet been raised. Dulles, however, stuck to our point that German reunification and security were a single item. When would the Russians give us their views about the first part of the question which had been remitted to us by the Heads of Government?

When we met after the weekend, Item III—that is, 'contacts' between East and West—came under discussion and we each delivered a little speech with an exchange of formal papers. This was easy going. Then, after a short recess, we came back to the real issue. Molotov now proposed that both the leaders of the East and West German Governments should be invited to the conference— that is, Otto Grotewohl and Adenauer. After a long dispute, very courteously conducted by Dulles, Molotov got tired of it and dropped his suggestion. He had made his demonstration and thought he could end the incident. However, we felt he should be taught a lesson. We did not see why he should take up subjects and then drop them again at will. So Dulles continued the debate, much to Molotov's surprise and displeasure, by requesting that

[1] 29 October 1955.

although the conference had decided not to call the East German Government into consultation, we ought to call on the West German Government. This was because they represented three-quarters of the German people and were freely elected. They were also now recognised by all the nations round the table.

> Molotov, rather nettled, replied and said that the East German Government was just as freely elected as the West.[1]

I could not resist joining in:

> 'Mr. Molotov says that the East German Government were elected by free elections. I remember that they were elected by over 99 per cent of the votes. It is 32 years since I first contested an election in my country and I have taken part in ten contested Parliamentary elections in that time. All I can say is that any man or any party that can get 99 per cent of the votes in a free election are not politicians — they're walking miracles.'[1]

This naturally caused great glee among the Americans and some polite amusement among the French.

> I also observed that the Russians laughed — and then suddenly stopped, looking to Molotov and Gromyko to see whether it was all right to laugh. Molotov, replying, turned it off by saying 'Mr. Macmillan is pleased to indulge in witticisms.' The subject then dropped.[1]

It was nearly seven o'clock, and Dulles suggested that Molotov should circulate his additional proposals on security. But he replied that he would rather read them out, which he proceeded to do at considerable length. His new security treaty was in a way an advance, for it abandoned the demand that NATO must be wound up. But it had the defect of being based on a permanent partition of Germany. When he finished, Molotov obviously thought that we should prefer dinner to argument; but I did not like the idea of this new initiative holding the field in the world's Press, creating a bad impression in West Germany. I therefore thought it better to keep the session going for a bit longer. I welcomed some aspects of

[1] 31 October 1955.

the new plan. It had certainly taken account of the directive which instructed us to find means of promoting German reunification.

I then continued: 'There is a popular riddle which in my country has been put traditionally to every generation of our children. It may be that it is also popular in Russia, and thus may form a happy link between us. This is the riddle:
'Which comes first—the egg or the hen?
'This was really the problem presented to the Heads of Governments at the summer meeting in Geneva. Which comes first—German reunification or European security? How did they solve it?
'They solved it by deciding that, whatever their individual views as to their logical or political priority, both these morsels must be eaten and digested together.
'In conformity with these instructions, the Western powers have presented proposals covering both components of Item I. Even with these new proposals on security, which we welcome, the Soviet Government have not done their duty, because they have expressed no views on German reunification. The Western powers have presented a complete picture. Will not the Soviet Union do the same? For I must repeat that the new security proposals of the Soviet Government are still based on the partition of Germany. That is not in conformity with the directive.'[1]

In writing to Churchill at this time about the conference, I told him that I did not despair of making some progress if we had sufficient patience. But my hopes were destined to be unrealised, for, as each day passed, the sessions became more tedious and more unremunerative. We concentrated on trying to force the Russians to produce some kind of plan for Germany. Ours had been tabled for six days at this conference, and, in substance, for twenty months before the world. At last they did so on 2 November; but it was only a proposal for an all-German Council to reorganise the political, economic and cultural life of the people, without any question of ultimate reunification or free elections.

The usual round of dinners went on—with the usual playful humour. For instance, since I had already given notice that I would

[1] 31 October 1955.

have to return to England for a day or two, Molotov, at the end of the dinner at which he was the host, asked me what I was going back for.

I said, 'A debate in the House of Commons.' He said, 'What about?' I said, 'On a subject where you can really help me, if you would do so—on Maclean and Burgess. Can you tell me where they are?' He said, with real or assumed seriousness, 'That is a matter which would require investigation.'[1]

The days passed with the conference sitting for three to four hours, until 5 November, when I returned to London. Molotov also went back to Moscow for instructions, and there were strong rumours that he would reappear with some new plan. By 8 November I was back for the session in the afternoon, and the message that Molotov had brought from his colleagues was soon apparent.

[He] threw his bombshell—a most aggressive, non-conciliatory, and retrograde speech, delivered in the old phraseology—monopolists and Junkers—in a *cassant* tone. He refused free elections for Germany altogether. He practically claimed that Germany could only be united as a Communist and satellite state.[2]

This was a cruel blow to our hopes, but we persevered.

Pinay was sadly harassed by continual journeys to Paris and back in order to sustain the French Government, which was in almost daily danger of defeat. But he played his part loyally. We were in close touch with the West Germans, now represented by Dr. Heinrich von Brentano, who began to urge us to break off the conference 'with a bang' and declare that we would never hold another.

I asked him to consider this very carefully. If Geneva was over and done with for ever at the first serious hitch, the Allies, not the Russians, would be blamed. Federal Germany would be under still greater pressure, both internally and from Moscow, to meet and agree with East Germany.[3]

Accordingly we agreed to take the line of speaking with firmness,

[1] 2 November 1955. [2] 8 November 1955. [3] 9 November 1955.

but more in sorrow than in anger. On the whole we succeeded. Unfortunately, on one occasion Pinay was betrayed by genuine anger into a long and somewhat turgid oration which Molotov answered with great skill. On a motion for the adjournment of Item I he was able to raise all sorts of irrelevant questions, covering a wide field. It was a really brilliant performance. I could not resist telling him that he was such a successful debater that he really ought to try his hand in a free parliament.

It was now only a question of how and when to bring the conference to an end. We must avoid the Russians being able to blame it on us. We must equally try to avoid difficulties for Adenauer and his friends.

Before the final stages, I had the good fortune to have a talk with one of the ablest and most well-informed men on Russian affairs—a Swiss diplomat. He had made a profound study of Soviet policy and believed that a *détente* was something which, in the long run, was historically inevitable; for Russia must in time be dominated by fear of China. 'They will try,' he declared, 'for a situation of peace with the West and, especially, friendship with other Asiatic peoples who also view China's potential with alarm.' But in the short term, he thought the policy of *détente* had considerable dangers for the Soviet system, so they would keep oscillating between a softer and stiffer line. He seemed equally well informed about the internal situation in Moscow. Although Malenkov had been demoted and Molotov appeared to be going down in authority, there was still only a small balance in favour of Khrushchev and Bulganin. With regard to Germany, the Russians were confident. My informant had

> heard a very high Russian commissar say: 'If we want to, we can always bring the Germans out of the arms of the West. We can offer them East Germany. If that is not enough, we can offer them the Oder–Neisse territory. If that does not do the trick, we can have another partition of Poland.[1]

At the same time, my Swiss friend thought that the *détente* was having a bad effect on our side—perhaps worse than we realised. In France, West Germany and Italy people were beginning to go

[1] 11 November 1955.

neutralist. We must use the end of this conference and its failure to shock them into a sense of reality.

As a diversion, and perhaps to temper the disappointment to the Western world at Russian intransigence over German reunification and European security, Molotov now revived the disarmament question and tabled a resolution in much the old terms. We had therefore to deal with this and also to find the best way of ending the conference, for Molotov now became completely negative, even on the question of 'contacts'. It seemed that the Iron Curtain was to be lowered again.

On the afternoon of 15 November, the four Ministers held a restricted meeting to discuss the terms of the communiqué. On the 17th we met for a final session. The communiqué was short and objective, merely saying that the question of future meetings would be taken up through diplomatic channels.

We finished at 6.30 p.m. and, after the usual formalities, departed for our respective capitals. This Foreign Ministers' conference, therefore, ended in a sense of disillusionment after the high hopes raised in the summer. Nevertheless, although the official meetings were so unproductive, behind the scenes there were some useful talks. I could not help feeling that there was some conflict of view and purpose inside the Soviet Government. Molotov had seemed at first uncertain of what line to follow. It was only after his return from his visit to Moscow that he launched into the most intransigent and violent of his diatribes. At the end he was more subdued. But, this move away from 'the Geneva spirit' was depressing.

In my view, there were two reasons for the Soviet change of attitude. First, the fact that the Soviet authorities had found that, especially in the satellite countries, more liberal policies had awakened expectations and movements of opinion which were proving difficult to control. Secondly, the balance of forces in the Soviet Government was still precariously poised between those who supported the policies of Stalin and those who favoured a more liberal approach. I thought that the Russians, having established a stalemate in Europe and (which seemed to suit them) in the Far East, would concentrate their energies on the Middle East. Our main objective in Europe must now be to hold West German opinion firmly attached to the West; and it was therefore in our interest to press ahead with the inclusion of German forces in NATO. The mistaken tactic of the Russians in indicating that they would not agree to German unity except on a basis which would preserve Communist gains in East Germany would assist us in holding West German opinion firm.

I made a formal report to the Queen and to all the Commonwealth countries. It only remained to answer a charming suggestion which I had from Mr. C. B. Fry, to which I made an appropriate reply as follows:

> Thank you for your letter about teaching the Russians to play cricket.
>
> I think that your proposal would represent an admirable form of East–West contact which it is certainly Her Majesty's Government's policy to foster. But I hope that in anything that you do, you will be careful that no damage ensues to the spirit of the game.

Finally, there was a broadcast statement to be made to the public. This was on the whole well received. Even *The Times* was largely favourable to my work in the Foreign Office. While feeling that I may have carried the debating manner of the House of Commons too far by appealing to Mr. Molotov's reason, the writer admitted that I had forced him to declare openly the Russian refusal to allow free elections and their determination to uphold—at all costs—the Communist regime in all the satellite countries.

Perhaps my greatest gain during all these weeks had been to get a closer picture of Dulles and his way of working. One afternoon after luncheon I drove out with him into the country. He told me of his talk with Molotov in the morning which had lasted two hours and made him miss church. 'Futile,' he described it—over and over again. (He pronounced it 'footle' but I knew what he meant.) They had discussed membership of the United Nations, the conference itself, East–West contacts, the Far East and the Middle East without any progress on any of these issues.

Dulles and I then had some talk about the 'China list'. This phrase covered a long list of commodities, of the most varied kinds, which the Western countries, under American pressure, had agreed not to supply to China. But in our view the catalogue included items which could not really be said to assist China's war effort. I told him that because exports were not vital to America, they failed to realise how important they were to us. He promised to consider favourably a reduction in the list. He then said, in a rather detached way, that he had heard that we were having difficulties about the balance of payments; to which I replied:

> 'Yes, indeed. We are still struggling with the results of having sold all our foreign investments, in two successive wars, before we got American aid.' He said nothing to this, but it seemed to strike him as a new idea.[1]

Dulles next discussed the future. The President would probably decide to 'run' again; if so, he would certainly win. Dulles thus looked forward to working with me for a long period—four years or more.

> We might together change the history of the world. (He grew quite excited and eloquent over this.) We must start a 'Counter-Reformation'. We must disprove the slanders against the old Western civilisations; show that 'Colonialism' was a fake charge; prove the immense benefit that the British Empire had been and was; and lead the young nations to our side. Much study should be given to this, and to the philosophic attack on the heresies and falsity of the Communist doctrines. All this was very surprising and impressive.[1]

This strange man had moments of vision, but also of relapse into obscurantism. Moreover, he weakened his reputation by his over-legalistic and often seemingly devious approach. Nevertheless, I was to regret that I was to lose contact with him, for I had not found it too difficult to bring him round to our point of view. But it needed a lot of patience and a great capacity for listening.

All this time tension between Israel and her Arab neighbours was

[1] 13 November 1955.

increasing alarmingly. Our dilemma remained. If we armed Israel, we would lose all hold upon the Arabs; if we refused to do so, Israel might be tempted into a preventive war. Nor, even before the Russian intervention, was it easy to co-ordinate Western policies regarding arms deliveries. On 9 November, by a speech at the Guildhall, Eden tried 'to break out of the ring'. He declared that

> if some arrangement could be reached between Israel and her Arab neighbours about their boundaries, the United States and Britain, and perhaps other powers also, would be prepared to give a formal guarantee to both sides.[1]

In spite of American support the response proved disappointing. Any fruitful negotiations must require the Arabs to abandon the 1947 position as a basis of negotiation and the Israelis to surrender the line which they had achieved in 1949. The latter naturally protested that the conditions of 1947 were obsolete while the frontier achieved in 1949 was a fact. The Arab countries, stimulated by Egyptian propaganda and seduced by Saudi Arabian money, maintained an intransigent position. We were back in the old difficulty –how could Britain and America, or any other countries, guarantee frontiers which had not been agreed?

My next task was to go to Baghdad for a meeting of the Ministerial Council of the new organisation. In the old days Foreign Secretaries seldom left their desk in Whitehall. Today they have become of necessity peripatetic salesmen. Whether there has been gain or loss in this development is certainly arguable; but no Foreign Minister, least of all the British, can avoid the necessity.

How far the formation of the Baghdad Pact, or the 'Northern Tier' as it was often called, was a prudent move or how far a hazardous adventure can still be argued. Even at the time, some countries felt that the Russians had grounds for regarding the Pact as 'provocative'. Yet it was Russian aggression which had forced the non-Communist world into defensive organisations such as NATO and SEATO. At the same time the British Government had a reasonable complaint against American vacillations. They had first

[1] The Earl of Avon, *Full Circle*, p. 330.

With Eden at Geneva, July 1955

Nicosia: British troops round up rioting youths, October 1955

led us along this path and then hesitated to follow themselves. It was too late to complain that the Russians were sensitive about Iran or anxious about Turkey. The die was cast. Turkey, Iraq, Iran and Pakistan were now leagued together, and we had given our formal adherence. Nevertheless, in view of all the uncertainties throughout the Middle East, the project had become more perilous without full American support. The most I could do was to persuade Dulles to allow the American Ambassador in Baghdad to attend as an observer, accompanied by Admiral Cassidy of the United States Navy. Both gave us all the assistance in their power.

On 20 November, accompanied by Evelyn Shuckburgh and Patrick Hancock, my private secretary, as well as the C.I.G.S., Sir Gerald Templer, I arrived in Baghdad. Michael Wright, our Ambassador, came to meet us.

On the afternoon of our arrival King Feisal II and the Regent, Crown Prince Abdul – the King's uncle – received all the delegations, and there followed a wreath-laying ceremony on the tomb of King Feisal I, the King's grandfather. The British Embassy was

> a fine old Turkish house in the old style which has been the Residency and is now the Embassy. . . . It is ugly and comfortable – but its ugliness is pleasant and traditional. The walls are immensely thick, which keeps it cool in summer. It rambles about, with lots of buildings, including the old harem, and has a fine garden. It is on the river Tigris and in general position and style reminds me a little of our Embassy in Cairo.[1]

The Iraqi Foreign Minister, M. Burhanuddin Bashayan, and the American Ambassador, Mr. Waldemar J. Gallman, came to dinner. The latter was very helpful and highly critical of his Government for not having joined the Pact. I was particularly struck by the deep respect in which Sir Gerald Templer was held. It was particularly encouraging to see the friendship between the British officers of the old Indian Army and the Pakistani soldiers.

The morning session on 21 November was mainly formal, with speeches of welcome, resolutions to constitute the Ministerial Council and the like. In the afternoon we met in private session

_____
[1] 20 November 1955.

Y

with Nuri Pasha, the Prime Minister of Iraq, in the chair, and at his request I gave a review of the world situation. A lot of trouble had been taken in the preparation of this speech, which was well received by my colleagues. The Turkish Prime Minister, M. Adnan Menderes, was, however, pessimistic. He thought the Russians had got a firm foothold in the Middle East and would be halted only with great difficulty.

On the following day the Council met to receive a number of reports from the various committees on military and economic affairs. After this the five representatives (three Prime Ministers and two Foreign Secretaries with one adviser each) had an informal meeting without the usual host of attendants.

> This led to an excellent discussion, unbriefed and uninhibited. Each head of delegation spoke with an apparent sincerity. It was a most useful two hours of talk. The general view was: (1) That a settlement of the Israel question ought to be got as soon as possible. Some of the Arab states (even those hostile to the Pact . . .) were coming round in favour of an early settlement. Eden's [Guildhall] speech was warmly approved. (2) Until the Israel question could be settled, the Arab world would be split over the Pact. (3) That Saudi Arabian gold was the cause of endless trouble.[1]

All the representatives agreed that pressure should be put on Jordan to join the Pact. The Turks as usual took a very firm line. This was my first meeting with Menderes, whom I was to see on many other occasions before his lamentable end. He struck me as

> agreeable; affable; smiling; voluble—not at all what I expected. But I suspect that behind this exterior he is a strong character.[1]

It was clear that the main problem was how to obtain the adherence of Jordan, confused by conflicting pressures.

On 23 November the Regent called on me at his own request. He was very anxious to bring in the Jordanians and offered to pay a visit himself to King Hussein and the Queen Mother and to bring all his influence to bear.

Nuri Pasha was the most striking of all the Ministers, with his

[1] 22 November 1955.

great experience and fine open character. The King and the Regent were equally loyal. All these devoted men were to be brutally murdered within a few years.

I returned through the Lebanon, arriving in Beirut in the evening of 23 November. It was clear that the Prime Minister, M. Rashid Karame, was a keen Arab partisan who was so preoccupied by desire of revenge upon the Israelis that he seemed unaware of the danger of Communism and Russian intervention. He received me courteously with a set speech about the wickedness of the Jews.

> I replied in a speech in French, about the importance of (*a*) keeping Soviet influence out of the Middle East—hence the Baghdad Pact; (*b*) a settlement in Palestine—hence Sir Anthony Eden's Guildhall speech. It was all rather a waste of time.[1]

I then went to see the President, Camille Chamoun, a most civilised and intelligent man.

> He agrees absolutely with us, but repeated the same story—the Saudis have bought up the Middle East![1]

I now began to wonder about the benefits to the countries concerned of the exploitation of oil. If these large sums were used, as Nuri Pasha was doing in Iraq, for the improvement of agriculture and the development of irrigation, well and good. But in many other countries the money was not so prudently employed.

On my return I reported my impressions to the Prime Minister. The Baghdad meeting had been a success, and if we could follow it up we might use the opportunity to create strong ties both in the military and economic field. The Pact might become a powerful link between Moslem countries and the West. At any rate our prestige was now involved. What we needed was a permanent secretariat, with a good chief, to play in a minor way the part which Lord Ismay carried out so successfully at NATO. We needed a budget, not extravagant but sufficient for the task. Above all, we must bring pressure upon the Americans to get them fully into the Pact and we must confront them with reality. Either they must back up our attempt to shore up the Middle East or risk it being lost in

[1] 23 November 1955.

the end to Communism. Finally, Nuri Pasha felt somewhat isolated with Iraq the only Arab country in the Pact. We could perhaps work out a package offer to Jordan, including a revision of the present treaty, which would hasten their decision. After all, we were paying large subsidies. Why should we continue our support, both financial and military, if they would do nothing in return? Naturally a settlement of the dispute between Egypt and Israel was the indispensable condition of lasting peace. Could we not now make a fresh attempt to draw the Arab world away from the growing ambitions of Nasser and the increasing temptations dangled before them by the Soviet Government?

It was agreed that Sir Gerald Templer should go out himself to see what he could do to bring in Jordan. But I began now to fear that the continuation of inflammatory propaganda and corruption would be too strong for us; and so it was to prove. A friendly Jordanian Government was forced to resign by continued outbreaks of disorder, fanned from outside sources.

I sent a full report to Dulles about the Baghdad meeting, with a tribute to Ambassador Gallman's notable contribution and with a fresh appeal. If America could not become a full partner by a formal treaty, could they not do so by a 'Congressional Resolution'? Their adherence would make success a certainty. It would be a message of hope and confidence throughout the whole area and have the same kind of effect as when NATO was formed after the fall of Czechoslovakia and the New World came into full partnership with Europe. I reminded Dulles that it was the support of the Atlantic Powers that had removed the hesitations of many European waverers.

I saw Dulles at the end of the month in Paris, but still could not make much impression upon him. The Americans now seemed to be oppressed by the

> news about the President's health, and the electoral disaster which hangs over them, if he doesn't run.[1]

The relations between Israel and her Arab neighbours, already tense, were subjected to further strains by an incident which took place on 11 December. The Israeli forces made a strong and well-

[1] 13 December 1955

prepared attack on Syrian positions on the east bank of Lake Tiberias. The casualties on both sides were heavy. Although the Israelis defended their action as a retaliation for Syrian attacks on Israeli fishing-boats on the lake, the Security Council, with the approval of the four Great Powers, found that the Israeli action was not justified. But there the matter rested.

Meanwhile a more difficult question had begun to emerge which was afterwards to assume almost decisive importance in the struggle between the Soviets and the Western countries. This concerned the construction of the new Aswan Dam.

In the summer of 1955 the Egyptian Government proposed an ambitious scheme to improve the irrigation of the Nile Valley and to develop hydro-electric power. This involved the building of a new High Dam across the Nile a few miles south of the existing construction. We had every sympathy with their desire to improve their agricultural production and meet the needs of their rapidly growing population. Nevertheless serious financial problems were involved. It would take sixteen years or more to build the dam; during that time Egypt seemed likely to face a formidable foreign exchange deficit. Even if they were to practise a rigid economy over this long period, it was quite impossible for Britain alone to guarantee the whole operation; nor could Egypt's sterling balances provide sufficient security. The first concept was a consortium of British, French and German firms. But more finance would be required, and we immediately began negotiations with the American Government and the International Bank to fill the gap. There were naturally many technical difficulties to be overcome, and regard had to be paid to the formal procedures and requirements of the Bank. Nevertheless, this negotiation was going along smoothly when we heard that Nasser was now in negotiation with the Soviet Government, who seemed willing to undertake to build the dam themselves and take payment over a period of fifty years. We felt that this was a most serious development, and the Prime Minister therefore sent urgent telegrams to President Eisenhower soliciting his help with the International Bank negotiations. We made it clear that we would contribute our fair proportion of financial aid, and in due course the Americans agreed to do the same. Together we would advance

$70 million for the first stage, of which we were to bear $14 million. Unhappily, the Western Powers were outmanœuvred and outbid by the Russians. Although on 20 December the Egyptian Minister of Finance, Dr. Abdel el-Kaysouni, who was visiting London, assured me that he was satisfied with the progress of the negotiation, early in the new year Nasser began to raise more and more difficulties and objections, even declaring that any conditions were an incursion upon Egyptian sovereignty. In view of the fact that all that the Bank required was an undertaking that the dam should have priority over other projects, and the contract should be awarded on a competitive basis, this was an obvious subterfuge.

Nasser was subsequently to claim that the failure of this negotiation was one of the reasons for the seizure of the Canal. This allegation was manifestly false. Unhappily, as in the case of the arms deal, he fell to the wiles of Soviet diplomacy, which encouraged him in his ambitious and dangerous dreams of Arab imperialism. Certainly both the British and American Governments used all their efforts to conclude their agreement on reasonable and even generous terms. Nasser's was a political and not a financial decision.

One other development in the Valley of the Nile was to cause us both anxiety and, in the end, some satisfaction—the evolution of the Sudan to independence. We had every right to be proud of the success which British administrators had achieved in this tortured area during the preceding seventy years. They had rescued the people from a terrible condition of internal strife and confusion, and had built, by their devoted efforts, the beginnings of a nation destined to take its place with comparable countries in the world.

In 1953 an Anglo-Egyptian agreement provided for a transitional period of not more than three years' 'self-government' for the Sudan, with an elected Parliament. After this interval a Constituent Assembly was to be elected to decide the future state of the country— independence, or union with Egypt. During these years, a British Governor-General was still in charge, but the British officials were being rapidly replaced by Sudanese, and the general movement towards self-government was fostered by our efforts.

For the next two years a virulent campaign of propaganda was carried on by the Egyptians in an attempt to persuade the Sudanese to agree to union with Egypt. In August 1955 there was some desire in Whitehall to protest vigorously against Egyptian actions, but in view of the fact that Egypt had suggested leaving it to the Sudanese to settle the composition of the Electoral Commission which was to preside over the creation of the Constituent Assembly, I felt it would be best to let things ride. The Egyptians looked like being hoist with their own petard; and, in spite of a campaign of pressure and bribery, the Sudanese would probably choose independence. This view was soon to be justified. Towards the end of August the famous, or infamous, Major Salem—the dancing major—who had been the Egyptian Minister in charge of Sudanese affairs, was sent 'on indefinite leave'. At the same time the Egyptian campaign of abuse against the Sudanese Government was suddenly brought to an end. Unhappily there had been a serious rebellion in the southern Sudan, where the people, of quite different race and character, protested against northern domination. The rising was put down after much slaughter; but it was an evil omen for the future.

Later in the year there seemed to be a general view that the laborious process envisaged in the treaty, of electing a Constituent Assembly and a subsequent plebiscite on the future of the Sudan, to be controlled by a commission of representatives of seven countries, might well be set aside. When the Egyptian Parliament reassembled it was clear that Sudanese opinion wished the matter to be settled, one way or another, without delay. On 13 November 1955 the last British and Egyptian forces were withdrawn from the Sudan in accordance with the 1953 agreement. A period of uncertainty followed. At the beginning of December the Sudanese Government appeared ready to carry out the original plan. But on 19 December the Parliament passed a unanimous resolution in favour of immediate and full independence. One of my last acts as Foreign Secretary was to recommend acceptance of this as an expression of the general will. It was the independence of the Sudan which we wanted and, since the whole Sudanese Parliament were agreed, it seemed pedantic to insist on the complicated machinery which had been devised three years before. The Egyptian Government was induced to accept this view and, on 1 January 1956, both Britain and Egypt recognised the independence of the Sudan. So ended a by no means inglorious episode in our imperial story. British blood, British money and devoted British administrators had raised this people out of a state of savagery and slavery and set them on the path to civilisation.

During the greater part of my short tenure of the Foreign Office my thoughts were concentrated on one or other aspect of world problems: Western Europe, Germany, Russia, the Middle East and the Far East. At the same time there were a number of other difficulties which could not be ignored. One of the most painful of these was the tense situation developing in Cyprus.

This beautiful island, one of the most lovely in the Eastern Mediterranean, has enjoyed—or suffered—a strange and romantic history. The fabled home of the Goddess of Love and Beauty, it has been from time to time the scene of many ugly rivalries and hatreds. Had these conflicts taken place in a spot less important strategically and politically, they would have proved of minor importance. Now the increasing nationalism in Greece after the pressures of nearly forty years of continuous warfare—internal and external—together with the growing awareness of the Turkish Government of the aggressive policies of Soviet Russia, enhanced the tension between two traditional enemies. Greeks began more and more to regard Cyprus as the last of the unredeemed Hellenic territories to be rescued and incorporated in the Greek State; Turks became increasingly aware of it as an off-shore island of considerable military significance, lying only a few miles from their coasts and pointing dangerously at the mainland. At the same time, British strategic interests, long dormant, had been suddenly revived.

On a basis of international law, Greece's position was weak. She could put forward no claims to sovereignty except those of sentiment, language and race. But these were strong indeed. Yet Cyprus had never belonged to Greece, although it had certainly formed part of the Byzantine Empire. It had been conquered in the twelfth century by Richard Cœur de Lion; but this, like so many of that

gallant monarch's victories, had proved an ephemeral gain. The old
Greek tradition had been further enriched by the culture of Western
Europe both under the Lusignan dynasty of the Latin kingdom of
Cyprus and under the Republic of Venice. For the next four
centuries Cyprus, like Greece itself and so many of the Balkan
countries, formed part of the Ottoman Empire.

By agreement with the British Government, the island was
assigned by the Sultan in 1878 to be 'occupied and administered by
England'. The purpose of this concession was to enable British
imperial power to be available to support the countries of the Near
East and above all Turkey against Russian imperialist aggression.
To this end the island was regarded by Disraeli and his colleagues as
a convenient *place d'armes*. Although the growing size of battle-
ships, cruisers and their accompanying flotillas had made the
harbours no longer suitable for modern navies, by a strange turn of
events the island had now once more become essential both for the
defence of our vital communications and to enable us to carry out
our obligations to NATO and similar leagues. The abandonment of
Egypt caused our military authorities to choose Cyprus as the alternative base, and we were busily occupied in organising—perhaps on
too ambitious a scale—a replica of the old installations that we had
so long enjoyed in Cairo and on the Canal. Furthermore, the new
importance of air power made the island, although unsuitable
for modern ships, highly desirable as a base for modern military
aircraft.

The sovereignty of Cyprus, left by Disraeli—at least nominally—in
Turkish hands, had formally passed to Britain under Article 20 of
the Treaty of Lausanne, signed in July 1923, by which Turkey
recognised the annexation of Cyprus proclaimed by the British
Government on 5 November 1914. This treaty had not merely been
signed by the British and Turkish Governments; it had also been
signed by the Greeks. It bore, indeed, the famous and honoured
name of Venizelos. Nor had the Greek Government made any
reservations at the time. Nevertheless, as a result of the Graeco-
Turkish war of 1920–22, Greek refugees from Asia Minor had
fled into Cyprus in such numbers as to destroy the old balance
between the populations. There were now 400,000 Greeks against

some 100,000 Turks. A new situation had thus emerged, in which no diplomacy, however patient or imaginative, seemed able to reconcile the conflicting claims.

Clearly British rights in Cyprus could not be challenged under international law. Yet under the developing pressures at work throughout the old British Empire, the principle of self-government and, ultimately, of self-determination was being generally applied. If our strategic position could be effectively guaranteed, we had no desire to prevent this evolutionary process applying to Cyprus as well as elsewhere. Our whole interest, therefore, lay in a peaceful solution; all the more did we desire this, since both the Greeks and the Turks were our allies and friends, bound together by the recent engagements of NATO and constituting the eastern flank of that defensive system.

The Greek patriots were now winning general support both in the island and throughout the Hellenic world, as well as much sympathy outside. They were supported by the Orthodox Church, which controlled a great part of the agricultural and urban land and had the sympathy of the people. The Church had long been respected as defenders of Hellenic tradition during the centuries of Ottoman occupation. Successive Archbishops of Cyprus had protected the interests of their people, as had leading ecclesiastics in other parts of the Ottoman Empire. The Turks had nevertheless kept tolerable order in the island by their own methods of casual administration alternating with fierce repression. The British authorities, in the first two generations of their rule, had met with little difficulty; but now in Cyprus, as elsewhere, they were coming up against a new spirit and new methods of terrorism, made possible by modern weapons. It used to be said that, in the early centuries of the Ottoman Empire, the Turkish governors kept the peace by hanging an Archbishop at suitable intervals. In spite of occasional temptations, recourse to such simple methods was now impracticable.

The claim for self-government was matched by a further demand for 'self-determination'. Although self-determination might, in theory, result in independence, it involved in practice the incorporation of Cyprus in the Greek State by a vote either of the Parliament or the people. This, known as 'Enosis', was the inspiration of many sincere patriots. It was based upon the same emotions which had moved the Governments of Europe to action, and their peoples to sympathy, more than a century before. Greek Cypriots were only repeating for their own island the claims that other Greeks had made throughout the Hellenic world and successfully enforced at intervals against the old and decaying Ottoman Empire. To no people did they make a more natural appeal than to our own. But, while the Cypriot Turks might be willing to accept a self-governing Cyprus if a method could be devised by which their community could be effectively guaranteed against inequality and repression, the Turkish Government at Ankara would never willingly allow an island, lying off their vital coasts and threatening their main harbours, to pass into the hands of a nation which, although at the moment allied, might become politically hostile. The Turks had watched recent Communist attempts to seize power in Greece. These had only been contained at first by the courage and tenacity of Churchill, who, in this cause, did not fear to offend his American allies; and later by similar support from the Americans after their eyes had been opened to the true purposes of the revolutionary Left-wing movements in Greece. My Turkish friends sometimes used to say to me, with a certain exaggeration but not without an element of reality, 'If Cyprus were to fall into hostile hands, it would have the same effect on us as it would have had on you if the Isle of Wight had been held by your enemies through two world wars.' Certainly the Turkish Government were concerned for the welfare of the Turkish population in Cyprus; but above all they were determined never to permit the island to become a threat to their own security.

On arrival at the Foreign Office I learned of the disturbed state of Cyprus. Archbishop Makarios was carrying on a strenuous campaign for Enosis, culminating in his appearance in April at the Bandung Conference of African and Asian states. In words, at least, he deprecated terrorism. But whatever might be the Archbishop's views about violence as a churchman, he could only retain his position of control as a politician by countenancing the terrorist organisations. EOKA was now to become as much a household word to us as the old I.R.A. had been to our predecessors.

In the early days of April, when I was still Minister of Defence, I recorded:

> Very bad news from Cyprus. In spite of the confidence of the Governor and the Colonial Office that there would be no trouble, there have been serious bomb outrages, including the destruction of the new wireless station (which has cost H.M.G. an immense sum).[1]

The Colonial Office seemed surprised and mildly pained; but the intelligence and security system was certainly inadequate and I could only hope that General Templer's organisation[2] would soon bring about an improvement.

In spite of the distractions of a General Election and the major problems which we were facing all over the world, I devoted much thought to the position in Cyprus. The Greek Government was certainly inspiring the recent terrorism, partly by inflammatory broadcasts from the Government-controlled Athens station and through the Press, partly by more covert means. Their next move was to bring the dispute before the United Nations—a project which was to cause us considerable embarrassment. I was fortunate in having an able, imaginative and generous colleague in the Colonial Secretary—Alan Lennox-Boyd; and after much consideration we made a joint proposal to the Cabinet. Any attempt to raise the 'Cyprus Question' in the Assembly of the United Nations would of course be contrary to the terms of their U.N. Charter, which precluded the discussion of the internal responsibilities of any individual state. Nevertheless, in view of the repercussions throughout the Eastern Mediterranean, we felt that we should find difficulty in maintaining this position without some positive action of our own. In any case, we needed the support and sympathy of the people and Government of the United States, both on the narrower issue of inscription on the Agenda of the United Nations, and on the wider implications. We proposed, therefore, that a fresh initiative should be taken which would at least demonstrate the sincerity of British policy. As a first step we decided to invite both Greece and Turkey to a tripartite discussion. We expected the Turks to accept. If the Greeks also

[1] 3 April 1955.   [2] See above, p. 573.

agreed, we would put forward definite proposals for constitutional progress in the island. If the Greeks refused, at least Britain's position at the United Nations would be strengthened. Naturally the idea of a conference at which the future of a British colony would be discussed with two neighbouring powers raised many doubts. This might prove a dangerous precedent and make it difficult to resist pressure to submit other colonial problems to a similar procedure. Nevertheless, it was only common sense to recognise the fact that no new arrangement in Cyprus could work successfully unless it was acceptable to both the Greek and Turkish Governments.

Continuing disorders throughout June virtually forced the Cabinet to choose between a policy of repression and the offer of a conference. It was finally agreed that the plan for the conference should be launched, and invitations were sent accordingly. The Prime Minister announced this decision to the House of Commons and we awaited the result. As expected, the Turks immediately accepted 'in principle', but the Greeks hesitated. However, I was pleased to receive a friendly personal message from King Paul, welcoming what he called a 'bold and imaginative gesture'.

In sending out our invitation we were careful to emphasise not merely the need for constitutional advance in Cyprus but the importance of protecting the strategic and political interests of the three Governments in the Eastern Mediterranean. When I was at Strasbourg in July I was able to have a talk with the Greek Foreign Minister, M. Stephanos Stephanopoulos. Rather to my astonishment, he accepted our invitation without any conditions or reservations, even saying that they would be glad to meet their Turkish friends.

> The only point which the Greeks made was that the Turks had surrendered their rights in Cyprus by the Treaty of Lausanne. This hardly seemed very relevant; for the Greeks have never had any rights in Cyprus at all.[1]

Since the Turkish Ambassador in Paris, M. Numan Menemencioglu, was representing his Government at the Council of Europe, we

[1] 5 July 1955.

were able immediately to agree on a suitable communiqué. A few days later M. Stephanopoulos came to see me in a rather excited mood, complaining that the conference was not to meet until 29 August. He explained in some detail the difficulties with which he was confronted. He and his friends were fighting a tremendous battle against the extremists. Archbishop Makarios had been in Athens stirring up trouble and had engaged in a bitter dispute with the Greek Prime Minister, Field-Marshal Papagos, now an ageing man.[1] If the conference could not meet until 29 August, the Greek Government, itself under great pressure, must insist upon putting the question of Cyprus on the Agenda of the United Nations; for this, according to the Minister, notice had to be given by 20 August. I told him that I thought he would be making a serious error in agreeing to such a move, and that the British Parliament and people would be affronted.

This was not the way to get concessions out of us. He was very apologetic, but said that the Greek Government was torn apart already about the conference. Only the influence of Papagos (it was really the King acting on Papagos) had persuaded him to accept.[2]

Unhappily, the situation in the island continued to cause anxiety, and acts of terrorism had become serious. Although we thought it unwise to allow the Governor to proclaim a full State of Emergency, special powers were given to him to detain suspected terrorists. But the prospects were not good. The Greek radio broadcasts from Athens even caused some doubts to be raised as to whether we should go ahead. I felt, however, that the conference could not do us any harm and might do us some good.

My plan was to reserve our proposals until the Greeks and the Turks had spoken on the wider issues involved. This would mean an opening speech confined to the historical and strategic reasons for the British presence. If a deadlock ensued, at least it would be clear to the world that it was due to Greek and Turkish intransigence, rather than to the obstinacy of British colonialism—our sole

[1] Papagos died in October and was succeeded as head of the Greek Government by Constantine Karamanlis.
[2] 16 July 1955.

'*How happy could I be with either, were t'other dear charmer away!*'
Cartoon by Illingworth

desire being now, as it had been in 1878, to protect the Eastern Mediterranean from Russian aggression. After any necessary adjournment, I would reveal our precise proposals. This plan seemed generally acceptable to my colleagues.

A talk which I had with M. Fatin Zorlu, the Turkish Foreign Minister, two days before the official opening was at least unambiguous.

> [Turkey] would never agree to Cyprus being in Greek hands. The fact is, they are already surrounded by Greek islands; Cyprus is at their back door, and they are afraid that sooner or later the Greeks will go 'fellow traveller' or Communist.[1]

The representatives of the three Governments duly met on 29 August at Lancaster House under the title of 'the Eastern Mediterranean and Cyprus Conference'. There was little difficulty in arranging the formalities, the chief discussion being about the Press and publicity. It was agreed that during each of the first four days only the most anodyne communiqués should be issued, and at the end we should try to agree on a joint statement, setting out the main positions taken up by the three Governments. On the morning of 30 August we began the real business.

> ... I made a portentous speech, lasting nearly an hour, setting out the whole military, historical, economic, and geographical complex of the Eastern Mediterranean and the island of Cyprus. (Everything was included, except a tribute to Aphrodite.)[2]

In reply, M. Stephanopoulos argued his case moderately and skilfully. He demanded self-government but abandoned 'Enosis' in the sense that the sovereignty of Cyprus should be transferred to Greece without more ado. He urged that the principle of self-determination should be applied in three years' time, when a free Government could make its own choice. He added that all the necessary arrangements would be made for the British base and the protection of the interests of the Turkish minority. This attitude, although implying the absorption of Cyprus by Greece in due course, represented some success for the moderates against the extremists.

[1] 27 August 1955.   [2] 30 August 1955.

Archbishop Makarios in Cyprus, 1955

The Cyprus talks in London, August 1955
Above: The Turkish delegation, led by M. Zorlu (left)
Below: The Greek delegation, led by M. Stephanopoulos (right)

Fundamentally, the division among laymen is between the older Greek politicians and civil servants and soldiers (who look back with pride to generations of friendship with England) and the younger men who are beginning to revive some old and foolish dreams of expansion. They *are* foolish, because if 7 or 8 million Greeks come up against 20 million (and more) Turks, they will get a bloody nose. Of course, the Church is unrepentant and chauvinist. This is, in a way, understandable. For, with all its faults, the Ethnarchy kept alive the concept of Greek nationhood and Greek civilisation through 400 years of Turkish domination.[1]

On the following day M. Zorlu replied. He argued that in accordance with the Treaty of Lausanne, the sovereignty of Cyprus must remain with Britain or revert to Turkey. He claimed that the historical connection of Cyprus with the mainland of Asia Minor was the one thing common to Cyprus through all its changes.

> Whoever held the Anatolian peninsula must, because of geographical and strategical considerations, hold Cyprus. It was the back door to Anatolia.[2]

In private conversation he suggested that we might proceed with some degree of self-government if we could only secure an 'armistice for five years' on the question of sovereignty. He seemed genuinely alarmed at the prospect of a serious deterioration in relations between Turkey and Greece.

In spite of a great deal of 'coffee-housing' and some excellent dinners, I did not feel very hopeful.

> The Turks are too tough, the Greeks are too weak, to make a concession. So poor old England will get the blame—and the bombs.[2]

Nevertheless, there seemed to be some improvement on the question of the form of self-government and the guarantees for minorities. For the Turks were beginning to make some rumbling menaces about counter-claims in Thrace, which had some effect.

On Saturday 3 September M. Stephanopoulos, together with the Greek Ambassador and some of his staff, came to luncheon with me

[1] 31 August 1955.   [2] 1 September 1955.

at Birch Grove House. Sir Charles Peake, the British Ambassador in Athens, came with them. The Minister was depressed but voluble.

> He gave half an hour or so of outpouring of his troubles and his country's wrongs. He explained the internal difficulties and rivalries of the Greek Government. The Marshal (Papagos) was seriously ill, and although they now had hopes for his recovery, his absence from the daily work of the Government was a tremendous handicap. The King was away and would not return till early November. All this immense burden lay upon him (Stephanopoulos).[1]

I did my best to soothe him, promising that we should put forward some new thoughts in a day or two. Meanwhile the vital thing was not to break off the conference. Let us make a little progress and thus keep together. He seemed relieved, and we then had some more relaxed talk about the Second World War, about Archbishop Damaskinos, and about Communism. But my impression was that the Greek Government was worried at the consequences of all the trouble which they had started. He was frank in his view that Makarios could not control the fire, still less put it out.

The next day, Sunday 4 September, I entertained M. Zorlu, the Turkish Foreign Minister, and M. Nuri Birgi, the Director-General of the Turkish Foreign Office. The Turks were in great contrast to the Greeks—confident, assertive and tough. They begged me not to give an inch. Self-government was perhaps tolerable, but self-determination could never be accepted. In addition to handing over the Turkish population in Cyprus to the Greeks, it would endanger the safety of the mainland. Nevertheless, they felt the conference had done them a lot of good, for it enabled them to publicise their case, which up till then had gone by default. There should now be a moratorium; after that, perhaps some solution could be found. In reply, I referred to our own difficulties. Apart from the rough time our administrators and soldiers would have in Cyprus, and the many casualties they would suffer, we had to face world opinion.

---

[1] 3 September 1955.

At this point we decided to put forward our own compromise. It was on the following lines.

We proposed the introduction of a new and liberal constitution, leading to the fullest measure of internal self-government compatible with the strategic requirements of the international situation. The constitution would provide for an Assembly with an elected majority, a proportionate quota of seats being reserved for the Turkish-speaking minority. All departments of the Cyprus Government would be progressively transferred to Cypriot Ministers, responsible to the Assembly, except Foreign Affairs, Defence and Public Security, which would be reserved for the Governor. There would be safeguards for the integrity and independence of the public service and a proportion of Ministerial portfolios would be reserved for the Turkish community. In addition to these constitutional arrangements, which followed the usual pattern of the progressive development of self-government in other colonies, we put forward a novel suggestion. Recognising the divergence of view between the three delegations, we suggested that a special tripartite committee of the conference should be set up in London for the purpose of helping to apply the new constitution, considering the necessary guarantees for the minority communities, and protecting the status and rights of Cypriot citizens within the United Kingdom, Greece and Turkey. We also proposed the appointment of representatives of the Greek and Turkish Governments to reside in Cyprus with special access to the Governor. This plan would at any rate meet the immediate needs. Although there might be disagreement as to the ultimate solution, all parties should co-operate for the introduction of the first instalment. When self-government was in working order, the full conference should be reconvened to reconsider the situation.

Although I felt that this offer of a tripartite committee and a partnership between the three powers ought to appeal to reasonable people, I was not sanguine of success. It was therefore necessary to send substantial reinforcements immediately to the island.

At this point trouble began to start. A bomb was thrown in Salonika at the Turkish Consulate and Atatürk's house was damaged. In reprisal, there were serious anti-Greek demonstrations, with a good deal of rioting, in both Smyrna and Istanbul. The police seemed unable or perhaps unwilling to interfere.

In my private and preliminary talks I was endeavouring merely to persuade the Greeks and Turks to take note of our proposals and to send a reply by their respective Governments. When the full conference met, I pointed out that the argument for self-determination was one which could not be a principle of universal application to all communities whatever their size, location, history and strategical importance. I was able to remind the members that even Austria with her seven million people was specifically denied the right of Enosis or union with Germany by the treaty only recently signed. Fortunately the tone of both the Greek and Turkish replies enabled me to say that I would await the formal decision of their Governments. Meanwhile I declared the conference 'suspended'.

Although the result was disappointing, I felt that the effort had been justified.

> It has at least proved that Cyprus is not a 'colonial' problem but a great international issue. The Turkish position has never been understood. Most English people do not look at maps and few have realised its key position both for us and for the Turks. Whoever holds Cyprus, commands the port of Alexandretta and the back door to Turkey.[1]

On the other hand, it could not be denied that the conference had perhaps increased rather than lowered the tension. The Turkish riots in Istanbul and Smyrna, which were undoubtedly connived at if not promoted by the Government, had temporarily made the Turks rather ashamed of themselves. As the sensational news of the vast amount of damage done began to be reported, the Greeks talked about abandoning NATO, but this I did not believe.

> The only thing for us to do now is to go quietly on our course. We have heard (from the Americans) that although the Greeks will continue to refuse a 'tripartite' committee on preparing for self-government in Cyprus, they will be ready to talk to us. We can, at the right moment, agree to this and then ask the Turks for

[1] 7 September 1955.

their views. Thus the 'tripartite' plan will change into a 'Trieste-type' negotiation.[1]

The general view of the British Press was that our plan was reasonable and should have been accepted. But Archbishop Makarios denounced the new proposals and the situation in the island became increasingly tense.

Happily, as a result of Dulles's decision to stand by us, it was decided on 23 September by 28 votes to 22, with 10 abstentions, not to inscribe Cyprus in the Agenda of the United Nations.

Field-Marshal Sir John Harding had now in a most patriotic spirit accepted the position of Governor and arrived in the island on 3 October, determined to do his best to restore order and to reach some solution. He was to pursue this dual policy with determination and patience.

The Field-Marshal soon began his negotiations with the Archbishop, and Eden seemed anxious to try a new formula for these talks. But this was not easy to devise without some weakening in our position. The search for a new basis of negotiation continued throughout October and November. I kept Dulles informed, sometimes by telegram and sometimes by letter. One of the main difficulties was to discover how far the Archbishop and the Greek Government played their hands jointly or separately. I had to deal with this changing situation sometimes from London, sometimes from Paris, sometimes from Geneva and sometimes from Baghdad. The whole thing reminded me of one of those irritating puzzles that we had as children, when it was almost impossible to get all the balls into their respective holes at the same time. One could perhaps get in the Turks and then the Greeks; but immediately Archbishop Makarios would suddenly pop out. Sometimes one could get other combinations; but never all at once. If the Turks were reassured, Athens would be alarmed. If Athens was reasonably quiet, Ankara would be in flames. If by any chance Athens and Ankara seemed passive, the Archbishop would be on the war-path.

We had definitely promised a wide measure of self-government and asked for the co-operation of the people and of the Greek and

[1] 14 September 1955.

Turkish Governments. On this our words were clear and forth-coming. With regard to the famous question of self-determination, we devised the following:

> It is not [H.M.G.'s] position that the principle of self-determination can never be applicable to Cyprus. It is their position that it is not now a practical proposition both on account of the present strategic situation and on account of the consequences on relations between NATO powers in the Eastern Mediterranean.[1]

In our plans for constitutional progress we now had the active help of the United States and we were assured that both Karamanlis, the Greek Prime Minister, and Spyros Theotokis, the Minister for Foreign Affairs, would agree to the formula on self-determination, although they were doubtful as to the Archbishop and suggested various methods by which he might be cajoled into acceptance. But we had all underrated or forgotten the capacity of Greeks, laymen and clerics alike, to prolong a discussion of phrases and definitions with infinite ingenuity and refinement. Since one of the many advantages of an Eton education in my time was to acquire some knowledge of the controversies which tore apart the early Christian Church and the extravagances into which men of learning can be drawn, especially when inspired by personal rivalries, I should have known better.

On 22 November Makarios broke off the negotiations. The Greek Government were deeply concerned. A public breach with Makarios seemed impossible, especially at a time when elections were proceeding in Greece. I was in Baghdad when I heard the news and had a talk with Menderes (the Turkish Prime Minister) and Zorlu (the Foreign Minister), who had accepted the new formula without enthusiasm but without bitterness. Both of them deplored the deterioration of their relations with Greece.

> The work of 26 years has been ruined by the Greek Government's adoption of Enosis, and the violence of their propaganda.[2]

However, these Turkish Ministers suspected that we knew a good

---

[1] For the full text of the final formula, see Appendix Three.   [2] 22 November 1955.

deal about their share in abetting the Istanbul riots, which had gone further than they wished. This perhaps made them a little less truculent than usual. Nevertheless, their fears were genuine. Unless something could be agreed, the minorities in both countries would be victimised.

> The Turkish minorities in Thrace had been very badly treated. If this continued, the rich and prosperous Greek minority in Turkey (mostly in Istanbul) would inevitably suffer.[1]

In view of the conditions in Cyprus itself, it was necessary to accept the Governor's proposal for a State of Emergency. But in spite of the pressure which the Greek Government and the Americans were trying to bring upon Makarios, he remained firm in his irresolution. In view of the impending debate in the House of Commons it was clear that our own formula, hitherto confidential, would now have to be published.

The debate took place on 5 December, and it was decided that I should open it and the Colonial Secretary (Lennox-Boyd) wind up. My speech was long but served its purpose, which was to lower the temperature.

> The fact that there was still a hope of settlement made responsible members unwilling to say things which would exacerbate feelings. Even [James] Griffiths . . . seemed to want not to be too unhelpful.[2]

At the conference we had all agreed on self-government – the Turks with some reservations; but still we all agreed.

> On self-determination, to adapt the old doggerel, the Greeks said, 'This year' or, at any rate, 'in a year or two,' the Turks said 'Never' and we said 'Some time'.[3]

(Although I knew I was trailing my coat, since an Under-Secretary for the Colonies had recently committed himself to the phrase 'Never', it was important that this declaration, made in reply to a supplementary question, should be firmly put aside.) Half-way

[1] Ibid.   [2] 5 December 1955.   [3] *Hansard*, 5 December 1955.

through the debate, the Socialists decided not to force a division. But debates, alas, cannot settle great issues.

When I saw the Greek and Turkish Ambassadors I was relieved to find that they had no particular objection to what I had said in the House of Commons or to the formula itself. But the Greek Government seemed to be suffering from a kind of moral paralysis, and for several days there was nothing but further quibbling and new drafts demanding 'fresh elucidations'. When I met Dulles on 16 December, he too thought that the Greeks would accept, subject to some minor changes. Eventually I agreed with M. Theotokis in Paris that the Greek Ambassador in London and Sir Harold Caccia should discuss 'elucidations and explanations' which might be useful, but I refused to do more.

In my last days at the Foreign Office I received a telegram from Athens from which it was clear that the Greek Government was still wavering. On this equivocal note ended my first experience of this painful and tangled dispute. The last words of my speech in the House of Commons were as follows:

> It would be very easy to win the sympathy and even the support of unthinking people, were we to make a gesture of abdication in conformity with a vague feeling of sentiment. But I must warn the House that were we to do so the consequences would be grave and even disastrous. We should be abdicating our duty not only to ourselves, but to the Greek as well as to the Turkish people. I am sure that we should be bringing about not peace in the Eastern Mediterranean, but bitter war and strife. We should be failing in our obligation to all other peoples who depend on us as one of the main buttresses in the defence of freedom and democracy, both in NATO and the Middle East, and we should, in this sense, be abandoning our task. . . .[1]

This deep sense of British responsibility continued to guide us through succeeding years. It has since proved possible to give full independence to Cyprus while maintaining the British Government's strategic interest in the base, and—so far—avoiding a direct conflict between Greece and Turkey. Cyprus is now an independent self-governing member of the Commonwealth. In spite of all the

[1] *Hansard*, 5 December 1955.

conflicts and the fierce guerrilla warfare, led by determined men, neither the Archbiship nor the Greek Government has taken the fatal step of Enosis, that is absorption of Cyprus by Greece, which, unless preceded by a successful negotiation between the two nations, must produce a violent reaction from Turkey. This lesson, at least, was learned from the events of 1955 and has not yet been forgotten.

On a very different level from the troubles of Cyprus, the question of the election of new members to the United Nations and to the Security Council was a cause of long and wearisome arguments. It is perhaps worth putting on record the story of this strange and confusing affair.

For five years there had been a deadlock because the candidates for membership of the United Nations proposed by the Soviet Union had failed to achieve the necessary seven votes in the Security Council. In retaliation, the Russians vetoed all the proposals made by the Western Powers. A new consideration arose when the Italian Foreign Minister pointed out to me that Italy's candidature for membership of the United Nations had been vetoed four times by Russia, and if there was to be a further failure the Italian Government would be disappointed and weakened. Would it not be possible to make a deal? But the Allied view was that each candidature should be considered on its merits, and this was still our position throughout the summer.

At the beginning of August it became necessary to elect the successor to Turkey on the Security Council. There were certain conventions which had hitherto been respected. There was an Eastern European seat and a Commonwealth seat, and I was anxious to maintain this tradition. I therefore proposed Yugoslavia as the Eastern European candidate. The Soviets were pressing hard for Poland.

There were thus two issues, the question of the seat on the Security Council and the question of elections to the United Nations itself. As regards the first, Dulles was committed to supporting the Philippines, but I doubted how firmly he would press this view. However, by the middle of October it appeared that Yugoslavia and the

Philippines were running neck and neck. The Americans now began to bring great pressure on us to support the latter, but we felt that the balance of advantage would be secured by backing Yugoslavia. In a talk towards the end of October Dulles argued that the issue of the election of the Philippines had been elevated into a United States–Soviet contest. If the United States were defeated there would be a corresponding loss of prestige and authority. Since an earlier discussion in August, when he had admitted that he did not regard the Philippine candidature as more than a gesture, there had developed a real chance that they would be elected. Moreover, since Yugoslavia was now supported by the Russians, she was no longer a compromise candidate. I still felt inclined in the general context of world affairs not to abandon Yugoslavia but to encourage her in her growing independence.

> I could not agree to withdraw our support for Yugoslavia's candidature for the Security Council seat in favour of the Philippines. [Dulles] did not seem unduly disappointed, for I was able to remind him that I was sticking to the plan on which he had agreed, while he wished to alter it.[1]

However, Dulles wrote to me on 3 December with a further plea for the Philippines, threatening that if they were not elected, his clients would be prepared to stand down in favour of Greece. He added that in view of the Cyprus matter we might be prepared to change our position. I rather resented this attempt at something approaching blackmail and refused his proposal. I maintained that the Yugoslavs

> really do hold a key position and it would be a great error for us both to antagonise them. They are always apt to be sensitive, and when the conditions of the struggle have been forgotten we may easily be accused of having let them down.[2]

In the last weeks of December the position became almost farcical. There had been altogether in two months thirty-five unsuccessful ballots for election to the Security Council. Since in the case of the smaller powers the election was for a period of two years, the President of the Assembly, Dr. José Maza of Chile, made a

[1] 25 October 1955.   [2] Letter to Foster Dulles, 5 December 1955.

suggestion worthy of Solomon. He proposed that the two candidates should divide the two-year term and serve one year each. As a result Yugoslavia was elected, with an informal understanding that she would retire after one year.

This affair had lasted some four or five months and involved a vast number of telegrams and conversations, but the outcome thus far may be said to have resulted in a drawn match slightly in our favour.

On the larger question of membership there was equally bitter controversy. The Canadian Government in the middle of September put forward an idea said to have come from Nehru. It was that all sixteen or—if Japan were included—seventeen applications should be agreed *en bloc*, with the hope that this could be done without any public wrangling. From our point of view this naturally meant backing a number of countries strongly opposed to Britain and the British Colonial Empire. We therefore still preferred some degree of selection. Moreover, Dulles maintained firmly that the United States would never vote for Bulgaria, Hungary or Roumania, whom they regarded as mere clients of the Communist bloc. The four Foreign Ministers discussed this matter at Geneva on 27 September, when Molotov made a strong plea for supporting the election of sixteen candidates *en bloc* and thus overcoming the icejam of recent years. However, the number was now not sixteen but eighteen, Spain and Japan having been added to the list. It became necessary for me to consult my colleagues and to give them a picture of the difficulties. If we were to support the full election there was a danger that the anti-colonial vote would be a source of trouble. On the other hand, if the Western Powers opposed them for no apparent reason except prejudice, this might swing them and their friends more and more into the Communist camp. In the end it was agreed to fall in with the general view. The only hope of getting over the Russian veto was to adopt the principle of universality, and the balance of opinion seemed to be to make the best of it. I had a further discussion with Dulles before the second Geneva meeting of Foreign Ministers broke up. I told him

that we were committed to vote for 18 (the principle of 'univer-sality') in spite of our dislike of Outer Mongolia, Albania and others. But we could not let down Ceylon, Italy, etc. Dulles cannot swallow Outer Mongolia. The French will veto *everyone*, unless the motion on Algeria is withdrawn![1]

On the next day Dulles told me that he had had a talk with Molotov, who was still sticking out over Outer Mongolia.

The Canadian resolution, supported by twenty-seven other countries and urging the election of the eighteen new members, was formally put forward in the middle of November. A special political committee of the Assembly asked the Security Council to approve this proposal; but an orgy of vetoing immediately broke out between the Soviet Union and Nationalist China, the latter no doubt acting for the Americans. Finally, on 14 December, a so-called compromise was reached. Sixteen countries were to be elected, only Outer Mongolia and Japan being for the moment excluded.

A great effort and a vast amount of bargaining and counter-bargaining led to a result which, if inevitable, was not greatly to our advantage. Looking back on it, I think that perhaps we were too anxious to please our own clients and in order to help them agreed too readily to the admission of unsuitable members. Nevertheless, it is not the election of increasing numbers of members to the Assembly which has injured the authority of the United Nations. The real error has been the enlargement of the Security Council beyond the number of the major powers, to which it was the founders' idea to limit the membership. This, and the fatal division of the world into hostile blocs, has destroyed the original conception. Only by a real *détente* between the West and Russia can the Security Council be made an effective instrument for carrying out the agreed policies of the Great Powers. The ultimate tragedy of a Third World War will no doubt be avoided by the nuclear deterrent. But, beneath this umbrella of fear, many minor conflicts will continue to distract the world unless and until some real Council of Great Powers can reassert its authority.

One further complication, painful and personal, still awaited me. It was another stage in the case of Burgess and Maclean. Although

[1] 12 November 1955.

these two men defected to the Russians on 25 May 1951, it was not till the last months of 1955 that the sordid story was blown up again to full heat.

Vladimir Petrov, a Russian agent who defected in Australia in April 1954, published his memoirs serially in the *People*, and the first article of his disclosures appeared on 18 September 1955. This, together with the report of the Royal Commission appointed by the Australian Government which appeared the same month, brought the whole matter again to the attention of the general public.

> The first instalment appeared yesterday. Even the more reputable journals are in a 'hue and cry' against the Foreign Office. The *Express*, the *Mirror* and the *Sketch* lead the baser part of the pack. . . . Of course we shall be attacked for having kept silent all these years.[1]

I had been too busy to pay much attention to a matter about which no further action seemed possible or desirable. Petrov's disclosures, followed by the violent Press campaign, made it necessary to decide upon some definite course.

> Burgess and Maclean all the morning. This squalid story is being worked up by the Press into a major scandal. There is a bitter attack on me by Crossman in the *Mirror*.[2]

I could hardly be blamed for the appointment, employment or even for the circumstances attending the flight of these two men. It seemed that the best course would be to publish a White Paper, setting out the whole story. This duly appeared on 23 September.[3] At the same time, a statement was put out from No. 10 that the Government would afford an opportunity for an early debate. Fortunately, the sensationalist Press

> has rather overplayed its hand . . . and people are getting rather disgusted. I have had one or two letters from Labour M.P.s urging me to stand firm in resisting an inquiry into the Foreign Office [which] Herbert Morrison has now publicly demanded.[4]

Nevertheless, this unhappy affair brought discredit on a great

---

[1] 19 September 1955.   [2] 20 September 1955.
[3] Cmd. 9577.   [4] 1 October 1955.

department and raised again the general question of security. We had not merely to settle our line for the debate, but also to do what we could to prevent a repetition of such a disaster.

Eden gave me much assistance, based upon his unique knowledge of the Foreign Service both before and after the Bevin reforms. I prepared for my colleagues in the Cabinet an outline of my opening speech and the suggested approach. It would not, of course, be easy to make a convincing defence of what had happened in the past, although I felt that it should be possible to show some of the inherent difficulties in a situation in which the principles of security and freedom could be in conflict.

The chief question to be decided was whether or not some form of inquiry should be held. Some Members of Parliament had proposed a Select Committee of the House of Commons, others an inquiry under the Tribunals Act. Finally, Herbert Morrison, who had been Foreign Secretary during the last months of the Labour administration, wanted a general inquiry into the Foreign Office and the system of security. I was strongly opposed to any inquiry into the past, which would merely lead to a lot of muck-raking and innuendo. This view was shared by all my colleagues. The real question was how to avoid such disasters in the future. For this purpose it was worth considering an inquiry into the whole problem of security within the framework of the existing law in relation to those employees of the State who had access to secret information. For the real difficulty was that almost all the demands for stricter precautions amounted, in practice, to encroachments on traditional British liberties. This matter was discussed at length and the final decision, taken while I was at Geneva in October, was against any inquiry at the present time.

When the debate took place on 7 November Members seemed divided between those who would be prepared to give the Executive far more drastic powers and those who preferred to run some risks in order to maintain the older traditions of the British system of law and equity. I began by pointing out that at the time of the Spanish Civil War and later when Hitler made his pact with Stalin and the Second World War began, many men and women had found that their ideological beliefs exerted a pull which was to prove stronger than their patriotism. Although this phase was ended, so far as the Communists were concerned, by the German attack on Russia, when later an estrangement began between Britain and the Soviet Government, the conflict of loyalties revived.

> Thus it was that men could be found in Britain who could put the interests of another country before those of their own, and could commit the horrible crime of treachery. This occurred not only among criminals and degenerates, but in men holding high technical and scientific posts, among men of philosophic and literary attainments, and, finally, these two cases, the subject of this debate, in the Foreign Service.[1]

I next made it clear that full Ministerial responsibility must be accepted by those who presided over the Foreign Office during all this period. It would be quite wrong to elevate any Department of State into a separate entity, uncontrolled by Ministers and not subject to full Parliamentary authority. Ministers, and Ministers alone, must bear the burden for what went wrong. After all, they were not slow to take credit for anything that went right. Of the Ministers concerned, Ernest Bevin and Hector McNeil were dead. Morrison, Eden and I survived, and therefore we must each carry our share.

This opening had the intended effect of preventing Morrison from turning this into a party matter.

In addition to the question of Burgess and Maclean, accusations had been freely made in the Press against a so-called 'Third Man' – alleged to be 'Kim' Philby. In view of subsequent developments, it is worth while putting on record what I then said. Philby was asked to resign in July 1951:

> Since that date his case has been the subject of close investigation. No evidence has been found to show that he was responsible for warning Burgess or Maclean. While in Government service he carried out his duties ably and conscientiously. I have no reason to conclude that Mr. Philby has at any time betrayed the interests of this country, or to identify him with the so-called 'third man', if, indeed, there was one.[1]

[1] *Hansard*, 7 November 1955.

It would have been quite wrong for me to have made any other answer to the direct question which was put to me in the House of Commons. Since there was no evidence available which could have justified a prosecution, I had surely no right to blacken this man's character. As is well known, he was subsequently to make a full confession when in a foreign country.

After dealing with the history of Burgess and Maclean and their record, I referred to the reforms of the Foreign Office which had been introduced by Bevin during his five-year tenure.

> He was certainly not the man to be unduly impressed by the outward semblance of things; he went to the inner core. He was not a defender of privilege, and, at the same time, was not a man to yield to prejudice. It fell to him to implement the scheme which had been laid down by the Act of 1943. If he had not been satisfied with it, I am sure that in his five years at the Foreign Office he would not have hesitated to propose some amendment or alteration. Actually, he felt for the Foreign Service a loyalty and devotion which has been amply rewarded by the respect and affection in which his name will always be held at the Foreign Office.[1]

At the end of my speech I indulged in some general reflections, reminding Members that we had now to face something completely different from anything which any of us had believed possible. Since 1688 in England, and since 1745 in Scotland, there had been no real dispute about the character of the regime. There had been bitter political conflicts, but no question of treason.

> We have to go back to the period of the wars of religion to find any parallel for the new ideological conflicts which divide the world and which may continue to divide it for many years to come.[1]

It was difficult for us to conceive of a son betraying his father or a father denouncing his own children, or to imagine a state of mind which regarded spying as a virtue and treachery as a duty. Perhaps we must study again the problems that confronted the Elizabethan statesmen, Burghley and Walsingham,

[1] *Hansard*, 7 November 1955.

With Lady Dorothy at Birch Grove House

when the Secret Service first developed, when espionage and counter-espionage, plot and counter-plot were inseparable from international politics.[1]

What we had to consider was whether the methods available to us under the law were sufficient, or whether we ought to ask for new powers.

> Here, may I say that I was struck by a criticism which appeared recently in one of the popular papers. Why, asked this critic, was Mrs. Maclean not prevented from leaving England. This is what it said. I quote from the article:
> '. . . the authorities said they would have no legal power to stop her. There is no law for this.'
> Then it goes on:
> 'Could not they have found one?'
> There we have the very hub of the problem. Could not they—that is, the authorities—have found one? Hitler would have found one, of course. Mussolini would have found one. Stalin had got one.[1]

We would certainly do everything possible to avoid such disasters in the future—to make them improbable but not, I feared, impossible. Before greater powers were granted to the Executive, I begged my fellow Members to weigh carefully the balance of advantage and disadvantage, for indeed it would be a tragedy if we destroyed our freedom in an effort to preserve it.

Morrison answered, in a speech which was critical of the Foreign Office but added little of value. He excused himself and by implication blamed Bevin. This contribution was not well received. After this Members seemed to lose interest. Eden wound up the debate admirably, offering talks about the whole problem with leading Privy Councillors of all parties, especially on the question of the state of the law and the limitations necessarily involved.

It was a great relief when this affair, on which a disproportionate amount of time had been spent, was finally over. On the whole the Press was favourable, and the mood of the country had swung away from the more violent demand for methods to be adopted in

[1] Ibid.

z

peace which had hitherto been thought only defensible in time of war.

Although the question was thus disposed of for the moment, the fundamental difficulties have remained; and, as I was to find in subsequent years, it was not altogether possible to avoid the temptations either of money or of ideology by which men of different types and with varying access to major secrets were from time to time seduced. Some of these proved, alas, far more damaging than anything that could have resulted from the defection of Burgess or Maclean, and we were forced to adopt more vigorous methods of defence. Yet even so the bias has remained in favour of continuing to accept certain risks rather than use methods which are distasteful to our national sentiment and contrary to our long traditions.

CHAPTER XX

A New Commission

O N 21 December a reorganisation of the Government which the Prime Minister had been for some time contemplating was officially announced. Some of the changes marked the end of an era and were therefore, for me at least, a cause of deep regret. Harry Crookshank, my oldest friend from childhood, was to resign his position as Lord Privy Seal and Leader of the House of Commons in order to make room for Butler.

> They wanted him to be Chancellor of the Duchy and 'assistant' to the Leader of the House of Lords. When one has been 'Leader' of the House of Commons for five years, this is not a good idea. He talked it all over with me and made his final decision . . . this morning.[1]

Harry was not being removed because of any failures of his own. He had proved himself able and resourceful, and the best manager of Parliamentary business in living memory. Woolton was also to retire and be replaced as Chancellor of the Duchy by Lord Selkirk. Although my friendship with Woolton was of much shorter duration, it was close and intimate. I knew how sorely we should miss his wise counsel and his unswerving loyalty. Woolton was anxious to leave; nevertheless Eden undoubtedly lost by this change, all the more since he had already parted with Lord Swinton, who possessed the ablest and most versatile brain in the Conservative Party. Osbert Peake, another old friend from pre-war days, also left us. But naturally the changes in the highest offices were the most sensational. Butler was to give up the Treasury, over which he had presided for four years, to become Leader of the House of Commons in place of Crookshank. I was to succeed Butler and thus be moved from the

[1] 20 December 1955.

Foreign Office after a short spell of nine months. Selwyn Lloyd, who had formerly been Minister of State at the Foreign Office and was now Minister of Defence, was to take my place.

I had first heard of this proposal on 23 September, the day after the debate on Cyprus. I was talking to Eden about the situation in the island and the proposed appointment of Sir John Harding as Governor. Just as I was leaving the Prime Minister threw a bombshell.

> How would I like to leave the Foreign Office and go to the Treasury? I confess I was somewhat staggered. 'When?' 'At once.' 'What about Rab?' 'He can be Lord Privy Seal—and Leader of the House.' 'Have you spoken to him?' 'Yes, last night. He seemed rather to like the idea.' We then discussed the effect on Rab's position and the prestige of the Government. Would it not seem a confession of failure? Would not the whole Government suffer accordingly? What about the autumn Budget?[1]

Eden seemed anxious to settle the matter promptly, but I said I must think about it most carefully. I refused to be rushed. Later in the day I had a talk with the Chief Whip, Patrick Buchan-Hepburn, about this, as it seemed to me, astonishing suggestion. He said that the Prime Minister was worried about 'the economic front' and felt that after four years of slogging work, with many ups and downs, Butler was tired and depressed. He had also suffered a grievous personal loss through the death of his wife. I replied that to lead the House of Commons was no sinecure. In any case I thought the political effect would be shattering. We had won an election only a few months before on Butler's triumphant cry 'Invest in Success'. If, as seemed likely, there was trouble ahead of us, surely we ought to defend our position without a change of guard. Both the Government's and Butler's reputation would suffer. The rest of the plan was then unfolded. Selwyn Lloyd, Eden's old subordinate and in whom he had great confidence, would follow me.

> I asked if the Prime Minister's purpose was really to get back control of the Foreign Office. [The] Chief Whip thought not. But he [Eden] was happy about foreign affairs and he understood

[1] 23 September 1955.

them. He thought I was the only person whom he could trust with finance, economics, etc. The last few weeks had shaken his confidence in the Treasury.[1]

It was certainly true that—as so often happens after a recovery from depression—an inflationary position had begun to develop. Unless firmly handled it might become alarming. Towards the end of August, at Eden's request, I had prepared for him a memorandum on this subject. I had not felt the situation to be by any means desperate, and suggested certain remedies. It was no doubt unwise of me to have acceded to this request, but I agreed in all innocence. A few days later, on 26 August, Eden and Butler lunched with me, and we went through my paper together.

> I thought the Prime Minister in good heart, but Butler seemed very tired and rather more *distrait* than usual. But I have no doubt that he will rise to the new challenge.[2]

I continued to feel that some action was necessary.

> The economic and financial position is not improving. August exports are up—really splendid. But imports continue to grow at a still greater rate. I have just seen a return of the reserves. In the first fortnight of September we have lost nearly $170 million. About half of this, I am told, is 'hot money'. The sooner Parliament meets and our measures are put through, the better it will be. I wish we did not have to wait another fortnight. Yet I am still convinced that the margin of inflation is not so great as to be beyond control.[3]

During August and September I had naturally taken some share in the various discussions on this subject at Cabinet and other meetings. But it was a shattering blow when Eden disclosed this new plan. Since my introduction to diplomacy during the Mediterranean campaign,[4] I had regarded the Foreign Office as the summit of my ambitions. If only I could achieve this post and hold it for three or four years I could then happily retire. I never felt that any of us should cling too long to public life or show any resentment if

[1] 23 September 1955.   [2] 26 August 1955.
[3] 14 September 1955.   [4] *The Blast of War*, pp. 189 ff.

changes were made to admit younger blood. If the Prime Minister had felt that I had failed at the Foreign Office I should of course have accepted his verdict. But it was clear that this was not his view. I had therefore to judge what was his real motive, and this I did not find easy to do. Apart from my conversation with the Chief Whip I spoke to no one about this, except my wife. She urged me to continue at least until some of the immediate tasks were completed. There was our policy on Cyprus to be developed; there was the Foreign Ministers' meeting at Geneva; there were many other issues of the highest importance to be faced. If I were to leave after only a few months, it would both be and seem to be a strange and inexplicable proceeding. Could I not tell the Prime Minister that I would think it over but that certainly no change should be made until the end of the year? I took her advice and when Eden next spoke to me about this plan on 11 October he agreed to wait.

Meanwhile, Butler had already given at the Bankers' dinner on 4 October an analysis of the current economic situation. We were suffering from the effect of 'buoyant expansion, coupled with insufficient restraint at home'. This restraint would be intensified, and his proposals to that end would be announced in Parliament as soon as it met. In the middle of October the Chancellor's plans were approved by all his colleagues; they involved the introduction of an autumn Budget, an unusual proceeding at that time and generally associated with a severe crisis. Yet the present difficulties were altogether unlike the great troubles of the past, such as 1931 or 1947. All that was needed was a slight application of the brake. The rates of purchase tax were increased by one-fifth, and certain goods previously exempt were now made subject to tax. The rate of tax on distributed profits was raised from $22\frac{1}{2}$ to $27\frac{1}{2}$ per cent. The volume of lending to local authorities was to be checked, and the Exchequer housing subsidy reduced except in cases of slum clearance and rehousing of excess population. Telephone charges and rentals were increased. All this was expected to produce £112·5 million in a full year.

I was in Geneva during these weeks and I noted that

According to the English papers, the Opposition are making

no end of a hullabaloo about the Budget. The cutting of the housing subsidies and the new measures to control local authority borrowing seem to annoy them still more. But the indignation seems rather synthetic.[1]

Gaitskell, bidding for the leadership and no doubt wishing to avoid the stigma of 'Butskellism',[2] made an unusually violent speech, attacking not merely the proposals but the political honour of the Chancellor of the Exchequer. The weight of the onslaught was directed to the fact that these new measures came only six months after the April Budget, in which income tax had been reduced. As the English papers came in I read the accounts in my villa at Geneva.

> ... the Labour Opposition is working itself up into a great state of excitement, attacking Rab and his 'honour'. But I am sure everyone will rally round. ...[3]

At any rate Eden, in closing the discussion, was able to make a good debating point. The April Budget was now described by the Labour Party as an 'electioneering deception'. But at the time and during the election it had been denounced as 'robbing the poor'. It could scarcely be both.

In spite of Butler's decision to grasp the economic nettle for good or ill, Eden began to press me for an answer. I now consulted Woolton.

> I told him how much I preferred the Foreign Office. I am on much surer ground, with a good staff (whom I trust) and a subject which I can more or less understand.[4]

Nevertheless, he thought I must do what the Prime Minister wanted.

The next day I had to go to Paris, and my wife came with me. I

[1] 28 October 1955.
[2] 'Mr. Gaitskell was, like Mr. Butler, a man of academic distinction, educated at a famous public school, and some mischievous person had a few years back invented a symbolical figure called 'Mr. Butskell', the suggestion being that these two politicians, though sitting on opposite sides of the House, were really very much of a muchness. The Labour Party would not want to be led by a 'Mr. Butskell', and Mr. Gaitskell was out to show that there was no such person': *Annual Register, 1955*, p. 55.
[3] 30 October 1955.   [4] 21 October 1955.

had composed the draft of a letter to the Prime Minister which I took with me. I would sleep on it, and send it from the Embassy. I had also received some good advice from Gwilym Lloyd George, whom I consulted.

He said that it was no good writing a letter setting out the arguments 'for' and 'against'. The only thing to do was to make up my own mind, and let the Prime Minister know my decision, and any conditions.[1]

After much thought and with many regrets I despatched my letter from Paris on 24 October. It was in the following terms:

Dear Anthony,

I have thought, for several weeks, over your proposal that I should leave the Foreign Office and go to the Treasury.

Naturally, I am not at all anxious to do so, for I love the Foreign Office—the work and the people. It is the fulfilment of a long ambition.

I would like to be clear about certain points from the start, because you are asking me to take on a very difficult job, which may involve some rather painful decisions.

1. I may want to make considerable changes in the set-up.

2. I may want to bring in outside advisers.

3. The organisation of the Bank of England may require attention.

For there is no point in my leaving the Foreign Office to be an orthodox Chancellor of the Exchequer. I must be, if not a revolutionary, something of a reformer. However, to reform the Treasury is like trying to reform the Kremlin or the Vatican. These institutions are apt to have the last laugh.

So I must ask for certain conditions without which it would be hopeless to try.

(a) Your firm support, especially through the early troubles.

(b) A position in the Government not inferior to that held by the present Chancellor. As Foreign Secretary, I am the head of the Foreign Front, under you as Prime Minister. As Chancellor I must be undisputed head of the Home Front under you.

If Rab becomes Leader of the House and Lord Privy Seal that

[1] 23 October 1955.

will be fine. But I could not agree that he should be Deputy Prime Minister. (Incidentally, this post does not exist constitutionally, and was invented by Churchill to suit quite exceptional situations.)

You will realise that the presence of a much respected ex-Chancellor, with all that this implies, in the Cabinet and in Whitehall must somewhat add to my difficulties, however loyal he will try to be. If he were also Deputy Prime Minister, my task would be impossible.

(c) I should like to be consulted about the Board of Trade. Treasury and Board of Trade must be partners (like Housing and Works, to get the 300,000 houses) otherwise, it won't work.

I thought it best to be quite frank. If you don't agree, I shall quite understand. If you do, I am willing to try.

Yours ever,

Harold

I sent with it a covering letter:

Dear Anthony,

Here is my reply. I thought you had better have it as soon as possible. Perhaps we could discuss it when I come back for the Maclean–Burgess Debate.

Yours ever,

Harold

Do not be alarmed. Dorothy typed it for me.

Anyone reading this letter with knowledge of subsequent events would not unnaturally assume that I was actuated by some degree of personal rivalry with Butler. This, in fact, was not the case. It never occurred to me at that time that there could be any question of a choice between him and me as successor to the Prime Minister. I had no reason to suppose that Eden would be struck down by illness and forced to resign his post a year later. He was three years younger than I, and there seemed no reason to doubt that he would complete the Parliament as Prime Minister and lead the party to the subsequent election in some four years' time. I was now sixty-one, and by the probable time of the election I would be sixty-five. Having finished a full term as Foreign Secretary I should be very happy to retire, whether we won the election or not, for I was already beginning to feel some of the results of the pressures, physical and mental, of an active life as a soldier, a publisher and a politician. I was only concerned that, if I was to leave the Foreign Office, where I had complete control under the Prime Minister, I should, in my new post, enjoy similar scope and authority. Butler had been for four years Chancellor of the Exchequer, and as Leader of the House and Lord Privy Seal would properly enjoy a powerful position. I had no objection to this, so long as I had an unchallenged control within my own sphere. I could not agree that he should be Deputy Prime Minister; partly because I felt that it would limit my powers, partly because it was really outside the constitution. When the time came for Eden to retire, Butler, who was five years younger than Eden and eight years younger than me, would be the natural successor.

The introduction of the Budget made it impossible for any change in Government to take place until the end of the autumn session. After a further exchange of letters, everything was amicably agreed. I withdrew my objections to a point which had arisen as to Butler presiding over the Cabinet in the Prime Minister's absence, since this had been the practice from the beginning of Eden's administration. Moreover, I remembered a phrase of Churchill's—'in order to heighten your dignity, it is not necessary to stand upon it'. Guidance to the Press was put out in the following form:

> Mr. Butler, as Leader of the House of Commons, will be responsible for planning and carrying through the Government's programme of legislation, and all other Government business in Parliament. He will be responsible, on behalf of the Leader of the Party, for the policy direction of the Conservative Central Office.
>
> Mr. Macmillan, as Chancellor of the Exchequer, in addition to his control over financial policy, will have, under the Prime Ministry, full responsibility for co-ordinating all aspects of economic policy, both internal and external.
>
> In the absence of the Prime Minister, Mr. Butler will continue as hitherto to preside over meetings of the Cabinet.

All these details would scarcely be worth recording had it not been that when—in wholly unexpected conditions—a successor to Eden had to be found, stories of a long-standing rivalry between Butler and myself were widely circulated.

On 15 December, a few days before the changes were formally announced, the *Daily Express* and the *Daily Telegraph*—but no other papers–published a pretty accurate forecast of the proposed changes, and the French Press carried the story about my leaving the Foreign Office. Since I was lunching at the American Embassy in Paris,

> I thought it best to tell Foster (in confidence). He was terribly distressed. He wanted to ask the President to call Anthony about it! I was rather touched.[1]

The genuineness of this feeling was confirmed in a letter from Roger Makins[2] (our Ambassador in Washington), written on 22 December:

> Foster had drawn me aside in the State Department and said how deeply distressed he was at the change, how well you had been working together, and what a pity it all was.
>
> When I got back to the Embassy I found your messages, so I asked to see Foster again, gave him the messages, and spoke as you had asked me to do in your telegram to me.
>
> Foster was obviously much touched and pleased, and after some further expressions of mutual regret we parted.
>
> I fear there may be a scarcely perceptible hardening of attitude towards us for a bit here, but we must try to break it down before it can set.

Many of my foreign friends, both politicians and diplomats, expressed similar sentiments, which I felt were more than mere formalities. There was also a letter from Gladwyn Jebb[3]–then our Ambassador in Paris–which I particularly valued. Apart from expressing his own regrets, he continued:

> I suppose you realise how popular you were with the Service as a whole? It was not only the head officials who appreciated your brilliant qualities; it was also the little people, right down to the typists and messengers, who thought you were the kindest and most considerate Secretary of State that they had ever known.

When it was too late I regretted my decision. I felt that six months at the Ministry of Defence and nine months at the Foreign Office were unsatisfactory experiences.

---

[1] 15 December 1955.   [2] Later Lord Sherfield.   [3] Later Lord Gladwyn.

Just as one is learning one job, one goes off to another. At my age, it is not quite so easy to switch the mind on to a completely new set of problems.[1]

What, then, were Eden's motives for making this sudden and drastic change, and why did I succumb to his arguments? In subsequent years I have naturally thought much about this matter. It is always difficult to analyse human motives, and to define them precisely. On reflection, I feel that Eden wished to have more control over foreign affairs, either in his own hands or in those of a Minister younger than himself and with less political experience. This was not because he wished to assume any stronger part than a Prime Minister is entitled to play in great issues of foreign policy. But his deep knowledge of foreign affairs and his long experience at the Foreign Office made him feel that he could exercise the influence which a Prime Minister can properly exert without involving himself in any of those conflicts of which he had only too much experience—first with Chamberlain, and then with Churchill. There had been a number of matters—not of any special importance—in which we had not seen altogether eye to eye, and I realised how natural it was that he should wish to keep his finger more closely upon the details of foreign negotiations than Prime Ministers such as Asquith, Baldwin or Attlee had ordinarily done. But if he was swayed by these considerations, consciously or unconsciously, I am certain that the reasons which he gave me were sincere and true. He was worried about financial and economic affairs, of which his experience was small, and of which he had not the same natural grasp as he had in the foreign field. He knew that the success of his Government, however well conducted its foreign policy might be, would depend ultimately upon our ability to ride out the series of economic storms which seemed the inevitable conditions of modern life, following two great wars which had gravely weakened our former strength. He felt that Butler, after his four years' unremitting labour, had temporarily lost his grip and needed some respite from the heavy load which he had been carrying. He thought that of all his colleagues, I would be the most likely—from my all-round

[1] 22 December 1955.

experience—to be able to carry the burden. In the Foreign Office he was happy with a less powerful Minister; but for the management of economic affairs he relied on a colleague who would shoulder the main responsibility and correspondingly relieve his own anxieties.

My motives in finally accepting Eden's proposal were more simple. I was sad indeed to leave the office where I had been very happy, and where I had found and renewed many friendships at home and abroad; where life, although strenuous, was agreeable and often, even among our anxieties, amusing. I was therefore, at first, most unwilling to consent. But I recognised Eden's difficulties and thought it my duty to help him in any way that I could. I believed that in politics, as in other walks of life, a simple rule should apply. If one has strong conscientious views one should not hesitate to express them freely and certainly never suppress them in order to obtain office or promotion. It was for this reason that I had followed my own somewhat solitary course in those inter-war years when I felt myself out of sympathy with the leadership of the Conservative Party.[1] But apart from such considerations, when in doubt one should do whatever one is asked to do for the general good of one's friends and associates, and in this one must follow the judgement of those in authority who presumably know best what it is that will help them to achieve the common purpose.

My wife, who was extremely unhappy at the final decision, nevertheless fully consented to this formula. She had thrown herself, with great vigour, into the work of the Foreign Office and the many duties which fell upon her. She was to do the same in the years that lay ahead. But instinctively—for she had an inborn and inherited shrewdness about public affairs—she felt that the change was a mistake. On looking back upon it, I feel sure that she was right.

[1] *Winds of Change*, pp. 355 ff.

Appendixes

Appendixes

Appendix One

Extract from Minute of 21 October 1942
from Winston S. Churchill to Anthony Eden,
used by Harold Macmillan
at Meeting of Assembly of Council of Europe,
5 September 1949

I must admit that my thoughts rest primarily in Europe—the revival of the glory of Europe, the parent continent of the modern nations and of civilisation. It would be a measureless disaster if Russian barbarism overlaid the culture and independence of the ancient States of Europe. Hard as it is to say now, I trust that the European family may act unitedly as one under a Council of Europe. I look forward to a United States of Europe in which the barriers between the nations will be greatly minimised and unrestricted travel will be possible. I hope to see the economy of Europe studied as a whole. I hope to see a Council consisting of perhaps ten units, including the former Great Powers[, with several confederations—Scandinavian, Danubian, Balkan, etc.—which would possess an international police and be charged with keeping Prussia disarmed].[1] Of course we shall have to work with the Americans in many ways, and in the greatest ways, but Europe is our prime care[, and we certainly do not wish to be shut up with the Russians and the Chinese when] Swedes, Norwegians, Danes, Dutch, Belgians, Frenchmen, Spaniards, Poles, Czechs, and Turks will have their burning questions, their desire for our aid, and their very great power of making their voices heard. It would be easy to dilate upon these themes. Unhappily the war has prior claims on our attention.

[1] Passages within square brackets were omitted when the Minute was quoted at the Council of Europe.

Appendix Two

*Invitation to the Government of the USSR from the
three Western Allies, May 1955*

The Governments of France, the United Kingdom and the United States
believe that the time has now come for a new effort to resolve the great problems
which confront us. We therefore invite the Soviet Government to join with us
in an effort to remove sources of conflict between us.

We recognise that the solution of these problems will take time and patience.
They will not be solved at a single meeting nor in a hasty manner. Indeed, any
effort to do so could set back real progress towards their settlement. Accordingly,
we think it would be helpful to try a new procedure for dealing with these
problems. In view of their complexity and importance, our suggestion is that
these problems be approached in two stages. We think it would be fruitful to
begin with a meeting of the Heads of Government, accompanied by their
Foreign Ministers, for an exchange of views. In the limited time for which the
Heads of Government could meet, they would not undertake to agree upon
substantive answers to the major difficulties facing the world. Such a meeting
could, however, provide a new impetus by establishing the basis for the detailed
work which will be required.

For this purpose the Heads of Government could devote themselves to
formulating the issues to be worked on and to agreeing on methods to be
followed in exploring solutions.

We further propose that the Foreign Ministers, to assist the Heads of
Government in their task, should come together shortly in advance of the
meeting of the Heads of Government and at the same place. This first stage
would lay the foundation for the second stage in which the problems would
be examined in detail by such methods, organs, and participants as it appears
will be most fruitful according to the nature of the issues. This work should be
started as soon as practicable after the meeting of the Heads of Government.
This procedure would facilitate the essential preparation and orderly negotiation
most likely to bring about agreements by progressive stages. The important
thing is to begin the process promptly and to pursue it with patience and
determination.

We hope that this proposal will commend itself to the Soviet Union as a useful basis for progress towards better relations between us. If the Soviet Union agrees that an early meeting of Heads of Government to explore such a programme would be useful, we suggest that our Foreign Ministers settle, through diplomatic channels or otherwise, upon a time and place for such a meeting. The forthcoming meeting of the Foreign Ministers at Vienna for the signing of the Austrian State Treaty might provide an opportunity for preliminary discussion of this proposal.

May 1955

Appendix Three

*Formula for Cyprus
presented to Greek and Turkish Governments
and to Archbishop Makarios,
November* 1955

Her Majesty's Government adhere to the principles embodied in the Charter of the United Nations, the Potomac Charter and the Pacific Charter, to which they have subscribed. It is not therefore their position that the principle of self-determination can never be applicable to Cyprus. It is their position that it is not now a practical proposition both on account of the present strategic situation and on account of the consequences on relations between NATO powers in the Eastern Mediterranean. They will therefore have to satisfy themselves that any final solution safeguards the strategic interests of the United Kingdom and her Allies.

Her Majesty's Government have offered a wide measure of self-government now. If the people of Cyprus will participate in the constitutional development, it is the intention of Her Majesty's Government to work for a solution which will satisfy the wishes of the people of Cyprus, within the framework of the treaties and alliances to which the countries concerned in the defence of the Eastern Mediterranean are parties. Her Majesty's Government will be prepared to discuss the future of the island with representatives of the people of Cyprus when self-government has proved itself a workable proposition and capable of safeguarding the interests of all sections of the community.

Index

HOME AND COMMONWEALTH AFFAIRS	FOREIGN AFFAIRS

1950

	Oct. 19	Gaitskell replaces Cripps as Chancellor of the Exchequer

1951 March 9 Bevin resigns
Morrison Foreign Secretary

July 1 Colombo Plan comes into force

Oct. 25 General Election
    Conservative Government
      Prime Minister: Churchill
      Foreign Secretary: Eden
      Chancellor: Butler
      (Macmillan Minister of Housing)

1952 Feb. 6 Death of King George VI
Elizabeth becomes Queen

Oct. 3 First British atomic bomb explosion

1953

May 11 Churchill's speech proposing talks with Russia

June 23 Churchill's illness begins

Oct. 23 Federation of Rhodesia and Nyasaland inaugurated

1954

July 3 Food rationing ends in Britain

FOREIGN AFFAIRS column:

1950
July 7 European Payments Union set up
Oct. Chinese invade Tibet

Dec. 19 Eisenhower appointed N.A.T.O. Supreme Commander

April 18 European Coal and Steel Treaty signed
May 2 Iran nationalises oil industry

Sept. 8 Peace Treaty with Japan
Oct. 6 U.S.S.R. admits exploding atomic bomb
Oct. 8 Egypt denounces Anglo-Egyptian Treaty of 1936

July 23 Neguib seizes power in Egypt
Aug. 10 European Coal and Steel Community inaugurated

Nov. 4 Eisenhower elected President of U.S.A.
Nov. 16 U.S.A. explodes hydrogen bomb

Feb. 12 Anglo-Egyptian Agreement on Sudan
March 5 Death of Stalin
Malenkov succeeds

June 17 Anti-Communist riots in E. Germany

July 27 Armistice in Korea
Aug. 12 U.S.S.R. explodes H-bomb

Dec. 4–7 Bermuda Conference, France, U.K., U.S.A.

Jan. 25–Feb. 18 Berlin Conference of Foreign Ministers
April 26–June 19 Geneva Conference of Foreign Ministers

July 21 Armistice signed in Geneva between warring parties in Indo-China. Vietnam partitioned
Aug. 5 Agreement reached between Iranian Government and oil companies
Aug. 22 Breakdown of Brussels Conference on E.D.C.
Sept. 8 South-East Asia Collective Defence Treaty signed at Manila
Sept. 28–Oct. 3 Nine-Power London Conference